# COMPUTERS AND INFORMATION SYSTEMS

## Fifth Edition

Sarah E. Hutchinson

Stacey C. Sawyer

### *IRWIN*

Chicago • Bogotá • Boston • Buenos Aires • Caracas
London • Madrid • Mexico City • Sydney • Toronto

*Sponsoring Editor:* Paul Ducham
*Associate Editor:* Garrett Glanz
*Production:* Stacey C. Sawyer, Sawyer & Williams
*Text and Cover Design:* Rogondino & Associates
*Cover Art:* Tim Jessell, *The Computer Factory* (James Conrad, Agent)
*Art and Composition:* GTS Graphics
*Photo Research:* Monica Suder
*Photo Setups:* Frank Bevans
*Typeface:* 10/12 Garamond Light
*Printer:* Wm. C. Brown

ISBN: 0-256-16719-2

Printed in the United States of America

5 6 7 8 9 0 WCB 0 9 8 7

# Brief Contents

# Preface to the Instructor

*Computers and Information Systems, Fifth Edition,* is written for future computer users—people for whom the computer will be an everyday tool for working with reports, spreadsheets, databases, and the like. It is not intended for specialists who will write programs or design computer systems.

## Why We Wrote This Book: Meeting the Needs of Users

We wrote this book in order to provide instructors and students with the most useful information possible in an introductory computer course. Specifically, we offer the following five important features:

1. Complete coverage, avoiding unnecessary detail
2. Practical orientation
3. Interesting, readable style
4. Learning reinforcement
5. Complete course solutions: supplements that work

We elaborate on these features below.

## FEATURE #1: COMPLETE COVERAGE, AVOIDING UNNECESSARY DETAIL

This book attempts to offer complete coverage of core concepts of computers and information systems. We have tried to be neither too brief nor too encyclopedic, offering users just what they need to know to use a computer competently. Moreover, we have avoided the cluttered, over-illustrated look and style that many instructors tell us they find objectionable in other texts. Thus, you will not find icons, margin notes, cartoons, or similar distractions.

## FEATURE #2: PRACTICAL ORIENTATION

The text presents information on capabilities of microcomputers that users can apply at work, home, and school. For example, we provide up-to-date, practical discussion of . . .

- PC and Macintosh hardware, addressing upgrading and compatibility issues
- Buying and maintaining a microcomputer system—an entire chapter
- Computer-related health and safety matters
- Ethics, privacy, and security
- Object-oriented programming, expert systems, virtual reality, and digital convergence

. . . and "bonus" topics readers will find useful on the job, such as different RAM requirements of color monitors.

## FEATURE #3: INTERESTING, READABLE STYLE

We are gratified that over many editions reviewers, instructors, and students have found our writing style praiseworthy. Our primary goal is to reach students by making our explanations of concepts as clear, relevant, and interesting as possible.

## FEATURE #4: LEARNING REINFORCEMENT

We have developed a variety of learning aids to provide learning reinforcement:

- *Chapter previews and outlines:* Each chapter opens with a list of chapter *learning objectives,* a brief *preview* of the chapter's contents, and an introductory section entitled *Why Is This Chapter Important?*

- *Section previews:* Each section heading is followed by a short *preview* of the text to come.

- *Chapter summaries:* Each chapter concludes with a *Summary* section to help students review.

- *Key terms:* All the important terms appearing in a chapter—and the page numbers where they appeared—are presented in a *Key Terms* section at the end of the chapter.

- *Self-tests and exercises: End-of-chapter fill-in-the-blank tests, short-answer exercises,* and *critical thinking questions* enable students to test their comprehension and encourage them to learn more about microcomputers on their own. Starting with Chapter 6, we also include end-of-chapter hands-on exercises called **In the Lab with Microsoft Windows.**

- *"The Clipboard" boxes:* One- and two-page boxes called *The Clipboard* show students how computers are used in some common and uncommon ways in the workplace.

- *Internet cross-references:* Throughout the text in the margins readers will find references to the Instructor's Resource Guide *Internet* appendix, which provides Internet addresses where users can research additional information on topics related to the text.

- *Episodes:* Four *Episodes,* or case studies, appear in the Instructor's Resource Guide to provide students with practical insights into changing over to computer-based information systems.

- *Time-line chart:* The *time-line chart* in the back of the book provides an overview of the historical development of information processing and related events, staring with the beginning of recorded history and projecting into the 21st century.

- *Glossary:* The *glossary* includes not only the book's key terms and their definitions but other important terms that students may encounter.

## FEATURE #5: COMPLETE COURSE SOLUTIONS—SUPPLEMENTS THAT WORK

Computer concepts are only one part of the course experience. Our instructional package also includes **lab tutorials, interactive software, lecture enhancement software, instructor support materials,** and a **software support program.** We elaborate on these below.

### Lab Tutorials

Our publisher, Richard D. Irwin, offers three different series of lab manuals, which present three different hands-on approaches to learning software. An Irwin sales representative can explain the specific software covered in each series.

- *The **Irwin Advantage Series** by Glen Coulthard and Sarah Hutchinson:* Averaging 224 pages per volume, the *Irwin Advantage Series* provides software tutorials for a large number of popular software packages. Each tutorial leads students through step-by-step instructions not only for the most common methods of executing commands but also for alternative methods.

   Each lesson within a volume begins with a case example and concludes with case problems showing the real-world application of the software. Quick-reference guides appear throughout. Boxes introduce unusual functions that will enhance the user's productivity. Exercises allow student practice.

- *The **Erickson & Vonk Series:*** Written specifically for the first-time computer user, the *Erickson & Vonk Series* is based on the premise that success breeds confidence and confident students learn more effectively. Exercises embedded within each lesson allow students to experience success before moving on to a more advanced topic. The "why" as well as the "how" is always carefully explained. Each lesson features several applications projects and a comprehensive problem for student solution.

- *The **ACT Series:*** Standing for *Accelerated Computer Training,* the *ACT Series* consists of manuals originally developed for professional training. The ACT manuals are perfect when lab time is limited and exercises are less important than quick comprehension.

**IMPORTANT NOTE—CUSTOM PUBLISHING:** The contents of these products can be tailored to meet your course needs through **custom publishing**. Titles or specific lessons from several titles in these series can be combined. *Irwin will happily send you an examination copy of the custom-published text you want so you can see exactly what your students will get.* Ask your Irwin sales representative for details.

## Interactive Software

CD-ROM-based software, **InfoTech Interactive,** developed by Irwin New Media, Tony Baxter, and The Human Element, provides students with 16 self-paced learning modules, on topics from mouse basics to security. Combining text, illustrations, and animation, this tool may also be used by instructors for bringing real-time activity into a lecture setting.

InfoTech Interactive includes coverage of:

| | |
|---|---|
| *Mouse Basics* | *Multimedia* |
| *Data Into Information* | *Data Representation* |
| *Application Software* | *Networks* |
| *User Interfaces* | *The Internet* |
| *Processors* | *Querying a Database* |
| *Secondary Storage* | *Client/Server* |
| *Peripheral Devices* | *Encryption/Decryption* |
| *Backing Up Data* | *Security* |

Each module provides three levels of learning: (1) The *introduction level* provides text and animated enhancement of computer concepts. (2) The *exploratory level* allows the user to experiment with various scenarios and see the immediate results. (3) The *practice level* poses cases and problems for which the user must provide solutions.

*System requirements:* (a) IBM PC or compatible with at least 2 MB of RAM running Windows 3.1, or (b) Macintosh with at least 2 MB of RAM running System 6.01 or later; CD-ROM drive.

## Lecture Enhancement Software

The **PowerPoint Presentation Package** is a graphics-intensive set of images created to enhance any lecture. This package, developed by Lewis Hershey, helps to explain topics that may otherwise be difficult to present.

*System requirements:* IBM PC or compatible with at least 2 MB of RAM running Windows 3.1. An LCD panel is needed if the images are to be shown to a large audience.

## Instructor Support Material

We offer the instructor the following other kinds of supplements and support to complement the text:

- ***Instructor's Resource Guide:*** This complete guide, prepared by Linda Behrens, supports instruction in any course environment. The Instructor's Resource Guide includes: *a student questionnaire, course planning and evaluation grid, suggestions for writing course objectives, suggested pace and coverage for courses of various lengths, suggestions for using the exercises in various class structures,* and *projects for small and large classes.*

  For each chapter, the IRG provides an overview, chapter outline, lecture notes, notes regarding the boxes (The Clipboard) from the text, solutions, and suggestions and additional information to enhance the project and critical thinking sections.

- ***Transparencies:*** There are 74 full-color transparency acetates available to the instructor. Transparencies have been specially *upsized*—enlarged and enhanced for clear projection.

- ***Test bank:*** The test bank, prepared by Catherine Keenan, contains 1,500 different questions, all referenced to the text. Specifically, it contains *true/false, multiple-choice,* and *fill-in questions,* categorized by difficulty and by type; *short-essay questions; sample midterm exam; sample final exam;* and *answers to all questions.*

- ***Computerized testing software:*** Called *Computest,* Irwin's popular computerized testing software is a user-friendly, menu-driven, microcomputer-based test-generating system that is free to qualified adopters. Containing all the questions from the test bank described above, Computest's Version 4 allows instructors to customize test sheets, entering their own questions and generating review sheets and answer keys.

  Available for DOS, Windows, and Macintosh formats, Computest has advanced printing features that allow instructors to print all types of graphics; Windows and Macintosh versions use easily remembered icons. All versions support over 250 dot-matrix and laser printers.

  System requirements: (a) IBM PC or compatible with at least 2 MB of RAM running Windows 3.1, or (b) Macintosh with at least 2 MB of RAM running System 6.01 or later; CD-ROM drive or 3.5-inch floppy-disk drives.

- ***Videos:*** A broad selection from 21 videos of the acclaimed PBS television series, *Computer Chronicles,* is available. Each video is approximately 30 minutes long. The videos cover topics ranging from computers and politics, to CD-ROM, to visual programming languages, to the Internet.

- ***Instructor's data disks:*** For instructors whose students are using the tutorials for software education, in the Irwin Advantage Series for Computer Education, instructor's data disks are available. These are floppy disks containing files used in the DOS- and Windows-based software labs. Specifically, the diskettes contain the letters and memos that the student will use in the word processing labs, sample budgets and other files that the students will retrieve and modify in the spreadsheet labs, and the data and reports that the student will work with in the database labs.

- ***Phone and fax instructor support services:*** Richard D. Irwin's College New Media Department offers telephone-linked support services to instructors in matters related to Irwin software, such as Computest and data disks used for the student tutorials in the Irwin Advantage Series. Software support analysts are available to help solve technical questions not covered in the documentation for any Irwin software product.

  Two kinds of support are offered: (1) toll-free telephone numbers, available 9:00 A.M. to 5 P.M. Central, Monday through Friday (except holidays); (2) support-on-demand FAX-BACK service, available 24 hours a day, seven days a week. Both the toll-free and fax numbers appear in the *Instructor's Resource & Lecture Guide.*

## ACKNOWLEDGMENTS

Two names are on the front of the book, but a great many others are powerful contributors to its development.

We are particularly grateful to many people at Richard D. Irwin: Tom Casson, Paul Ducham, and Garrett Glanz in Editorial and Gladys True, Lara Feinberg, Charlene Breedon, and all others in the Production Department who helped us get this book out on time. Cathy Crowe and Burrston House provided invaluable assistance by analyzing manuscript reviews and establishing revision needs. Anita Wagner once again did an excellent copyediting job. As usual, Pat and Michael Rogondino provided excellent design and electronic makeup services. Monica Suder was our invaluable photo researcher, and David Sweet took professional care of permissions fulfillment. GTS Graphics in Los Angeles provided the best prepress services in the business (special thanks go to Donna Machado).

Finally, we appreciate the helpful comments and suggestions provided by the following reviewers:

Nancy Alderdice, Murray State University
David Allen, San Antonio College
James Bode, Manatee Community College
Mark Bowman, Lansing Community College
Tim Gottleber, North Lake College
Ratan Guha, University of Central Florida
Catherine Leach, Henderson State University
Simon Li, Douglas College
Saundra May, Angelina Junior College
Janis Motsinger, Henry Ford Community College
Robert Otto, Western Kentucky University
Cindy Pryke, Commonwealth College
Lew Schmitt, Shasta College
Al Schroeder, Richland College
Wayne Snyder, Boston University
Dianne Vaught, National Business College

Professor Catherine Leach was particularly helpful in providing some of our critical-thinking questions.

*SEH*
*SCS*

# Contents

## Chapter 8  Communications and Connectivity  261

## Chapter 9  Systems Development 309

**Chapter 10    Database Management 347**

# Chapter 14 Purchasing and Maintaining a Microcomputer System 473

# Chapter Topics

# CHAPTER 1

# Overview

*Plug and play*—that's the kind of machine that computer makers ultimately hope to create. With such a device, people could simply take it out of the box, plug it in, and play it, just as we do now with stereos.

However, at present, computers still have features reflecting their technical origins. To use them, we must meet them halfway, just as drivers in the early days of the automobile had to know more about cars than drivers need to know today.

In this chapter we give you a brief overview of what a computer system is by focusing on hardware, software, data/information, procedures, people, and communications. Then we describe some major events in the development of computers, and how you can expect to use computers now and in the future.

## Preview

*When you have completed this chapter, you will be able to:*

- Define who the user is and what it means to be computer literate and computer competent

- Explain what a computer system is by focusing on hardware, software, data/information, procedures, people, and communications

- Describe the five categories of computer hardware: input, processing, storage, output, and communications

- Describe the four main types of computer systems: supercomputers, mainframe computers, minicomputers, and microcomputers

- Describe the main components of a microcomputer system

- Describe some of the major events in the development of computers

- Describe computing trends: connectivity, online access, and interactivity

**Why Is This Chapter Important?**

*The automated teller machine. The supermarket checkout scanner. The library online book-search system. The cheerful but flat-sounding telephone voice system that tells you "Please hang up and dial your call again."*

*These are all special-purpose computer devices. If you did not come into contact with one of these today, no doubt you encountered something similar. Like most people, then, you are already a computer user, interacting directly or indirectly with these devices several times a day. (See Figure 1.1.)*

*We assume you're reading this book, however, because you want to become a true computer user—to become "computer literate" and "computer competent." You want to go beyond pushbuttons and artificial voices and learn to use this technology as a problem-solving tool in your own career. This chapter will start you on your way by giving you a brief overview of computers, computer systems, and data processing. Subsequent chapters will cover these topics in greater detail.*

## Who Is the User?

**There is a difference between a "computer professional" and a general computer user.**

To help you better understand who the computer user is, consider the following distinction:

- A **computer professional** is a person who has had formal education in the technical aspects of using computers. For example, a *computer programmer* designs, writes, tests, and implements the programs that process the data in the computer system.

- The **user** (or **end-user**) is a person perhaps like yourself—someone without much technical knowledge of computers but who uses computers to perform professional or personal tasks, enhance learning, or have fun. The user is not necessarily a computer expert and may never need to become one. Most companies, for example, prefer to train new employees in the specific computer uses applicable to their job—and these applications may never require the user to have much technical knowledge.

As a person living in what is now often called the *Information Age,* you know that computers aren't just a passing fad. Businesses depend on computers. You will use computers in your job as well as in the pursuit of private interests. To use them efficiently, you must become computer literate and computer competent.

## Becoming Computer Literate and Computer Competent

**By learning certain terminology, concepts, and skills, you can become computer literate and computer competent.**

*Computer literacy* is having an understanding of what a computer is and how it can be used as a resource. Literacy, which refers to having knowledge and understanding, needs to be distinguished from competency, which refers to having a skill. *Computer competency* is applying your skill with computers to meet your information needs and improve your productivity.

**Figure 1.1**

Computers in daily life. As these examples show, today it is almost impossible to avoid using a computer: (a) computers scoring a hockey game at the 1994 Olympics, (b) analyzing medical problems, (c) classroom instruction, (d) in a college library, (e) patient monitoring and treatment, (f) portable data collection.

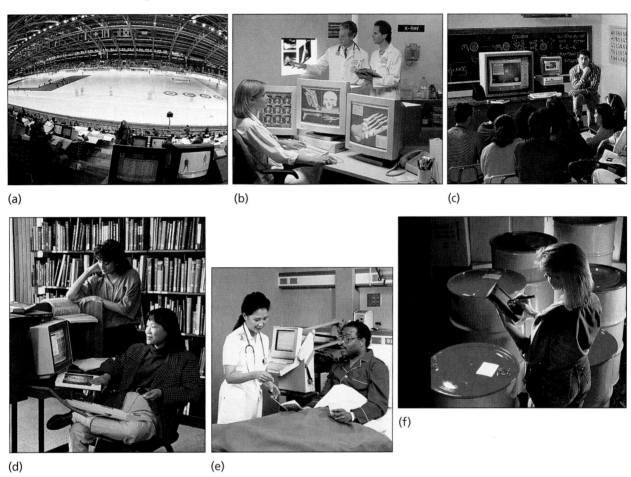

(a)　　　　　　　　　　　　　(b)　　　　　　　　　　　　　(c)

(d)　　　　　　　　　(e)　　　　　　　(f)

To help you become computer literate and computer competent, this textbook and its accompanying computer lab tutorials will help you learn the following:

- *Terms:* You should master the terminology used to describe computers and their operations.

- *Functions:* You should learn the functions of the parts of a computer system.

- *Uses:* You should learn how to use a computer to produce the information or perform the tasks you need done.

## What Is a Computer System?

**A computer system is made up of six parts: hardware, software, data/information, procedures, people, and communications.**

The term **computer** is used to describe a device made up of a combination of electronic and electromechanical (part electronic and part mechanical) components. By itself, a computer has no intelligence and is referred to as **hardware,** which means simply the physical equipment. A computer can't be used until it is connected to other parts of a computer system.

A **computer system** is a combination of six elements (see Figure 1.2):

1. Hardware
2. Software
3. Data/information
4. Procedures
5. People
6. Communications

**Software** is the term used to describe the instructions that tell the hardware how to perform a task. Without software, the hardware is useless.

The purpose of a computer system is to convert data into information. Data can be considered the raw material—whether in paper, electronic, or other form—that is processed by the computer. In other words, **data** consists of the raw facts and figures that are processed into information. **Information** is summarized data or otherwise manipulated (processed) data. Thus, the raw data of employees' hours worked and wage rates is processed by a computer into the information of paychecks and payrolls.

Actually, in ordinary usage, the words *data* and *information* are often used synonymously. After all, one person's information may be another person's data. The "information" of paychecks and payrolls may become "data" that goes into someone's yearly financial projections or tax returns.

**Figure 1.2**
A computer system typically combines six elements: hardware, software, data/information, procedures, people, and communications. Communications is a sixth element when two or more separate computer systems are set up to communicate.

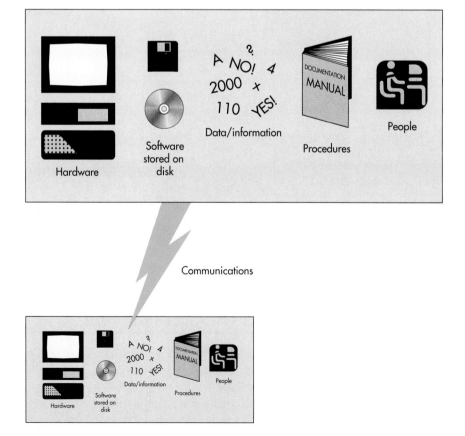

*People,* however, constitute the most important component of the computer system. People operate the computer hardware, and they create the computer software. They also follow certain procedures when using the hardware and software. (See Figure 1.3.) **Procedures** are descriptions of how things are done, steps for accomplishing a result. Procedures for computer systems appear in **documentation manuals,** also known as *reference manuals,* which contain instructions, rules, and guidelines to follow when using hardware and software. When you buy a microcomputer or software package, it comes with one or more documentation manuals.

When one computer system is set up to share data and information electronically with another computer system, **communications** becomes a sixth system element. In other words, the manner in which the various individual systems are connected—for example, by phone lines, microwave transmission, or satellite—is an element of the total computer system.

Now we'll focus on the basics of the first part of the typical computer system—the hardware devices. For now, use the following discussion to gain an overall perspective of computer hardware. Just focus on the large concepts. We provide you with more specific hardware discussions in Chapters 2–5.

## Computer Hardware

Computer hardware can be divided into five categories: (1) input, (2) processing, (3) storage, (4) output, and (5) communications. Common input devices are the keyboard and the mouse. Processing and memory hardware components include the central processing unit (CPU) and main memory (RAM). Storage hardware stores data and information in a relatively permanent form, such

**Figure 1.3**

People and procedures. This computer user—one element in a computer system—is reading an instruction manual, or set of procedures— another element in the system.

as on disk. **Output hardware** provides information printed out on paper (hardcopy) or displayed on a computer screen (softcopy). **Communications hardware,** such as modems, facilitates the connections between individual computers and groups of computers.

### Input Hardware

The function of **input hardware** is to collect data and convert it into a form suitable for computer processing. (See Figure 1.4.) An example of data for input would be sales figures for different musical instruments sold by different sales people in different states.

**Figure 1.4**

The five categories of computer hardware are input, processing, storage, output, and communications.

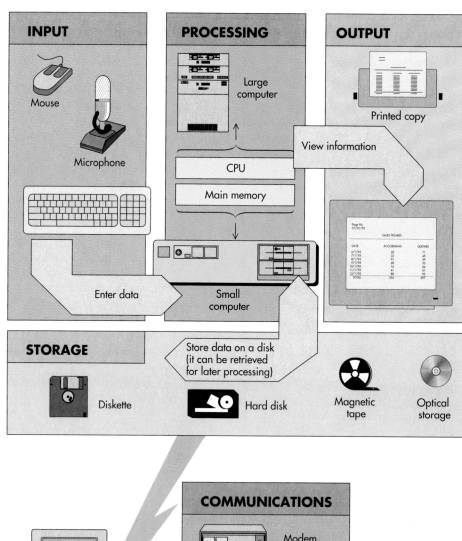

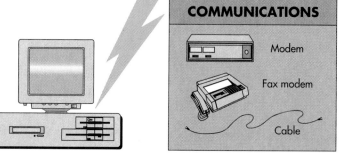

**Figure 1.5**
Keyboard and mouse.
The main computer cabinet,
which holds the processing
circuitry, is the system unit.

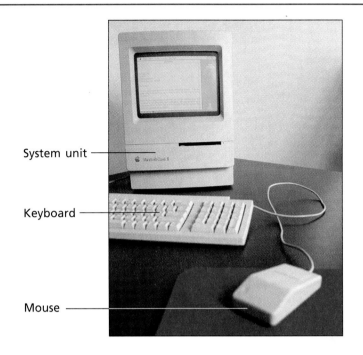

System unit

Keyboard

Mouse

The most common input device is a **keyboard.** It has rows of keys in the typical typewriter layout, as well as a number of additional keys used to enter special computer codes. Another common input device is the **mouse,** which is moved by hand over a flat surface to direct a pointer on the computer's display screen. (See Figure 1.5.) A pointer is a symbol, usually an arrow, on the computer screen that is used to select items from menus or to position the **cursor,** which marks where data may be entered next. In Chapter 2, we describe input devices in detail.

**Processing Hardware**

The function of **processing hardware** is to retrieve and execute (interpret) instructions (software) provided to the computer. Processing may consist of performing calculations and other logical activities, such as comparing sales figures to see which musical instruments or which salespeople have higher sales. The most essential components of processing hardware are the central processing unit and main memory.

The **central processing unit (CPU)** is the brain of the computer. It reads and interprets software and coordinates the processing activities that must take place. The design of the CPU affects the processing power and the speed of the computer, as well as the amount of main memory it can use effectively. The CPU is also referred to as a *processor*.

Main memory can be thought of as an electronic desktop. **Main memory** is also called **random access memory (RAM), internal memory, primary storage,** or just **memory.** All instructions and/or data ready for processing are held in memory. The more desk surface you have in front of you, the more you can place on it. Similarly, the amount of memory available determines whether you can run simple or sophisticated software; a computer with a large memory is capable of holding the thousands of instructions that are contained in more sophisticated software programs. In addition, a lot of memory allows you to work with and manipulate great amounts of data and information at one time. Typically, the more main memory you have in your computer, the more you can accomplish. However, since RAM is **volatile**—that is, all contents are lost when the computer's power is shut off—the data and instructions should be saved to a storage device before the computer is turned off (and to protect data in case of a power outage).

## Storage Hardware

optical disk storage

The function of **storage hardware** is to provide a means of storing software and data in a form that is relatively permanent, or **nonvolatile**—that is, the data is not lost when the power is turned off—and easy to retrieve when needed for processing. Storage hardware serves the same basic functions as do office filing systems except that it stores data as electromagnetic signals or laser-etched spots, commonly on magnetic disk or optical disk storage devices, rather than on paper.

## Output Hardware

The function of **output hardware** is to provide the user with the means to view information produced by the computer system. The jumble of unorganized sales figures now processed into meaningful form is displayed on a computer screen or printed out on paper. We are now able to tell whether guitars outsell accordions and whether Dinah sells more than Ian.

Information is output in either hardcopy or softcopy form. *Hardcopy output* can be held in your hand—an example is paper with text (words or numbers) or graphics printed on it. *Softcopy output* is typically displayed on a monitor, a television-like screen on which you can read text and graphics. Another type of softcopy output is audio output, such as a voice.

## Communications Hardware

The function of **communications hardware** is to facilitate the connections between computers and between groups of connected computers (networks). You would use communications hardware to receive on your computer the guitar sales data from computers located throughout the United States and Canada. You could then use the data to create a summary report. Common communications hardware components are the modem, cable, and fax modem.

Before describing what modems do, we must first explain the terms *digital* and *analog*. **Digital** refers to communications signals or information that is represented in a binary or two-state way. With a two-state on/off, open/closed, present/absent, positive/negative, yes/no arrangement, the "on" state can be coded as a 1 digit, the "off" state as a 0 digit. Computers use digital signals—strings of on and off electrical pulses represented in codes of 1s and 0s—to represent software instructions and data. However, most phenomena of the world are **analog,** representing continuously variable quantities. Sound, light, temperature, and pressure values, for instance, can fall anywhere on a continuum or range. Standard telephone lines are an analog medium—that is, they transmit only analog signals, such as voice messages and "on-hold" music.

### Modems

To convert a computer's digital signals to analog signals, and vice versa, you need a device called a **modem** (pronounced "moh-dem"). A modem allows computers to communicate with each other over telephone lines. (See Figure 1.6.) Many microcomputers come with a modem already built in. Otherwise, for $100 or less you can buy one that you simply plug into the computer and connect to the telephone jack. We describe modems, and digital and analog signals, in greater detail in Chapter 8, Communications and Connectivity.

**Figure 1.6**
The modem shown here is called an *external modem*. Today most modems are installed inside the computer.

### Cable

Computers can communicate directly with each other, via a cable, if the signal doesn't go over the traditional telephone lines. This is common when computers are part of a specially wired small network (a *local area network*) on a college campus, for example.

### Fax Modem

The standard fax machine scans a paper document and converts its image into code for transmission over a telephone line to another fax machine. The receiving fax machine then reconverts the codes and prints out a facsimile (duplicate) of the original.

There is another kind of fax hardware, however, that can be installed inside the computer cabinet. This kind is much quicker and may be ideal for anyone who regularly writes and faxes reports. A fax modem is a modem with a fax capability that enables you to send signals directly from your computer to someone else's fax machine or computer fax modem. That is, you don't have to print out the material before you send it. The fax modem allows you to transmit information much more quickly than if you had to feed it page by page into a fax machine.

Ultimately, it is hoped, such communications devices will free us from the torrent of paper with which most of us do business. Indeed, for years experts have been predicting the arrival of the "paperless office" once electronic communications are fully phased in.

## Computer Software

Computer hardware is useless without electronic instructions—software—that tell it what to do. There are two kinds of software: applications software, which performs general-purpose tasks for users, and systems software, which runs the basic computer operations, manages computer resources, and enables applications software to run on the computer. Software generally comes on disk—purchased "off the shelf" or custom written.

A computer has no intelligence of its own and must be supplied with instructions that tell it what to do and how and when to do it. These instructions are called *software*. The importance of software can't be overestimated. Without software to instruct the computer to do what you want it to do, the computer will only take up space.

Software is made up of a group of related *programs*. In turn, each program is made up of a group of related instructions that perform specific processing tasks. Software acquired to perform a general business function is often referred to as a *software package*. Software is usually created by professional software programmers and comes on disk.

Software can generally be divided into two categories:

1. Systems software
2. Applications software

## Systems Software

Software designed to allow the computer to manage its own resources and run basic operations is called **systems software.** This software runs the basic operations; it tells the hardware what to do and how and when to do it. However, it does not solve specific problems relating to a business or a profession. For example, systems software will not process a prediction of what your company's tax bill will be next year, but it will tell the computer where to store and retrieve the data used during the processing of that tax bill. Systems software will not process the creation of the animation strip for your next film, but it will manage how it is output. Examples of systems software are DOS, Windows, OS/2, Macintosh Operating System, and UNIX. (We describe systems software in greater detail in Chapter 6.)

## Applications Software

**Applications software** is software that can perform tasks. Examples are programs that do word processing, desktop publishing, or payroll processing. (We describe applications software in greater detail in Chapter 6.)

Applications software can be purchased "off the shelf" of a computer store or from a supplier—that is, already programmed—or it can be created, or customized, to order by qualified programmers. If, for example, a company has fairly routine payroll processing requirements, it can probably purchase one or more payroll software packages off the shelf to handle the job. However, if a company has unique payroll requirements, such as a need to handle the records of hourly employees, salaried employees, and commissioned employees, then off-the-shelf software may not be satisfactory. It may be more cost-effective to have the payroll programs customized, or written, to exact specifications by a computer programmer.

Figure 1.7 shows a store where you can buy software. Many of these products are also available through vendors and mail-order sources.

## Types of Computer Systems: What's the Difference?

Computers are classified—according to size and level of power—into supercomputers, mainframe computers, minicomputers, and microcomputers. General users most commonly deal with the microcomputer, which uses a chip as its CPU and has three basic hardware components: keyboard, monitor, and system unit. Monitors can be monochrome or color. The system unit houses the power supply, the system board, and some storage devices.

**Figure 1.7**
The software store.
Software packages are
sold on racks like music
CDs or paperback books.

"Thoreau's Theory of
Adaption: After months
of training and you
finally understand all of
a program's commands,
a revised version of the
program arrives with
an all-new command
structure."

—*Computer Industry
Almanac*

# THE CLIPBOARD

## Computers for College

You may still hear the sounds of late-night typing in a college residence hall. However, it's certainly not the smart way to work anymore. Indeed, coping with a typewriter actually detracts from learning. You're worrying about making mistakes and avoiding retyping a whole paper rather than concentrating on content and educational principles. Using a computer to write your papers not only makes life easier but it also opens up new areas of freedom and knowledge and helps prepare you for the future.

Thus students who come to college with a personal computer as part of their luggage are ahead of the game. If you don't have one, however, there are other options.

### IF YOU DON'T OWN A PERSONAL COMPUTER

If you don't have a PC, you can probably borrow someone else's occasionally. However, if you have a paper due the next day, you may have to defer to the owner, who may also have a dead-line. When borrowing, you need to plan ahead and allow yourself plenty of time.

Virtually every campus now makes computers available to students, either at minimal cost or essentially free as part of the regular student fees. This availability may take two forms:

- *Library or computer labs:* Even students who have their own PCs may sometimes want to use the computers available at the library or campus computer lab. These may have special software or better printers.

- *Dormitory computer centers or dorm-room terminals:* Some campuses provide dormitory-based computer centers (for example, in the basement). More and more campuses are also providing computers or terminals within students' dormitory rooms. These are usually connected by a campuswide local area communications network (LAN) to lab computers and administrative systems. Many also allow students to communicate over phone lines to people in other states.

Of course, the system cannot accommodate a large number of students. All the computers may be in high demand come term-paper time. Clearly, owning a computer offers you convenience and a competitive advantage.

### IF YOU DO OWN A PERSONAL COMPUTER

If you acquired a personal computer before you came to college, it is probably one of three types: (1) an IBM or IBM-compatible such as a Compaq, AST, Radio Shack, Zenith, or Dell; (2) an Apple Macintosh; (3) an Apple II. Is it adequate?

If all you need to do is write term papers, nearly any microcomputer, new or used, will do. Indeed, you may not even need to have a printer, if you can find other ways to print things out. The University of Michigan, for example, offers "express stations," or drive-up windows. These allow students to use diskettes or connect to a printer to print out their papers. Or, if a friend has a computer that is compatible with yours—that is, the same type—you could ask to borrow it and the printer for a short time in order to print out your work.

You should, however, take a look around you to see if your present system is appropriate for your campus and your major.

■ *The fit with your campus:* Some campuses are known as "IBM (or IBM-compatible) schools," others as "Mac (Macintosh) schools." Apple IIs and Commodores are not used much at the college level.

■ Why should choice of machine matter? The answer is that, without special conversion software, diskettes generally still can't be used interchangeably among the three main types of microcomputer. Thus, if you own a system not generally used by your school, you may find it difficult to swap files or print out on its equipment, for example.

■ *The fit with your major:* Speech communications, foreign language, physical education, political science, biology, and English majors probably don't need a fancy computer system. However, business, engineering, architecture, and journalism majors may have special requirements. For instance, an architecture major doing computer-aided design (CAD) projects or a journalism major doing desktop publishing will need a fairly powerful system. A history major who will mainly be writing papers will not. You should check with advisors in the areas in which you wish to major to determine special computer-related requirements.

Computers come in a variety of sizes and shapes and with a variety of processing capabilities. The earliest computers were very large because of the technologies used. However, as technological improvements were made in computer components, the overall size of computers began to shrink—and continues to do so. To provide a basis for comparing their capabilities, computers are generally grouped into four basic categories (see Figure 1.8):

1. Supercomputers
2. Mainframe computers
3. Minicomputers
4. Microcomputers

It's hard to assign a precise definition to each type of computer because definitions can get bogged down in potentially confusing technical jargon. Nevertheless, the following definitions can suffice:

■ A **supercomputer** can handle gigantic amounts of scientific computation. It's maintained in a special room or environment, may be about 50,000

**Figure 1.8**
The principal types of computers. Shown are examples of a (a) supercomputer, (b) mainframe computer, (c) minicomputer (center), and two kinds of microcomputers—(d) a personal computer (PC) and (e) a workstation.

(a)     (b)

(c)     (d)     (e)

times faster than a microcomputer, and may cost as much as $20 million. As a user in business, you probably would not have contact with a supercomputer. However, you might if you worked in the areas of defense and weaponry, weather forecasting, or scientific research; at one of several large universities; or for the National Aeronautics and Space Administration. For example, Gregory and David Chudnovsky broke the world record for pi calculations by using two supercomputers to calculate pi to 480 million decimal places (the printout would be 600 miles long).

■ A **mainframe computer** is a large computer, usually housed in a controlled environment, that can support the processing requirements of hundreds and often thousands of users and computer professionals. It is smaller and less powerful than a supercomputer. It may cost from several hundred thousand dollars up to $10 million. If you go to work for an airline, a bank, a large insurance company, a large accounting company, a large university, or the Social Security Administration, you may have contact—through your individual workstation—with a mainframe computer. However, mainframes are being purchased less frequently now. Instead, new, powerful minicomputer and microcomputer systems—often hooked together in networks—are being used in place of mainframes. (This trend is called *downsizing*.)

■ A **minicomputer,** also known as a *mid-size* or *mid-range computer,* is similar to but smaller and less powerful than a mainframe computer. It can support 2 to about 50 users and computer professionals. Minicomputers and mainframe computers can work much faster than microcomputers and have many more storage locations in main memory. Minicomputers cost from about $10,000 to several hundred thousand dollars. Many small and medium-size companies today use minicomputers, which can fit in the corner of a room or on the floor next to a desk.

■ The **microcomputer** is the type of computer that you will most likely be dealing with as a user. You may already be familiar with the microcomputer, also known as a **personal computer (PC).** Fully functional microcomputers cost between $1,000 and about $20,000. They vary in size from small portables, such as palmtop (handheld) computers, notebook computers, and laptop computers that you can easily carry around, to powerful desktop workstations, such as those used by engineers and scientists. (See Figure 1.9.) A microcomputer is generally used by only one person at a time but can often support more; it uses a *chip* as its CPU. This chip is

**Figure 1.9**
Microcomputers come in various sizes: Desktop models, laptops, notebooks, subnotebooks, and palmtops.

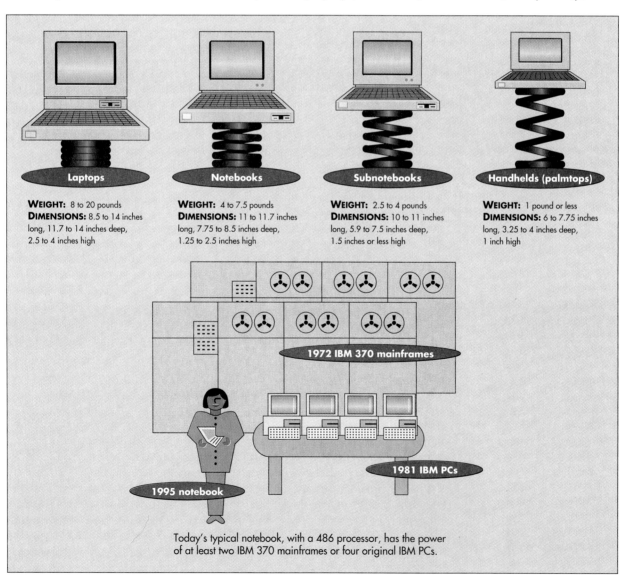

Today's typical notebook, with a 486 processor, has the power of at least two IBM 370 mainframes or four original IBM PCs.

**Figure 1.10**
This photo of a micro-processor gives you an idea of how small a chip is.

referred to as the *microprocessor*. As small as ¼ inch square and ¹⁄₁₀₀ inch thick (see Figure 1.10), a chip is made of silicon, a material made from sand. Silicon is referred to as a *semiconductor* because it sometimes conducts electricity and sometimes does not.

It's difficult to say exactly what kind of computer you'll be using in the business or professional environment. Some companies use a combination of computers. For instance, a company with branch offices around the country might use a mainframe computer to manage companywide customer data. To access information from the mainframe, the user might use a microcomputer that sits on his or her desktop. In addition to accessing information from the mainframe computer, the microcomputer can be used to perform specialized tasks such as generating invoices or drafting letters to customers. Although it is still relatively easy to find a company that doesn't use a supercomputer, a mainframe, or a minicomputer to process data, it is difficult to locate a company that doesn't use microcomputers for some of its processing. Because microcomputers are generally versatile, increasingly powerful, and more affordable than the other types of computers, they provide a practical tool for the organization that wants to computerize or improve the efficiency and flexibility of an existing computer system.

Chances are that, when you enter the business or professional environment, you will be required to know how to use a microcomputer to perform many of your responsibilities. In the following section, we concentrate a bit more on microcomputer components. (*Note:* We describe different types of computer systems in more detail in Chapter 3.)

## The Anatomy of a Microcomputer

To understand the tremendous role microcomputers now play in business and the professions, it's helpful to look at how that role has developed. With the introduction of the Apple II and the Radio Shack Model I and II systems in the late 1970s, the business community began to adopt microcomputers. Then a number of additional vendors, including Atari, Commodore, Osborne, and Kaypro, entered the marketplace with computers designed to be used in the office or in the home. The interest in microcomputers grew rather slowly at first for several reasons: (1) The initial cost for some microcomputer systems was quite high, ranging up to $6,000; (2) only a limited amount of applications software was commercially available; (3) the average person did not have sufficient background in computer-related subjects to use the computer without difficulty; and (4) there were no industrywide standards to ensure the *compatibility*—that is, the common usability—of data and software on different types of microcomputer systems.

However, when IBM introduced the IBM PC in 1981, so many businesses adopted the product that an industry standard was set. Most vendors now design their products to be compatible with this standard; these products are referred to as IBM *clones*. The only relatively successful microcomputer product line today that has maintained a different standard is the Apple Macintosh. To bridge the gap between IBM computers and Apple computers, the new PowerPC line of computers was designed to support both the IBM and Apple standards.

The large number of competing microcomputer systems in the marketplace makes it difficult to select one best system. As a result, our discussion of the microcomputer will center on the three basic hardware components found in most desktop microcomputer systems (see Figure 1.11):

1. The keyboard
2. The monitor
3. The system unit

**Figure 1.11**
(a) This illustration shows the basic parts of the microcomputer's system unit. (b) If the system unit is built to stand vertically, it is called a *tower unit*.

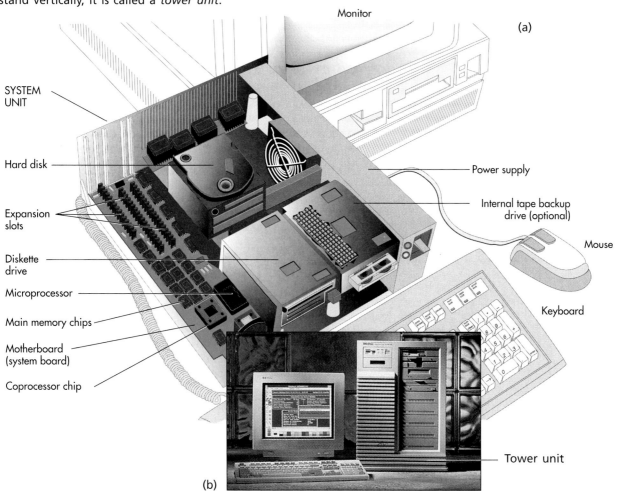

# THE CLIPBOARD

## The High-Tech House

The rapid growth of increasingly powerful microcontrollers and microprocessors coupled with the acceptance and integration of computers into our homes and offices are triggering both an evolution and revolution in the way we interact with our homes. No longer considered an expensive toy, your PC is the key to a futuristic doorway that promises to link household appliances such as televisions and dishwashers, thermostats and microwaves, and telephones and lighting systems into one big happy electronic family capable of digitally chatting with each other.

This "future" is closer than you think. Just about every coffee machine, microwave, fax machine, TV, dishwasher, VCR, thermostat, dryer, clock radio, exercise machine, and car has a tiny computer chip controlling their specific functions. Missing is a command center—such as a PC—to make each unit "smarter" and interconnect them all.

Industry analysts predict that new and retrofitted intelligent home systems will reach a market penetration level of 12% to 15% of houses by the year 2000, exceeding $6 billion. Already on board are such industry giants as Microsoft, Hewlett-Packard, Motorola, Bell-Atlantic, Time-Warner, NEC, Mitsubishi, Sharp, Toshiba, Xerox, Intel, and Texas Instruments. The stage is set for a new generation of programmable household systems. . . .

[An example] on the grand scale is the trademarked Smart House, a complete home automation system from Smart House Limited Partnership and developed by the National Association of Home Builders (NAHB).

The NAHB has been demonstrating the Smart House system, which took about a decade and $40 million to develop, in prototype model homes across the country, including Texas, California, and Florida. The Smart House system is similar to installing a local-area network inside your house. The built-in proprietary whole-house system consists of integrating telephone, power, and audio-visual items using a touch-tone phone, remote control units, and a keypad or personal computer. Price depends on features, and ranges from $5,000 to $25,000.

Michael Cahlin, "The High-Tech House," *PC Novice*, March 1995, pp. 78–81

### Keyboard

The microcomputer input device that you will use the most—the keyboard—is made up of a circuit board and related electronic components that generate a unique electronic code when each key is pressed. The code is passed along the keyboard cord to the computer system unit, where it is translated into a usable form for processing. The number of keys and their positions on the keyboard vary among machines. You should select a keyboard that is comfortable for you to use. (A mouse is also frequently used to input data.)

### Monitor

The term **monitor** is used interchangeably with *screen, video display screen,* and *cathode-ray tube (CRT)*. This output device provides your principal visual contact with the microcomputer system. When you enter commands or data from the keyboard, you see the results on the monitor. A *monochrome monitor* displays text and, in some cases, graphics in a single color—commonly green or amber—usually on a dark background, or in black and white. A *color monitor* can display text and graphics in various colors.

### System Unit

The main computer system cabinet, called the **system unit,** usually houses the power supply, the system board, and the storage devices (although some storage devices—disk drives, for example—are often housed in cabinets outside the system unit). These elements can be defined as follows:

motherboard

1.  The *power supply* provides electrical power to all components housed in the system unit. In some microcomputers—such as older Macintoshes—it also provides power to the monitor.

2.  The **system board,** also known as the **motherboard** or the *logic board,* is the main circuit board of the microcomputer system. It normally includes:

    — The microprocessor chip (or CPU)

    — Main memory chips (RAM)

    — All related support circuitry

    — The expansion slots where additional components can be plugged in

3.  The *storage devices* are usually one or more diskette drives and usually a high-capacity hard disk drive. (A "drive" is the equipment that encloses the disk and runs it.) A **diskette,** or **floppy disk,** is a thin plastic disk enclosed in a paper or plastic covering that can be magnetically encoded with data. **Hard disks** are rigid disks capable of storing much more data than a diskette. (And hard disk drives access data faster than do diskette drives.) Hard disks are more expensive than diskettes. Since most hard disks are permanently installed in the system unit, diskettes, which can be carried around, are often used to move data from one computer to another. (Other types of storage devices such as backup tape drives and optical disk drives may also be installed in the system unit; we discuss these in detail later.)

4.  *Additional components:* The expansion slots on the system board allow users to add new components and to customize their computer systems. The most frequently used add-on components include:

    — A memory card containing main memory chips that give the user additional main memory

    — An internal modem to facilitate data communications between computers over phone lines and similar cables

    — Additional printer ports (socket-like hook-ups) that allow the computer to communicate with several types of output devices

    — Specialized processing chips—called *coprocessors*—that support (assist) the microprocessor chip

    — A video display board (card) that enables the user to improve the display capacity of the monitor

    — A sound board that enables the user to record and play audio data, such as music

Don't worry about remembering what all these components are right now. They will be explained in detail later in the book. This overview of a computer system and its hardware components is just meant to get you started.

Now we present a brief overview of the history of computer processing so that you may better understand the nature of information technology and the information explosion.

## Advances Toward the Paper-Free Workplace

Recently the Aetna Life & Casualty Co. in Hartford, Connecticut, donated 10,000 three-ring binders to schools around the country in a small gesture of charity.

Aetna didn't over-order or buy the binders with largesse in mind. It made them obsolete in one of the largest-scale successes to date in the push toward the paperless office.

The paper-free workplace has been one of the great unfulfilled promises of the information age. It will probably never come. But intracompany computer networking and new software are finally beginning to staunch the document deluge that swamps many offices.

Aetna says it is saving at least $6 million a year by creating insurance manuals and other texts that exist only in computers. For example, Aetna saves $2000 a month in storage costs for extra manuals and binders; recently it also avoided distributing 100 million pages of addenda and updates at a cost of 4.5 cents a sheet. . . .

Some companies scan and store all customer orders and correspondence electronically. But the biggest successful conversions from paper are internal—such as replacing memos with electronic mail while retaining paper for letters and other essential outside communication.

"Paper in a service business is like cholesterol in the blood stream," says John Loewenberg, who heads information services for Aetna. "Good paper is what you need to communicate with others—claims checks and premium notices. Bad paper is the internal stuff that clogs up the arteries."

William M. Bulkeley, "Advances in Networking and Software Push Firms Closer to Paperless Office," *The Wall Street Journal,* August 5, 1993, p. B1.

## Milestones in Computer Development

People have been processing data and information in some form since prehistoric times. However, it was the development of the computer that recently revolutionized information processing. Since the first generation of computers were built, the subsequent three computer generations have produced smaller, more powerful, and less expensive machines—mostly as the result of the development of the integrated circuit.

In this section, we go back almost 5,000 years to show the tremendous effect that computers have had on data processing in general, which in turn has profoundly affected the society of which you are a part.

### Data Processing Before Computers

To record and communicate data and information, prehistoric cave dwellers painted pictures on the walls of their caves, and the ancient Egyptians wrote on a crude form of paper called *papyrus*. Around 3000 B.C., the Sumerians created a device for representing numbers that consisted of a box containing stones. About 2,000 years later, in 1000 B.C., the Chinese took that idea one step further when they strung stones on threads in a wooden frame. The

Chinese device was named after their word for box, *baccus*. The *abacus*, as we know it, remains in wide use and is still considered a powerful tool for performing mathematical computations.

Over the centuries, people have developed an amazing variety of data processing tools and techniques. Some of the most notable tools in use between the mid-1600s and the early 1900s are described in Figure 1.12.

## The Evolution of Computers

The first large-scale electronic computer, the Electronic Numerical Integrator and Computer (ENIAC), became operational in 1946. (See Figure 1.13, p. 22.) It contained approximately 18,000 electronic vacuum tubes—the size of light bulbs—that controlled the flow of electric current. The ENIAC, which weighed 30 tons and occupied about 1,500 square feet of floor space—a huge machine by today's standards—was able to perform a scientific calculation involving the multiplication of four numbers in approximately 9 milliseconds (9/1,000 of a second). Since that time, the technology used in the design and production of computers has accelerated at a remarkable pace.

Since the days of ENIAC, computers have developed in three directions:

- Smaller size
- More power
- Less expense

The term *computer generation* was applied to different types of computers to help identify the major technological developments in hardware and software. To date, computer technology has evolved through four generations.

### First Generation (1944–1958)

In the earliest general-purpose computers, most input and output media were punched cards and magnetic tape. Main memory was almost exclusively made up of hundreds of vacuum tubes—although one computer used a magnetic drum for main memory. These computers were somewhat unreliable because the vacuum tubes failed frequently. They were also slower than any microcomputer used today, produced a tremendous amount of heat, and were very large. They could run only one program at a time. ENIAC and UNIVAC I—the UNIVersal Automatic Computer, which was used by the U.S. Bureau of the Census from 1951 to 1963—are examples of first-generation computers. The UNIVAC was priced at $500,000 in 1950; today, you could purchase the same processing power for under $100.

# Computer Technology

| 3000 BC | | 200 BC |
|---|---|---|
| Abacus, used for arithmetic calculations, developed in Orient | | Chinese artisans develop an entire mechanical orchestra |

**Figure 1.12**
Which came first—computers or data processing? Many people think that we have been turning data into information only since computers came into use. The truth is that people have been processing data since prehistoric times. This illustration shows a few of the data processing methods used between the mid-1600s and the early 1900s. (a) Pascaline calculator (mid-1600s), the first automatic adding and subtracting machine; (b) Leibniz Wheel (early 1700s), the first general-purpose calculating machine; (c) Jacquard loom (1801), run by punched cards; (d) Thomas's arithnometer (1860), the first commercially successful adding and subtracting machine; (e) Hollerith's tabulating machine, used in the 1890 U.S. census; and (f) early IBM calculating machine (circa 1930).

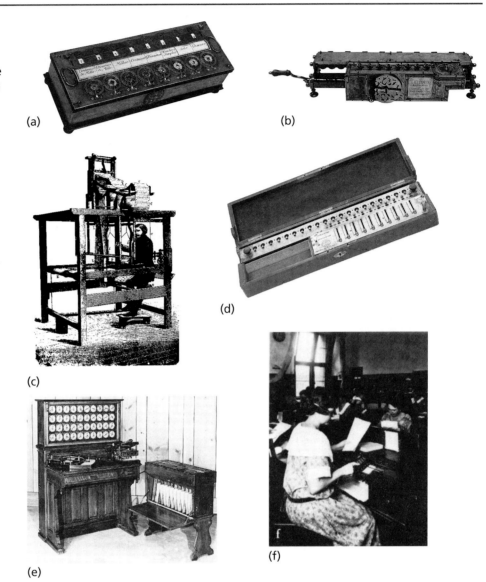

(a)

(b)

(c)

(d)

(e)

(f)

| 1642 AD | 1832 | 1843 |
|---|---|---|
| First automatic adding machine (Blaise Pascal) | Babbage's analytical engine (first "computer") | World's first computer programmer, Ada Lovelace, publishes her notes |

**Figure 1.13**
ENIAC. The first large-scale electronic computer. ENIAC weighed 30 tons, filled 1,500 square feet, included 18,000 vacuum tubes—and it failed about every 7 minutes.

Software was written using *machine language* or *assembly language*. Machine language contained instructions composed of a series of 1s and 0s; obviously this language was very cumbersome to use. In the 1950s, assembly language became the preferred programming language because programmers could write instructions in a kind of shorthand. Assembly language instructions were then converted, or compiled, into machine language before being used as software.

**Second Generation (1959–1963)**

By the early 1960s, transistors and some other solid-state devices that were much smaller than vacuum tubes were being used for much of the computer circuitry. (A transistor is an electronic switch that alternately allows or does not allow electronic signals to pass.) Magnetic cores, which looked like very small metal washers strung together by wires that carried electricity, became the most widely used type of main memory. Removable magnetic disk packs, stacks of disks connected by a common spindle (like a stack of records), were introduced as storage devices. Second-generation machines tended to be smaller, more reliable, and significantly faster than first-generation computers.

## Computer Technology (cont.)

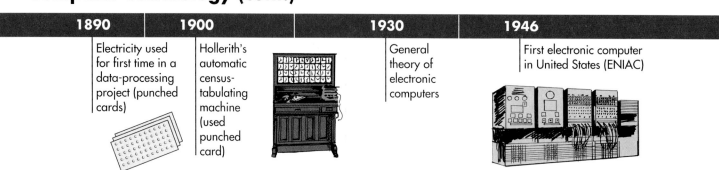

| 1890 | 1900 | 1930 | 1946 |
|---|---|---|---|
| Electricity used for first time in a data-processing project (punched cards) | Hollerith's automatic census-tabulating machine (used punched card) | General theory of electronic computers | First electronic computer in United States (ENIAC) |

### Third Generation (1964–1970)

In the third period, the **integrated circuit**—a complete electronic circuit that packages transistors and other electronic components on a small silicon chip—replaced traditional transistorized circuitry.

The use of magnetic disks for data storage became widespread, and computers began to support such capabilities as multiprogramming (processing several programs simultaneously) and timesharing (people using the same computer simultaneously). Minicomputers, priced around $18,000, were being widely used by the early 1970s and were taking some of the business away from the established mainframe market. Processing that formerly required the processing power of a mainframe could now be done on a minicomputer.

### Fourth Generation (1971–Now)

**H**

Intel

Large-Scale Integrated (LSI) and Very-Large-Scale Integrated (VLSI) circuits were developed that contained hundreds to millions of transistors on a tiny chip. Also, in 1971, Ted Hoff, from a company in the Silicon Valley named Intel, developed the *microprocessor,* which packaged an entire CPU—complete with memory, logic, and control circuits—on a single chip. The microprocessor and VLSI circuit technology helped to fuel today's trend towards *miniaturization* (smaller and smaller computers).

Also during this time, computers' main memory capacity increased, which directly affected the types and usefulness of software that could be used. Software applications like WordPerfect (word processing), Lotus (electronic spreadsheet), and dBASE (database management) became commercially available, giving more people a reason to use a computer.

## What Does All This Mean to the User?

To date, the net effect of the tremendous increase in processing power provided by the computer is that more data can be processed faster than ever before. This means that all the information you need to make decisions is quickly available.

The catch to all this, however, is that the power of the computer has grown so much that it can often generate more information than people can effectively deal with at one time. Indeed, in this society, knowledge is the primary resource for individuals and for the economy overall. As a result, we must be selective about the type of data and information we process. It must be concise, relevant, and accurate so that we avoid getting buried under an avalanche of unnecessary information. And we need to start thinking about the difference between data and information we *really* need and what we

| 1952 | 1964 | 1970 | 1971 | 1977 |
|---|---|---|---|---|
| UNIVAC computer correctly predicts election of Eisenhower as U.S. President | IBM introduces 360 line of computers | Microprocessor chips come into use; floppy disk introduced for storing data | First pocket calculator | Apple II computer (first personal computer sold in assembled form) |

*think* we need—especially in our professional lives. Being bogged down in a swamp of unnecessary details and inaccurate information is frustrating and time-consuming. The problem of being overloaded with information is being discussed more and more in business and computer publications.

Fortunately, thanks to the science of **ergonomics** (also called *human engineering*), which designs things to be used easily by people, the convenience of computer use has improved over the years. Many people have been afraid of computers, but great strides have been made in transforming the computer into a friendly, familiar tool. Input devices have become easier to use, and software is easier to understand than ever before.

In the next sections, we describe the trends in the computer industry that will affect users now and in the future.

## Computing Trends: Connectivity, Online Access and Interactivity

**Three trends in computers and communications technology are connectivity, online information access, and interactivity.** *Connectivity* **is the ability to connect computers and other information devices to each other by communications lines. Connectivity provides the benefits of telecommuting, teleshopping, and e-mail and voice mail.** *Online* **refers to being connected by modem or network to other computers. Being online provides users with access to databases, online services and networks, and electronic bulletin board systems.** *Interactivity* **refers to the ability to respond to and affect a computer or communications device. Interactive devices include multimedia computers, TV/PC "smart boxes" and set-top boxes, and personal digital assistants (PDAs).**

Lee Taylor is what is known as a "lone eagle." Once he was the manager of several technical writers for a California information services company. Then, taking a one-third pay cut, he moved with his wife to a tiny cabin near the ski-resort town of Telluride, Colorado. There he operates as a freelance consultant for his old company, using a phone, computer network, and fax machine to stay in touch.[1]

"Lone eagles" like Taylor constitute a growing number of professionals who, with information technology, can work almost anywhere they want. Many operate out of resort areas and backwoods towns. Although their income may be less, it is offset by such "quality of life" advantages as weekday skiing or reduced housing costs.

## Computer Technology (cont.)

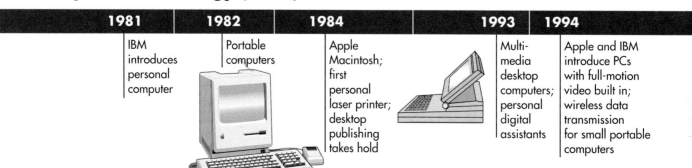

| 1981 | 1982 | 1984 | 1993 | 1994 |
|---|---|---|---|---|
| IBM introduces personal computer | Portable computers | Apple Macintosh; first personal laser printer; desktop publishing takes hold | Multimedia desktop computers; personal digital assistants | Apple and IBM introduce PCs with full-motion video built in; wireless data transmission for small portable computers |

Taylor is one beneficiary of several trends that will probably intensify as information technology continues to proliferate. These trends are:

■ Connectivity

■ Online information access

■ Interactivity

## Connectivity: The Examples of Telecommuting, Teleshopping, and E-Mail and Voice Mail

As we've just seen, small communications, or telecommunications, networks may be connected to larger ones. This is called **connectivity,** the ability to connect computers and telephones by telecommunications lines to other devices and sources of information. It is this connectivity that is the foundation of the Information Age.

The connectivity of telecommunications has made possible many kinds of activities, among them telecommuting, teleshopping, and electronic and voice mail. Here we discuss these topics only briefly; they are covered in detail in Chapter 8.

**H**

telecommuting

■ *Telecommuting:* In standard commuting, one takes transportation (car, bus, train) from home to work and back. In *telecommuting,* one works at home and communicates with ("commutes to") the office by phone, fax, and computer. Already an estimated 8.3 million people telecommute at least part of the time. (See Figure 1.14.)

Telecommuters may be full-time employees—insurance claims processors, typesetters, travel agents—who work at home and seldom go in to the company's main office. Or they may work at home some days and make the trek to the office on others.

Consultants or freelancers like Lee Taylor resemble these kinds of telecommuters. The difference is that, instead of being tied to headquarters by high technology, they are headquarters. That is, they run their own businesses from wherever they want and "telecommute" with clients and suppliers by telephone, fax, and computer.

■ *Teleshopping:* You may already be familiar with some of the cable-TV shop-at-home services such as QVC and Home Shopping Network. These services exist mainly to sell products at prices discounted from those normally found in retail stores. Merchandise such as jewelry or appliances is displayed on your TV screen, along with the price and a toll-free 800 number. You may call the phone number and order the merchandise charged to your credit card. It is then delivered to you a few days later by a package-delivery system.

Teleshopping is the computer version of the same thing. With *teleshopping,* microcomputer users dial into a telephone-linked computer-based

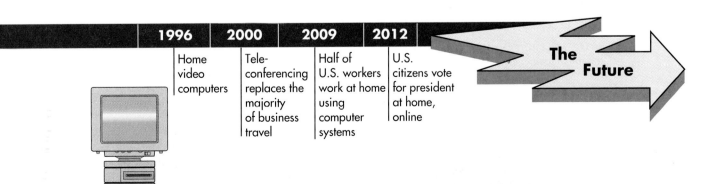

| 1996 | 2000 | 2009 | 2012 | |
|---|---|---|---|---|
| Home video computers | Tele-conferencing replaces the majority of business travel | Half of U.S. workers work at home using computer systems | U.S. citizens vote for president at home, online | **The Future** |

**Figure 1.14**

Telecommuting. The number of employees who telecommute—use computer and phone technology to work from home—for at least part of their working time has greatly increased. Telluride, Colorado, has become a testing site for telecommuting and other new communications ideas.

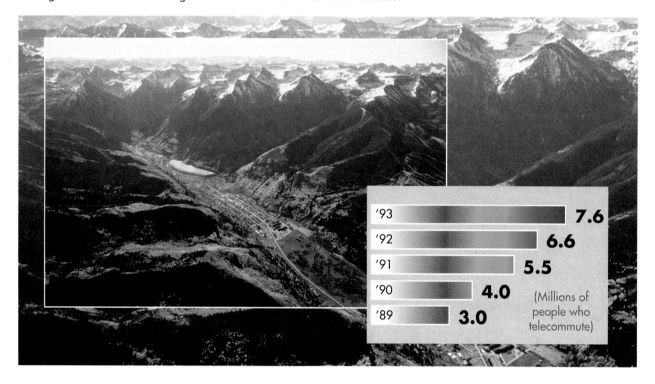

'93   **7.6**
'92   **6.6**
'91   **5.5**
'90   **4.0**
'89   **3.0**

(Millions of people who telecommute)

shopping service that lists prices and descriptions of products, which may be ordered through the computer.

- *E-mail and voice mail: E-mail,* or *electronic mail,* is a system that links computers by wired or wireless connections. It allows users, through their keyboards, to post messages and to read responses on their computer screens. Whether the network is a company's small local area network or a worldwide network, e-mail allows users to send messages anywhere on the system.

  An alternative system is voice mail. *Voice mail* acts like a telephone answering machine; incoming voice messages are digitized and stored for your retrieval later. Retrieval is accomplished by dialing into your "mailbox" number from any telephone. The advantage over answering machines is that you don't have to worry about the machine running out of message tape or not functioning properly.

### Online Information Access: The Examples of Databases, Online Services and Networks, and BBSs

The term **online,** or *on-line* (with a hyphen), refers to being connected via modem or network to other computers. That is, you are "on the line" with them. Online connections usually are of the wired kind but rapidly are becoming wireless also.

Being online gives you access to resources far beyond those available with a computer sitting by itself unconnected to anything else. The word *access* means the ability to connect to a particular database, network, online service, or electronic bulletin board system (BBS). Being able to access modern information systems can significantly enhance your professional abilities.

■ *Databases:* A database may be a large collection of data located within your own unconnected microcomputer. Here, however, we are concerned with databases located elsewhere. These are libraries of information at the other end of a wired or wireless connection and available to you through your microcomputer. A **database** is a collection of integrated, or cross-referenced, data, which different people may access to use for different purposes.

    For example, suppose that a company offered you a job, but you didn't know much about it. To find out about your prospective employer, you could go online to gain access to some helpful databases. Examples are Business Database Plus, Magazine Database Plus, or TRW Business Profiles (all available through the online service CompuServe). You could then study the company's products, review financial data, identify major competitors, or learn about recent sales increases or layoffs. You might even get an idea of whether or not you would be happy with the "corporate culture."[2]

■ *Computer online services and networks:* Established major commercial online services include America Online, CompuServe, Delphi, GEnie, and Prodigy. A **computer online service** is a commercial information service that, for a fee, makes available to subscribers various services through their telephone-linked microcomputers.

    Among other things, consumers can research information in databases, make airline reservations, or send messages through e-mail to others using the service.

    Through a computer online service you may also gain access to the greatest network of all, the Internet. The *Internet* is a network of approximately 11,000 local and regional computer networks that link computers at academic, industrial, and scientific institutions. Internet members are found in more than 200 countries.

■ *Electronic bulletin board systems:* An electronic *bulletin board system (BBS)* is a centralized information source and message-switching system for a particular computer-linked interest group. For example, there are BBSs on such varying subjects as fly-fishing, clean air, ecology, genealogy, San Diego entertainment, Cleveland city information, and adult chat.

**H**
BBSs

    BBSs have become wildly popular. For instance, the San Francisco Bay Area alone has more than 300 BBSs. One called The WELL (for Whole Earth 'Lectronic Link) has 7,000 subscribers, half outside the Bay Area. The WELL offers several "conferences," or special-interest categories. The Homeowner's conference alone features 147 topics. (Sample subjects: Country Living vs. City Living, 220-Volt Wiring, Favorite Home Products.)[3]

### Interactivity: The Examples of Multimedia Computers, TV/PC "Smart Boxes," and Personal Digital Assistants

The movie rolls on your TV/PC screen. The actors appear. Instead of passively watching the plot unfold, however, you are able to determine different plot developments by pressing keys on your keyboard.

    This is an example of interactivity, one of the hottest features of the new technology. **Interactivity** means that the user is able to make an immediate response to what is going on and modify the processes. That is, there is a dialog between the user and the computer or communications device. Video games, for example, are interactive. Interactivity allows users to be active rather than passive participants in the technological process.

    Among the types of interactive devices are multimedia computers, PC/TV "smart boxes" and set-top boxes, and personal digital assistants.

■ *Multimedia computers:* The word *multimedia* has been variously defined. Essentially, however, *multimedia* refers to technology that presents information in more than one medium, including text, graphics, animation, video, music, and voice. "Multimedia" has become one of the hot buzzwords of the '90s.

Multimedia personal computers are fairly powerful microcomputers that include sound capability, run CD-ROM disks, and allow playing games or performing interactive tasks. The first, the MPC (for Multimedia Personal Computer), was unveiled in 1991 by Tandy and Microsoft.

■ *TV/PC "smart boxes" and set-top boxes:* Already envisioning a world of crossbreeding among televisions, telephones, and computers, enterprising manufacturers are bringing to market various forerunners of TV/PC "smart boxes." (See Figure 1.15.) A *TV/PC* is a device that combines the television and the personal computer.

Perhaps a leading indicator is the Interactive Multiplayer, designed by 3DO and made by Panasonic. This computer, which plays CDs and offers high-quality graphics on the screen, is promoted as a central commander for home entertainment centers. Eventually, marketers hope, people will use such devices to listen to CDs, watch movies, do computing, and browse multiple cable channels. Smart boxes would provide two-way interactivity not only with video games but also with entertainment, news, and educational programs.

Gadgets that would perform similar functions are set-top control boxes for cable television offered by General Instrument and by Time Warner Cable.

■ *Personal digital assistants:* In 1988, handheld electronic organizers were introduced, which consisted of tiny keypads and barely readable screens. They were unable to do much more than store phone numbers and daily "to do" lists.

---

**Figure 1.15**

The TV/PC. Microsoft founder and chairman William Gates has called the device that fuses the television (TV) and the personal computer (PC) a "TV/PC." The Apple Computer device, called a *Macintosh TV,* represents one of the initial attempts. It features a television set with keyboard and built-in stereo speakers that accepts CD-ROM computer disks and plays music CDs. It can run word processing and other serious computer programs but can also tune in to television shows.

The device we're talking about here has all the benefits of a TV. It is fairly inexpensive; you can stick it in your living room and use a little remote control to control it. But inside are chips that are even more powerful than today's PCs. And if you add a keyboard or printer you can do PC-like things. So it's a device that needs a new name. If I say it's a PC, people will say "Oh, that's for a limited set of people—too hard to use." If I say TV, people will think it's just a passive device that doesn't let you store your preferences or take your pictures and send them up so they can be stored or mailed around to other people. . . . We call it the TV/PC. I'm sure there will be better names that come along.

—William Gates, chairman of Microsoft Corp., interviewed by Richard M. Smith, "Bill's Excellent Future," *Newsweek,* October 11, 1993, p. 43.

**H**

PDAs

In 1993, electronic organizers began to be supplanted by personal digital assistants. *Personal digital assistants (PDAs)* are small pen-controlled, handheld computers that, in their most developed form, can do two-way wireless messaging. Instead of pecking at a tiny keyboard, you can use a special pen to write out commands on the computer screen. PDAs can be used to send and receive faxes and e-mail, to write memos, and to keep an appointment calendar. (See Figure 1.16.)

The earliest version of the PDA was Apple's Newton. The Newton was criticized—probably unfairly—for being unable to quickly translate handwritten scrawls into typed text. Since then, BellSouth and IBM have introduced the PDA known as Simon.

Now that we've given you an overview of computer systems from large to small and past to present, in Chapter 2 we will focus on the first category of hardware, input hardware.

## Suggestions for Further Reading

*Electronic Computer Glossary.* 5521 State Park Road, Point Pleasant, PA 18950: The ComputerLanguage Company. (215) 297-5999. Offers several software versions of a dictionary-encyclopedia on a disk with more than 5,000 definitions of computer terms and phrases. Current price about $30 plus shipping, or about $40 for the disk and the book plus shipping.

Freedman, A. *The Computer Glossary: The Complete Illustrated Desk Reference* (6th ed.). New York: AMACOM, 1993. Defines more than 4,300 words; also provides background on technology breakthroughs, history, and important people and companies.

Walter, R. *The Secret Guide to Computers* (20th ed., 1995). Russ Walter, 22 Ashland Street #2, Somerville, MA 02144-3202. (617) 666-2666. Hailed by reviewers, librarians, and computer clubs, this is an extraordinarily good book for beginners.

*PC Novice.* P.O. Box 85380, Lincoln, NE 68501-9807. (800) 848-4600. Subtitled "Personal Computers in Plain English," this magazine provides excellent introductory articles on all subjects related to personal computing; $24 a year.

**Figure 1.16**

The personal digital assistant (PDA). *Left:* The Apple Newton. *Right:* Simon, offered by BellSouth and IBM, a handheld wireless computer that can send and receive phone calls and electronic mail. Simon can also store the user's handwriting, although (unlike Newton) it merely replicates the appearance of the scribbling rather than tries to turn the handwriting into typed text.

Ultimately, the PDA holds out the promise of "any-where, anytime" access to the staff, on-line data and computers back at the office. Experts have a favorite example: As you wait at the airport, your pocket gizmo emits an electronic chirp. You answer, and an assistant says your flight is canceled. You punch a few buttons on the "touch screen," scroll through other flights, press a key to reserve tickets and charge them, and zap an electronic-mail message about the delay to the person you are meeting. The device updates the change in your calendar back at the office, as you check voice mail, call up morning stock quotes and, what the heck, rip out the heart of a bad guy in the video game Mortal Kombat while waiting for the next takeoff.

—Dennis Kneale, "IBM, BellSouth Team Up to Sell 'Simon,'" *The Wall Street Journal,* October 29, 1993, p. B1

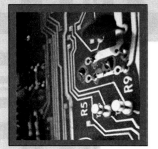

# S U M M A R Y

■ A *computer professional* is a person in a profession involving computers who has had formal education in the technical aspects of using computers; examples are computer programmer, systems analyst, and network administrator. (p. 2)

■ A *user* is someone without much technical knowledge of computers but who uses computers to produce information for professional or personal tasks, enhance learning, or have fun. (p. 2)

■ People in business and the professions generally must be computer literate or computer competent. *Computer literacy* is having an understanding of what a computer is and how it can be used as a resource. *Computer competency* is applying some skill using a computer to meet your information needs and improve your productivity. (p. 2)

■ A computer must be part of a system to be useful. A computer system has six parts (p. 4):

1. Hardware
2. Software
3. Data/information
4. Procedures
5. People
6. Communications

■ *Hardware* comprises the electronic and the electromechanical parts of the computer system. (p. 4)

■ *Software* is the term for electronic instructions that tell the hardware how to perform a task. (p. 4)

■ *Data* consists of the raw facts and figures that are processed into information. *Information* is summarized data or otherwise manipulated (processed) data. (p. 4)

■ *Procedures* are descriptions of how things are done, steps for accomplishing a result. Procedures for computer systems appear in *documentation manuals,* which contain the guidelines for using the hardware and software. (p. 5)

■ *People*—the most important part of the computer system—design and develop computer systems, operate the computer hardware, create the software, and establish procedures for carrying out tasks. (p. 5)

■ *Communications* becomes an element of the computer system when one computer system is set up to share data and information electronically with another computer system. (p. 5)

■ *Digital* refers to communications signals or information that is represented in a binary or two-state way. With a two-state on/off, open/closed, present/absent, positive/negative, yes/no arrangement, the "on" state can be coded as the digit 1, the "off" state as the digit 0. Computers use digital signals—strings of on and off electrical pulses represented in codes of 1s and 0s—to represent software instructions and data. (p. 8)

■ Most phenomena of the world are in *analog* form, representing continuously variable quantities—examples are sound, light, temperature, and pressure values. Standard telephone lines are an analog medium—that is, they transmit only analog signals, such as voice messages. Digital computer signals must be converted, by a modem, to analog form in order to be transmitted over standard telephone lines. (p. 8)

■ Computer hardware is categorized as follows:

1. *Input hardware*—used to collect data and input it into the computer system in computer-usable form. The keyboard and mouse are the most common input devices. (p. 6)

2. *Processing hardware*—retrieves and executes (interprets) instructions (software) provided to the computer. The main components of processing hardware are the central processing unit (CPU), which is the brain of the computer, and main memory, where all instructions and/or data ready for processing are held. Since main memory is *volatile,* all contents are lost when the computer's power is turned off. (p. 7)

3. *Storage hardware*—provides a means of storing software and data in a form that is relatively permanent, or *non-volatile.* (p. 8)

4. *Output hardware*—provides a means for the user to view information produced by the computer system. Output is either in hardcopy form, such as printouts from a printer, or softcopy form, such as a display on a monitor, a TV-like screen that can be color or monochrome. (p. 8)

5. *Communications hardware*—facilitates connections between computers and computer systems over phone lines and other channels. Examples are *modems, cable,* and *fax modems*. (p. 8)

■ *Software* is made up of a group of related programs. Each program in turn is made up of a group of related instructions that perform very specific processing tasks. Software that runs the hardware and allows the computer to manage its resources is *systems software;* software that is acquired to perform a general business function is referred to as *applications software* or a *software package*. Software is accompanied by documentation, or users' manuals. (p. 10)

■ Computers are categorized from the largest and most powerful to the smallest and least powerful (p. 12):

1. Supercomputer

2. Mainframe computer

3. Minicomputer

4. Microcomputer

■ *The microcomputer (personal computer, or PC)* is the computer used most by business professionals. Microcomputers range in size from small palmtops, notebooks, and laptops to powerful desktop workstations, which are hooked up to a larger computer. The microcomputer has a small silicon chip, or microprocessor, as its CPU. (p. 14)

■ A microcomputer system cabinet—the *system unit*—usually houses the power supply, the system board (motherboard), and some storage devices, such as one or more diskette drives and a high-capacity hard disk drive. The system board includes the micro-processor chip, main memory chips, related support circuitry, and expansion slots. (p. 18)

■ The term *computer generation* was applied to different types of computers to help delineate the major technological developments in hardware and software. To date, computer technology has evolved through four distinct generations. With each generation, computers became smaller, more powerful, and less expensive. (p. 20)

1. *First Generation* (1944–1958): These are the earliest general-purpose computers. Most input and output media were punched cards and magnetic tape, and main memory was almost exclusively made up of hundreds of vacuum tubes. These computers were slow and large and produced a tremendous amount of heat. They could run only one program at a time. (p. 20)

2. *Second Generation* (1959–1963): By the early 1960s, transistors and some other solid-state devices that were much smaller than vacuum tubes were being used for much of the computer circuitry. Second-generation machines tended to be smaller, more reliable, and significantly faster than first-generation computers. (p. 22)

3. *Third Generation* (1964–1970): During this period, the integrated circuit—a complete electronic circuit on a silicon chip—replaced transistorized circuitry. The use of magnetic disks became widespread, and computers began to support such capabilities as multiprogramming (processing several programs simultaneously) and timesharing (people using the same computer simultaneously). The size of computers continued to decrease. (p. 23)

4. *Fourth Generation* (1971–Now): In 1971, the first electronic computers were introduced that used Large-Scale Integrated (LSI) and Very-Large-Scale Integrated (VLSI) circuits—thousands to millions of transistors on a tiny chip—for main memory and logic circuitry. These computers had a much larger capacity to support main memory. The *microprocessor,* introduced in 1971,

combined all the circuitry for the central processing unit on a single chip of silicon. Useful software applications pushed the microcomputer into the mainstream. (p. 23)

■ As information technology continues to proliferate, several trends will intensify, including connectivity, online information access, and interactivity. (p. 24)

■ *Connectivity* is the ability to connect computers and telephones by telecommunications lines to other devices and sources of information. Connectivity provides the foundation for the Information Age. The connectivity of *telecommunications* has made possible many kinds of activities, among them *telecommuting, teleshopping,* and *electronic* and *voice mail.* (p. 25)

■ Being online gives you access to resources far beyond those available with a computer sitting by itself unconnected to anything else. The word *access* means the ability to connect to a particular *database, network, online service,* or *electronic bulletin board system (BBS).* Being able to access modern information systems can significantly enhance your professional abilities. (p. 26)

■ *Interactivity* means that the user is able to make an immediate response to what is going on and modify the processes. That is, there is a dialog between the user and the computer or communications device. Among the types of interactive devices are multimedia computers, PC/TV "smart boxes" and set-top boxes, and personal digital assistants. (p. 27)

## KEY TERMS

analog, p. 8
applications software, p. 10
central processing unit (CPU), p. 7
communications, p. 5
communications hardware, p. 8
computer, p. 3
computer online service, p. 27
computer professional, p. 2
computer system, p. 4
connectivity, p. 25
cursor, p. 7
data, p. 4
database, p. 27
digital, p. 8

diskette (floppy disk), p. 18
documentation manual, p. 5
ergonomics, p. 24
hard disk, p. 18
hardware, p. 4
information, p. 4
input hardware, p. 6
integrated circuit, p. 23
interactivity, p. 27
keyboard, p. 7
mainframe computer, p. 13
main memory, p. 7
microcomputer (personal computer), p. 14
minicomputer, p. 13
modem, p. 8

monitor, p. 17
mouse, p. 7
nonvolatile, p. 8
online, p. 26
output hardware, p. 8
procedures, p. 5
processing hardware, p. 7
software, p. 4
storage hardware, p. 8
supercomputer, p. 12
system board (motherboard), p. 18
systems software, p. 10
system unit, p. 18
user (end-user), p. 2
volatile, p. 7

## EXERCISES

### SELF-TEST

1. The term _hardware_ COMPUTER is used to describe a device made up of electronic and electromechanical parts.

2. List five main categories of hardware:

    a. _Input_    c. _Storage_    e. _Communication_

    b. _processing_    d. _output_

3. Main memory is a software component. (true/**false**)

4. _Operating System software_ includes programs designed to enable the computer to manage its own resources.

5. Softcopy output can be displayed on a ~~paper~~ _Monitor_, or TV-like screen.

6. _Teleshopping_ refers to microcomputer users dialing into a telephone-linked computer-based shopping service listing prices and descriptions of products, which may be ordered through the computer.

7. Related programs designed to be carried out by a computer to satisfy a user's specific needs are called _application software_.

8. Computers are generally grouped into one of the following four basic categories:

    a. _Supercomp_    c. _Mini comp_

    b. _Mainframe_    d. _Microcomp_

9. You are more likely to use a microcomputer in business than a supercomputer. (**true**/false)

10. The _System Unit_ of a microcomputer usually houses the power supply, the system board (motherboard), and the storage devices.

11. _Monogram_ _Monochrome_ monitors display images only in a single color or black and white.

12. Hard disks have greater storage capacities than diskettes. (**true**/false)

13. A(n) _Modem_ allows computers to communicate over telephone lines.

14. Users' manuals that accompany computer hardware and software are referred to as _soft-ware documentation_.

15. Mainframe computers process faster than microcomputers. (**true**/false)

16. The CPU of a microcomputer is referred to as the _microprocessor_. _brain processor_.

17. As a result of computer processing, _input data_ (what you put into the computer) is often processed into _output information_ (what is output by the computer).

18. List the six main parts of a computer system:

_hardware_    a. ~~Input~~    c. _processing_    e. _people_    _procedure_

_software_    b. _Data/Infor._    d. _output_    f. _comm_.

19. Computers are continually getting larger and more expensive. (true/*false*)

20. _Multimedia PC_ refers to technology that presents information in more than one medium, including text, graphics, animation, video, music, and voice.

21. Computers generate signals in _digital_ form, which must be converted to _analog_ form in order to be transmitted over standard telephone lines.

*Solutions:* (1) computer; (2) input, processing, storage, output, communications; (3) false; (4) systems software; (5) monitor; (6) teleshopping; (7) applications software; (8) supercomputer, mainframe, minicomputer, microcomputer; (9) true; (10) system unit; (11) monochrome; (12) true; (13) modem; (14) documentation; (15) true; (16) microprocessor; (17) data, information; (18) hardware, software, data/information, procedures, people, communications; (19) false; (20) multimedia; (21) digital, analog

## SHORT-ANSWER QUESTIONS

1. Briefly describe the function of each of the six main components of a computer system.
2. What does it mean to be *computer literate*? *computer competent*?
3. What is the difference between systems software and applications software?
4. What is the meaning of the term *connectivity*?
5. What is the purpose of communications hardware? Name three communications hardware components.
6. What is a microprocessor?
7. What is the function of storage hardware in a computer system?
8. What is the purpose of main memory?
9. Why is it better to have a computer with more main memory rather than less?
10. What is the purpose of the system unit in a microcomputer system?
11. How is a computer user different from a computer professional?
12. What are the two most common input devices?

## PROJECTS AND CRITICAL THINKING EXERCISES

1. Look in the job opportunities section of several newspapers to see if many jobs require applicants to be familiar with using microcomputers. What types of experience are required? What kinds of computer skills do you think you'll need in your chosen job or career?

2. Although more new information has been produced in the last 30 years than in the previous 5,000, information isn't knowledge. In our quest for knowledge in the Information Age, we are often overloaded with information that doesn't tell us what we want to know. Richard Wurman identified this problem in his book *Information Anxiety;* John Naisbitt, in his books *Megatrends* and *Megatrends 2000,* said that "uncontrolled and unorganized information is no longer a resource in an information society. Instead, it becomes the enemy of the information worker."

    Identify some of the problems of information overload in one or two departments in your school or place of employment—or in a local business, such as a real estate firm, health clinic, pharmacy, or accounting firm. What types of problems are people having? How are they trying to solve them? Are they rethinking their use of computer-related technologies?

3. Determine what types of computers are being used where you work or go to school. Microcomputers? Minicomputers? Mainframes? Any supercomputers? In which departments are the different types of computers used? What are they being used for? How are they connected to other computers?

4. In an article for the *Harvard Business Review* (Sept./Oct. 1992, p. 97), Peter Drucker predicted that, in the next 50 years, schools and universities will change more drastically than they have since they assumed their present form more than 300 years ago, when they reorganized themselves around the printed book. What will force these changes is, in part, new computer and communications technology and, in part, the demands of a knowledge-based society in which organized learning must become a life-long process.

   How do you feel about the prospect of bookless reading and learning? What advantages and disadvantages can you think of in using computers instead of books? And how do you feel about perhaps having to renew your fund of knowledge about your job or profession every four or five years?

5. Many people are afraid of or resistant to learning about computers. Are you one of them? If so, make a list of all the factors that you think are affecting your attitude, then list reasons to refute each point. Keep your list and review it again after you have finished the course. What do you still agree with? Have you changed your mind about computers?

6. Imagine a business you could start and run at home. What type of business is it? What type of computer do you think you'll need? Describe the computer system in as much detail as possible, including hardware components in all the six areas we discussed. Keep your notes and then refine your answers after you have completed the course.

7. Should we allow the workplace to be computerized if it "de-skills" the workforce and/or increases depersonalization, boredom, and fatigue? Or do you think the workplace can be computerized without incurring these negative side effects? Explain your point of view.

8. Should computer professionals be bound by a code of conduct and, if so, what should it include?

# Chapter Topics

# CHAPTER 2

# Input Hardware

Learning to benefit from information technology means becoming comfortable with the input devices that constitute some of the computer's main interfaces with people.

## Preview

*When you have completed this chapter, you will be able to:*

■ Describe the difference between keyboard input and direct-entry input

■ Discuss the fundamentals of using a keyboard for input

■ List the three different types of terminals used for data input and describe some of the ways they are used

■ Describe the different categories of direct-entry input devices used with computer systems: pointing devices, scanning devices, smart cards, optical cards, and voice recognition devices

■ Describe audio-input and video-input devices, electronic cameras, sensors, and human-biology input devices

■ Describe the importance of input controls

*As a computer user, you will not be able to avoid entering data of some
sort into a computer system. However, be glad you are not entering the
job market when the principal means of inputting data to a computer
system was on punched cards—the so-called IBM cards that a generation of college students were admonished never to "fold, spindle, or
mutilate." Every year in the 1960s, 150,000 tons of cards were used—
enough, put end to end, to stretch 8 million miles.*

*Now many different types of input devices exist, and each is better
suited for some purposes than for others. This chapter will explain what
these input devices are and how they are used.*

## Categorizing Input Hardware

**Input hardware is classified as keyboard entry or direct entry.**

**Input hardware** consists of devices that take data and programs that people
can read or comprehend and convert them to a form the computer can
process. The people-readable form may be words like the ones in these sentences, but the computer-readable form consists of 0s and 1s, or off and on
signals.

Input devices are of two types: *keyboard entry* and *direct entry*. (See
Figure 2.1.)

In a computer, a **keyboard** is a device that converts letters, numbers,
and other characters into electrical signals that are machine-readable by the
computer's processor. The keyboard may look like a typewriter keyboard to
which some special keys have been added. Or it may look like the keys on
a bank's automatic teller machine or the keypad of a pocket computer used
by a bread-truck driver.

**Direct-entry device** refers to the many forms of data-entry devices that
are not keyboards. Direct-entry devices create machine-readable data on magnetic media or paper or feed it directly into the computer's processor. Direct-
entry devices include the following:

- Pointing devices
- Scanning devices
- Smart cards and optical cards
- Voice-recognition devices
- Audio-input devices
- Video-input devices
- Electronic cameras
- Sensors
- Human-biology input devices

Often keyboard and direct-entry input devices are combined in a single
computer system. A desktop-publishing system, for example, uses a keyboard,
a mouse, and an image scanner.

## Keyboard Input

**Keyboard-type devices include computer keyboards and termi-
nals. Computer keyboards consist of typewriter keys, cursor-**

**Figure 2.1**
Summary of input devices.

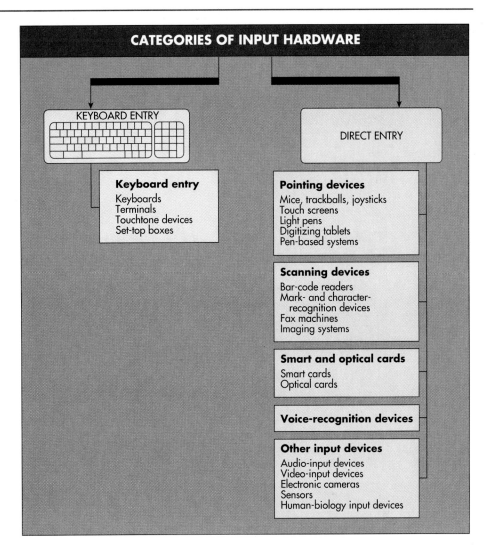

**CATEGORIES OF INPUT HARDWARE**

KEYBOARD ENTRY

DIRECT ENTRY

**Keyboard entry**
Keyboards
Terminals
Touchtone devices
Set-top boxes

**Pointing devices**
Mice, trackballs, joysticks
Touch screens
Light pens
Digitizing tablets
Pen-based systems

**Scanning devices**
Bar-code readers
Mark- and character-
    recognition devices
Fax machines
Imaging systems

**Smart and optical cards**
Smart cards
Optical cards

**Voice-recognition devices**

**Other input devices**
Audio-input devices
Video-input devices
Electronic cameras
Sensors
Human-biology input devices

**movement keys, numeric keys, function keys, and special-purpose keys. Terminals are of three types: dumb, smart, and intelligent.**

Even if you aren't a ten-finger typist, you can use a keyboard. Yale University computer scientist David Gelernter, for instance, lost the use of his right hand and right eye in a mail bombing. However, he expressed not only gratitude at being alive but also recognition that he could continue to use a keyboard even with his limitations. "In the final analysis," he wrote in an online message to colleagues, "one decent typing hand and an intact head is all you really need. . . ."[1]

Here we describe the following keyboard-type devices:

■ Computer keyboards

■ Terminals

## Keyboards

Conventional computer keyboards, such as those for microcomputers, have all the keys that typewriter keyboards have plus others unique to computers. (See Figure 2.2.) You should not feel intimidated by the number of keys.

**Figure 2.2**
Two popular computer keyboards. Pictured are keyboards for the IBM PS/2 (*top*) and the Apple Macintosh (*bottom*). The 101-extended keyboard layout is common with IBM-style desktop microcomputers, but there are variations. In order to fit the keyboard into limited space, portable computers of necessity have fewer keys or position the keys in different areas.

IBM

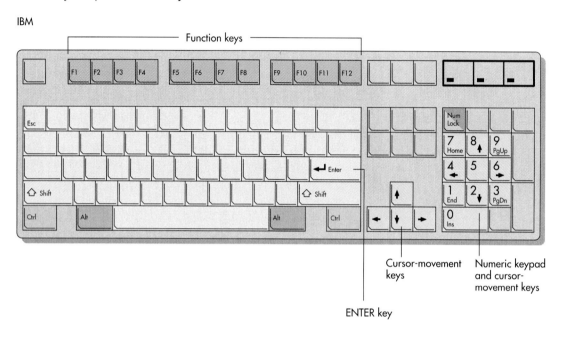

Cursor-movement keys

Numeric keypad and cursor-movement keys

ENTER key

Macintosh

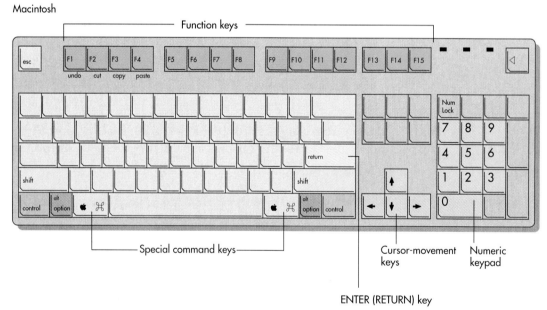

Special command keys

Cursor-movement keys

Numeric keypad

ENTER (RETURN) key

Actually, computer keyboards are easier to use than most typewriter keyboards because you can so easily undo mistakes.

■ *Standard typewriter keys: Typewriter keys* are the same familiar QWERTY arrangement of letter, number, and punctuation keys found on any typewriter. QWERTY refers to the alphabet keys in the top left row on a standard typewriter keyboard.

The space bar and Shift, Tab, and Caps Lock keys do the same things on the computer that they do on a typewriter. (When you press the Caps Lock key, a light on your keyboard shows you are typing ALL CAPITAL LETTERS until you press the Caps Lock key again.)

An exception is the Enter (bent left arrow) key, which occupies the place where a carriage-return key would be on a typewriter. The **Enter key,** sometimes called the *Return key,* is used to enter commands into the computer. (There is no such thing as a "carriage return" on a computer.)

■  *Cursor-movement keys:* The **cursor** is the symbol on the display screen that shows where data may be entered next. The **cursor-movement keys,** or arrow keys, are used to move the cursor around the text on the screen. These keys move the cursor left, right, up, or down.

The key labeled *PgUp* stands for *Page Up,* and the key labeled *PgDn* stands for *Page Down.* These keys move the cursor the equivalent of one page or one screen at a time up (backward) or down (forward). Some software lets you use the Home key to move the cursor to the top of the page and the End key to move to the bottom of the page.

The numeric keys, as we discuss next, may also be used as arrow keys to move the cursor around.

■  *Numeric keys:* A separate set of keys, 0 through 9, known as the **numeric keypad,** is laid out like the keys on a calculator. The numeric keypad has two purposes.

Whenever the Num Lock key is off, the numeric keys may be used as arrow keys for cursor movement.

When the Num Lock key is on, the keys may be used for typing numbers, as on a calculator. A light is illuminated on the keyboard when the Num Lock key is pressed once and goes off when the Num Lock key is pressed again.

For space reasons, portable computers often lack a separate numeric keypad—or the numeric keys may be superimposed on the typewriter letter keys and activated by the Num Lock key.

■  *Function keys:* **Function keys** are the keys labeled with an F and a number, such as F1 and F2. They are used for tasks that occur frequently. Desktop microcomputers usually have 12 function keys, portables often only 10.

The purpose of each function key is defined by the software you are using. For example, in one program, pressing F2 may print your document; in a different program, pressing F2 may save your work to disk. The documentation manual that comes with the software tells you how to use the function keys. Also, some companies make small templates that fit around or above the function keys and list the commands that the function keys correspond to.

■  *Special-purpose keys:* Special-purpose keys include Backspace, Del, Ins, Esc, Ctrl, and Alt.

—*Backspace* (indicated by a left-pointing arrow) erases as you move left over the preceding text you have typed.

—*Del* (Delete) erases text to the right.

—*Ins* (Insert) allows you to type over (or push right) existing text to insert new text.

—*Esc* (Escape) may be used to cancel whatever task you are currently performing.

—The purposes of *Ctrl* (Control) and *Alt* (Alternate) are defined by the software you are using. Some computers may have other special-purpose keys.

IBM claims that its under-$1000 Personal Dictation System . . . has a surprising 95% to 98% accuracy rate.

The software is simple to operate. Users just speak into a microphone, and the software converts speech to text on screen. The spec sheets for the Personal Dictation System say that the system accepts about 70 words per minute, but in reality, Elton Sherwin, IBM's development manager for speech recognition, says that users can push it to 110 words per minute (wpm) before it starts to lag behind the user. People usually speak at about 100 to 120 wpm, so some folks may have to slow down a little. . . .

Like other voice recognition systems, the Personal Dictation System has to be trained to recognize an individual voice. Users train the system by reading "A Ghost Story" by Mark Twain for about 90 minutes. From the story, the software learns a user's dialect, pitch, and voice fluctuations.

After it's been trained, the system can distinguish between homophones—words that sound alike but are spelled differently, like "to," "two," and "too." The Personal Dictation System puts in its best guess for a word, but, as the user speaks, it can backtrack and correct mistakes based on the words surrounding it. For example, if it originally enters "We need to order to PCs," it can recognize that the second "to" actually refers to a quantity and can correct the mistake to read "two."

The system inserts capitalization and punctuation as the user speaks, so the text is relatively clean in the first stages. If the operator needs to make changes, he or she can simply edit the document as if it had been typed directly into the PC.

The Personal Dictation System has a vocabulary of 32,000 words out of the box, and up to 2000 more words can be added. After that, the system will discard the word used the least for each new word added. So, if a user composed a memo containing the word *downsizing* and then never used the word again, *downsizing* would eventually be discarded from the vocabulary. . . .

Users should remember this is a personal dictation system. Because of the unique sound of an individual's voice, it may be difficult for more than one person to use the same system.

IBM cites this customization as one of the main reasons that the product will be successful. It's a valuable tool, the company claims, because good language skills are not necessary for the product to work well. People who have strong foreign accents and for whom English is a second or third language will also be able to train the product because the Personal Dictation System doesn't care about mispronunciation. The word just needs to be consistently mispronounced.

Wendy Pickering, *Datamation,* January 7, 1994, pp. 51–52.

Different keyboards may have a different "feel" or touch to them. *Soft-touch keyboards* press down easily and make almost no sound. *Regular-touch keyboards* emit audible clicks when you press down on them.

As computers have become more widespread, so has the incidence of various hand and wrist injuries. Accordingly, keyboard manufacturers have been giving a lot of attention to ergonomics. **Ergonomics** is the study of the

**Figure 2.3**
Microsoft Natural keyboard. The Natural keyboard is ergonomically designed to provide you with greater comfort, a more natural posture, and an easier way to type.

physical relationships between people and their work environment. Various attempts are being made to make keyboards more ergonomically sound in order to prevent injuries. (See Figure 2.3.)

## Terminals

A **terminal** is an input device that consists of a keyboard, a video display screen, and a communications line to a mainframe computer system.

Terminals are of three types: dumb, smart, and intelligent.

- *Dumb:* A **dumb terminal** can be used only to input data to and receive information from a computer system. That is, it cannot do any processing on its own.

  An example of a dumb terminal is that used by airline clerks at airport ticket and check-in counters. Another example is a kind of portable terminal. A **portable terminal** is a mobile terminal that can be connected to a main computer system through wired or wireless communications. A parking control officer might use a handheld wireless dumb terminal to send data about cars to a central computer in order to identify those with unpaid parking tickets.

- *Smart:* A **smart terminal** can do input and output and has some limited processing capability. It may be able to edit or verify data before it is sent to a larger computer. However, it cannot be used to do programming—that is, create new instructions.

  Three examples of smart terminals are automatic teller machines, point-of-sale terminals, and Minitel Terminals. An *automatic teller machine (ATM)* is used to retrieve information on bank balances, make deposits, transfer sums between accounts, and withdraw cash. Usually the cash is disbursed in $20 bills. (Some Nevada gambling casinos have machines that dispense only $100 bills.)

  A variant on the ATM is the ETM, or electronic ticket machine, in which you insert your credit card and an airline or train ticket pops out.

  A **point-of-sale (POS) terminal** is a smart terminal used much like a cash register. It records customer transactions at the point of sale but also stores data for billing and inventory purposes. POS terminals are found in most department stores. (See Figure 2.4.)

  The *Minitel* is a terminal used in most homes in France to link citizens with an electronic phone directory and dozens of information services. In the United States, Minitels have been used in some localities to

**Figure 2.4**
POS terminal. *Right:* This point-of-sale terminal is being used at a clothing store. The system not only prints out the customer's receipt but also updates sales records and inventory records. *Left:* A hand-held POS terminal.

**Figure 2.5**
A Minitel. In France, this terminal is used in most homes in place of a telephone directory and Yellow Pages, but it offers other online services as well.

let children, teachers, and parents communicate, as well as to connect with electronic encyclopedias.[2] (See Figure 2.5.)

*Intelligent:* An **intelligent terminal** is essentially a full-fledged microcomputer with a communications link. That is, an intelligent terminal is a "stand-alone" device with its own input, output, processing, and storage capacity and its own software.

Microcomputers increasingly are being used in business as terminals—and in place of dumb and smart terminals. This trend is occurring not only because their prices have come down but also because they reduce the processing and storage load on the main computer system.

An example of an intelligent terminal is what is called an executive workstation. An **executive workstation** is a microcomputer that performs not only as a stand-alone computer but also connects with a main computer. It usually has voice and data communications capabilities.

Now we turn from keyboard entry and terminals to various types of direct entry, in which data is converted into machine-readable form as it is entered into the computer or other device.

## Pointing Devices

**Pointing devices include mice, trackballs, and joysticks; touch screens; light pens; digitizing tablets; and pen-based systems.**

One of the most natural of all human gestures, the act of pointing, is incorporated in several kinds of input devices. The most prominent ones are the following:

- Mice, trackballs, and joysticks
- Touch screens
- Light pens
- Digitizing tablets
- Pen-based systems

**Figure 2.6**
Giving a few pointers: mouse, trackball, and joystick.

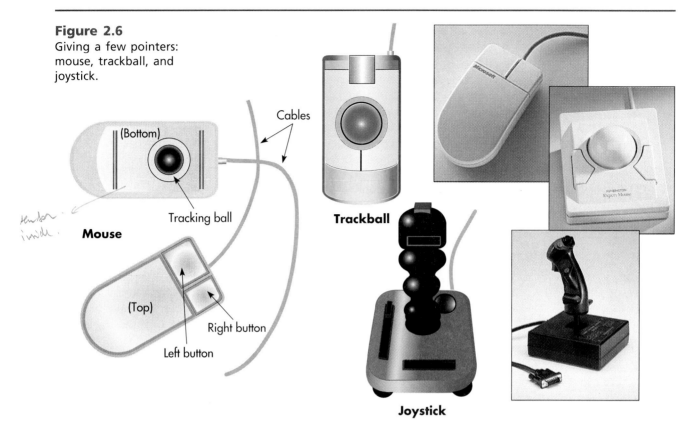

## Mice, Trackballs, and Joysticks

The principal pointing tools used with microcomputers are the mouse, the trackball, and the joystick, all of which have variations. (See Figure 2.6.)

■ *Mouse:* A **mouse** is a device that is rolled about on a desktop to direct a pointer on the computer's display screen. The pointer may sometimes be, but is not necessarily the same as, the cursor. The **mouse pointer** is the symbol that indicates the position of the mouse on the display screen. (See Figure 2.7.) It may be an arrow, a rectangle, or even a representation of a person's pointing finger. The pointer may change to the shape of an I-beam to indicate that it is a cursor indicating the place where text or other data may be entered.

**Figure 2.7**
Mouse and mouse pointer. Movement of the mouse on the desktop causes a corresponding movement of the mouse cursor on the display screen. A mouse may have one to three buttons, used for common or special functions.

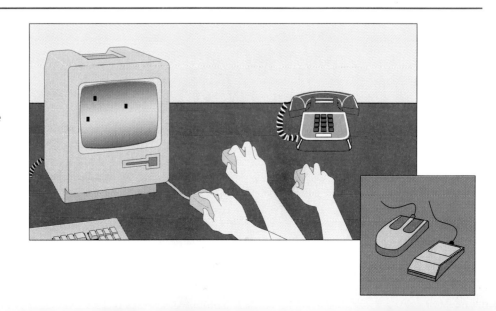

The mouse has a cable that is connected (by being plugged into a special port, or socket) to the microcomputer's system unit. This tail-like cable and the rounded "head" of the instrument are what suggested the name mouse.

On the bottom side of the mouse is a ball that translates the mouse movement into digital signals. On the top side are one, two, or three buttons. Depending on the software, these buttons are used for common or special functions, such as *clicking* and *dragging*. (See Table 2.1.)

Gently holding the mouse with one hand, you can move it in all directions on the desktop (or on the mouse pad, which may provide additional traction). This will produce a corresponding movement of the mouse pointer on the screen.

Depending on the software, many commands that can be done with a mouse can also be performed through the keyboard. The mouse may make it easy to learn the commands for, say, a word processing program. However, you may soon find that you can execute those commands more quickly through a combination of keystrokes on the keyboard.

■ *Trackball:* Another form of pointing device, the trackball, is a variant on the mouse. A **trackball** is a movable ball, on top of a stationary device, that is rotated with the fingers or palm of the hand. In fact, the trackball looks like a mouse turned upside down. Instead of moving the mouse around on the desktop, you move the trackball with the tips of your fingers.

Trackballs are especially suited to portable computers, which are often used in confined places, such as on airline tray tables. Trackballs may appear on the keyboard centered below the space bar, as on the Apple PowerBook, or built into the right side of the screen. On some portables the trackball is a separate device that is clipped to the side of the keyboard.

■ *Joystick:* A **joystick** is a pointing device that consists of a vertical handle like a gearshift lever mounted on a base with one or two buttons. Named for the control mechanism that directs an airplane's fore-and-aft and side-to-side movement, joysticks are used principally in video games and in some computer-aided design systems.

■ *Other pointing controllers:* The IBM ThinkPad, a portable computer, uses a pointing controller that resembles a small stick. It protrudes through the keyboard amid the G, H, and B keys.

**Table 2.1**
Learning mouse language.

| TERM | DEFINITION |
| --- | --- |
| Point | Move the pointer to the desired spot on the screen, such as over a particular word or object. |
| Click | Tap—that is, press and quickly release—the left mouse button. |
| Double-click | Tap—press and release—the left mouse button twice, as quickly as possible. |
| Drag | Press and hold the left mouse button, while moving the pointer to another location. |
| Drop | Release the mouse button after dragging. |
| Point-and-shoot | Point, then click. |

## One Negative Side to Computer Use . . . ?

. . . Computers should be in the schools. They have the potential to accomplish great things. With the right software, they could help make science tangible or teach neglected topics like art and music. They could help students form a concrete idea of society by displaying on screen a version of the city in which they live—a picture that tracks real life moment by moment.

In practice, however, computers make our worst educational nightmares come true. While we bemoan the decline of literacy, computers discount words in favor of pictures and pictures in favor of video. While we fret about the decreasing cogency of public debate, computers dismiss linear argument and promote fast, shallow romps across the information landscape. While we worry about basic skills, we allow into the classroom software that will do a student's arithmetic or correct his spelling.

Take multimedia. The idea of multimedia is to combine text, sound, and pictures in a single package that you browse through on screen. You don't just *read* Shakespeare; you watch actors performing, listen to songs, view Elizabethan buildings. What's wrong with that? By offering children candy-coated books, multimedia is guaranteed to sour them on unsweetened reading. It makes the printed page look even more boring than it used to look. Sure, books will be available in the classroom, too—but they'll have all the appeal of a dusty piano to a teen who has a Walkman handy. . . .

Hypermedia, multimedia's comrade in the struggle for a brave new classroom, is just as troubling. It's a way of presenting documents on screen without imposing a linear start-to-finish order. Disembodied paragraphs are linked by theme; after reading one about the First World War, for example, you might be able to choose

another about the technology of battleships, or the life of Woodrow Wilson, or hemlines in the '20s. This is another cute idea that is good in minor ways and terrible in major ones. Teaching children to understand the orderly unfolding of

a plot or a logical argument is a crucial part of education. Authors don't merely agglomerate paragraphs; they work hard to make the narrative read a certain way, prove a particular point. To turn a book or document into hypertext is to invite readers to ignore exactly what counts—the story.

The real problem, again, is the accentuation of already bad habits. Dynamiting documents into disjointed paragraphs is one more expression of the sorry fact that sustained argument is just not our style. If you're a newspaper or magazine editor and your readership is dwindling, what's the solution? Shorter pieces. If you're a politician and you want to get elected, what do you need? Tasty sound bites. Logical presentation be damned.

Excerpted from David Gelernter, professor of computer science at Yale University, "Unplugged," *The New Republic,* September 19 & 26, 1994, pp. 14–15.

**Figure 2.8**
A touch screen. *Below:*
A touch screen at
Boston Chicken that
allows customers to rate
service and food. *Right:*
Waitress using a touch
screen POS terminal.

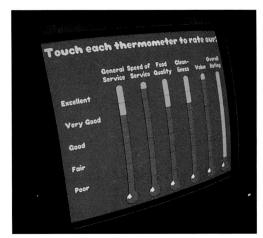

## Touch Screens

A **touch screen** is a video display screen that has been sensitized to receive
input from the touch of a finger. (See Figure 2.8.) The screen is covered with
a plastic layer, behind which are invisible beams of infrared light.

Because touch screens are easy to use, they can convey information
quickly. They are used more often in automatic teller machines, in directories
conveying tourist information in airports and hotels, and in fast-food restaurants to display menus. Some applications are also available for microcomputers, although touch screens are of limited use because they cannot display
large amounts of information.

## Light Pen

The **light pen** is a light-sensitive stylus, or pen-like device, connected by a
cable to the computer terminal. The user brings the pen to a desired point
on the display screen and presses the pen button, which identifies that
screen location to the computer. (See Figure 2.9.) Light pens are used by
engineers, graphic designers, and illustrators.

## Digitizing Tablets

A **digitizing tablet** consists of a tablet connected by a cable to a stylus or
puck. A stylus is a pen-like device with which the user "sketches" an image.

**Figure 2.9**
Light pen. *Left:* Light pen and Controller card, which is installed inside the computer. *Right:* This person is using a light pen to create a cartoon.

**Figure 2.10**
Digitizing tablet. *Left:* Calcomp Drawingboard digitizer (puck); *right:* digitizing tablet (and stylus) used in engineering.

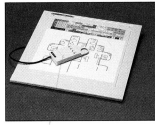

*like mouse but more precise*

A puck is a copying device with which the user copies, or traces, an image. (See Figure 2.10.)

When used with drawing and painting software, a digitizing tablet and stylus allow you to do shading and many other effects similar to those artists achieve with pencil, pen, or charcoal. Alternatively, when you use a puck, you can trace a drawing laid on the tablet, and a digitized copy is stored in the computer.

Digitizing tablets are used primarily in design and engineering.

### Pen-Based Systems

**Pen-based computer systems** use a pen-like stylus to enter handwriting and marks into a computer. (See Figure 2.11.) There is a good chance you will use one of these systems if you haven't already.

**Figure 2.11**
Pen-based systems. Two types are shown. *Left:* AT&T EO Personal Communicator; *Right:* The Apple Newton MessagePad, a personal digital assistant, was designed to be able to recognize handwriting and convert it to typed text. Initial versions were not wholly successful, but later versions have been improved.

There are four types of pen-based systems:

- *Gesture recognition or electronic checklists: Gesture recognition* refers to a computer's ability to recognize various check marks, slashes, or carefully printed block letters and numbers placed in boxes. This type of pen-based system is incorporated in devices that resemble simple forms or checklists on handheld electronic clipboards that have an accompanying electronic pen or stylus.

  An example of a gesture recognition device is Go Corporation's Pen-Point. This type of small computer is used by meter readers, package deliverers, and insurance claims representatives.

- *Handwriting stored as scribbling:* A second type of pen-based system recognizes and stores handwriting. The handwriting is stored as a scribble and is not converted to typed text.

  This kind of handwriting recognition is found in some kinds of electronic organizers, such as the Sharp Wizard.

- *Handwriting converted, with training, to typed text:* Some pen-based devices can recognize your handwriting and transform it into typed text. These systems require that the machine be "trained" to recognize your particular (or even peculiar) handwriting. Moreover, the writing must be neat printing rather than script. The advantage of converting writing to typed text is that after conversion the text can be retrieved and later edited or further manipulated.

  An example of this kind of handwriting recognition is found in IBM's pen-based ThinkPad computer, which consists of a tablet screen and a stylus.

- *Handwriting converted, without training, to typed text:* The most sophisticated—and still mostly elusive—application of pen-based computers converts script handwriting to typed text without training. This was the claim originally made by Apple Computer for its Newton MessagePad, a personal digital assistant. **Personal digital assistants (PDAs)** are small pen-controlled, handheld computers that, in their most developed form, can do two-way wireless messaging. In addition, the Newton users were supposed to be able to use handwritten commands to send and receive faxes and electronic mail, to write memos, and to keep an appointment calendar.

Initial versions of the Newton failed to live up to their advance billing for recognizing handwriting. A later version is better because it recognizes letters independently, whereas the original typically tried to identify words from letter groups. It also allows users to defer translation of their scribbling until later, so that they can take notes at full speed.

Clearly, it is not too difficult to design a pen-based computer system that will store handwriting as it is scrawled, and several of these exist. What is more difficult is to convert a person's distinctive handwriting into typescript, particularly without training the computer. After all, when you're trying to read someone else's notes, you may have to ask "Is that an *e,* an *a,* or an *o?*"

## Scanning Devices

**Scanning devices include bar-code readers, mark- and character-recognition devices, fax machines, and imaging systems. Mark- and character-recognition devices include magnetic-ink character recognition (MICR), optical mark recognition (OMR), and optical character recognition (OCR). Fax machines may be dedicated machines or fax modems. Imaging systems convert text and images to digital form.**

**Scanning devices** translate images of text, drawings, photos, and the like into digital form [✔ p. 8]. The images can then be processed by a computer, displayed on a monitor, stored on a storage device, or communicated to another computer. Scanning devices include:

- Bar-code readers
- Mark- and character-recognition devices
- Fax machines
- Imaging systems

### **H** Bar-Code Readers

bar-code readers

**Bar codes** are the vertical zebra-striped marks you see on most manufactured retail products—everything from candy to cosmetics to comic books. In North America, supermarkets, food manufacturers, and others have agreed to use a bar-code system called the *Universal Product Code.* Other kinds of bar-code systems are used on everything from Federal Express packages to railroad cars. (See Figure 2.12.)

Bar codes are read by **bar-code readers,** photoelectric scanners that translate the bar code symbols into digital forms. The price of a particular item is set within the store's computer and appears on the sales-clerk's point-of-sale terminal and on your receipt. Records of sales are input to the store's computer and used for accounting, restocking store inventory, and weeding out products that don't sell well.

A recent innovation is the self-scanning bar-code reader, which grocers hope will extend the concept of self-service and help them lower costs. Here customers bring their groceries to an automated checkout counter, where they scan them and bag them. They then take the bill to a cashier's station to

**Figure 2.12**
Bar codes. Bar codes, which are converted by bar-code scanners into computer-acceptable digital input, appear on FedEx packages, grocery products, and price tags, among other things.

pay. To guard against theft, the bar-code scanner is able to detect attempts to pass off steak as peas.[3]

## Mark-Recognition and Character-Recognition Devices

There are three types of scanning devices that "read" marks or characters. They are usually referred to by their abbreviations MICR, OMR, and OCR.

- *Magnetic-ink character recognition:* **Magnetic-ink character recognition (MICR)** reads the strange-looking numbers printed at the bottom of checks. (See Figure 2.13.) MICR characters, which are printed with magnetized ink, are read by MICR equipment, producing a digitized signal. This signal is used by a bank's reader/sorter machine to sort checks.

- *Optical mark recognition:* **Optical mark recognition (OMR)** uses a device that reads pencil marks and converts them into computer-usable form. The most well-known example is the OMR technology used to read the College Board Scholastic Aptitude Test (SAT) and the Graduate Record Examination (GRE).

- *Optical character recognition:* **Optical character recognition (OCR)** uses a device that reads special preprinted characters and converts them into machine-readable form. Examples that use OCR characters are utility bills

**Figure 2.13**
MICR technology. Checks use magnetized ink that can be read by a bank's magnetic-ink character-recognition equipment.

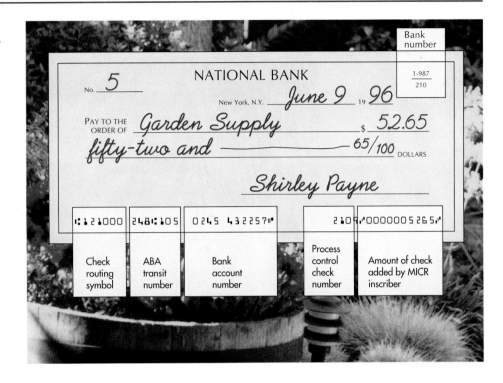

Bank number

NATIONAL BANK

1-987 / 210

No. 5

New York, N.Y. _____ June 9 19 96

PAY TO THE ORDER OF _Garden Supply_ $ 52.65

_fifty-two and_ ———————— 65/100 DOLLARS

_Shirley Payne_

Check routing symbol | ABA transit number | Bank account number | Process control check number | Amount of check added by MICR inscriber

and price tags on department-store merchandise. The wand reader is a common OCR scanning device. (See Figure 2.14.)

### Fax Machines

A **fax machine**—or **facsimile transmission machine**—scans an image and sends it as electronic signals over telephone lines to a receiving fax machine, which re-creates the image on paper. (*Facsimile* means "an exact copy.")

There are two types of fax machines: dedicated (stand-alone) fax machines and fax modems.

■ *Dedicated fax machines:* Generally called simply "fax machines," **dedicated fax machines** are specialized devices that do nothing except send

**Figure 2.14**
Optical character recognition. The typefaces can be read by a special scanning device called a wand.

ABCDEFGHIJKLMN
OPQRSTUVWXYZ,.
$/*-1234567890

**Figure 2.15**
Car fax. Fax machines can be installed beneath a car's dashboard.

**Figure 2.16**
Fax in a PDA. This portable digital assistant, the Simon, not only is a notepad and address book but also can send and receive fax messages.

and receive fax documents. They are found not only in offices and homes but also alongside regular phones in public places such as airports.

For the status-conscious or those needing to work from their cars (such as salespeople on the road), fax machines can be installed in an automobile. (See Figure 2.15.) The movie *The Player*, for example, contains a scene in which the stalker of a movie-studio executive faxes a threatening note. It arrives through the fax machine housed beneath the dashboard in the executive's Range Rover.

The scanner in a fax machine can also be used to scan graphics and other items and then send them to a computer to be saved as an electronic file and later manipulated.

■ *Fax modem:* A **fax modem** is installed as a circuit board inside the computer's system cabinet. It is a modem with fax capability that enables you to send signals directly from your computer to someone else's stand-alone fax machine or internal computer fax modem. With this device, you don't have to print out the material from your computer printer and then run it through a fax-machine scanner. The fax modem allows you to send information much more quickly than if you had to feed it page by page into a fax machine.

The fax modem is another feature of mobile computing. Fax modems are installed inside portable computers, including pocket PCs and PDAs. (See Figure 2.16.) You can also link up a cellular phone to the fax modem in your portable computer and thereby receive wireless fax messages. Indeed, faxes may be sent and received all over the world.

The main disadvantage of a fax modem is that you cannot scan in outside documents. Thus, if you have a photo or a drawing that you want to fax to someone, you need an image scanner, as we describe next.

Communication by fax has become cheaper than first-class mail for many purposes.

## Imaging Systems

An **imaging system**—or image scanner or graphics scanner—converts text, drawings, and photographs into digital form that can be stored in a computer system and then manipulated. The system scans each image with light and breaks it into light and dark dots, which are then converted to digital code.

An example of an imaging system is the type used in desktop publishing. This device scans in artwork or photos that can then be positioned within a page of text. Other systems are available for turning paper documents into electronic files so that people can reduce their paperwork.

Imaging-system technology has led to a whole new art or industry called *electronic imaging*. Electronic imaging is the combining of separate images, using scanners, digital cameras, and advanced graphic computers. This technology has become an important part of multimedia.

## Smart Cards and Optical Cards

*CPU
inside
↓
for
future*

**A smart card contains a microprocessor and a memory chip. An optical card is a plastic, laser-recordable card used with an optical card reader.**

It has already come to this: Just as many people collect stamps or baseball cards, there is now a major worldwide collecting mania for used wallet-sized telephone debit cards. (See Figure 2.17.) These are the cards by which telephone time is sold and consumed in many countries. Generally the cards are collected for their designs, which bear likenesses of anything from Elvis Presley to Felix the Cat to Martin Luther King, Jr.[4] The cards have been in use in Europe for about 15 years, although about 500 U.S. phone companies are now selling them.

**H**

optical card

Most of these telephone cards are examples of "smart cards." An even more sophisticated technology is the optical card.

### Figure 2.17
Future collectibles? Many of these "smart-card" telephone debit cards are of interest to collectors because of their designs and messages.

## Smart Cards

A **smart card** looks like a credit card but contains a microprocessor and memory chip. In France, where the smart card was invented, you can buy telephone debit cards at most cafes and newsstands. You insert the card into a slot in the phone, wait for a tone, and dial the number. The time your call lasts is automatically calculated on the chip inside the card and deducted from the balance of time paid for. The French also use smart cards as bank cards, and some people carry their medical histories on them.

The United States has been slow to embrace smart cards because of the prevalence of the conventional magnetic-strip credit card. Moreover, the United States has a large installed base of credit-card readers and phone networks with which merchants can check on these cards. However, in other countries phone lines are scarce, so that merchants cannot easily check over the phone with a centralized credit database. In these places, smart cards make sense because they carry their own spending limits.[5]

Already planners have envisioned a host of future uses for smart cards. For instance, the Department of Defense is looking at replacing traditional military dog tags with smart cards that include service and family data. Some observers think that business travelers will soon have a personal smart card that can be used for many purposes. This includes buying airline tickets, reserving rental cars, checking into hotels—even opening the door to their hotel rooms. Once back at the office, they will be able to transfer all their travel expenses electronically onto an expense report. There will be no need to keep paper receipts.[6]

## Optical Cards

The conventional magnetic-strip credit card holds the equivalent of a half page of data. The smart card with a microprocessor and memory chip holds the equivalent of 30 pages. The optical card presently holds about 2,000 pages of data. Optical cards use the same type of technology as music compact disks but look like silvery credit cards. **Optical cards** are plastic, laser-recordable, credit-card-size cards used with an optical card reader. Because they can cram so much data (6.6 megabytes) into so little space, they may become popular in the future. With an optical card, for instance, there's enough room for a person's health card to hold not only his or her medical history and health-insurance information but also digital images. Examples are electrocardiograms, low-resolution chest X-rays, and ultrasound pictures of a fetus. A book containing 1,000 pages of text plus 150 detailed drawings could be mailed on an optical card in a 1-ounce first-class letter. One manufacturer of optical library-card systems suggested that people might wish to store personal information on their cards, such as birth certificates and insurance policies.[7]

 *not good yet.*

## Voice-Recognition Systems

**Voice-recognition systems, which convert human speech into digital code, still have several limitations.**

Sprint Corporation took the telephone calling card to a new level in early 1994, when it introduced its Voice Fōncard. Actually, the system doesn't require a card at all to make the calls. You dial an 800 number and then say your Social Security number (preceded by one digit for added protection). When your voice is recognized, you can then automatically direct the system—with verbal commands such as "Call home" or "Call agent"—to dial up to ten numbers.[8]

The Sprint system is an example of voice-recognition technology. A **voice-recognition system** converts a person's speech into digital code by comparing the electrical patterns produced by the speaker's voice with a set of prerecorded patterns stored in the computer. (See Figure 2.18.)

Voice-recognition systems are finding many uses. Warehouse workers are able to speed inventory-taking by recording inventory counts verbally. Blind people can give verbal commands to their PCs rather than use the keyboard. Traders on stock exchanges can communicate their trades verbally. Astronauts who need to use two hands to make repairs in space can activate display screens in their helmet visors with spoken commands.

So far, however, most voice-recognition technology has been hindered by three limitations:

- *Speaker dependence:* Most systems need to be "trained" by the speaker to recognize his or her distinctive speech patterns and even variations in the way a particular word is said. Systems that are "speaker independent" are beginning to appear, but consider the hurdles to be overcome: different voices, pronunciations, and accents.

- *Single words versus continuous speech:* Most systems can handle only single words and have vocabularies of 1000 words or less. However, some new technology, such as DragonDictate, now offers continual-speech recognition so that one need not artificially pause between words when speaking, and 30,000-word dictionaries (vocabularies).[9]

- *Lack of comprehension:* Most systems merely translate sounds into characters. A more useful technology would be one that actually comprehends the *meaning* of spoken words. You could then ask a question, and the system could check a database and formulate a meaningful answer. Some such systems are being developed for the military.

**Figure 2.18**
How a voice-recognition system works. Voice recognition begins with a person speaking into a microphone attached to a computer system.

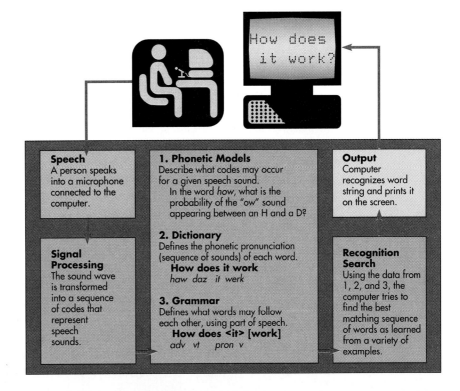

## Other Input Devices: Audio, Video, Cameras, Sensors, and Human-Biology Devices

**Five other types of input devices are audio-input devices, video-input devices, electronic cameras, sensors, and human-biology input devices. Audio-input devices may digitize sound by means of an audio board or a MIDI board. Video-input devices may use frame-grabber or full-motion video cards. Electronic cameras are still-video or digital cameras; the latter use light-sensitive silicon chips to capture photographic images. Sensors collect specific kinds of data directly from the environment. Human-biology input devices include biometric systems, line-of-sight systems, cyber gloves and body suits, and brainwave devices.**

"The machine never grew impatient, never gave up," reported journalist Jerry Adler about The Miracle Piano Teaching System. This combination of electronic keyboard and software for an IBM-compatible computer promises to teach novices Handel's "Water Music" in only 40 lessons. "It simply devised new exercises, sent me back to practice again, issued wildly inflated praise at the slightest signs of improvement, until at last I made it through all 15 bars of 'Mary Had a Little Lamb' and was rewarded with a heart-felt WHEW! YOU'RE BECOMING A MUSICIAN!"[10]

As this example suggests, there are all kinds of input devices beyond those we have mentioned. Here we describe five types:

- Audio-input devices
- Video-input devices
- Electronic cameras
- Sensors
- Human-biology input devices

### Audio-Input Devices

Voice-recognition devices are only one kind of audio input, which can include music and other sounds. An **audio-input device** records or plays analog sound and translates it for digital storage and processing. As we mentioned in Chapter 1, an *analog sound signal* represents a continuously variable wave within a certain frequency range. Such continuous fluctuations are usually represented with an analog device such as a cassette player. For the computer to process them, these variable waves must be converted to digital 0s and 1s, the language of the computer.

There are two ways in which audio is digitized:

- *Audio board:* Analog sound from, say, a cassette player goes through a special circuit board called an *audio board*. An *audio board* is an add-on circuit board in a computer that converts analog sound to digital sound and stores it for further processing.

- *MIDI board:* A *MIDI* (pronounced "middie") *board*—MIDI stands for *M*usical *I*nstrument *D*igital *I*nterface—is an add-on board that creates digital music. That is, the music is created in digital form as the musician performs, for example, on a special MIDI keyboard.

The principal use of audio-input devices such as these is to provide digital input for multimedia PCs. A **multimedia system** is a microcomputer that incorporates text, graphics, sound, video, and animation in a single digital presentation. Video input is also often used for this purpose, as we describe next.

## Video-Input Devices

As with sound, most film and videotape is in analog form, with the signal a continuously variable wave. Thus, to be used by a computer, the signals that come from a VCR or a camcorder must be converted to digital form through a special video card installed in the computer.

Two types of video cards are the frame-grabber video and the full-motion video:

■ *Frame-grabber video card:* Some video cards, called *frame grabbers,* can capture and digitize only a single frame at a time.

■ *Full-motion video card:* Other video cards, called *full-motion video cards,* can convert analog to digital signals at the rate of 30 frames per second, giving the effect of a continuously flowing motion picture.

The main limitation in capturing full video is not input but storage. It takes a huge amount of storage space to store just 1 second of video.

## Electronic Cameras

The electronic camera is a particularly interesting piece of hardware because it foreshadows major change for the entire industry of photography. Instead of using traditional (chemical) film, an electronic camera captures images in electronic form for immediate viewing on a television or computer display screen.

Electronic cameras are of two types: still-video and digital.

■ *Still-video cameras:* Still-video cameras are like camcorders. However, they capture only a single video image at a time. Because the cameras are meant to display images only on a television screen, the pictures must be converted (by a video capture board) before they can be stored in a computer. In addition, compared to the digital camera, picture resolution and color range are limited. An example of a still-video camera is the RC-570 from Canon.

■ *Digital cameras:* More interesting is the digital camera. A *digital camera* uses a light-sensitive processor chip to capture photographic images in digital form. The bits of digital information can then be copied onto a computer's hard disk for manipulation and printing out. Examples of digital cameras are Apple Computer's QuickTake 100, Logitech's Fotoman, and Dycam's Model 4.

In February 1994, Eastman Kodak and the Associated Press (AP) introduced an electronic camera specifically designed for news photographs, the NewsCamera 200. The camera stores 30–50 digitized images in a battery-backed memory. Later a photographer can download (transfer) these images to his or her microcomputer or transmit them by modem or even via satellite uplink to a photo editor at the AP's New York office.

## **H** Sensors

sensor

A *sensor* is a type of input device that collects specific kinds of data directly from the environment and transmits it to a computer. Although you are unlikely to see such input devices connected to a PC in an office, they exist all around us, often in invisible form. Sensors can be used for detecting all kinds of things: speed, movement, weight, pressure, temperature, humidity, wind, current, fog, gas, smoke, light, shapes, images, and so on.

Beneath the pavement, for example, are sensors that detect the speed and volume of traffic. These sensors send data to computers that can adjust traffic lights to keep cars and trucks away from gridlocked areas. In aviation, sensors are used to detect ice buildup on airplane wings or to alert pilots to sudden changes in wind direction. In California, sensors have been planted along major earthquake fault lines in an experiment to see if scientists can predict major earth movements. Sensors are also used by government regulators to monitor whether companies are complying with air-pollution standards.

## Human-Biology Input Devices

Characteristics and movements of the human body, when interpreted by sensors, optical scanners, voice recognition, and other technologies, can become forms of input. Some examples are as follows:

- *Biometric systems: Biometric security devices* identify a person through a fingerprint, voice intonation, or other biological characteristic. For example, retinal-identification devices use a ray of light to identify the distinctive network of blood vessels at the back of one's eyeball. Biometric systems are used, for example, in lieu of typed passwords to identify people authorized to use a computer system.

- *Line-of-sight systems:* Line-of-sight systems enable a person to use his or her eyes to "point" at the screen, a technology that allows physically handicapped users to direct a computer. This is accomplished by a video camera mounted beneath the monitor in front of the viewer. When the user looks at a certain place on the screen, the video camera and computer translate the area being focused on into screen coordinates.

- *Cyber gloves and body suits:* Special gloves and body suits—often used in conjunction with "virtual reality," or the computer-generated simulation of reality—use sensors to detect body movements. The data for these movements is sent to a computer system. Similar technology is being used for human-controlled robot hands, which are used in nuclear power plants and hazardous-waste sites.

- *Brainwave devices:* Perhaps the ultimate input device analyzes the electrical signals of the brain and translates them into computer commands. Experiments have been successful in getting users to move a cursor on the screen through sheer power of thought. Other experiments have shown users able to type a letter by slowly spelling out the words in their heads. Although there is a very long way to go before brainwave input technology becomes practicable, the consequences could be tremendous, not only for handicapped people but for all of us.

## Input Controls: Preserving Data Integrity

**Input controls are necessary to ensure the accuracy of input data; otherwise the output may not be accurate.**

No matter how sophisticated your input hardware is and how well thought out your input methods are, you still run the risk of generating inaccurate or even useless information. The completeness and accuracy of information produced by a computer system depend to a great extent on how much care was taken in capturing the raw data that served as input to the processing procedures. An old computer-related saying summarizes this point: "Garbage In, Garbage Out" (GIGO). If you—the user—input incomplete and inaccurate data (Garbage In), then you can expect the information that is produced to be correspondingly incomplete and inaccurate (Garbage Out). How do you ensure that input data is accurate and complete?

**Input controls** include a combination of manual and computer-based control procedures designed to ensure that all input data has been accurately put into computer-usable form. A variety of control techniques can be used, depending on the design of the computer system and the nature of the processing activities taking place. Systems designers study these techniques and build them into systems. .

How important are input controls? Consider the modest-living couple who got a phone bill or a local store's invoice for $450,000 and spent months trying to convince the company it was a mistake. The customer service personnel and the data processing staff were probably trying to identify the glitch in the input control procedures. The computer doesn't make mistakes; the people who input data and monitor input procedures do. Even software writers are not infallible. Without input controls, mistakes might be impossible to detect or correct. Imagine the consequences this could have at the level of international trade, politics, and military activities. Of course, input controls are not the only controls involving data accuracy, completeness, and security.

# SUMMARY

■ *Input hardware* consists of devices that take data and programs that people can read or comprehend and convert them to a form the computer can process. Input hardware is classified as keyboard entry or direct entry. (p. 38)

■ The *keyboard* is the most widely used input device. It includes five basic types of keys (p. 38):

1. *Standard typewriter keys*—used to type in text and special characters.

2. *Cursor-movement keys*—used to move the cursor, which marks the position of the next character to be typed, around on the screen. The keys for cursor movement are sometimes combined with the numeric keypad.

3. *Numeric keys*—used to enter numbers.

4. *Function keys*—used to issue commands. The purpose of each function key is defined by the software you are using.

5. *Special-purpose keys*—Backspace, Del, Ins, Esc, Ctrl, and Alt.

■ Keyboards are used with terminals hooked up to a large computer system. A terminal consists of a video display screen, a keyboard, and a communications link. (p. 43)

■ Terminals can be "dumb," "smart," or "intelligent." (p. 43)

—A *dumb terminal* is entirely dependent for all its capabilities on the computer system to which it is connected.

—A *smart terminal* can input data to and receive data from the main computer system and also do some limited processing on its own. An example of a smart terminal is an ATM.

—An *intelligent terminal* is essentially a full-fledged microcomputer with a communications link.

■ *Pointing devices* include mice, trackballs, and joysticks; touch screens; light pens; digitizing tablets; and pen-based systems.

■ The principal pointing tools used with microcomputers are:

1. The *mouse*—a small, hand-held device connected to the computer by a cable and rolled about on the desktop to direct the *mouse pointer* on the computer's display screen. (p. 45)

2. The *trackball*—essentially an upside-down mouse. A trackball is a movable ball, on top of a stationary device, that is rotated with the fingers or palm of the hand. Trackballs are used where space is limited. (p. 46)

3. The *joystick*—a pointing device that consists of a vertical handle like a gearshift lever mounted on a base with one or two buttons. (p. 46)

■ The *touch screen* is a special display screen that is sensitive to touch. The user touches the screen at desired locations, often marked by labeled boxes, to "point out" choices to the computer. (p. 48)

■ The *light pen* is a light-sensitive stylus, or pen-like device, connected by a cable to the computer. The user brings the pen to the desired point on the display screen and presses the pen button, which identifies that screen location to the computer. (p. 48)

■ The *digitizing tablet* is a tablet connected by a cable to a stylus or puck. A stylus is a pen-like device with which the user "sketches" an image. A puck is a copying device with which the user copies an image. Digitizing tablets are used primarily in design and engineering. (p. 48)

■ *Pen-based computer systems* use a pen-like stylus to enter handwriting and marks into a computer. There are four types of pen-based systems (p. 49):

1. *Gesture recognition or electronic checklists:* Gesture recognition refers to a pen-based computer system's ability to recognize various check marks, slashes, or carefully printed block letters and numbers placed in boxes.

2. *Handwriting stored as scribbling:* This type of pen-based system stores handwriting as scribble and doesn't convert it into typed text.

3. *Handwriting converted to typed text with training:* This type of pen-based system stores handwriting as text. These systems require that the machine be "trained" to recognize handwriting.

4. *Handwriting converted to typed text without training:* This type of pen-based system stores handwriting as text without training.

■ *Scanning devices* include bar-code readers, mark- and character-recognition devices, fax machines, and imaging systems. (p. 51)

■ A *bar-code reader* is a special type of scanner that "reads" bar codes on products such as grocery items and translates the codes into electrical signals for the computer system. (p. 51)

■ There are three types of scanning devices that read marks or characters (p. 52):

1. *Magnetic-ink character recognition (MICR)* equipment is used to read the strange-looking numbers printed at the bottom of checks, and then produce a digitized signal.

2. *Optical mark recognition (OMR)* uses a device that reads pencil marks such as those entered on college SAT tests, and converts them into computer-usable form.

3. *Optical character recognition (OCR)* uses a device that reads special preprinted characters and converts them into machine-readable form. Examples that use OCR characters are utility bills and price tags.

■ A *fax (facsimile) machine* is a type of scanner that "reads" text and graphics and then transmits them over telephone lines to another fax machine, which re-creates the image. There are two types of fax machines (p. 53):

1. *Dedicated fax machine*—a specialized device that does nothing except send and receive fax documents.

2. *Fax modem*—modem with fax capability installed as a circuit board inside a computer; it can send and receive electronic signals via telephone lines directly to/from a computer similarly equipped or to/from a dedicated fax machine.

■ An *imaging system*—also known as an image scanner, or graphics scanner—converts text, drawings, and photographs into digital form that can be stored in a computer system. (p. 55)

■ A *smart card* is a wallet-type card that contains a microprocessor and memory chip that can be used to input data. In some countries, telephone users may buy a smart card allowing them to make telephone calls until the programmed total cost is used up. (p. 56)

■ An *optical card* is a plastic, credit-card-size card using laser technology, like music compact disks, which can be used to input data. Because they hold so much data, optical cards have considerable potential, such as a health card holding a person's medical history including digitized X-rays. (p. 56)

■ A *voice-recognition system* converts a person's speech into digital code; the system compares the electrical patterns produced by the speaker's voice with a set of prerecorded patterns stored in the computer. (p. 56)

■ Five other types of input devices are (p. 58):

1. *Audio-input devices* record or play analog sound and translate it for digital storage and processing.

2. *Video-input devices* convert video from analog to digital form. Two types of video cards are the frame-grabber video and the full-motion video.

3. *Electronic cameras* capture images in electronic form, which can be manipulated by a computer, for immediate viewing on a television or computer display screen. Two types of electronic cameras are still-video and digital-video.

4. *Sensors* collect specific kinds of data directly from the environment and transmit it to a computer.

5. *Human-biology input devices* convert characteristics and movements of the human body into a form of input. Some examples include biometric systems, line-of-sight systems, cyber gloves and body suits, and brainwave devices.

■ Input controls are manual and computer-based procedures designed to ensure that input data is entered accurately. Without controls, erroneous data can be entered, resulting in unreliable output: "Garbage In, Garbage Out" (GIGO). (p. 60)

## KEY TERMS

audio-input device, p. 58
bar code, p. 51
bar-code reader, p. 51
cursor, p. 41
cursor-movement keys, p. 41
dedicated fax machine, p. 53
digitizing tablet, p. 48
direct-entry device, p. 38
dumb terminal, p. 43
Enter key, p. 41
ergonomics, p. 42
executive workstation, p. 44
fax (facsimile) machine, p. 53
fax modem, p. 54
function keys, p. 41
imaging system, p. 55
input controls, p. 61

input hardware, p. 38
intelligent terminal, p. 44
joystick, p. 46
keyboard, p. 38
light pen, p. 48
magnetic-ink character recognition (MICR), p. 52
mouse, p. 45
mouse pointer, p. 45
multimedia system, p. 58
numeric keys (keypad), p. 41
optical card, p. 56
optical character recognition (OCR), p. 52
optical mark recognition (OMR), p. 52

pen-based computer system, p. 49
personal digital assistant (PDA), p. 50
point-of-sale (POS) terminal, p. 43
portable terminal, p. 43
scanning device, p. 51
smart card, p. 56
smart terminal, p. 43
terminal, p. 43
touch screen, p. 48
trackball, p. 46
voice-recognition system, p. 57

## EXERCISES

### SELF-TEST

1. One of the easiest ways to categorize input hardware is whether or not it uses a(n) _key board_ .

2. Most keyboards used with microcomputers include the following types of keys:

   a. ALPHABET        standard type writer key
   b. NUMBER.        function key.
   c. function.        number key
   d. arrow        special purpose key.
   e. space bar.        cursor movement key.

3. What determines what the function keys on a keyboard do?
    _OR appl. software_

4. Cursor-movement keys are used to execute commands. (true/**false**)

5. A smart card looks like a credit card but contains a microprocessor and memory chip. (true/false)

6. A(n) ~~hard disk scanner~~ enables users to convert hardcopy text and graphics into computer-usable code.

7. List the three most common pointing devices used with microcomputers.
   a. Mice
   b. Track ball
   c. ~~Pen~~ Joy stick

8. A(n) __direct__-__entry__ device is used for data entry and doesn't use a keyboard.

9. Ergonomics is the study of the physical relationships between people and their work environment. (**true**/false)

10. A(n) __Joy stick__ is a pointing device that consists of a vertical handle like a gearshift lever mounted on a base with one or two buttons.

11. Trackballs are used to input data when the user has a great deal of space to work in. (true/**false**)

12. A(n) __CRT dump__ terminal is entirely dependent for all its processing activities on the computer system to which it is hooked up.

13. The most popular input hardware device is the __key board__.

14. QWERTY describes a common keyboard layout. (**true**/false)

15. Personal digital assistants (PDAs) are small pen-controlled, handheld computers that, in their most developed form, can do two-way wireless messaging. (**true**/false)

16. __INPUT__ __CONTROL__ are designed to ensure the accuracy of input data.

17. Function keys are used the same way with every software application. (true/**false**)

18. A dedicated fax machine is installed as a circuit board inside the computer's system cabinet. (true/**false**)

19. A code is sent to the computer every time a keyboard key is pressed. (**true**/false)

20. There are three types of scanning devices that read marks or characters. They are usually referred to by their abbreviations MICR, OMR, and OCR. (**true**/false)

## SHORT-ANSWER QUESTIONS

1. What are the two main categories of input hardware?
2. What is a fax machine?
3. What is a mouse and how is it used?
4. What is a terminal?
5. What are audio-input and video-input devices used for?
6. What is an imaging system?
7. What are human-biology input devices?
8. What is the importance of input controls?
9. What is the difference between a dedicated fax machine and a fax modem?
10. What is a voice-recognition system?

## PROJECTS AND CRITICAL THINKING EXERCISES

1. Write a few paragraphs describing how you think the input devices described in this chapter might be used in your planned profession.
2. What kinds of input devices would you use to update a design of an appliance created before the use of computers? Why?
3. Research scanning technology. What differentiates one scanner from another? Is it the clarity of the scanned image? Price? Software? If you were going to buy a scanner, which do you think you would buy? Why? What do you need to run a color scanner? How do you think scanners are used in your chosen profession?
4. During the next week, make a list of all the input devices you notice—in stores, on campus, at the bank, in the library, on the job, at the doctor's, and so on. At the end of the week, report on the devices you have listed and name some of the advantages you think are associated with each device.
5. Interview someone in your school or business's computer center and find out what kinds of input controls are used to minimize the amount of errors input to the system. Give a short report.
6. Reread the Clipboard box on p. 47 by David Gerlernter. Do you agree with his opinions? What other problems regarding the use of computers in the classroom can you identify? What can be done to solve these problems while at the same time promoting appropriate use of computers in education? Prepare a one-page statement.
7. Since magnetic-strip cards are so popular in the United States, how soon do you think it will take for smart cards and optical cards to "catch on" in this country? Or will they ever become widely used? If smart cards and/or optical cards do become available how do you think you might use one?

# THE CLIPBOARD
## Of Things to Come

What technological advances will we see in the next decade? Researchers at Battelle (a Columbus, Ohio, company that develops, commercializes, and manages technology) say they have a fairly good idea. They identified 10 technologies they think will evolve in the next decade that meet three criteria: People will want to buy the technology, the technology will have a competitive advantage, and it will support business goals. Their predictions include:

1. Scientific researchers will map the human genome for genetic-based identification and diagnostics, so perhaps diseases can be treated before they occur.

2. Manufacturers will develop "super materials" designed on the molecular level for high-performance in transportation, computers, energy, and communications.

3. Longer-lasting and portable energy sources, such as fuel cells and batteries, will be produced.

4. Digital, high-definition television is expected to be a huge breakthrough for better pictures and more channels.

5. Electronics will be miniaturized for personal use, so perhaps wireless devices the size of a pocket calculator will serve as a fax, telephone, and computer.

6. "Smart computerized systems" will control manufacturing processes.

7. Anti-aging products and services will be the rage.

8. Medical treatments will target illnesses more precisely; for instance, chemotherapy will target just the cancer cells and reduce side effects.

9. Motor vehicles will use more than one type of fuel, selecting the appropriate fuel for various conditions.

10. Children will expect more from education and require more edutainment/multimedia products for learning.

# Chapter Topics

# CHAPTER 3

# Processing Hardware

How is it possible that today's portable computers are now as powerful as former mainframes? This development is the result of technology that can cram increasing numbers of tiny electrical switches called *transistors* onto a thumbnail-size sliver of mineral called *silicon*. In this chapter we describe how the silicon chip works as a processor in PCs, workstations, minicomputers, mainframes, and supercomputers. We also show how it has become a powerful force behind portable technology.

## Preview

*When you have completed this chapter, you will be able to:*

- Distinguish between the four types of computer systems: microcomputers, minicomputers, mainframes, and supercomputers

- Identify the two main parts of the central processing unit and describe their functions

- Explain how data is represented in a computer system

- Describe the processing components found in a microcomputer's system unit

- Describe some future processing technologies

**Why Is This Chapter Important?**

*You may never have to look inside a computer, although, if a computer technician comes to your office to fix your microcomputer, we recommend that you look over his or her shoulder and ask the technician to identify some of the internal components, just so you can get a general idea of what's going on inside. But why do you need to know anything about the processing hardware and activities any more than you need to know how the engine of a car works?*

- *Just as some people like to work on their own cars, you may decide, for example, that it's economical for you to do some work on your microcomputer. For instance, you may find that some new software programs are too sophisticated for your computer, that your computer cannot hold enough data or instructions or process them fast enough, and that you need to add some more random access memory. This may well be something you can do yourself.*

- *More likely, you will some day need to make a buying decision about a computer, either for yourself or for an organization. And, just as when you buy a car, you should learn something about the topic first. It is important to understand processing facts and trends so you can purchase a computer that indeed meets your needs and avoid purchasing a machine that will be obsolete in the near future.*

  *In Chapter 1 we gave you a brief overview of the four types of computer systems. We would like to start now by describing these systems in more detail so you will have a basis for understanding and comparing processing hardware components.*

## Four Types of Computer Systems

Computers are classified as microcomputers, minicomputers, mainframe computers, and supercomputers. Microcomputers may be either personal computers (PCs) or workstations. PCs include desktop and floor-standing units, luggables, laptops, notebooks, subnotebooks, pocket PCs (electronic organizers, palmtops, personal digital assistants), and pen computers. Workstations are sophisticated desktop microcomputers used for

**Figure 3.1**

Different sizes of computers. Shown are several types of microcomputers (*left to right*)—desktop microcomputer, workstation, floor-standing (tower) microcomputer, luggable microcomputer, laptop, notebook, subnotebook, pocket PC, and pen computer—plus a minicomputer, a mainframe, and a supercomputer.

| Desktop | Workstation | Floorstanding (tower) micro | Luggable | Laptop | Notebook |

technical purposes. **Minicomputers are intermediate-size machines that have become important as "servers," for holding databases and programs for many PCs. Mainframes are large computers used in large companies to handle millions of transactions. The high-capacity machines called *supercomputers* are the fastest calculating devices and are used for large-scale projects. Supercomputers have two designs: vector processing and massively parallel processing.**

Generally speaking, the larger the computer, the greater its processing power. As we described in Chapter 1, computers are often classified into four sizes—small, medium, large, and super-large, which (though the sizes overlap) are given the following names:

- Microcomputers—both personal computers and workstations
- Minicomputers
- Mainframe computers
- Supercomputers

The differences among these categories are illustrated in Figure 3.1.

## Microcomputers: Personal Computers

We have little doubt that you will become familiar with this type. **Microcomputers** are small computers that can fit on or beside a desktop or are portable. Often microcomputers are used as terminals connected to a larger computer system (network). A **terminal** may or may not do processing by itself. However, it provides a keyboard for input and a display screen and perhaps a printer for output from a computer system.

Microcomputers can be personal computers and workstations.

**Personal computers (PCs)** are desktop, floor-standing, or portable computers that can run easy-to-use programs such as word processing or spreadsheets. PCs come in several sizes, as follows.

- *Desktop and floor-standing units:* Even though many personal computers today are portable, even buyers of new PCs often opt for nonportable systems, for reasons of price, power, and flexibility. For example, the television-tube-like monitors that come with desktops have display screens that are easier to read than those of many portables. Moreover, you can stuff a desktop's roomy system cabinet with add-on circuit boards (to extend the computer's capabilities) and other extras, which is not possible with portables.

    *Desktop PCs* are those in which the system cabinet sits on a desk, the monitor often on top and the keyboard in front. A difficulty with this

| Subnotebook | Pocket computer | Pen PC | Minicomputer | Mainframe | Supercomputer |
|---|---|---|---|---|---|

arrangement is that the system cabinet's "footprint" can deprive you of a fair amount of desk space. *Floor-standing PCs* are those in which the system cabinet sits as a "tower" on the floor next to the desk, giving you more usable desk space. The IBM PS/2 (for Personal System/2) is available in both desktop and floor-standing versions.

■ *Luggables*: A *luggable computer* weighs between 20 and 25 pounds. The typical luggable has processor, monitor, disk drives, and keyboard combined in one unit. Sometimes the unit will include the printer also. Although 25 pounds may not seem like much to lift, as one source points out, "carrying that much onto an airplane or to work every day may make you think you bought a cruise ship's anchor!"[1]

Today luggables have largely been superseded by laptops, notebooks, subnotebooks, and pocket PCs. An example of a luggable is the IBM PS/2 Model P75.

■ *Laptops*: A **laptop computer** is a portable computer equipped with a flat display screen and weighing 8–20 pounds. The top of the computer opens up like a clamshell to reveal the screen.

We describe the differences between display screens elsewhere. Here we will simply say that flat screens don't provide the quality of the monitors found with desktop computers (although that is changing). However, most laptops can be hooked up to standard desktop-type monitors so that you don't lose display quality.

Some laptops, such as Toshiba's T48450CT or T6400MM and the Dell Dimension XPS P90, carry multimedia systems. (See Figure 3.2.) A **multimedia system** has the capacity to incorporate text, sound, video, graphics, and animation in computer-based presentations.

**Figure 3.2**
Multimedia laptop. The Toshiba T6400MM multimedia laptop computer is shown here between two speakers. It offers the capacity to present not only color graphics and text but also sound, video, and animation. Portable multimedia systems are useful for education, training, and sales presentations.

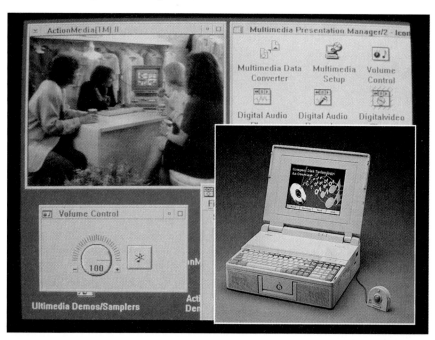

■ *Notebooks*: A **notebook computer** is a portable computer that weighs 4–7.5 pounds and is roughly the size of a thick notebook, perhaps 8½ × 11 inches. Notebook PCs can easily be tucked into a briefcase or backpack or simply under your arm.

Notebook computers can be just as powerful as some desktop machines. However, because they are smaller, the keys on the keyboard are closer together and harder to use. Also, as with laptops, the display screens are more difficult to read.

An example of a notebook is the Zenith Z-Note, which weighs 5.9 pounds. Another is the Macintosh PowerBook 170, which has a color display screen and weighs less than 7 pounds.

■ *Subnotebooks:* A **subnotebook computer** weighs 2.5–4 pounds. Clearly, subnotebooks have more of both the advantages and the disadvantages of notebooks.

Examples of subnotebooks are Hewlett-Packard's Omnibook 300 (2.9 pounds), IBM's ThinkPad 500 (3.8 pounds), Zenith's Z-Lite 320L (3.9 pounds), and Apple's Macintosh PowerBook Duo (less than 4 pounds). The Duo has an optional docking unit that converts the PowerBook into a desktop unit. (*Docking* means that the subnotebook unit slips into a slot in the desktop unit, thereby becoming the desktop unit's processing system.)

■ *Pocket PCs:* **Pocket personal computers,** or **handhelds,** weigh 1 pound or less. These PCs are useful in specific situations, as when a driver of a package-express truck must send hourly status reports to company headquarters. Another use is when police officers must check out suspicious car license numbers with a central computer. Other pocket PCs have more general applications as electronic diaries and pocket organizers.

Pocket PCs may be classified as three types:
1. **Electronic organizers** are specialized pocket computers that mainly store appointments, addresses, and "To do" lists. Recent versions feature wireless links to other computers for data transfer. Some electronic organizers can share stored data with an IBM-compatible PC through a connecting wire. One model transmits data via infrared light, resembling a TV remote control. An example of an electronic organizer is the Sharp Wizard (15.2 ounces).
2. **Palmtop computers** are PCs that are small enough to hold in one hand and operate with the other. They also use the same software as IBM PCs. Examples of palmtop computers are the Hewlett-Packard 95LX (11 ounces) and the Atari Portfolio.
3. **Personal digital assistants (PDAs),** or *personal communicators,* are small, pen-controlled, handheld computers that, in their most developed form, can do two-way wireless messaging. With these devices one uses a special pen (stylus) to write out commands on the computer screen instead of pecking at a tiny keyboard. Examples of PDAs are the Apple Newton MessagePad 120 (1.3 pounds), the Casio Z-7000 (1 pound), and the Sony Magic Link (20 ounces).

■ *Pen computers:* Often the size of a subnotebook or pocket computer, a **pen computer** lacks a keyboard or mouse but allows you to input data by writing directly on the screen with a stylus, or pen. Pen computers are useful for inventory control, as when a store clerk has to count merchandise; for package-delivery drivers who must get electronic signatures as proof of delivery; and for more general purposes, like those of electronic organizers and PDAs.

Pen computers range from the 3-pound AT&T EO (no longer manufactured) to the lightweight Sharp Expert Pad (15.5 ounces) and the Amstrad PDA (14 ounces).

Peter Ferrara, chief operating officer of Granum Communications, which owns five radio stations, used to use a paper organizer to keep track of meetings, deals, and other events. Then he bought a Newton MessagePad, made by Apple Computer. He told a magazine interviewer how it works.

### How does [the Newton] differ from the paper organizer you gave up?

My old organizer had a calendar section, a telephone and address section, and a "to do" section, and so does the Newton. The difference is that I would fill my organizer with yellow sticky notes and airline schedules, and pretty soon the whole thing was bulging with paper. With my Newton, everything is there and put away in one place. I don't have to wonder, "Now, where did that little piece of paper go?"

Also, the Newton does some things automatically that I used to have to do myself. If I don't get a "to do" item on a certain day and check it off, the Newton moves it to the following day so I won't forget it. . . .

### How hard was it to get the Newton to work smoothly?

The Newton either converts your handwriting to type or stores an image of what you've written as "electronic ink." I started with the first Newton, and it took about a month of practicing every day before it could recognize my handwriting at an acceptable level. Recently I upgraded my system with a chip that comes with the new MessagePad 110. The handwriting recognition is vastly improved, and it also lets you choose letter-by-letter recognition for unfamiliar words instead of limiting you to words in its dictionary. But even before the upgrade, the Newton was getting better at recognizing my handwriting—and I was learning to write more neatly.

### What advice would you give a prospective Newton user?

The Newton requires patience, but it can be a very powerful and useful tool. You have to be organized or be willing to get organized, or it will frustrate you. Because handwriting recognition takes time, it forces you to be brief and orderly in your thoughts. I use things the Newton does well to make my life simpler. When it doesn't work as well for other things, such as taking notes during a meeting, I don't force it.

Alison L. Sprout, "Getting the Most Out of Newton," *Fortune,* July 25, 1994, p. 237.

What is the one thing besides their light weight that makes portable computers truly portable? The answer: batteries. A typical notebook's batteries will keep it running about 3–5 hours, a subnotebook's about 3 hours; Dell's lithium-ion batteries last 6–8 hours. Then the PC must be plugged into an AC outlet and charged up again. Some travelers carry spare battery packs.

### Microcomputers: Workstations

Workstations look like desktop PCs but are far more powerful. Traditionally, **workstations** were sophisticated machines that fit on a desktop, cost $10,000–$150,000, and were used mainly by engineers and scientists for technical purposes. Workstations have caught the eye of the public mainly for their graphics capabilities, such as those that film director Steven Spielberg used to breathe life into dinosaurs for the movie *Jurassic Park*. (See Figure

3.3.) However, workstations have also been used for computer-aided design and manufacturing (CAD/CAM), software development, and scientific modeling. Well-known makers of workstations have been Sun Microsystems, Hewlett-Packard, IBM, Digital Equipment, and Silicon Graphics.

Two recent developments have altered the differences between workstations and PCs:[2]

- *Decline in workstation prices:* A workstation that not long ago cost $15,000 or more is now available for under $5,000, which puts it within range of many PC buyers.

- *Increase in PC power:* In 1993 Intel Corporation introduced the Pentium chip, and in 1994 Motorola (with IBM and Apple) introduced its Power PC chip. Both of these very powerful microprocessors are now found in PCs. In addition, IBM's OS/2 and Microsoft Corporation's Windows NT, are among the first operating systems designed to take advantage of more powerful microprocessors. (Also, another full-featured operating system from Microsoft, Windows 95, should be released in the second half of 1995.)

It might be deduced that, if PCs are becoming more powerful, then workstations are becoming more powerful still—and indeed they are. Over the past 15 years the fastest workstations have increased in speed a thousandfold.[3] They have been cutting into the sales not only of minicomputers and mainframes but even of supercomputers. These large machines have become vulnerable particularly because workstations can now be harnessed in "clusters" to attack a problem simultaneously.

**Figure 3.3**

Workstation. Steven Spielberg, through the Marin County, California, company Industrial Light and Magic, used workstations to create the special effects for his dinosaur epic, *Jurassic Park*.

We turn now from the microcomputer to what is called "big iron"—computers of greater size and power: minicomputers, mainframes, and supercomputers.

## Minicomputers

**Minicomputers** are machines midway in cost and capability between microcomputers and mainframes. They can be used either as single workstations or as a system tied by network to several hundred terminals for many users. (See Figure 3.4.) Costing between $20,000 and $250,000, the minicomputer overlaps with other categories of computers. A low-end minicomputer may be about as powerful as a high-end microcomputer (called a *supermicro*) and cost about the same. A high-end minicomputer (called a *supermini*) may equal a low-end mainframe. Launched in 1959 by Digital Equipment Corp. (DEC), minicomputers are also made by Data General, Hewlett-Packard, Tandem, AT&T, and IBM, as well as by newer companies like Sequent Computer Systems and Pyramid Technology.

Traditionally, minicomputers have been used to serve the needs of medium-size companies or of departments within larger companies, often for accounting or design and manufacturing (CAD/CAM). Minis are also becoming more important as "servers."[4] A **server** is a central computer that holds databases and programs for many PCs, workstations, or terminals, called *clients*. These clients are linked by a computer network. The entire network is called a client-server network.

## Mainframes

The large computers called *mainframes* are the oldest category of computer system. The word "mainframe" probably comes from the metal frames, housed in cabinets, on which manufacturers mounted the computer's electronic circuits.

Occupying specially wired, air-conditioned rooms and capable of great processing speeds and data storage, **mainframes** are air-cooled computers that are about the size of a jeep and range in price from $50,000 to $5 million. (See Figure 3.5.) Such machines are typically operated by professional programmers and technicians in a centrally managed department—often known as the "glass house"—within a large company. Examples of such companies are banks, airlines, and insurance companies, which handle millions of transactions. The principal makers of mainframes have been IBM, Fujitsu, Hitachi, NEC, Unisys, and Amdahl; more recent competitors are AT&T and Encore Computer Corp.[5]

Today, one hears, "mainframes are dead," being supplanted everywhere by small computers connected together in networks in a trend known as "downsizing." Is this true? The world has an estimated $1 trillion invested in this kind of "big iron"—perhaps 50,000 mainframes, 60% of them made and sold by IBM.[6] But what are the future prospects for people working in a company's glass house? Although mainframe manufacturers will probably promote new uses for their equipment (such as to make them servers), there appear to be three trends:[7,8]

- *Old mainframes will be kept for some purposes:* Massive and repetitive computing chores, such as maintaining a company's payroll, may best be left on a mainframe rather than moved to a new system.

- *Networks of smaller computers will grow:* Mainframes usually cannot be reprogrammed quickly to develop new products and services, such as to pull together information about single customers from different divisions

**Figure 3.4**
Minicomputer. The VAX is made by Digital Equipment Corp.

**Figure 3.5**
Mainframe. The IBM ES/9000.

of a bank. Networks offer the flexibility that mainframes lack because they are not burdened with an accumulation of out-of-date programming.

■ *Mainframes will be reinvented:* IBM has worked to redesign mainframes, which formerly were essentially custom-built. Now they are being manufactured on an assembly-line basis, making them less expensive. In addition, the automobile-size machines will be reduced to the size of a desk. Using more recent technology, new mainframes will not require water cooling. As a result, a $1 million machine will come down in price to only $100,000.

## Supercomputers

Gregory Chudnovsky, 39, with the help of his older brother, David, built a supercomputer in the living room of his New York City apartment. Seven feet tall and 8 feet across, the supercomputer was put together from mail-order parts and cost only $70,000 (compared to $30 million for some commercial supercomputers).

The brothers, both mathematicians and former citizens of the Soviet Union, have found some drawbacks to their homemade machine, which they named "m zero." They must keep the computer, along with 25 fans, running day and night. They must make sure the apartment's lights are turned off as much as possible, to prevent blowing the wiring in their living unit. "The building superintendent doesn't know that the Chudnovsky brothers have been using a supercomputer in Gregory's apartment," reports journalist Richard Preston, "and the brothers haven't expressed an eagerness to tell him."[9] Still, the machine makes their lives more convenient. The "m zero" performs computations that make up the basis of many of the scholarly papers and books they write on number theory and mathematical physics.

Most supercomputer users aren't as resourceful as the Chudnovskys and must buy their equipment from manufacturers. Typically priced from $225,000 to more than $30 million, **supercomputers** are high-capacity machines that require special air-conditioned rooms and are the fastest calculating devices ever invented. (See Figure 3.6.) Makers of supercomputers include Cray Research, Intel Supercomputers, Convex, Hitachi, nCube, Fujitsu, NEC, MasPar, and Thinking Machines (filed for bankruptcy protection).

**Figure 3.6**
Supercomputer. Cray Y-MP/C90.

Supercomputer users are those who need to model complex phenomena. Examples are automotive engineers who simulate cars crashing into walls, military scientists modeling nuclear explosions, and airplane designers simulating air flowing over an airplane wing. "Supers," as they are called, are also used for oil exploration and weather forecasting. They can even help managers in department-store chains decide what to buy and where to stock it. Finally, they have been used to help redesign parachutes, which are surprisingly complex from the standpoint of aerodynamics. The supercomputer simulates the flow of air in and around the parachute during its descent.

Supercomputers are designed in two ways:

■ *Vector processors:* The traditional design, now 20 years old, is vector processing. In vector processing, a relatively few (1–16) large, highly specialized processors run calculations at high speeds. The drawback is that tasks are accomplished by a single large processor (or handful of processors) one by one, in serial fashion, creating potential bottlenecks. In addition, the processors are costly to build, and they run so hot that they need elaborate cooling systems.

■ *Massively parallel processors:* The newer design is called *massively parallel processing (MPP),* which spreads calculations over hundreds or even thousands of standard, inexpensive microprocessors of the type used in PCs. Tasks are parceled out to a great many processors, which work simultaneously. The reason the Chudnovsky brothers were able to build their super so cheaply was that they used standard microprocessors available for PCs in an MPP design.

A difficulty is that MPP machines are notoriously difficult to program. Still, with the right software, 100 small processors can often run a large program in far less time than the largest supercomputer running it in serial fashion, one instruction at a time.[10]

Massively parallel processing might seem as powerful as one could expect. However, fiber-optic (glass fiber) communications lines have made possible supercomputing power that is truly awesome. Scientists at the National Science Foundation are attempting to link 21 supercomputers at four locations throughout the United States into what they call a nationwide "metacenter." With this arrangement a scientist sitting at a terminal or workstation anywhere in the country could have access to all the power of these fast machines simultaneously.[11] (See Figure 3.7.)

The four kinds of computers are compared in the table on the next page. (See Table 3.1.)

## The CPU and Main Memory

**The central processing unit (CPU) consists of the control unit and the arithmetic/logic unit (ALU). Main memory holds data in storage temporarily; its capacity varies in different computers. Registers are staging areas that store data during processing. The operations for executing a single program instruction are called the machine cycle, which has an instruction cycle and an execution cycle. Processing speeds are expressed in three ways: fractions of a second, MIPS, and flops.**

How is the information in "information processing" in fact processed? As we indicated, this is the job of the circuitry known as the *microprocessor.* This

**Figure 3.7**
Powerful supercomputer network. In the National Science Foundation plan,
21 supercomputers at four locations are linked into a "metacenter." This is a
national network that allows scientists anywhere in the United States to
have access to the computers' combined processing power.

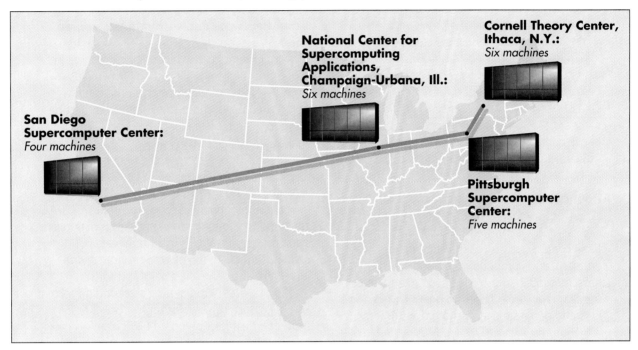

**Table 3.1**  Four types of computers compared. Figures are approximate,
owing to rapid technological changes and blurring of distinctions.

|  | MICROCOMPUTER | MINICOMPUTER | MAINFRAME | SUPERCOMPUTER |
|---|---|---|---|---|
| **Main memory (RAM)** | 512,000– 32,000,000 characters | 8,000,000– 50,000,000 characters | 32,000,000– 200,000,000 characters | 100,000,000– 2,000,000,000 characters |
| **Storage** | 360,000– 300,000,000 characters | 120,000,000– 1,000,000,000+ characters | 500,000,000–? characters | No limitation |
| **Processing speed** | 800,000– 10,000,000 instructions per second | 8–40 MIPS* | 30 MIPS and up | 200 MIPS and up |
| **Cost** | $500–$20,000 | $20,000– $250,000 | $50,000 and up | $225,000 and up |

*MIPS: millions of instructions per second

device, the "processor-on-a-chip" found in a microcomputer, is also called the
CPU. The CPU works hand in hand with other circuits known as *main memory* to carry out processing.

*Al Cohn is an engineer who is also a marketing manager for a division of Akron-based Goodyear, Tire & Rubber. Part of his job is to call on big customers to sell tires used for fleets of vehicles. One of his tools is a portable IBM ThinkPad with software that helps him connect via phone lines to the company's mainframe. He told an interviewer how this arrangement helps him with sales calls.*

**How can a mainframe help land a sale?**

We've got six years' worth of performance data, such as statistics on tread wear, durability, and fuel economy, as well as information on pricing, tire sizes, and competitors' products. When you have that much information, you need a mainframe: no portable system can crunch the numbers and generate charts and graphs that fast.

During a sales call we hook into the mainframe by phone and can answer specific questions from the customer—for example, how a particular tire performs on Mack trucks that haul coal in Kentucky with an average load of 6,000 pounds per tire. In 8 to 10 seconds we can generate a graph with the answer and print it out. In the old days people would ask questions like these, and we'd say, "Sure, let us look in our files, and we'll get back to you in two weeks."

**What hardware and software lets you do this?**

The equipment I carry depends on what we're trying out. Right now I have an IBM ThinkPad 702C, which is a notebook computer with a color screen. We chose the ThinkPad in part because of its removable hard-disk drive, which makes it possible to carry around several different drives loaded with presentation material. The ThinkPad's optional credit-card-size modem lets me call the mainframe back in Akron.

We use software called Attachmate EXTRA! for Windows to make the ThinkPad function like a mainframe terminal. Attachmate lets you switch from PC to mainframe programs with ease, and also sends files back and forth. . . .

To put everything in nice presentation form I use Microsoft Powerpoint for Windows or IBM Storyboard LIVE! Storyboard LIVE! also lets me add animation. Sometimes I bring an nVIEW MediaPro LCD [liquid crystal display] panel that fits on an overhead projector so I can show everything I'm doing on a big screen. If the customer has a VCR and TV, I'll use that to show clips of a truck rolling down the highway. It's my own kind of multimedia show.

Alison Sprout, "Getting Mileage from a Mainframe," *Fortune*, January 10, 1994, p. 85.

## The CPU

bus

The **CPU,** for **central processing unit,** follows the instructions of the software to manipulate data into information. The CPU consists of two parts: (1) the control unit and (2) the arithmetic/logic unit. The two components are connected by a kind of electronic roadway called a *bus.* (See Figure 3.8.)

- *Control unit:* The **control unit** tells the rest of the computer system how to carry out a program's instructions. It directs the movement of electronic signals between main memory and the arithmetic/logic unit. It also directs these electronic signals between main memory and the input and output devices.

- *Arithmetic/logic unit:* The **arithmetic/logic unit,** or **ALU,** performs arithmetic operations and logical operations and controls the speed of those operations.

**Figure 3.8**
The control unit and the arithmetic/logic unit. The two components are connected by a kind of electronic roadway called a *bus*. A bus also connects these components to main memory. Temporary data storage holding/computation working areas called *registers* are located in the arithmetic/logic unit.

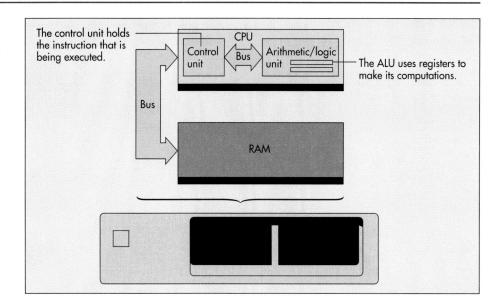

As you might guess, *arithmetic operations* are the fundamental math operations: addition, subtraction, multiplication, and division.

*Logical operations* are comparisons. That is, the ALU compares two pieces of data to see whether one is equal to (=), greater than (>), or less than (<) the other. (The comparisons can also be combined, as in "greater than or equal to" and "less than or equal to.")

The CPU, or microprocessor, is made of silicon. What is silicon, and why use it? *Silicon* is an element that is widely found in clay and sand. It is used not only because its abundance makes it cheap but also because it is a *semiconductor*. A *semiconductor* is material whose electrical properties are intermediate between a good conductor of electricity and a nonconductor of electricity. (An example of a good conductor of electricity is copper in household wiring; an example of a nonconductor is the plastic sheath around that wiring.) Because it is only a semiconductor, silicon has partial resistance to electricity. As a result, when good-conducting metals are overlaid on the silicon, the electronic circuitry of the integrated circuit can be created. (See Figure 3.9.)

In brief, chips are created like this:

1. A large drawing of electrical circuitry is made that looks something like the map of a train yard. The drawing is photographically reduced hundreds of times so that it is of microscopic size.

2. That reduced photograph is then duplicated many times so that, like a sheet of postage stamps, there are multiple copies of the same image or circuit.

3. That sheet of multiple copies of the circuit is then printed (in a printing process called *photolithography*) and etched onto a 3-inch-diameter piece of silicon called a wafer.

4. Subsequent printings of layer after layer of additional circuits produce multilayered and interconnected electronic circuitry built above and below the original silicon surface.

5. Later an automated die-cutting machine cuts the wafer into separate *chips,* which are usually less than 1 centimeter square and about half a millimeter thick. A **chip,** or **microchip,** is a tiny piece of silicon that

**Figure 3.9**
Making of a chip. *Top:* Silicon wafer imprinted with many microprocessors. *Bottom:* Microprocessor chip mounted in a protective frame with pins that can be connected to an electronic circuit board in a computer.

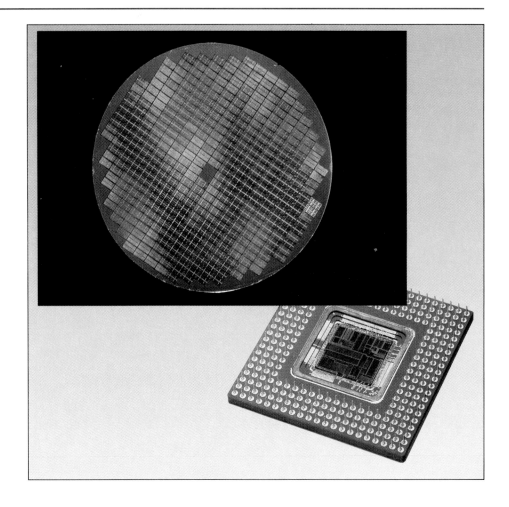

contains thousands of microminiature electronic circuit components, mainly transistors. (A transistor is like an electronic "gate," or switch, that opens and closes to transmit or stop electrical current. It can alternate between "on" and "off" millions of times per second.)

6. After being tested, each chip is then mounted in a protective frame with extruding metallic pins that provide electrical connections through wires to a computer or other electronic device.

## Main Memory

**Main memory**—also known as **memory, primary storage, internal memory,** or **RAM** (for **random access memory**)—is working storage. It has three tasks. (1) It holds data for processing. (2) It holds instructions (the programs) for processing the data. (3) It holds data that has been processed (become useful information) and is waiting to be sent to an output or storage device. Main memory is contained on chips called *RAM chips,* as we describe shortly. This memory is in effect the computer's short-term storage capacity. It determines the total size of the programs and data files it can work on at any given moment.

There are two important facts to know about main memory:

■ *Its contents are temporary:* Once the power to the computer is turned off, all the data and programs within main memory simply vanish. This is why data must also be stored on disks and tapes—called *secondary storage* to distinguish them from main memory's *primary storage.*

Thus, main memory is said to be *volatile*. As mentioned earlier, *volatile storage* is temporary storage; the contents are lost when the power is turned off. Consequently, if you kick out the connecting power cord to your computer, whatever you are currently working on will immediately disappear. This impermanence is the reason why you should *frequently* save your work in progress to a secondary-storage medium such as a diskette or hard disk. By "frequently," we mean every 3–5 minutes.

■ *Its capacity varies in different computers:* The size of main memory is important. It determines how much data can be processed at once and how big and complex a program may be used to process it. This capacity varies with different computers, with older machines holding less.

For example, the original IBM PC, introduced in 1979, held only about 640,000 characters of data or instructions. By contrast, the later IBM PS/2e can hold over 16 *million* characters. The old IBM PC was fine for the software of its day. Since then, however, programs have begun to require much more memory.

## Registers: Staging Areas for Processing

The control unit and the ALU also contain registers, or special areas that enhance the computer's performance. (Refer back to Figure 3.8.) **Registers** are high-speed staging areas that temporarily store data during processing and provide working areas for computation. It could be said that main memory holds material that will be used "a little bit later." Registers hold material that is to be processed "immediately." The computer loads the program instructions and data from main memory into the registers just before processing, which helps the computer process faster. (There are several types of registers, including an instruction and address register, a storage register, and an accumulator.)

## The Machine Cycle: How a Single Instruction Is Processed

How does the computer keep track of the characters of data or instructions in main memory? Like a system of post-office mailboxes, it uses addresses. An *address* is the location, designated by a unique number, in main memory in which a character of data or an instruction is stored during processing. To process each character, the control unit of the CPU retrieves that character from its address in main memory and places it into a register. This is the first step in what is called the *machine cycle.*

The **machine cycle** is a series of operations performed to execute a single program instruction. The machine cycle consists of two parts: an instruction cycle, which fetches and decodes, and an execution cycle, which executes and stores. (See Figure 3.10.)

■ *Instruction cycle:* In the **instruction cycle,** or **I-cycle,** the control unit (1) fetches (gets) an instruction from main memory and (2) decodes that instruction (determines what it means).

■ *Execution cycle:* During the **execution cycle,** or **E-cycle,** the arithmetic/logic unit (3) executes the instruction (performs the operation on the data) and (4) stores the processed results in main memory or a register.

The details of the machine cycle are actually a bit more involved than this, but our description shows the general sequence. What's important for you to know is that the entire operation is synchronized by a *system clock,* as we will describe. The microprocessor clock speed is an important factor to consider when you are buying a computer.

**H** system clock

**Figure 3.10**
The machine cycle. *Left:* The machine cycle executes instructions one at a time during the instruction cycle and execution cycle, through four steps: fetch, decode, execute, store. *Right:* Example of how the addition of two numbers, 50 and 75, is processed and stored in a single machine cycle.

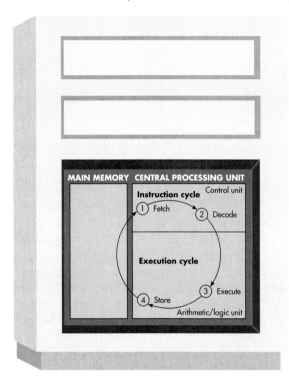
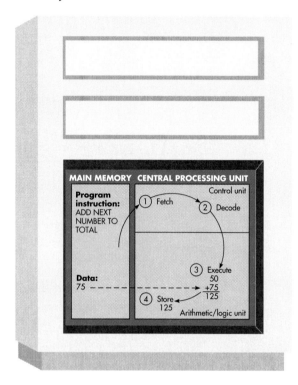

## Processing Speeds

With transistors switching off and on at perhaps millions of times per second, the tedious repetition of the machine cycle occurs at blinding speeds.

There are three ways in which processing speeds are measured:

- *Time to complete one machine cycle, in fractions of a second:* The speeds for completing one machine cycle are measured in milliseconds for older and slower computers. They are measured in microseconds for most microcomputers and in nanoseconds for mainframes. Picoseconds occur only in some experimental machines.

  A *millisecond* is one-thousandth of a second. A *microsecond* is one-millionth of a second. A *nanosecond* is one-billionth of a second. A *picosecond* is one-trillionth of a second.

- *Time to complete instructions, in millions of instructions per second (MIPS):* Another measurement is the number of instructions per second that a computer can process, which today is in the millions. **MIPS** is a measure of a computer's processing speed; it stands for **m**illions of **i**nstructions **p**er **s**econd that the processor can perform. A microcomputer (with an 80486 chip) might perform 54 MIPS, a mainframe 240 MIPS.

- *Time in floating-point operations per second (flops):* The abbreviation **flops** stands for **flo**ating-**p**oint operations per **s**econd, a floating-point operation being a special kind of mathematical calculation. This measure, usually expressed in *megaflops*—millions of floating-point operations per second —is used mainly with supercomputers. A Thinking Machines CM-2 super-computer might do 5200 megaflops.

## How Data and Programs are Represented in the Computer

Computers use the two-state, 0/1 binary system to represent data. Capacity of a computer is expressed in bits, bytes, kilobytes, megabytes, gigabytes, or terabytes. Two common binary coding schemes are ASCII-8 and EBCDIC. Parity-bit schemes are used to check for accuracy. Human programming languages are processed as 0s and 1s by the computer in machine language.

Electricity is the basis for computers and communications, but how is it used to represent data? We start with a simple fact: electricity can be either *on* or *off.*

Other kinds of technology also use this two-state on/off arrangement. An electrical circuit may be open or closed. The magnetic pulses on a disk or tape may be present or absent. Current may be high voltage or low voltage. A punched card or tape may have a hole or not have a hole. This two-state situation allows computers to use the *binary* system to represent data and programs. (*Bi-* means "two.")

### The Binary System: Using Two States

The decimal system that we are accustomed to has 10 digits (0, 1, 2, 3, 4, 5, 6, 7, 8, 9). By contrast, the **binary system** has only two digits: 0 and 1. Thus, in the computer the 0 can be represented by the electrical current being off (or at low voltage) and the 1 by the current being on (or at high voltage). All data and programs that go into the computer are represented in terms of these numbers. (See Figure 3.11.) For example, the letter *H* is a translation of the electronic signal 01001000, or off-on-off-off-on-off-off-off. When you press the key for *H* on the computer keyboard, the character is automatically converted into the series of electronic impulses that the computer recognizes.

**Figure 3.11**
Binary representation. How the letters *H-E-R-O* are represented in one type of off/on, 0/1 binary code.

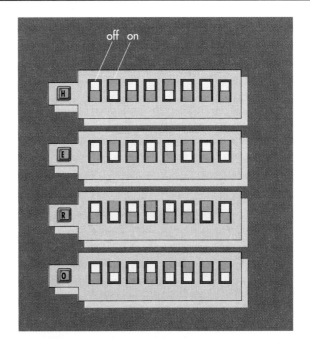

## How Capacity Is Expressed

How many 0s and 1s will a computer or a storage device such as a hard disk hold? This is a very important matter. The following terms are used to denote capacity:

- *Bit:* In the binary system, each 0 or 1 is called a **bit,** which is short for **b**inary dig**it.**

- *Byte:* To represent letters, numbers, or special characters (such as ! or *), bits are combined into groups. A group of 8 bits is called a **byte,** and a byte represents one character, digit, or other value. (For example, in one scheme, 01001000 represents the letter *H*.) The capacity of a computer's memory or a diskette is expressed in numbers of bytes or generally in multiples such as kilobytes and megabytes.

- *Kilobyte:* A **kilobyte (K, KB)** is about 1,000 bytes. (Actually, it's precisely 1,024 bytes, but the figure is commonly rounded.) The kilobyte was a common unit of measure for memory or secondary-storage capacity on older computers. The original IBM PC, for example, had 640 K (about 640,000 characters) of memory.

- *Megabyte:* A **megabyte (M, MB)** is about 1 million bytes (1,048,576 bytes). Most measures of microcomputer capacity today are expressed in megabytes.

- *Gigabyte:* A **gigabyte (G, GB)** is about 1 billion bytes (1,073,741,824 bytes). This measure is used with "big iron" types of computers.

- *Terabyte:* A **terabyte (T, TB)** represents about 1 trillion bytes (1,009,511,627,776 bytes).

## Binary Coding Schemes

Letters, numbers, and special characters are represented within a computer system by means of *binary coding schemes.* That is, the off/on 0s and 1s are arranged in such a way that they can be made to represent characters, digits, or other values. Two popular binary coding schemes are *ASCII-8* and *EBCDIC.* Both use 8 bits to form each byte. (See Figure 3.12.)

- *ASCII-8:* Pronounced "*as*-key," **ASCII,** which stands for **A**merican **S**tandard **C**ode for **I**nformation **I**nterchange, is the most widely used binary code with microcomputers.

    ASCII originally used 7 bits, but a zero was added in the left position to provide an 8-bit code, which offers more possible combinations with which to form characters, such as math symbols and Greek letters.

- *EBCDIC:* Pronounced "*eb*-see-dick," **EBCDIC,** which stands for **E**xtended **B**inary **C**oded **D**ecimal **I**nterchange **C**ode, is the most popular code for IBM and IBM-compatible mainframes.

    When you type a word on the keyboard (for example, *HERO*), the letters are converted into bytes—eight 0s and 1s for each letter. The bytes are represented in the computer by a combination of eight transistors, some of which are closed (representing the 0s) and some of which are open (representing the 1s).

## The Parity Bit

Dust, electrical disturbance, weather conditions, and other factors can cause interference in a circuit or communications line that is transmitting a byte. How does the computer know if an error has occurred? Detection is accom-

**Figure 3.12**

Two binary coding schemes: ASCII-8 and EBCDIC. There are many more characters than those shown here. These include punctuation marks, Greek letters, math symbols, and foreign language symbols.

| Character | ASCII-8 | EBCDIC | Character | ASCII-8 | EBCDIC |
|---|---|---|---|---|---|
| A | 0100 0001 | 1100 0001 | N | 0100 1110 | 1101 0101 |
| B | 0100 0010 | 1100 0010 | O | 0100 1111 | 1101 0110 |
| C | 0100 0011 | 1100 0011 | P | 0101 0000 | 1101 0111 |
| D | 0100 0100 | 1100 0100 | Q | 0101 0001 | 1101 1000 |
| E | 0100 0101 | 1100 0101 | R | 0101 0010 | 1101 1001 |
| F | 0100 0110 | 1100 0110 | S | 0101 0011 | 1110 0010 |
| G | 0100 0111 | 1100 0111 | T | 0101 0100 | 1110 0011 |
| H | 0100 1000 | 1100 1000 | U | 0101 0101 | 1110 0100 |
| I | 0100 1001 | 1100 1001 | V | 0101 0110 | 1110 0101 |
| J | 0100 1010 | 1101 0001 | W | 0101 0111 | 1110 0110 |
| K | 0100 1011 | 1101 0010 | X | 0101 1000 | 1110 0111 |
| L | 0100 1100 | 1101 0011 | Y | 0101 1001 | 1110 1000 |
| M | 0100 1101 | 1101 0100 | Z | 0101 1010 | 1110 1001 |
| 0 | 0011 0000 | 1111 0000 | 5 | 0011 0101 | 1111 0101 |
| 1 | 0011 0001 | 1111 0001 | 6 | 0011 0110 | 1111 0110 |
| 2 | 0011 0010 | 1111 0010 | 7 | 0011 0111 | 1111 0111 |
| 3 | 0011 0011 | 1111 0011 | 8 | 0011 1000 | 1111 1000 |
| 4 | 0011 0100 | 1111 0100 | 9 | 0011 1001 | 1111 1001 |
| ! | 0010 0001 | 0101 1010 | ; | 0011 1011 | 0101 1110 |

parity bit

plished by use of a parity bit. A **parity bit,** also called a *check bit,* is an extra bit attached to the end of a byte for purposes of checking for accuracy.

Parity schemes may be *even parity* or *odd parity.* In an even-parity scheme, for example, the ASCII letter *H* (01001000) consists of two 1s. Thus, the ninth bit, the parity bit, would be 0 in order to make the byte come out even. With the letter *O* (01001111), which has five 1s, the ninth bit would be 1 to make the byte come out even. (See Figure 3.13.) The system software in the computer automatically and continually checks the parity scheme for accuracy. (If the message "Parity Error" appears on your screen, you need a technician to look at the computer to see what is causing the problem.)

## Machine Language

Why won't word processing software that runs on an Apple Macintosh run (without special arrangements) on an IBM PS/2? It's because each computer has its own machine language. **Machine language** is a binary-type programming language that the computer can run directly. To most people an instruction written in machine language is incomprehensible, consisting only of 0s and 1s. However, it is what the computer itself can understand, and the 0s and 1s represent precise storage locations and operations.

How do people-comprehensible program instructions become computer-comprehensible machine language? Special systems programs called *language translators* rapidly convert the instructions into machine language. This translating occurs virtually instantaneously, so that you are not aware of its happening. (Language translators are discussed in more detail in Chapter 6.)

**Figure 3.13**
Example of a parity bit. This example uses an even-parity scheme.

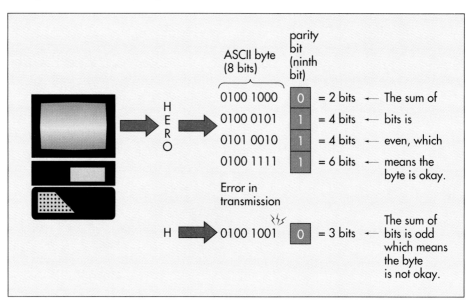

## The System Unit

**The system unit, or cabinet, contains the following electrical components: the power supply, the motherboard, the CPU chip, specialized processor chips, the system clock, RAM chips, ROM chips, other forms of memory (cache, VRAM, flash), expansion slots and boards, bus lines, ports, and PCMCIA slots and cards.**

What is inside the gray or beige box that we call "the computer"? The box or cabinet is the **system unit;** it contains the electrical components that make the computer work. These components actually do the processing in information processing.

The system unit of a desktop microcomputer does not include the keyboard or printer. Quite often it also does not include the monitor or display screen (although it does in some Apple Macintoshes and the Compaq Presario). It usually does include a hard-disk drive and one or two diskette drives, and sometimes a tape drive. We describe all these and other *peripheral devices*—hardware that is outside the central processing unit—in other chapters on storage and output devices. Here we are concerned with the following parts of the system unit. (See Figure 3.14.)

- The power supply
- The motherboard
- The CPU
- Specialized processor chips
- The system clock
- RAM chips
- ROM chips
- Other forms of memory—cache, VRAM, flash

**Figure 3.14**
The system unit.

**An IBM PS/2**          **An Apple Macintosh**

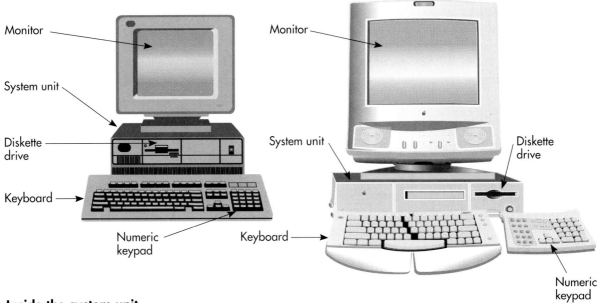

**Inside the system unit**

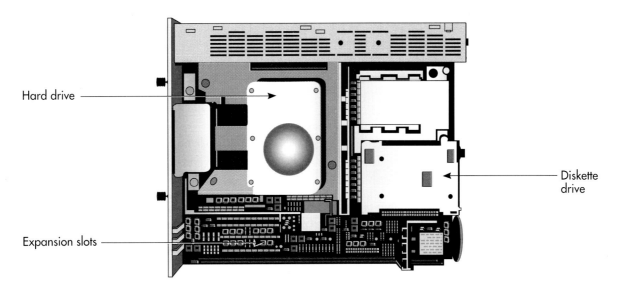

- Expansion slots and boards
- Bus lines
- Ports
- PCMCIA slots and cards

These are terms that appear frequently in advertisements for microcomputers. After reading this section, you should be able to understand what these ads are talking about.

## Giving Your CPU a Boost

Many computer companies are looking to the future, when the whiz-bang system you buy today will become old and outdated.

To give your microprocessor an added boost, most computer companies are making their systems upgradeable. By plugging an additional chip into your computer's motherboard or replacing the motherboard with a new one, you may be able to boost your CPU's performance or upgrade it to the next generation of microprocessor.

A complete upgrade may require replacing the microprocessor with one with a faster clock speed and a better architecture available from the same microprocessing company (like Intel, Apple, or Cyrix) or from a third-party vendor (like Kingston Technology or Evergreen Technologies). Or, it may require plugging an additional chip into the motherboard.

For example, if you own an Intel-based system and you want a little extra processing power, Intel offers a special OverDrive processor for its 486 line and Pentium processors. The OverDrive doesn't replace the exisiting microprocessor but rather pops into a vacant socket on the system's motherboard.

Debbie Hoffman, Intel's channel marketing manager for the Pentium processor group, says the OverDrive processor was designed to give users a little more performance from their PCs. . . .

"It will boost your performance, not necessarily up to the next generation of CPUs, but it will give it a mid-life kick," she says.

The OverDrive processor may or may not be a solution for you. Since they cost from $200 to $650 and are verified to work only with Intel microprocessors, you may want to buy a new system when the time comes.

Rumor has it that IBM is developing a chip to fit into the overdrive slots of Pentium motherboards, thus upgrading Pentium PCs into Power-PCs. . . .

Macintosh buyers who purchased an Apple system without the PowerPC microprocessor are also in luck. For around $650, Macintosh Quadra or Macintosh Centris owners can install a Power Macintosh Upgrade Card inside their computers to run PowerMac programs four times faster along with the existing Mac programs. . . .

*PC Novice,* February 1995, p. 24.

### The Power Supply

The electricity available from a standard wall outlet is AC (aternating current), but a microcomputer runs on DC (direct current). The *power supply* is a device that converts power from AC to DC to run the computer. The on/off switch in your computer turns on or shuts off the electricity to the power supply. Because electricity can generate a lot of heat, a fan inside the computer keeps the power supply and other components from becoming too hot.

Electrical power drawn from a standard AC outlet can be quite uneven. A sudden surge, or "spike," in AC voltage can burn out the low-voltage DC circuitry in your computer ("fry the motherboard"). Instead of plugging your computer directly into the wall electrical outlet, it's a good idea to plug it into a power protection device. The two principal types are *surge protectors* and *UPS units.*

- *Surge protector:* A *surge protector,* or *surge suppressor,* is a device that protects a computer from being damaged by momentary surges (spikes) of high voltage. The computer is plugged into the surge protector, which in turn is plugged into a standard electrical outlet.

■ *UPS:* A *UPS,* for *u*ninterruptable *p*ower *s*upply, is a battery-operated device that provides a computer with electricity if there is a power failure. The UPS will keep a computer going from 5 to 30 minutes or more. It kicks into operation as soon as the power to your computer fails.

### The Motherboard

The **motherboard,** or **system board,** is the main circuit board in the system unit. (See Figure 3.15.) The motherboard consists of a flat board that fills the bottom of the system unit. (It is installed with the power-supply unit and fan and one or more disk drives.) This board contains the "brain" of the computer, the CPU or microprocessor; electronic memory that assists the CPU, known as RAM; and some sockets, called *expansion slots,* where additional circuit boards, called *expansion boards,* may be plugged in. The processing is handled by the CPU and main memory (RAM), as we explain next.

### The CPU Chip

Most personal computers today use CPU chips (microprocessors) of two kinds—those made by Intel and those by Motorola—although that situation may be changing. (See Table 3.2.) Workstations generally use RISC chips.

■ *Intel-type 86-series chips:* Intel makes chips for IBM and IBM-compatible computers such as Compaq, Dell, Gateway, Tandy, Toshiba, and Zenith. Variations of Intel chips are made by other companies, such as Advanced Micro Devices (AMD), Cyrix Inc., and Chips and Technologies.

### Figure 3.15

The motherboard. The main circuit board in the system unit, the motherboard includes the CPU or microprocessor, the computer's "brain." It also includes electronic memory, called *RAM,* and sockets, or expansion slots, for plugging in additional circuit boards to connect other hardware.

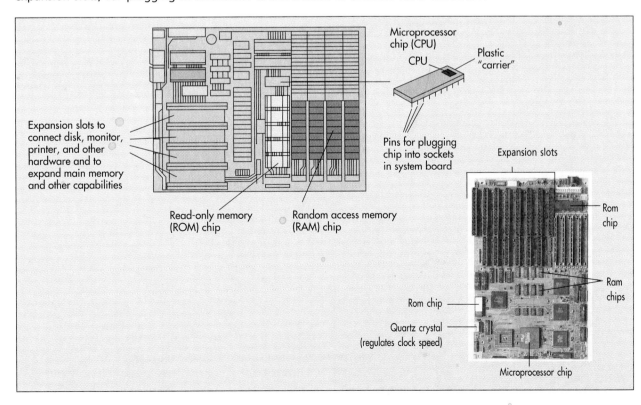

**Table 3.2** Microcomputers and microprocessors. Some widely used micro-computer systems and their chips.

| MANUFACTURER AND CHIP | DATE INTRODUCED | SYSTEMS USING CHIP | CLOCK SPEED (MHz) | BUS WIDTH |
|---|---|---|---|---|
| Intel 8088 | 1979 | IBM PC, XT | 4–8 | 8 |
| Motorola 6800 | 1979 | Macintosh Plus, SE; Commodore Amiga | 8–16 | 16 |
| Intel 80286 | 1982 | IBM PC/AT, PS/2 Model 50/60; Compaq Deskpro 286 | 8–28 | 16 |
| Motorola 68020 | 1984 | Macintosh II | 16–33 | 32 |
| Sun Microsystems RISC | 1985 | Sun Sparcstation 1, 300 | 20–25 | 32 |
| Intel 80386DX | 1985 | IBM PS/2; IBM-compatibles | 16–33 | 32 |
| Motorola 68030 | 1987 | Macintosh IIx series, SE/30 | 16–50 | 32 |
| Intel 80486DX | 1989 | IBM PS/2; IBM-compatibles | 25–66 | 32 |
| Motorola 68040 | 1989 | Macintosh Quadras | 25–40 | 32 |
| IBM RISC 6000 | 1990 | IBM RISC/6000 workstation | 20–50 | 32 |
| Sun Microsystems MicroSparc | 1992 | Sun Sparcstation LX | 50 | 32 |
| Intel Pentium | 1993 | Compaq Deskpro; IBM-compatibles | 60–100 | 64 |
| IBM/Motorola/Apple PowerPC RISC | 1994 | Power Macintoshes | 60–80 | 64 |

Intel has identified its chips by numbers—8086, 8088, 80286, 80386, 80486—although it is now marketing its 80586 chip under the name Pentium, or P5. In early 1995 Intel announced a new chip under development that it calls the P6; plans for the P7 chip are already underway. The higher the number, the newer and more powerful the chip and the faster the processing speed, which means that software runs more efficiently. The chips are commonly referred to by their last three digits, such as 386 and 486.

Some chips have different versions—for example, 386SX or 486DX. SX chips are usually less expensive than DX chips and run more slowly. Thus, they are more appropriate for home use, whereas DX chips are more appropriate for business use. SL chips are designed to reduce power consumption and so are used in portable computers. DX2 and DX4 chips are usually used for heavy-duty information processing.

■ *Motorola-type 68000-series chips:* Motorola makes chips for Apple Macintosh computers. These chip numbers include the 68000, 68020, 68030, and 68040. More recently, Motorola joined forces with IBM and Apple and produced the PowerPC chip.

■ *RISC chips:* Sun Microsystems, Hewlett-Packard, and Digital Equipment use RISC chips in their desktop workstations, although the technology is also showing up in some portables.

**RISC** stands for **r**educed **i**nstruction **s**et **c**omputing. With RISC chips a great many needless instructions are eliminated. Thus, a RISC computer system operates with fewer instructions than those required in conventional computer systems. RISC-equipped workstations have been found to work 10 times faster than conventional computers. A problem, however, is that software has to be modified to work with them.

Most new chips are "downward compatible" with older chips. *Downward compatible,* or *backward compatible,* means that you can run the software written for computers with older chips on a computer with a newer chip. For example, the word processing program and all the data files that you used for your 386 machine will continue to run on a 486 machine. However, the reverse compatibility is not necessarily true. *Upward compatible* means that software written for a machine with a newer chip will run on a machine with an older chip. Thus, if you have a 486-powered desktop PC and buy an old 286 portable, you may or may not be able to run your software on both.

The capacities of CPUs are expressed in terms of *word size.* A **word** is the group of bits that may be manipulated or stored at one time by the CPU. Often the more bits in a word, the faster the computer. An 8-bit word computer will transfer data within each CPU chip in 8-bit chunks. A 32-bit word computer is faster, transferring data in 32-bit chunks. *> a thick piece.*

## Specialized Processor Chips

A motherboard usually has slots for plugging in specialized processor chips. (Refer back to Figure 3.15.) Two in particular that you may encounter are math and graphics coprocessor chips. A **math coprocessor chip** helps programs using lots of mathematical equations to run faster. A **graphics coprocessor chip** enhances the performance of programs with lots of graphics and helps create complex screen displays. Specialized chips significantly increase the speed of a computer system.

## The System Clock

When people talk about a computer's "speed," they mean how fast it can do processing—turn data into information. Every microprocessor contains a system clock. The **system clock** controls how fast all the operations within a computer take place. The system clock uses fixed vibrations from a quartz crystal to deliver a steady stream of digital pulses to the CPU. The faster the clock, the faster the processing, assuming the computer's internal circuits can handle the increased speed.

Processing speeds are expressed in **megahertz (MHz)**, with 1 MHz equal to 1 million beats (cycles) per second. An old IBM PC had a clock speed of 4.77 MHz, whereas computers with 486 chips may run at 66 MHz. The high-end Power Macintosh 8100, from Apple Corp., uses a PowerPC microprocessor running at 80 MHz. Some Intel Pentium chips, used in IBM-style computers, run at speeds of 90 or 100 MHz.

Interestingly, a 486 chip running at 25 MHz still processes information faster than a 386 chip running at the faster speed of 33 MHz. For reasons too technical to go into here, newer chips run at slower speeds than older chips but still process the information at a faster rate.[12]

## RAM Chips

**RAM,** for **r**andom **a**ccess **m**emory, is memory that temporarily holds data and instructions that will be needed shortly by the CPU. RAM is what we have been calling *main memory* or *primary storage;* it operates like a chalkboard that is constantly being written on, then erased, then written on again. (The term *random access* comes from the fact that data can be stored and retrieved at random—from anywhere in the electronic RAM chips—in approximately equal amounts of time, no matter what the specific data locations are.)

Like the microprocessor, the RAM consists of circuit-inscribed silicon chips attached to the motherboard. RAM chips are often mounted on a small circuit board, such as a *SIMM* (for *s*ingle *i*nline *m*emory *m*odule), which is plugged into the motherboard. (Refer back to Figure 3.15.) The two principal types of RAM chips are *DRAM* (for *d*ynamic *r*andom *a*ccess *m*emory) chips, used for most main memory, and *SRAM* (for *s*tatic *r*andom *a*ccess *m*emory) chips, used for some specialized purposes within main memory.

Microcomputers come with different amounts of RAM. In many cases, additional RAM chips can be added by plugging a memory-expansion card into the motherboard, as we will explain. The more RAM you have, the faster the computer operates, and the better your software performs. If, for instance, you type such a long document in a word processing program that it will not all fit into your computer's RAM, the computer will put part of the document onto your disk (either hard disk or diskette). This means you have to wait while the computer swaps data back and forth between RAM and disk.

*Having enough RAM has become a critical matter!* Before you buy any software package, look at the outside of the box to see how much RAM is required. For example, Windows 3.1 software requires at least 640 kilobytes of RAM and 1 megabyte of extended memory (a type we explain next). Although the actual amount of RAM installed on a microcomputer may well be less, an Intel 8088 microprocessor can access up to 640 kilobytes of RAM. A 286 processor can access up to 16 megabytes, and a 386 or 486 up to 4 gigabytes. (If you have an IBM-style PC, you can fairly easily find out how much RAM you have. You simply use the operating system software's CHKDSK or MEM command following the system prompt, such as C:>. This will cause the screen to display the number of bytes of memory installed and available.)

In IBM-type PCs, RAM is of four types. (See Figure 3.16.)

- *Conventional memory:* **Conventional memory** consists of the first 640 kilobytes of RAM. This area is used by all PCs for running the operating system and applications programs. Today most microcomputers come with 640 kilobytes of conventional memory installed.

- *Upper memory:* **Upper memory** is the memory located between 640 kilobytes and 1 megabyte of RAM. Microcomputers with 286 or higher chips use this area for storing parts of the operating system, leaving conventional memory available for running application programs.

- *Extended memory:* **Extended memory** is all memory over 1 megabyte. If your microcomputer has 4 megabytes of memory, it will be apportioned as follows: conventional memory—640 kilobytes; upper memory—384 kilobytes; extended memory—3 megabytes.

  The older chips, 8088 and 8086, weren't made to access extended memory. Only computers with 286 chips and higher give you the opportunity to use this memory. Some microcomputers with 386 chips and above can use up to 4 gigabytes of extended memory.

  Not all programs can use extended memory. For programs to be able to use it, they must be so-called *DOS (disk operating system) extended* programs. More and more programs are now being written with DOS extenders. (They are able to switch to something called *protected mode,* which can access the more advanced features of 286 and higher CPUs.)

- *Expanded memory:* **Expanded memory** lets 8088-chip-based PCs access memory over the limit of 640-kilobyte conventional memory, up to 32 megabytes. Expanded memory requires that you buy hardware and software—an *expanded memory board* with an *expanded memory manager*

**Figure 3.16**
Types of RAM. In IBM-type PCs the four types of RAM are conventional, upper, extended, and expanded.

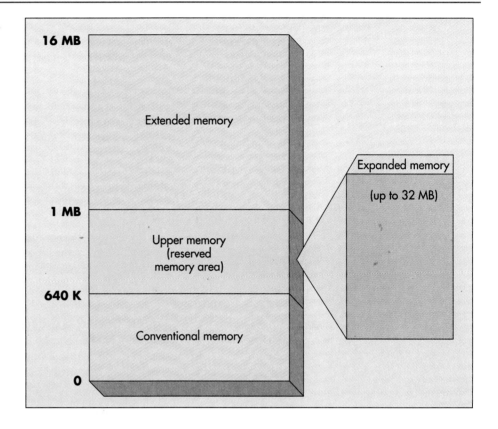

program. Users with 386SX or higher CPUs don't need to make this purchase.

### ROM Chips

Unlike RAM, which is constantly being written on and erased, **ROM,** which stands for **r**ead-**o**nly **m**emory and is also known as *firmware,* cannot be written on or erased by the computer user. ROM chips contain programs that are built in at the factory; these are special instructions for computer operations, such as those that start the computer or put characters on the screen.

Three variations on ROM chips are *PROM, EPROM,* and *EEPROM:*

- *PROM: PROM chips,* for *p*rogrammable *r*ead-only *m*emory, are blank chips on which the buyer, using special equipment, writes the program. Once the program is written, it cannot be erased.

- *EPROM: EPROM chips,* for *e*rasable *p*rogrammable *r*ead-only *m*emory, are like PROM chips except that the contents can be erased, using special equipment, and new material can be written. Erasure is done with a special device that uses ultraviolet light.

- *EEPROM: EEPROM chips,* for *e*lectrically *e*rasable *p*rogrammable *r*ead-only *m*emory, can be reprogrammed using special electrical impulses. The advantage of EEPROM chips is that they need not be removed from the computer to be changed.

### Other Forms of Memory

The performance of microcomputers can be enhanced further by adding other forms of memory, as follows:

■ *Cache memory:* Pronounced "cash," **cache memory** is a special high-speed memory area that the CPU can access quickly. Cache memory is used in computers with very fast CPUs, so that these CPUs don't have to wait for data to be delivered from RAM. The most frequently used instructions are kept in the cache memory so the CPU can look there first. This allows the CPU to run faster because it doesn't have to take time to swap instructions in and out of RAM. Large, complex programs benefit the most from having a cache memory available.

Cache memory can be built into the microprocessor chip. At least 8 kilobytes of cache memory generally come with 486 processors. If you plan to run large spreadsheets or database management programs, you may want to have greater amounts of cache, such as 16 or 32 kilobytes. Cache memory can also be installed on the system board (motherboard) as a separate chip.

■ *Video memory:* **Video memory** or **video RAM (VRAM) chips** are used to store display images for the monitor. The amount of video memory determines how fast images appear and how many colors are available. Video memory chips are particularly desirable if you are running programs that display a lot of graphics.

■ *Flash memory:* Used primarily in notebook and subnotebook computers, **flash memory,** or **flash RAM cards,** consist of circuitry on credit-card-size cards that can be inserted into slots connecting to the motherboard. Unlike standard RAM chips, flash memory is *nonvolatile.* That is, it retains data even when the power is turned off. Flash memory can be used not only to simulate main memory but also to supplement or replace hard disk drives for permanent storage.

## Expansion Slots and Boards

For a long time some microcomputers, principally the Apple Macintoshes (but not the Apple IIs), were said to have *closed architecture,* meaning that the system cabinet could not be opened, except by a technician. IBM and IBM-compatible microcomputers, on the other hand, were said to have *open architecture*—that is, they could easily be opened, so that users could add new devices. Today most new microcomputers can be opened up, which permits expandability.

*Expandability* refers to a computer's capacity for adding more memory or peripheral devices. Having expandability means that when you buy a PC you can later add devices to enhance its computing power. This spares you from having to buy a completely new computer.

expansion cards

Expandability is made possible with expansion slots and expansion boards. **Expansion slots** are sockets on the motherboard into which you can plug expansion cards. **Expansion cards,** or *add-on boards,* are circuit boards that provide more memory or control peripheral devices. The words card and board are used interchangeably. Some slots may be needed right away for ordinary functions, but if your system unit leaves enough slots open, you can use them for expansion later.

Among the types of expansion cards are the following. (See Figure 3.17.)

■ *Expanded memory:* Memory expansion cards (or SIMMs) allow you to add several additional RAM chips, giving you more main memory.

■ *Display adapter or graphics adapter cards:* These cards allow you to adapt different kinds of color video display monitors for your computer.

■ *Controller cards:* **Controller cards** are circuit boards that allow your CPU to work with the computer's various peripheral devices. For example, a

**Figure 3.17**
Expansion cards for microcomputers. Expansion cards fit into slots in the motherboard.

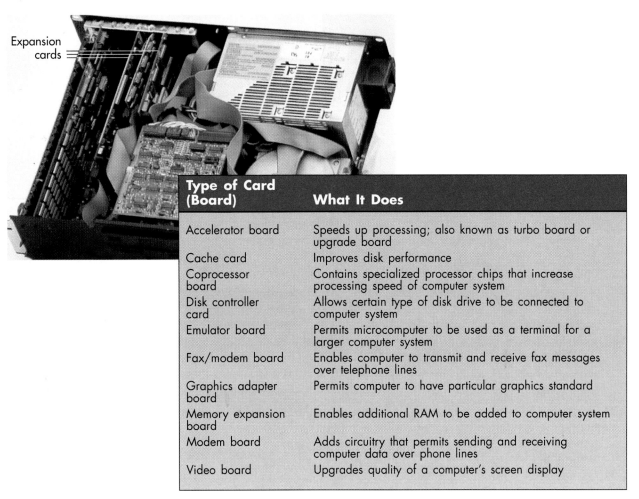

Expansion cards

| Type of Card (Board) | What It Does |
|---|---|
| Accelerator board | Speeds up processing; also known as turbo board or upgrade board |
| Cache card | Improves disk performance |
| Coprocessor board | Contains specialized processor chips that increase processing speed of computer system |
| Disk controller card | Allows certain type of disk drive to be connected to computer system |
| Emulator board | Permits microcomputer to be used as a terminal for a larger computer system |
| Fax/modem board | Enables computer to transmit and receive fax messages over telephone lines |
| Graphics adapter board | Permits computer to have particular graphics standard |
| Memory expansion board | Enables additional RAM to be added to computer system |
| Modem board | Adds circuitry that permits sending and receiving computer data over phone lines |
| Video board | Upgrades quality of a computer's screen display |

disk controller card allows the computer to work with different kinds of hard disk and diskette drives.

■ *Other add-ons:* You can also add special circuit boards for modems, fax, sound, and networking, as well as math or graphics coprocessor chips.

## Bus Lines

A **bus line,** or simply **bus,** is an electrical pathway through which bits are transmitted within the CPU and between the CPU and other devices in the system unit. There are different types of buses (address bus, control bus, data bus), but for our purposes the most important is the **input/output bus,** which links the CPU to every hardware device.

A bus resembles a multilane highway: The more lanes it has, the faster the bits can be transferred. The old-fashioned 8-bit bus of early microprocessors had only eight pathways. It was therefore four times slower than the 32-bit bus of later microprocessors, which had 32 pathways. Intel's Pentium chip is a 64-bit processor, although in less expensive machines it may be installed on a motherboard with a 32-bit bus. Some supercomputers contain buses that are 128 bits.

## The BIOS Chip

The BIOS chip in your PC is a strange beast. Part software, part hardware, it's one of the most frequently used and least understood components of your computer. . . .

BIOS stands for *basic input-output system*. It's a set of instructions permanently encoded on a computer chip. Computer operating systems (like DOS) and other applications can use the BIOS instructions to communicate with the computer's input and output devices such as keyboards and printers. . . .

The BIOS instructions are "burned," or permanently encoded, onto a *ROM chip*. ROM stands for *read-only memory*, which means that the computer can read instructions from the chip, but cannot write to it. Writing, or adding information to the chip, would alter or erase the instructions. Sometimes the BIOS is referred to as the *ROM BIOS*. Unlike *RAM*, or *random-access memory*, which is temporary electrical storage space, ROM and its contents are permanent components of your computer. Although you cannot see them, the BIOS instructions spring into memory as soon as you turn on your computer.

Because the ROM BIOS contains coded instructions, it's like software. Because the instructions are a permanent component of your PC, the BIOS is like hardware. . . .

When you turn on your PC, the computer's brain chip, called the *central processing unit (CPU)*, hands over controls to the BIOS. The first job the BIOS has at start-up is to run the *power-on self-test*, or *POST*.

The POST makes sure all the chips on the computer's system board are working. It runs diagnostic tests on the CPU, on various timers and controllers, and on the computer's memory chips. One test you can see is the memory test. When you see the computer "counting" its

bytes of memory at start-up, that's the BIOS testing for errors in your memory chips.

Next, the BIOS tries to communicate with all the hardware devices, the keyboard, the monitor, the mouse. If it can't find a particular device, an error will usually register on-screen. . . .

Finally, the BIOS boots (starts) the computer's operating system. Here's how it works: The BIOS first checks the floppy drive for a diskette with an operating system on it. If it can't find an operating system there, the BIOS then searches the hard disk. You'll see the *drive indicator lights* (usually located on the front panel of your PC) flicker when the BIOS searches the respective drives. When the BIOS finds the operating system, whether on hard disk or floppy diskette, the BIOS hands over control of the machine to the operating system. . . .

But the BIOS doesn't leave the picture after start-up. The BIOS offers important services to DOS and other software programs. The BIOS allows software to communicate with input and output devices such as the floppy diskette drive, hard disk, printer, screen, and keyboard. . . .

Marti Remington, "BIOS Basics," *PC Novice*, January 1992, pp. 72–73.

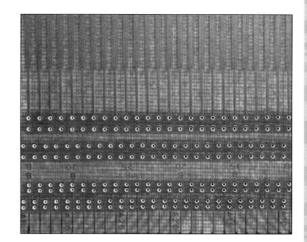

Today there are several principal bus standards, or "architectures":

■ *ISA:* **Industry Standard Architecture (ISA)** is a bus standard developed for the IBM Personal Computer; it was first 8 bits, then 16 bits. ISA is the most common PC bus and works satisfactorily for 286 microprocessors and expansion boards.

■ *MCA:* IBM's **Micro Channel Architecture (MCA),** used in IBM's PS/2 line of microcomputers and supporting the 386 chip, is a 32-bit bus. Expansion boards cannot simply be plucked from an older IBM (PC, XT, or AT) and plugged into newer machines with MCA; they will not work. Nor will EISA cards run in MCA slots.

■ *EISA:* The **Enhanced Industry Standard Architecture (EISA)** is a 32-bit bus used on many IBM-compatible computers, such as the Compaq. ISA cards will run in EISA slots.

■ *NuBus:* Apple's **NuBus** is a 32-bit bus used in recent Apple Macintoshes.

■ *PCMCIA:* Short for **P**ersonal **C**omputer **M**emory **C**ard International **A**ssociation, **PCMCIA** is a completely open, nonproprietary bus standard for new notebooks, subnotebooks, and palmtops. It allows users to insert credit-card-size peripherals (about 2.1 by 3.4 inches), typically memory cards or modems. These cards are now called *PC cards.*

To bypass existing standard bus systems—in other words, to connect peripheral computer components directly to the microprocessor—some microcomputer companies have added so-called *local bus extensions* to new machines:

■ *VESA:* The **VESA,** for **V**ideo **E**lectronics **S**tandard **A**ssociation, was the first of the local bus extensions to connect peripherals directly to the microprocessor. The VL-Bus, as it is also known, carries data in 32-bit chunks. If you buy a PC with VESA, it means that the video circuitry has been installed right next door to the microprocessor. This makes everything on the video screen move faster. VESA is used with most 486 systems.

■ *PCI:* The **PCI,** for **P**eripheral **C**omponent **I**nterconnect, is a local bus using a 64-bit data path. It is used in high-end Pentium-based systems.

## Ports

A **port** is a socket on the outside of the system unit that is connected to an expansion board on the inside of the system unit. A port allows you to use a cable to connect a peripheral device, such as a monitor, printer, or modem, so that it can communicate with the computer system.

Ports are of five types (see Figure 3.18):

■ *Parallel ports:* A **parallel port** allows lines to be connected that will enable 8 bits to be transmitted simultaneously, like cars on an eight-lane highway. Parallel lines move information faster than serial lines do, but they can transmit information efficiently only up to 15 feet. Thus, parallel ports are used principally for connecting printers.

■ *Serial ports:* A **serial port,** or **RS-232 port,** enables a line to be connected that will send bits one after the other on a single line, like cars on a one-lane highway. Serial lines are used to link equipment that is not close by. Serial ports are used principally for communications lines, modems, and mice. (They are frequently labeled "COM" for communications.)

■ *Video adapter ports:* **Video adapter ports** are used to connect the video display monitor outside the computer to the video adapter card inside the

**Figure 3.18**
Different types of ports. Shown are the backs of an IBM-style computer and an Apple Macintosh.

**IBM-compatible**

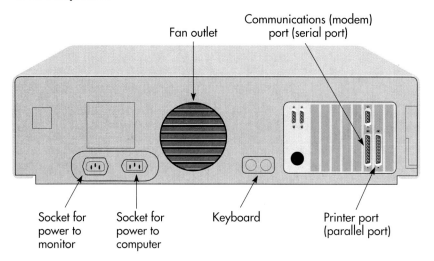

**Apple Macintosh**

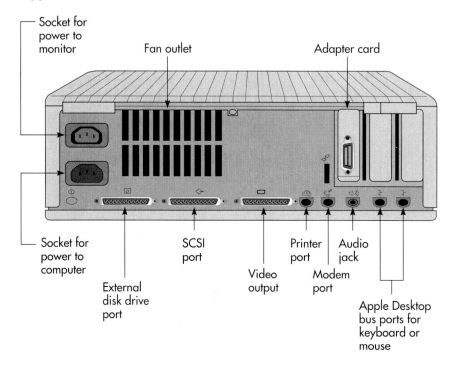

system unit. Monitors may have either a 9-pin plug or a 15-pin plug. The plug must be compatible with the number of holes in the video adapter card.

■ *SCSI ports:* Pronounced "scuzzy" (and short for *S*mall *C*omputer *S*ystem *I*nterface), a **SCSI port** provides an interface for transferring data at high speeds for up to eight SCSI-compatible devices. These devices include external hard disk drives, magnetic-tape backup units, and CD-ROM drives.

■ *Game ports:* Game ports allow you to attach a joystick or similar game-playing device to the system unit.

### PCMCIA Slots and Cards

**H**

PCMCIA

"Although its name doesn't exactly roll off the tongue," says one writer, "PCMCIA is changing mobile computing more dramatically than any technology today."[13] As we mentioned, PCMCIA represents a new bus standard for notebooks, subnotebooks, and pocket computers. However, even desktop systems and printers with PCMCIA slots are becoming available. These allow you to plug in credit-card-size peripherals such as memory cards using flash memory chips (mentioned earlier) and holding up to 100 megabytes of data. They will also accept modems, hard drives, and adapters for communicating over networks.

Not all slots will take all kinds of peripherals. There are four types of PCMCIA slots, each accepting a different thickness of card. (See Figure 3.19.) Type I is used primarily for memory cards. Type II is used for fax modems, LAN adapters, and other slim media. Type III is for rotating disk devices, such as hard disk drives. Type IV is for large-capacity hard-disk drives.

**Figure 3.19**

Four sizes of PCMCIA cards, now called *PC cards*. Cards are about 2 × 3 inches, but thicknesses vary.

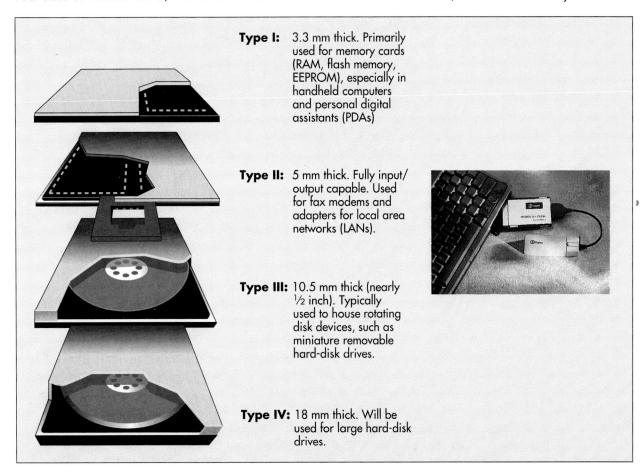

**Type I:** 3.3 mm thick. Primarily used for memory cards (RAM, flash memory, EEPROM), especially in handheld computers and personal digital assistants (PDAs)

**Type II:** 5 mm thick. Fully input/output capable. Used for fax modems and adapters for local area networks (LANs).

**Type III:** 10.5 mm thick (nearly ½ inch). Typically used to house rotating disk devices, such as miniature removable hard-disk drives.

**Type IV:** 18 mm thick. Will be used for large hard-disk drives.

## Possible Coming Attractions: From Gallium Arsenide to Nanotechnology to Biochips

**Future processing technologies may use gallium arsenide, superconductors, optical processing, nanotechnology, and biochips.**

The old theological question of how many angels could fit on the head of a pin has become the technological question of how many circuits could fit there. Computer developers are obsessed with speed, constantly seeking ways to promote faster processing. Some of the most promising directions, already discussed, are RISC chips and parallel processing. Some other research paths being explored are the following:

- *Gallium arsenide:* Silicon is the material of choice today for microprocessors, but there are other contenders. One is *gallium arsenide,* which allows electrical impulses to be transmitted several times faster than silicon can. Gallium arsenide also requires less power than silicon chips and thus can operate at higher temperatures. However, chip designers at present are unable to squeeze as many circuits onto a chip as they can with silicon.

- *Superconductors:* Silicon, we stated, is a semiconductor: Electricity flows through the material with some resistance. This leads to heat buildup and the risk of circuits melting down. A *superconductor,* by contrast, is material that allows electricity to flow through it without resistance. The superconducting materials so far discovered are considered impractical because they are superconductors only at subzero temperatures. Nevertheless, the search continues for a superconductor at room temperature—which would lead to circuitry 100 times faster than today's silicon chips.

**H**

opto-electronic processing
- *Opto-electronic processing:* Today's computers are electronic, tomorrow's might be *opto-electronic*—using light, not electricity. With optical-electronic technology, a machine using lasers, lenses, and mirrors would represent the on-and-off codes of data with pulses of light.

  Light is much faster than electricity. Indeed, fiber-optic networks, which consist of hair-thin glass fibers, can move information at speeds 3,000 times faster than conventional networks. However, the signals get bogged down when they have to be processed by silicon chips. Opto-electronics chips would remove that bottleneck.

- *Nanotechnology:* Nanotechnology, nanoelectronics, nanostructures, nanofabrication—all start with a measurement known as a nanometer. A *nanometer* is a billionth of a meter, which means we are operating at the level of atoms and molecules. A human hair is approximately 100,000 nanometers in diameter.

  *Nanotechnology* is a science based on using molecules to create tiny machines to hold data or perform tasks. Experts attempt to do "nanofabrication" by building tiny "nanostructures" one atom or molecule at a time. When applied to chips and other electronic devices, the field is called "nanoelectronics."

- *Biotechnology:* Another possibility is using biotechnology to grow cultures of bacteria, such as one that, when exposed to light, emits a small electrical charge. The properties of this "biochip" could be used to represent the on/off digital signals used in computing.

Imagine millions of nanomachines grown from microorganisms processing information at the speed of light and sending it over far-reaching pathways. What kind of changes could we expect with computers like these?

## Suggestions for Further Reading

Bow, L. *How to Use Your Computer*. Emeryville, CA: Ziff-Davis Press, 1993.

*Compute*. P.O. Box 5052, Harlan, IA 51593-2552. (800) 727-6937. Subscriptions: About $20 for 12 months.

*Home Office Computing*. P.O. Box 51322, Boulder, CO 80321-1344. (800) 288-7812. Subscriptions: About $20 for 12 months.

Murray, K. *Introduction to Personal Computers*. Carmel, IN: Que Corporation, 1993.

Norton, P. *Inside the PC* (5th ed.). New York: Brady Publishing, 1993.

Rizzo, J., and Clark, K. Daniel. *How Macs Work*. Emeryville, CA: Ziff-Davis Press, 1993.

White, R. *How Computers Work*. Emeryville, CA: Ziff-Davis Press, 1993.

# S U M M A R Y

- Computers are classified into *microcomputers, minicomputers, mainframe computers,* and *supercomputers.* (p. 71)

- *Personal computers (PCs)* are microcomputers that run easy-to-use software programs such as word processing or spreadsheets. Different sizes of PCs are available including *desktop* and *floor-standing units, luggables, laptops, notebooks, subnotebooks, pocket PCs,* and *pen computers.* (p. 71)

- *Workstations* are microcomputers that are more powerful than personal computers and more expensive. They are used mainly by engineers and scientists. (p. 74)

- *Minicomputers* are more powerful than microcomputers and can be used as either single workstations or tied to a network of several hundred terminals. Minicomputers are less powerful and expensive than mainframe computers. (p. 76)

- *Mainframe computers* are more expensive and more powerful than minicomputers. They range in price from $50,000 to $5 million. Mainframe computers are used by companies that need to handle millions of transactions. Increasingly, mainframes are being supplanted by smaller computers connected together in networks. (p. 76)

- *Supercomputers* are more expensive than mainframe computers, costing from $300,000 to over $30 million. They are the fastest calculating machines ever invented and are used for such tasks as simulating car crashes into walls and modeling nuclear explosions. *Vector processing* and *massively parallel processing (MPP)* are two types of supercomputer design. (p. 77)

- The *central processing unit (CPU)* is the "brain" of the computer. It has two main parts (p. 80):

    1. *Control unit*—directs and coordinates most of the computer system activities

    2. *Arithmetic/logic unit (ALU)*—performs arithmetic and logical (comparison) functions and controls the speed of these operations

- *Main memory,* also called *memory, primary storage, internal memory,* or *random access memory (RAM),* refers to working storage. Main memory (p. 82):

    1. Holds data for processing

    2. Holds instructions for processing the data

    3. Holds data after it is processed

- The contents of main memory are temporary, meaning that if you turn off your computer before saving your work, you will lose your latest edits. (p. 82)

- Memory capacity varies in different computers. The amount of memory you have in your computer determines the level of software sophistication your computer can handle. When it comes to memory, more is better. (p. 83)

- *Registers* are high-speed staging areas that temporarily store data and instructions that will be used immediately by the CPU. (p. 83)

- To process an instruction, the control unit of the CPU retrieves it from memory and places it in a register. The *instruction cycle (I-cycle)* refers to the retrieval of the instruction from memory and its subsequent decoding. The *execution cycle (E-cycle)* refers to the processing of the instruction and subsequent storing of the result in a register. Together, the instruction cycle and the execution cycle are called the *machine cycle.* (p. 83)

- There are three ways to measure computer processing speeds (p. 84):

    1. Time to complete one machine cycle, in fractions of a second. A *millisecond* is one-thousandth of a second. A *microsecond* is one-millionth of a second. A *nanosecond* is one-billionth of a second. A *picosecond* is one-trillionth of a second.

    2. Time to complete instructions, in *millions of instructions per second (MIPS).*

    3. Time in *floating-point operations per second (flops).* Supercomputer speeds

are usually measured in *megaflops, millions of floating-point operations per second.*

■ In a computer system, data is represented using the *binary system,* combinations of binary digits (bits). There are only two binary digits: 1 ("on") and 0 ("off"). During processing, 0 is represented by the electrical current being off (or at low voltage) and 1 by the current being on (or at high voltage). When you type a letter on the keyboard, the character is automatically converted into a series of 1s and 0s that the computer can recognize. (p. 85)

■ It typically takes 8 *bits* (binary digits) to represent a character, or *byte,* of data. A *kilobyte (K, KB)* is about 1,000 bytes (1,024 bytes). A *megabyte (M, MB)* is about 1 million bytes (1,048,576 bytes). A *gigabyte (G, GB)* is about 1 billion bytes (1,073,741,824 bytes). A *terabyte (T, TB)* represents about 1 trillion bytes (1,009,511,627,776 bytes). (p. 86)

■ Two common binary coding schemes are *ASCII-8* and *EBCDIC. ASCII* stands for American Standard Code for Information Interchange and EBCDIC stands for Extended Binary Coded Decimal Interchange. ASCII is typically used to represent data for microcomputers, and EBCDIC is used on larger computers. (p. 86)

■ A *parity bit* is an extra bit attached to a byte for purposes of checking the accuracy of the stored byte. Parity schemes may be *even parity* or *odd parity.* The computer's system software continually checks the parity scheme for accuracy. When an error occurs, a message displays on the screen. At this point, you may need a technician to look at your computer. (p. 87)

■ The CPU understands only *machine language,* in which data and instructions are represented by 0s and 1s—the off and on states of electrical currents. Software instructions are converted into machine language by a *language translator,* a type of systems software program. (p. 87)

■ The *system unit* contains the electrical components that make a computer work.

   1. The *power supply*—device that converts AC power to DC to run the computer.

The power supply can generate a lot of heat; therefore a fan inside the system unit keeps the power supply (and other components) from getting too hot. (p. 90)

2. The *motherboard*—main circuit board in the system unit, which houses the CPU chip, main memory chips, and expansion slots where additional components, such as add-on circuit boards, can be plugged in. (p. 91)

3. The *CPU*—microprocessor chip, the "brain" of the computer. Three types of microprocessor are Intel-type 86-series chips, Motorola-type 68000-series chips, and RISC chips. (p. 91)

4. Specialized processor chips—The motherboard usually has slots for plugging in specialized processor chips such as a *math coprocessor chip* and a *graphics coprocessor chip.* These chips help to speed up your computer system. (p. 93)

5. The *system clock*—clock that controls how fast all operations within a computer are performed. Speeds are measured in *megahertz (MHz),* with 1 MHz equal to 1 million beats (cycles) per second. (p. 93)

6. *RAM chips*—chips that temporarily hold data and instructions that will be needed shortly by the CPU. These chips are plugged into the motherboard. RAM chips may be mounted on a small circuit board, such as a *SIMM (single inline memory module).* Your computer may contain four types of RAM: *conventional memory, upper memory, extended memory,* and *expanded memory.* (p. 93)

7. *ROM chips*—chips containing programs that are built into the computer at the factory. These chips contain special instructions including those that execute when you turn on your computer. Three variations on ROM chips are *PROM, EPROM,* and *EEPROM.* (p. 95)

8. Other forms of memory (cache, VRAM, flash)—*Cache memory* is special high-speed memory that the CPU can access quickly. *Video memory* or *video RAM (VRAM)* chips are used to store display

images for the monitor. *Flash memory,* or *flash RAM cards,* consist of circuitry on credit-card-size cards that can be inserted into slots on the motherboard. (p. 96)

9. Expansion slots and boards—*Expansion slots* are sockets on the motherboard into which you can plug *expansion cards,* or *boards.* Among the types of expansion cards are *expanded memory, display adapter* or *graphics adapter cards, controller cards,* and other add-ons. (p. 96)

10. *Bus lines*—electrical pathways through which bits are transmitted within the CPU and between the CPU and other devices in the system unit. The most important is the *input/output bus,* which links the CPU to every hardware device. (p. 97)

11. *Ports*—sockets on the outside of the system unit that each connect to an expansion board on the inside of the system unit. Ports are of five types: *parallel ports, serial ports, video adapter ports, SCSI ports,* and *game ports.* (p. 99)

12. PCMCIA slots and cards—*PCMCIA* represents a new bus standard for notebooks, subnotebooks, and pocket computers. PCMCIA cards—for memory, disk storage, a modem, or a local area network adapter—are used to upgrade your existing system by simply sliding the card into a PCMCIA slot. (p. 101)

■ Future processing technologies may include the following: gallium arsenide, superconductors, opto-electronic processing, nanotechnology, or biotechnology. (p. 102)

## KEY TERMS

arithmetic/logic unit (ALU), p. 80
ASCII, p. 86
binary system, p. 85
bit (binary digit), p. 86
bus (line), p. 97
byte, p. 86
cache memory, p. 96
central processing unit (CPU), p. 80
chip (microchip), p. 81
controller card, p. 96
control unit, p. 80
conventional memory, p. 94
EBCDIC, p. 86
electronic organizer, p. 73
Enhanced Industry Standard Architecture (EISA), p. 99
execution cycle (E-cycle), p. 83
expanded memory, p. 94
expansion card, p. 96
expansion slot, p. 96
extended memory, p. 94
flash memory, p. 96
flops, p. 84
gigabyte (G, GB), p. 86
graphics coprocessor chip, p. 93

Industry Standard Architecture (ISA), p. 99
input/output bus, p. 97
instruction cycle (I-cycle), p. 83
kilobyte (K, KB), p. 86
laptop computer, p. 72
machine cycle, p. 83
machine language, p. 87
mainframe, p. 76
main memory, p. 82
math coprocessor chip, p. 93
megabyte (M, MB), p. 86
megahertz (MHz), p. 93
Micro Channel Architecture (MCA), p. 99
microcomputer, p. 71
minicomputer, p. 76
MIPs, p. 84
motherboard, p. 91
multimedia system, p. 72
notebook, p. 73
NuBus, p. 99
palmtop computer, p. 73
parallel port, p. 99
parity (check) bit, p. 87
PCI, p. 99
PCMCIA (PC cards), p. 99

pen computer, p. 73
personal computer (PC), p. 71
personal digital assistant (PDA), p. 73
pocket PC (handheld PC), p. 73
port, p. 99
random access memory (RAM), pp. 82, 93
register, p. 83
RISC, p. 92
ROM, p. 95
SCSI port, p. 100
serial port, p. 99
server, p. 76
subnotebook, p. 73
supercomputer, p. 77
system clock, p. 93
system unit, p. 88
terabyte (T, TB), p. 86
terminal, p. 71
upper memory, p. 94
VESA, p. 99
video adapter port, p. 99
video RAM (VRAM), p. 96
word, p. 93
workstation, p. 74

**SELF-TEST**

1. Luggables, laptops, notebooks, subnotebooks, and pen computers are all types of personal computers (PCs). (true/false)

2. The _____ALU_____ performs all the computer's arithmetic and logical functions.

3. In machine language, data and instructions are represented with 0s and 1s. (true/false)

4. A(n) __WORK STATION__ is a type of microcomputer that fits on a desktop, costs $10,000–$150,000, and is used mainly by engineers and scientists for technical purposes.

5. __MINI COMP__ are computers midway in cost and capability between microcomputers and mainframes.

6. A(n) __SYSTEM BUS__ connects the different components of the CPU.

7. Read-only memory is a nonvolatile form of storage. (true/false)

8. List three types of ROM chips:

   a. PROM

   b. EPROM

   c. EEPROM

9. A(n) ____byte____ is composed of 8 ____bits____.

10. Data and instructions in RAM are lost when the computer is turned off. (true/false)

11. The instruction cycle and the execution cycle together are called the __MACHINE CYCLE__.

12. __SUPER COMP__ are high-capacity machines and are the fastest calculating devices ever invented.

13. A(n) ____K____ is about 1,000 bytes (1,024 bytes). A(n) ____MEG____ is about 1 million bytes (1,048,576 bytes). A ____GIGA____ is about 1 billion bytes (1,073,741,824 bytes).

14. EBCDIC is the most popular binary coding scheme used with microcomputers. (true/false)

15. A(n) __PARITY__ bit is an extra bit attached to a byte for purposes of checking for accuracy.

16. __MACHINE LANGUAGE__ is a binary programming language that the computer can run directly.

17. Conventional memory consists of the first 640 kilobytes of RAM. Extended memory is all memory over 1 megabyte. (true/false)

18. Cache memory is a special high-speed memory area that the CPU can access quickly. (true/false)

19. ___Expansion___ ___slot___ are sockets on the motherboard into which you can plug expansion cards.

20. PCMCIA represents a new bus standard for notebooks, subnotebooks, and pocket computers. (true/false)

*Solutions:* (1) true; (2) arithmetic/logic unit (ALU); (3) true; (4) workstation; (5) minicomputers; (6) bus; (7) true; (8) PROM, EPROM, EEPROM; (9) byte, bits; (10) true; (11) machine cycle; (12) supercomputers; (13) kilobyte, megabyte, gigabyte; (14) false; (15) parity; (16) machine language; (17) true; (18) true; (19) expansion slots; (20) true.

## SHORT-ANSWER QUESTIONS

1. What is the function of the ALU in a microcomputer system?
2. What is the difference between vector processing and massively parallel processing (MPP)?
3. Describe why having more RAM in your computer (as opposed to less) is useful.
4. What is the function of the control unit in a microcomputer system?
5. What is the function of registers in a microcomputer system?
6. What is the purpose of a parity scheme? How does one work?
7. What is ASCII? EBCDIC?
8. What is the function of a surge protector? UPS?
9. What is a motherboard?
10. As it relates to computer processing, what do gallium arsenide, superconductors, opto-electronic processing, nanotechnology, and biotechnology have in common?
11. What is the main difference between a 386 processor and a 486 processor?

## PROJECTS AND CRITICAL THINKING EXERCISES

1. If you were a real estate salesperson, what kind(s) of computer would you buy? Why? What if you were a lawyer? A hardware store owner? A physician in private practice?
2. As a student, what could you use a PDA for?
3. Develop a binary system of your own (use any two states, objects, or conditions) and encode the following: I am a rocket scientist.
4. Research the current uses of and the latest advances in ROM technology. How do you think ROM technology will affect the way we currently use microcomputers?
5. Advances are made almost every day in microprocessor chip technology. What are some of the most recent advances? In what computers are these chips being used? How might these advances affect the way we currently use microcomputers? Research the latest advances by reviewing the most current computer magazines and periodicals.
6. Visit a well-equipped computer store and, with the help of a salesperson, decide what microcomputer might be the best one for you to use based on your processing requirements (if necessary, pick a hypothetical job and identify some probable processing requirements). Describe the microcomputer you would choose and explain why. Compare this microcomputer to the others you were shown. Use the following categories:

Name and brand of computer:

Microprocessor model:                clock speed:

Cache? (yes/no):                  if yes, how much?

RAM capacity:                   (upgradable to:      )

Uses extended memory?

Data bus capacity:

Register (wordsize) capacity:

Any coprocessors?              if so, what kind:

Cost:

7. What does it mean for a microcomputer and related equipment to be "IBM compatible"? Look through some computer magazines and identify advertised microcomputer systems that are IBM compatible. What are their clock speeds? microprocessor model numbers and manufacturers? RAM capacities? register (wordsize) and data bus capacities? Do you think there are any risks involved in buying an IBM-compatible system instead of an IBM PC?

8. Can you envision yourself using a supercomputer in your planned profession or job? How?

9. Look through several computer magazines and list all the coprocessor chips and add-on boards mentioned. Next to each listed item, write down what it does and what type of computer system it's compatible with. Then note an application (task) for which each item could be useful.

10. The oldest source of used microcomputers in the United States is the Boston Computer Exchange (800/262-6399 or 617/542-4414). It will give you free information, by phone, about 1,000 used computers you can buy. If you send $10, it will also send you a copy of the complete 1,000-computer master list. Another used-computer exchange is the National Computer Exchange in Atlanta (800/786-0717 or 404/250-0050). Choose a microcomputer model and "comparison shop," using these resources. Compare price, warranty, hot-line help resources, and delivery procedures.

# Chapter Topics

CHAPTER 4

# Storage Hardware

We have already described how data is input and processed. Now let us consider how this computerized data is stored and retrieved. In this chapter we describe secondary storage hardware, which stores data in a permanent form. Such storage includes magnetic tape, diskettes, hard disks, and optical disks. We also discuss compression and decompression, and other forms of secondary storage such as flash memory cards and bubble memory.

## Preview

*When you have completed this chapter, you will be able to:*

■ Describe the difference between primary and secondary storage and other basic concepts relating to storage

■ Explain how data is represented on magnetic tape

■ Describe the characteristics of diskettes and how to take care of them, and explain why backup is important

■ Describe hard disks for microcomputers and large computer systems

■ Describe optical storage technology by focusing on CD-ROM disks, CD-R disks, WORM disks, erasable optical disks, and interactive and multimedia CD-ROM formats

■ Explain why compression techniques are important and describe how compression works

**111**

**Why Is This Chapter Important?**

*Two of the most overused marketing terms of recent times are "interactivity" and "multimedia." Interactivity refers to users' ability to have a back-and-forth dialog with whatever is on their screen. Multimedia refers to the use of a variety of media—text, graphics, sound, video—to deliver information, whether via computer or (as the phone and cable companies plan) via the anticipated union of computers, telecommunications, and broadcasting technologies.*

*Both interactivity and multimedia, however, require machines that can store complicated programs and enormous amounts of data. This kind of hardware is called secondary storage. Secondary storage media can range from a small diskette holding the text of a few letters to a giant video server such as those being planned to store and distribute thousands of first-run movies over cable channels.*

*Let us look at how these functions work. We begin by describing storage fundamentals, including the data storage hierarchy, and then consider various forms of secondary storage.*

## Storage Fundamentals

**Storage is categorized as primary or secondary. Primary storage is RAM (main memory), which is volatile. Secondary storage is permanent storage, which is nonvolatile. The capacity of storage devices is measured in bytes, kilobytes, megabytes, gigabytes, and terabytes. Files are classified as program files or data files, which in turn are classified as master files or transaction files. Data may remain in secondary storage for a while before being processed (batch processing), or it may be processed immediately (real-time processing).**

As you learned in the previous chapter, the data you are working on—such as a document—is stored in RAM (primary storage) in an electrical state during processing. Because RAM exists through electricity, when you turn off the power to your computer, data in RAM disappears. Therefore, before you turn your microcomputer off, you must save your work onto a storage device that stores data magnetically (permanently)—such as a diskette or a hard disk—rather than electrically. When stored on a secondary storage device, your data will remain intact even when the computer is turned off.

secondary storage

In addition to data, computer software must be stored in a computer-usable form. A copy of software instructions must be retrieved from a permanent storage device and placed into RAM before processing can begin.

Before we describe the characteristics of secondary storage devices, let's look at a few storage fundamentals, including:

■ The difference between primary and secondary storage

■ How data is represented and units of measurement for storage

■ Different types of files

### Primary and Secondary Storage

The term **primary storage** (main memory) refers to RAM, where both data and instructions are temporarily held for immediate access and use by the computer's microprocessor. Although the technology is changing, most primary storage is considered a *volatile* form of storage, meaning that the data and instructions are lost when the computer is turned off. **Secondary storage** (or **auxiliary storage**) is any storage device designed to retain data and instructions (programs) in a relatively permanent form. Secondary storage is *nonvolatile,* meaning that saved data and instructions remain intact when the computer is turned off.

The easiest way to differentiate between primary and secondary storage is to consider the reason data is placed in them. Data is placed in primary storage only when it is needed for processing. Data in secondary storage remains there until overwritten with new data or deleted, and it is accessed when needed. In very general terms, a secondary storage device can be thought of as a file cabinet. We store data there until we need it. Then we open the drawer, take out the appropriate folder (file), and place it on the top of our desk (in primary storage, or RAM), where we work on it—perhaps writing a few things in it or throwing away a few papers. When we are finished with the file, we take it off the desktop (out of primary storage) and return it to the cabinet (secondary storage).

## Data Representation and Data Storage Capacity

Computers, we have said, are based on the principle that electricity may be "on" or "off," or "high-voltage" or "low-voltage," or "present" or "absent." Thus, individual items of data are represented by 0 for off and 1 for on. A 0 or 1 is called a **bit.** A unit of 8 bits is called a **byte;** it may be used to represent a character, digit, or other value, such as *A, ?,* or *3.* Bits and bytes are the building blocks for representing data, whether it is being processed, stored, or telecommunicated.

In Chapter 3, we explained the meanings of kilobytes, megabytes, gigabytes, and terabytes in conjunction with the capacities of processing hardware components. The same terms are also used to measure the data capacity of storage devices. To repeat:

- *Kilobyte:* A **kilobyte** (abbreviated **K** or **KB**) is equivalent to 1,024 bytes. Kilobytes are a common unit of measure for storage capacity.

- *Megabyte:* A **megabyte** (abbreviated **M** or **MB**) is 1 million bytes (rounded off).

- *Gigabyte:* A **gigabyte** (**G** or **GB**) is 1 billion bytes (rounded off).

- *Terabyte:* A **terabyte** (**T** or **TB**) is about 1 trillion bytes.

The amount of data being held in a file or a database in your personal computer might be expressed in kilobytes or megabytes. The amount of data being held by a remote database accessible to you over a communications line could well be expressed in gigabytes or terabytes.

## Types of Files

A **file** is a collection of information treated as a unit. (We discuss the organization of data within files in Chapter 10.) There are many kinds of files, but the principal division is between program files and data files.

- *Program files:* **Program files** are files containing software instructions. In a word processing program, for example, you may see files listed (with names such as INSTALL.EXE) that perform specific functions associated with word processing. These files are part of the software package.

- *Data files:* **Data files** are files that contain data. Often you will create and name these files yourself, such as DOCUMENT.1 or PSYCH.RPT (for "Psychology Report").

Among the several types of data files two are commonly used in business and organizations to update data: a master file and a transaction file.

■ *Master file:* The **master file** is a data file containing relatively permanent records that are generally updated periodically. An example of a master file would be the address-label file for all students currently enrolled at your college.

■ *Transaction file:* The **transaction file** is a temporary holding file that holds all changes to be made to the master file: additions, deletions, revisions. For example, in the case of the address labels, a transaction file would hold new names and addresses to be added (because over time new students enroll) and names and addresses to be deleted (because students leave). It would also hold revised names and addresses (because students change their names or move). Each month or so, the master file would be updated with the changes called for in the transaction file.

## Batch Versus Real-Time Processing

Although the title of this section, Batch Versus Real-Time *Processing,* might make you think this topic belongs in Chapter 3, Processing Hardware, we are referring here to how long data remains in secondary storage. Data may be taken from secondary storage and processed in either of two ways: (1) "later" for *batch processing,* or (2) "right now" for *real-time processing:*

■ *Batch processing:* In **batch processing,** data is collected over several days or weeks and then processed all at one time, as a "batch." Thus, if users need to make some request of the system, they must wait until the batch has been processed. Batch processing is less expensive than real-time processing and is suitable for work in which immediate answers to queries are not needed.

An example of batch processing is that done by banks for balancing checking accounts. When you deposit a check in the morning, the bank will make a record of it. However, it will not compute your account balance until the end of the day, after all checks have been processed in a batch.

■ *Real-time processing:* **Real-time processing** records information immediately and responds to user requests at the time transactions occur. For example, when you use your ATM card to withdraw cash from an automated teller machine, the system automatically computes your account balance then and there. Airline reservation systems also use real-time processing.

Now let's take a look at the following forms and elements of secondary storage:

■ Tape

■ Diskette

■ Hard disk

■ Optical disk

■ Data storage and retrieval methods

■ Data compression and decompression

■ Other forms of secondary storage

## Tape Storage

**Magnetic tape is thin plastic tape on which data can be represented with magnetized spots. On large computers, tapes are used on magnetic-tape units. On microcomputers, tapes are used in cartridge tape units.**

Movie makers used to love to represent computers with banks of spinning reels of magnetic tape. Indeed, with early mainframes, "tape" was the principal method of secondary storage.

The magnetic tape used for computers is made from the same material used for audiotape and videotape. **Magnetic tape** is thin plastic tape coated with a substance that can be magnetized; data is represented by the magnetized or nonmagnetized spots. Today tape is used mainly to provide backup, or duplicate storage.

### Representing Data on Magnetic Tape

Traditional magnetic tape stores each character, or byte, of data in a row of magnetic spots arranged in tracks, or channels, running the length of the tape. The 0 or 1 bits making up a byte are represented by a magnetized spot for a 1 bit and a nonmagnetized spot for a 0 bit. (See Figure 4.1.) (As described earlier, a byte is made up of 8 bits, with a 9th bit representing a parity bit to check for errors.) The capacity, or storage density, is represented in bytes per inch, or bpi.

The two principal forms of tape storage of interest to us are *magnetic-tape units,* traditionally used with mainframes and minicomputers, and *cartridge tape units,* which are often used for backup on microcomputers.

**Figure 4.1**
How data is stored on traditional magnetic tape. A character (byte) is represented as a row of magnetized and nonmagnetized spots arranged in nine tracks.

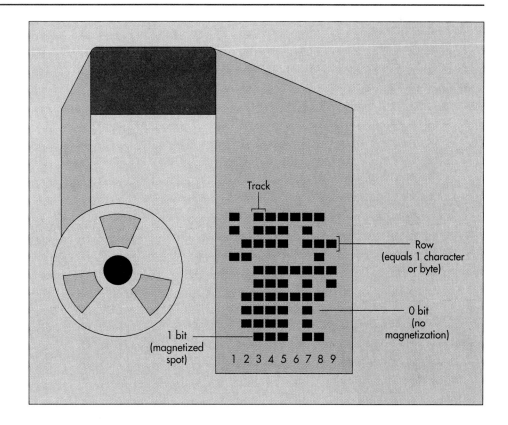

**Figure 4.2**
Magnetic-tape unit. Tape reels are mounted on spindles, which turn the reels. Tape is unreeled off the supply reel, fed past the read/write heads that read (retrieve) or write (record) data, and wound up on the take-up reel.

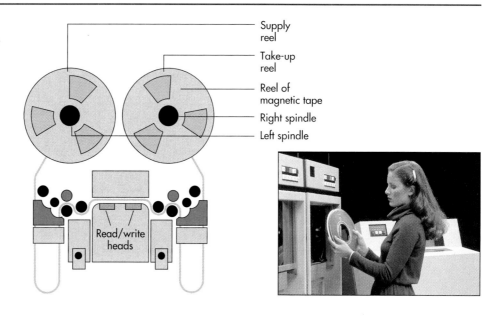

## Magnetic-Tape Units for Large Computers

The kind of cassette tapes you use for an audiotape recorder are 200 feet long and record 200 bytes per inch. By contrast, a reel of magnetic tape used in mainframe and minicomputer storage systems is ½ inch wide, 3,600 feet long, and can hold 1,600–6,250 bpi. A traditional 10½-inch tape reel can hold up to 250 megabytes of data.

Tapes are used on **magnetic-tape units (drives),** which consist of a read/write head and spindles for mounting two tape reels: a supply reel and a take-up reel. (See Figure 4.2.) The tape is reeled off the supply reel, fed through pulleys that regulate its speed and hold it still long enough for data to be read from it or written to it by the read/write heads, and then wound up on the take-up reel. During the writing process, any existing data on the tape is automatically written over, or erased.

Large organizations, such as public utilities, often use reels of magnetic tape for storing backup records of essential data, such as customer names and account numbers. Usually these reels are housed in tape libraries, or special rooms, and there are strict security procedures governing their use.

## Cartridge Tape Units

**Figure 4.3**
Cartridge tape unit. This device is used with microcomputers to back up data on a hard disk.

You may never see the traditional reel-to-reel tape systems used with mainframes (except in 1960s movies), but you may encounter cartridge tape units because they are often used with microcomputers. **Cartridge tape units,** also called **tape streamers,** are used to back up data from a hard disk onto a tape cartridge. (See Figure 4.3.)

A cartridge tape unit using quarter-inch cassettes (QIC), which fits into the standard hard disk drive bay of a microcomputer, uses minicartridges that store 40, 80, 120, or even 250 megabytes of data on a single tape. A high-density 1,000-foot tape cartridge can hold up to 1.35 gigabytes. An advanced form of cassette, adapted from technology used in the music industry, is the *digital audio tape (DAT),* or *R-DAT,* which uses 2- or 3-inch cassettes and stores 2 gigabytes or more. (See Figure 4.4.) Future R-DATs are expected to hold as much as 8 gigabytes.

**Figure 4.4**
How much is backup worth?

" 'When you lose a disk, you're not only losing the hardware and software,' said John L. Copen, president of Integ, an information protection company in Manhattan. 'The information has to be reproduced, and if you have to reproduce it without a backup. . . .'

Mr. Copen demonstrates the point by holding up a digital audio tape (DAT) cassette, one of the newer technologies used for backing up data on larger hard disk drives, the kind that act as hubs for networks of personal computers in an office.

'I ask people in the audience what it's worth,' he said. 'It's a little cassette, about the size of a credit card. The cassette costs about $16. I ask them to guess how much it can store. Forty megs? Eighty megs? It stores four gigabytes.' A gigabyte is roughly a thousand megabytes, or a billion characters of information.

'How much information can you put in four gigs?' Mr. Copen continued. 'About 20,000 big spreadsheets, which translates to about 100,000 days of work, or 800,000 hours. At $20 an hour, that's $16 million. Never before have people been able to reach down, pick up a cassette and walk out the door with $16 million of data in their pocket.' "

—Peter H. Lewis, "Finding an Electronic Safe-Deposit Data Box," *The New York Times,* January 11, 1994, p. B10.

## Diskette Storage

Diskettes are round pieces of flat plastic that store data and programs as magnetized spots. The two principal sizes are 3½-inch and 5¼-inch. A disk drive copies, or reads, data from the disk and writes, or records, data to the disk. Components of a diskette include tracks and sectors; disks come in various densities. All have write-protect features. Care must be taken to avoid destroying data on disks, and users are advised to back up, or duplicate, the data on their disks.

A **diskette,** or **floppy disk,** is a removable round, flat piece of mylar plastic that stores data and programs as magnetized spots. More specifically, data is stored as electromagnetic charges on a metal oxide film that coats the mylar plastic. Data is represented by the presence or absence of these electromagnetic charges, following standard patterns of data representation (such as ASCII). The disk is contained in a square paper envelope or plastic case to protect it from being touched. Diskettes are often called "floppy" because the disk within the envelope or case is flexible, not rigid.

Two sizes of diskettes are commonly used for microcomputers. (See Figure 4.5.)

**Figure 4.5**
Diskettes. The two most popular sizes are 3½-inch and 5¼-inch. The latter size is becoming less common.

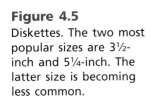

- *3½-inch:* The smaller size, now the more popular, is 3½ inches across. This size comes inside a hard plastic jacket, so that no additional protective envelope is needed.

- *5¼-inch:* The older and larger size is 5¼ inches across. The disk is encased inside a flexible plastic jacket. The 5¼-inch disk is often inserted into a removable paper or cardboard envelope or sleeve for protection when it is not being used.

Larger and smaller sizes of diskettes also exist, although they are not standard on most microcomputers.

Incidentally, you should never try to jam a 3½-inch disk into a 5¼-inch disk drive slot. Not only will the arrangement not work, but it will damage both the disk and possibly the internal drive mechanisms (read/write heads, discussed shortly).

### The Disk Drive

To use a diskette, you need a disk drive. A **disk drive** is a device that holds, spins, and reads data from and writes data to a floppy disk.

The words *read* and *write* have exact meanings:

■ *Read:* **Read** means that the data represented in the magnetized spots on the disk (or tape) is converted to electronic signals and transmitted to the primary storage (memory) in the computer. That is, *read* means the disk drive *copies* data—stored as magnetic spots—from the diskette.

■ *Write:* **Write** means that the electronic information processed by the computer is recorded magnetically onto a disk (or tape). *Write* means the disk drive transfers data—represented as electronic signals within the computer's memory—onto the disk.

Whereas *reading* simply makes a copy of the original data, without altering the original, *writing* actually replaces the data underneath it. With writing, it is as though you recorded on an audio tape recorder a new song, obliterating the original song already on the tape.

### Figure 4.6

Disk drives. *Top:* Separate external disk drive (3½-inch). *Bottom:* Disk drives built into system cabinet.

Disk drives

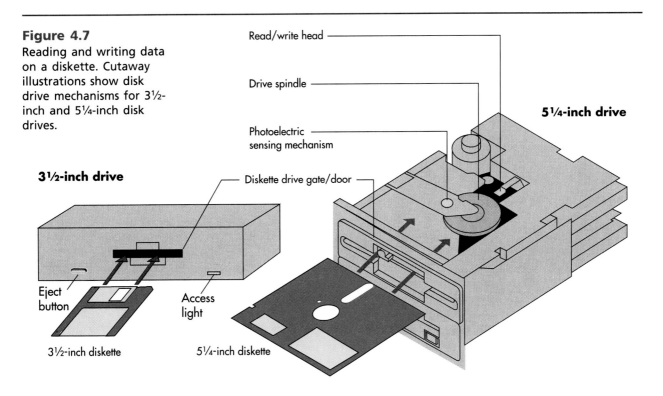

**Figure 4.7**
Reading and writing data on a diskette. Cutaway illustrations show disk drive mechanisms for 3½-inch and 5¼-inch disk drives.

A diskette drive may be a separate unit attached to the computer, particularly on older models. Usually, however, it is built into the computer's system cabinet. (See Figure 4.6.)

## How a Disk Drive Works

A diskette is inserted into a slot, called the *drive gate* or *drive door,* in the front of the disk drive. (See Figure 4.7.) Sometimes a door or a latch must be closed after the disk is inserted. This clamps the diskette in place over the spindle of the drive mechanism so the drive can operate. In newer drives, however, the diskette is simply pushed into the drive until it clicks into place. An access light goes on when the disk is in use. After using the disk, you can retrieve it either by pressing an eject button beside the drive or by opening the drive gate.

The device by which the data on a disk is transferred to the computer, and from the computer to the disk, is the disk drive's **read/write head.** The diskette spins inside its jacket, and the read/write head moves back and forth over the data access area. The **data access area** is an opening in the disk's jacket through which data is read or written.

## Characteristics of Diskettes

Both 5¼-inch and 3½-inch disks work in similar ways, although there are some differences. (See Figure 4.8.) The characteristics of diskettes are as follows:

■ *Tracks and sectors:* On a diskette, data is recorded in rings called **tracks.** Unlike on a phonograph record, these tracks are neither visible grooves nor a single spiral. Rather, they are closed concentric rings.

Each track is divided into eight or nine sectors. **Sectors** are invisible wedge-shaped sections used for storage reference purposes. When you

**Figure 4.8**

Parts of a diskette. *Top:* A 5¼-inch disk. *Bottom:* A 3½-inch disk.

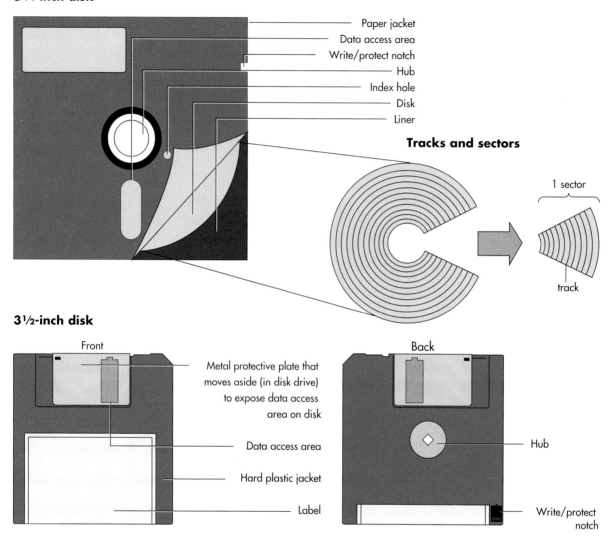

**5¼-inch disk**

Paper jacket
Data access area
Write/protect notch
Hub
Index hole
Disk
Liner

**Tracks and sectors**

1 sector

track

**3½-inch disk**

Front

Metal protective plate that moves aside (in disk drive) to expose data access area on disk

Data access area

Hard plastic jacket

Label

Back

Hub

Write/protect notch

save data from your computer to a diskette, it is distributed by tracks and sectors on the disk. That is, the systems software uses the point at which a sector intersects a track to reference the data location in order to spin the disk and position the read/write head.

■ *Unformatted versus formatted disks:* When you buy a new box of diskettes to use for storing data, the box may state that it is "unformatted" (or say nothing at all). This means you have a task to perform before you can use the disks with your computer and disk drive. *Unformatted disks* are manufactured without tracks and sectors in place. **Formatting**—or **initializing,** as it is called on the Macintosh—means that you must prepare the disk for use so that the computer's operating system software can write information on it. This includes defining the tracks and sectors on it.

The software documentation (user's manual) that comes with your microcomputer tells you what commands to enter to format your disks. Alternatively, when you buy a new box of diskettes, the box may state that it is "formatted IBM." This means that you can simply insert a diskette into the drive gate of your IBM or IBM-compatible microcomputer and use it without any effort. It's just like plunking an audiotape into a standard tape recorder.

■ *Data capacity—sides and densities:* Not all disks hold the same amount of data, because the characteristics of microcomputer disk drives differ. For example, on some boxes of 5¼-inch disks you will see "2S/2D" or "DS, DD," which means *double-sided, double-density.*

The first diskettes were *single-sided,* or diskettes that store data on one side only. Now all diskettes are *double-sided,* capable of storing data on both sides. They therefore hold twice as much data as single-sided disks. For double-sided diskettes to work, the disk drive must have read/write heads that will read both sides simultaneously. Disk drives have been built this way for some time now.

A diskette's capacity also depends on its recording density. **Recording density** refers to the number of bytes per inch that can be written onto the surface of the disk. There are three densities: *single-density, double-density,* and *high-density.* A double-sided, double-density 5¼-inch disk can store 360 kilobytes (equal to 260 typewritten pages). A 3½-inch double-sided, double-density disk can store 720 kilobytes. A high-density 5¼-inch disk can store 1.2 megabytes. A high-density 3½-inch disk can store 1.44 megabytes. (See Figure 4.9.)

■ *Write-protect features:* The 5¼-inch and 3½-inch disks have features to prevent someone from accidentally writing over—and thereby obliterating—data on the disk. (This is especially important if you're working on your only copy of a program or a document that you've transported from somewhere else.) This **write-protect** feature allows you to protect a diskette from being written to.

The write-protect feature works a bit differently for the two sizes of disks. With a 5¼-inch disk, there is a write-protect notch, a small, square cutout on the side of the disk. This notch is covered by a piece of tape in order to protect it. With a 3½-inch disk, you press a slide lever toward the edge of the disk, uncovering a hole (which appears on the lower right side, viewed from the back). (See Figure 4.10.)

Disks have additional features (such as the index hole, for positioning the disk over a photoelectric sensing mechanism within the disk drive). However, these are of no concern for our present purposes.

**Figure 4.9**
Diskette capacity. Common capacities of 5¼-inch and 3½-inch diskettes.

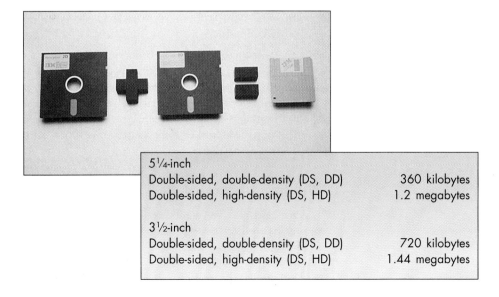

| 5¼-inch | |
| --- | --- |
| Double-sided, double-density (DS, DD) | 360 kilobytes |
| Double-sided, high-density (DS, HD) | 1.2 megabytes |
| | |
| 3½-inch | |
| Double-sided, double-density (DS, DD) | 720 kilobytes |
| Double-sided, high-density (DS, HD) | 1.44 megabytes |

**Figure 4.10**
Write-protect features.
*Top:* 5¼-inch disk—For
data to be written to the
disk, the write-protect
notch must be uncovered,
as shown in the diskette
at left. To protect the
disk from being mis-
takenly written over, you
must fold a small piece
of tape around the
notch. (The tape comes
with a box of new disks.)
*Bottom:* 3½-inch disk—
For data to be written to
this disk, a small piece of
plastic must be closed
over the tiny window on
one side of the disk. To
protect the disk from
being written to, you
must open the window
(using the tip of a pen
helps).

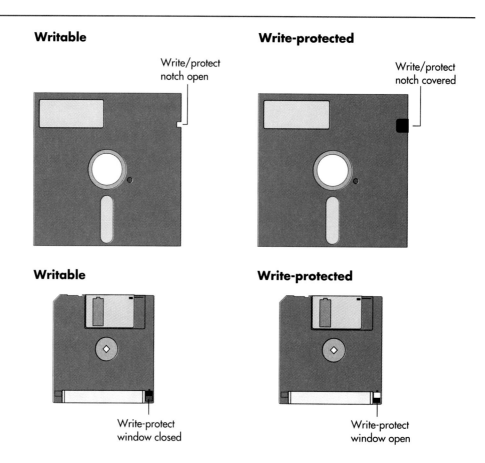

**Writable**

Write/protect
notch open

**Write-protected**

Write/protect
notch covered

**Writable**

Write-protect
window closed

**Write-protected**

Write-protect
window open

## Taking Care of Diskettes

Diskettes need at least the same amount of care that you would give to an
audiotape or music CD. (See Figure 4.11.) In fact, they need more care than
that if you are dealing with difficult-to-replace data or programs. There are a
number of rules for taking care of diskettes. In general, they boil down to
the following:

■ *Don't touch disk surfaces:* Don't touch anything visible through the protective jacket, such as the data access area.

■ *Handle 5¼-inch diskettes gently:* Don't bend them, put weights on them,
or stick them with sharp objects (as in writing on them by bearing down
on a ballpoint pen).

■ *Avoid risky physical environments:* Disks don't do well in sun or heat
(such as in glove compartments or on top of steam radiators). They
should not be placed near magnetic fields (including those created by
nearby telephones or electric motors). They also should not be exposed
to chemicals (such as cleaning solvents) or spilled coffee or alcohol. Keep
5¼-inch diskettes in their paper envelopes and store them in a file box
when not in use.

## The Importance of Backup

Having said all this, we hasten to point out that diskettes are surprisingly
hardy. Every day people send thousands of disks through the mail in cardboard mailing envelopes. They also pass them in luggage through airport-
security X-ray machines. They even violate many of the rules we've just cited,
and still the disks continue working.

**Figure 4.11**
Avoiding disk risks.

### Don't touch disk surfaces

Do not touch the disk surface. It is easily contaminated, which causes errors.

Disk drive

Insert carefully, by grasping upper edge of disk and placing it into the disk drive.

Do not use rubber bands or paper clips on the disk.

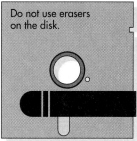

Do not use erasers on the disk.

### Handle disks gently

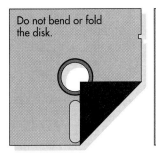

Do not bend or fold the disk.

Do not place heavy objects on the disk.

Write on the index label with felt tip pen only, not pencil or ball-point pen.

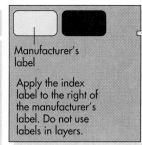

Manufacturer's label

Apply the index label to the right of the manufacturer's label. Do not use labels in layers.

### Avoid risky physical environments

Do not expose the disk to excessive heat or light.

Do not use near magnetic field, including that of a telephone. Data can be lost if exposed.

Do not use alcohol, thinners, or freon to clean the disk.

Keep disk in its protective envelope when not in use.

Even with the best of care, however, a disk can suddenly fail for reasons you can't understand. Many computer users have had the experience of being unable to retrieve data from a diskette that worked perfectly the day before, because some defect has damaged a track or sector.

Thus, you should always be thinking about backup. As we've mentioned, **backup** is the name given to a tape or diskette that is a duplicate or copy of another form of storage. The best protection if you're writing, say, a make-or-break research paper is to make two copies of your data. One copy may be on your hard disk, certainly, but duplicates should be on tape and diskette or on two diskettes.

# THE CLIPBOARD

## When Technology Brings Pressure, Not Convenience

I am a lawyer who works in a modern office. I can transport reams of documents across continents in an instant or close a multi-million-dollar deal in a flash. I know I should feel grateful. So why do I feel enslaved?

In the pre-fax, pre-computer, pre-FedEx days . . . life was less complicated, expectations were more reasonable. Deals were done at a temperate pace. The corporate merger that we now race through in weeks was cautiously closed in months. Another day or two rarely mattered. . . .

Computers and facsimile machines . . . come in handy when time is running short. But the problem is that as soon as a technological advance is made, it becomes not a frill but an imperative.

Progress should bring us ease and convenience. Instead it dispenses pressure. We can cut complex deals on fast-forward, so we do just that. Within hours of a handshake we produce 20 sets of 60 word-processed pages memorializing the transaction. We process words faster than we can read them. Then comes the battle of the faxes. Revision requests surge through phone lines—often at the end of a long day as we're bolting out the door. . . .

Jumping through computerized hoops may seem impressive. But sometimes it only encourages people to raise those hoops even higher.

Madeleine Begun Kane, "When Executives Should Just Say No," *The New York Times,* April 4, 1991, sec. 3, p. 11.

## Hard Disks

**Hard disks are rigid metal platters that hold data as magnetized spots. Usually a microcomputer hard disk drive is built into the system unit, but external hard disk drives are available, as are removable hard disk cartridges. Large computers use removable hard disk packs, fixed disk drives, or RAID storage systems.**

Switching from a microcomputer that uses only diskettes to one containing a hard disk is like discovering the difference between moving your household in several trips in a small sportscar and doing it all at once with a moving van. Whereas a high-density 3½-inch diskette holds 1.44 megabytes of data, a hard disk in a personal computer may hold 40, 80, 100, 200, 500 megabytes, or a gigabyte or more. Indeed, at first with a hard disk you may feel you have more storage capacity than you'll ever need. However, after a few months, you may worry that you don't have enough. This feeling may be intensified if you're using graphics-oriented programs, with pictures and other features requiring immense amounts of storage.

Diskettes are made out of flexible material, which makes them "floppy." By contrast, **hard disks** are thin but rigid metal platters covered with a substance that allows data to be held in the form of magnetized spots. Hard disks are also tightly sealed within an enclosed unit to prevent any foreign matter from getting inside. Data may be recorded on both sides of the disk platters.

We'll now describe the following aspects of hard disk technology:

- Microcomputer hard disk drives

- Microcomputer hard disk variations

- Hard-disk technology for large computer systems

### Microcomputer Hard Disk Drives

In microcomputers, hard disks are one or more platters sealed inside a **hard disk drive** that is built into the system unit and cannot be removed. The drive is installed in a **drive bay,** a slot, or opening, in the computer cabinet. From the outside of a microcomputer, a hard disk drive is not visible; it looks simply like part of the front panel on the system cabinet. Inside, however, is a disk or disks on a drive spindle, read/write heads mounted on an actuator (access) arm that moves back and forth, and power connections and circuitry. (See Figure 4.12.) The disks may be 5¼ inches in diameter, although today they are more often 3½ inches, with some even smaller. The operation is

**Figure 4.12**
Microcomputer hard disk drive. *Top:* Photo and cutaway view of drive. *Bottom inset:* An IBM PS/2 computer; the hard disk drive is sealed inside the system cabinet and not accessible. The drive gate is for inserting a diskette.

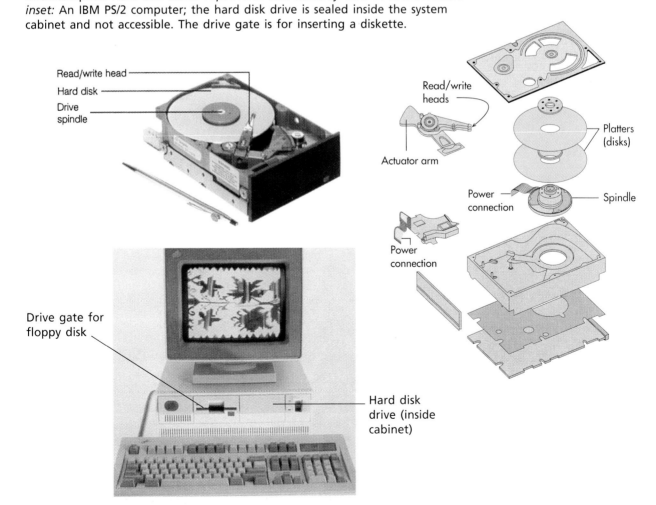

much the same as for a floppy disk drive, with the read/write heads locating specific pieces of data according to track and sector.

Hard disks have a couple of real advantages over diskettes—and at least one significant disadvantage.

■ *Advantages—capacity and speed:* We mentioned that hard disks have a data storage capacity that is significantly greater than that of diskettes. Microcomputer hard disk drives typically hold 40–500 megabytes and some newer ones are in the 1–3 gigabyte range.

As for speed, hard disks allow faster access to data than do diskettes because a hard disk spins several times faster than a diskette.

■ *Disadvantage—possible "head crash":* In principle a hard disk is quite a sensitive device. The read/write head does not actually touch the disk but rather rides on a cushion of air about 0.000001 inch thick. The disk is sealed from impurities within a container, and the whole apparatus is manufactured under sterile conditions. Otherwise, all it would take is a smoke particle, a human hair, or a fingerprint to cause what is called a *head crash*.

A **head crash** happens when the surface of the read/write head or particles on its surface come into contact with the disk surface, causing the loss of some or all of the data on the disk. An incident of this sort could, of course, be a disaster if the data has not been backed up. There are firms that specialize in trying to retrieve (for a hefty price) data from crashed hard disks, though this cannot always be done.

In recent years, computer magazines have evaluated the durability of portable computers containing hard disks by submitting them to drop tests. Most of the newer machines are surprisingly hardy. However, with hard disks—whether in portable or in desktop computers—the possibility of disk failure always exists.

## Microcomputer Hard Disk Variations: Power and Portability

If you have an older microcomputer or one with limited capacity in its existing hard disk, some variations are available that can provide additional power or portability:

■ *Miniaturization:* Newer hard disk drives are less than half the height of older drives ($1\frac{1}{2}$ inches versus $3\frac{1}{2}$ inches high) and so are called *half-height drives*. Thus, you could fit two disk drives into the bay in the system cabinet formerly occupied by one.

In addition, the diameter of the disks has been getting smaller. Instead of $5\frac{1}{4}$ or $3\frac{1}{2}$ inches, some platters are 2.5, 1.8, or even 1.3 inches in diameter. The half-dollar-size 1.3-inch Kittyhawk microdisk, which is actually designed for use in handheld computers, holds 21 megabytes of data.

■ *External hard disk drives:* If you don't have room in the system unit for an internal hard disk but need additional storage, consider adding an external hard disk drive. Some detached external hard disk drives, which have their own power supply, can store gigabytes of data.

■ *Hard disk cartridges:* The disadvantages of hard disks include the difficulty of removing them and their finite amount of storage. **Hard disk cartridges** consist of one or two platters enclosed along with read/write heads in a hard plastic case. The case is inserted into a detached external cartridge system connected to a microcomputer. (See Figure 4.13.) A cartridge, which is removable and easily transported in a briefcase, may hold as much as 1.2 gigabytes of data. An additional advantage of hard disk cartridges is that they may be used for backing up data.

**Figure 4.13**
Removable hard disk cartridge. Each cartridge has self-contained disks and read/write heads. The entire cartridge, which may contain as much as 1.2 gigabytes of data, may be removed for transporting or may be replaced by another cartridge.

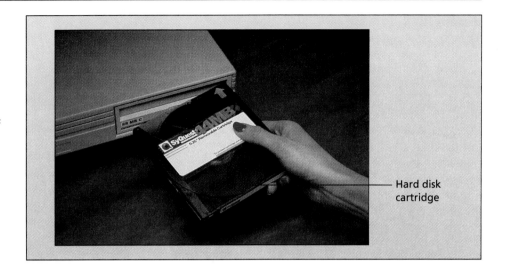

Hard disk cartridge

## Hard Disk Technology for Large Computer Systems

As a microcomputer user, you may regard secondary-storage technology for large computer systems as of only casual interest. However, this technology forms the backbone of the revolution in making information available to you over communications lines. The large databases offered by such organizations as CompuServe, America Online, or Dialog, as well as the predicted movies-on-demand through cable and wireless networks, depend on secondary-storage technology.

Secondary-storage devices for large computers consist of the following:

■ *Removable packs:* A **removable-pack hard disk system** contains 6–20 hard disks, of 10½- or 14-inch diameter, aligned one above the other in a sealed unit. Capacity varies, with some packs ranging into the gigabytes.

These removable hard disk packs resemble a stack of phonograph records, except that there is space between disks to allow access arms to move in and out. Each access arm has two read/write heads—one reading the disk surface below, the other the disk surface above. However, only one of the read/write heads is activated at any given moment.

Secondary storage systems that use several hard disks don't use the sector method to locate data. Rather they use what is known as the *cylinder method*. Because the access arms holding the read/write heads all move together, the read/write heads are always over the same track on each disk at the same time. All tracks with the same track number, lined up one above the other, thus form a **cylinder.** (See Figure 4.14.)

■ *Fixed disk drives:* **Fixed disk drives** are high-speed, high-capacity disk drives that are housed in their own cabinets. Although not removable or portable, they generally have greater storage capacity and are more reliable than removable packs. A single mainframe computer might have 20 to 100 such fixed disk drives attached to it.

**H**

RAID

■ *RAID storage system:* A fixed disk drive sends data to the computer along a single path. A **RAID storage system,** which consists of over 100 5¼-inch disk drives within a single cabinet, sends data to the computer along several parallel paths simultaneously. Response time is thereby significantly improved. (*RAID* stands for *r*edundant *a*rray of *i*nexpensive *d*isks.)

The advantage of a RAID system is that it not only holds more data than a fixed disk drive within the same amount of space, it also is more reliable, because if one drive fails, others can take over.

**Figure 4.14**

Disk packs. *Top right:* These sealed units of 6–12 disks are removable.
*Bottom:* Access arms slide in and out to a specific track. Tracks with the same
track number lined up vertically one above the other on the several stacked
disks constitute a cylinder.

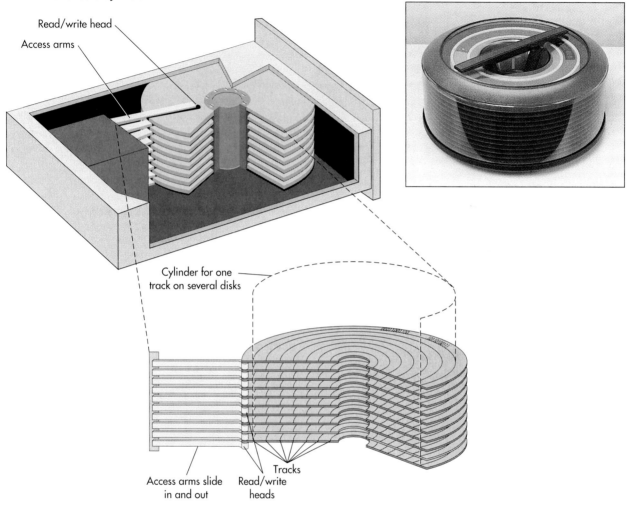

Read/write head

Access arms

Cylinder for one
track on several disks

Access arms slide
in and out

Read/write
heads

Tracks

## Optical Disks

**Optical disks are removable disks on which data is written and read using laser technology. Four types of optical disks are CD-ROM disks, CD-R disks, WORM disks, and erasable optical disks. CD-ROM formats may be interactive and multimedia. Variants of CD-ROMs are CD-I, CDTV, and MPC.**

By now optical disk technology is well known to most people. An **optical disk** is a removable disk on which data is written and read through the use of laser beams. The most familiar form of optical disk is the one used in the music industry. A **compact disk,** or **CD,** is an audio disk using digital code that is like a miniature phonograph record. A CD holds up to 72 minutes of high-fidelity stereo sound.

The optical disk technology that has revolutionized the music business with music CDs is doing the same for secondary storage with computers. A single optical disk of the type called CD-ROM can hold 650 megabytes of data. This works out to 250,000 pages of text, or more than 7,000 photos or graphics, or 19 hours of speech, or 72 minutes of video.[1] Although some disks are used strictly for digital data storage, many combine text, visuals, and sound.

In the principal types of optical disk technology, a high-power laser beam is used to represent data by burning tiny pits into the surface of a hard plastic disk. To read the data, a low-powered laser light scans the disk surface: Pitted areas are not reflected and are interpreted as 0 bits; smooth areas are reflected and are interpreted as 1 bits. (See Figure 4.15.) Because the pits are so tiny, a great deal more data can be represented than is possible in the same amount of space on a magnetic disk, whether floppy or hard.

The optical disk technology used with computers consists of four types:

- CD-ROM disks
- CD-R disks
- WORM disks
- Erasable optical disks

We will also describe some variations on these, such as video CDs, which offer the prospect of putting movies on CD-ROM disks.

### CD-ROM Disks

For microcomputer users, the best-known type of optical disk is the CD-ROM. **CD-ROM,** which stands for compact disk–read-only memory, is an optical

**Figure 4.15**
Optical disks. *Top: writing data.* A high-powered laser beam records data by burning tiny pits onto the surface of the disk. *Bottom: reading data.* A low-powered laser beam reads data by reflecting smooth areas, which are interpreted as 1 bits, and not reflecting pitted areas, which are interpreted as 0 bits.

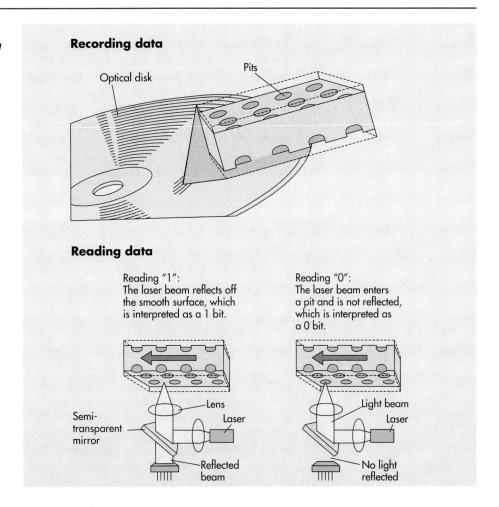

**Figure 4.16**
CD-ROM. *Left:* Panasonic laptop computer with built-in CD-ROM drive. *Right:* NEC separate CD-ROM drive, with CD-ROM disks and speakers for outputting sound.

disk format that is used to hold prerecorded text, graphics, and sound. Like music CDs, a CD-ROM is a read-only disk. **Read-only** means the disk cannot be written on or erased by the user. You as the user have access only to the data imprinted by the disk's manufacturer.

More and more microcomputers are being made with built-in CD-ROM drives. (See Figure 4.16.) However, many microcomputer users buy their CD-ROM drives separately and connect them to their computers. This requires installation of an audio circuit board and speakers if you wish to be able to play the kind of CD-ROM disks that offer music and sound.

Whereas at one time a CD-ROM drive was only a single-speed drive, now there are double-, triple-, and even quadruple-speed drives. A single-speed drive will access data at 150 kilobytes per second, a double-speed drive at 300 kilobytes per second. This means that a double-speed drive spins the compact disk twice as fast. The faster the drive spins, the more quickly it can deliver data to the processor. Some truly fast CD-ROM drives (such as the NEC MultiSpin 4X Pro) will access data at 600 kilobytes per second.

At present, CD-ROMs are a standard 120 millimeters in diameter, which is considered a bit bulky to fit in most notebook and handheld personal computers [✓ p. 73]. Several companies, including Panasonic and Kodak, are supporting a new type of CD-ROM drive that will use a smaller size—80 millimeters. This size would have only one-third the capacity of regular CD-ROM disks but would play on standard CD-ROM drives, using an adapter ring.

Clearly, CD-ROM has become an important medium. Among the uses are the following:

■ *Data storage:* Originally, computer makers thought that CD-ROM "would be good for storing databases, documents, directories, and other archival information that would not need to be altered," said one report. "Customers would be libraries and businesses."[2]

In this vein, among the top-selling titles are road maps (*Street Atlas U.S.A.*), typeface and illustration libraries for graphics professionals (*Key*

*Fonts Pro* and *Key Clipmaster Pro*), and video and audio clips (*MPC Wizard*). Publishers are also mailing monthly "publications" of CD-ROMs on such subjects as medical literature, patents, and law.[3]

- *Encyclopedias:* The principal CD-ROM encyclopedias are *The Grolier Multimedia Encyclopedia, Compton's New Century Encyclopedia,* and Microsoft's *Encarta.* Each packs the entire text of a traditional multivolume encyclopedia onto a single disk, accompanied by pictures, maps, animation, and snippets of audio and video.

- *Catalogs:* Publishers have also discovered that CD-ROMs can be used as electronic catalogs, or even "megalogs." One, for instance, combines the catalogs of several companies. "A single disk now holds the equivalent of 7,000 pages of information on almost 50,000 different products from salad-bar sneeze-guards to deep-fat fryers," noted one report.[4] *Cinemania* offers a multimedia catalog of movies available on videotape.

- *Games:* As you might expect, CD-ROM has been a hugely successful medium for games. Early bestsellers on the CD-ROM hit parade included *7th Guest, Battle Chess,* and *Kings Quest V.* The CD-ROM program called *Sherlock Holmes, Consulting Detective,* features three different murder mysteries to choose from. Each offers you the opportunity, with a Shakespearean actor playing Sherlock Holmes, to solve a murder with as few clues as possible.

- *Edutainment: Edutainment* software consists of programs that look like games but actually teach in a way that feels like fun. An example for children aged 3–6 is *Yearn 2 Learn Peanuts,* which teaches math, geography, and reading. *Multimedia Beethoven: The Ninth Symphony,* an edutainment program for adults, plays the four movements of the symphony while the on-screen text provides a running commentary and allows you to stop and interact with the program.

- *Magazines and books:* Several magazines, including *Newsweek* and *Business Week,* are publishing multimedia issues. Book publishers have produced several CD-ROM titles, including *Time-Life 35mm Photography* and *From Alice to Ocean,* about a young woman's 1,700-mile trip by camel through the Australian Outback.

- *Movies:* As we describe shortly, using CD-ROMs for movies has some limitations. Nevertheless, you can watch films ranging from the 1954 *White Christmas* with Bing Crosby to Tom Cruise's *Top Gun* on home video CD.

  One company has taken a movie called *The Discoverers,* which plays on a giant five-story-high IMAX screen at Chicago's Museum of Science and Industry, and put it on CD-ROM. The disk uses the hypertext technique of the "hot link" to enable viewers to click on a word or picture and jump to related material.[5]

  Some companies are using CD-ROM jukeboxes as a means of increasing archive storage capacity. Based on the same principles as coin-operated music jukeboxes. *CD-ROM jukeboxes* can hold as few as six CDs and a single drive to as many as 1,400 CDs and 32 drives.

## CD-R Disks

*CD-R,* which stands for *c*ompact *d*isk–*r*ecordable, is a CD format that allows you to write data onto a specially manufactured disk that can then be read by a standard CD-ROM drive. One of the most interesting examples of CD-R technology is the Photo CD system. Developed by Eastman Kodak, **Photo CD** is a technology that allows photographs taken with an ordinary 35-millimeter camera to be stored digitally on an optical disk. (See Figure 4.17.) You can

**Figure 4.17**
Photo CD. With Kodak's Photo CD system, ordinary snapshots can be stored on CD-ROM disks, then viewed on a computer display screen or on a television screen.

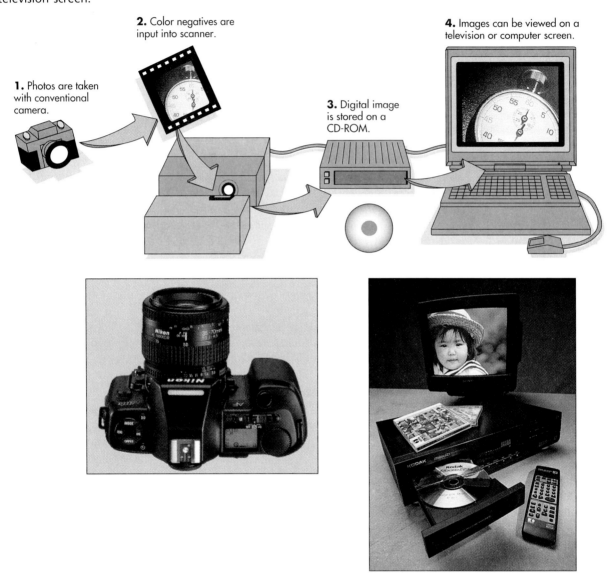

**2.** Color negatives are input into scanner.

**4.** Images can be viewed on a television or computer screen.

**1.** Photos are taken with conventional camera.

**3.** Digital image is stored on a CD-ROM.

shoot up to 100 color photographs and take them to a local photo shop for processing. A week later you will receive back not only conventional negatives and snapshots but also the images on a CD-ROM disk. Depending on your equipment, you can then view the disk using any compatible CD-ROM drive. The drive could be for an IBM PC or Macintosh, a CD-I device (described shortly), or one of Kodak's own Photo CD players, which attaches directly to a television set.

Photo CD is particularly significant for the impact it will have on the manipulation of photographs. With the right software, you can flip, crop, and rotate photos, incorporate them into desktop-publishing materials, and print them out on laser printers. Commercial photographers and graphics professionals can manipulate images at the level of pixels. **Pixels,** or picture elements, are the dots of color that make up a picture. For example, they can easily merge images from different sources, such as superimposing the heads of show-business figures in the places of the U.S. presidents on Mount Rushmore. "Because the image is digital," says one writer, "it can be taken apart pixel by pixel and put back together in many ways."[6] This helps photo professionals further their range, although at the same time it also presents a danger that photographs will be compromised in their credibility.

## WORM Disks

**WORM** stands for "write once, read many." A WORM disk can be written, or recorded, onto just once and then cannot be erased; it can be read many times. WORM technology is useful for storing data that needs to remain unchanged, such as that used for archival purposes. WORM disks hold 122–6,400 megabytes of data.

## Erasable Optical Disks

magneto-optical disk

An **erasable optical disk** allows users to erase data so that the disk can be used over and over again. An erasable optical disk can store 281–3,200 megabytes of data. The most common type of erasable and rewritable optical disk is probably the *magneto-optical disk,* which uses aspects of both magnetic disk and optical disk technologies. Such disks are useful to people who need to save successive versions of large documents, handle enormous databases, or work in multimedia production or desktop publishing.

## Interactive and Multimedia CD-ROM Formats

As use of CD-ROMs has burgeoned, so has the vocabulary, creating difficulty for consumers. Much of this confusion arises in conjunction with the words *interactive* and *multimedia.*

As we mentioned at the beginning of the chapter, **interactive** means that the user controls the direction of a program or presentation on the storage medium. That is, there is back-and-forth interaction, as between a player and a video game. You could create an interactive production of your own on a regular 3½-inch diskette. However, because of its limited capacity, you would not be able to present full-motion video and high-quality audio. The best interactive storage media are those with high capacity, such as CD-ROMs.

**Multimedia** refers to technology that presents information in more than one medium, including text, graphics, animation, video, sound, and voice.

There are perhaps 20 different CD-ROM formats, some of which work on computers and some of which work only on TVs or special monitors. Most are not mutually compatible right now. The majority of nongame CD-ROM disks are available for Macintosh or for Windows- or DOS-based microcomputers. Among the kinds of variations on CD-ROM technology used for interactive and multimedia purposes are the following:

■ *Game CD-ROMs:* Both Sega and 3DO offer video game machines that play their own types of CD-ROM disks. (Nintendo is sticking with cartridges for the moment.)

■ *CD-I:* CD-I, for *c*ompact *d*isk-*i*nteractive, is a disk format that stores data, audio, still video pictures, and animated graphics. Developed by Philips Consumer Electronics and Sony Corp. of America, CD-I is mainly used for home entertainment, including interactive games and educational and reference uses. The CD-I drive is connected to a television set, and a remote control can be used to interact with the program. A CD-I disk will not play on a CD-ROM player.

Philips touts its CD-I system as being useful not only for games, music, and Photo CDs but also for video CDs. *Video CDs* are compact disks that contain movies or music videos. At present, video CDs have several limitations. They can be played only on properly equipped Philips or Magnavox CD-I systems, are visually no better than VHS (and inferior in quality to laser disk), can't be recorded on, and require two CDs to hold a movie.

However, video CDs also have several advantages. They don't break or wear out. They offer the ability to divide a movie into chapters, so that the viewer can jump quickly from one section to another. Finally, they offer fast-forward, fast-backward, and freeze-frame capability.

- *CDTV:* CDTV, for *c*ompact *d*isk *t*elevision, is another home entertainment system that connects directly to a TV set. Available from Commodore, it has an advantage over CD-I in that it can be expanded into a home computer system. A Philips CD-I disk will not play on a CDTV unit or vice versa.

- *MPC:* The term *MPC* indicates that hardware or software meets the industry standard for connecting CD-ROM drives to IBM-compatible microcomputers and supporting multimedia input, processing, storage, and output requirements. An **MPC machine** is a multimedia personal computer that adheres to standards set by the Multimedia PC (MPC) Marketing Council. This organization consists of important hardware and software companies, including Intel, Microsoft, IBM, NEC, and Fujitsu. Advanced software requires PCs with at least a 386 microprocessor, although less powerful machines can play many CD-ROM disks.

Besides knowing the basics about secondary-storage devices, users should be familiar with two concepts relating to secondary storage: data storage and retrieval methods and data compression.

## Naming Disk Drives

On IBM-style microcomputers, disk drives are referred to by letter. Sometimes there are three or more disk drives, although more often these days there are only two: A and B or A and C. The first diskette drive is *drive A*. The second diskette drive is *drive B*. The hard disk drive is *drive C*. A CD-ROM drive might be *D* or *E*. (See Figure 4.18.) On Macintoshes, users can name various disk drives anything they want—such as hard drive, new disk, CD disk, mongo disk.

It is possible to operate a microcomputer with just one diskette drive and with no hard disk drive, although it is quite cumbersome. Copying from one diskette to another, for example, would require constantly switching the diskettes back and forth in the single drive. Also, modern software programs require greater storage capacity than that offered by diskettes.

If an IBM-type computer has two diskette drives (and no hard disk drive), the first drive (drive A) is used for the program disk. The **program disk** is the diskette that holds the software program, such as a spreadsheet program. The second diskette drive (drive B) is used for the data disk. The **data disk** is the diskette that holds the data being manipulated, such as the spreadsheet numbers.

Today a typical microcomputer has a single diskette drive (drive A), usually for 3½-inch disks, and a hard disk drive (drive C). It may also, however, have an additional diskette drive (drive B) that accepts the larger, 5¼-inch disks.

**Figure 4.18**
Disk drive names.

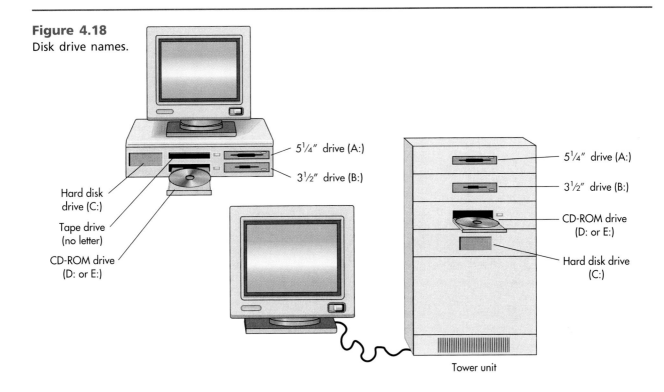

5¼" drive (A:)

3½" drive (B:)

Hard disk
drive (C:)

Tape drive
(no letter)

CD-ROM drive
(D: or E:)

5¼" drive (A:)

3½" drive (B:)

CD-ROM drive
(D: or E:)

Hard disk drive
(C:)

Tower unit

## File Organization: Data Storage and Retrieval Methods

Three methods of file organization are sequential, direct, and indexed-sequential.

**Sequential storage** means that data is stored in sequence, such as alphabetically. Tape storage falls in the category of sequential storage. Thus, you would have to search a tape past all the information from A to J, say, before you got to K. This process may require running several inches or feet off a reel of tape, which takes time.

Disk storage, by contrast, generally falls into the category of direct access storage (although data can be stored sequentially). **Direct access storage** means that the computer can go directly to the information you want. The process resembles what you would do if you moved the arm on a record player directly to a song you wished to play on an LP record (or on a programmed CD player) to play a certain song. Because you can directly access information, retrieving data is much faster with magnetic disk than with magnetic tape.

A third type of data storage is *indexed-sequential,* which has some of the advantages of both sequential and direct forms of storage. Files on secondary-storage devices are organized according to one of these three methods. (See Figure 4.19.)

- *Sequential file organization:* **Sequential file organization** stores records in sequence, one after the other. This is the only method that can be used with magnetic tape. Data can be retrieved only in the sequence in which it was stored. This method can also be used with disk.

   For example, if you are looking for employee number 8888, the computer will have to start with record 0001, then go past 0002, 0003, and so on, until it finally comes to record 8888.

**Figure 4.19**
Three methods of file organization: sequential, direct, and indexed-sequential.

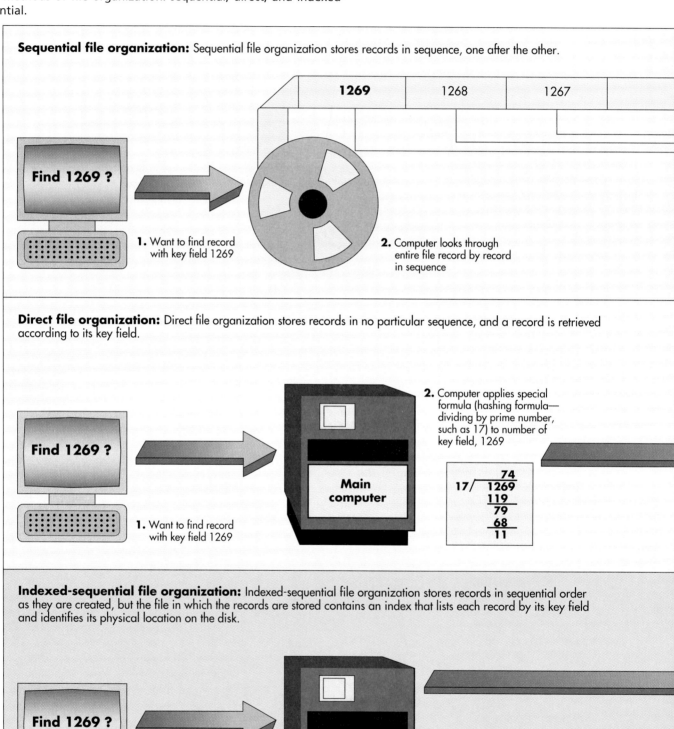

**Sequential file organization:** Sequential file organization stores records in sequence, one after the other.

1269 | 1268 | 1267

**Find 1269 ?**

**1.** Want to find record with key field 1269

**2.** Computer looks through entire file record by record in sequence

**Direct file organization:** Direct file organization stores records in no particular sequence, and a record is retrieved according to its key field.

**Find 1269 ?**

**1.** Want to find record with key field 1269

**Main computer**

**2.** Computer applies special formula (hashing formula— dividing by prime number, such as 17) to number of key field, 1269

$$\begin{array}{r} 74 \\ 17\overline{)1269} \\ 119 \\ \overline{79} \\ 68 \\ \overline{11} \end{array}$$

**Indexed-sequential file organization:** Indexed-sequential file organization stores records in sequential order as they are created, but the file in which the records are stored contains an index that lists each record by its key field and identifies its physical location on the disk.

**Find 1269 ?**

**1.** Want to find record with key field 1269

**Main computer**

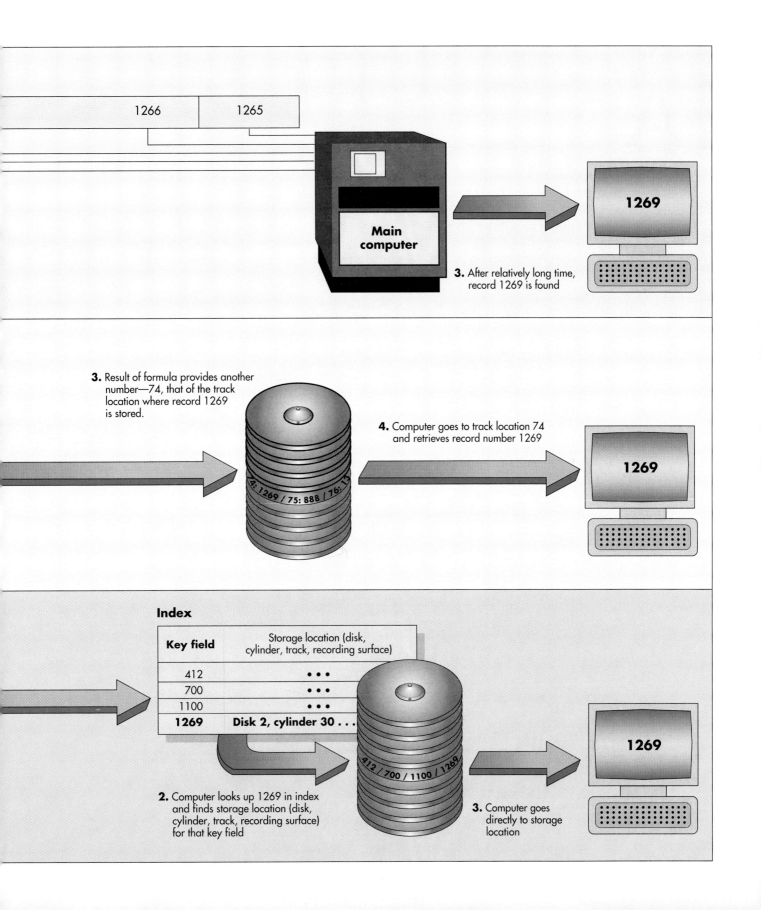

1266    1265

**Main computer**

**3.** After relatively long time, record 1269 is found

1269

**3.** Result of formula provides another number—74, that of the track location where record 1269 is stored.

4: 1269 / 75: 888 / 76: 13

**4.** Computer goes to track location 74 and retrieves record number 1269

1269

**Index**

| Key field | Storage location (disk, cylinder, track, recording surface) |
|-----------|-------------------------------------------------------------|
| 412 | • • • |
| 700 | • • • |
| 1100 | • • • |
| **1269** | **Disk 2, cylinder 30 . . .** |

412 / 700 / 1100 / 1269

**2.** Computer looks up 1269 in index and finds storage location (disk, cylinder, track, recording surface) for that key field

**3.** Computer goes directly to storage location

1269

# THE CLIPBOARD

## Computers Manipulate Old Photos

*tlanta* . . . Rex Hartman breaks into tears when he sees the once-faded and wrinkled portrait of his grandmother, who died young in 1907. Now restored, the life-size photo that hangs in his den looks almost real.

"I never knew her, but my mother always made her sound full of love and laughter," says Hartman, a retired Atlanta accountant. "We're grateful to have her back in the family."

Such photo magic is made possible by digital imaging, a process that blends photo and computer technology.

The Christmas season brought a flood of requests for digital imaging. Stores classify the requests in three groups: restoration of old photos; alteration to eliminate "red eye" or blemishes, or to add color; and manipulation, to add or wipe out people and objects.

While the technology is welcomed unabashedly in private life, some media uses have stirred howls of protest.

A January cover of the *National Enquirer* tabloid showed an altered photo of a "battered" Nicole Brown Simpson. The bruises,

scratches, and bloodshot eye, identified as a "photo re-creation," are far more severe than those in the real pictures shown in court.

*National Geographic* moved the Giza pyramids to get a better framed cover. *TV Guide* gave Oprah Winfrey's head a new body. *Time* featured a darkened O. J. Simpson police mug shot. Each incident generated a flurry of ethical concerns.

But no one complains about using imaging magic to produce a personal keepsake. Other unusual imaging tricks include:

- Replacing the old with the new. For example, adding a new arrival to an office staff or plugging in missing relatives at a family reunion.

- Adjusting the hands of time by posing generations together—a grandmother, mother, and daughter—or placing a newborn in a photo of a great-great-grandma.

Cox News Service, "Computers Manipulate Old Photos," *San Jose Mercury News,* Feb. 19, 1995, p. 5H.

Sylvester Stallone and Groucho Marx join Joseph Stalin, Winston Churchill, and Franklin D. Roosevelt at the Yalta Conference in 1945.

Sequential file organization is useful, for example, when a mail-order house is sending out catalogs to all names on a mailing list. The method also is less expensive than other methods because it uses magnetic tape, which is cheaper than disk. The disadvantage of sequential file organization is that data must be ordered in a particular way and so searching for data is slow.

■ *Direct file organization:* Instead of storing data in sequence, **direct file organization,** or **random file organization,** stores data in no particular sequence. The data is retrieved (accessed) according to a unique identifier called a **key field.** This method of file organization is used with hard disks and other types of disks. It is ideal for applications such as airline reservations systems or computerized directory-assistance operations. In these cases there is no fixed pattern to the requests for data.

Direct file organization is much faster than sequential file organization for finding specific data. However, because the method requires hard-disk or optical disk storage, it is more expensive than magnetic tape.

■ *Indexed-sequential file organization:* A compromise has been developed between the preceding two methods. **Indexed-sequential file organization** stores data in sequential order. However, the file in which the data is stored contains an index that lists the data by key fields and identifies the physical locations on the disk. This type of file organization requires magnetic or optical disk.

For example, a company could index certain ranges of employee identification numbers—0000 to 1000, 1001 to 2000, and so on. For the computer to find the key field 8888, it would go first to the index. The index would give the location of the range in which the key field appears (for example, 8001 to 9000). The computer would then search sequentially (from 8001) to find the key field 8888.

This method is slower than direct file organization because of the necessity of having to do an index search. The index-sequential method is best when large batches of transactions occasionally must be updated, yet users want frequent, rapid access to records. For example, bank customers and tellers want to have up-to-the-minute information about checking accounts, but every month the bank must update bank statements to send to customers.

## Compression and Decompression

**Compression is a method of removing redundant elements from a computer file so that it requires less storage space. Compression and decompression techniques are called codec techniques. The two principal compression techniques are "lossless" and "lossy."**

"Like Gargantua, the computer industry's appetite grows as it feeds. . . . ," says one writer. "The first symptoms of indigestion are emerging. So the smartest software engineers are now looking for ways to shrink the data-meals computers consume, without reducing their nutritional value."[7]

What this writer is referring to is the "digital obesity" brought on by the requirements of the new multimedia revolution for putting pictures, sound, and video onto a CD-ROM or sending them over a communications line. For example, a two-hour movie contains so much sound and visual information that, if stored on CD-ROM disks, it would require 360 disk changes during a single showing. A broadcast of *Oprah* that presently fits into one conventional, or analog, television channel would require 45 channels if sent in digital language.[8]

The solution for putting more data into less space comes from the mathematical process called compression. **Compression, or digital-data compression,** is a method of removing redundant (repetitive) elements from a computer's file, or collection, of data so that the file requires less storage space or can be easily transmitted. After the data is stored or transmitted and is to be used again, it is decompressed. The techniques of compression and decompression are referred to as **codec (for compression/decompression) techniques.**\* Codec works so efficiently that digital TV broadcast signals actually take up less room than analog TV signals. For example, 150 channels of compressed digital television will handle the work of 32 uncompressed analog ones.

## "Lossless" Versus "Lossy" Compression

There are two principal methods of compressing data:

- *Lossless techniques: Lossless compression techniques* achieve compression by avoiding repetition but preserve every bit of data that was input. That is, the data that comes out is every bit the same as what went in; it has merely been repackaged for purposes of storage or transmission.

  Lossless techniques are used for computer data. Microcomputer users, for example, can double the amount of data they store on their hard disks by using software products such as Stacker, Superstor, and Drive-Space. These programs store text by eliminating irrelevant letters and redundant spaces between words. Some techniques can shrink a file of text by 70% or more.

- *Lossy techniques:* It is much easier to compress text than to compress sounds, pictures, or videos. "Here, reconstructive surgery is not enough," commented one article. "Some information has to be thrown away forever. The trick is to work out what will not be missed."[9] This is the problem for lossy techniques.

  *Lossy compression techniques* permanently discard some data during compression. Thus, a lossy codec might discard shades of color that a viewer would not notice or soft sounds that are masked by louder ones. In general, most viewers or listeners would not notice the absence of these details.

**H**

lossy compression

The major difficulty now is that several standards exist for compression, particularly of visual data. If you record in one standard, you cannot play it back in another. The main reason for the lack of agreement is that different industries have different priorities. What will satisfy the users of still photographs, for instance, will not work for the users of moving images. Even so, the vast streams of bits and bytes of text, audio, and visual information threaten to overwhelm us. Compression/decompression has become a vital technology for rescuing us from the swamp of digital data.

If you plan to send files via modem, you can use compression programs to minimize your phone bill. Downloaded programs and files from electronic bulletin boards are often in compressed form, so you may have to learn about decompression programs to expand them back to their original size—you cannot use files in their compressed form.

Some software packages come with codec programs built in. As we mentioned, codec software can also be purchased separately. You may also be able to download free codec software from a bulletin board service.

---

\**Note:* In telecommunications, "codec" is used to refer to "coder-decoder."

## Other Forms of Secondary Storage

**Other types of secondary storage include flash memory, bubble memory, and advanced storage technology.**

Blockbuster Entertainment, which has nearly 3,500 video and music stores, and IBM have teamed up to develop an idea—a jukebox and record factory rolled into one. This device would enable any small-town record shop or video store to offer all the titles of recordings or movies now carried by a big-city megastore.[10]

The concept works like this: A customer enters a computerized kiosk or retail booth and runs a credit card through a credit-card-swipe reader. The display screen built into the booth then presents a menu of choices. The customer can play video clips and sample cuts and then make selections from a vast library of digitally recorded music, video games, movies, or other kind of digital information. The information is delivered in seconds over connecting communications lines from a computer thousands of miles away and reproduced on a CD in about 6 minutes. As one research analyst points out, such technology "could well change the economics of retailing for record stores and video rental shops."[11]

The revolution in secondary-storage technology will probably continue throughout our lifetimes and will have a profound effect on the way information is handled and business is conducted. In the next section we describe flash memory, a variation on conventional computer-memory chips that we mentioned in Chapter 3. Some noteworthy developments to which we should pay close attention are bubble memory and advanced storage technology.

### Flash Memory

**H**

flash memory

Disk drives, whether for diskettes or for CD-ROMs, all involve moving parts—and moving parts can break. Flash-memory cards, by contrast, are variations on conventional computer-memory chips, which have no moving parts [✓ p. 93]. **Flash-memory** or **flash RAM** cards consist of circuitry on credit-card-size cards that can be inserted into slots connecting to the motherboard [✓ p. 91]. They can hold up to 100 megabytes of data.

A videotape produced for Intel Corp., which makes flash-memory cards, demonstrates their advantage, as one report makes clear:

> In it, engineers strap a memory card onto one electric paint shaker and a disk drive onto another. Each storage device is linked to a personal computer, running identical graphics programs. Then the engineers switch on the paint shakers. Immediately, the disk drive fails, its delicate recording heads smashed against its spinning metal platters. The flash-memory card takes the licking and keeps on computing.[12]

Flash-memory cards are not infallible. Their circuits wear out after repeated use, limiting their lifespan. Still, unlike conventional computer memory (RAM or primary storage), flash memory is *nonvolatile*. That is, it retains data even when the power is turned off.

As we describe elsewhere, flash memory is only one of the options available with PCMCIA slots, which were designed primarily for small portable computers. **PCMCIA** (for **P**ersonal **C**omputer **M**emory **C**ard **I**nternational **A**ssociation) slots allow users to insert credit-card-size peripherals (called *PC* cards) measuring about 2.1 by 3.4 inches into slots in a computer's system cabinet [✓ p. 88]. Besides flash-memory cards, you can plug PC cards in modems, hard drives, and adapters for communicating over local area networks (LANs).

## Bubble Memory

Many forms of secondary storage, such as tape and disk, don't do well under extreme environmental conditions, such as heat, cold, dirt, and vibrations. Such conditions are encountered during warfare, environmental cleanup, and some kinds of communications. How, then, can data be safeguarded?

One answer is bubble memory, which, though more expensive than other kinds of secondary storage, is able to survive rugged conditions. A secondary-storage device that is only a couple of square inches in size, bubble memory consists of electromagnetic bubbles that move in a circular motion past the equivalent of a read/write head. The presence of a bubble is considered a binary 1, its absence a binary 0. Even when power to the device is turned off, bubble memory continues to hold its data (that is, it is *nonvolatile*).

## Advanced Storage Technology

Scientists keep finding new ways to put more and more data on storage media. In 1993, IBM announced development of an optical recording system capable of storing 350 million bits per square inch. The company said it expects to reach densities of 10 billion bits a square inch by the year 2000. Such densities would mean that a 3½-inch disk drive could contain all the text of 10,000 300-page novels.[13] In 1994, IBM demonstrated a technique by which CDs or CD-ROMs could store information in multiple layers. This would allow several feature-length movies to be stored on a single optical disk.

In what has been called "the world's smallest Etch-a-Sketch," physicists at NEC Corp. in Tokyo said in 1993 that they had used a sophisticated probe—a tool called a *scanning tunneling microscope (STM)*—to paint and erase tiny lines roughly 20 atoms thick.[14] This development could someday lead to ultra-high-capacity storage devices for computer data.

## Suggestions for Further Reading

*CD-ROM Today.* P.O. Box 51478, Boulder, CO 80322-1478. About $50 for 12 issues.

*PC Novice: Personal Computers in Plain English.* P.O. Box 85380, Lincoln, NE 68501-9807. About $24 for 12 issues.

Rathbone, A. *Multimedia and CD-ROMs for Dummies.* Boston: IDG, 1994.

Vaughan, Tay. *Multimedia: Making It Work.* Berkeley, CA: Osborne McGraw-Hill, 1993. Includes 3½-inch disk.

Wodaski, Ron. *Multimedia Madness.* Indianapolis: Sams, 1994. Includes a CD-ROM disk.

# SUMMARY

■ *Primary storage* refers to main memory (RAM), which is volatile; *secondary storage* refers to storage devices that retain data and instructions in a relatively permanent (nonvolatile) form. (p. 113)

■ As in main memory (primary storage), data on a secondary storage device is measured in *kilobytes, megabytes, gigabytes,* and *terabytes*. (p. 113)

■ Data is often stored as files. A *file* is a collection of data treated as a unit. *Program files* contain software instructions; *data files* contain data. (p. 113)

■ Two common types of data files are *master files,* which contain relatively permanent files that are generally updated periodically, and *transaction files,* which are holding files that temporarily hold changes to be made to the master file. (p. 114)

■ Data may remain in secondary storage for a predetermined amount of time and then be processed as a batch (*batch processing*), or it may be processed immediately as it is input (*real-time processing*). (p. 114)

■ On magnetic tape, data is stored using magnetized spots in sequential fashion. On microcomputers, tapes are used in cartridge tape units. On large computers, tapes are used in *magnetic-tape units*. (p.115)

■ The *diskette,* or *floppy disk,* is a storage medium frequently used with microcomputers. Diskettes are made of a flexible plastic that is coated with a material that is easily magnetized. The disk is enclosed in a protective paper or hard plastic jacket. (p. 117)

■ Diskettes have the following characteristics:

—Data is recorded in rings called *tracks.* Each track is divided into eight or nine *sectors,* which are wedge-shaped sections used for storage reference purposes. (p. 119)

—If you buy unformatted diskettes, you must *format,* or *initialize,* them before they can store data. (p. 120)

—A disk's capacity depends on whether it is single- or double-sided and on its *recording density* (single-density, double-density, and high-density). (p. 121)

—A diskette's *write-protect* feature allows you to protect a diskette from being written to; that is, the data on the disk can't be changed. (p. 121)

—Although other diskette sizes are available, diskettes come in two standard sizes: *5¼ inches* (with paper jackets) and *3½ inches* (with hard plastic jackets). (p. 117)

■ *Hard disks* can store more data than can diskettes—from 40 MB to more than a gigabyte of data. Hard disk drives can be internal (inside the computer) or external (outside the computer, connected to it by a cable). (p. 124)

■ The disadvantage of using a hard disk is the possibility of having a head crash, which causes the loss of some or all of the data on the disk. A *head crash* happens when the read/write heads or particles come into contact with the disk surface. (p. 126)

■ Hard disks for large computer systems come in the following forms (p. 127):

1. Removable packs

2. Fixed disk drives

3. RAID storage systems

■ *Optical storage* technologies use a laser beam to pack information densely on a removable disk. The optical storage technology used with computers consists of four types (p. 129):

1. CD-ROM disk

2. CD-R disks

3. WORM disks

4. Erasable optical disks

■ *Compact disk—read-only memory (CD-ROM)* is an optical (laser) technology capable of storing huge amounts of data on a disk. The data is prerecorded on the disk by the

**143**

manufacturer, so the user can only read it (p. 129)

■ *CD-R,* which stands for compact disk–recordable, is a CD format that allows you to write data onto a specially manufactured disk that can then be read by a standard CD-ROM drive. (p. 131)

■ *Write once, read many (WORM),* an optical storage technology, is like CD-ROM, except that the user can determine what the manufacturer records on the disk. Once recorded, however, the data can then only be read. (p. 133)

■ *Erasable optical disks* allow the user both to record data on an optical disk and to erase it. An erasable optical disk can store 281–3,200 megabytes of data. (p. 133)

■ CD-ROM formats may be *interactive* or *multimedia.* Variants of CD-ROMs are *CD-I (compact disk-interactive), CDTV (compact disk television),* and *MPC (multimedia personal computer).* (p. 133)

■ Other types of secondary storage:

—*Flash memory* uses circuitry on credit-card-size cards (PC cards) that can be inserted into slots connecting to the motherboard. A card holds up to 100 megabytes of data. (p. 141)

—*Bubble memory* uses electromagnetic bubbles that move in a circular motion past the equivalent of a read/write head. The presence of a bubble is considered a binary 1, its absence a binary 0. (p. 142)

—*Advanced storage technology* refers to new ways scientists keep finding to store more in a smaller space. For example, in 1993 IBM announced that it is developing an optical recording system capable of storing 350 million bits per square inch. (p. 142)

■ *Compression* techniques are used to remove redundant elements from a computer file so that it requires less storage space. The two principal compression techniques are *lossless* and *lossy.* (p. 140)

■ *Lossless compression techniques* achieve compression by avoiding repetition but preserve every bit of data that was input. *Lossy compression techniques* permanently discard some data during compression. (p. 140)

■ The three main types of file organization are:

1. *Sequential*—Data is stored in sequence, one after the other. This method is typically used with magnetic tape, although it can be used with a magnetic or optical disk. (p. 135)

2. *Direct*—Data is stored in no particular sequence, and a record is retrieved according to its key field. This method is used with hard disks. (p. 139)

3. *Indexed sequential*—Data is stored in sequential order along with an index that lists data according to key fields and identifies the physical locations on the disk. This method requires a magnetic or optical disk. (p. 139)

## KEY TERMS

backup, p. 123
batch processing, p. 114
bit, p. 113
byte, p. 113
cartridge tape unit (tape streamer), p. 116
CD-ROM, p. 129
codec techniques, p. 140
compact disk (CD), p. 128
compression, p. 140
cylinder, p. 127
data access area, p. 119
data disk, p. 134
data file, p. 113
direct access storage, p. 135
direct (random) file organization, p. 139
disk drive, p. 118
diskette (floppy disk), p. 117
drive bay, p. 125
erasable optical disk, p. 133
file, p. 113
fixed disk drive, p. 127

flash memory, p. 141
formatting (initializing), p. 120
gigabyte, p. 113
hard disk, p. 124
hard disk cartridge, p. 126
hard disk drive, p. 125
head crash, p. 126
indexed sequential file organization, p. 139
interactive, p. 133
key field, p. 139
kilobyte, p. 113
magnetic tape, p. 115
magnetic tape unit (drive), p. 116
master file, p. 114
megabyte, p. 113
MPC machine, p. 134
multimedia, p. 133
optical disk, p. 128
PCMCIA, p. 141
Photo CD, p. 131
pixel, p. 132

primary storage, p. 112
program disk, p. 134
program file, p. 113
RAID storage system, p. 127
read, p. 118
read-only, p. 130
read/write head, p. 119
real-time processing, p. 114
recording density, p. 121
removable-pack hard disk system, p. 127
secondary storage (auxiliary storage), p. 113
sector, p. 119
sequential file organization, p. 135
sequential storage, p. 135
terabyte, p. 113
track, p. 119
transaction file, p. 114
WORM disk, p. 133
write, p. 118
write-protect, p. 121

## EXERCISES

### SELF-TEST

1. Magnetic tape can handle only sequential data storage and retrieval. (true/false)

2. On an IBM-PC, the hard disk drive is referred to as drive A and the first diskette drive is referred to as drive B. (true/false)

3. 1,024 bytes is equal to 1 _____ KILO BYTE _____.

4. Secondary-storage devices for large computers consist of removable packs, fixed disk drives, and RAID storage systems. (true/false)

5. All diskettes must be _____ FORMATED = INITIAL _____ before they can store data.

6. Diskettes come in two standard sizes: _____ 3½ _____ and _____ 5 ¼ _____.

7. A(n) _____ _____ is a removable disk on which data is written and read through the use of laser beams. optical device

8. List four types of optical disk technology:
   a. CD ROM    c. WORM
   b. CD R    d. ERASABLE OPTICAL DISK.

9. Diskettes are often referred to as _____ FLOPPY _____ disks.

10. _____ is the name given to a diskette (or tape) that is a duplicate or copy of another form of storage.

[handwritten: BACK UP]

11. Hard disks may be affected by a head crash, when particles on the read/write heads come into contact with the disk's surface. (true/false)

*Solutions:* (1) true; (2) false; (3) kilobyte; (4) true; (5) formatted (or initialized); (6) 3½ inches, 5¼ inches; (7) optical disk; (8) CD-ROM, CD-R, WORM, erasable optical disks; (9) floppy; (10) backup; (11) true

## SHORT-ANSWER QUESTIONS

1. What is the significance of the terms track and sector?
2. What are the advantages of a hard disk over a diskette?
3. What is the difference between lossy compression and lossless compression techniques?
4. What kinds of secondary storage do large computer systems use?
5. What does *formatting (initializing)* mean? Why do users need to know about it?
6. What happens to data stored in bubble memory when the power to your computer is turned off?
7. What is a PCMCIA slot? What can PCMCIA cards be used for?
8. What are some of the uses for CD-ROM technology?
9. What does the term *multimedia* mean? Why is storage such an important consideration for multimedia technologies?
10. Why is backup important?
11. What is the difference between a program disk and a data disk?
12. A disk drive can *read* and *write*. What does that mean? What does *read only* mean?
13. What does the term *interactive* mean?

## PROJECTS AND CRITICAL THINKING EXERCISES

1. You want to purchase a hard disk for use with your microcomputer. Because you don't want to have to upgrade your secondary storage capacity in the near future, you are going to buy one with the highest storage capacity you can find. Use computer magazines or visit computer stores and find a hard disk you would like to buy. What is its capacity? How much does it cost? Who is the manufacturer? What are the system requirements? Is it an internal or an external drive? Can you install/connect this unit yourself? Why have you chosen this unit and this storage capacity?
2. What types of storage hardware are currently being used in the computer you use at school or at work? What is the storage capacity of these hardware devices? Would you recommend alternate storage hardware be used? Why or why not?
3. Do you think books published on CD-ROMs will ever replace printed books? Why or why not? Look up some recent articles on this topic and prepare a short report.
4. The Bureau of Electronic Publishing's product guide lists many products and publications available on CD-ROM, such as *Compton's New Century Encyclopedia, The Grolier Multimedia Encyclopedia,* National Geographic's *Mammals, CD Fun House, U.S. History, Birds of America, Microsoft Bookshelf 1994,* and *Mayo Clinic Family Health Book.* Write for a copy of the catalog and identify some business and professional uses for some of the products. What hardware and software would you need to run the programs you are interested in?

Bureau of Electronic Publishing
141 New Road
Parsippany, NJ 07054
(800)828-4766

5. Sometimes users forget to back up their work, or their backup tape/diskettes are lost or destroyed. What can you do, then, if your hard disk crashes and you have forgotten to back up your work? Look in the Yellow Pages of your phone book under Computer Disaster Recovery or Data Recovery. Call up the services listed and find out what they do, how they do it, and what they charge. Give a short report on this topic.

6. CD-recordable (CD-R) drive technology is improving with each year. Research the "state of the art" of CD-R technology. How much does a CD-R drive cost? Using a CD-R drive, how long does it take to write data onto a CD-ROM disk? Do you need special software to use the drive? When do you think CD-R drives will be a standard component in microcomputer systems?

# Chapter Topics

# CHAPTER 5

# Output Hardware

Presentation can be important—how you present yourself, your product, your information. Although computers may not be able to help you with your wardrobe or your public speaking skills, they can help you create clear and attractive informational presentations quickly. But because computers can produce beautiful, professional, seemingly error-free printouts or exciting colorful graphics on a screen, we are apt to believe that the information is more truthful than the same results scribbled on a yellow pad. In fact, the information that is output—the basis on which you and others will be making decisions—is no better than the quality of the data that was input.

## Preview

*When you have completed this chapter, you will be able to:*

■ Describe the basic forms of output and categories of output media and hardware

■ Describe hardcopy output devices including printers and plotters

■ Describe softcopy output devices including CRTs and flat-panel displays

■ Describe the audio-output technologies that enable voice and sound output

**Why Is This Chapter Important?**

*To be effective, information must be produced in a usable form. To achieve this goal, you may need to generate the output using more than one output device, such as a video display screen, a sound card, and a printer. Each type of output device has characteristics that determine whether it is useful. For example, is the hardware going to make a lot of noise? What is the quality of the output produced? Is the hardware slow? Is the hardware expensive? Is it compatible with the equipment you already have? Can it handle large volumes of output? Can it handle color? Not all software programs work with all types of output devices. How do you know which output hardware device to use? This chapter will help you learn how to decide.*

## Output Hardware: Hardcopy Versus Softcopy

**Output devices translate information processed by the computer into a form that humans can understand. The two principal kinds of output are hardcopy, which is printed, and softcopy, such as material shown on a display screen. Output devices include printers, plotters, and multifunction devices; display screens; and audio-output devices.**

**Output hardware** consists of devices that translate information processed by the computer into a form that humans can understand. The computer-processed information consists of 0s and 1s, which need to be translated into words, numbers, or pictures that people can comprehend.

The two kinds of output are hardcopy and softcopy:

microfilm, microfiche

- *Hardcopy:* **Hardcopy** refers to printed output. The principal examples are printouts, whether text or graphics, from printers. Film, including microfilm and microfiche, is also considered hardcopy output.

- *Softcopy:* **Softcopy** refers to data that is shown on a display screen or is in audio or voice form. This kind of output is not tangible; it cannot be touched.

There are several types of output devices. (See Figure 5.1.) We begin by describing the following hardcopy output devices: printers, plotters, and multifunction devices.

## Hardcopy Output Hardware

**Printers, plotters, and multifunction devices produce printed text or images on paper. Printers may be desktop or portable, impact or nonimpact. Impact printers include daisy wheel and dot-matrix printers. Nonimpact printers include laser, ink-jet, and thermal printers. Plotters are pen, electrostatic, and thermal. Multifunction devices combine capabilities such as printing, scanning, copying, and faxing.**

Among the wide variety of hardcopy output devices used with computers, printers and plotters are used the most. A **printer** is an output device that prints characters, symbols, and perhaps graphics on paper. Printers are categorized according to whether or not the image produced is formed by physical contact of the print mechanism with the paper. *Impact printers* have contact;

**Figure 5.1**
Summary of output devices.

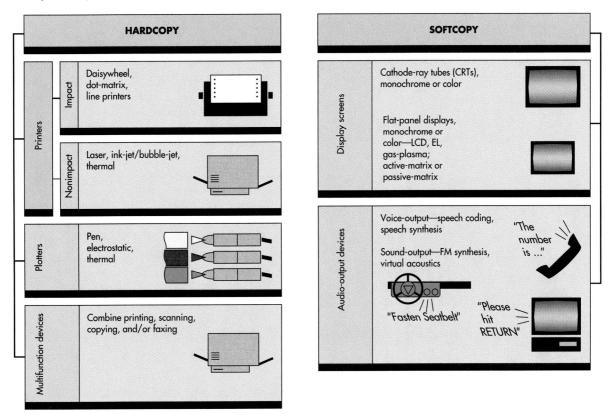

*nonimpact printers* do not. A **plotter** is used most often for outputting graphics and complex designs because it can produce specialized, free-form drawings on paper. To suit the needs of various different users, various types of printers and plotters are available that have slightly different characteristics and capabilities as to cost, quality, and speed.

### Desktop Versus Portable Printers

Technologies used for printing range from those that resemble typewriters to those that resemble photocopying machines. An important question you need to ask yourself in this era of mobility is: Will a desktop printer be sufficient, or will you need a printer that is portable?

- *Desktop printers:* Many people, perhaps including most students, find portable computers useful but have no need for a portable printer. You can do your writing or computing wherever you can tote your portable PC, then print out documents back at your regular desk. The advantage of desktop printers is that there is a wide range in quality and price available.

- *Portable printers:* Portable printers are of two types: those that plug into an AC electrical outlet and those that run on batteries. Built-in batteries (as in Canon's Bubble Jet 10ex) last for perhaps 25–30 pages. Unless they are on a wilderness trip, most people who need a portable printer find the one that plugs into the wall to be sufficient.

  As you might expect, most portable printers have some limitations. Depending on the type, you may need to pack along extra printer ribbons or ink-jet cartridges. Many require that you feed the paper in laboriously one sheet at a time if you don't want to haul around a bulky multiple-sheet feeder. An important exception is the Hewlett-Packard Deskjet Portable Printer, which includes a sheet feeder that does not take up excess space.

In the final analysis, do you really need a portable printer? Even business travelers, says portable-computing expert Jim Seymour, don't usually require an immediate printout for most of the work they're doing while away from the office. Moreover, it's often easy, he says, to simply borrow someone else's printer. "For years, I've carried a . . . printer cable in the bottom of the case containing the portable PC of the moment," says Seymour. "When I'm traveling and need the occasional quick printout, I just look around for someone in the office or hotel where I'm working who does have a PC printer."[1] Having his own printer cable makes it easier to hook his computer up to someone else's printer. (Seymour also carries six basic, widely interchangeable printer *drivers* on disk. This is software that runs most common printers he is likely to encounter.) Another option when traveling is to rent a printer for a couple of days. What would seem to be the most elegant solution for the traveler is one that brings us almost full circle to the old days of the portable typewriter: a 7.7-pound laptop [✔ p. 72] with a built-in printer. (See Figure 5.2.) The printer portion of the Canon Note Jet 486 adds only 2 pounds to what is essentially a notebook PC.

## Impact Printers

An impact printer has mechanisms resembling those of a typewriter. That is, an **impact printer** forms characters or images by striking a mechanism such as a print hammer or wheel against an inked ribbon, leaving an image on paper. Two types of printers used with microcomputers are the daisy wheel printer (being phased out) and the dot-matrix printer.

■ *Daisy wheel printer:* A **daisy wheel printer** has a removable print wheel—the flower-like daisy wheel—consisting of spokes. Each spoke ends with a raised character. The wheel turns to align the desired letter with the next printing position, and a hammer strikes the spoke end.

   Daisy wheel printers produce clear and precise print images of text, which is why they are often called *letter-quality printers*. They are useful for important correspondence and reports and for printing onto three-copy carbon-type forms. However, they are slower (at 10–75 characters per second) and noisier than dot-matrix printers, and they cannot produce graphics. Daisy wheel printers are no longer being manufactured because better and cheaper dot-matrix and laser printers have been introduced.

■ *Dot-matrix printer:* A **dot-matrix printer** contains a print head of small pins that strike an inked ribbon, forming characters or images. Print heads are available with 9, 18, or 24 pins, with the 24-pin head offering the best print quality. Dot-matrix printers can print *draft quality,* a coarser-looking 72 dots per inch vertically, or *near-letter-quality (NLQ),* a crisper-looking 144 dots per inch vertically. (See Figure 5.3.) Students and others find draft quality acceptable for doing drafts of papers and reports. They then usually switch to near-letter-quality when they are preparing a finished product to be shown to other people.

   Dot-matrix printers are faster (150–300 characters per second) than daisy wheel printers and print graphics as well as text. Although not as noisy as daisy wheels, dot-matrix impact printers are still somewhat noisy.

There is another type of impact printer that is not used with microcomputers. Large computer installations use high-speed **line printers,** which print

**Figure 5.2**
Reinventing the portable typewriter: PC with printer inside. The Canon Note Jet 486 weighs 7.7 pounds, measures 10 × 12.2 × 2.2 inches, and has a 9.5-inch monochrome screen. Paper is fed into the computer from a slot in front that can hold up to 10 pages at a time; printed documents exit from the rear.

## Figure 5.3

Dot-matrix printer. *Top:* The print head of small pins strikes the ribbon, forming a character or image on the paper. *Bottom:* Examples of draft-quality and near-letter-quality printing. The near-letter-quality image is printed twice. On the second pass the print head is positioned slightly to the right of the original image, producing a character like the *E* shown here.

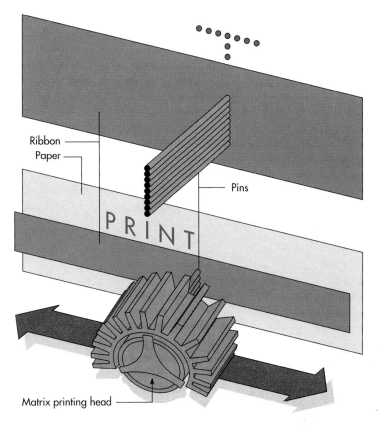

Ribbon
Paper
Pins

PRINT

Matrix printing head

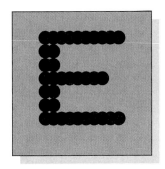

```
This is a sample of draft quality.
```
**This is a sample of near-letter quality.**

a whole line of characters at once rather than a single character at a time. Some of these can print up to 3,000 lines a minute. Two types of line printers are **chain printers,** which contain characters on a rotating chain, and **band printers,** which contain characters on a rotating band. (See Figure 5.4.)

### Nonimpact Printers

Nonimpact printers are faster and quieter than impact printers because they have fewer moving parts. **Nonimpact printers** form characters and images without making direct physical contact between printing mechanism and paper.

Two types of nonimpact printers often used with microcomputers are *laser printers* and *ink-jet printers.* A third kind, the *thermal printer,* is seen less frequently.

- *Laser printer:* Similar to a photocopying machine, a **laser printer** uses the principle of dot-matrix printers of creating images with dots. However, these images are created on a drum, treated with a magnetically charged ink-like toner (powder), and then transferred from drum to paper. (See Figure 5.5.)

**Figure 5.4**

High-speed line printers. Used in large computer installations, line printers print an entire line at a time. Two types are chain printers and band printers. Chains and bands can be changed for different typeface styles.

**Chain printer**　　　　　　　　　**Band printer**

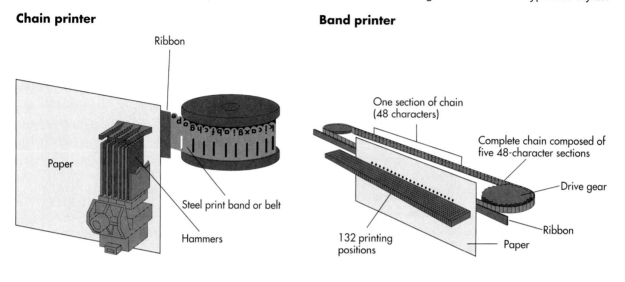

**Figure 5.5**

Laser printer. A small laser beam is bounced off a mirror millions of times per second onto a positively charged drum. The spots where the laser beam hits become neutralized, enabling a special toner (powder) to stick to them and then print out on paper. The drum is then recharged for the next cycle.

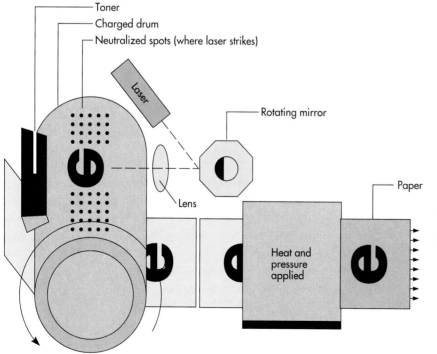

There are good reasons why laser printers are the most common type of nonimpact printer. They produce sharp, crisp images of both text and graphics. They are quieter and faster than dot-matrix printers. They can print 4–20 pages per minute for individual microcomputers (and over 120 pages per minute for mainframes). [✓ p. 76] They can print in different **fonts**—that is, type styles and sizes. The more expensive models can print in different colors.

One particular group of laser printers has become known as *Post-Script printers*. **PostScript** is a printer language, or page description language, that has become a standard for printing graphics on laser printers. A **page description language (PDL)** is software that describes the shape and position of letters and graphics to the printer. PostScript printers are essential if you are printing a lot of graphics or want to generate fonts in various sizes. Another page description language used with laser printers is *Printer Control Language (PCL),* which has resolutions and speeds similar to those of PostScript.

■ *Ink-jet printer:* Like laser and dot-matrix printers, ink-jet printers also form images with little dots. **Ink-jet printers** spray small, electrically charged droplets of ink from four nozzles through holes in a matrix at high speed onto paper. (See Figure 5.6.)

Most color printing is done on ink-jets because the nozzles can hold four different colors. Moreover, ink-jet printers can match the speed of dot-matrix printers (120–240 characters per second, or 1–4 pages per minute). They are even quieter than laser printers and produce an equally high-quality image.

**Figure 5.6**
Ink-jet printer.

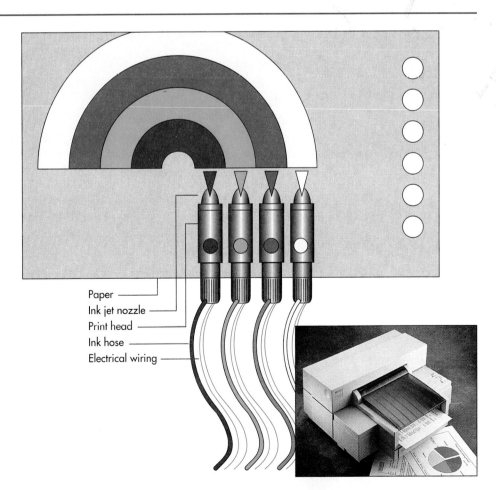

Paper
Ink jet nozzle
Print head
Ink hose
Electrical wiring

## The War on Information Clutter

Too often, what we want to find in documents, manuals, graphs, maps, and computer screens is all but lost in a mishmash of visual junk," point out *Business Week* writers John Verity and Jessie Nathan [April 29, 1991]. Says Richard Saul Wurman in *Information Anxiety*, "As the only means of comprehending information are through words, numbers, and pictures, the two professions that primarily determine how we receive it are writing and graphic design. Yet the orientation and training in both fields are more preoccupied with stylistic and aesthetic concerns."

As a result, a new field has emerged in recent years called *information design* or *information graphics*. "Infographics" is dedicated to searching for ways to display information for clarity and lucidity rather than looks. The discipline uses principles formulated over centuries by artists, mapmakers, and typographers.

Practitioners of information design are concerned with furthering human understanding of information on all levels, whether making graphical sense of the cascade of data poured forth by giant computer systems, redesigning telephone books and newspapers for more reader accessibility, or discovering comprehensible icons for road signs and computer interfaces.

A pioneer in infographics is Yale University statistician and political science professor Edward Tufte. The author of two influential books, *The Visual Display of Quantitative Information* and *Envisioning Information,* Tufte says that good graphics should communicate complex ideas with "clarity, precision, and efficiency." He writes:

Graphical displays should:

■ show the data

■ induce the viewer to think about the substance rather than about methodology, graphic design, the technology of graphic reproduction, or something else

■ avoid distorting what the data has to say . . .

■ encourage the eye to compare different pieces of data

■ reveal the data at several levels of detail

Edward R. Tufte, *The Visual Display of Quantitative Information* (Cheshire, CT: Graphics Press, 1983), p. 13.

A variation on ink-jet technology is the *bubble-jet printer,* which uses miniature heating elements to force specially formulated inks through print heads with 128 tiny nozzles. The multiple nozzles print fine images at high speeds. This technology is commonly used in portable printers.

■ *Thermal transfer printer:* **Thermal transfer printers** use colored waxes and heat to produce images by burning dots onto special paper. (See Figure 5.7.) The colored wax sheets are not required for black-and-white output because the thermal print head will register the dots on the paper. For people who want the highest-quality color printing available with a desktop printer, thermal printers are the answer. However, they are expensive, and they require expensive paper. Thus, they are not generally used for jobs requiring a high volume of output. (See Table 5.1.)

It's not uncommon these days to receive a crisply printed letter rendered on a word processor—in an envelope with a handwritten address. Why? Because the person writing the letter doesn't have, or doesn't know how to

**Figure 5.7**
Thermal transfer printer. A thermal printer produces color images by using colored waxes and heat to burn dots onto special paper.

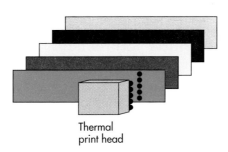

Thermal
print head

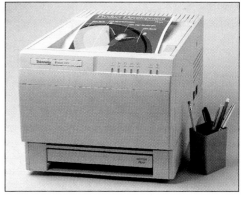

use, a printer envelope feeder for printing addresses. Envelope feeders and label printers are only one of several considerations to make when buying a printer. (Specialty printers are also available, useful for businesses that do large mailings, that print nothing but envelopes and labels.)

(*Note:* Printers use parallel ports; see [✔ p. 99], for a review of ports.)

## Plotters

A **plotter** is a specialized output device designed to produce high-quality graphics in a variety of colors. Plotters are especially useful for creating maps and architectural drawings, although they may also produce less complicated charts and graphs.

The three principal kinds of plotters are *pen, electrostatic,* and *thermal.* (See Figure 5.8.)

■ *Pen plotter:* A **pen plotter** is designed so that paper lies flat on a table-like surface (flatbed plotter) or is mounted on a drum (drum plotter). Between one and four pens move across the paper, or the paper moves beneath the pens. This is the most popular type of plotter; can produce up to four colors.

■ *Electrostatic plotter:* Instead of using pens, an **electrostatic plotter** uses electrostatic charges to create tiny dots on specially treated paper. The

**Table 5.1**  Laser, ink-jet, and thermal printers compared.

| TYPE | TECHNOLOGY | ADVANTAGES | DISADVANTAGES | TYPICAL SPEED | APPROXIMATE COST |
|---|---|---|---|---|---|
| Laser | Laser beam directed onto a drum, "etching" spots that attract toner, which is then transferred to paper | Quiet; excellent quality; output of text and graphics; very high speed | High cost, especially for color | 4–25 pages per minute | $600–$20,000 |
| Ink-Jet | Electrostatically charged drops hit paper | Quiet; prints color, text, and graphics; less expensive; fast | Relatively slow; clogged jets; fewer dots per inch | 1–4 pages per minute | $500–$8,000 |
| Thermal | Temperature-sensitive; paper changes color when treated; characters are formed by selectively heating print head | Quiet; high quality color output of text and graphics; can also produce transparencies | Special paper required; expensive; slow | 4–5 pages per minute | $5,000–$22,000 |

**Figure 5.8**
Plotters. Two types of plotters, pen and electrostatic.

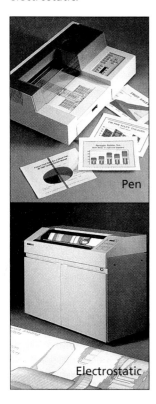

Pen

Electrostatic

paper is then run through a developer to produce the image, which may be four-color.

■ *Thermal plotter:* A **thermal plotter** uses electrically heated pins and heat-sensitive paper to create images. Thermal printers are capable of producing only two colors rather than four.

## Multifunction Printer Technology

Everything is becoming something else, and even printers are becoming devices that do more than print. For instance, plain-paper fax machines are now available (such as several from Ricoh) that can also function as laser or ink-jet printers. Since 1990, Xerox Corp. has sold an expensive printer-copier-scanner that can be hooked into corporate computer networks.

Some recent hardware can do even more. **Multifunction devices** combine several capabilities, such as printing, scanning, copying, and faxing, all in one device. An example is Okidata's Doc-It, which combines four pieces of office equipment—photocopier, fax machine, scanner, and laser printer—in one. (See Figure 5.9.) By doing the work of four separate office machines at a price below the combined cost of buying these devices separately, the Doc-It offers budgetary and space advantages.

## Softcopy Output Hardware

**Display screens are either CRT (cathode-ray tube) or flat-panel display. CRTs use a vacuum tube like that in a TV set. Flat-panel displays are thinner, weigh less, and consume less power but are not as clear. Flat-panel displays are liquid-crystal display (LCD), electroluminescent (EL) display, or gas-plasma display. Users must decide about screen clarity, monochrome versus color, and text versus graphics (character-mapped versus bit-mapped). Various video display adapters (such as VGA, SVGA, and XGA) allow various kinds of resolution and colors.**

Softcopy output generally refers to the display on a monitor, the output device that many people use the most. The two main types of monitors are the cathode-ray tube (CRT) and the flat panel.

**Figure 5.9**
The multifunction device. Okidata's Doc-It combines four machines in one: printer, copier, fax machine, and scanner.

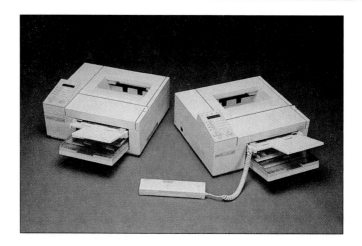

## Understanding Fonts

Aknowledge of fonts is essential for obtaining quality printed output. A *font* is a set of characters in a particular typeface, such as Times Roman or Courier, and in a particular size, such as 10-point or 12-point. [Typeface sizes are designated in points. Each point measures .0138 of an inch. There are approximately 72 points to 1 inch.]

| Typeface | Times Roman 10 pt |
| --- | --- |
| Typeface | Times Roman 12 pt |
| Typeface | Times Roman 14 pt |
|  |  |
| Typeface | Courier 10 pt |
| Typeface | Courier 12 pt |
| Typeface | Courier 14 pt |

There are three types of fonts: *resident fonts,* built into the printer at the factory; *cartridge fonts,* located on a card that fits into a special slot in the printer; and *soft fonts,* which are downloaded to the printer from the microcomputer before printing.

■ Resident fonts are usually limited in number.

■ Cartridge-based fonts are usually many but cannot be changed by the user.

Since both of these font types are contained on ROM chips, printer output is produced rapidly. Cartridge fonts are sold by manufacturers to expand a printer's capabilities.

■ Soft fonts are generated by the microcomputer and then downloaded to the printer's RAM. It is a slow process but needs to be performed just once daily, since the fonts remain in printer RAM until the printer is turned off. Sufficient memory is required by laser printers to store both the downloaded fonts and the contents of each printed page.

Soft fonts do not usually come in any one point size but as outline fonts. *Outline fonts* are descriptions (or calculations) that enable different font sizes to be created from one typeface. *PCL* [*Printer Control Language*] *4* and *PCL 5* from Hewlett-Packard and *PostScript* from Adobe Software are the leading page description languages (PDLs) used to produce outline fonts and print them on paper. PCL is used primarily on Hewlett-Packard's laser printers. PostScript is licensed by Adobe to various printer manufacturers and is used on a wide range of printers. A newer PDL, *TrueType,* is being promoted by Microsoft and Apple and is used with Windows systems software.

Printer buyers must ensure that adequate printer RAM exists to download soft fonts. They should also be aware of the speed differences between resident fonts and soft fonts. PostScript printers are an important print standard and are favored for high-quality printing. Additionally, buyers must ensure that appropriate *printer drivers,* software that interfaces between the printer and the user's application, are available. (Microcomputer systems software comes with a large of assortment of printer drivers so that users can use almost any commercially available printer.)

Adapted from Bay Arinze, *Microcomputers for Managers.* Belmont, CA: Wadsworth, 1994, p. 118.

The size of a screen is measured diagonally from corner to corner in inches, just like television screens. For desktop microcomputers, 14-inch screens are a common size. Portable computers of the notebook and subnotebook sizes [✓ p. 73] may have screens ranging from 7.4 inches to 10.4 inches. Pocket-size computers [✓ p. 73] may have even smaller screens. To give themselves a larger screen size, some portable-computer users buy a larger desktop monitor (or a separate "docking station") to which the portable can be connected. Near the display screen are control knobs that, as on a television set, allow you to adjust brightness and contrast.

### Cathode-Ray Tubes (CRTs)

The **cathode-ray tube (CRT)** is a vacuum tube used as a display screen in a computer or video display terminal. CRTs are the most common softcopy output devices used with computer systems; this technology is also used in TV sets. The CRT's screen display is made up of small picture elements (dots), called *pixels* for short. A **pixel** is the smallest unit on the screen that can be turned on or off or made different shades. A stream of bits defining the image is sent from the computer (from the CPU, ✓ p. 80) to the CRT's electron gun, where the bits are converted to electrons. (See Figure 5.10.) The inside of the front of the CRT screen is coated with phosphor. When a beam of electrons from the electron gun (deflected through a yoke) hits the phosphor, it lights up selected pixels to generate an image on the screen.

**Figure 5.10**

How a CRT works. *Top:* A stream of bits from the computer's CPU is sent to the electron gun, which converts the bits into electrons. The gun then shoots a beam of electrons through the yoke, which deflects the beam in different directions. When the beam hits the phosphor coating on the inside of the CRT screen, a number of pixels light up, making the image on the screen. *Bottom:* Each character on the screen is made up of small dots called *pixels,* short for *picture elements.*

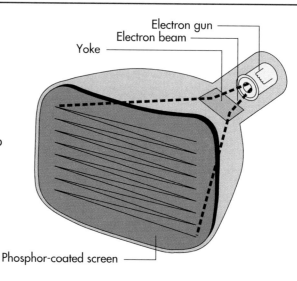

Electron gun
Electron beam
Yoke
Phosphor-coated screen

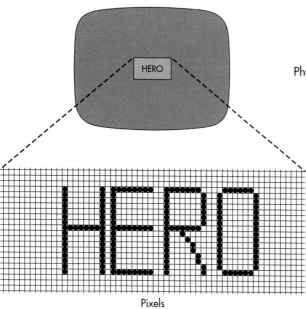

HERO

Pixels

## Flat-Panel Displays

If CRTs were the only existing technology for computer screens, we would still be carrying around 25-pound "luggables" instead of lightweight notebooks, subnotebooks, and pocket PCs. CRTs provide bright, clear images, but they consume space, weight, and power.

**H**

flat panel displays

Compared to CRTs, **flat-panel displays** are much thinner, weigh less, and consume less power. Thus, they are better for portable computers. Flat-panel displays are made up of two plates of glass with a substance in between them, which is activated in different ways.

Flat-panel displays are distinguished in two ways: (1) by the substance between the plates of glass and (2) by the arrangement of the transistors in the screens.

■   *Substances between plates—LCD, EL, or gas plasma:* There are three types of technology used in flat-panel display screens: *liquid-crystal display, electroluminescent display,* and *gas-plasma display.* (See Figure 5.11.)

   **Liquid-crystal display (LCD)** consists of a substance called *liquid crystal,* the molecules of which line up in a way that alters their optical properties. As a result, light—usually backlighting behind the screen—is blocked or allowed through to create an image.

   **Electroluminescent (EL) display** contains a substance that glows when it is charged by an electric current. A pixel is formed on the screen when current is sent to the intersection of the appropriate row and column. The combined voltages from the row and column cause the screen to glow at that point.

   **Gas-plasma display** is like a neon bulb, in which the display uses a gas that emits light in the presence of an electric current. That is, the

---

**Figure 5.11**
Three flat-panel display technologies. *Top:* A liquid-crystal display (LCD) in an IBM PS/2 CL57. *Middle:* An electroluminescent (EL) display in a Hewlett-Packard Integral computer. *Bottom left:* A gas-plasma display in a Toshiba T5100.

technology uses predominantly neon gas and electrodes above and below the gas. When electric current passes between the electrodes, the gas glows.

At present, EL and gas-plasma technology are more expensive and thus are not used as often as LCD technology.

■ *Arrangement of transistors—active-matrix or passive-matrix:* Flat-panel screens are either active-matrix or passive-matrix displays.

In an **active-matrix display,** each pixel on the screen is controlled by its own transistor. Active-matrix screens are much brighter and sharper than passive-matrix screens, but they are more complicated and thus more expensive.

In a **passive-matrix display,** a transistor controls a whole row or column of pixels. The advantage is that passive-matrix displays are less expensive and use less power than active-matrix displays.

## Screen Clarity

Whether for CRT or flat-panel, screen clarity depends on three qualities: *resolution, dot pitch,* and *refresh rate.*

■ *Resolution:* The clarity or sharpness of a display screen is called its **resolution;** the more pixels there are per square inch, the better the resolution. Resolution is expressed in terms of the formula *horizontal pixels ✕ vertical pixels.* A screen with 640 ✕ 480 pixels multiplied together equals 307,200 pixels. This screen will be less clear and sharp than a screen with 800 ✕ 600 (equals 480,000) or 1,024 ✕ 768 (equals 786,432) pixels.

■ *Dot pitch:* **Dot pitch** is the amount of space between pixels; the closer the dots, the crisper the image.

■ *Refresh rate:* **Refresh rate** is the number of times per second that the pixels are recharged so that their glow remains bright. In dual-scan screens, the tops and bottoms of the screens are refreshed independently at twice the rate of single-scan screens, producing more clarity and richer colors.

## Monochrome and Color Screens

Display screens can be either *monochrome* or *color.*

■ *Monochrome:* **Monochrome display screens** display only two colors—usually black and white, amber and black, or green and black. If your principal applications are word processing or number manipulation, a monochrome monitor will probably suit your needs nicely.

■ *Color:* **Color display screens** can display between 16 and 16.7 million colors, depending on their type. Most software today is developed for color, and—except for some pocket PCs—most microcomputers today are sold with color display screens.

## Character-Mapped Displays

**Character-mapped display** screens, such as the IBM monochrome monitor, can display only characters. (*Note:* As described in the next section, a character-mapped display screen may be able to display graphics if a video adapter card is plugged into the motherboard.) The patterns of pixels used to represent the standard characters displayed on a monitor (the alphabetic characters, numbers, and special symbols) in character-mapped displays are drawn from prerecorded templates (guides) stored in a video display ROM chip. [✔ p. 95]

When the user's software sends a request to display, for example, the letter at a specific location, the template for that pixel pattern is looked up in the video display ROM chip. The electron gun then uses this pattern when it fires at the phosphor in the appropriate character box. The screen of a personal computer has 25 lines with 80 characters per line; this means that there are 2,000 positions on the screen where a predefined character can be placed.

### Bit-Mapped Displays

**Bit-mapped display screens** permit the computer to manipulate pixels on the screen individually rather than as blocks, enabling the software to create a greater variety of images. Today most screens can display text and graphics— icons, charts, graphs, and drawings.

For a computer to display bit-mapped graphics, the display screen must have a video display adapter. A **video display adapter,** also called a *graphics adapter card,* is a circuit board that determines the resolution, number of colors, and how fast images appear on the display screen. Video display adapters come with their own memory chips, which determine how fast the card processes images and how many colors it can display. A video display adapter with 256 K of memory will provide 16 colors; one with 1 megabyte will support 16.7 million colors.

The video display adapter is often built into the motherboard, although it may also be an expansion card that plugs into an expansion slot. [✔ p. 96] Video display adapters embody certain standards. (See Figure 5.12.) The MDA and CGA standards are no longer favored; newer computer displays tend to favor VGA, SVGA, or XGA standards:

■ *VGA:* Perhaps the most common video standard today, **VGA,** for **v**ideo **g**raphics **a**rray, will support 16 to 256 colors, depending on resolution. At 320 × 200 pixels it will support 256 colors; at the sharper resolution of 640 × 480 pixels it will support 16 colors.

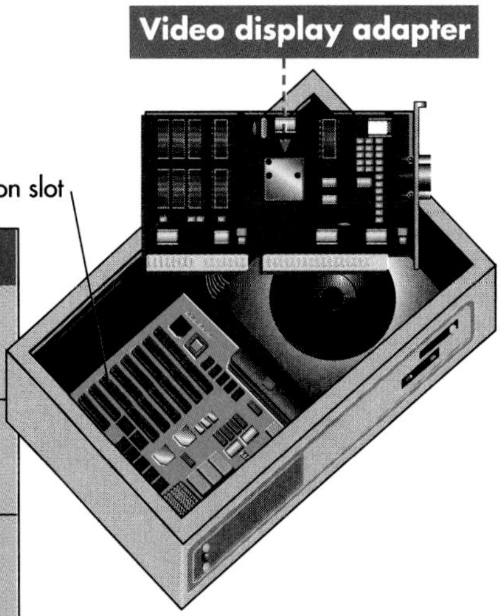

### Figure 5.12
Different types of video display adapters. The video display adapter, which enables the screen to display information, may be built into the motherboard. It may also be added as an expansion card to an expansion slot inside the computer.

Video display adapter

Expansion slot

| Monitor Type | Remarks |
|---|---|
| MDA (Monochrome Display Adapter) | Designed for monochrome monitors. Does not support color or graphics. Displays 80 lines of text. Introduced for the IBM PC in 1981. |
| CGA (Color Graphics Adapter) | Supports monochrome at 640-by-200-pixel resolution or 4 colors at 320 by 300 pixels. The original low-resolution color standard, introduced for the IBM PC in 1981. |
| VGA (Video Graphics Array) | Displays 16 colors in 640-by-480-pixel resolution and 256 colors at 320 by 200 pixels. This color bitmapped graphics display standard was introduced in 1987 for IBM PS/2 computers. |
| SVGA (Super Video Graphics Array) | Supports 256 colors with 800-by-600-pixel resolution and a 1024-by-768 resolution. This is a higher-resolution version of VGA. |
| XGA (Extended Graphics Array) | Displays up to 16,777,216 colors at resolutions up to 1024 by 768 pixels. |

■ *SVGA:* **SVGA,** for **s**uper **v**ideo **g**raphics **a**rray, will support 256 colors at higher resolution than VGA. SVGA has two graphics modes: 800 × 600 pixels and 1,024 × 768.

■ *XGA:* Also referred to as *high resolution display,* **XGA,** for e**x**tended **g**raphics **a**rray, supports up to 16.7 million colors at a resolution of 1,024 × 768 pixels. Depending on the video display adapter memory chip, XGA will support 256, 65,536, or 16,777,216 colors.

For any of these displays to work, video display adapters and monitors must be compatible. Your computer's software and the video display adapter must also be compatible. Thus, if you are changing your monitor or your video display adapter, be sure the new one will still work with the old.

## Audio-Output Hardware

**Audio output includes voice-output technology (speech coding and speech synthesis) and sound-output technology (FM synthesis, virtual acoustics).**

In the following sections we describe the hardware devices that enable voice output and sound output.

### Voice Output

**Voice-output devices** convert digital data into speech-like sounds. These devices are no longer very unusual. You hear such forms of voice output on telephones ("Please hang up and dial your call again"), in soft-drink machines, in cars, in toys and games, and recently in vehicle-navigation devices.

Two types of voice-output technology exist: *speech coding* and *speech synthesis.*

*Speech coding* uses actual human voices speaking words to provide a digital database of words that can be output as voice sounds. That is, words are codified and stored in digital form. Later they may be retrieved and translated into voices as needed. The drawback of this method is that the output is limited to whatever words were previously entered into the computer system. However, the voice-output message does sound more convincingly like real human speech.

speech synthesis

*Speech synthesis* uses a set of 40 basic speech sounds (called *phonemes*) to electronically create any words. No human voices are used to make up a database of words; instead, the computer converts stored text into voices. For example, with one Apple Macintosh program, you can type in *Wiyl biy ray5t bae5k*—the numbers elongate the sounds. The computer will then speak the synthesized words, "We'll be right back." Such voice messages are usually understandable, though they don't sound exactly human.

Some uses of speech output are simply frivolous or amusing. You can replace your computer start-up beep with the sound of James Brown screaming "I feel goooooood!" Or you can attach a voice annotation to a spreadsheet to say "I know this looks high, Bob, but trust me."[2]

But some uses are quite serious. For the disabled, for example, computers help to level the playing field. A 39-year-old woman with cerebral palsy had little physical dexterity and was unable to talk. By pressing keys on the laptop computer bolted to her wheelchair, she was able to construct the following voice-synthesized message: "I can do checkbooks first time in my life. I cannot live without my computer."[3]

## Sound Output

**Sound-output devices** produce digitized sounds, ranging from beeps and chirps to music. All these sounds are nonverbal. PC owners can customize their machines to greet each new program with the sound of breaking glass or to moo like a cow every hour. Or they can make their computers express the distinctive sounds available (from the book/disk combination *Cool Mac Sounds*) under the titles "Arrgh!!!" or "B-Movie Scream." To exercise these possibilities, you need both the necessary software and the sound card, or digital audio circuit board (such as the popular Sound Blaster and Sound Blaster Pro cards). The sound card plugs into an expansion slot in your computer.

A sound card is also required in making computerized music. There are two types of sound-output technology for music: *FM synthesis* and *virtual acoustics.*

In *FM synthesis,* a synthesizer mimics different musical instruments by drawing on a library of stored sounds. Sounds are generated by combining wave forms of different shapes and frequencies. This is the kind of music-synthesis technology embodied in the pioneering Moog synthesizer, invented in 1964, and the best-selling Yamaha DX-7 synthesizer. It is also used in 95% of the circuit boards that offer advanced sound in IBM-compatible computers. The drawback, however, is that even the best synthesized music doesn't sound truly life-like; electronic instruments can't capture all the nuances of real instruments.

In *virtual acoustics,* instead of storing a library of canned sounds, the device stores a software model of an actual instrument, such as a clarinet. Thus, a set of formulas in the software represent how tightly a musician's lips press against the clarinet's mouthpiece reed (what's called *embouchure*). On a virtual-acoustics synthesizer, the musician can simulate "blowing" on the instrument either by breathing into a sensor or by pushing a pedal. This triggers a special microprocessor that simulates the airflow and resonances of an actual clarinet.

In either case, the digital sound outputs go to a mixer, a device that balances and controls music and sounds. They can then flow through stereo speakers or be recorded. Microcomputers often come with a sound speaker, although these speakers have a rather tinny quality.

Clearly, the various kinds of audio outputs and their devices are important components of multimedia systems. Some software developers are working on applications not only for entertainment but also for the business world.

The advances and refinements in output devices are producing more and more materials in *polymedia* form. That is, someone's intellectual or creative work, whether words, pictures, sound, or animation, may appear in more than one form or medium. For instance, you could be reading this chapter printed in a traditional bound book. Or you might be reading it in a "course pack," printed on paper through some sort of electronic delivery system. Or it might appear on a computer display screen. Or it could be in multimedia form, adding sounds, animated graphics, and video to the text.

Thus information technology changes the nature of how ideas are communicated.

## Suggestions for Further Reading

See popular computer-user magazines such as *PC Magazine, PC Computing, Macworld, Computer Shopper,* and *PC Novice* for articles that rate output devices for various computer systems and explain how to use them.

# S U M M A R Y

■  *Output hardware* consists of devices that translate information processed by the computer into a form that humans can understand. ( p. 150)

■  Output is available in two forms (p. 150):

1. *Hardcopy* is information that has been recorded on a tangible medium (you can touch it), such as paper or microfilm. When computer display devices are not readily available and information has some value over time, it is best produced as hardcopy.

2. *Softcopy* is the output displayed on the computer screen. When computer display devices are readily available and information must be quickly accessible, it is best produced as softcopy.

■  A *printer* is capable of printing characters, symbols, and perhaps graphics on paper. Two categories of printers are impact and nonimpact. The print mechanism of an *impact printer* has contact with the paper; the print mechanism of a *nonimpact printer* doesn't. (p. 150)

■  For microcomputer users, the most common types of impact printers are daisy wheel printers and dot-matrix printers (p. 152):

1. *Daisy wheel printers* produce a high-quality print image because the entire character is formed with a single impact by a print wheel with a set of characters on the outside tips of the wheel's spokes. Daisy wheel printers are no longer being manufactured because better and cheaper dot-matrix and laser printers have been introduced.

2. *Dot-matrix printers* produce images with a print head composed of a series of little print hammers (usually 9, 18, or 24) that look like the heads of pins. Dot-matrix printers are more flexible, quieter, and faster than daisy wheel printers, and they can print graphics.

■  *Line printers* are typically used with large computer systems (not microcomputers). A line printer prints a whole line of characters at once rather than a single character at a time. Two types of line printers are *chain printers* and *band printers*. (p. 152)

■  The two types of nonimpact printers often used with microcomputers are laser printers and ink-jet printers. Thermal printers aren't used as frequently.

1. *Laser printers* create images on a drum, which is then treated with a magnetically charged ink-like toner (powder), and the image is transferred from drum to paper. Laser printers are fast, quiet, have low maintenance requirements, and produce high-quality images, including graphics. They can also output text in a variety of fonts—type sizes and styles. Laser printers that have a built-in page description language (such as PostScript by Adobe Systems) provide greater flexibility to produce different fonts and special graphics. (p. 154)

2. *Ink-jet printers* form images by spraying tiny electrically charged droplets of ink (black or colors) from four nozzles through holes in a matrix at high speed onto paper. These printers are as fast as dot-matrix printers, and they are quieter than laser printers. (p. 155)

3. *Thermal printers* use heat to produce images on special paper. No ribbon or ink is involved. Thermal printers are expensive and require expensive paper. Therefore they aren't used often in jobs requiring a high volume of output. (p. 156)

■  *Plotters* are specialized output devices that can produce high-quality graphics in a variety of colors. The three principal types of plotters are:

1. *Pen plotter*—The most popular type of plotter, pen plotters move between one and four pens across paper to form images. (p. 157)

2. *Electrostatic plotter*—Electrostatic charges create tiny dots on specially treated paper. The paper is then run through a developer to produce the image. Images can be four-color. (p. 157)

3. *Thermal plotter*—Electrically heated pins are used with heat-sensitive paper to produce images. Images can be two-color. (p. 158)

■ *Multifunction printing devices* combine several capabilities such as printing, scanning, copying, and faxing. (p. 158)

■ The *cathode-ray tube (CRT)* is the most popular softcopy output device used with microcomputers. The CRT's screen is made up of *pixels* (picture elements); the smaller the pixels and the closer together they are, the better the image clarity, or resolution. The pixels are illuminated under software control by electron guns to form images. (p. 160)

■ *Flat-panel displays,* used with portable computers, are much thinner, weigh less, and consume less power than CRTs. Flat-panel displays are distinguished by (p. 161):

1. *The substance between the plates of glass*—The three types of flat-panel displays each use different substances between the plates of glass. They are *liquid-crystal display (LCD), electroluminescent (EL) display,* and *gas-plasma display.*

2. *The arrangement of the transistors on the screen*—In *active-matrix displays,* each pixel on the screen is controlled by its own transistor. In *passive-matrix displays,* a transistor controls a whole row or column of pixels.

■ Display screens can be color or monochrome and/or character-mapped or bit-mapped. *Character-mapped displays* can display characters only, according to template grid information stored in a video

display ROM chip. Other displays are *bit-mapped;* they can display characters and free-form graphics because the electron beam can illuminate each individual pixel. (p. 162)

■ To have bit-mapping capability, your computer must be configured with a *video display adapter,* also called a *graphics adapter card.* A video display adapter card determines the resolution, number of colors, and how fast images appear on the display screen. Video display adapters embody certain standards including *video graphics array (VGA), super VGA,* and *extended graphics array (XGA).* (p. 163)

■ *Voice-output devices* convert digital data into speech-like sounds. Two types of voice-output technology are (p. 164):

1. *Speech coding*—Human voices are used to provide a digital database of words that can be output as voice sounds.

2. *Speech synthesis*—A set of 40 basic speech sounds (called *phonemes*) is used to electronically create words.

■ *Sound-output devices* produce digitized sounds, ranging from beeps and chirps to music. Two types of sound-output technology are used for outputting music (p. 165):

1. *FM synthesis*—A synthesizer is used to mimic different musical instruments by drawing on a library of stored sounds. Sounds are generated by combining wave forms of different shapes and frequencies.

2. *Virtual acoustics*—Software models of actual instruments are stored.

## KEY TERMS

active-matrix display, p. 162
band printer, p. 153
bit-mapped display, p. 163
cathode-ray tube (CRT),
 p. 160
chain printer, p. 153
character-mapped display,
 p. 162
color display screen, p. 162
daisy-wheel printer, p. 152
dot-matrix printer, p. 152
dot pitch, p. 162

electroluminescent (EL)
 display, p. 161
electrostatic plotter, p. 157
extended graphics array
 (XGA), p. 164
flat-panel display, p. 161
font, p. 155
gas-plasma display, p. 161
hardcopy, p. 150
impact printer, p. 152
ink-jet printer, p. 155
laser printer, p. 153

line printer, p. 152
liquid-crystal display (LCD),
 p. 161
monochrome display screen,
 p. 162
multifunction device, p. 158
nonimpact printer, p. 153
output hardware, p. 150
page description language
 (PDL), p. 155
passive-matrix display, p. 162
pen plotter, p. 157

(*cont.*)

# EXERCISES

## SELF-TEST

1. Output is available in two forms: _____ and _____ .

   *— hand — soft copy*

2. A(n) _____ printer contains a print head of small pins, which strike an inked ribbon, forming characters or images.

   *dot matrix*

3. Printers are either ___IMPACT___ or ___NON IMPACT___ .

4. _____ are used most often for outputting graphics because they can produce specialized and free-form drawings on paper.

   *→ PLOTTER*

5. Two types of printers used with large computer systems are chain printers and band printers. (true/false)

6. Two types of nonimpact printers often used with microcomputers are laser printers and ink-jet printers. (true/false)

7. _____ printers are nonimpact and use colored waxes and heat to produce images by burning dots onto special paper.

   *thermal*

8. PostScript is a printer language, or _____ _____ language, that has become standard for printing graphics on laser printers.

   *page pres graphics*

9. _____ printers spray small, electrically charged droplets of ink from four nozzles through holes in a matrix onto paper.

   *ink jet*

10. The most popular type of plotter available is the pen plotter. (true/false)

11. The image on a CRT is made up of _____ , short for _____ _____ .

    *pixel picture element*

12. _____ devices combine several capabilities, such as printing, scanning, copying, and faxing.

    *multi function*

13. Flat-panel displays are either active-matrix or passive-matrix displays. (true/false)

14. Three main types of flat-panel technologies are:

    a. LCD

    b. Electroluminescent display

    c. Gas plasma display

15. A(n) _____ _____

_____ is a circuit board that determines the resolution, number of colors, and how fast images appear on the display screen. *[handwritten: graphic display adapter]*

16. Newer computer displays tend to favor the CGA standard. (true/(false))

17. _____ devices convert digital data into speech-like *[handwritten: voice output]* sounds.

18. Some computer screens can display more than 16 million colors. ((true)/false)

19. _____ devices produce digitized sounds, ranging from *[handwritten: sound output]* beeps and chirps to music.

20. The more pixels that can be displayed on the screen, the better the *[handwritten: RESOLUTION]* _____ of the image.

*Solutions:* (1) hardcopy, softcopy; (2) dot-matrix; (3) impact, nonimpact; (4) plotters; (5) true; (6) true; (7) thermal; (8) page description; (9) ink-jet; (10) true; (11) pixels, picture elements; (12) multifunction; (13) true; (14) liquid-crystal display, electroluminescent display, gas-plasma display; (15) video display adapter (or graphics display adapter); (16) false; (17) voice-output; (18) true; (19) sound-output; (20) resolution

## SHORT-ANSWER QUESTIONS

1. What are some ways that sound output is used?
2. What is meant by the terms *resolution, dot pitch,* and *refresh rate?*
3. In voice-output technology, what is the difference between speech coding and speech synthesis?
4. What is the difference between a character-mapped display and a bit-mapped display?
5. What is a page description language? What is it used for?
6. What is the difference between hardcopy and softcopy? When might each be needed?
7. In what two ways can all flat-panel displays be distinguished?
8. What are plotters best used for?
9. What determines how many colors your monitor will display? What determines the monitor's resolution?
10. What is the difference between an active-matrix and a passive-matrix flat-panel display?

## PROJECTS AND CRITICAL THINKING EXERCISES

1. If you could buy any printer you want, what type (make, model, etc.) would you choose? Does the printer need to be small (to fit in a small space)? Does it need to print across the width of wide paper (11 × 14 inches)? In color? On multicarbon forms? Does it need to print graphics and typeset-quality (high-resolution) text? How much printer RAM would you need to support a PDL? Analyze what your needs might be and choose a printer (if necessary, make up what your needs might be). Review some of the current computer publications for articles or advertisements relating to printers. What is the approximate cost of the printer you would buy? Your needs should be able to justify the cost of the printer.
2. Visit a local computer store to compare the output quality of the different printers on display. Then obtain output samples and a brochure on each printer sold. After comparing output quality and price, what printer would

you recommend to a friend who needs a printer that can output resumes, research reports, and professional-looking correspondence with a logo?

3. What uses can you imagine for voice output and/or sound output in your planned job or profession?

4. *Paperless office* is a term that has been appearing in computer-related journals and books for the past 5 years or more. However, the paperless office has not yet been achieved. Do you think the paperless office is a good idea? Do you think it's possible? Why do you think it has not yet been achieved?

5. Do you think that flat-panel displays will replace CRTs by the year 2000? Why? If not, when?

6. Pretend that you have $2,000 to spend on a home-office computer that includes the input, processing, storage, and output components (including a printer). Explore current computer publications and identify a system you would purchase. Explain why you chose the system.

7. Personal computers with CD-ROM drives and sound cards can play regular audio compact disks. A video card will allow you to view moving pictures on your computer screen. Some movies have even been recorded on CD. Do you think the PC will replace stereos and/or VCRs in the near future? If so, how soon do you think it will happen? Why would this succeed when laser disks have not been the success they were supposed to be?

# Chapter Topics

# CHAPTER 6

# Software

Why can't you simply buy a diskette with the software program you need, put it into your microcomputer's disk drive, start it up, and have it run? Unfortunately, it's often not that easy; buying software is not like buying an audio cassette of your favorite music and slapping it into a tape deck, or renting a movie to play on your VCR. Computer software comes in two forms: applications software and systems software. Systems software is designed for various purposes and some applications software is not compatible with some systems software. Thus, it is important for users to understand the fundamental concepts and features of these two types of software and to learn to effectively evaluate software.

## Preview

*When you have completed this chapter, you will be able to:*

- Explain what applications software is and categorize the types of applications software

- Describe some features common to all types of applications software

- Define systems software by focusing on operating systems, utility programs, and language translators

- Name and describe some popular microcomputer operating systems and operating environments

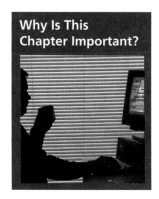

**Why Is This Chapter Important?**

*No such thing as software existed in the earliest computers. Instead, to change computer instructions, technicians would actually have to rewire the equipment. Then, in the 1950s, computer research began to use punched cards to store program instructions. In the mid-1950s, high-speed storage devices that were developed for ready retrieval eliminated the need for hand-wired control panels. Since that time, the sophistication of computer hardware and software has increased exponentially.*

*The appearance of the microcomputer in the late 1970s made computer hardware and software accessible to an increased number of people because they became more affordable, easier to use, and flexible enough to handle very specific job-related tasks. Because of this accessibility, a large pool of applications software has been created to satisfy almost any user's requirements. In other words, you do not have to be a specialist to use computer software to solve complicated and tedious problems. However, you will be entering the job race without your running shoes if you do not understand the uses of—and the differences among—types of software.*

## What Software Is Available and How Good Is It?

**Software consists of the step-by-step instructions that tell the computer how to perform a task. There are two basic types of software: applications software and systems software. Applications software, which may be custom written or packaged, enables users to perform their work. Systems software enables the computer to run applications software.**

To help you begin to understand the differences among types of software, let us repeat the definitions for applications and systems software.

- **Applications software** consists of computer programs designed to satisfy a user's specific needs. (See Figure 6.1.) The task or problem may require, for example, computations for payroll processing, the maintenance of different types of data in different types of files, or the preparation of forms and documents.

**Figure 6.1**
Applications software programs exist for almost every business. Here sous chef Jean-Jacques Pereira of Gaucho Rotisserie in Oakland, California, changes a menu and his restaurant's food positioning using a software program for planning menus, determining inventory levels, and pricing.

■ **Systems software** "underlies" applications software; these programs start up the computer and function as the principal coordinator of all hardware components and applications software programs. Without systems software loaded into the RAM [✓ p. 93] of your computer, your hardware and applications software are useless.

Every application works through "layers" in the computer to get to the hardware and perform the desired result. Think of the applications software layer as what the computer is doing and the systems software as how the computer does it. Both systems software and applications software must be purchased by the user (systems software is usually included in the price of a microcomputer).

Many people will buy an applications software program just because it was recommended by a friend. They do not bother to evaluate whether the program offers all the features and processing capabilities necessary to meet their needs. It's much easier in the short run to simply take the friend's recommendation, but in the long run a lot of extra time and money may be spent. Knowing what software is available—and how to evaluate it—is vital to satisfy processing requirements.

For large computer systems, the choice of systems software tends to be made by computer specialists, and the applications software is usually custom-written for the system; this type of software is called **custom software.** For microcomputer systems, applications software is usually purchased at a store or from a catalog. (There is much more applications software to choose from than systems software.) Applications software purchased off the shelf is often referred to as **off-the-shelf,** or **packaged, software.** (See Figure 6.2.) Microcomputer users generally receive systems software along with the computer they purchase or use at work.

*If you are a microcomputer user starting from scratch, you should choose your applications software first, after you identify your processing needs. Then choose compatible hardware models and systems software that will allow you to use your applications software efficiently and to expand your system if necessary. By choosing your applications software first, you will ensure that all your processing requirements will be satisfied. You won't be forced to buy a software package that is your second choice simply because your first choice wasn't compatible with the hardware or systems software already purchased.*

**Figure 6.2**
Packaged applications software. Something for everyone.

When you go to work in an office, chances are that the computer hardware and systems software will already be in operation; so if you have to choose anything, it will most likely be applications software to help you do your job. If you do find yourself in a position to choose applications software, make sure not only that it will satisfy the processing requirements of your job, but also that it is compatible with your company's hardware and systems software.

## Applications Software

**Applications software may be divided into "basic tools" and "advanced tools." Many applications software packages share common features such as cursors, scrolling, menus, Help screens, dialog boxes, macros, OLE, tutorials, and documentation. Popular types of applications software include word processing, desktop publishing, spreadsheet, database management, graphics, communications, and integrated programs. Groupware, software suites, desktop accessories, project management software, and computer-aided design/manufacturing programs are also common. As software packages are updated by their manufacturers, new versions are released; all software versions must be "installed" by users.**

Computer software has become a multibillion-dollar industry. More than a thousand companies have entered the applications software industry, and they have developed a wide variety of products. As a result, the number of sources of applications software has grown. Applications software can be acquired directly from a software manufacturer or from the growing number of businesses that specialize in the sale and support of microcomputer hardware and software. Most independent and computer chain stores devote a substantial amount of shelf space to applications software; some businesses specialize in selling only software.

If you can't find off-the-shelf software to meet your needs, you can develop—or have someone else develop—your own. If you don't know how to do it yourself, you can have the computer professionals within your own organization develop the software, or you can hire outside consultants to do it. Unfortunately, hiring a professional to write software for you usually costs much more than off-the-shelf software.

### Basic Tools Versus Advanced Software Tools

Whatever your occupation, you will probably find it has specialized software programs available to it. This is so whether your career is dairy farmer, building contractor, police officer, dance choreographer, or chef. Before you get to those, however, there are two levels of programs to know about—*basic software tools* and *advanced software tools.*

- *Basic software tools:* These are the programs found in most offices and probably all campuses. Their purpose is simply to make users more productive at performing general tasks. This category includes word processors, spreadsheets, database managers, graphics programs, communications programs, integrated programs, groupware, software suites, and desktop accessories.

It may still be possible to work in an office somewhere in North America today without knowing any of these programs. However, that won't be the case in the 21st century.

**H**

CAD/CAM

■ *Advanced software tools:* Knowledge of advanced programs is a necessity in some occupations (as desktop publishing is for people in publications work). You should have at least a nodding acquaintance with them because they are general enough to be used in many vocations and professions. Many advanced software tools exist today. Examples of some tools that fall into this category include desktop publishing, project management, and computer-aided design/manufacturing software (CAD/CAM).

Don't worry if you don't know all these terms; you will by the end of the chapter. However, before we discuss the different types of basic and advanced software tools, we need to go over some of the features common to most kinds of applications software packages.

## Common Features of Applications Software

Although applications software packages differ in their use of specific commands and functions, most of them have some features in common: cursors, scrolling, menus, Help screens, dialog boxes, macros, OLE, and tutorials and documentation. (See Figure 6.3.)

■ *Cursor:* The **cursor** is the movable symbol on the display screen that shows you where you may enter data next. You can move the cursor around using either the keyboard's directional arrow keys [✔ p. 41] or an electronic mouse.

■ *Scrolling:* **Scrolling** is the activity of moving quickly upward or downward through the text or other screen display. Normally a computer screen contains 20–22 lines of text. Using the directional arrow keys or a mouse, you can move ("scroll") through the display screen and into the text above and below. (*Note:* Sometimes what you are working on is too wide to fit on the screen. The term *panning* is used to describe the process of scrolling to the right and left.)

**Figure 6.3**
Common features of applications software.

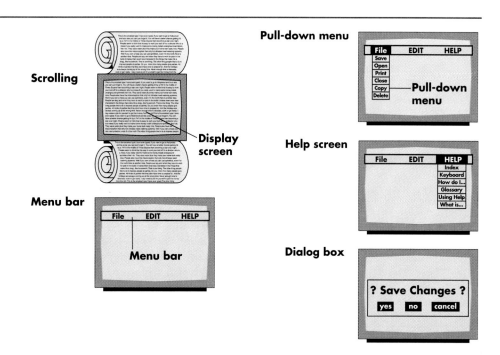

■ *Menu bar:* This is a row of menu options displayed across the top or the bottom of the screen. (A **menu** is a list of command options, or choices.)

■ *Pull-down menu:* A **pull-down menu** is a list of command options, or choices, that is "pulled down" out of the menu bar. Pull-down menus can be opened by keystroke commands or by "clicking" (pressing) the mouse button while pointing to the title in the menu bar and then dragging the mouse pointer down. (Some menus "pop up" from the menu bar and so are called *pop-up menus.*)

■ *Help menu or screen:* A **Help menu** offers a choice of **Help screens,** specific explanations on how to perform various tasks, such as printing out a document. Having a set of Help screens is like having a built-in electronic instruction manual.

■ *Dialog box:* A **dialog box** is a box that appears on the screen and displays a message requiring a response from you, such as pressing Y for "Yes" or N for "No."

■ *Macros:* A **macro** is a feature that allows you to use a single keystroke or command to automatically issue a predetermined series of keystrokes or commands. Thus, you can consolidate several keystrokes for a command into only one or two keystrokes. Although many people have no need for macros, others who have been continually repeating complicated patterns of keystrokes find them quite useful.

■ *OLE:* Many software applications have the ability to integrate applications using a feature called **OLE** (pronounced **"olé"**), or **object linking and embedding.** This feature enables you to embed an object created using one application (such as graphics) into another application (such as word processing). It thus facilitates the sharing of information. An *object* may be a document, worksheet, chart, picture, or even a sound recording.

■ *Tutorials and documentation:* How are you going to learn a given software program? Most commercial packages come with tutorials. A *tutorial* is an instruction book or program that takes you through a prescribed series of steps to help you learn the product. Tutorials must be contrasted with documentation. **Documentation** is a user manual or reference manual that is a narrative and graphical description of a program. Documentation may be instructional, but features and functions are usually grouped by category for reference purposes. For example, in word processing documentation, all cut-and-paste features are grouped together so you can easily look them up if you have forgotten how to perform them.

Now that we have taken a look at some of the features shared by many different types of applications software packages, let's briefly examine the most common types of applications software.

## Word Processing Software

**Word processing software** allows you to use computers to create, edit, revise, store, and print documents. It enables the user to easily insert, delete, and move words, sentences, and paragraphs—without ever using an eraser. Word processing programs also offer a number of features for "dressing up" documents with variable margins, type sizes, and styles. The user can do all these manipulations on screen, before printing out hardcopy [✓ p. 150].

Table 6.1 provides a list of some of the common features of word processing software packages. Figure 6.4 shows a screen for Microsoft Word 6.0 for Windows. The three leading programs for IBM-style Windows computers are WordPerfect, Microsoft Word, and Ami Pro; for Macintoshes they are Word and MacWrite.

**Table 6.1**  Some Common Word Processing Software Features

---

**Editing Features**

*Correcting:* Deleting and inserting; simply place the cursor where you want to correct a mistake and press either the Delete key or the Backspace key to delete characters. You can then type in new characters.

*Check grammar:* Word processing packages often include programs that check and highlight, for example, incomplete sentences, awkward phrases, wordiness, over-long sentences, and poor grammar.

*Check spelling:* Many packages come with a spelling checker program that, when executed, will alert you to misspelled words and offer correct versions.

*Cut, Copy, and Paste (block move, block copy):* Selecting and changing the position of a block (one or more characters) of text; this can be done within the same document or between different documents. To move a paragraph, for example, select it and then "cut" it from the document. The "cut" text is removed from the document and temporarily stored in memory. Then move the cursor to the new location and "paste" or copy the text from memory into the document. (The procedure for copying text is the same except that the original text isn't removed from the document.)

*Scrolling:* This feature, described earlier, allows the user to move up or down through a document until you can see the text you're interested in. Most packages allow you to "jump" over many pages at a time—for example, from the beginning of a document straight to the end.

*Search and replace:* You can easily search through a document for a particular word—for example, a misspelled name—and replace it with another word.

**Formatting Features**

*Boldface / italic / underline:* Word processing software makes it easy to emphasize text by using **bold**, *italic*, or underlining.

*Font choice:* Many packages allow you to change the font, or the typeface and the size of the characters, to improve the document's appearance.

*Justify/unjustify:* This feature allows you to print text aligned on both right and left margins or unaligned.

**Word Processing Functions**

*File format exchange:* A file format is the structure that defines the way a file is stored and the way it appears on the screen or in print. In addition to text, word processing files also contain these formatting codes. Every word processing program has a different format. To exchange word processing files (for example, to work on a document in WordPerfect that was originally created in Microsoft Word), you use the program's file format conversion feature.

*Footnote placement:* This feature allows the user to build a footnote file at the same time he or she is writing a document; the program then places the footnotes at appropriate page bottoms when the document is printed.

*Index creation:* Using this feature, you can create an index for your document that includes page numbers for words or phrases that can be easily looked up.

*Mail merge:* Most word processing programs allow the user to combine parts of different documents (files) to make the production of form letters much easier, faster, and less tedious than doing the same thing using a typewriter. For example, you can combine address files with a letter file that contains special codes where the address information is supposed to be. The program will insert the different addresses in copies of the letter and print them out.

*Outlining:* Some packages automatically outline the document for you; you can use the outline as a table of contents.

*Split screen:* This feature allows you to work on two documents at once—one at the top of the screen and one at the bottom. You can scroll each document independently and move and copy text between the documents.

*Thesaurus:* Thesaurus programs allow the user to pick word substitutions. For example, if you are writing a letter and want to use a more exciting word than *impressive*, you can activate your thesaurus program and ask for alternatives to that word—such as *awe-inspiring* or *thrilling*.

*Word wrap:* As you type, the text insertion point automatically moves to the beginning of the next line when the end of the current line is reached. In other words, you may type a paragraph continuously without pressing Return or Enter.

**Figure 6.4**
Microsoft Word 6.0 for
Windows screen. This
pull-down Edit menu
offers, among other
things, several options for
moving text around in a
document and finding
and replacing words.

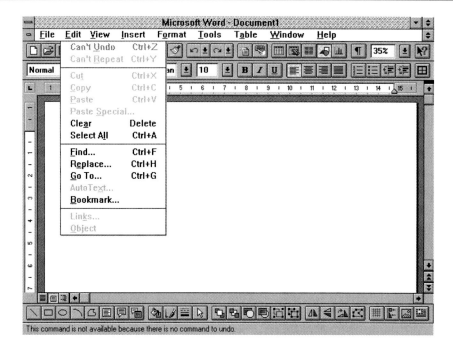

Some word processing packages, including WordPerfect, Microsoft Word, and Ami Pro, provide desktop publishing features that enable users to integrate, or combine, graphics and text on a professional-looking page. Compared to dedicated desktop publishing packages (described shortly), word processing packages lack the ease with which different elements in a document can be placed and rearranged. However, the line that differentiates word processing packages and desktop publishing packages is blurring.

## Desktop-Publishing Software

The availability of microcomputers and reasonably inexpensive software has opened up a career area formerly reserved for professional typographers and printers. **Desktop publishing,** abbreviated **DTP,** involves using a microcomputer and mouse, scanner [✓ p. 51], laser printer [✓ p. 153], and DTP software for mixing text and graphics to produce high-quality printed output. Often the laser printer is used primarily to get an advance look before the completed job is sent to a typesetter for even higher-quality output. Principal desktop-publishing programs are Aldus PageMaker, QuarkXPress, and First Publisher. Microsoft Publisher is a low-end DTP package. Some word processing programs, such as Word and WordPerfect, also have many DTP features.

Desktop publishing has the following characteristics:

■ *Mix of text with graphics:* Unlike traditional word processing programs, desktop-publishing software allows you to manage and merge text with graphics. Indeed, while laying out a page on screen, you can make the text "flow," liquid-like, around graphics such as photographs.

Software used by many professional typesetters shows display screens full of formatting codes. In this case, what they see on the screen is not what they will see when the job is printed out. By contrast, DTP programs can display your work in WYSIWYG form. WYSIWYG (pronounced "wizzy-wig") stands for "What You See Is What You Get." It means that the text and graphics appear on the display screen exactly as they will print out. (See Figure 6.5.)

**Figure 6.5**

WYSIWYG. *Top:* How a desktop publishing document—a restaurant menu—looks on a display screen. *Bottom:* How the page looks when printed out. Because the display screen uses the "What You See Is What You Get" (WYSIWYG) form, the user can make changes in the appearance before printing the document out.

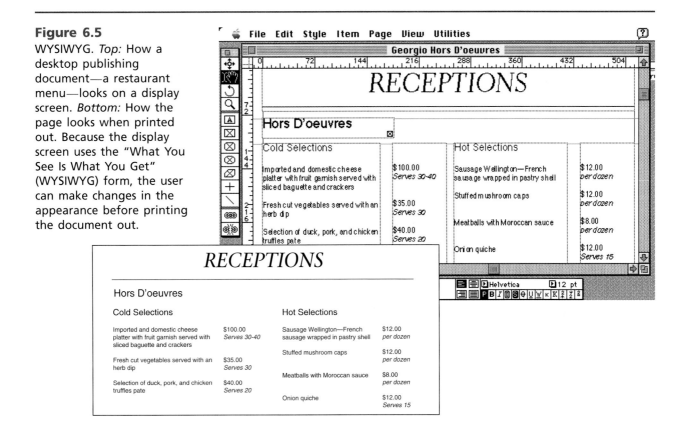

- *Varied type and layout styles:* DTP programs provide a variety of fonts [✓ p. 159], or character sets in particular type styles and sizes, from readable Times Roman to staid Tribune to wild Jester and Scribble. You can also create all kinds of rules, borders, columns, and page numbering styles. A *style sheet* in the DTP program enables you to make design decisions and record them in a file. You can then apply the same codes over and over again to document areas to determine the basic appearance of the pages.

- *Use of files from other programs:* Most DTP programs don't have all the features of full-fledged word processing or computer-based drawing and painting programs. Thus, text is usually composed on a word processor, artwork is created with drawing and painting software, and photographs are scanned in with a scanner. Prefabricated art may also be obtained from disks containing *clip art,* or "canned" images, that can be used to illustrate DTP documents. The DTP program is used to integrate all these files. You can look at your work on the display screen as one page or as two facing pages in reduced size.

- *Page description language:* Once you have finished your composition and layout, you can send the document to the printer for printing out. Much of the shaping of text characters and graphics is done within the printer rather than in the computer. For instance, instead of sending the complete image of a circle from the computer to the printer, you send a command to the printer to draw a circle. The printer uses *page description language* software to describe the shape and position of characters and graphics. An example of a page description language is Adobe's PostScript [✓ p. 155], which is used with Aldus PageMaker.

## Electronic Spreadsheet Software

What is a spreadsheet? Traditionally, it was simply a grid of rows and columns, printed on special green paper, that was used by accountants and others to produce financial projections and reports. A person making up a spreadsheet often spent long days and weekends at the office penciling tiny numbers into countless tiny rectangles. When one figure changed, all the rest of the numbers on the spreadsheet had to be recomputed—and ultimately there might be wastebaskets of jettisoned worksheets.

In the late 1970s, Daniel Bricklin was a student at the Harvard Business School. One day he was staring at columns of numbers on a blackboard when he got the idea for computerizing the spreadsheet. The result, VisiCalc, was the first of the electronic spreadsheets or electronic worksheets. The **electronic spreadsheet** allows users to create tables and financial schedules by entering data into rows and columns arranged as a grid on a display screen. Its automatic calculation abilities can save the user almost a lifetime of tedious arithmetic. The small spreadsheet shown in Figure 6.6 was created by a beginner in less than an hour. This spreadsheet is designed to calculate expense totals and percentages. Some of the terms you will encounter when using spreadsheets are listed in Table 6.2.

One of the most useful features of spreadsheet software is the ability to perform "what if" analyses. The user can say: "What if we change this num-

**Figure 6.6**
Electronic spreadsheets (*right*) look much like spreadsheets created manually (*below*). However, when a number is changed in an electronic spreadsheet, all totals can be automatically updated—certainly not the case when you work with a spreadsheet by hand!

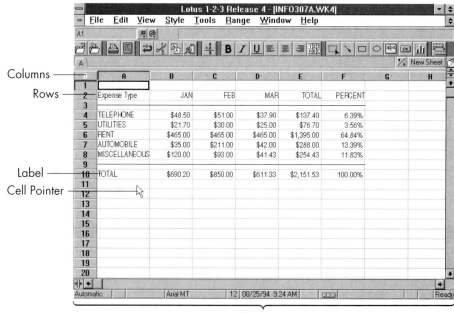

Worksheet area

**Table 6.2**  Common Spreadsheet Terminology (listed in alphabetical order)

*Cell:* The intersection of a column and a row; a cell holds a single unit of information.

*Cell address:* The location of a cell. For example, B3 is the address of the cell at the intersection of column B and row 3.

*Cell pointer:* Indicates the position where data is to be entered or changed; the user moves the cell pointer around the spreadsheet, using the particular software package's commands.

*Column labels:* The column headings across the top of the worksheet area.

*Formula:* Instructions for calculations; these calculations are executed by the software based on commands issued by the user. For example, a formula might be SUM(A5:A15), meaning "Sum (add) all the numbers in the cells with cell addresses A5 through A15."

*Graphics:* Most spreadsheets allow users to display data in graphic form, such as bar, line, and pie charts.

*Recalculation:* Automatic reworking of all the formulas and data according to changes the user makes in the spreadsheet.

*Row labels:* The row headings that go down the left side of the worksheet area.

*Scrolling:* Moving the cell pointer up and down, and right and left, to see different parts of the spreadsheet.

*Value:* The number within a cell.

ber? How will the bottom line be affected?" and get an immediate answer by having the spreadsheet software automatically recalculate all numbers based on the one change. For example, let's say you're considering buying a new car. Any number of things can be varied: total price ($10,000?, $15,000?), down payment ($2,000?, $3,000?), interest rate on the car loan (7%?, 8%?), or number of months to pay (36? 48?). You can keep changing the "what if" possibilities until you arrive at a monthly payment figure that you're comfortable with.

Most spreadsheet packages enable you to link spreadsheets together—this is called *dynamic file linking.* If a number, such as an expense amount, is changed in one spreadsheet, the change is automatically reflected in other spreadsheet files that might be affected by the change. Thus, the amount of data being manipulated can be enormous.

Spreadsheets can also display data in graphic form, such as in pie charts or bar charts, which are easier to read than columns of numbers.

Today the principal spreadsheets are Excel, Lotus 1-2-3, and Quattro Pro.

## Database Management System Software

**Database management system (DBMS) software,** also known as a **database manager,** consists of programs for storing, cross-indexing, retrieving, and manipulating large amounts of data. With database management system software, you can compile huge lists of data and manipulate, store, and retrieve it without having to touch a single file cabinet or folder. Table 6.3 lists some common features of database management software.

Because they can access several files at one time, database management systems are much better than the old flat-file management systems that used to dominate computing. A *flat-file management system* or *file manager* is a software package that organizes data into records but can access information only one file at a time. Thus, with a flat-file system, you could use the Student database and call up a list of, say, all students at your college majoring in English. Likewise, you could use the Instructor database and display

**Table 6.3** Common Features of Database Management System Software
(listed in alphabetical order)

*Calculate and format:* Many database management programs contain built-in mathematical formulas. This feature can be used, for example, to find the grade-point averages for students in different majors or in different classes. Such information can then be organized into different formats and printed out.

*Fields:* A *field* is a unit of data consisting of one or more characters. Examples of a field are your name, your address, or your driver's license number.

*File:* A *file* is a collection of related records. An example of a file could be one in your state's Department of Motor Vehicles. The file would include all the people who received driver's licenses on the same day, including their names, addresses, and driver's license numbers.

*Records:* A *record* is a collection of related fields. An example of a record would be your name and address and driver's license number.

*Select and display:* The beauty of database management programs is that you can select specific records in a file quickly and display them. For example, suppose you use a database manager to keep track of names and addresses that were originally stored in your address book. To select and then display a list of those friends who live in Texas, for example, you could type "Texas" into the State field. After completing the command, a list of those friends who live in Texas would display on the screen.

*Sort:* Data is entered into the database in a random fashion; however, the user can easily change the order of records in a file—for example, alphabetically by employee last name, chronologically according to date hired, or by zip code. The field according to which the records are ordered is the *key field,* or *key.*

**Figure 6.7**
Graphics data. Database managers are increasingly being used to store not only text but also graphics, sound, and animation.

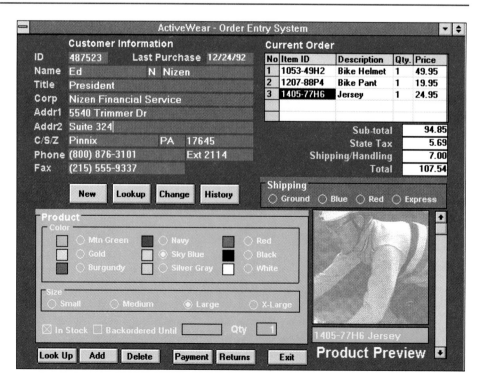

information about each instructor (name, address, salary, courses taught, and so on). But you could not call up a list of English majors along with the names of their instructors. Database management systems allow you to do that.

Databases are a lot more interesting than they used to be. Once they included only text. The Digital Age has added new kinds of information—not only documents but also pictures, sound, and animation. (See Figure 6.7.)

Today, the principal DOS-type database manager is dBASE. The major ones that run under Microsoft Windows are Access and Paradox, followed by FileMaker Pro, FoxPro, Q&A, Approach, and dBASE. In Chapter 10, Database Management, we explore concepts relating to databases and DBMSs in greater detail.

## Graphics Software

Which would you rather read—a list of numbers or the same information displayed as a graph or bar chart? Information is conveyed much more quickly, and retained and remembered longer, in graphic, or visual, form than in words or numbers. **Graphics software** enables users to produce many types of graphic creations, which come in two forms:

- **Analytical graphics** are basic graphical forms used to make numerical data easier to understand. The most common analytical graphic forms are bar graphs, line charts, and pie charts—or a combination of these forms. (See Figure 6.8.) The user can view such graphics on the screen (color or monochrome) or print them out.

   Most analytical graphics are features of spreadsheet programs, such as Lotus 1-2-3. Whether viewed on a monitor or printed out, analytical graphics help make sales figures, economic trends, and the like easier to comprehend and analyze.

presentation graphics

- **Presentation graphics** are graphics used to communicate or make a presentation of data to others, such as clients or supervisors. Presentations may make use of analytical graphics, but they look much more sophisticated. They use different texturing patterns (speckled, solid, cross-hatched),

**Figure 6.8**

Analytical graphics. Bar charts, line graphs, and pie charts are used to display numerical data in graphical form.

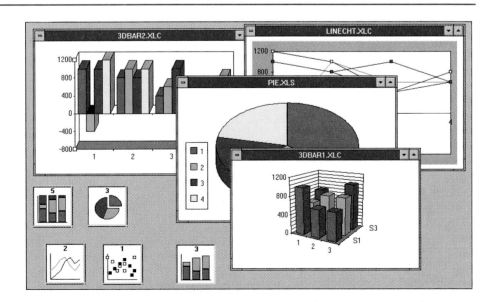

color, and three-dimensionality. Examples of well-known graphics packages are Curtain Call, Freelance Plus, Harvard Graphics, Hollywood, Persuasion, Microsoft PowerPoint, and Presentation Graphics.

Some presentation graphics packages provide artwork (clip art) that can be electronically cut and pasted into the graphics. These programs also allow you to use electronic painting and drawing tools for creating lines, rectangles, and just about any other shape. Depending on the system's capabilities, you can create multimedia presentations by adding text, animated sequences, and sound. (Multimedia software presentations are discussed in more detail in an upcoming section.)

With special equipment you can do graphic presentations on slides, transparencies, and videotape. With all these options the main problem may be simply restraining yourself. (See Figure 6.9.)

## Communications Software

**Communications software** includes programs that access software and data from, and transmit data to, a computer in a remote location. Popular microcomputer communications programs include Smartcom, Crosstalk, ProComm, PC-Dial, Blast, and PC Talk.

Besides the communications software, the computer user usually needs a telephone line connected to a modem in his or her microcomputer. A **modem** is a device for translating digital signals from a computer into the analog signals [✓ p. 8] required to transmit over a telephone line. A modem is also required in the microcomputer at the other end of the telephone line to translate the analog signals back into computer-usable digital signals. (We describe modems and other types of communications hardware in greater detail in Chapter 8, Communications and Connectivity.)

In recent years, communications has changed the world of computing, bringing connectivity to many computer users. *Connectivity* is the name given to the electronic connections between computer systems or between information resources. The connection may be by means of telephone lines, microwave transmission, or satellite.

**Figure 6.9**
Presentation graphics. These graphics programs allow sophisticated visual presentations of data— much more sophisticated than those created with analytical graphics.

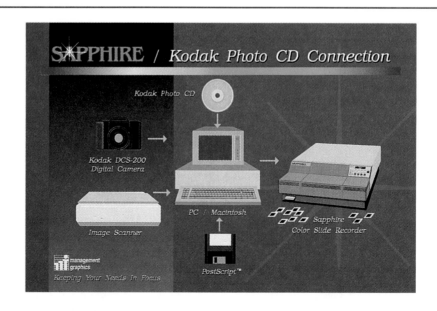

# THE CLIPBOARD

## Try Before You Buy with Shareware and Freeware

There are software programs that are designed to let the user try them out before buying. Two examples are *shareware* and *freeware*.

Shareware is copyrighted software that is distributed mainly through online bulletin board systems (BBSs) and information services free of charge. (Bulletin board systems and information services are services that let computer users tap in to a central computer where they can obtain information on specific topics.) Satisfied users will usually make some type of payment to cover costs and registration for documentation and other benefits.

Freeware is also distributed free of charge. You can sometimes find freeware on bulletin board systems or through computer users

groups. A users group is a group of computer users who share interests and information and ideas concerning systems and software. Some users groups also distribute catalogs that let you know what is available in shareware and freeware.

A freeware developer might offer a program to observe how users respond. The developer has control over the rights and distribution of his or her program, so the user may not be able to change information in the program.

Software programs such as these give users a chance to work with a program to see if it is right for them before investing any money.

Jennifer Larson, "Try Before You Buy," *PC Novice*, March 1993, p. 41.

### Integrated Software

**Integrated software** is a collection of several applications in a single package with a common set of commands and the ability to work together and share data. The objective is to allow the user to perform a variety of tasks without having to switch software programs and learn different commands and procedures to run each one. Integrated software combines the capabilities of word processing, electronic spreadsheets, database management systems, graphics, and data communications (using telephone lines, satellites, and other communications technology to transmit data and information) into a single program.

Examples of integrated packages are Claris Works, Eight-in-One, Lotus Works, Microsoft Works, PFS:First Choice, and WordPerfect Works. In general, integrated packages are less powerful than separate programs used alone, such as a word processing or spreadsheet program used by itself. Moreover, some systems software (discussed later in this chapter) makes integrated programs unnecessary; such systems allow users to shift easily between applications programs that are *completely different*. Finally, integrated programs are largely being replaced by *software suites,* discussed shortly.

### Groupware

Most microcomputer software is written for people working alone. **Groupware** is software that is used on a network and serves a group of users working together on the same project. Groupware improves productivity by keeping you continually notified about what your colleagues are thinking and doing, and they about you. "Like e-mail [electronic mail]," one writer points out, "groupware became possible when companies started linking PCs into networks. But while e-mail works fine for sending a message to a specific person or group—communicating one-to-one or one-to-many—groupware allows a new kind of communication: many-to-many."[1]

Groupware is essentially of four types:

workflow software

■ *Basic groupware:* Exemplified by Lotus Notes, this kind of groupware uses an enormous database containing work records, memos, and notations and combines it with a messaging system. Thus, a company like accounting giant Coopers & Lybrand uses Lotus Notes to let co-workers organize and share financial and tax information. It can also be used to relay advice from outside specialists, enabling audits to be done more quickly and complex questions from clients to be answered sooner.[2]

■ *Workflow software:* Workflow software, exemplified by ActionWorkflow System and ProcessIt, helps workers understand and redesign the steps that make up a particular process. It also routes work automatically among employees and helps reduce the paper flow in organizations.

■ *Meeting software:* An example of meeting software is Ventana's Group Systems V, which allows people to have computer-linked meetings. With this software, people "talk," or communicate, with one another by typing on microcomputer keyboards. As one writer describes it, "Because people read faster than they speak, and don't have to wait for others to finish talking, the software can dramatically speed progress toward consensus."[3]

■ *Scheduling software:* Scheduling software uses a microcomputer network to coordinate co-workers' electronic datebooks or appointment calendars so they can figure out a time when they can all get together. An example is Network Scheduler 3 from Powercore.

With groupware, technology has changed the kind of behavior that is required for success in an organization. For one thing, such software requires workers to take more responsibility. Obviously, when your contribution to a group project is clearly visible to all, you need to do your best. For another thing, using e-mail or groupware means learning to be sensitive to the manners of being online.

## Software Suites

Integrated packages should not be confused with software "suites." **Suites** are applications—like spreadsheets, word processing, graphics, communications, and groupware—bundled together and sold for a fraction of what the programs would cost if bought individually. "Bundled" and "unbundled" are jargon one encounters in software and hardware merchandising. **Bundled** means that components of a system are sold together for a single price. **Unbundled** means that a system has separate prices for each component.

The principal suites are Microsoft Office from Microsoft Corp., SmartSuite from Lotus Corp., and PerfectOffice from Novell, Inc. Microsoft's Office suite consists of programs that separately would cost $1,565. Lotus's SmartSuite programs separately would cost $1,730. In both cases the suites cost less than half those prices—$750, and retailers' discounted prices are usually under $500.

Although cost is what makes suites attractive to many corporate customers, they have other benefits as well. Microsoft and Lotus have taken pains to integrate the "look and feel" of the separate programs within the suites to make them easier to use. "The applications mesh more smoothly in the package form," says one writer, "and the level of integration is increasing. More and more, they use the same commands and similar icons in the spreadsheet, word processor, graphics, and other applications, making them easier to use and reducing the training time."[4]

### Desktop Accessories and PIMs

Is there any need to have an electronic version of the traditional appointment calendar, clock, and file of phone numbers and addresses? Many people find ready uses for this kind of software, called *desktop accessories* or *PIMs*.

■ *Desktop accessories:* A **desktop accessory,** or desktop organizer, is a software package that provides an electronic version of tools or objects commonly found on a desktop: calendar, clock, card file, calculator, and notepad. (See Figure 6.10.) Some desktop-accessory programs come as standard equipment with some systems software (such as on Microsoft's Windows). Others, such as Borland's SideKick or Lotus Agenda, are available as separate programs to run in your computer's primary storage at the same time you are running other software. Some are principally scheduling and calendar programs; their main purpose is to enable you to do time and event scheduling.

Suppose, for example, you are working on a word processing document and someone calls to schedule lunch next week. You can simply type a command that "pops up" your appointment calendar, type in the appointment, save the information, and then return to your interrupted work. Other features, such as a calculator keypad, a "scratch pad" for typing in notes to yourself, and a Rolodex-type address and phone directory (some with automatic telephone dialer), can be displayed on the screen when needed.

■ *PIMs:* A more sophisticated program is the **PIM,** or **personal information manager,** a combination word processor, database, and desktop accessory program that organizes a variety of information.[5] Examples of PIMs are Ascend, CA-UpToDate, DayMaker Organizer, DateBook Pro, Dynodex, Instant Recall, Lotus Organizer, OnTime for Windows, and Personal Reminder System.

**Figure 6.10**
Desktop accessory with daily schedule displayed.

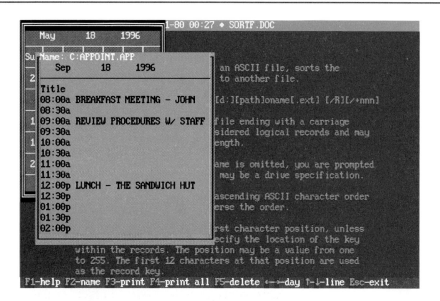

Lotus Organizer, for example, looks on the screen much like a paper datebook—down to simulated metal rings holding simulated paper pages. The program has screen images of section tabs labeled Calendar, To Do, Address, Notepad, Planner, and Anniversary. The Notepad section lets users enter long documents, including text and graphics, that can be called up at any time.[6] Whereas Lotus Organizer resembles a datebook, the PIM called *Dynodex* resembles an address book, with spaces for names, addresses, phone numbers, and notes.

## Project Management Software

A desktop accessory/PIM can help you schedule your appointments and do some planning. That is, it can help you to manage your life. But what if you need to manage the lives of others to accomplish a full-blown project, such as steering a political campaign or handling a nationwide road tour for a band? Strictly defined, a project is a one-time operation consisting of several tasks that must be completed during a stated period of time. The project can be small, such as an advertising campaign for an in-house advertising department, or large, such as construction of an office tower or a jetliner.

**Project management software** is a program used to plan, schedule, and control the people, costs, and resources required to complete a project on time. For instance, the associate producer on a feature film might use such software to keep track of the locations, cast and crew, materials, dollars, and schedules needed to complete the picture on time and within budget. The software would show the scheduled beginning and ending dates for a particular task—such as shooting all scenes on a certain set—and then the date that task was actually completed. Examples of project management software are Harvard Project Manager, Microsoft Project for Windows, Project Scheduler 4, SuperProject, and Time Line.

Two important tools available in project management software are Gantt charts and PERT charts. (See Figure 6.11.)

 Gantt chart

- *Gantt charts:* A *Gantt chart* uses lines and bars to indicate the duration of a series of tasks. The time scale may range from minutes to years. The Gantt chart allows you to see whether tasks are being completed on schedule.

- *PERT charts:* PERT stands for *Program Evaluation Review Technique*. A *PERT chart* shows not only timing but also relationships among the tasks of a project. The relationships are represented by lines that connect boxes describing the tasks.

Even project management software has evolved into new forms. For example, a program called *ManagePro for Windows* is designed to manage not only goals and tasks but also the people charged with achieving them. "I use it to track projects, due dates, and the people who are responsible," says the manager of management information systems at a Lake Tahoe, Nevada, timeshare condominium resort. "And then you can get your reports out either on project information, showing progress on all the steps, or a completely different view, showing all the steps that have to be taken by a given individual."[7]

## Computer-Aided Design (CAD)

Industry, especially manufacturing, has probably experienced the greatest economic impact of computer graphics. Mechanical drawings that used to take days or weeks to complete can now be done in less than a day. Among other things, the drawings can be three-dimensional, rotated, shown in

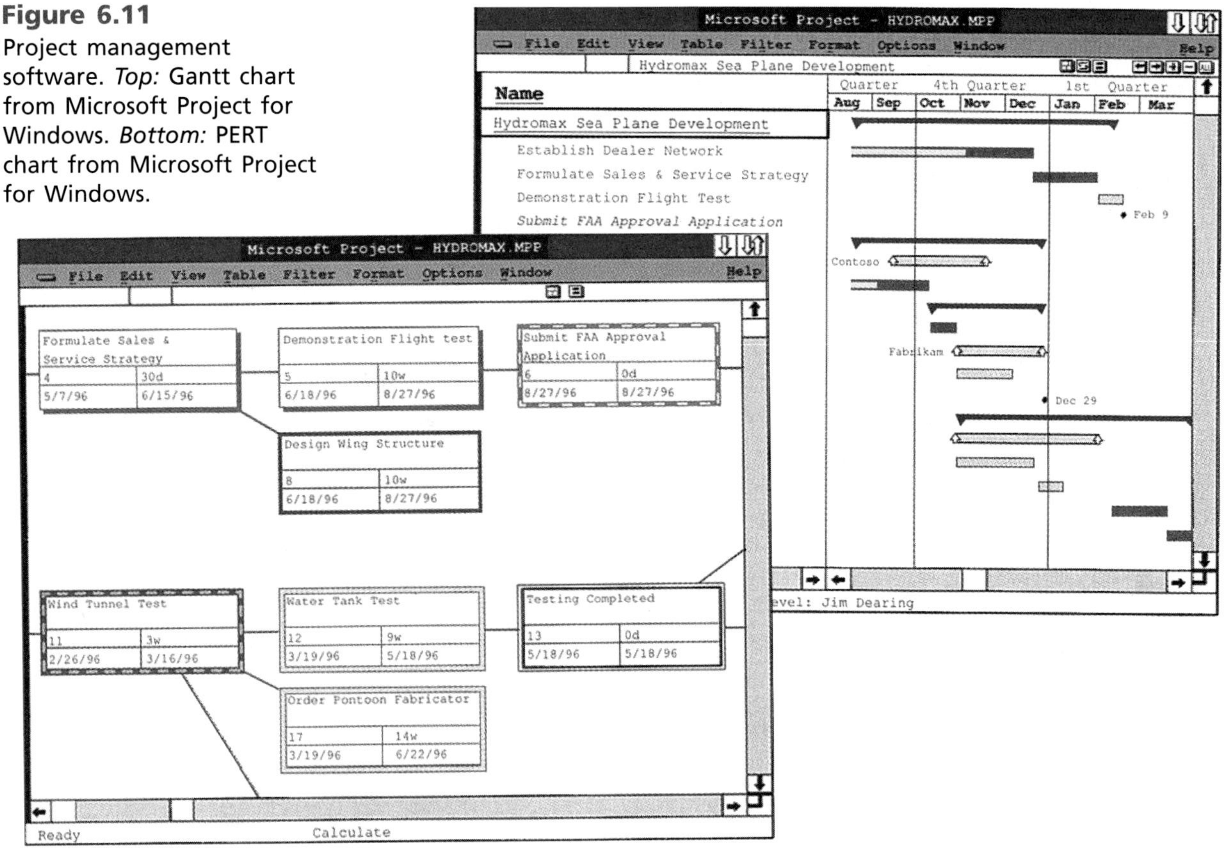

**Figure 6.11**
Project management
software. *Top:* Gantt chart
from Microsoft Project for
Windows. *Bottom:* PERT
chart from Microsoft Project
for Windows.

detailed sections or as a whole, automatically rendered on a different scale, and easily corrected and revised. But the use of computer graphics has evolved beyond the rendering of drawings; it is now used to help design, engineer, and manufacture products of all kinds, from nuts and bolts to computer chips to boats and airplanes.

**Computer-aided design (CAD)** shortens the design cycle by allowing manufacturers to shape new products on the screen without having to first build expensive models. (See Figure 6.12.) Examples of CAD programs for beginners are Autosketch, EasyCAD2 (Learn CAD Now), and TurboCAD.

**CAD/CAM**—for **computer-aided design/computer-aided manufacturing**—software allows products designed with CAD to be input into an automated manufacturing system that makes the products. For example, CAD and its companion, CAM, brought a whirlwind of enhanced creativity and efficiency to the fashion industry. Some CAD systems, says one writer, "allow designers to electronically drape digital-generated mannequins in flowing gowns or tailored suits that don't exist, or twist imaginary threads into yarns, yarns into weaves, weaves into sweaters without once touching needle to garment."[8] The designs and specifications are then input into CAM systems that enable robot pattern-cutters to automatically cut thousands of patterns from fabric, with only minimal waste. Whereas previously the fashion industry worked about a year in advance of delivery, CAD/CAM has cut that time to 8 months.

## Multimedia Presentations

**Multimedia software**—also called *multimedia production tools* or *authorware*—enables users to combine not only text and graphics but animation,

**Figure 6.12**

CAD: example of computer-aided design. *Left:* Screens from Autodesk CAD system. *Right:* CAD screen of automobile brake assembly. A designer can draw in three dimensions and rotate the figure on the screen.

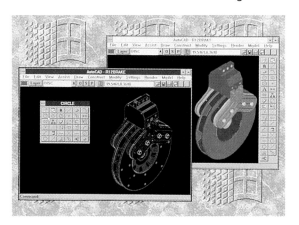

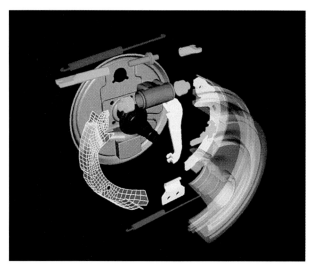

video, music, voice, and sound as well. (See Figure 6.13.) A multimedia system, however, is not just a single technology or software application but instead a combination of hardware and software that incorporates multiple media within a desktop computer system.

Figure 6.13 shows the basic components of a multimedia system—both for a PC and for a Macintosh. Some older microcomputer systems may be

**Figure 6.13**

Basic components of a multimedia system

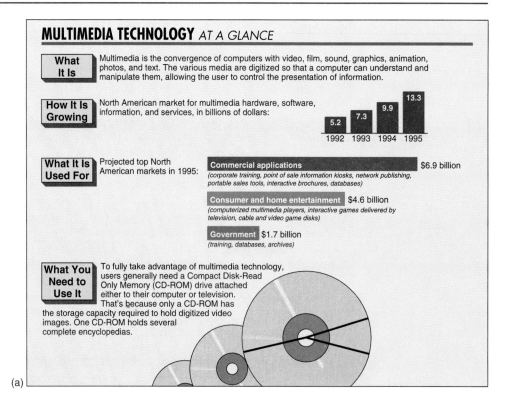

(a)

**Figure 6.13**
(Continued)

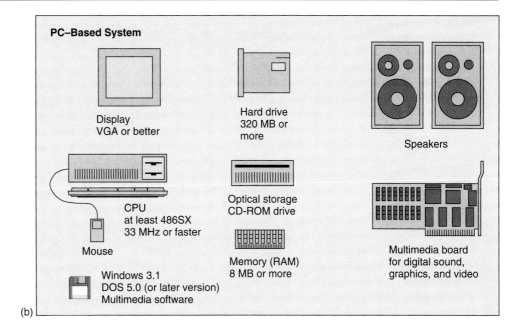

(b)

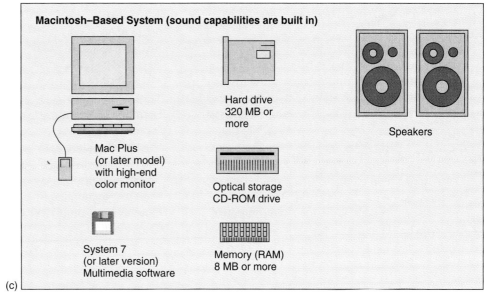

(c)

upgraded to handle multimedia; other, newer systems are multimedia-ready. (Remember, however, that all the components of any system must be designed to run together—must be compatible—for the system to work.)

■ *Processing power:* You need a microcomputer with a recent-model CPU [✓ p. 80] and a speed of at least 33 MHz [✓ p. 93]; the more power and speed, the better. For PCs, the recommendation is a 486 or later microprocessor; for Macintoshes, a Macintosh Plus or later model.

■ *Memory (RAM):* You need at least 8 MB of RAM to work effectively with most multimedia programs; some require 16 MB.

■ *Input:* You need a hard drive of 320–500 MB and a double- or quad-speed CD-ROM drive [✓ p. 129]. Your computer should also have at least one diskette drive.

## Brainstorming Software

You're working on an important project. The deadline is rapidly approaching . . . and . . . you're . . . stuck. . . .

All you need is a little more time. And maybe, just a little help from your computer. At this point, it's time for some brainstorming! . . .

While they differ in price and features, most brainstormers work on the same basic principles. By providing lists of related and unrelated words and concepts, they try to channel your thinking down avenues your brain has never (or rarely) walked through unescorted. The hope is that new insights and thoughts will be triggered by different or unusual word associations. They assume your brain kettle has been stewing and just needs a lightning bolt of inspiration to release it. . . .

Certainly the grandaddy of brainstorming software is *IdeaFisher* for Windows, DOS, and Macintosh. . . . Composed of two uniquely cross-referenced and linked databases, the Idea-Bank embodies 65,000 idea words with a staggering 775,000 association links, while the Question Bank (referred to as QBank) houses 6,000 questions to identify and simplify problems and shape ideas. The third important component is the Idea and Answer Notepad.

These three tools can be used separately or in any combination. To start, type in any word or phrase and the IdeaBank begins providing associated word listings. In most cases, clicking on Ideas, Words, and Phrases produces a prodigious amount of words to start you thinking. Click on any word and you see a Topical Categories List. From there you can delve deeper into the next level of Section Titles. At every step of the way, word associations, concepts, subconcepts, and word groupings are stimulating your creative process. Material can be saved in the Notepad and your own text added at any time.

QBank hones ideas by asking a series of questions about the idea or immediate problem. . . .

As information is transferred to the Notepad, IdeaFisher automatically strips out prepositions, conjunctions, and other little words, brewing your ideas down to a filtered list of Key Concepts. . . .

[A] word of caution about all brainstorming or creativity programs. No matter how wonderful, how technologically advanced the software is, you're not going to be able to push a button, click a mouse, or rub a lamp and instantly receive a breakthrough solution to your problem. Each one is meant to be used as a springboard for ideas, a departure point where technology and your innate creativity and knowledge meet and create a new idea, thought, or concept that wasn't in your brain just a second ago.

Like everything else, your output is only as good as your input. You still have to do the work.

Michael Cahlin, "Fresh Out of Ideas?" *PC Novice*, September 1994, pp. 69–71.

- *Output:* You need a sound board [✔ p. 165] and speakers for a PC. Macintoshes come with sound capabilities built in, but you can connect speakers for sound amplification.

- *Display:* You need at least a VGA color monitor [✔ p. 163] and graphics board [✔ p. 163] for a PC. For some programs, you need a super VGA monitor. For a Mac, you need a high-end color monitor.

- *Software:* For a PC, you need Windows 3.1 and DOS version 5.0 or higher systems software. For a Mac, you need System 7.0 or a later version (systems software from Apple). You will also need multimedia software for producing projects or presentations. Examples are Multimedia ToolBox, Authorware, and Multimedia Works. (Of course, you must be sure that the software and the hardware are compatible.) Also, users who develop multimedia presentations often use data-compression [✓ p. 139] utility software to make the huge files for graphics, sound, and video manageable.

If you are using a scanner, video recorder, or other special peripheral devices, you must be sure to purchase the software that enables the computer to use them.

If you don't want to create multimedia presentations but do want to run packaged multimedia programs, you won't need multimedia production software; instead, you can purchase CD-ROMs with everything on them.

■ *Communications:* If you want to transmit parts of your multimedia projects to another computer user in a distant location, you'll need a modem. (However, because so many multimedia files are huge, users often purchase removable hard disk cartridges to transport compressed files on disk.)

## What Can You Do with Multimedia?*

■ Browse through an encyclopedia and check out animations on everything from the circulatory system to an atomic nucleus during fission.

■ Explore the intimate details of a musical selection, moving from discussions of the historical period, to explanations of the themes, to pictures of the composer, to a game that tests your knowledge of music.

■ Build a business presentation that includes sound effects, music, still pictures, animation, video, and text.

■ Explore your creative musical interests, even recording and editing music on your PC.

■ Add sounds to files or tasks.

■ Hold up a part for a complex machine in front of a video camera and have the video appear on someone else's computer far, far away while you explain how to install the part.

■ Explore the topography of the Atlantic Ocean for a geology paper.

■ Create 3-D effects.

■ Create animated birthday cards for your friends who have computers.

■ Call up a map of the country you're visiting next week and, with the click of a mouse, look up sights to see.

■ Capture a video image from your wedding videotape.

■ Record your thoughts about a letter, and insert the recording right into the document for later review.

■ Explore medical terminology, using pictures and animations to help out with the hard parts.

■ Look up the history of the word *set* (all 150 or so pages) in the *Oxford English Dictionary* on CD-ROM.

■ Make a sale using life-like animation of your product in use on your color portable computer in your client's office.

■ Learn a new language by interacting with the written and spoken words.

---

*Adapted from Ron Wodaski, *Multimedia Madness*. Englewood Cliffs, NJ: Sams Publishing, 1994.

This section has provided only the basics about multimedia capabilities. In the near future, you will see multimedia applications being used in all walks of life—from business to the home, and in education, entertainment, and recreation.

### Applications Software Versions

Many software developers sell different versions of the same software application. Each version is usually designated by a different number—generally, the higher the number, the more current the version and the more features included with the package. In some cases, different versions are written to be used with particular microcomputer systems such as IBM compatibles or Macintosh microcomputers. If you buy a software package, make sure you have the version that goes with your microcomputer.

A user who buys a certain version of a software application may after a few months find that a later version of the same application is now available. This user has two choices: either stay with the purchased version or upgrade (usually for a fee) to the later version. A user may choose to upgrade in order to use the updated features present in the new version or to be compatible with other users of the same version. Often, however, it isn't necessary to upgrade. The current version may already satisfy current processing requirements.

If you want to try to keep track of all the software available, you can read software catalogs and directories. For example, magazines such as *PC World* (for the PC) and *Macworld* (for the Macintosh) provide general users with reviews of many different kinds of software.

### Installing Applications Software

You can buy a videotape, CD-ROM, or audiotape, insert it into its player, and view or listen to it by simply pressing a button. This is not the case with applications software. To use it in your microcomputer, you must first *install* it. Installation means the user "tells" the application program what the characteristics of the hardware are so the program will run smoothly. Directions for installing come with the instructions (documentation) accompanying applications software. Additional advice is available (usually through a toll-free 800 number) from the software manufacturer.

Why all this bother? Consider, for instance, that there are many types, brands, and models of printers on the market. To be effective, a word processing program must be told which one will print its output. (See Figure 6.14.) The means for doing this is the printer *driver*. A printer driver is a file stored on a disk containing instructions that enable a software program to print on the user's printer. The installation directions will show you how to specify which printer driver to use.

The installation program may also ask you to specify what kind of microcomputer and monitor you are using, whether you are using a hard disk, and so on. Once you have completed the installation procedure, which takes 5–30 minutes, the application program will store most of your responses in a special file on the disk. This file is referred to by the applications program every time you load the software.

## Systems Software

Systems software runs the computer's basic operations, allows the computer to run applications software, and allows the user

**Figure 6.14**
Printer driver selection screen (during software installation). A PostScript printer has been chosen as the default printer. (The default printer is the one always used by the system unless the user gives other instructions.) (LPT1 refers to the parallel port 1, the port where the printer is plugged into the back of the computer.)

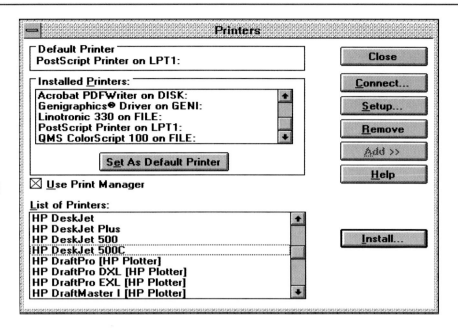

to interact with the computer. Systems software comprises three parts: the operating system, utility programs, and language translators. Popular microcomputer operating systems include DOS, Macintosh Operating System, Windows, OS/2 (Warp), Windows NT, UNIX, and NetWare.

Without systems software you won't be able to use any applications software. **Systems software** tells the computer how to interpret data and instructions; how to run peripheral equipment like printers, keyboards, and disk drives; and how to use the hardware in general. Also, it allows you, the user, to interact with the computer. Systems software comprises a large number of instructions that can be grouped into the following categories:

1. Operating systems
2. Utility programs
3. Language translators

As a computer user, you will have to use systems software, so it is important to understand the role it plays in the computer system.

## Operating Systems

The **operating system (OS)** consists of the master system of programs that manage the basic operations of the computer. These programs provide resource management services of many kinds, handling such matters as running and storing programs and storing and processing data. The operating system allows you to concentrate on your own tasks or applications rather than on the complexities of managing the computer. It interprets the commands you give to run programs and allows you to interact with the programs while they are running.

The operating system is automatically loaded into main memory as soon as you turn on, or "boot," the computer. The term *booting* refers to the process of loading an operating system into a computer's main memory from diskette or hard disk. This loading is accomplished by a program (called the *bootstrap loader* or *boot routine*) that is stored permanently in the computer's electronic circuitry. When you turn on the machine, the program obtains the operating system from your diskette or hard disk and loads it into memory. Other programs (called *diagnostic routines*) also start up and test the main memory, the central processing unit, and other parts of the system to make sure they are running properly. As these programs are running, the display screen may show the message "Testing RAM" (main memory). Finally, other programs (indicated on your screen as "BIOS," for basic input-output system) will be stored in main memory to help the computer interpret keyboard characters or transmit characters to the display screen or to a diskette.

All these activities create a jumble of words and numbers on your screen for a few seconds before they finally stop. At that point, you may see the system prompt, such as "A:\>" or "C:\>". Or you may see the graphical interface of another operating system. In any case, you know the operating system is successfully loaded.

The operating system performs the following types of tasks:

- Coordinates processing
- Manages the use of main memory
- Allocates use of peripheral devices
- Checks equipment malfunction and displays error messages
- Manages files stored on disk

## Utility Programs

**Utility programs** are generally used to support, enhance, or expand existing programs in a computer system. Many operating systems have utility programs built in for common purposes such as copying the contents of one disk to another. Other utility programs (such as The Norton Utilities) are available on separate diskettes, for example, to recover damaged files. Examples of utility programs are:

- *Screen saver:* A screen saver is a utility that supposedly prevents a monitor's display screen from being etched by an unchanging image. Some people believe that if a computer is left turned on without keyboard or mouse activity, whatever static image is displayed may burn into the screen. Screen savers automatically put some moving patterns on the screen, supposedly to prevent burnout. Actually, burnout doesn't happen on today's monitors. Nevertheless, people continue to buy screen savers, often for other reasons. Some of these can be quite entertaining, such as flying toasters.

- *Data recovery:* A *data recovery utility* is used to undelete a file or information that has been accidentally deleted. *Undelete* means to restore the last delete operation that has taken place. The data or program you are trying to recover may be on a hard disk or a diskette. (Data in a deleted file may remain on the surface of a disk until that area has been written over with new data. Therefore, deleted data may still be recovered in some cases.)

- *Backup:* Suddenly your hard disk drive fails, and you have no more programs or files. Fortunately, we hope, you have used a utility to make a backup, or duplicate copy, of the information on your hard disk. DOS has commands to help you make backups on diskettes, but they are not easy to use. Other utilities are more convenient. Moreover, they also condense (compress) the data, so that fewer diskettes are required.

## How Software Suites Change Users' Preferences for Application Programs

Many [corporate information systems] directors may wonder if their users are actually using all the applications in those suites they're buying. They may have found that some users have no need for the presentation package the vendor threw into the bundle. Others users may have been quite vocal in their demand for WordPerfect and are now running WordPerfect with Microsoft's Office suite, meaning the company is paying for two word processors for each user.

But the good news for vendors is that the users are being won over to the benefits of their suites in ever increasing numbers. Few users are loyal enough to stick with any one application now that suites offer a comparable application with tight integration to other apps in the suite.

Some 90% of suite owners use the word processor supplied with the suite, and another 90% use the spreadsheet. As a result, suites coexist with stand-alone applications less often.

According to Will Reynolds, director of development for SmartSuite, the days of users mixing and matching applications is gone. Best of breed has lost out to the compelling economics of suites. Mike Fulton, group manager of research at Microsoft, says users are much more concerned about using applications to share data, which creates a greater need for products from one vendor.

According to Fulton, 72% of Office users typically have two or three applications open simultaneously; some 13% typically have all the applications open at once. The remaining 15% use only one application at a time. . . .

Jeffrey Henning, "Suites Sway User Habits," *Computerworld,* October 31, 1994, p. 48.

---

**H**

viruses

Examples of backup utilities are Norton Backup from Symantec Corp. and Fastback Plus from Fifth Generation Systems, Inc.

■ *Virus protection:* Few things can make your heart sink faster than the sudden failure of your hard disk. One exception may be the realization that your computer system has been invaded by a virus. A **virus** consists of hidden programming instructions that are buried within an application or systems program. They copy themselves to other programs, causing havoc. Sometimes the virus is merely a simple prank that pops up a message. Sometimes, however, it can destroy programs and data. Viruses are spread when people exchange diskettes or download (make copies of) information from computer networks. (We discuss viruses in more detail in Chapter 13.)

Fortunately, antivirus software is available. **Antivirus software** is a utility program that scans hard disks, diskettes, and the microcomputer's memory to detect viruses. Some utilities destroy the virus on the spot. Others notify you of possible viral behavior, in case the virus originated after the software was released.

Examples of antivirus software are Anti-Virus from Central Point Software, Inc., The Norton AntiVirus from Symantec Corp., and ViruCide from Parsons Technology.

■ *Data compression:* As you continue to store files on your hard disk, it will eventually fill up. You then have three choices. You can delete old files to make room for the new. You can buy a new hard disk with more capacity and transfer the old files and programs to it. Or you can buy a data compression utility. Data compression removes redundant elements, gaps, and unnecessary data from a computer's storage space so less space is required to store or transmit data.

■ *Memory management:* Different microcomputers have different types of memory, and different applications programs have different memory requirements. *Memory-management utilities* are programs that determine how to efficiently control and allocate memory resources.

Memory-management programs may be activated by software drivers. A **driver** is a series of program instructions that standardizes the format of data transmitted between a computer and a peripheral device, such as a mouse or printer. (We described printer drivers earlier in this chapter.) Electrical and mechanical requirements differ among peripheral devices. Thus, software drivers are needed so that the computer's operating system will know how to handle them. Many basic drivers come with the operating system. If you buy a new peripheral device, however, you need to install the appropriate software driver so the computer can operate it.

■ *Defragmentation:* When a file is stored on a disk, the computer tries to put the elements of data next to one another. However, this is not always possible because previously stored data may be taking up locations that prevent this. Then, after the user has saved and deleted many files, there remain many scattered areas of stored data that are too small to be used productively. (This is called *fragmentation.*) This situation causes the computer to run slower than if all the data in a file were stored together in one location. Utility programs are available to *defragment* the disk, thus rearranging the data so that the data units of each file are repositioned together in one location on the disk.

Many other utilities exist. They are often offered by companies other than those making the operating system. Later the operating system developers incorporate these features as part of the upgrade of their product.

## Language Translators

A **language translator** is software that translates a program written by a programmer in a language such as BASIC into machine language [✓ p. 87], which the computer can understand. We describe language translators later, in Chapter 7.

## Other Systems Software Capabilities

### Multitasking

As we have mentioned, the first operating systems were designed for computers with limited processing speed and limited RAM and storage capacity. These early operating systems were referred to as single-user operating systems because they could accept commands from only a single terminal [✓ p. 43] or other input source and could manage only a single program in RAM at one time. Although most operating systems for microcomputers are considered single-user/single-program operating systems, some microcomputer operating systems are single-user but can also do multitasking. **Multitasking,** or **multiprogramming,** is the execution of two or more programs by one user concurrently on the same computer with one central processor. (See Figure 6.15.) You may be writing a report on your computer with one program while another program searches an online database for research material. How does the computer handle both programs at once?

**Figure 6.15**
Multitasking. An operating system that can execute more than one program at a time (concurrently) is capable of multitasking—in other words, the user can run several different application programs at the same time. Although it may seem as if the programs are being processed at exactly the same time, they are actually being processed one after the other, extremely quickly.

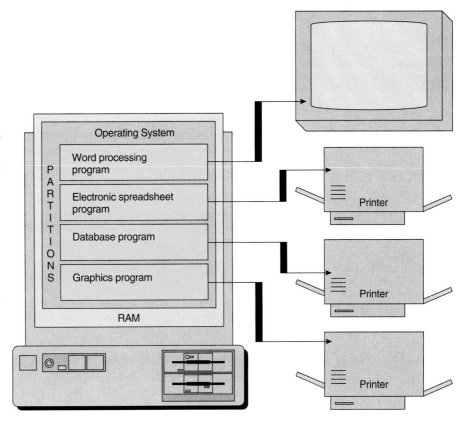

The operating system directs the microprocessor to spend a predetermined amount of time (according to programmed priorities) executing the instructions for each program, one at a time. In essence, a small amount of each program is processed, and then the microprocessor moves to the remaining programs, one at a time, processing small parts of each. This cycle is repeated until processing is complete. The processing speed of the microprocessor is usually so fast that it may seem as if all the programs are being executed at the same time. However, the microprocessor is still executing only one instruction at a time, no matter how it may appear to users.

**Timesharing**

**Timesharing** is a single computer's processing of the tasks of several users at different stations in round-robin fashion. Timesharing is used when several users are linked by a communications network to a single computer. A timesharing computer system supports many users simultaneously by enabling users to share time on the computer, based on assigned *time slices*. Timesharing is like multitasking, except that multitasking computers shift tasks based on program priorities, whereas timesharing systems assign each program a slice of time and then process the programs in small increments one after the other. The processing requirements of an operating system with timesharing capabilities are great.

From the user's perspective, timesharing isn't much different from multitasking except that, with timesharing systems, usually more than one user is sharing the processing power of a central microcomputer (main computer) by using terminals connected to it.

### Multiprocessing

Multiprocessing goes beyond multitasking, which works with only one microprocessor. In both cases, the processing should be so fast that, by spending a little bit of time working on each of several programs in turn, a number of programs can be run at the same time. With both multitasking and multiprocessing, the operating system keeps track of the status of each program so that it knows where it left off and where to continue processing. But the multiprocessing operating system is much more sophisticated than multitasking. **Multiprocessing** is processing done by two or more computers or processors linked together to perform work simultaneously. (See Figure 6.16.) This can entail processing instructions from different programs or different instructions from the same program. Multiprocessing configurations are very popular in large computing systems.

Microcomputer users may encounter an example of multiprocessing in specialized microprocessors called *coprocessors* [✓ p. 93]. Working simultaneously with a computer's CPU microprocessor, a coprocessor will handle such specialized tasks as display-screen graphics and high-speed mathematical equations.

## Popular Operating Systems and Operating Environments

Operating systems aren't just a topic of academic interest. As a microcomputer user, you'll have to learn not only whatever applications software you want to use but also, to some degree, the operating system with which they work.

**Figure 6.16**
Multiprocessing. Some computers use two or more microcomputers and sophisticated systems software to process different programs simultaneously.

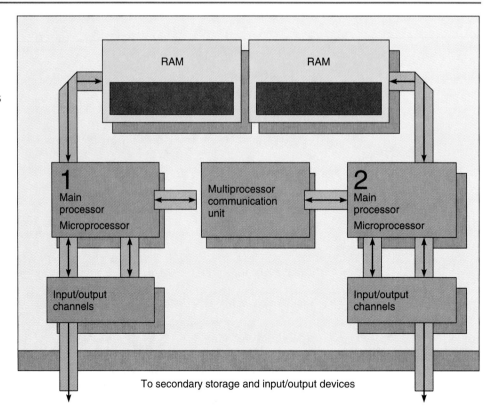

Moreover, when buying a PC, you have to choose which operating system you want.

In this section, we describe the following systems:

■ DOS

■ Macintosh System Software

■ Windows

■ OS/2

■ Windows NT

■ UNIX

■ NetWare

### DOS

There are reportedly over 100 million users of DOS. This makes it the most popular software of any sort ever adopted, and certainly the most popular systems software.[9] **DOS**—short for **D**isk **O**perating **S**ystem—runs primarily on IBM and IBM-compatible microcomputers, such as Compaq, Zenith, AST, Dell, Tandy, and Gateway.

There are three operating systems calling themselves DOS:

■ *Microsoft's MS-DOS:* DOS is sold under the name MS-DOS by software maker Microsoft Corp. The "MS" stands for Microsoft. Microsoft launched its original version, MS-DOS 1.0, in 1981, and there have been several upgrades since then. MS-DOS 6.2 was issued in November 1993.

■ *IBM's PC-DOS:* Microsoft licenses a version to IBM called PC-DOS. The "PC" stands for "Personal Computer." The most recent version is PC-DOS 6.1.

■ *Novell's DOS:* Famous for its network software, Novell, Inc. acquired DR-DOS from Digital Research, upgraded it, and renamed it Novell DOS 7. Its most prominent feature is its built-in networking capabilities.

What do these numbers mean? The number before the period refers to a *version.* The number after the period refers to a release, which has fewer refinements than a new version. The most recent versions are all backward compatible. Backward compatible means that users can run the same applications on the later versions of the operating system that they could run on earlier versions.

Recent versions of DOS have expanded the range of the operating system. For example, version 4.0 changed MS-DOS from a command-driven interface to a menu-driven interface. Version 5.0 added a graphical interface. Version 6.0 added features that took advantage of a computer's main memory.

No doubt DOS will be around for years. After all, there are a great many old but still useful microcomputers running it and a great many application programs written for it. Nevertheless, as a command-driven, single-user program, DOS is probably a fading product. Although satisfactory for many uses, it will be succeeded by other, more versatile operating systems.

### DOS and Windows

MS-DOS was designed principally to perform a single task for a single user. That is, it can switch back and forth between different applications, but it can't run two or more applications simultaneously. **Windows** is an operating environment made by Microsoft that lays a graphical user interface shell around the MS-DOS and PC-DOS operating systems and extends DOS's capabilities. (An *operating environment,* also known as a *windowing environment* or *shell,* adds an outer layer to an operating system.)

Windows (uppercase W) lets you display your work in windows (lowercase w). A **window** is a portion of the video display area dedicated to some specific purpose. With Windows, which supports multitasking, you can display several windows on a computer screen, each showing a different application, such as word processing or spreadsheet. You can easily switch between the applications and move data between them. Windows also provides users with a graphical user interface (GUI, pronounced "goo-ey"), which makes IBM-type PCs easier to use. (See Figure 6.17.) (DOS uses a character user interface—CUI, or "coo-ey"—meaning that the user must type words into the computer to get it to perform a function.) **Graphical user interfaces** enable users to select menu options by choosing pictures, called **icons,** that correspond to the appropriate processing option. For software that includes a graphical, or graphic, user interface, users typically use a mouse rather than a keyboard to choose menu options.

To effectively use Windows, you should have a reasonably powerful microcomputer system. This would include a 386 microprocessor or better, at least four times as much main memory as is required for DOS, and a hard disk drive.

For a long time, Microsoft labored on its newest version of Windows for release in 1995. **Windows 95,** the upgrade from Windows 3.1, should be released about the same time this book goes to print. Windows 95 is a true operating system, not requiring the separate MS-DOS program. Thus it does not have the residual feel of an operating system written for programmers rather than for regular users. Like Windows, it has a graphical user interface, called the *Desktop.* (See Figure 6.18.) Among the many new features included in Windows 95 are support for e-mail, voice mail, fax transmission, multimedia, and game building. Windows 95 comes bundled with Microsoft Net-

**Figure 6.17**
Windows' graphic user interface. Most software developed now and in the future will incorporate a graphic user interface that uses many of the components labeled here.

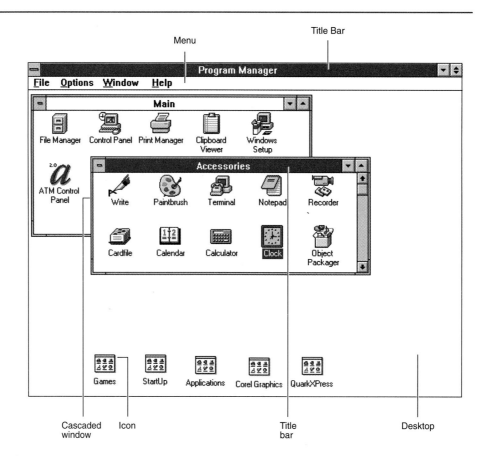

**Figure 6.18**
Windows 95 graphical
user interface.

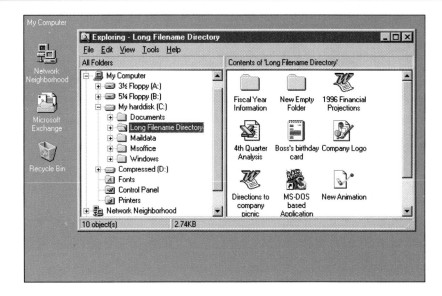

work software, which, among other things, will let Microsoft market its applications software without going through retail channels.

During the Windows 95 development, Microsoft also worked with several hardware manufacturers to develop an industrywide hardware standard to produce so-called plug-and-play products. Thus, users should be able to easily connect and use ("plug and play") hard disk drives, printers, and other peripheral equipment. This is a significant change from the dozen or so frustrating steps required to configure earlier IBM-style equipment running DOS and Windows programs, a difficulty not true of Macintoshes.[10]

Microsoft has also introduced a new kind of user interface—called *Bob,* a "social interface"—into the marketplace. (See Figure 6.19.) Bob is an attempt to make computers even easier to use by replacing icons with cartoon images and animated characters to lead users through programs. It does away with keyboard commands and pull-down menus. Users theoretically do not even need to use a manual to use Bob; instead, "personal guides" like Rover, the dog, and Scuzz, the rat, hang out on the PC screen to help users learn to use

**Figure 6.19**
Bob screen shot. Rover,
the dog: the user's guide.

the program. Over time, these guides offer help only when they think the user needs it. (Bob is equipped with a database that lets it "learn," so that the guides offer less help to users who demonstrate some level of skill.) Some people think that Bob is little more than a cute and somewhat condescending introduction to using computers; others feel that it is easy to use and practical.

Bob requires 8 MB of RAM, takes up 30 MB on a hard disk, and requires a 486 or higher processor to run.

### OS/2

OS/2 (there is no OS/1) was initially released in April 1987 as IBM's contender for the next mainstream operating system. **OS/2**—for **O**perating **S**ystem/**2**—is designed to run on many recent IBM and compatible microcomputers. Like Windows 95, OS/2 does not require DOS to run underneath it and has a graphical user interface, called the *Workplace Shell (WPS),* which uses icons resembling documents, folders, printers, and the like. (See Figure 6.20.) OS/2 can also run most DOS, Windows, and OS/2 applications programs simultaneously. This means that users don't have to throw out their old applications to take advantage of new features. In addition, OS/2 is the first microcomputer operating system to take full advantage of the power of the newest Intel microprocessors, such as I486 and Pentium chips. Lastly, this operating system is designed to connect everything from small handheld personal computers to large mainframes [✓ p. 76].[11]

OS/2 can perform some advanced feats. It can, for example, receive a fax and run a video while at the same time recalculating a spreadsheet. This is the kind of multitasking (and even multimedia) activity that is increasingly important for networked computers. It is also the first operating system created just for today's new "workgroup" environments. In workgroups, individuals work in groups sharing electronic files and databases over communications lines. IBM also offers a version called OS/2 for Windows, which can run on both systems. In late 1994 it unveiled a souped-up version of OS/2 with the Star Trek-like name of OS/2 Warp. (See Figure 6.21.) Although Warp can be tricky to install and needs at least 8 MB of RAM to run well, it has many devoted users (although not nearly as many as Windows: 6 million Warp users versus 80 million Windows users in March 1995). Warp's GUI is easier to use than Windows', and it provides an Internet gateway and automatically saves users' work.

---

**Figure 6.20**
OS/2. The Workplace Shell.

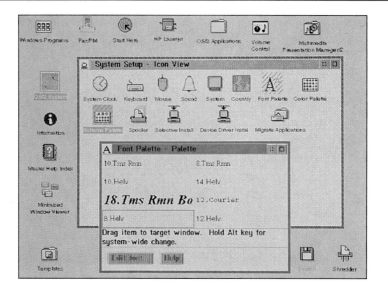

**Figure 6.21**
Warp screen shot showing
an Internet access window
(World Wide Web).

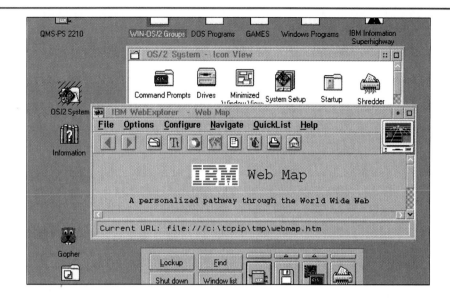

It may be that the battle for the operating system to rule the desktop has just begun.

### Windows NT

Unveiled by Microsoft in May 1993, **Windows NT,** for New Technology, is an operating system intended to support large networks of computers. Examples of such networks are those involved in airline reservations systems. Like Windows 95 and OS/2, Windows NT is a true operating system, interacting directly with the hardware. Windows NT is designed to run on workstations [✔ p. 74] or other more powerful computers.

Most PC owners will find Windows NT far more than they need. The people most benefiting are engineers and others who use workstations and who require massive amounts of computing power at their desks. A second category of users consists of those tied together in "client/server" networks with "file server" computers. A *client/server network* is a type of local area network (LAN). The "client" is the requesting PC or workstation and the "server" is the supplying file-server or mainframe computer, which maintains databases and processes requests from the client. A *file server* is a high-speed computer in a LAN that stores the programs and files shared by the users. (These topics are discussed in more detail in Chapter 8.)

Despite its power, Windows NT hasn't been very popular. To run Windows NT, a computer must be configured with at least 16 MB of main memory and 60 MB of extra hard disk space. Some industry onlookers think Windows NT's lagging sales are the result of its large memory and disk requirements.

### UNIX

UNIX was invented more than two decades ago by American Telephone & Telegraph, making it one of the oldest operating systems. **UNIX** is an operating system for multiple users, with built-in networking capability, the ability to run multiple tasks at one time, and versions that can run on all kinds of computers. Because it can run with relatively simple modifications on different types of computers—from micros to minis to mainframes—UNIX is called a *portable* operating system. (See Figure 6.22.) The primary users of UNIX are large corporations and banks, which use the software for everything from airplane-parts design to currency trading.

**Figure 6.22**
UNIX screen shot.

For a long time, AT&T licensed UNIX to scores of companies that make minicomputers [✓ p. 76] and workstations. As a result, the operating system was modified and resold by several companies, producing several versions of UNIX. Recent versions include NextStep, from Next, Inc.; Solaris, by Sun Microsystems; and Motif, by a coalition of companies (including IBM, Digital Equipment Corp., and Hewlett-Packard) called the *Open Software Foundation*. Repeated attempts to unify the various UNIX versions into one standard came to naught.

Finally, galvanized by the threat that Microsoft's Windows NT might become the standard for large microcomputer networks, UNIX suppliers struggled toward agreement. Over 50 companies have agreed to adhere to a single standard for a common interface linking UNIX to applications like word processing and spreadsheet programs.[12] More significant, Novell Inc. purchased the UNIX trademark from AT&T. To promote standardized approaches to UNIX, Novell gave away the UNIX brand name to an independent foundation and declared that it would be responsible for maintaining UNIX specifications.

Will UNIX prevail? It is a popular operating system in Europe, where users have discovered that its applications can survive changes in hardware, so that business is not unduly disrupted when new hardware is introduced. Perhaps, with agreement on UNIX standards, the same thing will be discovered in North America.

## Macintosh Operating System

Apple Computer Corporation introduced its popular Apple II personal computer system in the late 1970s. Because the Apple machines were based on entirely different microprocessors than those used in the IBM microcomputers, their operating systems were incompatible and unable to share data and instructions. The disk operating system used on many Apple computers was called Apple DOS and was designed to perform a single task for a single user.

Many current Macintosh users are using System 7.1. (See Figure 6.23.) The most recent systems software for the Macintosh is System 7.5, which supports multitasking and enables users to read MS-DOS and Windows files, even if they don't have the software to create such files. In addition, System 7.5 has a feature called *Apple Guide,* which offers "active assistance." Active assistance

**Figure 6.23**
Macintosh screen.
System 7.1.

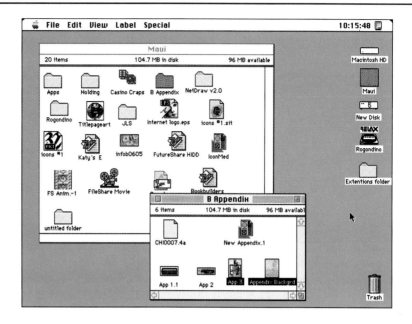

helps users accomplish different tasks on the computer—for example, it explains how to share files with other users. System 8, code-named Copland, expected in 1995 or early 1996, will add improved active assistance, among other features.[13]

The principal characteristics of the operating systems we have described thus far are summarized in Table 6.4.

**Table 6.4**
Microcomputer Operating Systems

| OPERATING SYSTEM | TYPES OF MICROPROCESSORS | SINGLE USER | MULTITASK | MULTIUSER |
|---|---|---|---|---|
| MS-DOS & PC-DOS | Intel 8088, 8086 80286, 80386 80486, Pentium | Yes | | Yes |
| Macintosh System Software | Motorola 8030, 8040, PowerPC | Yes | Yes | |
| Windows 3.1 | Intel 80286, 80386, 80486, Pentium | Yes | Yes | Yes |
| Windows 95 | Intel 80386, 80486, Pentium | Yes | Yes | Yes |
| Windows NT | Intel 80386, 80486, Pentium, PowerPC | Yes | Yes | Yes |
| OS/2 | Intel 80286, 80386, 80486, Pentium, PowerPC | Yes | Yes | Yes |
| UNIX | Intel 8086, 82486, 80386, 80486, Pentium | | Yes | Yes |
| NetWare | Intel 80386, 80486, Pentium | | Yes | Yes |

**Figure 6.24**
NetWare screen shot.

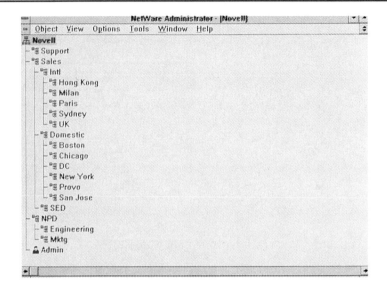

### NetWare

Developed by Novell, Inc. during the 1980s, **NetWare** has become the most popular operating system for orchestrating microcomputer-based local area networks (LANs) throughout a company or campus. (See Figure 6.24.) LANs allow PCs to share data files, printers, and file servers. Indeed, NetWare controls a reported 65% of the local area network market.[14] The unveiling of NetWare 4.0 in March 1993 allows organizations to extend the scope of their networks from under 250 microcomputers connected to one file server to thousands of users connected to multiple servers.

Can you continue to use, say, MS-DOS on your office personal computer while it is hooked up to a LAN running NetWare? Indeed you can. NetWare provides a shell around your own operating system. If you want to work "off network," you run the PC's regular operating system. If you want to work "on network," you respond to another prompt and type in whatever password will admit you to the network.

## Suggestions for Further Reading

Any of the Dummies books put out by IDG Books—such as *DOS for Dummies, Windows for Dummies, UNIX for Dummies,* and so on.

*Computer Shopper Magazine.* 5970 South Vivian Street, Littleton, CO 80127. (303) 973-6038. Subscription: about $36 per year.

"Computer Shopping Secrets," *Home Office Computing,* November 1994.

**Applications Software Manufacturers—Toll-Free Numbers**

Aldus Consumer Division. (800) 888-6293. *DateBook Pro.*

Approach Software Corp. (800) 277-7622. *Approach.*

Autodesk Retail Products. (800) 228-3601. *Autosketch.*

Borland International Corp. (800) 331-0877. *dBase, Office, Paradox, Quattro Pro, Sidekick.*

Campbell Services, Inc. (800) 345-6747. *OnTime for Windows.*

Claris Corp. (800) 3CLARIS. *Claris Works, FileMaker Pro.*

Computer Associates International. (800) CALL CAL. CA-*UpToDate, Kiplinger's CA-Simply Money.*

Fox Software Inc. (800) 837-3692. *FoxBase, FoxPro.*

Franklin Quest Co. (800) 654-1776. *Ascend.*

Intuit, Inc. (800) 624-8742. *Quicken.*

Lotus Development Corp. (800) 343-5414. *Agenda, Ami Pro, Improv, 1-2-3, Organizer, SmartSuite.*

MECA Software, Inc. (800) 820-7457. *Managing Your Money.*

Microsoft Corp. (800) 426-9400. *Access, Bookshelf, EasyCAD2, Excel, Money, Office, Word, Works.*

Pastel Development Corp. (800) 249-8316. *DayMaker Organizer.*

PRS Software. (800) 942-6777. *Personal Reminder System.*

Spinnaker Software Corp. (800) 826-0706. *Eight-in-One, PFS: First Choice.*

Symantec Corp. (800) 441-7234. *Q&A.*

WordPerfect Corp. (800) 321-4566. *WordPerfect, Works.*

WordStar Writing Tools Group. (800) 843-2204.

# S U M M A R Y

■ *Applications software* is a collection of related programs designed to perform a specific task, such as word processing or payroll management. Applications software is either purchased *off the shelf (packaged)* at a computer store or from a software outlet, or it is custom written for the user. Applications software cannot run without systems software. (p. 174)

■ *Systems software* "underlies" applications software; it starts up the computer and coordinates the hardware components and the applications software programs. Systems software usually comes with the microcomputer. (p. 175)

■ The following are popular types of applications software:

—*Word processing software* enables the user to easily create and edit documents, including inserting, deleting, and moving words, sentences, and paragraphs, and to easily alter the appearance of documents through the use of different type sizes and styles and through different text arrangements. (p. 178)

—*Desktop-publishing software* uses a combination of hardware and software to enable the user to combine text and graphics on the same page in a professional-looking, publishable format, and print it, using a page description language. (p. 180)

—*Spreadsheet software* allows users to create tables and financial schedules by entering data into rows and columns arranged as a grid on a display screen. When one or more numbers are changed, such reports can be automatically recalculated to provide "what if" analyses. (p. 182)

—*Database management system (DBMS) software,* also known as a *database manager,* consists of programs for storing, cross-indexing, retrieving, and manipulating large amounts of data. (p. 183)

—*Graphics software* gives the user the ability to make reports and other presentations more effective through the use of

*analytical graphics,* common graph forms that make numerical information easier to understand, and *presentation graphics* that can dress up graphs and use freeform drawings. (p. 185)

—*Communications software* allows users to access software and data from, and transmit data to, a computer in a remote location. (p. 186)

—*Integrated software* enables the user to perform a wide variety of tasks that typically include creating documents, spreadsheets, databases, and graphs. Most integrated software packages also include communications capabilities. (p. 187)

—*Groupware* is software that is used on a network and serves a group of users working together on the same project. Groupware is of four types: (a) basic groupware, (b) workflow software, (c) meeting software, and (d) scheduling software. (p. 187)

—*Software suites* are applications—like spreadsheets, word processing, graphics, communications, and groupware—bundled together and sold for a fraction of what the programs would cost if bought individually. (p. 188)

—*Desktop accessories* are software for organizing your computer "desktop" using such electronic tools as a calendar, clock, card file, calculator, and notepad. (p. 189)

—A *PIM,* or *personal information manager,* provides software tools that enable you to organize a variety of personal information, such as addresses. PIMs generally provide you with word processing and database capabilities. (p. 189)

—*Project management software* is used to help manage large-scale projects that involve a number of people. This software helps with planning many aspects of a project including scheduling, costs, resources, and people. Project management software often uses two tools: *Gantt charts* and *PERT charts.* (p. 190)

—*Computer-aided design (CAD) software* enables manufacturers to save much time and money because they can design products on the screen without having to construct expensive models. *CAD/CAM*—for *computer-aided design/computer-aided manufacturing*—software allows products designed with CAD to be input into an automated manufacturing system that makes the products. (p. 191)

—*Multimedia software* enables users to combine not only text and graphics but animation, video, music, voice, and sound as well. A multimedia system, however, is more than just a single technology or software application—it requires a combination of hardware and software that incorporates multiple media within a desktop computer system. (p. 191)

- Systems software comprises a large number of instructions that can be grouped as follows:

  1. *Operating systems:* The master system of programs that manage the basic operation of the computer. (p. 197)

  2. *Utility programs:* Used to support, enhance, or expand existing programs in a computer system. Utility programs are available for data recovery and backup, virus protection, compression, and memory management. Screen-saver utilities are also available. (p. 198)

  3. *Language processors (translators):* Software that translates a program written by a programmer in a language such as BASIC into machine language, which the computer can understand. (p. 200)

- Other systems software capabilities include *multitasking (multiprogramming), timesharing,* and *multiprocessing.* (p. 200)

- *DOS*—short for *Disk Operating System*—was designed for a single user to perform one task at a time. It is a very popular operating system because so many applications programs have been written to be used with it. However, the use of DOS has been declining in recent years because more powerful operating systems have become available. (p. 203)

- *Microsoft Windows* was developed to be used with DOS to take advantage of sophisticated microprocessors. Microsoft Windows provides users with a *graphical user interface (GUI),* allows users to multitask, and allows users to address an increased amount of main memory. (p. 203)

- *Microsoft Windows 95* is a new version of Windows that is a true operating system; that is, it doesn't run as a layer on top of DOS. Among its new features are support for e-mail, voice mail, and fax transmission. (p. 204)

- *Operating System/2 (OS/2),* initially introduced by IBM in 1987, supports multitasking and workgroup computing. OS/2 also includes a graphic user interface. The new version of OS/2 is called *Warp;* it adds an Internet interface, automatic saving capability, and an improved GUI to OS/2. (p. 206)

- *Microsoft Windows NT,* for *New* Technology, is an operating system intended to support large networks of computers. (p. 207)

- The *UNIX operating system* is one of the oldest operating systems. It is a multitasking operating system that includes built-in networking support. It is a popular operating system in universities, where a multiuser environment is often needed. (p. 207)

- The *Macintosh operating system (System 7)* was designed to be used on Apple Macintosh computers. This operating system supports multitasking and enables users to read MS-DOS and Windows files. (p. 208)

analytical graphics, p. 185
antivirus software, p. 199
applications software, p. 174
bundled, p. 188
communications software,
  p. 186
computer-aided design
  (CAD), p. 191
computer-aided
  design/computer-aided
  manufacturing (CAD/CAM),
  p. 191
cursor, p. 177
custom software, p. 175
database management system
  (DBMS) software, p. 183
database manager, p. 183
desktop accessory, p. 189
desktop publishing (DTP),
  p. 180
dialog box, p. 178
Disk Operating System
  (DOS), p. 203

documentation, p. 178
driver, p. 200
electronic spreadsheet, p. 182
graphical user interface
  (GUI), p. 204
graphics software, p. 185
groupware, p. 187
Help menu, p. 178
Help screen, p. 178
icon, p. 204
integrated software, p. 187
language translator, p. 200
macro, p. 178
menu, p. 178
modem, p. 186
multimedia software, p. 191
multiprocessing, p. 202
multitasking, p. 200
NetWare, p. 210
object linking and embedding
  (OLE), p. 178
off-the-shelf (packaged)
  software, p. 175

operating system (OS), p. 197
Operating System/2 (OS/2)
  (Warp), p. 206
personal information
  manager (PIM), p. 189
presentation graphics, p. 185
project management
  software, p. 190
pull-down menu, p. 178
scrolling, p. 177
suites, p. 188
systems software, pp. 175, 197
timesharing, p. 201
unbundled, p. 188
UNIX, p. 207
utility programs, p. 198
virus, p. 199
window, p. 204
Windows, p. 203
Windows 95, p. 204
Windows NT, p. 207
word processing software,
  p. 178

## SELF-TEST

1. ___APPL_____ ___SOFTWARE_____ is a collection of
   related programs designed to perform a specific task for the user.

2. List three components of systems software:
   a. OPERATING SYSTEM.
   b. UTILITY PROGRAM.
   c. LANGUAGE TRANSLATOR.

3. ___WORD_____ ___PROCESSING____
   ___SOFTWARE_____ offers capabilities that enable the user to easily
   create and edit documents.

4. Applications software starts up the computer and functions as the principal
   coordinator of all hardware components. (true/false)

5. ___DESKTOP_____ ___PUBLISHING_____ involves using a
   microcomputer and mouse, scanner, laser printer, and ___DESKTOP_____
   ___PUBLISHING_____ software for mixing text and graphics to produce high-quality printed output.

6. Printers often use a page description language, which is software, to
   describe the shape and position of characters and graphics. (true/false)

7. _MULTIMEDIA_ presentation software enables you to include text, graphics, sound, and video in a presentation.

8. If you need to develop a report that involves performing extensive calculations on financial data, what type of software should you use? _SPREAD SHEET_

9. _COMM_ _SOFTWARE_ includes programs that access software and data from, and transmit data to, a computer in a remote location.

10. New applications software must be _INSTALLED_ by the user before it can be used.

11. Groupware is a collection of several applications in a single package with a common set of commands and the ability to work and share data. (true/false)

12. _BUNDLING_ means that components of a computer system are sold together for a single price.

13. Gantt charts and PERT charts are used by _PROJECT_ _MANAGEMENT_ _SOFTWARE_.

14. The Macintosh operating system and Windows for the PC both use pictures called _ICON_ to represent processing functions.

15. A(n) _OPERATING_ _SYSTEM_ consists of the master system of programs that manage the basic operations of the computer.

16. The term _BOOTING_ refers to the process of loading an operating system into a computer's main memory from diskette or hard disk.

17. List three systems software capabilities that affect whether more than one user and/or more than one application can run at a time.
    a. _Multi tasking_
    b. _Multi sharing_
    c. _Multi processing_

18. UNIX is one of the oldest operating systems. (true/false)

19. Microcomputer users may encounter an example of multiprocessing in specialized processors called _CO PROCESSOR_.

20. Microsoft Windows is an operating environment that lays a(n) _GRAPHICAL_ _USER_ _INTER FACE_ shell around the DOS operating system.

*Solutions:* (1) applications software; (2) operating systems, utility programs, language translators; (3) word processing software; (4) false; (5) desktop publishing (twice); (6) true; (7) multimedia; (8) electronic spreadsheet software; (9) communications software;

(10) installed; (11) false; (12) bundling; (13) project management software; (14) icons; (15) operating system; (16) booting; (17) multitasking, timesharing, multiprocessing; (18) true; (19) coprocessors; (20) graphical user interface

## SHORT-ANSWER QUESTIONS

1. What is the difference between word processing software and desktop publishing software?
2. Why does a computer need systems software?
3. What does spreadsheet software do?
4. What is the purpose of communications software?
5. What is a page description language used for?
6. What does the term *booting* mean?
7. What would be a good use for database management system software?
8. Provide some examples of utility programs that are used to support or enhance existing programs in a computer system.
9. Why do some people prefer using integrated software to other types of applications software?
10. What do the abbreviations CAD and CAM mean?
11. What is a computer virus? How might you detect the existence of a virus?
12. What is the difference between applications software and systems software?
13. What is the significance of object linking and embedding (OLE)?
14. What is an icon? What is it used for?
15. What is the difference between multitasking and timesharing?
16. What is scrolling?
17. What is the difference between integrated software and a software suite?
18. What does multimedia presentation software enable you to do?
19. What is a *driver*?

## PROJECTS AND CRITICAL THINKING EXERCISES

1. If you have been using a particular microcomputer for two years and are planning to upgrade the version of systems software you are using, what issues must you consider before you go ahead and buy the new version?
2. Prepare a short report about how you would use an electronic spreadsheet to organize and manage your personal finances and to project outcomes of changes. What column headings (labels) would you use? Row headings? What formula relationships would you want to establish among which cells? (For example, if your tuition increased by $2,000, how would that affect the monthly amount set aside to buy a car or take a trip?)
3. Locate an individual or a company that is using some custom-written software. What does this software do? Who uses it? Why couldn't it have been purchased off the shelf? How much did it cost? Do you think there is an off-the-shelf program that can be used instead? Why/why not?
4. Attend a meeting of a computer users' group in your area. What is the overall purpose of the group? Software support? Hardware support? In what ways? Does it cost money to be a member? How many members are there? How does the group get new members? If you were looking to join a user group, would you be interested in joining this group? Why/why not?
5. Make a list of all the ways a student could use word processing software to make life easier. Look at Table 6.1 to get some ideas, read some reviews of word processing software in computer magazines, and read the copy on word processing packages in a computer store.
6. Use current computer publications to research the use of OS/2 in the business environment. On what types of computers is it being used? What types of businesses are using it? Is it easy to use? What do you think the future is for OS/2? How does the use of OS/2 compare to that of UNIX?

7. Go to a large computer store and find out how many microcomputers (and what types) run on these operating systems: MS-DOS, MS-DOS/Windows, Windows 95, OS/2, UNIX, Macintosh System 7. Ask the salesperson for his or her opinion about which disk operating system is the most powerful and flexible. Ask why.

8. Picture yourself in your future job. What types of current applications software do you see yourself using? What are you producing with this software? What kinds of new applications software would you invent to help you do your job better?

9. Look at the Help-Wanted section of several newspapers. Do the ads require only general types of applications software knowledge such as word processing skills, or do they require knowledge of specific packages such as WordPerfect? Make a list of the required packages and the types of jobs needing these skills.

10. Pen-based computing [✓ p. 73] uses its own particular type of systems software. Check some articles in computer magazines to find out what makes this type of systems software different from regular microcomputer systems software. Is pen-based systems software compatible with DOS? How would pen-based systems software limit a traditional microcomputer user?

## IN THE LAB WITH MICROSOFT WINDOWS

### Mouse Practice

1. In this section you learn how to use a mouse. We assume that the Microsoft Windows Program Manager is displaying.

2. First, locate the Help menu option on the top of the Program Manager window. Then, to display the Help menu:
CLICK: Help menu option

3. To start the Microsoft Windows tutorial:
CLICK: Windows Tutorial option

4. Read the instructions on the screen. As indicated, type **M** to learn how to use a mouse.

5. Follow the instructions on the screen.

6. When you have completed the mouse portion of the tutorial, Microsoft Windows will display three option boxes. To exit the tutorial, click the "Exit the Tutorial" box. Then type **Y**. The Program Manager window is displaying.

### Windows Basics

1. In this section you learn how to use the Microsoft Windows graphical-user interface. Right now, the Microsoft Windows Program Manager should be displaying.

2. First, locate the Help menu option on the top of the Program Manager window. Then, to display the Help menu:
CLICK: Help menu option

3. To start the Microsoft Windows tutorial:
CLICK: Windows Tutorial option

4. Read the instructions on the screen. As indicated, type **W** to learn the basics of Microsoft Windows.

5. Follow the instructions on the screen.

6. When you have completed the tutorial, Microsoft Windows will display two option boxes. To exit the tutorial, click the "Exit the Tutorial" box. Then type **Y**. The Program Manager window is displaying.

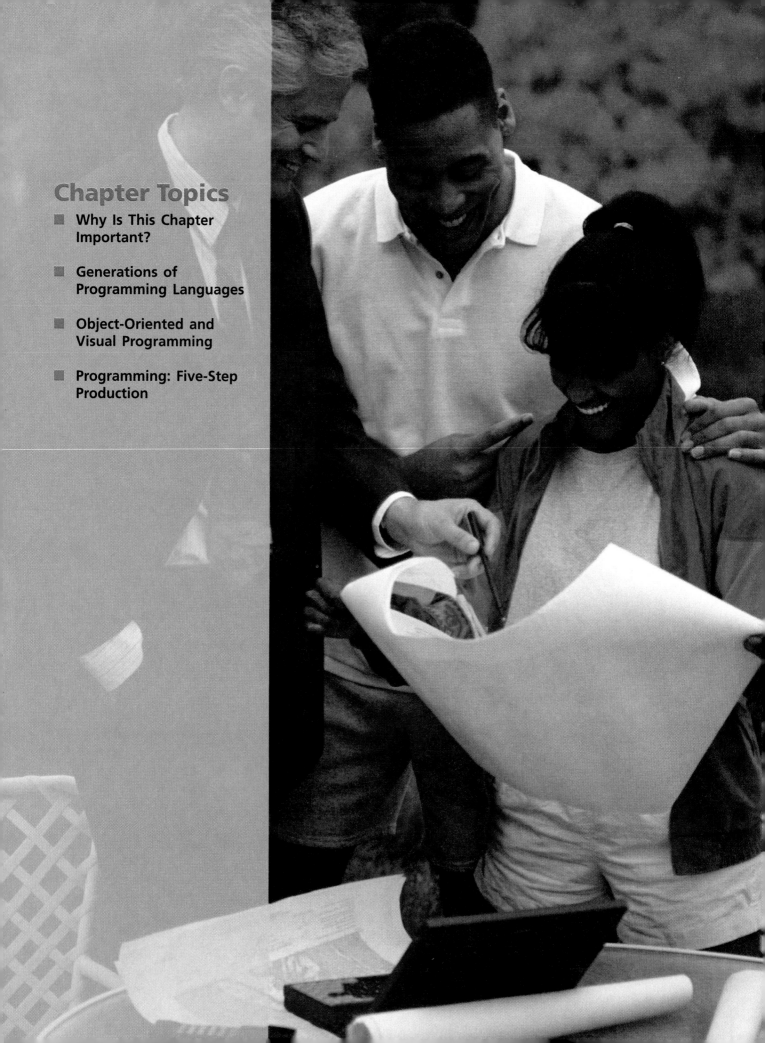

# Chapter Topics

# CHAPTER 7

# Software Development and Programming Languages

At this point, just learning how to use computer hardware and software may seem challenging enough. Yet there often comes a day when users suddenly discover that the ready-made, off-the-shelf programs available to them won't do everything they want. People renovate their houses or modify their clothes for the same reasons that software users fiddle with their programs. Would you ever be able to create applications software yourself? Or be able to help someone else do so? Are you curious about where software comes from—how it is created? In this chapter, we describe ways to develop or modify applications software through the use of programming languages, techniques, and tools, and through existing software.

## Preview

*When you have completed this chapter, you will be able to:*

■ Name and describe the generations of programming languages

■ Describe the uses for some of the most popular high-level programming languages

■ Describe concepts relating to object-oriented and visual programming

■ Name and discuss the five basic steps in developing a computer program and describe some software development tools

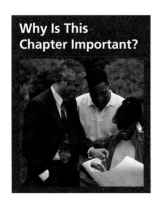

**Why Is This Chapter Important?**

*One day at work you are tinkering with your database management program on your microcomputer when you suddenly realize you can't make it produce a sales report in just the right format. As new computer users gain experience, they find it easier to identify areas where software can be modified or created to provide more useful and sophisticated processing capabilities. To obtain custom-made software, the user can work with a computer specialist to develop it or in special cases do it alone. Regardless of the approach you take, you need to understand the process by which software is developed and be familiar with the tools available for you to use.*

*In addition, users need to understand the basic programming process so that they can effectively deal with programmers who are creating software for them. If users can't specify their requirements properly, they may end up with software they are not happy with.*

*Many tools exist for building a house; likewise, many tools are available for creating, or writing, software. These tools include different types of programming languages used to write detailed sets of instructions that enable users to process data into information. Because the topics of software programming and software languages are the subjects of entire courses, the following sections can necessarily offer only the basic principles with which users should be familiar.*

## Generations of Programming Languages

**Programming languages are said to have evolved in "generations." There are five generations of programming languages: (1) machine language, (2) assembly language, (3) high-level (procedural) languages, (4) very-high-level (nonprocedural) languages, and (5) natural language. Some common high-level languages used by programmers to create applications are FORTRAN, COBOL, PL/1, BASIC, RPG, C, Pascal, Modula-2, and Ada.**

A **programming language** is a set of rules that tells the computer what operations to perform. In other words, it is an artificial language for expressing computer programs. Programming languages can best be categorized as falling into one of five generations. (See Figure 7.1.) Programming languages are said to be *lower level* when they are closer in form to the language the computer itself uses—the binary system of 1s and 0s [✔ p. 85]. They are called *higher level* when they are closer to the language people use.

The languages in each of the successive five generations represent an improvement over those of the prior generation—just as the electric saw was an improvement over the manual one. Languages of later generations are easier to learn than earlier ones, and they can produce results (software) more quickly and more reliably. But just as a builder might need to use a manual saw occasionally to cut a tricky corner, professional programmers still need to use some early-generation languages to create software.

Compared with later generations, the early-generation programming languages (first, second, and third) require the use of more complex vocabulary and syntax to write software; they are therefore used only by computer professionals. The term **syntax** refers to the precise rules and patterns required for the formation of the programming language sentences, or encoded statements, that tell the computer what to do and how to do it. Programmers must use a language's syntax to write a program in that language—just as

**Figure 7.1**
The five generations of programming languages.

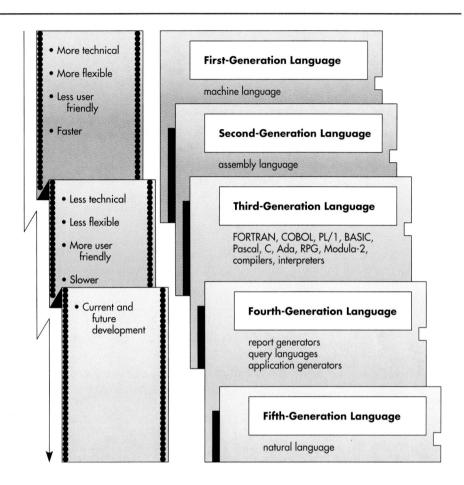

- More technical
- More flexible
- Less user friendly
- Faster

- Less technical
- Less flexible
- More user friendly
- Slower

- Current and future development

**First-Generation Language**

machine language

**Second-Generation Language**

assembly language

**Third-Generation Language**

FORTRAN, COBOL, PL/1, BASIC, Pascal, C, Ada, RPG, Modula-2, compilers, interpreters

**Fourth-Generation Language**

report generators
query languages
application generators

**Fifth-Generation Language**

natural language

you would use the rules of German, not French, grammar to communicate in German.

In addition to the five generations of programming languages, some microcomputer software packages are widely used for creating software. Although these packages generally cannot be categorized into one of the five generations, many people consider some of the database management systems software [✓ p. 183] used on microcomputers, such as Microsoft Access dBASE, as belonging to the fourth generation.

The following sections examine programming languages a bit more closely.

## First and Second Generations: Machine Language and Assembly Language

A programmer can use machine language—that is, first-generation language—to write software programs. In contrast to later-generation languages, machine-language programs do not need to be translated before they can be run on the computer. A programmer can also write software programs in higher-level languages; however, these programs must be converted (translated) into machine language before they can be run on the computer. **Machine language** is the basic language of the computer, representing instructions and data as binary digits (a series of 1s and 0s corresponding to on and off electrical states or on and off magnetic pulses). (See Figure 7.2.) Because the specific format and content of machine-language instructions vary according to computer architecture (usually determined by the central processing unit

**Figure 7.2**

*Top:* Machine language is all binary 1s and 0s—very difficult for people to work with. *Middle:* Assembly language uses abbreviations for major instructions, such as MP for MULTIPLY. This is easier for people to use, but still quite difficult. *Bottom:* COBOL, a third-generation language, uses English words, for example, that can be understood by people.

**First generation**
Machine language

```
11110010 01110011 1101 001000010000 0111 000000101011
11110010 01110011 1101 001000011000 0111 000000101111
11111100 01010010 1101 001000010010 1101 001000011101
11110000 01000101 1101 001000010011 0000 000000111110
11110011 01000011 0111 000001010000 1101 001000010100
10010110 11110000 0111 000001010100
```

**Second generation**
Assembly language

```
                    PACK 210(8,13),02B(4,7)
                    PACK 218(8,13),02F(4,7)
                    MP   212(6,13),21D(3,13)
                    SRP  213(5,13),03E(0),5
                    UNPK 050(5,7),214(4,13)
Third generation    OI   054(7),X'F0'
Cobol
```

```
        MULTIPLY HOURS-WORKED BY PAY-RATE GIVING GROSS-PAY ROUNDED
```

[✓ p. 80]), machine-language programs are considered *machine dependent;* that is, they run only on the computer for which they were designed.

The first step in making software development easier and more efficient was the creation of assembly languages, also known as *second-generation languages.* (See Figure 7.2.) **Assembly languages** use symbols as abbreviations for major instructions instead of long combinations of binary digits. This means a programmer can use abbreviations instead of having to remember lengthy binary instruction codes. For example, it is much easier to remember L for Load, A for Add, B for Branch, and C for Compare than the binary equivalents—strings of different combinations of 0s and 1s.

Although assembly languages represented an improvement, they have obvious limitations. They can be used only by computer specialists familiar with the architecture of the computer being used. Also, assembly languages are not easily converted to run on other types of computers.

## Third Generation

**Third-generation languages,** also known as *high-level languages,* are very much like everyday text and mathematical formulas in appearance. They are designed to run on a number of different computers with few or no changes. Among the most commonly used high-level programming languages are COBOL, FORTRAN, BASIC, and C. A large number of additional languages have been developed, each with its own strengths. High-level languages were developed for several reasons:

■ To relieve the programmer of the detailed and tedious task of writing programs in machine language and assembly language

■ To provide programs that can be used on more than one type of machine with very few changes

■ To allow the programmer more time to focus on understanding the user's needs and designing the software required to meet those needs

Most high-level languages are considered to be procedure-oriented languages, or *procedural languages,* because the program instructions comprise lists of steps, or procedures, that tell the computer not only *what* to do but *how* to do it. High-level language statements generate, when translated, a comparatively greater number of assembly-language instructions and even more machine-language instructions. (See Figure 7.2.) The programmer spends less time developing software with a high-level language than with assembly or machine language because fewer instructions have to be created.

However, because a computer can execute programs only in machine language, a language translator is needed to convert programs written in any other type of language [✓ p. 200]. A **language processor,** or **language translator,** is required to convert (translate) a high-level language program (**source code**) into machine language (**object code**), so that the program will work on the computer. (See Figure 7.3.) As a general user, you will need to use a language processor only if you create a program using a high-level language such as BASIC (Beginner's All-purpose Symbolic Instruction Code), which is commonly taught in university-level courses.

Programmers use three types of language processors: assemblers, compilers, and interpreters. An **assembler** is a program that translates an assembly language program into machine language. A **compiler** is a language processor that translates an entire high-level language program into a machine-language version of the program in a single process. If no programming errors exist in the source code, the program becomes operative.

An **interpreter** is a language processor that translates and executes high-level language instructions one instruction statement at a time. If an error is detected in the source code, the interpreter displays immediate feedback on the screen. Interpreters are commonly used when developing small and simple programs and in educational settings because the user receives immediate feedback.

**Figure 7.3**
A language processor translates the high-level language program (source code) into a machine-language version of the program (object code) before the computer can execute the program.

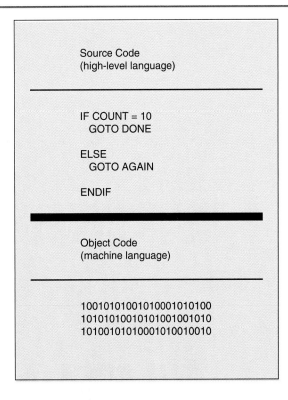

Source Code
(high-level language)

IF COUNT = 10
    GOTO DONE

ELSE
    GOTO AGAIN

ENDIF

Object Code
(machine language)

1001010100101000101010100
1010101001010100100101010
1010010101000101001010010

The most important difference between using compiled or interpreted software is speed. Programs that are compiled (such as COBOL) tend to execute up to five times faster than programs that are interpreted (such as BASIC). However, if you are working with microcomputers at home or in the office, you won't have to worry about compiling or interpreting—the software packages have already been compiled, and you will not even be able to look at the machine-level language the computer uses.

By the early 1960s, most computer manufacturers were working on a version of FORTRAN, the first widely used high-level language, for their computers. Various manufacturers' versions of FORTRAN were similar; however, their efforts to make one package better than the others resulted in a number of small differences. The problems associated with resolving these differences led to the realization that industry standards were needed to ensure complete compatibility of high-level language programs with different computers. The task of establishing such standards was turned over to the American Standards Association, and in 1966 the association released the first FORTRAN standards.

Since the late 1960s, the association—now known as the **American National Standards Institute (ANSI)**—worked with the **International Standards Organization (ISO)** to develop, among other things, standards for all high-level programming languages. All versions of programming languages that developers wish to have designated as meeting the standards must accommodate all the commands, syntax, and processing requirements formulated by the ANSI and the ISO.

Following is a list of the most commonly used high-level programming languages (there are over 500 languages in use today):

- FORTRAN
- COBOL
- PL/1
- BASIC
- RPG
- C
- Pascal
- Modula-2
- Ada

**FORTRAN**

**FORTRAN**—short for **FOR**mula **TRAN**slator—was first made available in 1954 by IBM. One of the very first high-level languages, FORTRAN was designed for technical and scientific applications. (See Figure 7.4.) Its popularity grew

**Figure 7.4**
FORTRAN. Here, a FORTRAN statement calculates a discount (7% of the invoice amount) if the invoice is greater than $500. Otherwise, no discount is given to the customer.

```
IF (XINVO .GT. 500.00) THEN
    DISCNT = 0.07 * XINVO
ELSE
    DISCNT = 0.0
ENDIF
XINVO = XINVO - DISCNT
```

rapidly, and by the 1960s a version of the language was available for almost all types of computers; however, it is used primarily on minicomputers and mainframes. Because the language was designed to handle research and analytical problems definable in terms of mathematical formulas and relationships, the majority of people using FORTRAN are mathematicians, scientists, and engineers. The newest version of FORTRAN is FORTRAN 90.

Some advantages of FORTRAN:

■ It can handle complex mathematical and logical expressions.

■ Its statements are relatively short and simple.

■ Programs developed in FORTRAN on one type of computer can often be easily modified to work on other types.

Some disadvantages:

■ It does not handle input and output operations to storage devices as efficiently as some other high-level languages.

■ It has only a limited ability to express and process nonnumeric data.

■ It is not as easy to read and understand as some other high-level languages.

### COBOL

**CO**mmon **B**usiness **O**riented **L**anguage, or **COBOL** for short, was released in 1960. (See Figure 7.5.) The U.S. Department of Defense, which is one of the world's largest buyers of data processing equipment, no longer wanted to commission the development of software in unalterable assembly language, so it funded the development of this programming language for business. The leader of the team that developed COBOL was naval officer Grace Hopper. The concern over the differences among versions of FORTRAN—all machine dependent—led the developers of COBOL to adopt machine independence as one of the primary objectives. The U.S. government then adopted a policy that required a computer to have the COBOL programming language available if the vendor wanted to sell or lease the equipment to the government. In 1968, COBOL was approved as the standard business programming language in the United States; the latest ANSI standards for COBOL were released in 1985.

The commands and syntax of COBOL's instruction statements resemble sentences you would use when speaking English, Spanish, French, or German, for example. As a result, it is sometimes easier for a programmer to

---

**Figure 7.5**
COBOL. This COBOL statement shows the same discount calculation given in Figure 7.4.

```
OPEN-INVOICE-FILE.
     OPEN I-O INVOICE FILE.

READ-INVOICE-PROCESS.
     PERFORM READ-NEXT-REC THROUGH READ-NEXT-REC-EXIT UNTIL END-OF-FILE.
     STOP RUN.

READ-NEXT-REC.
     READ INVOICE-REC
          INVALID KEY
               DISPLAY 'ERROR READING INVOICE FILE'
               MOVE 'Y' TO EOF-FLAG
               GOTO READ-NEXT-REC-EXIT.
     IF INVOICE-AMT > 500
          COMPUTE INVOICE-AMT = INVOICE-AMT - (INVOICE-AMT * .07)
          REWRITE INVOICE-REC.

READ-NEXT-REC-EXIT.
     EXIT.
```

read and understand COBOL than FORTRAN. COBOL is used primarily on minicomputers and mainframes but is also available for microcomputer use, and it is the language most used for business applications.

Some advantages of COBOL:

■ It is machine independent.

■ Its English-like statements are easy to understand.

■ It can handle many files, records, and fields.

■ It easily handles input and output operations.

Some disadvantages:

■ Because it is so readable, it is wordy; thus even simple programs are lengthy, and programmer productivity is slowed.

■ It cannot handle mathematical processing as well as FORTRAN, BASIC, or C.

In spite of the drawbacks, many programmers believe that COBOL will remain the most widely used language for writing business applications. Many companies are using applications written in COBOL that represent a huge investment that the business community is not yet prepared to throw away.

### PL/1

The intended uses of FORTRAN and COBOL were always very clear. However, as the complexity and sophistication of the applications being developed for business increased, a language was needed that would be capable of dealing with computation and heavy-duty file handling. For this reason, IBM and two international organizations of computer users began to develop a general-purpose programming language, which was designated **Programming Language 1,** or **PL/1.** PL/1 was released in the mid-1960s for use on the IBM System 360 series of computers and has since been used primarily on mainframe computer systems. Figure 7.6 shows an extract from a PL/1 program.

Some advantages of PL/1:

■ It combines text and mathematical processing capabilities.

■ It is very flexible—the programmer using it has few coding restrictions.

■ It automatically identifies and corrects common programming errors.

Some disadvantages:

■ It runs more slowly than COBOL and FORTRAN.

■ It requires a substantial amount of main memory (twice as much as COBOL and four times as much as FORTRAN).

■ Its list of options is long and difficult to memorize.

■ It is harder to learn than COBOL.

**Figure 7.6**
PL/1. The discount calculation of Figures 7.4 and 7.5 is shown here in PL/1.

```
/*CALCULATE DISCOUNT*/

GET LIST (INVOICE);

IF INVOICE > 500 THEN DISCOUNT = INVOICE * .07;

ELSE DISCOUNT = 0;

END;
```

## Programmer Profiles

Following are profiles of a few programmers—out of many—who helped shape the computer industry.

### CHARLES SIMONYI

Born on September 10, 1948 in Budapest, Hungary, Charles Simonyi was introduced to computers and programming while attending high school, when his father arranged for him to assist an engineer who was working on one of the few computers in Hungary at the time.

By 1966 Charles had not only completed high school but also his first compiler. With the experience gained from writing the compiler, he was able to obtain employment at A/S Regnecentralen in Copenhagen, Denmark. In 1968 Charles left Denmark to study in the United States at the University of California at Berkeley, where he received his bachelor of science degree in 1972 and his doctorate degree from Stanford University in 1977.

Simonyi has worked at the UC Berkeley Computer Center, the Berkely Computer Corporation, the ILLIAC 4 Project, Xerox PARC, and Microsoft Corporation. . . . At Microsoft, Charles organized the Application Software Group, which has produced Multiplan, Microsoft Word, Microsoft Excel, and other popular application products.

*Quote:* "What is programming? People argue about it all the time. Some people call it a *science,* some people call it an *art,* some people call it a *skill* or a *trade.* I think it has aspects of all three. We like to pretend that it has a lot of art in it, but we know it has a lot of science."

### JOHN WARNOCK

Born in 1940 and raised in Utah, John Warnock was educated at the University of Utah, where he received both a bachelor's and master's degree in mathematics and a Ph.D. in computer science. . . . After completing his studies, Warnock tried his hand at being an entrepreneur with a company in Vancouver, British

Columbia, for a short time; then he joined Computer Sciences of Canada and worked in Toronto. After that he traveled to Washington, D.C., where he was employed at the Goddard Space Flight Center.

In 1972, Warnock moved to California to work with Dave Evans and Ivan Sutherland on the ILLIAC 4 Project, the NASA space flight shuttle simulator, and airplane simulators. In 1978, Warnock went to Xerox PARC, where he spent four years working in the Computer Sciences Laboratory. While at Xerox PARC, Warnock worked on improving the typographic quality of computer gray-scale displays.

In 1982, Drs. John Warnock and Charles Geschke formed Adobe Systems to develop software that integrates text and graphics and is also output-device independent. Their effort resulted in PostScript, Adobe Systems' first product.

*Quote:* "I think a lot before I do anything, and once I do something, I'm not afraid to throw it away. It's very important that a programmer be able to look at a piece of code like a bad chapter of a book and scrap it without looking back. Never get too enamored with one idea, never hang onto anything tenaciously without being able to throw it away when necessary; that should be the programmer's attitude."

### TORU IWATANI

Game designer Toru Iwatani was born on January 25, 1955 in the Meguro Ward of Tokyo, Japan. He is totally self-taught, without any formal training in computers, visual arts, or graphic design. In 1977, at the age of 22, Iwatani joined NAMCO Limited, a computer software company in Tokyo that produces video games. Once within the company, Iwatani eventually found his place designing games. He completed Pac Man with the help of four others, after working on it for a year and five months, taking it from concept to finished product.

The game was first introduced in Japan, where it was very successful. When the game was exported, Pac Man captured the imaginations of Americans and Europeans as well.

*Quote:* "I must tell you, I don't have any particular interest in [computers]. I'm interested in creating images that communicate with people. A computer is not the only medium that uses images; I could use the movies or television or any other visual medium. It just so happens I use the computer."

### JARON LANIER

From New Mexico and West Texas, where he grew up, Jaron Lanier moved to California in 1981 with the intention of carving out, as he says, "some sort of hippie-like lifestyle in Santa Cruz, playing flute in the mall." But it never worked out. Instead, at the age of 25, Lanier was running his own company called Visual Programming Languages and developing products most of us never dreamed could exist. He initially entered the computer world by programming the sound portion of video games. Eventually, he developed whole video games while working at Atari. [Lanier has since worked as one of the major developers of virtual reality programs.]

*Quote:* "Everyone in programming today is talking about different ways of telling the computer what to do. My programming language doesn't do that. With mine, you actually look at what the program is doing and you mess with it until it's right. It's really a different process.

"For example, you have a recipe, which a person follows to make a cake or something.

That's what current programming is like. On the other hand, there's tuning your car's engine. You watch the thing running and see what it does and change it until it works the way you want it to. My programming is more like the latter."

### MICHAEL HAWLEY

Working as a digital audio programmer for the Droid Works, an affiliate of Lucasfilm Ltd., charged with the monumental task of computerizing the filmmaking process, Michael Hawley has been involved in the development of software for the SoundDroid, which is the all-digital sound studio in a box. It is capable of storing, recording, editing, and mixing sound, as well as reproducing it for immediate feedback.

Hawley got involved with computers and programming as a youth growing up in New Providence, a suburb of New York City. Throughout high school and college, he worked at the neighboring Bell Labs offices in Murray Hill. While cultivating his interest in computers at Bell Labs, Hawley pursued serious studies in music and the piano at Yale University, where, in 1983, he earned his bachelor's degree in music and computer science.

*Quote:* "What I like about programming is that it really helps you think about how we communicate, how we think, how logic works, how creative arts work."

From Susan Lammers, *Programmers at Work,* Redmond Washington: Tempus Books of Microsoft Press, 1989.

### BASIC

**B**eginner's **A**ll-purpose **S**ymbolic **I**nstruction **C**ode, or **BASIC,** was developed in the mid-1960s by John Kemeny and Tom Kurtz at Dartmouth College, where the large computer timesharing system supported many student terminals that allowed interactive testing of the new computer language. BASIC was intended to be a programming language that was easy to learn and flexible enough to solve a variety of simple problems. It is the most popular microcomputer language and is used primarily to teach people how to program. BASIC is an interactive language—user and computer can communicate with each other during the writing and running of programs.

By the late 1970s and early 1980s, BASIC had become so popular that it was selected as the primary language for implementation on microcomputers, although it can be used on all types of computers. Because of its popularity,

**Figure 7.7**
BASIC. The discount calculation is shown here in QuickBASIC.

```
10   REM   This Program Calculates a Discount Based on the Invoice Amount
20   REM        If Invoice Amount is Greater Than 500, Discount is 7%
30   REM        Otherwise Discount is 0
40   REM
50   INPUT "What is the Invoice Amount"; INV.AMT
60   IF INV.AMT 500 THEN LET DISCOUNT = .07 ELSE LET DISCOUNT = 0
70   REM        Display results
80   PRINT "Original Amt", "Discount", "Amt after Discount"
90   PRINT INV.AMT, INV.AMT * DISCOUNT, INV.AMT — INV.AMT * DISCOUNT
100  END
```

a number of extensions have been added to the language to facilitate file creation and handling, as well as the creation of graphics. Popular versions of BASIC are True BASIC, QuickBASIC, and Visual BASIC. Figure 7.7 shows an excerpt from a BASIC program.

An advantage of BASIC:

- Ease of use

Some disadvantages:

- Slow processing speed (although newer versions of BASIC, such as Microsoft QuickBASIC, can be compiled as well as interpreted and so can run much faster than previous versions)

- Lack of standards

## RPG

The **Report Program Generator,** or **RPG,** language was introduced by IBM in 1964 to help small businesses generate reports and update files easily. RPG is not as procedure-oriented as other third-generation languages but is still often referred to as a programming language. The programmer fills out a number of very detailed coding forms that are easy to learn to use; however, because RPG is designed to be used to solve clear-cut and relatively simple problems, it is much more limited than FORTRAN, COBOL, BASIC, and some other programming languages. RPG is used on a variety of IBM minicomputers and has been enhanced, or improved, several times. The first revision, RPG 2, was released in the early 1970s and provided enhanced capabilities for handling tape and disk files. The latest version of the language, RPG 3 (released in 1979), added the capabilities necessary to extract reports from data stored in a database system. Figure 7.8 shows an RPG form with data entered (other forms exist for input, output, and file description specifications). After the data is entered on the form, it is typed into the computer.

Some advantages of RPG:

- Reports can be produced easily and in a short amount of time.
- Few formal rules for syntax and grammar

A disadvantage:

- RPG is being overshadowed by new languages that come with microcomputer applications, such as dBASE for database management.

## Figure 7.8
RPG. The discount calculation.

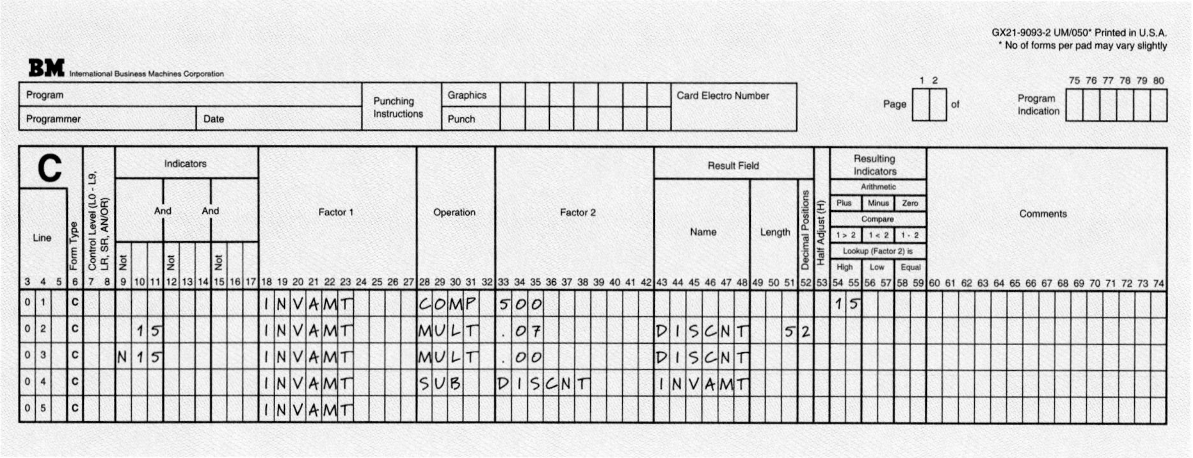

## C

**C,** which is quite sophisticated, was introduced by Brian Kernighan and Dennis Ritchie at Bell Laboratories in the early 1970s for use in writing systems software. It was used to create most of the UNIX operating system (assembly language was used to create the rest). Today, it is useful for writing operating systems, database management software, and some scientific applications. Increasingly, C has been used in commercial software development, including games, robotics, and graphics. It is now considered to be a necessary language for programmers to know.

Some advantages of C:

- It can be used on different types of computers, including microcomputers.
- It is fast and efficient.
- It enables the programmer to manipulate individual bits.
- It is useful for writing operating systems software, database management software, and a few scientific applications.

Some disadvantages:

- Because of its conciseness, the code can be difficult to follow.
- It is not suited to applications that require a lot of report formatting.

Figure 7.9 shows an example of the C programming language.

## Figure 7.9
C. The C version of the 7% discount. C has many characteristics of both assembly and high-level programming languages and can be used on a variety of machines.

```
if (invoice_amount > 500.00)

    DISCOUNT = 0.07 * invoice_amount;

else

    discount = 0.00;

invoice_amount = invoice_amount - discount;
```

### Pascal

The **Pascal** language, named after the 17th-century French mathematician Blaise Pascal, was developed by Swiss scientist Niklaus Wirth and introduced in the early 1970s. Available for both large and small computer systems, it was developed to teach programming as a systematic and structured activity. Pascal is taught at most universities and colleges because of its superior structured programming format. *Structured programming,* which we describe later in this chapter, is based on the principle that main programming functions can be broken down into smaller, more manageable units, called modules. Figure 7.10 shows an excerpt from a Pascal program.

Some advantages of Pascal:

- Pascal can be used for mathematical and scientific processing.

- It has extensive capabilities for graphics programming.

- It is easy to learn.

A disadvantage:

- It has limited input/output programming capability, which limits its use in business applications.

### Modula-2

Developed by Niklaus Wirth as an improvement of Pascal and introduced in 1980, **Modula-2** is better suited for business use than Pascal, and although it's used primarily to write systems software, it can be used as an applications software development tool. Many experts believe that it may become a popular business programming language.

### Ada

In 1975, the U.S. Department of Defense began to encourage the creation of a language that would facilitate the development and maintenance of large programs for any application—from business to missile launching—and that could be used and modified over a long period of time. This decision was prompted by the results of a study showing that lack of uniformity in the use of languages resulted in yearly software costs of billions of dollars. These costs were necessary to pay for the large staff of programmers required to support all the different languages used.

The programming language **Ada** was derived from Pascal and named after Augusta Ada, Countess of Lovelace, the daughter of the famous English poet Lord Byron. The Countess of Lovelace worked with the mathematician Charles Babbage in the mid-1800s to develop mechanical computing devices and is considered to be the world's first programmer. Ada is intended primarily for use in computer systems that are an integral part of another system for which they act as the control mechanism; that is, they are embedded systems. Many

**Figure 7.10**
Pascal. The customer discount calculation is shown in Pascal.

```
        if INVOICEAMOUNT > 500.00 then

            DISCOUNT := 0.07 * INVOICEAMOUNT

        else

            DISCOUNT := 0.0;

        INVOICEAMOUNT := INVOICEAMOUNT - DISCOUNT
```

**Figure 7.11**
Ada. The 7% solution
in Ada.

```
if INVOICE_AMOUNT > 500.00 then

    DISCOUNT := 0.07 * INVOICE_AMOUNT

else

    DISCOUNT := 0.00

endif;

INVOICE_AMOUNT := INVOICE_AMOUNT − DISCOUNT
```

military weapons systems and equipment, for example, have embedded computer systems. However, the language can be used for commercial as well as military applications. Ada combines the good qualities of Pascal with improved input/output capabilities. Figure 7.11 is a sample excerpt of an Ada program.

Some advantages of Ada:

■ Extensive support of real-time processing

■ Automatic error recovery

■ Flexible input/output operation

■ Structured and modular design (this design method is described shortly)

Some disadvantages:

■ High level of complexity and difficulty

■ Large storage requirements

■ Not as efficient as some other languages

Although Ada has great potential, it is not yet widely used outside the U.S. Department of Defense.

## Fourth Generation

Also known as very-high-level languages or problem-oriented languages, fourth-generation languages (4GLs) are as yet difficult to define in general, because they are defined differently by different vendors; sometimes these languages are tied to a software package produced by the vendor, such as a database management system. Basically 4GLs are easier for programmers—and users—to handle than third-generation languages. **Fourth-generation languages (4GLs)** are *nonprocedural languages,* so named because they allow programmers and users to specify what the computer is supposed to do without having to specify how the computer is supposed to do it, which, as you recall, must be done with third-generation, high-level (procedural) languages. Consequently, fourth-generation languages need approximately one tenth the number of statements that a high-level language needs to achieve the same result.

Because they are so much easier to use than third-generation languages, fourth-generation languages allow users, or noncomputer professionals, to develop certain types of applications software. It is likely that, in the business environment, you will at some time use a fourth-generation language. In the following sections we describe three types of fourth-generation language tools.

### Query Languages

**Query languages** allow users (nonprogrammers) to ask questions about, or retrieve information from, database files by forming requests in normal human-language statements (such as English). For example, a manager in charge of inventory may key in the following question of a database, using DB2, a database management program:

```
How many items in inventory have a quantity-on-hand that
is less than the reorder point?
```

The query language will do the following to retrieve the information:

1. Copy the data for items with quantity-on-hand that is less than the reorder point into a temporary location in main memory.
2. Sort the data into order by inventory number.
3. Present the information on the video display screen (or printer).

The manager now has the information necessary to proceed with reordering certain low-stock items. The important thing to note is that the manager didn't have to specify how to get the job done, only what needed to be done. In other words, in our example, the user needed only to specify the question, and the system automatically performed each of the three steps listed above.

Examples of query languages are SQL (Structured Query Language), QBE (Query-By-Example), and Intellect.

### Report Generators

**Report generators** are similar to query languages in that they allow users to ask questions of a database and retrieve information from it for a report (the output); however, in the case of a report generator, the user is unable to alter the contents of the database file. And with a report generator, the user has much greater control over what the output (or the result of a query) will look like. The user of a report generator can either specify that the software automatically determine how the output should look or create customized output reports using special report-generator command instructions.

An example of a report generator is RPG III.

### Applications Generators

Applications generators do more than query languages and report generators, both of which allow the user to specify only output-related processing tasks (and some input-related tasks, in the case of query languages). An **applications generator** is a programmer's tool that allows a person to give a detailed explanation of what data needs to be processed. The software then generates the code needed to create a program to perform the task. Applications generators basically consist of prewritten (preprogrammed) modules, or program "building blocks," that comprise fundamental routines that most programs use. These modules, usually written in a high-level language, constitute a "library" of routines to choose from. The programmer or user must key in the specifications for what the program is supposed to do. The resulting specification file is input to the applications generator, which determines how to perform the tasks and which then produces the necessary instructions for the software program.

Examples of applications generators are NOMAD and FOCUS, two database management systems.

4GLs will probably not replace third-generation languages because they are usually focused on specific tasks, and hence offer fewer options. Still, they improve productivity because programs are easy to write.

### Fifth Generation

Natural languages represent the next step in the development of programming languages—**fifth-generation languages. Natural language** is similar to query language, with one difference: it eliminates the need for the user or programmer to learn a specific vocabulary, grammar, or syntax. The text of a natural-language statement very closely resembles human speech, more than query languages do.

For example, with 4GLs, you can type in some rather routine inquiries. An example of a request in FOCUS, for instance, might be:

```
SUM SHIPMENTS BY STATE BY DATE.
```

Natural languages allow questions or commands to be framed in a more conversational way or in alternate forms. For example, with a natural language, you might be able to state:

```
I WANT THE SHIPMENTS OF PERSONAL DIGITAL ASSISTANTS FOR
ALABAMA AND MISSISSIPPI BROKEN DOWN BY CITY FOR JANUARY
AND FEBRUARY. ALSO, I NEED JANUARY AND FEBRUARY SHIPMENTS
LISTED BY CITIES FOR PERSONAL COMMUNICATORS SHIPPED TO
WISCONSIN AND MINNESOTA.
```

Natural language takes the user one step farther away from having to deal directly and in detail with computer hardware and software. These languages are also designed to make the computer "smarter"—that is, to simulate the human learning process.

**H**

artificial intelligence

The use of natural language touches on expert systems, computer-based collections of the knowledge of many human experts in a given field that are applied to solving problems, and *artificial intelligence,* independently smart computer systems—two topics that are receiving much attention and development and will continue to do so in the future.

## Object-Oriented and Visual Programming

**Object-oriented programming (OOP) is a programming method that combines data and instructions for processing that data into a self-sufficient "object," or block of preassembled programming code, that can be used in other programs. Three concepts of OOP are encapsulation, inheritance, and polymorphism. Some examples of OOP languages are Smalltalk, C++, Turbo Pascal, and Hypertalk. Visual programming enables the programmer to make connections between programming objects by drawing, pointing, and clicking on diagrams and icons.**

Consider how it was for the computer pioneers, programming in machine language or assembly language. Novices putting together programs in BASIC or Pascal can breathe a collective sigh of relief that they weren't around at the dawn of the Computer Age. Even some of the simpler third-generation languages represent a challenge. Fortunately, two new developments have made things easier—*object-oriented programming* and *visual programming*.

### Object-Oriented Programming

Imagine you're programming in a traditional third-generation language, such as BASIC, creating your coded instructions one line at a time. As you work on some segment of the program (such as how to compute overtime pay), you may think, "I'll bet some other programmer has already written something like this. Wish I had it. It would save a lot of time."

Fortunately, a kind of recycling technique now exists. This is object-oriented programming. Let us explain this in four steps:

1. *What OOP is:* **Object-oriented programming (OOP)** is a programming method that combines data with instructions for processing that data to make a self-sufficient "object" that can be used in other programs. The important thing here is the object.

2. *What an "object" is:* An **object** is a block of preassembled programming code that is a self-contained module. The module contains, or encapsulates, both (1) a chunk of data and (2) the processing instructions that may be called on to be performed on that data.

3. *When an object's data is to be processed—sending the "message":* Once the object becomes part of a program, the processing instructions may or may not be activated. Activiation happens only when a message is sent. A *message* is an alert sent to the object that it is needed for an operation.

4. *How the object's data is processed—the "methods":* The message need only identify the operation. How it is actually to be performed is embedded within the processing instructions that are part of the object. These instructions about the operations to be performed on data within the object are called the *methods*.

Once you've written a block of program code (that computes overtime pay, for example), it can be reused in any number of programs. Thus, unlike with traditional programming, with OOP you don't have to start from scratch each time. (See Figure 7.12.)

Object-oriented programming takes longer to learn than traditional programming because it means training oneself to a new way of thinking. Once

**Figure 7.12**

Conventional versus object-oriented programs. *Left:* When building conventional programs, programmers write every line of code from scratch. *Right:* With object-oriented programs, programmers can use blocks, or "objects," of preassembled modules containing data and the associated processing instructions.

**Conventional Programs**

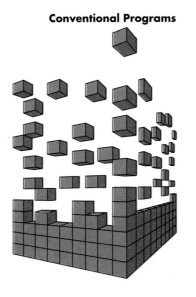

**Object-Oriented Programs**

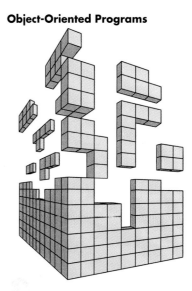

learned, however, the beauty of OOP is that an object can be used repeatedly in different applications and by different programmers, thereby speeding up development time and lowering costs.

## Three Important Concepts of OOP

Object-oriented programming involves three important concepts, which go under the jaw-breaking names of *encapsulation, inheritance,* and *polymorphism.* Actually, these terms are not as fearsome as they look:

- *Encapsulation: Encapsulation* means an object contains (encapsulates) both (1) data and (2) the instructions for processing it, as we have seen. Once an object has been created, it can be reused in other programs. An object's uses can also be extended through concepts of class and inheritance.

- *Inheritance:* Once you have created an object, you can use it as the foundation for similar objects that have the same behavior and characteristics. All objects that are derived from or related to one another are said to form a class. Each class contains specific instructions (methods) that are unique to that group.

    Classes can be arranged in hierarchies—classes and subclasses. *Inheritance* is the method of passing down traits of an object from classes to subclasses in the hierarchy. Thus, new objects can be created by inheriting traits from existing classes.

    Writer Alan Freedman gives this example: "The object MACINTOSH could be one instance of the class PERSONAL COMPUTER, which could inherit properties from the class COMPUTER SYSTEMS."[1] If you were to add a new computer, such as COMPAQ, you would need to enter only what makes it *different* from other computers. The *general* characteristics of personal computers could be inherited.

- *Polymorphism: Polymorphism* means "many shapes." In object-oriented programming, *polymorphism* means that a message (generalized request) produces different results based on the object that it is sent to.

    Polymorphism has important uses. It allows a programmer to create procedures about objects whose exact type is not known in advance but will be at the time the program is actually run on the computer. Freedman gives this example: "A screen cursor may change its shape from an arrow to a line depending on the program mode." The processing instructions "to move the cursor on screen in response to mouse movement would be written for 'cursor,' and polymorphism would allow the cursor to be whatever shape is required at runtime." It would also allow a new cursor shape to be easily integrated into the program.[2]

## Four Examples of OOP Languages

Some examples of object-oriented programming languages are Smalltalk, C++, Turbo Pascal, and Hypertalk.

Smalltalk

- *Smalltalk—the first OOP language:* Smalltalk was invented by computer scientist Alan Kay in 1970 at Xerox's Palo Alto Research Center in California. *Smalltalk,* the first OOP language, uses a keyboard for entering text, but all other tasks are performed with a mouse.

- *C++—more than C: C++*—the plus signs stand for "more than C"—combines the traditional C programming language with object-oriented capability. With C++, programmers can write standard code in C without the object-oriented features, use object-oriented features, or do a mixture of both.

■ *Turbo Pascal—object-oriented Pascal:* Designed in 1984 by Philippe Kahn of Borland International, Turbo Pascal is an object-oriented version of Pascal. The language allows a program to use removable modules, or objects, that can be replaced later when the program is changed.

■ *Hypertalk—the language for HyperCard:* HyperCard, the software introduced for the Apple Macintosh in 1987, is based on the concept of cards and stacks of cards—just like notecards, only they are electronic. A card is a screenful of data that makes up a single record; cards are organized into related files called *stacks.* Using a mouse, you can make your way through the cards and stacks to find information or discover connections between ideas.

HyperCard is not precisely an object-oriented programming language, but a language called Hypertalk is. *Hypertalk,* which uses OOP principles, is the language used in the HyperCard program to manipulate HyperCard stacks.

## Visual Programming

**Visual programming** is a method of creating programs in which the programmer makes connections between objects by drawing, pointing, and clicking on diagrams and icons.

The goal of visual programming is to make programming easier for programmers and more accessible to nonprogrammers. It does so by borrowing the object orientation of OOP languages but exercising it in a graphical or visual way. Visual programming enables users to think more about solving the problem than about handling the programming language. There is no learning of syntax or actual writing of code.

**H**
Visual BASIC

With one example, *ObjectVision* (from Borland), the user doesn't employ a programming language but simply connects icons and diagrams on screen. *Visual BASIC* (Microsoft) offers another visual environment for program construction, allowing you to build various components using buttons, scroll bars, and menus. (See Figure 7.13.)

**Figure 7.13**
Visual BASIC screen shot (right).

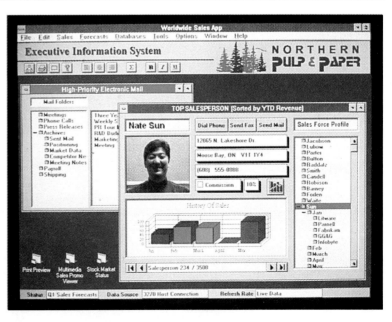

## Who's Writing Software Now?

Since the invention of computers, Americans have dominated the software market. Microsoft alone produces more computer code each year than do any of 100 nations, according to Capers Jones of Software Productivity Research in Burlington, Mass. U.S. suppliers hold about 70% of the worldwide software market.

But as international networks sprout and large corporations deflate, India, Hungary, Russia, the Philippines and other poorer nations are discovering in software a lucrative industry that requires the one resource in which they are rich: an underemployed, well-educated labor force. American and European giants are now competing with upstart Asian development companies for contracts, and in response many are forming subsidaries overseas. Indeed, some managers in the trade predict that software development will gradually split between Western software engineers who design systems and Eastern programmers who build them. . . .

So far India's star has risen fastest. "Offshore development [work commissioned in India by foreign companies] has begun to take off in the past 18 to 24 months," says Rajendra S. Pawar, head of New Delhi-based NIIT, which has graduated 200,000 Indians from its programming courses. . . . Indeed, India's software exports have seen a compound annual growth of 38% over the past five years. . . .

Offshore development certainly costs less than body shopping, and not merely because of saved airfare. "Thanks to the time differences between India and the U.S., Indian software developers can act the elves and the shoemaker," working overnight on changes requested by managers the previous day, notes Richard Heeks, who studies Asian computer industries at the University of Manchester in England.

W. Wayt Gibbs, "A Developing World," *Scientific American,* September 1994, pp. 94–95.

## Programming: Five-Step Production

Programming is done in an orderly, five-step process: (1) Define the problem. (2) Map out program logic and design a solution. (3) Code the program. (4) Test the program. (5) Collate the documentation. Programmers work out algorithms before the program is written, and they use many types of programming tools, such as flowcharts, pseudocode, top-down design, structure charts, and control structures.

For a number of important reasons, the user should understand the basic steps a computer programmer follows to create software. For example, the user may have to evaluate software vendors' claims about what their programs can do. More important, if the user fails to communicate clearly and precisely to the programmer the processing procedures and logic to be incorporated into a program, the programmer will have to make assumptions about what exactly should be done. If the assumptions are wrong, the user will probably end up with reports that contain erroneous information or reports that simply do not have the necessary information.

The orderly process that an organization goes through when identifying its applications software program requirements is referred to as the **software development cycle.** As mentioned earlier, you need to understand these steps so that you will be able to tell a programmer, in terms he or she can understand, exactly what your programming requirements are. Although this section on programming is not detailed enough to allow you to communicate on the level of a programmer, it will tell you the basics that you, as a user, need to understand about programming.

Briefly, the five steps of the software development cycle are as follows (see Figure 7.14):

■ *Step 1—Define the problem.*

—"Think first and program later." Consider all possible ways of solving a problem and specify the objectives of the intended program, including who (which departments) will use the information produced.

—Specify program objectives and program users.

—Specify output requirements.

—Specify input requirements.

—Specify processing requirements.

—Study the feasibility of the program.

—Document the analysis and objective specification process. This may involve using flowcharts, flow diagrams, data dictionaries that catalog and identify the data elements that will be used, sketches of display screen formats and report layouts, and so on.

Step 1 usually involves meetings that include the programmer(s), users, and the systems analyst/designer who designed the system of which the program will be a part. At this point a make-or-buy decision is made. If an off-the-shelf program exists that you can buy to solve your problems, you will not have to make (create) your own custom software [✓ p. 175]. However, if you do have to create your own software, you must then proceed to step 2.

**Figure 7.14**
The five steps of software development.

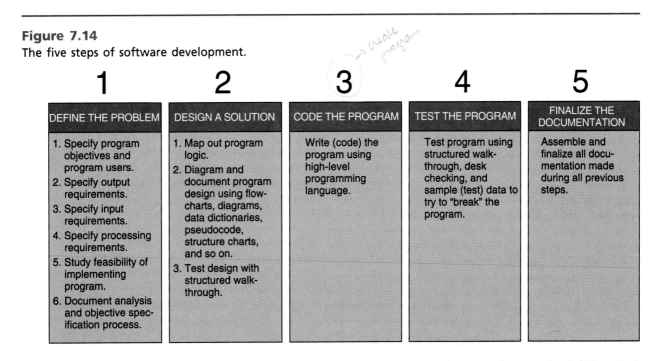

■ *Step 2—Map out the program logic and design a solution.*

After the problem has been defined, the program must be logically designed. This process is not unlike outlining a long term paper's organization before you actually begin to write it. The programmer must work out algorithms, or process specifications, before the program is written. An *algorithm* is a set of well-defined rules for the solution of a problem in a particular number of steps. (This type of problem-solving method is contrasted with *exploratory,* or trial-and-error, methods.) The programmer may use a variety of tools to do this, including flowcharts, pseudocode, and structure charts (discussed later in this chapter). You probably won't ever need to use any of these tools, because they are used mostly by programmers mapping out complex logic or by those using third-generation languages. However, you should have a basic idea of how they are used in order to appreciate the detail that is necessary for a programmer to create a program. The more detail you can give the programmer about your own processing requirements, the better the resulting program will be.

After the program has been designed, programmers, systems designers, and users check its logic and documentation by means of a "structured walk-through."

■ *Step 3—Code (write) the program.*

Translate the processing requirements of the program into the necessary programming (high-level) language statements and then enter the coded instructions into the computer. (This is usually done on a terminal, and the instructions are stored on disk. The programmer can modify the instructions as necessary.)

■ *Step 4—Test the program.*

Review the program carefully to ensure that it is doing exactly what it is supposed to. Repeat "structured walkthroughs," conduct "desk-checking" by proofreading a printout of the program, and, using test ("fake") data, review output reports to determine that they are in the correct format and contain all the required information ("logic testing"). The user can play an important role in identifying the problem areas, or "bugs," in a program by participating in tests to see how it handles the types of tasks it was asked to do—including trying to "break" the program by inputting unusual test data. The programmer can then fix the problems, or "debug" the program.

■ *Step 5—Collate and finalize the documentation.*

Clearly document all the steps, procedures, logic tools, and testing results, as well as the goals of the program and other specific facts. Although listed as step 5, the activity of *documenting the program should go on throughout the design and coding process.* The documentation, or manual, tells future program operators, users, and programmers (who may later have to modify the program) exactly what the program does, how it does it, and how to use it. Documentation also helps programmers track down errors. (Users must assume some responsibility to see that the new software is adequately documented.)

The following sections discuss the steps in the software development cycle in more detail.

## Step 1—Define the Problem

Say your company needs a computer-based payroll processing program. That's the problem. In specifying the objectives of the program, you and your employees would list in great detail everything you want the program to do, which means specifying output, input, and processing requirements. For example, do you want both hardcopy and softcopy output? How often? What information must reports and checks include? What will be the source and format of input data? You would also specify who in your company needs to see reports, in what form, and how often.

Let's say that after you have defined the problem, specified program objectives and program users, and listed the output, input, and processing requirements, you decide that none of the available off-the-shelf programs is adequate; you must have your software custom written. At this point, you should determine if the project is feasible—in other words, do the apparent benefits of the program outweigh the costs of preparing it? Should you proceed? Of course, you should document everything you do in step 1, as well as in all subsequent steps. (See Figure 7.15.)

## Step 2—Map Out the Program Logic and Design a Solution

During the programming process, users must know how to express their processing requirements in the detailed terms necessary for the computer specialist to convert them into program logic. (See Figure 7.16.) It may be easy to describe what you want accomplished to someone who is at least slightly familiar with the working of your department. However, you would be amazed at how much detail is required to communicate to a person unfamiliar with your work exactly what to do, when to do it, and how it is to be done. And exceptions must always be accounted for—a program has to be able to take care of the rare case as well as the routine ones.

A number of tools and techniques have been developed to assist in documenting the logic to be built into programs. We will discuss only program flowcharts, pseudocode, and top-down design, because it's unlikely that, as a general business user, you would come into direct contact with any other programming tools or techniques.

### Flowcharts

A program **flowchart** is a diagram that uses standard ANSI symbols to show the step-by-step processing activities and decision logic needed to solve a problem. (See Figure 7.17.) Flowcharts are created before a programmer

---

**Figure 7.15**

First step: Problem definition.
1. Specify program objectives and program users.
2. Specify output requirements.
3. Specify input requirements.
4. Specify processing requirements.
5. Study feasibility of implementing program.
6. Document the analysis.

**Figure 7.16**
Second step: program design.
1. Determine program logic through top-down approach and modularization, using hierarchy charts.
2. Design details using pseudocode and/or flowcharts, preferably involving control structures.
3. Test design with structured walkthroughs.

**Figure 7.17**
Standard flowchart symbols. Programmers use plastic templates (b) to trace standard ANSI flowchart symbols when preparing plans for program design (a). (c) Example of a program flowchart.

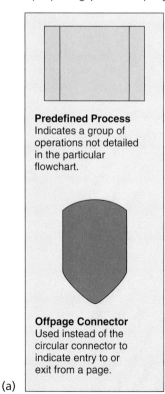

**Predefined Process**
Indicates a group of operations not detailed in the particular flowchart.

**Offpage Connector**
Used instead of the circular connector to indicate entry to or exit from a page.

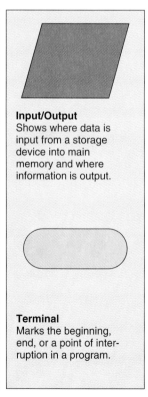

**Input/Output**
Shows where data is input from a storage device into main memory and where information is output.

**Terminal**
Marks the beginning, end, or a point of interruption in a program.

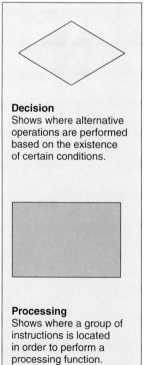

**Decision**
Shows where alternative operations are performed based on the existence of certain conditions.

**Processing**
Shows where a group of instructions is located in order to perform a processing function.

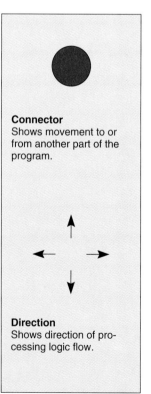

**Connector**
Shows movement to or from another part of the program.

**Direction**
Shows direction of processing logic flow.

(a)

**Figure 7.17**
(Continued)

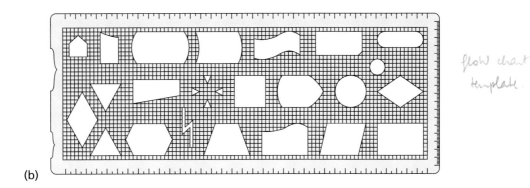

(b)

flow chart
template

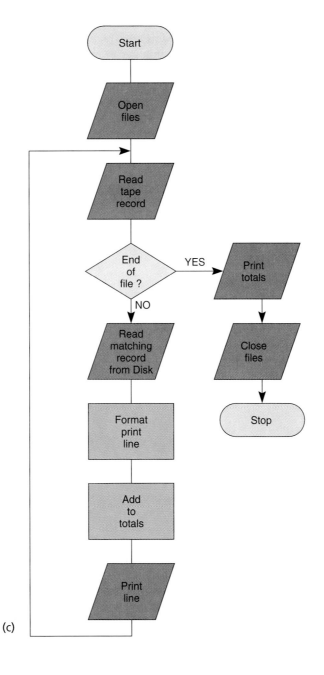

(c)

begins writing the program. In concept, flowcharts are similar to an architect's blueprint for a house. You need the blueprint before you can nail in the first 2 × 4 stud. After construction is underway, you may need to modify the blueprint. Similarly, the programmer may need to modify the flowchart during the process of creating the program.

The flow of logic in a program flowchart normally goes from top to bottom and left to right. Arrows are used to show a change from those directions.

Although program flowcharts have some disadvantages—their preparation may be time-consuming and they can be many pages long—they are considered to be good tools for documenting the procedures to be used in the program, and they are often included in a program's documentation package. Software packages are available that automate the process of drawing and modifying flowcharts.

## Pseudocode

The prefix *pseudo* means "fake"; *pseudocode,* therefore, literally means "fake code"—that is, not the code that is actually entered into the computer. **Pseudocode** uses human-language statements instead of symbols (such as flowchart symbols) to represent program logic. It is more precise in representing logic than regular, idiomatic English but does not follow a specific programming language's syntax. Pseudocode statements can be composed and edited by hand or by using a typical off-the-shelf word processing program. Some people would argue further that pseudocode is much closer to actual code than are flowcharts, which makes pseudocode more productive than flowcharting. However, some programmers don't like to use pseudocode because it doesn't depict the program logic visually like a flowchart does.

Pseudocode uses four statement keywords to portray logic: IF, THEN, ELSE, and DO. Repetitive processing logic is portrayed using the statements DO WHILE (repeat an activity as long as a certain condition exists), DO UNTIL (repeat an activity until a certain condition is met), and END DO (stop repeating the activity). The processing logic is written out in narrative sentences. The logic statement keywords are capitalized, and several levels of standard indentation are used to show decision processes and subprocesses. Figure 7.18 gives you an idea of how the keywords, statements, and indentation are used.

## Top-Down Design

Program flowcharts, pseudocode, and the rules of a high-level language enable a programmer to design and write software that leads to predictable results that solve a problem. However, for a long time many computer scientists felt that more structure and control were needed to standardize programming and make it more exact—to change it from an art to a science. Thus, in the mid-1960s, the concept of *structured programming* was developed. **Structured programming** uses top-down design to "decompose" (break down) main processing functions, called **modules,** into smaller ones for coding purposes.

**Top-down design** starts with the highest level of the program and works its way down to the lowest level of detail. The modules at the top of the structure are general and the ones identified at the bottom are very specific. Programming, on the other hand, always starts at the bottom of the structure; that is, the modules below a particular point must be completed (programmed) before programming begins at that level. (In some programming languages, modules are referred to as *subroutines*.) If possible, each module should have only a single function, just as an English paragraph should have

**Figure 7.18**
Example of pseudocode.

```
START
DO WHILE so long as there are records
        Read a customer billing account record
        IF today's date is greater than 30 days from
        date of last customer payment
                Calculate total amount due
                Calculate 5% interest on amount due
                Add interest to total amount due to calculate
                grand total
                Print on invoice overdue amount
        ELSE
                Calculate total amount due
        ENDIF
        Print out invoice
END DO
END
```

a single, complete thought; this forces a limit to a module's size and complexity.

*Structure charts,* often called *hierarchy charts,* are often used to picture the organization and breakdown of modules. (See Figure 7.19.) A program that is considered modular in design has the following characteristics:

1. Each module must be of managable size—have fewer than 50 program instructions.

2. Each module should be independent and have a single function.

3. Each module has a single entry point (execution of the program module always starts at the same place) and a single exit point (control always leaves the module at the same place).

4. If one module refers to or transfers control to another module, the latter module returns control to the point from which it was "called" by the first module.

Following are some of the advantages of a modular program:

■  Complex programs can be organized into smaller and more manageable pieces in a relatively standard way.

■  Programs can be modified with less effort than nonmodular programs because, when modular programming guidelines are followed carefully, each module is relatively independent and can be changed without affecting all the other parts of the program.

■  A collection or library of standardized modules can be created to use in various programs. (Similar processing tasks don't have to be programmed redundantly, which helps ensure accuracy because the same task is always

**Figure 7.19**
Structure (hierarchy) chart. This represents a top-down design for a payroll program. Here the modules are represented from the highest level of the program down to details. The three principal processing operations—input, processing, and output—are represented by the modules in the second layer: "Read input," "Calculate pay," and "Generate output." Before tasks at the top of the chart can be performed, all the ones below must be performed. Each module represents a logical processing step.

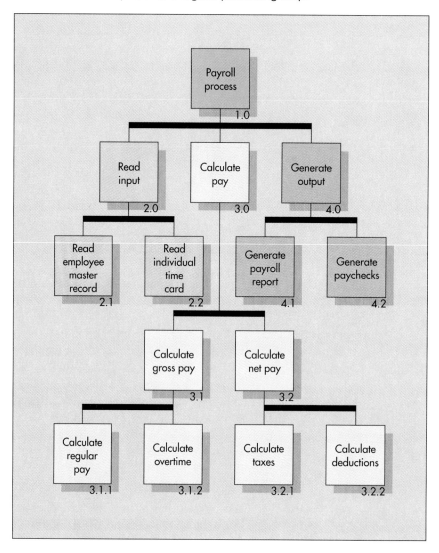

accomplished in the same way. Modular programming was the precursor to object-oriented programming, described earlier.)

■ Errors in logic can be quickly isolated and fixed.

A structure chart can be used as part of a *hierarchy plus input-process-output package*, also called *HIPO*. The HIPO concept was developed by IBM as a tool for program design and documentation.

### Check Work in Progress

Before the program is written, or coded (step 3), it should be subjected to initial testing to avoid costly and time-consuming changes "after the fact." This is usually done by a **structured walkthrough**—a group of programmers meet to review the logic and documentation of a program designed by another programmer in order to identify what is not clear or workable and to verify code. Systems designers and users often also attend such meetings.

### Step 3—Code the Program

In this step, the programmer actually writes out the program designed in step 2, using a high-level language. (See Figure 7.20.) The programmer may write the program out first, using pencil and paper, or he or she may key it in directly. The programmer will follow certain rigid rules and use *control structures.* A **control structure,** or **logic structure,** controls the logical sequence in which computer program instructions are executed. In structured program design, three control structures are used to form the logic of a program: *sequence, selection,* and *iteration.* (See Figure 7.21.) These are the tools with which you write structured programs and take a lot of the guesswork out of programming.

One thing that all three control structures have in common is *one entry* and *one exit.* The control structure is entered at a single point and exited at another single point. This helps simplify the logic so that it is easier for others following in a programmer's footsteps to make sense of the program. (In the days before this requirement was instituted, programmers could have all kinds of variations, leading to the kind of incomprehensible program known as *spaghetti code.*)

Let us consider the three control structures:

1. In the **sequence control structure,** one program statement follows another in logical order. In the example shown in Figure 7.21, there are two boxes—"statement" and "statement." The first statement might be "Open file," the other "Read a record." There are no decisions to make, no choices between "yes" and "no." The boxes logically follow one another in sequential order.

IF-THEN-ELSE

2. The **selection control structure**—also known as an **IF-THEN-ELSE structure**—represents a choice. It offers two paths to follow when a

---

**Figure 7.20**
The third step: program coding.
1. Select the appropriate high-level programming language.
2. Code the program in that language, following the syntax carefully.

**Figure 7.21**
The three control structures. The three structures used in structured program design to form the logic of a program are *sequence, selection,* and *iteration.*

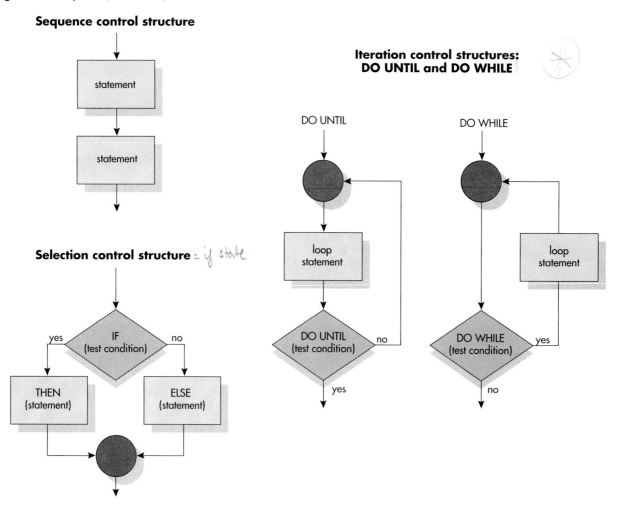

**Sequence control structure**

statement

statement

**Selection control structure** = *if state*.

IF
(test condition)

yes

no

THEN
(statement)

ELSE
(statement)

**Iteration control structures:
DO UNTIL and DO WHILE**

DO UNTIL

loop
statement

DO UNTIL
(test condition)

no

yes

DO WHILE

loop
statement

DO WHILE
(test condition)

yes

no

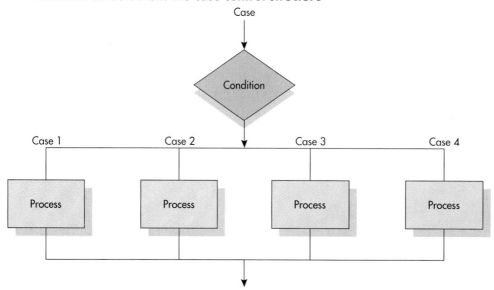

**Variation on selection: the case control structure**

Case

Condition

Case 1     Case 2     Case 3     Case 4

Process     Process     Process     Process

decision must be made by a program. An example of a selection structure is as follows:

```
IF a worker's hours in a week exceed 40
THEN overtime hours equal the number of hours
exceeding 40
ELSE the worker has no overtime hours.
```

A variation on the usual selection control structure is the case control structure. This offers more than a single yes-or-no decision. The case structure allows several alternatives, or "cases," to be presented. "IF Case 1 occurs, THEN do thus-and-so. IF Case 2 occurs, THEN follow an alternative course . . . " and so on. The case control structure saves the programmer the trouble of having to indicate a lot of separate IF-THEN-ELSE conditions.

3. The **iteration,** or **loop, control structure** represents a process that may be repeated as long as a certain condition remains true. There are two types of iteration structures—DO UNTIL (the most common form) and DO WHILE.

An example of a DO UNTIL structure is as follows:

```
DO read in employee records UNTIL there are no more
employee records.
```

An example of a DO WHILE structure is as follows:

```
DO read in employee records WHILE [as long as] there
continue to be employee records.
```

What seems to be the difference between the two iteration structures? It is simply this: If there are several statements that need to be repeated, you need to decide when to *stop* repeating them. You can decide to stop them at the *beginning* of the loop, using the DO WHILE structure. Or you can decide to stop them at the end of the loop, using the DO UNTIL structure. The DO UNTIL iteration means that the loop statements will be executed at least once before the statement to check whether to stop appears.

## Step 4—Test the Program: Getting the Bugs Out

**Program testing** involves running various tests, such as desk-checking and debugging, and then running real-world data to make sure the program works. (See Figure 7.22.)

Two principal activities are desk-checking and debugging.

- *Desk-checking:* **Desk-checking** is simply reading through, or checking, the program to make sure that it's free of errors and that the logic works. In other words, desk-checking is sort of like proofreading. This step should be taken before the program is actually run on a computer.

- *Debug the program:* Once the program is run on a computer, further errors, or "bugs," will doubtless surface. To **debug** means to detect, locate, and remove all errors in a computer program.

  Mistakes may be syntax errors or logic errors. **Syntax errors** are caused by typographical errors or incorrect use of the programming language. **Logic errors** are caused by incorrect use of control structures.

- *Run real-world data:* After desk-checking and debugging, the program may run fine—in the laboratory. However, it then needs to be tested with data from the real world. Indeed, it is even advisable to test it with bad data—data that is faulty, incomplete, or in overwhelming quantity—to see if you can make the system crash. Many users, after all, may be far more heavy handed, ignorant, and careless than programmers have anticipated.

**Figure 7.22**

The fourth step: program testing. The fourth step is to test the program and "debug" it so it will work properly. Programmers' use of the word bug dates from 1945, when a moth was discovered in the wiring of the Mark I computer. The moth disrupted the execution of the program.
1. Desk-check the program to discover errors.
2. Run the program and debug it.
3. Run real-world data.

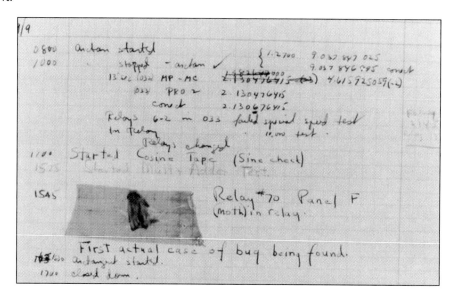

The testing process may take several trials using different data before the programming team is satisfied the program can be released. Even then, some bugs may remain, but there comes a point at which the pursuit of errors becomes uneconomical. This is one reason why many users are nervous about using the first version (version 1.0) of a commercial software package.

## Step 5—Collate the Documentation

Program documentation should have been going on since the very beginning of program development. The importance of this step cannot be overemphasized. (See Figure 7.23.) Without documentation, programmers may not be able to update the program in the future; diagnosis of problems will be difficult; identifying and eliminating any remaining bugs will be nightmarish; and users will have no instructions for using the program.

Program documentation should provide the following:

■ A permanent record of what the program does

■ Instructions for users on how to interact with the program

■ Instructions for computer operators on how to organize and control the processing of the program

■ Detailed documentation required for programmers to modify the program to meet new requirements

As you can see, program documentation is required at several levels: *user documentation, operator (technical) documentation,* and *programmer documentation.*

**User documentation** usually consists of simple step-by-step procedures that describe what the user is to do and how to do it plus report descriptions

**Figure 7.23**
The fifth step: program documentation. The fifth step is really the culmination of activity that has been going on all through the programming—documentation. Developing written descriptions and procedures about a program and how to use it needs to be done for different people—users, operators, and programmers.
1. Write user documentation.
2. Write operator documentation.
3. Write programmer documentation.

and sample output. User documentation is required for programs that have the user interacting directly with the computer during operation—such as entering data into the system, directing the processing, and requesting reports.

**Operator (technical) documentation** consists of a number of items prepared during the development of the program including:

- A narrative overview of what the program does

- A series of flowcharts or paragraphs of pseudocode depicting processing logic (or a combination of flowcharts and pseudocode)

- Examples of all reports produced by the program

- Examples of any display screen activity such as menus or softcopy reports

- A listing of the program language statements

**Programmer documentation** is required to train new programmers unfamiliar with the program to enable them to maintain it—that is, to keep it in working condition, error-free, and up to date.

As we have stated, the absence of good program documentation can create problems. Users can become frustrated when they try to work with the program. Programmers can have a very difficult time modifying programs they did not create if the documentation is inadequate. If a program is lost, it cannot be reconstructed without good documentation. And the need for good documentation doesn't apply just to custom-written programs: Be sure your microcomputer software comes with adequate documentation manuals!

## Programming's Future

The five-step structured programming techniques we have just discussed represent the traditional approach to creating programs. However, all that may change with the increased use of object-oriented programming languages. Indeed, some schools have already started teaching only object-oriented design techniques, which allow the design and ongoing improvement of working program models. Users can try out these models early in the development of new programs; thus they don't have to wait until the end of the entire process to discover what they said they wanted is really not what they want after all.

Object-oriented design uses a "fountain" model, in which programming stages overlap: Start at the bottom with analysis. Go up through design, coding, and testing; then fall back down through each stage to the bottom, and repeat the process.

This new approach to programming is not yet in place in business, but in a few years, it may be. If you are interested in becoming a computer programmer, this topic is worth paying attention to.

## Suggestions for Further Reading

Lammers, S. *Programmers at Work*. Redmond, WA: Microsoft Press, 1989.

Scott, D. F. *Programming Illustrated*. Indianapolis: Que Corp., 1994.

# S U M M A R Y

■ Programming languages can be divided into five generations (p. 220).

1. *Machine language*, the only language the computer's processor can understand, is *first-generation language*. Instructions and data are represented by binary digits (1s and 0s). Machine-language instructions run only on the computer for which they were designed—thus they are *machine dependent*. (p. 221)

2. *Assembly language* is easier to work with than machine language because it allows the programmer to use abbreviations. It is a *second-generation language*. (Both machine and assembly language are considered low-level languages.) (p. 222)

3. *High-level*, or *third-generation, languages* were developed to make writing software even easier by using human-language (for example, English-like) statements. High-level languages are *procedural languages;* that is, they tell the computer not only *what* to do but *how* to do it. Of the hundreds of high-level languages used today, the following are some of the popular ones:

   —*FORTRAN (FORmula TRANslator):* the first high-level language, formulated for scientific and technical applications; this language does not handle the input and output of large volumes of data efficiently. (p. 224)

   —*COBOL (COmmon Business Oriented Language):* its development as a common programming language for business applications was funded by the U.S. government; this language is noted for its machine independence and its data processing and file-handling capabilities. (p. 225)

   —*PL/1 (Programming Language 1):* designed to combine the computational capabilities of FORTRAN and the data processing and file-handling capabilities of COBOL. Although flexible, it is harder to learn than

COBOL and requires a great deal of main storage. (p. 226)

—*BASIC (Beginner's All-purpose Symbolic Instruction Code):* developed at Dartmouth College for instructional purposes, but now used on microcomputers and certain business systems to solve a variety of relatively simple problems. (p. 228)

—*RPG (Report Program Generator):* introduced by IBM as a program geared to deal with clear-cut problems and produce reports; users can produce reports by filling out special coding forms and then entering the recorded data. (p. 229)

—*C:* developed by Bell Laboratories as a tool for writing systems software such as UNIX. It works on a variety of different computers, including microcomputers. However, the code can be difficult to follow and it is not suited to applications that require a lot of report formatting. (p. 230)

—*Pascal:* named for 17th-century French mathematician Blaise Pascal. Developed to teach structured programming. Has strong mathematical, scientific, and graphics-processing capabilities and can be used on large and small computer systems; not used extensively in business. (p. 231)

—*Modula-2:* an improved version of Pascal; better suited for business; used primarily to write systems software, but can be used as an applications software development tool. (p. 231)

—*Ada:* named for Augusta Ada, Countess of Lovelace (the first programmer), and developed by the U.S. Department of Defense for use as an embedded system in computerized weapons systems. (p. 231)

4. *Fourth-generation languages* do not rely on a long list of detailed procedures that tell the computer how to do some-

thing. They just use human-language statements to tell the computer what to do, and so they are called *nonprocedural languages*. The three basic types of fourth-generation language tools are (a) *query languages*, (b) *report generators*, and (c) *applications generators*. (p. 232)

5. *Natural languages*, which some people refer to as *fifth-generation languages*, allow users and programmers to interact with the computer by using human language patterns that are much more natural than query languages. The use of natural language touches on *expert systems* and *artificial intelligence*. (p. 234)

■ Two new programming methods, object-oriented and visual programming, represent important developments for programmers.

1. *Object-oriented programming (OOP)* is a programming method that combines data with instructions for processing that data to make an *object* that can be reused in other programs. Object-oriented programming involves three important concepts: *encapsulation*, *inheritance*, and *polymorphism*. Examples of OOP programming languages are Smalltalk, C++, Turbo Pascal, and Hypertalk. (p. 234)

2. *Visual programming* is a method of creating programs in which the programmer makes connections between objects by drawing, pointing, and clicking on diagrams and icons. The goal of visual programming is to make programming easier for programmers and more accessible to nonprogrammers. (p. 237)

■ The *software development cycle* follows five steps:

1. Define the problem. (p. 239)

2. Map out the program logic—that is, work out the necessary algorithms. (p. 240)

3. Code the program. (p. 240)

4. Test the program. (p. 240)

5. Document the program. (p. 240)

■ Many tools and techniques are used to document program logic, including *program flowcharts, pseudocode, structure charts,* and *HIPO packages*. (p. 241)

■ *Program flowcharts* use standard symbols to represent the step-by-step activities and decision logic needed to solve a processing problem. Logic flow normally goes from top to bottom and left to right. (p. 241)

■ *Pseudocode* is a "fake" code—that is, it uses natural language statements instead of symbols. Pseudocode uses four keywords to portray logic: IF, THEN, ELSE, and DO. Repetitive processing logic is represented by DO WHILE, DO UNTIL, and END DO. (p. 244)

■ In an effort to bring more structure to the programming process than could be provided by flowcharts and pseudocode, the concept of structured programming was developed. *Structured programming* uses top-down design to break down main processing functions, called *modules*. Top-down design starts with the highest level of the program and works its way down to the lowest level of detail. *Structure charts* are often used to picture the organization and breakdown of modules. (p. 244)

■ When following the rules of structured programming, the programmer will use three control structures to form program code: (1) *sequence*, (2) *selection (if-then-else)*, and (3) *iteration*. (p. 247)

■ After a program has been designed, it must be tested by desk-checking, debugging, and running real-world data through the program. *Desk-checking* is simply reading through, or checking, the program to make sure that it's free of errors and that the logic works. To *debug* means to detect, locate, and remove all errors in a computer program. After desk-checking and debugging, the program should be tested with data from the real world and data that is faulty, incomplete, or in overwhelming quantity. (p. 249)

■ Documentation should be done throughout all steps of program development. *User documentation, operator (technical) documentation,* and *programmer documentation* provide guidance for all those who must use, maintain, and modify the program. (P. 250)

Ada, p. 231
American National Standards
  Institute (ANSI), p. 224
applications generator, p. 233
assembler, p. 223
assembly language, p. 222
BASIC, p. 228
C, p. 230
COBOL, p. 225
compiler, p. 223
control (logic) structure,
  p. 247
debug, p. 249
desk-checking, p. 249
fifth-generation languages,
  p. 234
flowchart, p. 241
FORTRAN, p. 224
fourth-generation languages
  (4GLs), p. 232
International Standards
  Organization (ISO), p. 224

interpreter, p. 223
iteration control structure
  (loop), p. 249
language processor, p. 223
logic error, p. 249
machine language, p. 221
Modula-2, p. 231
module, p. 244
natural language, p. 234
object, p. 235
object code, p. 223
object-oriented programming
  (OOP), p. 235
operator (technical)
  documentation, p. 251
Pascal, p. 231
PL/1, p. 226
programmer documentation,
  p. 251
programming language,
  p. 220
program testing, p. 249

pseudocode, p. 244
query language, p. 233
report generator, p. 233
RPG, p. 229
selection control structure,
  p. 247
sequence control structure,
  p. 247
software development cycle,
  p. 239
source code, p. 223
structured programming,
  p. 244
structured walkthrough,
  p. 246
syntax, p. 220
syntax error, p. 249
third-generation languages,
  p. 222
top-down design, p. 244
user documentation, p. 250
visual programming, p. 237

### SELF-TEST

1. The orderly process an organization goes through when identifying and developing its applications software program requirements is referred to as the ___SOFTWARE___ ___DEVELOPMENT___ ___CYCLE___.

2. The rules for using a programming language are called *syntax*. (true/false)

3. Machine language is a ___FIRST___-generation language.

4. ___BASIC___ is a relatively simple high-level language that was developed to help students learn programming.

5. Query languages, report generators, and applications generators are ___FOURTH___-generation languages.

6. Fifth-generation languages are often called ___NATURAL___ languages.

7. A query language allows the user to easily retrieve information from a database using English-like statements. (true/false)

8. A diagram that uses ANSI symbols to document a program's processing activities and logic is called a ___FLOW CHART___.

9. The ___OBJECT___ found in an object-oriented program can be reused in other programs.

10. Object-oriented programming involves encapsulation, inheritance, and polymorphism. (true/false)

*Solutions:* (1) software development cycle; (2) true; (3) first; (4) BASIC; (5) fourth; (6) natural; (7) true; (8) flowchart; (9) objects; (10) true

## SHORT-ANSWER QUESTIONS

1. How do third-generation languages differ from first- and second-generation languages? HUMAN LANGUAGE
2. What is natural language? FIFTH GENERATION
3. What is object-oriented programming, and what are its advantages over traditional programming methods?
4. What is visual programming? PROGRAM METHODS → MADE OBJECT BY DRAWING, POINT.
5. What are the three main types of fourth-generation language tools? query, report & appl. generator
6. What were the reasons behind the development of high-level programming languages?
7. What are flowcharts and pseudocode used for? Who developed the symbols used in flowcharts?
8. What is the difference between procedural and nonprocedural languages? WHAT TO DO
   WHAT & HOW TO DO ←
9. What are the five basic steps of software development? → DEFINE P, MAP LOGIC, CODE, TEST, DOCUMENT
10. Why is documentation important during program development?
11. Which high-level language is commonly used to create business applications? COBOL.

## PROJECTS AND CRITICAL THINKING EXERCISES

1. Some experts think that, before long, we will have only one *superapplication* to run on our computers instead of several separate applications packages. However, people in the computer industry are commonly overoptimistic about the speed at which new developments will occur. What do you think will be the obstacles to achieving such a superapplication?
2. Visit the computer laboratory at your school.
   a. Identify which high-level languages are available.
   b. Determine if each language processor identified is a compiler or an interpreter.
   c. Determine if the language processors are available for microcomputers, larger computers, or both.
   d. Identify any microcomputer-based electronic spreadsheet software and database management systems software. Have these been customized in any way? How and why?
3. Use the library and scan the employment ads in a few major newspapers from different areas of the country. Report on the high-level programming languages most in demand. What types of jobs require each language? Do any of these languages appear to be required in only certain regions of the country?
4. If you were a programmer, would you rather work on applications software or systems software? Think of as many reasons as you can to support your choice, and write a brief report.
5. Interview several students who are majoring in computer science and studying to become programmers. What languages do they plan to master? Why? What kinds of jobs do they expect to get? What kinds of future developments do they anticipate in the field of software programming?
6. Check the yellow pages in your phone book, and contact a company that develops custom-designed software. What languages do they use to write the software? Does this company follow the five stages of software development described in this book, or does it use another set of stages? If another set of software-development stages are used, what are they?

## IN THE LAB WITH MICROSOFT WINDOWS

(*Note:* If you aren't familiar with using a mouse and/or don't know how to use the Microsoft Windows graphical-user interface, complete the "In the Lab with Microsoft Windows" exercises in Chapter 6 before proceeding.)

### More Mouse Practice

1. One of the Windows exercises in Chapter 6 led you through using a mouse. In this section you get more practice using a mouse. Right now, the Microsoft Windows Program Manager should be displaying.
2. DOUBLE-CLICK: Games group icon
   DOUBLE-CLICK: Solitaire program icon
3. If you don't know how to play Solitaire:
   CHOOSE: Help, Contents
   CLICK: Rules of the Game *and then read the text in the Help window (press the Down arrow key to scroll the text upward)*
   When you're finished reviewing the rules:
   CHOOSE: File, Exit
4. Play the game by dragging cards to the correct locations.
5. When you're finished playing Solitaire:
   CHOOSE: Game, Exit
   The Program Manager window should be displaying.
6. To close the Games group window:
   DOUBLE-CLICK: Control-menu box *located in the upper-left corner of the Games window*

### Using Microsoft Write

1. In this section you learn the basics of using the Microsoft Write tool, which enables you to perform simple word processing tasks. Right now, the Microsoft Windows Program Manager should be displaying. In this exercise we lead you through creating a simple document.
2. DOUBLE-CLICK: Accessories group icon
   DOUBLE-CLICK: Write program icon
   The Write window should be displaying. The blinking cursor marks where the first character you type will appear.
3. Keep the following in mind when you type text using a word processing program:
   a. Most word processing programs operate in Insert mode. That is, the text you type and the commands you issue affect the document beginning at the current cursor position. In Insert mode, for example, you can insert a word in the middle of a sentence.
   b. When typing text, don't press Enter at the end of every line. When the right margin is reached, the text you're typing will automatically move to the next line. Press Enter to start a new paragraph.
   c. Press Backspace to delete the character to the left and Delete to delete the character to the right.
   d. Use the cursor-movement keys to move the cursor around a document. You can also use the mouse to position the cursor anywhere in a document. Just click where you want the cursor to be positioned.
   TYPE: Word processing software offers capabilities that greatly enhance the user's ability to create and edit documents. It enables the user to easily insert, delete, and move words, sentences, and paragraphs without ever using an eraser. Word processing programs also offer a number of features for "dressing up" documents with variable margins, type sizes, and styles. The user can do all these manipulations on screen, before printing out hardcopy.

4. Move the cursor to the top of the document by clicking at the beginning of the document before the "W" of "Word processing." The cursor should be blinking to the left of "W." (*Note:* If you accidentally selected the first line, click again to display a blinking cursor, and then repeat step 4.)

5. To insert a centered title at the top of the document:
   PRESS: Enter *twice*
   CLICK: *on the first blank line of the document*
   CHOOSE: Paragraph, Centered from the Menu bar
   TYPE: Word Processing Software

6. To boldface the title:
   SELECT: *the title by dragging the mouse over it*
   CHOOSE: Character, Bold

7. At this point, after reviewing your work, you would normally save the document onto the hard disk or a diskette. We will show you the save procedure now; however, you'll cancel the SAVE command before actually saving in case you don't have an available diskette.
   CHOOSE: File, Save
   Write is waiting for you to type in a name for the document. To name the document WP and save it onto a diskette in drive A:, for example, you would type **A:WP.** To save it into a diskette in drive B:, you would type **B:WP.** To complete the command you would press Enter. However, to cancel the SAVE command:
   CLICK: Cancel button

8. If your computer is connected to a printer, you can print the document you created:
   CHOOSE: File, Print
   PRESS: Enter

9. To close the Write program:
   DOUBLE-CLICK: Control-menu box *located in the upper-left corner of the Write window*
   CLICK: No *when asked if you want to save your work*

10. To close the Accessories group window:
    DOUBLE-CLICK: Control-menu box *located in the upper-left corner of the Accessories window*

# Chapter Topics

# CHAPTER 8

# Communications and Connectivity

Getting from here to there has always fascinated human beings, going farther and doing it faster. Aside from the thrills associated with speed, going places quickly means being able to stay connected with other people, to spread news and information and receive them in return—in other words, to *communicate*. Obviously, technology reached the point some time ago of allowing communication to occur without having to transport people from one place to another. In fact, today, computers, telephones, and wireless devices are being linked by invisible networks everywhere. In this chapter, we describe the data transmission media, hardware and software, and communications networks that have made this world of connectivity possible.

## Preview

*When you have completed this chapter, you will be able to:*

■ Identify four basic characteristics of data communications

■ Describe data transmission media and forms including twisted-pair and coaxial cable, fiber-optic cable, microwave and satellite systems, and wireless data transmission

■ Describe what modems, multiplexers, concentrators, and front-end processors are used for

■ Explain the purpose of communications software and protocols

■ Describe what a network is, and name and explain the common network types

■ List some practical uses of communications and connectivity

■ Explain what is meant by the terms *digital convergence* and *information superhighway*

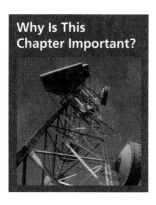

**Why Is This Chapter Important?**

*Technology often changes our society in ways that are hard to imagine beforehand. Elevators allowed skyscrapers in the city. Air-conditioning helped us settle the desert. Cars and interstate highways enabled people to commute from far away to work. Now computers and electronic communications—the movement of data and voice messages over long distances—promise another revolution.*

*One example is already seen in the rise of telecommuting, working at home and communicating with employer, co-workers, and clients by telephone-linked computer. Telecommuting spares employees the pressures and time of regular commuting, yet allows them to stay fully connected with and productive in their work world.*

*However, even non-telecommuters find that using communications to expand computer capabilities vastly increases their productivity. For example, connectivity allows them to exchange messages (electronic "mail") and computer files with users anywhere in the world, access a host of online services, post messages on bulletin board systems, participate in teleconferences, and travel the worldwide web of networks called the Internet.*

*In this chapter we describe the channels for data transmission, such as telephone lines and microwave dishes, and the hardware and software that let you use these transmission channels. We also explain networks and give some practical uses of communications and connectivity. We begin this chapter by describing four important characteristics of data transmission.*

## Characteristics of Data Communications

**Data communications signals can be in analog or digital form; in asynchronous or synchronous mode; flow in simplex, half-duplex, or full-duplex manner; and vary in frequency and bandwidth.**

All forms of data communications have certain characteristics:

1. Signal type: analog or digital
2. Transmission mode: asynchronous versus synchronous
3. Direction of flow: simplex, half-duplex, and full-duplex
4. Transmission rate: frequency and bandwidth

### Signal Type: Analog and Digital

As we described in Chapter 1, when we speak we transmit continuous sound waves, or **analog signals,** that form what we call the "voice." (See Figure 8.1.) Analog signals could be compared to a fairly steady stream of water coming out of a garden hose. Analog signals form a single, continuous wave that fluctuates a certain number of times over a certain time period; this fluctuation rate is called the **frequency,** measured in cycles per second, or **hertz.** Sometimes our voices sound high (composed of high-frequency sound waves: many wave fluctuations per second), and sometimes our voices sound low (composed of low-frequency sound waves: fewer wave fluctuations per second). Analog signals can also differ in **amplitude,** or loudness; a soft

**Figure 8.1**
Analog and digital signals. An analog signal represents a continuous electrical signal in the form of a wave. A digital signal is discontinuous, expressed as discrete bursts in on/off electrical pulses.

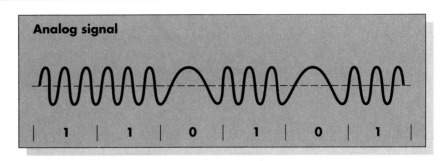

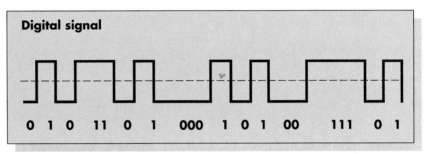

voice is at low amplitude. Most established telephone systems transmit data in analog form.

In contrast to human voices, computers communicate with each other in streams of binary digits (bits) [✔ p. 85] transmitted in patterns of **digital signals**—series of on and off pulses. These signals can be compared to the short bursts of water that shoot out of a timed garden sprinkler; they are discontinuous (discrete). For data to travel from one computer to another across the phone lines, the sending computer's digital data must first be converted into analog form and then reconverted into digital form at the receiving end. This process is called *modulation* and *demodulation*.

**Modulation** converts digital signals into analog form so that data can be sent over the phone lines. **Demodulation** converts the analog signals back into digital form so that they can be processed by the receiving computer. The hardware that performs modulation and demodulation is called a **modem** (**mo**dulate/**dem**odulate). The sending computer must be connected to a modem that modulates the transmitted data, while the receiving computer must be connected to a modem to demodulate the data. (See Figure 8.2.) Both modems are connected to the telephone line. (We describe modems in greater detail later in this chapter.)

**Figure 8.2**
How modems work. A sending modem translates digital signals into analog waves for transmission over phone lines. A receiving modem translates the analog signals back into digital signals.

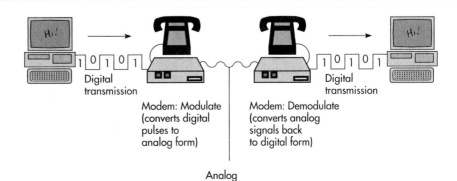

## Transmission Mode: Asynchronous and Synchronous

When signals are transmitted through modems from one computer to another, patterns of bits coded to represent data are sent one bit at a time. How does the receiving device know where one character ends and another starts? In **asynchronous transmission,** also called *start-stop transmission,* each string of bits that make up a character is bracketed by control bits (start and stop bits). (See Figure 8.3a.) In effect, each group of digital or analog signals making up the code for one character is individually "wrapped" in an electronic "envelope" made of a start bit (often symbolized by a 0), an error check bit (called a *parity bit*) [✔ p. 86], and one or two stop bits (often symbolized by a 1). Because asynchronous communication is inexpensive, it is widely used with microcomputers; however, it is also relatively slow, because of the number of error check bits that must be transmitted with the data bits.

In **synchronous transmission,** characters can be sent much faster because they are sent as blocks, or "packets." (See Figure 8.3b.) Header and trailer bytes are inserted as identifiers at the beginnings and the ends of blocks. In addition, error check bits are transmitted before the trailer bytes. Synchronous transmission is used by large computers to transmit huge volumes of data at high speeds. Expensive and complex timing devices must be used to keep the transmission activities synchronized. Synchronous transmission is rarely used in microcomputer-based communications lines.

## Direction of Transmission Flow: Simplex, Half-Duplex, and Full-Duplex

Besides signal type (analog or digital) and manner of data transmission (synchronous or asynchronous), data communications technology must also consider the direction of data traffic flow supported by communications links

**Figure 8.3**
Asynchronous and synchronous transmission. So that devices receiving data transmission can decode the beginnings and ends of data strings and check for transmission errors, the character strings are transmitted asynchronously or synchronously. Synchronous transmission takes less time because groups of characters are transmitted as blocks with no start and stop bits between characters.

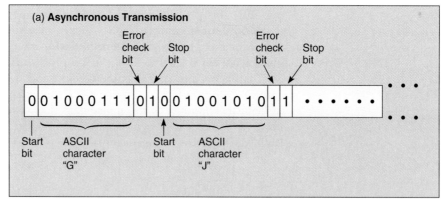
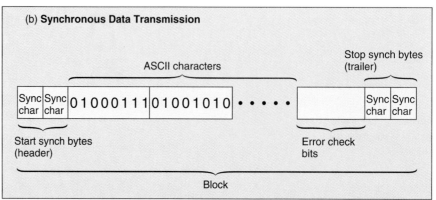

such as modems. In **simplex transmission,** data can travel in only one direction at all times. (See Figure 8.4.) For example, in some museum rooms, environmental devices send information about temperature, humidity, and other conditions to a computer that monitors and adjusts office environmental settings automatically. However, the computer does not send information back to the devices. The simplex mode is used occasionally in some local area networks, which we will discuss later.

In **half-duplex transmission,** data can travel in two directions, but in only one direction at one time. This mode of transmission is similar to using a CB (citizens' band) radio. When you press the transmit button you can talk, but you cannot receive. After you release the transmit button, you can receive, but you cannot transmit. Transmission of data in this mode over long distances can greatly increase the time it takes to communicate data. This delay is due to three factors: (1) the time needed for device A (at the receiving end) to change from receive to transmit mode, (2) the time required for device A to transmit to device B a request for confirmation that all is ready for transmission, and (3) the time required for device A to receive the confirmation that device B is ready to receive. The half-duplex transmission mode is frequently used for linking microcomputers via telephone lines.

In **full-duplex transmission,** data is sent in both directions simultaneously, similar to two trains passing in opposite directions on side-by-side tracks. This transmission mode eliminates the problem of transmission delay,

**H**

full-duplex

---

**Figure 8.4**
Data traffic moves in simplex, half-duplex, or full-duplex modes.

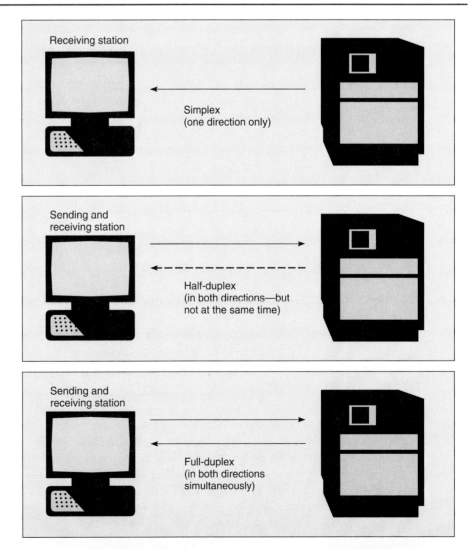

Receiving station

Simplex
(one direction only)

Sending and
receiving station

Half-duplex
(in both directions—but
not at the same time)

Sending and
receiving station

Full-duplex
(in both directions
simultaneously)

but it is more expensive than the other two modes because it requires special equipment. Full-duplex transmission is used primarily for mainframe [✓ p. 76] communications.

### Transmission Rate: Frequency and Bandwidth

Transmission rate is a function of two variables: frequency and bandwidth.

■ *Frequency:* The amount of data that can be transmitted on a channel depends on the wave **frequency**—the cycles per second. Frequency is expressed in hertz: 1 cycle per second equals 1 hertz. The more cycles per second, the more data that can be sent through that channel.

■ *Bandwidth:* **Bandwidth** is the difference between the highest and lowest frequencies—that is, the range of frequencies. Data may be sent not just on one frequency but on several frequencies within a particular bandwidth. Thus, the greater the bandwidth of a channel, the more frequencies it has available and hence the more data that can be sent through that channel. The rate of speed of data through the channel is expressed in bits per second (bps).

Channels that move data relatively slowly, like telegraph lines, are *narrowband* channels. Most telephone lines are *voiceband* channels, and they have a wider bandwidth than narrowband channels. *Broadband* channels (like coaxial cable, fiber-optic cable, microwave circuits, and satellite systems) transmit large volumes of data at high speeds.

## Data Transmission Media (Channels) and Forms

**(1) Electronic pulses (charges) transmit data over telephone lines and cables. (2) Electromagnetic waves transmit data through the air via microwave dishes and satellite. (3) Fiber-optic cable transmits data in the form of pulses of light. (4) Infrared, spread spectrum, and standard radio waves are used in wireless data transmission.**

To get from here to there, data must move *through* a medium. A telephone line, a cable, or the atmosphere are all transmission *media,* or *channels.* But before the data can be communicated, it must be converted into a form suitable for communication. The basic forms into which data can be converted for communication are as follows:

1. Electronic pulses or charges—used to transmit data over telephone lines or cable

2. Electromagnetic waves—used to transmit data through the air via microwave dishes and satellites

3. Light pulses—used to transmit data through glass fibers

4. Infrared, spread spectrum, or standard radio waves—used for some newer types of wireless data transmission

The form or method of communication affects the maximum rate at which data can be moved through the channel and the level of noise that will exist—for example, light pulses travel faster than electromagnetic waves, and some types of satellite transmission systems are less noisy than transmission over telephone wires. Obviously, some situations require that data be moved as fast as possible; others don't.

## Electronic Pulses: Telephone Lines and Coaxial Cable

### Telephone Lines

The earliest type of telephone line was referred to as *open wire*—unsheathed copper wires strung on telephone poles and secured by glass insulators. Because it was uninsulated, this type of telephone line was highly susceptible to electromagnetic interference; the wires had to be spaced about 12 inches apart to minimize the problem. Although open wire can still be found in a few places, it has almost entirely been replaced with cable and other types of communications media.

Cable is insulated wire. Insulated pairs of wires twisted around each other—called *twisted-pair cable* (see Figure 8.5)—can be packed into bundles of a thousand or more pairs. These wide-diameter cables are commonly used as telephone lines today and are often found in large buildings and under city streets. Even though this type of line is a major improvement over open wire, it still has many limitations. Twisted-pair cable is susceptible to various types of electrical interference (noise), which limits the practical distance that data can be transmitted without being garbled. (To be received intact, digital signals must be "refreshed," or strengthened, every 1 to 2 miles through the use of an amplifier and related circuits, which together are called *repeaters*. Although repeaters do increase the signal strength, which tends to weaken over long distances, they can be very expensive.) Twisted-pair cable has been used for years for voice and data transmission; however, newer, more advanced media are replacing it.

### Coaxial Cable

More expensive than twisted-pair wire, **coaxial cable** (also called *co-ax* or *shielded cable*) is a high-frequency transmission cable that replaces the multiple wires of telephone lines with a single solid copper core that is thickly insulated. (See Figure 8.5.) Coaxial cable has 80 times the transmission capacity of twisted-pair cable. The insulation is composed of a nonconductive material covered by a layer of woven wire mesh and heavy-duty rubber or plastic. Coaxial cable is similar to the cable used to connect your TV set to a cable TV service. Coaxial cables can also be bundled together into a much

---

**Figure 8.5**
Twisted-pair wire (a) does not protect well against electrical interference. Coaxial cable (b) is shielded against electrical interference. It can also carry more data than twisted-pair wire. When coaxial cable is bundled (c), it can carry more than 40,000 conversations at once.

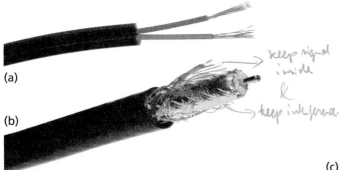

(a)

(b)

(c)

# THE CLIPBOARD

## Satellite Networks
## Rule the Skies

Few people exercise greater influence in the globe's daily business than the powerful but little-known group of men and women who manage the international satellite network.

They oversee a handful of consortia that finance research and operations, regulate use, and set prices in the fastest-growing sector of the telecommunications industry—effectively governing the aerial flow of broadcast images and telephone conversations worldwide.

One of the busiest players on this stage is John Tomlinson, 52, a 25-year veteran at British Telecommunications Plc, who represents the United Kingdom on the boards of the three leading satellite groups—Intelsat, Inmarsat, and Utelsat.

London-based British Telecom (BT) is the second largest corporate investor in the 1235-nation Intelsat, outranked only by Comsat, the body that acts jointly for all U.S. telecommunications firms in international negotiations.

Every phone call and fax transmission between the United States and Latin America or Africa, and a soaring percentage of its links to the rest of the world, rests on the deliberations of Tomlinson and his colleagues at Intelsat. Every live news image televised from the earthquake in Kobe, the Australian Open, and the Russian invasion of Chechnya was transmitted via Intelsat's 20 orbiting satellites.

Tomlinson describes the consortia that run international satellite communications:

> The leading members are clearly commercial rivals, and in many cases among the largest and most aggressive corporations around—BT, the Comsat companies, France Telecom, Deutsche Telekom, Telestra of Australia, KDD of Japan, Singapore Telecom, and Cable and Wireless of Hong Kong. But we all have to sit down at the same table and work together for the common good.

> It's a highly unusual situation. The board decides everything, on behalf of the entire membership: What sort of satellites to acquire. Where to put them in orbit. Who to purchase them from. Which rockets to launch them—American? Europeans? Russian? Chinese? Then we set a common wholesale price for satellite use. . . .

> Our product, quite simply, is satellite time, and our customers are telecom companies and television operators. Although developing companies remain the biggest users, traffic between Europe and North America is moving to fiber optic cables, which offer strong competition. But in other parts of the world, our business is growing very rapidly—by as much as 40% per year.

Excerpted from Frank Viviano, "Satellite Networks Rule the Skies," *San Francisco Chronicle,* Feb. 20, 1995, p. B2.

Satellite shop in the Indonesian capital, Jakarta.

larger cable. This type of communications line has become very popular because of its capacity and reduced need for signals to be refreshed (every 2 to 4 miles). Coaxial cables are most often used as the primary communications medium for locally connected networks in which all computer communication is within a limited geographic area, such as in the same building. Computers connected by coaxial cable do not need to use modems. Coaxial cable is also used for undersea telephone lines.

### Point-to-Point and Multipoint Lines

When devices are connected to a telephone line or coaxial cable line, one of two principal configurations is generally used: point-to-point and multipoint.

- *Point-to-point:* A *point-to-point line* is a single line that directly connects the sending and receiving devices, such as a terminal [✔ p. 43] and a central computer. There is no intermediate computer. This arrangement is appropriate for a private line whose sole purpose is to keep data secure by transmitting it only from one particular device to another.

- *Multipoint:* A *multipoint line* (also called a *multidrop line*) is a single line that interconnects several communications devices to one computer. Often on a multipoint line only one communications device, such as a terminal, can transmit at any given time.

## Electromagnetic Waves: Microwave and Satellite Systems

### Microwave Systems

electromagnetic waves

Instead of using wire or cable, **microwave systems** use the earth's atmosphere as the medium through which to transmit signals. These systems are extensively used for high-volume as well as long-distance communication of both data and voice in the form of electromagnetic waves. These waves are similar to radio waves but are in a higher frequency range.

Microwave signals are often referred to as "line of sight" signals because they cannot bend around the curvature of the earth; instead, they must be relayed from point to point by microwave towers, or relay stations, placed 20 to 30 miles apart. (See Figure 8.6.) The distance between the towers depends on the curvature of the surface terrain in the vicinity. The surface of the earth typically curves about 8 inches every mile. The towers have either a dish- or a horn-shaped antenna. The size of the antenna varies according to the distance the signals must cover. A long-distance antenna could easily be 10 feet or larger in size; a disk of 2 to 4 feet in diameter, which you often see on city buildings, is large enough for small distances. Each tower facility receives incoming traffic, boosts the signal strength, and sends the signal to the next station.

The primary advantage of using microwave systems for voice and data communications is that direct physical cabling is not required. (Obviously, telephone lines and other types of cable must physically connect all communications system points that can't receive atmospheric signals.) More than half of the telephone system now uses microwave transmission. However, in some areas, the saturation of the airwaves with microwave transmissions has reached the point where future needs will have to be satisfied by other communications methods, such as satellite systems.

### Satellite Systems

Satellite communications systems transmit signals in the gigahertz range—billions of cycles per second. The satellite must be placed in a geosynchronous orbit, 22,300 miles above the earth's surface, so it revolves once a day

**Figure 8.6**
Microwave systems. Microwaves cannot bend around corners or around the curvature of the earth. Therefore, microwave antennas must be in "line of sight" of each other—that is, unobstructed. Microwave dishes and relay towers are usually situated atop high places, such as mountains or tall buildings, so that signals can be beamed over uneven terrain.

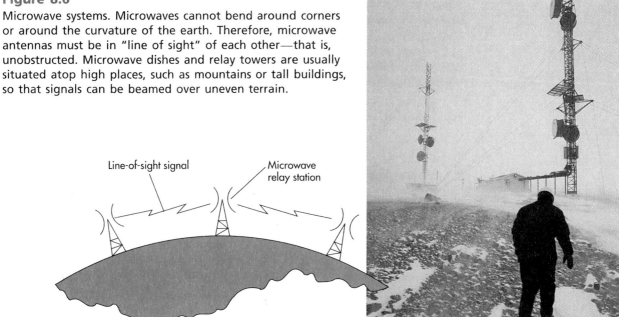

*with* the earth. (See Figure 8.7.) To an observer, it appears to be fixed over one region at all times. A **satellite** is a solar-powered electronic device that has up to 100 transponders (a *transponder* is a small, specialized radio) that receive, amplify, and retransmit signals; the satellite acts as a relay station between satellite transmission stations on the ground (called *earth stations*).

Although establishing satellite systems is costly (owing to the cost of a satellite and the problems associated with getting it into orbit above the earth's surface and compensating for failures), satellite communications systems have become the most popular and cost-effective method for moving large quantities of data over long distances. The primary advantage of satellite communications is the vast area that can be covered by a single satellite. Three satellites placed in particular orbits can cover the entire surface of the earth, with some overlap.

However, satellite transmission does have some problems:

1. The signals can weaken over long distances, and weather conditions and solar activity can cause noise interference.

2. A satellite is useful for only seven to ten years, after which it loses its orbit.

3. Anyone can listen in on satellite signals, so sensitive data must be sent in a secret, or encrypted, form.

4. Depending on the satellite's transmission frequency, microwave stations on earth can jam, or prevent, transmission by operating at the same frequency.

5. Signal transmission may be slow if the signals must travel over very long distances.

Companies must lease satellite communications time from suppliers such as Intelsat, Comsat, Inmarsat, Utelsat, and Telstar (AT&T). Large companies that have offices around the world benefit the most from satellite communications.

**Figure 8.7**
Satellite communications. (a) The satellite orbiting the earth has solar-powered transponders that receive microwave signals from the earth's surface, amplify the signals, and retransmit them to the earth's surface (b). Part (c) illustrates how various communications media can work together as communications links.

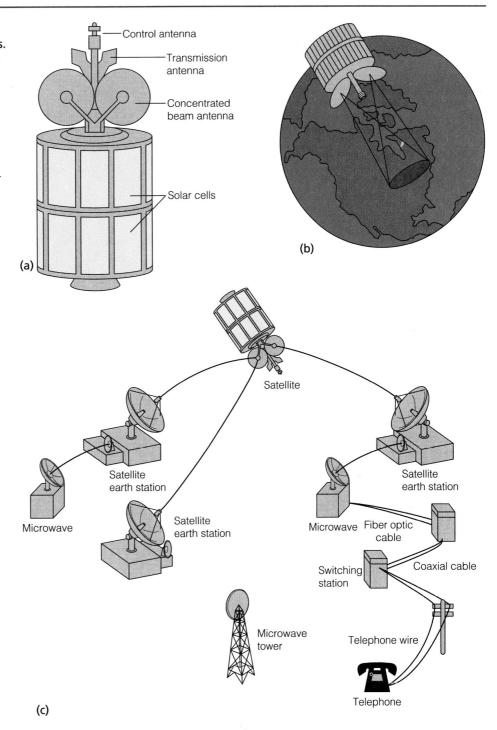

## Light Pulses: Fiber Optics

### Fiber Optics

Although satellite systems are expected to be the dominant communications medium for long distance during the rest of the 90s, fiber-optics technology is revolutionizing the communications industry because of its low cost, high transmission volume, low error rate, and message security. Fiber-optic cables are replacing copper wire as the major communications medium in buildings and cities; major communications companies are currently investing huge sums of money in fiber-optics communications networks that can carry *digital* signals, thus increasing communications capacity. (Computers connected by fiber-optic cables do not need to use modems.)

In **fiber-optics communications,** signals are converted to light form and fired by laser in bursts through insulated, very thin (2/1000 of an inch) glass or plastic fibers. (See Figure 8.8.) The pulses of light represent the "on" state in electronic data transmission and can occur nearly 1 billion times per second—up to 80 gigabytes of digital data per second can be sent through a fiber-optic cable. Equally important, fiber-optic cables aren't cumbersome in size: a fiber-optic cable (insulated fibers bound together) that is only 0.12 inch thick is capable of supporting nearly 250,000 voice conversations at the same time (soon to be doubled to 500,000). However, since the data is communicated in the form of pulses of light, specialized communications equipment must be used.

Fiber-optic cables are not susceptible to electronic noise and so have much lower error rates than normal telephone wire and cable. In addition, their potential speed for data communications is up to 10,000 times faster than that of microwave and satellite systems. Fiber-optic communications is also resistant to illegal data theft, because it is almost impossible to tap into it to listen to the data being transmitted or to change the data without being detected; in fact, it is currently being used by the Central Intelligence Agency. Another advantage to fiber-optic transmission is that electrical signals don't escape from the cables—in other words, the cables don't interfere with sensitive electrical equipment that may be nearby. Given its significant advantages, it is not surprising that fiber-optic cable is much more expensive than telephone wire and cable. (A twisted-pair telephone wire of 4 megahertz might send only 1 kilobyte of data in a second. A coaxial cable of 100 megahertz might send 10 megabytes. And a fiber-optic cable of 2 billion megahertz might send 1 gigabyte.)

AT&T has developed undersea optical fiber cables for transatlantic use in the belief that fiber optics will eventually replace satellite communications in terms of cost-effectiveness and efficiency. Japan has already laid an underwater fiber-optic cable. Sprint uses a fiber-optic communications network laid along railroad rights-of-way in the United States that carries digital signals (analog voice signals are converted to digital signals at company switching stations). Most of the "information superhighway" covered so much in the mass media today involves fiber-optic connections. (See The Clipboard: Digital Convergence and the Information Superhighway.)

**Figure 8.8**
Fiber-optic cable. Thin glass strands transmit pulsating light instead of electricity. These strands can carry computer and voice data over long distances.

# THE CLIPBOARD

## Digital Convergence and the Information Superhighway

The essence of all revolution, stated philosopher Hannah Arendt, is the start of a new story in human experience. For us, the "new story" is the fusion of several important industries in a unification called *digital convergence.*

**Digital convergence** is the technological merger of several industries through various devices that exchange information in the electronic, or digital, format used by computers. The industries are computers, communications, consumer electronics, entertainment, and mass media/publishing. Called "the mother of all industries," digital convergence has tremendous significance. It means that, from a common electronic base, information can be communicated in all the ways we are accustomed to receiving it. These include the media of newspapers, photographs, films, recordings, radio, and television. However, they also include newer technology—satellite, fiber-optic cable, cellular phone, fax machine, compact disk. More important, as time goes on, the same information may be exchanged among many kinds of equipment, all using the language of computers—0s and 1s.

This development signifies a shift from single, isolated technologies to a unified digital technology. This shift has given rise to the use of the term *information superhighway.* The **information superhighway,** which will be constructed mostly of fiber-optic cable, is a metaphor for a fusion of the two-way wired and wireless capabilities of telephones and networked computers with cable TV's capacity to transmit hundreds of programs. The resulting interactive [✓ p. 27] digitized traffic would include movies, TV shows, phone calls, databases, shopping services, and online services. This superhighway, it is hoped, would link all homes, schools, businesses, and government organizations. (See Figure 8.9.)

At present, this electronic highway remains a vision, much as today's U.S. interstate highway system was a vision in the 1950s. It is as though we still had old-fashioned Highway 40s and Route 66s, along with networks of one-lane secondary and gravel back roads. These, of course, have largely been replaced by high-speed blacktop and eight-lane freeways. In 40 years, will the world be as changed by the electronic highway as North America has been by the interstate highways of the past four decades?

However, before the new digital world is to be realized, much cooperation will be needed between hardware, software, and communications companies, along with agreement on standards for digitizing, integrating, storing, and manipulating all the information around us. In addition, it will take time to convert enough existing, nondigital materials for a broad base of information and to put in place the necessary fiber-optic networks and other equipment.

**Figure 8.9**
Information superhighway hookups of the future.

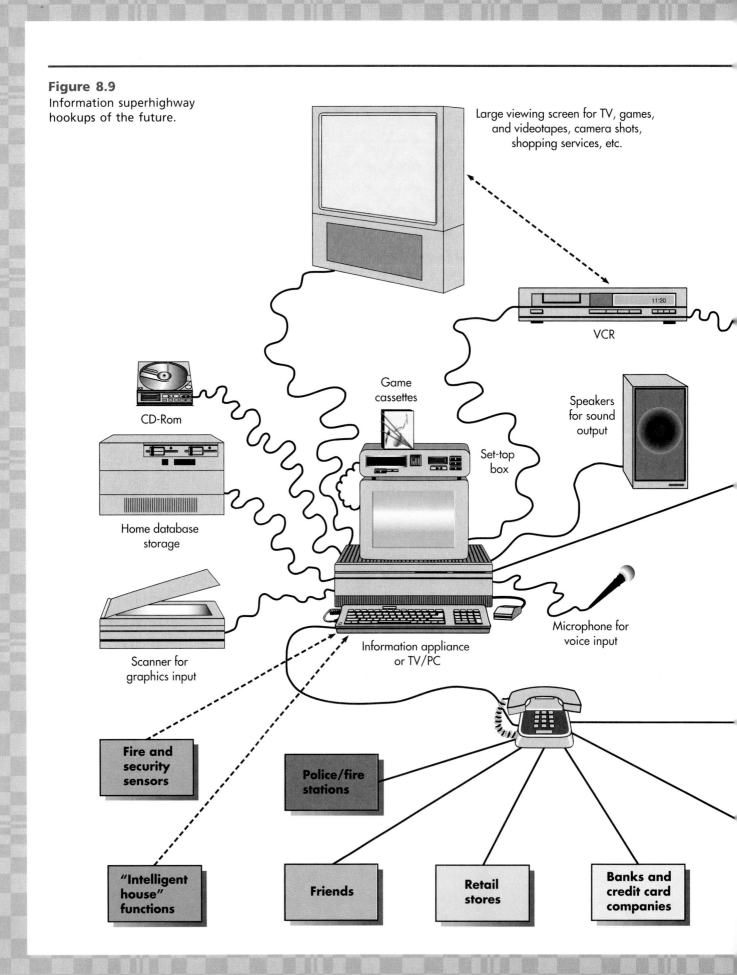

Large viewing screen for TV, games, and videotapes, camera shots, shopping services, etc.

VCR

CD-Rom

Game cassettes

Speakers for sound output

Set-top box

Home database storage

Scanner for graphics input

Information appliance or TV/PC

Microphone for voice input

Fire and security sensors

Police/fire stations

"Intelligent house" functions

Friends

Retail stores

Banks and credit card companies

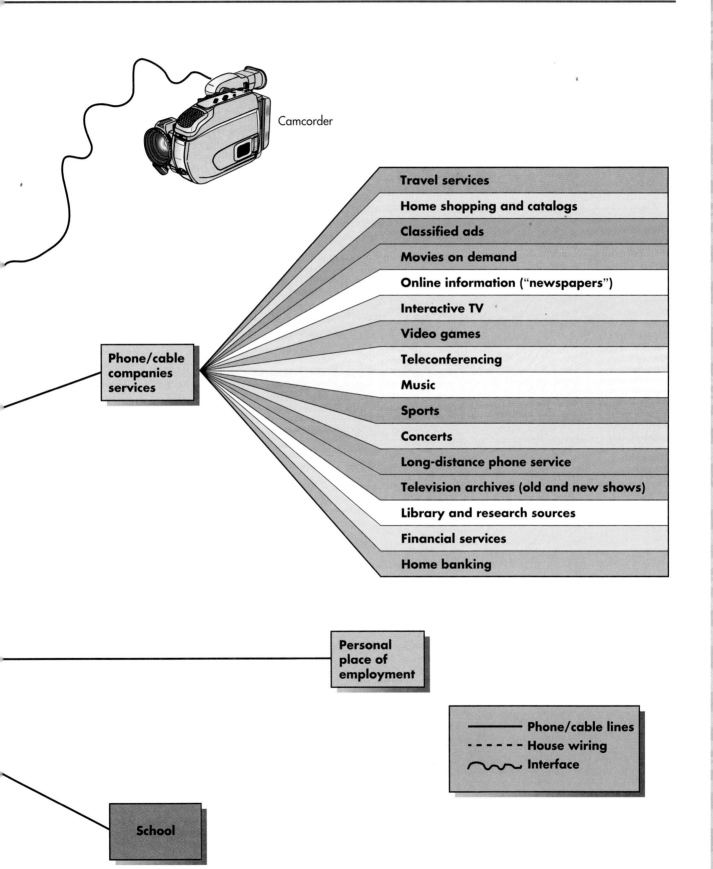

Camcorder

Phone/cable companies services

- Travel services
- Home shopping and catalogs
- Classified ads
- Movies on demand
- Online information ("newspapers")
- Interactive TV
- Video games
- Teleconferencing
- Music
- Sports
- Concerts
- Long-distance phone service
- Television archives (old and new shows)
- Library and research sources
- Financial services
- Home banking

Personal place of employment

——————— Phone/cable lines
- - - - - - House wiring
〜〜〜 Interface

School

### Wireless Transmission: Infrared, Spread Spectrum, and Standard Radio Waves

A new generation of wireless data communications devices is rapidly gaining attention. These devices use three basic technologies: infrared, spread spectrum, and standard radio transmission.

*Infrared (IR) technology* uses the same method as TV remote control units (invisible radiation at a particular frequency). However, transmission devices that use infrared must be within line of sight of one another and so cannot be used for mobile computing (objects may come between the transmission units).

*Spread spectrum* radio was developed by the U.S. Army during World War II for jam-proof and interception-proof transmissions. This technology is being used in small networks within individual buildings.

*Standard radio technology* is also being employed for data transmission in networks, but it involves some licensing difficulties. (Standard radio frequencies cannot be used without government licenses.)

### Communications Hardware, Software, and Protocols

**Communications hardware commonly used in business includes modems, fax modems, multiplexers, concentrators, and front-end processors. Communications software manages data transmission and controls error correction, data compression, remote control, and terminal emulation. Protocols set the standards for data transmission.**

Much of the hardware and software used in data communications is operated by technical professionals and is rarely of immediate consequence to the user unless it stops working—when you're calling from New York and can't reach your division office in London, for example. However, you should be familiar with certain types of communications hardware and the software that makes it run.

To access the transmission channels described in the last section, you must use communications hardware and software that adheres to certain standards for communicating, called *protocols*.

### Communications Hardware

First, let's discuss the communications hardware commonly used in business.

- Modems
- Fax modems
- Multiplexers, concentrators, and front-end processors

#### Modems

Modems are probably the most widely used data communications hardware. They are certainly the most familiar to microcomputer users who communicate with one another or with a larger computer. As you learned earlier in this chapter, the word *modem* is a contraction of *mo*dulate and *dem*odulate. A modem's basic purpose is to convert digital computer signals to analog signals for transmission over phone lines, then to receive these signals and convert them back to digital signals.

A modem allows the user to directly connect the computer to the telephone line. (See Figure 8.10.) Transmission speed is measured in **bits per second (bps).** Modems commonly transmit and receive data at 1,200 and

**Figure 8.10**

External versus internal modem. An external modem is a box that is outside the computer. An internal modem is a circuit board installed in an expansion slot inside the system cabinet.

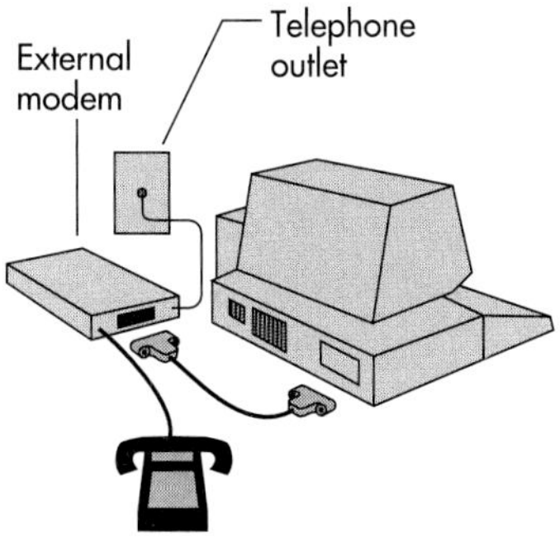

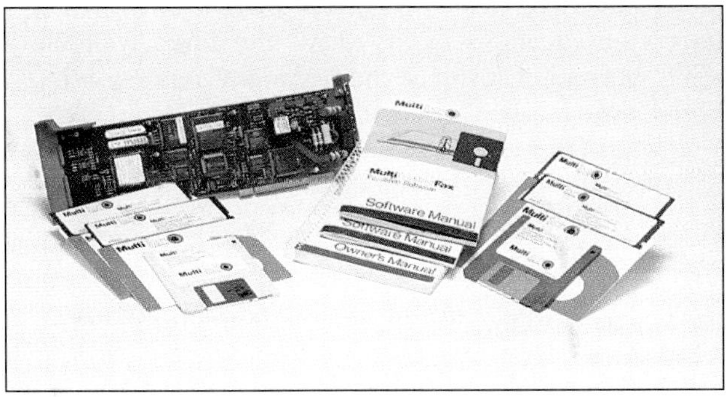

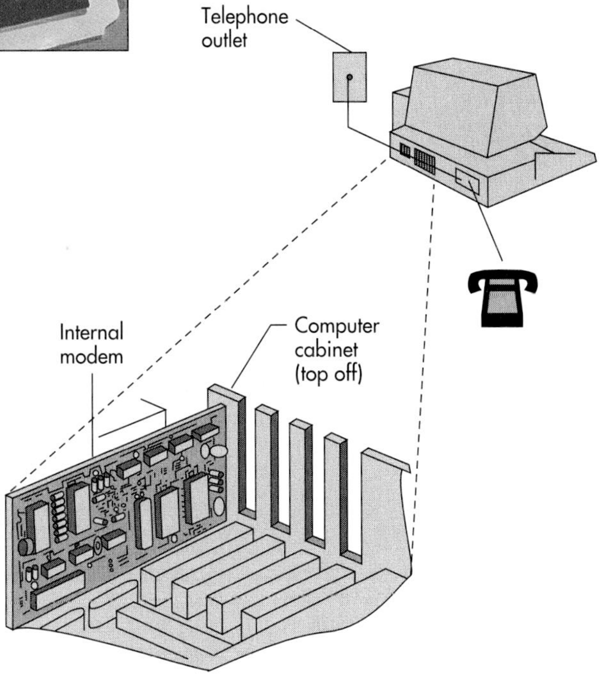

2,400 bps (considered slow); 4,800 and 9,600 bps (moderately fast); 14,400 and 19,200 bps (high speed); and 28,800 bps (very high speed). A 10-page single-spaced letter can be transmitted by a 2,400-bps modem in 2½ minutes. It can be transmitted by a 9,600-bps modem in 38 seconds and by a 19,200-bps modem in 19 seconds. (Note that high-speed modems will automatically adjust to run at slower speeds, but slower modems cannot adjust to run faster.)

Modems are either internal or external. An **internal modem** is located on a circuit board that is placed inside a microcomputer (plugged into an expansion slot) [✓ p. 96]. (See Figure 8.10.) The internal modem draws its power directly from the computer's power supply. No special cable is required to connect the modem to the computer. An **external** direct-connect **modem** is an independent hardware component—that is, it is outside the computer—and uses its own power supply. (See Figure 8.10.) The modem is connected to the computer via a serial cable plugged into a port [✓ p. 99].

IBM-type computers have four serial ports: COM1, COM2, COM3, and COM4. Since the mouse is connected to COM1, an external modem would be connected to COM2. The communications software (discussed shortly) that is used with the modem must also be set up to send transmitted data to COM2. (Macintosh computers have a serial modem port identified by an icon of a modem.)

### Fax Modems

A **fax modem,** which is installed as a circuit board inside the computer's system cabinet, is a modem with fax capability. It enables you to send data and scanned-in images directly from your computer to someone else's fax machine or fax modem. Fax modems are installed inside portable computers, including pocket PCs [✓ p. 73], as well as in desktop computers.

*Note:* Users who purchase modems and communications software should check the documentation [✓ p. 5] or ask the seller about compatibility. The modem and the software must be compatible with each other and with the user's computer.

### Multiplexers, Concentrators, and Front-End Processors

When an organization's data communications needs grow, the lines available for that purpose often become overtaxed, even if the company has leased one or more private telephone lines—called *dedicated lines*—used only for data communications. *Multiplexing* optimizes the use of communications lines by allowing multiple users or devices to share one high-speed line, thereby reducing communications costs. Multiplexing can be done by *multiplexers, concentrators,* or *front-end processors.*

multiplexer

- A **multiplexer** is a device that merges several low-speed transmissions into one high-speed transmission. Depending on the multiplexer model, 32 or more devices may share a single communications line. Messages sent by a multiplexer must be received by a multiplexer of the same type. The receiving multiplexer sorts out the individual messages and directs them to the proper recipient. High-speed multiplexers, called *T1 multiplexers,* which use high-speed digital lines, can carry as many messages, both voice and data, as 24 analog telephone lines. (See Figure 8.11.)

- Like a multiplexer, a concentrator is a piece of hardware that enables several devices to share a single communications line. However, unlike a multiplexer, a **concentrator** collects data in a temporary storage area. It then forwards the data when enough has been accumulated to be sent economically. Often a concentrator is a minicomputer.

- The most sophisticated of these communications-management devices is the front-end processor, a computer that handles communications for mainframes. A **front-end processor** is a smaller computer that is connected to a larger computer and assists with communications functions. The front-end processor is itself a minicomputer or even a mainframe. It transmits and receives messages over the communications channels, corrects errors, and relieves the larger computer of routine computational tasks.

  Sometimes the term *front-end processor* is used synonymously with the term *communications controller,* although this latter device is usually less sophisticated. (A communications controller handles communications between a computer and peripheral devices such as terminals and printer.)

**Figure 8.11**
How multiplexing works. With sending and receiving multiplexers, several low-speed transmissions may share a high-speed line; (*bottom*) multiplexer.

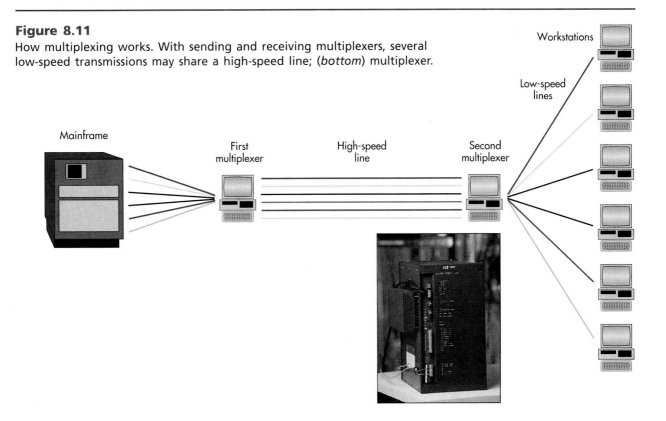

## Communications Software

Even with the best communications hardware, you won't be able to communicate with another computer without communications software. **Communications software** manages the transmission of data between computers and between computers and terminals. Popular microcomputer communications software packages include Smartcom, Crosstalk, ProComm, PC-Dial, Blast, and PC Talk. Often the software comes on diskettes bundled with (sold along with) the modem. Besides establishing connections between computers, communications software may perform other functions:

- *Error correction:* Static on telephone lines can introduce errors into data transmission, or "noise." *Noise* is anything that causes distortion in the signal when it is received. When acquiring a modem and its accompanying software, you should inquire whether it incorporates error-correction features.

- *Data compression:* **Data compression** reduces the volume of data in a message, thereby reducing the amount of time required to send data from one modem to another. The software does this by replacing repeating patterns with symbols that indicate what the pattern is and how often it is repeated. When the compressed message reaches the receiver, the symbols are then replaced and the full message is restored. With text and graphics, a message may be compressed to as much as one-tenth of its original size.

- *Remote control: Remote-control software* allows you to control a microcomputer from another microcomputer in a different location, perhaps even thousands of miles away. One part of the program is in the machine in front of you, the other in the remote machine. Such software is useful for travelers who want to use their home machines from afar. It's also helpful for technicians trying to assist users with support problems. Examples of remote-control software for microcomputers are Carbon Copy, Commute, Norton PCAnywhere, and Timbuktu/Remote.

■ *Terminal emulation:* Mainframes and minicomputers are designed to be accessed by terminals, not by microcomputers, which have different operating systems [✓ p. 197]. **Terminal emulation software** allows you to use your microcomputer to simulate a mainframe or minicomputer terminal. That is, the software tricks the large computer into acting as if it is communicating with a terminal. Terminal emulation is useful, for example, for microcomputer users who want to tap into a mainframe database for reference purposes.

## Protocols

Many of the terms you've come across in this chapter may seem unduly technical for an ordinary user. For example, terms like *simplex, half-duplex, full-duplex, asynchronous, synchronous,* and *multiplexing* are enough to make most people uneasy. Fortunately, when you sit down to send a message through a telecommunications system, you won't have to think about many of these terms. Experts will already have taken care of them for you in a set of rules called a protocol.

The word *protocol* is used in the military and in diplomacy to express rules of precedence, rank, manners, and other matters of correctness. (An example would be the protocol for who will precede whom into a formal reception.) Here, however, a **protocol,** or communications protocol, is a set of conventions (rules) governing the exchange of data between hardware and/or software components in a communications network.

Protocols are built into the hardware or software you are using. The protocol in your communications software, for example, will specify how receiver devices will acknowledge sending devices, a matter called *handshaking.* Protocols will also specify the type of electrical connections used, the timing of message exchanges, error-detection techniques, and so on.

In the past, not all hardware and software developers subscribed to the same protocols. As a result, many kinds of equipment and programs have not been able to work with one another. In recent years, more developers have agreed to subscribe to a standard of protocols called *OSI,* short for *Open Systems Interconnection.* Backed by the International Standards Organization, **OSI** is an international standard that defines seven layers of protocols for worldwide computer communications.

### ISDN

Traditional telephone lines are analog, but digital lines are also becoming available. Many common carriers offer ISDN, a technology that allows users to transmit data digitally through the traditional copper-based telephone network. *ISDN (Integrated Services Digital Network)* is a set of international communications standards for software control of transmitting voice, video, and data simultaneously as digital signals over twisted-pair telephone lines (traditionally an analog communications medium).

Basic rate ISDN provides better quality than analog connections and more reliable digital connections at higher speeds than those offered by traditional analog connections. ISDN has two types of access interfaces, or levels of service: basic rate interface (BRI) and primary rate interface (PRI). BRI and PRI were designed and priced for different levels of ISDN usage. BRI would suffice for most individual users; PRI would be used by large corporations with extensive dial-in requirements.

Research shows that ISDN usage is on the rise in both Europe and the United States. Dataquest—a company that does high-technology market analysis—projects the number of basic rate lines to grow from 790,000 in 1994 to 3.4 million in 1998. In January 1995, the Texas Public Utility Commission ordered that ISDN be available to all telephone customers in Texas by July 1, 1996.

# Networks

**Communications channels and hardware may have different layouts or networks, varying in size from large to small: wide area networks (WANs), metropolitan area networks (MANs), and local networks. Local networks may be private branch exchanges (PBXs) or local area networks (LANs). LANs may be client-server or peer-to-peer and include components such as cabling, network interface cards, operating system, other shared devices, and bridges and gateways. The topology, or shape, of a local area network may take five forms: star, ring, bus, hybrid, or FDDI.**

Information and resources gain in value if they can be shared. A **network,** or *communications network,* is a system of interconnected computers, telephones, and other communications devices that can communicate with one another and share applications and data. It is the tying together of so many communications devices in so many ways that is changing the world we live in.

### Types of Networks: Wide Area, Metropolitan Area, and Local

Networks are categorized principally in the following three sizes: *wide area, metropolitan area,* and *local.*

**H**

Acunet

A **wide area network (WAN)** is a communications network that covers a wide geographical area, such as a state or a country. Some examples of computer WANs are Tymnet, Telenet, Uninet, and Accunet. Of course, most telephone systems—long-distance, regional Bells, and local   are WANs.

A **metropolitan area network (MAN)** is a communications network covering a geographic area the size of a city or suburb. The purpose of a MAN is often to avoid long-distance telephone charges. Cellular phone systems are often MANs.

A **local network** is a privately owned communications network that serves users within a confined geographical area. The range is usually within a mile—perhaps one office, one building, or a group of buildings close together, as a college campus. In the following sections, we consider the following aspects of local networks:

■  Types of Local networks—PBXs and LANs

■  Types of LANs—client-server and peer-to-peer

■  Components of a LAN

■  Topology of LANs—star, ring, bus, hybrid, and FDDI

■  Impact of LANs

## Types of Local Networks: PBXs and LANs

The most common types of local networks are PBXs and LANs.

■ *Private branch exchange (PBX):* A **private branch exchange (PBX)** is a private or leased telephone switching system that connects telephone extensions in-house. (A *switched line* is a communications line that connects through a switching system to a variety of destinations.) A PBX also connects users to the outside telephone system.

A public telephone system consists of "public branch exchanges"— thousands of switching stations that direct calls to different "branches" of the network. A private branch exchange is essentially the old-fashioned company switchboard. You call in from the outside, the switchboard operator says "How may I direct your call?" and you are connected to the extension of the person you wish to talk to.

New PBXs can handle not only analog telephones but also digital equipment, including computers. However, because older PBXs use existing telephone lines, they may not be able to handle the volumes of electronic messages found in some of today's organizations. These companies may be better served by LANs.

■ *Local area network (LAN):* PBXs may share existing phone lines with the telephone system. Local area networks usually require installation of their own communication channels, whether wired or wireless. **Local area networks (LANs)** are local networks consisting of a communications link, network operating system software, microcomputers or workstations [✔ p. 74], servers, and other shared hardware. Such shared hardware might include printers, scanners, and storage devices. Unlike larger networks, LANs do not use a host computer.

## Types of LANs: Client-Server and Peer-to-Peer

Local area networks are of two principal types: client-server and peer-to-peer. (See Figure 8.12.)

■ *Client-server LANs:* A **client-server LAN** consists of the requesting microcomputers, called *clients,* and the supplying devices that provide a service, called *servers.* The server is a computer that manages shared devices, such as laser printers. The server microcomputer is usually a powerful one, running on a powerful chip such as a Pentium. Client-server networks, such as those run under Novell's NetWare [✔ p. 210] operating system, are the most common type of LAN.

There may be different servers for managing different tasks—files and programs, databases, printers. The one you may hear about the most often is the file server. A **file server** is a computer that stores the programs and data files shared by users on a LAN. It acts like a disk drive but is in a remote location.

A *database server* is a computer in a LAN that stores data. Unlike a file server, it does not store programs. A *print server* is a computer in a LAN that controls one or more printers. It stores the print-image output from all the microcomputers on the system. It then feeds the output to the printer or printers one document at a time. *Fax servers* are dedicated to managing fax transmissions, and *mail servers* manage electronic mail.

■ *Peer-to-peer LANs:* The word *peer* denotes one who is equal in standing with another (as in the phrases "peer pressure" or "jury of one's peers"). A **peer-to-peer LAN** is one in which all microcomputers on the network communicate directly with one another without relying on a server. Peer-to-peer networks are less expensive than client-server networks and work

**Figure 8.12**

Two types of LANs: client-server and peer-to-peer. *Top:* Client-server LAN. Individual microcomputer users, or "clients," share the services of a centralized computer called a server. In this case, the server is a file server, allowing users to share files of data and some programs. *Bottom:* Peer-to-peer LAN. Computers share equally with one another without having to rely on a central server.

**Client-server LAN**

File server

Shared network printer

Local printer

**Peer-to-peer LAN**

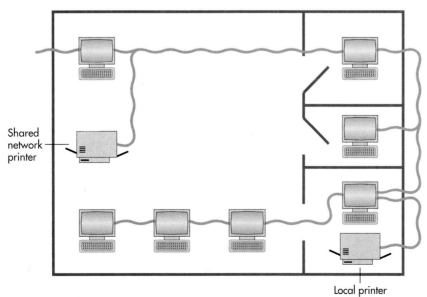

Shared network printer

Local printer

effectively with up to 25 computers. Beyond that they slow down under heavy use. They are thus appropriate for networking in small groups, as for workgroup computing. *Workgroup computing,* also called *collaborative computing,* enables teams of co-workers to use networks of microcomputers to share information and cooperate on projects.

Software used for peer-to-peer networking includes LANtastic by Artisoft, Localtalk by Apple, and Windows for Workgroups by Microsoft. Many LANs mix elements from both client-server and peer-to-peer models.

## Components of a LAN

Local area networks are made up of several standard components. (See Figure 8.13.)

■  *Connection or cabling system:* LANs do not use the telephone network. Instead, they use some other cabling or connection system, either wired or wireless. Wired connections may be twisted-pair wiring, coaxial cable, or fiber-optic cable. Wireless connections may be infrared or radio-wave transmission. Wireless networks are especially useful if computers are portable and are moved often. However, they are subject to interference.

---

**Figure 8.13**
Components of a typical LAN.

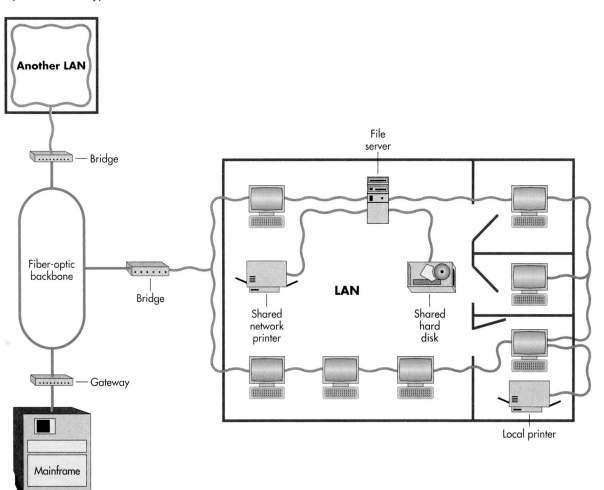

- *Microcomputers with interface cards:* Two or more microcomputers are required, along with network interface cards. A *network interface card,* which is inserted into an expansion slot in a microcomputer, enables the computer to send and receive messages on the LAN.

- *Network operating system:* The network operating system software manages the activity of the network. Depending on the type of network, the operating system software may be stored on the file server or on each microcomputer on the network. Examples of network operating systems are Novell's NetWare, Microsoft's LAN Manager, and IBM's PC LAN.

- *Other shared devices:* Printers, fax machines, scanners, storage devices, and other peripherals may be added to the network as necessary and shared by all users.

- *Bridges and gateways:* A LAN may stand alone, but it may also connect to other networks, either similar or different in technology. Hardware and software devices are used as interfaces to make these connections. A **bridge** is an interface that enables similar networks to communicate. A **gateway** is an interface that enables dissimilar networks to communicate, such as a LAN with a WAN.

## Topology of LANs

Networks can be laid out in different ways. The physical layout, or shape, of a network is called its *topology.* The five basic topologies are star, ring, bus, hybrid, and FDDI. (See Figure 8.14.)

- *Star network:* A **star network** is one in which all microcomputers and other communications devices are connected to a central hub, such as a file server or host computer. Electronic messages are routed through the central hub to their destinations. The central hub monitors the flow of traffic. A PBX system is an example of a star network.

  The advantage of a star network is that the hub prevents collisions between messages. Moreover, if a connection is broken between any communications device and the hub, the rest of the devices on the network will continue operating.

- *Ring network:* A **ring network** is one in which all microcomputers and other communications devices are connected in a continuous loop. Electronic messages are passed around the ring until they reach the right destination. There is not a central host computer or server. An example of a ring network is IBM's Token Ring Network.

  The advantage of a ring network is that messages flow in only one direction. Thus, there is no danger of collisions. The disadvantage is that if a connection is broken, the entire network stops working.

- *Bus network:* The bus network works like a bus system at rush hour, with various buses pausing in different bus zones to pick up passengers. In a **bus network,** all communications devices are connected to a common channel. There is no central computer or server. Each communications device transmits electronic messages to other devices. If some of those messages collide, the device waits and tries to retransmit again. An example of a bus network is Xerox's Ethernet.

  The advantage of a bus network is that it may be organized as a client-server or peer-to-peer network. The disadvantage is that extra circuitry and software are needed to avoid collisions between data. Also, if a connection is broken, the entire network may stop working.

**Figure 8.14**

Three LAN topologies: star, ring, bus. *Top:* Star network. This arrangement connects all the network's devices to a central host computer, through which all communications must pass. *Middle:* Ring network. This arrangement connects the network's devices in a closed loop. If one component fails, the whole system fails. *Bottom:* Bus network. A single channel connects all communications devices.

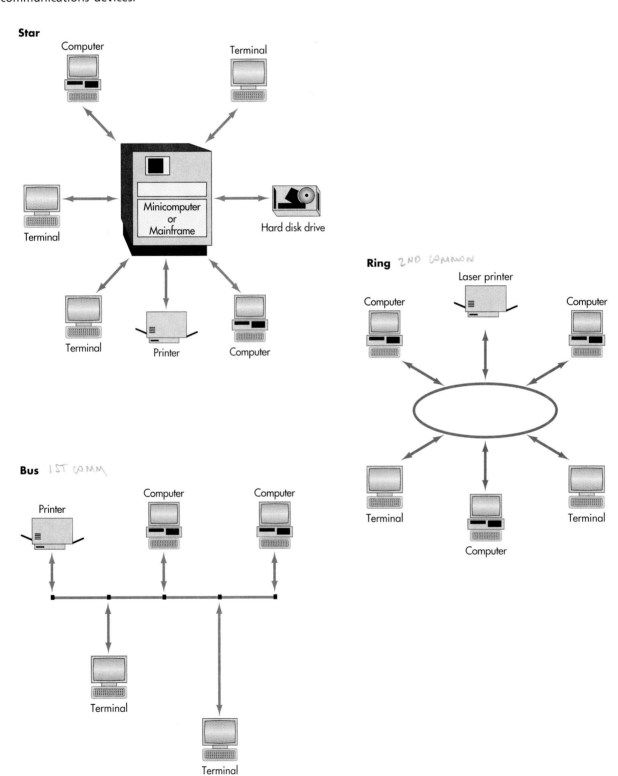

■ *Hybrid network:* **Hybrid networks** are combinations of star, ring, and bus networks. For example, a small college campus might use a bus network to connect buildings and star and ring networks within certain buildings.

■ *FDDI network:* A newer, higher-speed network is the FDDI, short for Fiber Distributed Data Interface. Capable of transmitting 100 megabits per second, an *FDDI network* uses fiber-optic cable with a dual counter-rotating ring topology. The FDDI network is being used for such high-tech purposes as electronic imaging, high-resolution graphics, and digital video.

### The Impact of LANs

Sales of mainframes and minicomputers have been falling for some time. This is largely because companies have discovered that LANs can take their place for many functions, and at considerably less expense. This situation reflects a trend known as *downsizing.* Still, a LAN, like a mainframe, requires a skilled support staff. Moreover, LANs have neither the great storage capacity nor the security that mainframes have, so they are not useful for some applications.

## Some Practical Uses of Communications and Connectivity

**With connected communications devices, or connectivity, users can access telephone-related services such as fax, voice mail, and electronic mail. They can do teleconferencing. They can share resources through workgroup computing and Electronic Data Interchange. They can use online services for research, electronic mail, games, travel services, and teleshopping. They can connect with the Internet. They can make their work portable with telecommuting and mobile workplaces.**

What kinds of options do communications and connectivity give you? Here are some possibilities:

■ Telephone-related communications services

■ Online information services

■ Electronic bulletin board systems

■ The Internet

■ Telecommuting

### Telephone-Related Communications Services: Voice Mail, E-Mail, and Teleconferencing

Phones and computers have begun to fuse together. On the one hand, there are computerized telephones, such as the Enhanced Telephone produced by Phillips Electronics. Computerized telephones have display screens (LCD screens), keyboards for typing in messages, and hardware for sending faxes. On the other hand, there are handheld computers or "personal communicators," which contain wired or wireless communications devices. An example is the Simon from IBM/BellSouth.

Services available through telephone connections, whether the conventional wired kind or the wireless cellular-phone type, include *voice mail, e-mail,* and *teleconferencing:*

■ *Voice mail:* Voice mail systems, or voice-messaging systems, are essentially computer-based answering machines. **Voice mail** digitizes incoming voice messages and stores them in the recipient's "voice mailbox" in digitized form. It then converts the digitized versions back to voice messages when they are retrieved.

Unlike conventional answering machines, voice mail systems allow callers to direct their calls within an office by pressing numbers on their touch-tone phone. No doubt you have dialed a company's number and gotten a recording that presented a "menu" of different options. ("If you wish to talk to someone in customer services, press 1; for other information, press 0.")

Voice mail systems also allow callers to deliver the same message to many people within an organization. They can forward calls to the recipient's home or hotel. They allow the person checking messages to speed through them or to slow them down. He or she can save some messages and erase others and can dictate replies that the system will send out.

The main benefit is that voice mail helps eliminate "telephone tag." That is, two callers can continue to exchange messages even when they can't reach each other directly.

- *E-mail:* **E-mail,** or **electronic mail,** links computers by wired or wireless connections and allows users, through their keyboards, to post messages and to read responses on their display screens. (See Figure 8.15.) E-mail allows "callers," or users, to send messages to a single recipient's "mailbox," which is simply a file stored on a computer system. Or they can send the same message to multiple users on the same system.

As with voice mail, e-mail helps users avoid playing "telephone tag." It also offers confidentiality. Recipients cannot get into their "mailboxes" to pick up messages unless they enter a *password,* a secret word or number that limits access.

To send a message, you access your communications software program. Then you type in the e-mail system's telephone number on your computer keyboard. You next type in the name or number of the recipient's mailbox, and then type in the message and send it by, for example, clicking with the mouse on the "send" box displayed on the screen. The

**Figure 8.15**
E-mail. This screen
appears on CompuServe.

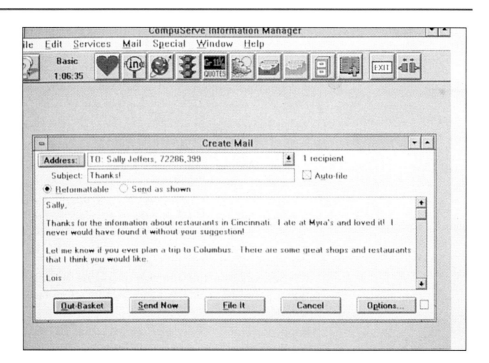

same message can be delivered to several other mailboxes on the system at the same time.

To gain access to your mailbox, you dial the e-mail system's telephone number and type in the name or number of your mailbox and your password. The display screen will then show a list of the senders, subjects, and dates and times of messages received. You can then read messages of interest, delete those not of interest, and transfer ("download") to your hard disk those messages you want to keep.

E-mail has jumped in use, especially in large organizations, where it helps to speed the exchange of memos and scheduling of appointments. Often a company will use its own specialized computer network. However, sometimes outside online information services such as CompuServe and Prodigy are used. E-mail not only speeds communications, it can also reduce telephone, postage, and secretarial costs. As a result, there has been a 3,000% increase in e-mail use within the last 10 years.

■ *Teleconferencing:* **Teleconferencing** is a meeting among people remote from one another who are linked by communications devices, usually computers and telephones. There are five types of teleconferencing: (1) *Audio conferencing,* which is often called a *conference call;* it links people in various locations by telephone only. (2) *Video teleconferencing,* usually called *video conferencing,* links people by phone lines and video cameras and monitors, so that the participants can see one another. (3) *Computer conferencing* is a keyboard conference among several users at microcomputers or terminals linked by a network. (4) *Document conferencing* allows meeting participants not only to see and hear one another but to work on text and graphics projects at the same time. (5) *Personal videoconferencing,* or *desktop videoconferencing,* combines video conferencing with computer and document conferencing.

## Online Information Services

"We have gone from sitting by the radio for fireside chats to seeing a war start while watching CNN one evening," wrote the contributor to a Seniornet Online electronic talk forum, "from hearing about the invasion of Poland a day later on the radio to watching the butchery in the former Yugoslavia nightly, from the agony of plucking and cleaning chickens to the joy of buying them bare-bottom clean. . . . The point is, we cannot stagnate."[1]

Whatever the truth of these comments about old patterns of perception, it's clear that not all older people are closed to new ideas and technologies. With 9,200 members 55 years of age or older, Seniornet has contradicted erroneous stereotypes about aging ever since it was founded in 1986. Seniornet Online is a section of America Online, an online information service or "information utility."

An **online information service** provides access to all kinds of databases and electronic meeting places for subscribers equipped with telephone-linked microcomputers. Says one writer:

> Online services are those interactive news and information retrieval sources that can make your computer behave more like a telephone; or a TV set; or a newspaper; or a video arcade, a stock brokerage firm, a bank, a travel agency, a weather bureau, a department store, a grocery store, a florist, a set of encyclopedias, a library, a bulletin board and more.[2]

There are many online services, but the five that are considered the most mainstream and have the most subscribers are *Prodigy, CompuServe, America Online, GEnie,* and *Delphi.*

Other important online services are considered valuable for their research capabilities. These include *Dialog*, which provides access to thousands of periodicals and specialized documents, and *Dow Jones News Retrieval*, which offers business news and information. *Nexis*, frequently used by journalists and other researchers, has an electronic library of hundreds of periodicals. *Lexis* is useful for lawyers for its comprehensive offerings of state, federal, and international law.

New information services seem to appear all the time. Apple Computer has formed an online service, *eWorld*, that uses a shopping mall format. Ziff-Davis, a publisher of computer magazines (*PC Week, MacWeek*), launched Interchange Online Network. This network is for serious PC users and requires more-than-ordinary computing power. Microsoft Corp. has also launched *The Microsoft Network*, which is expected to expand from a customer hotline into a full-blown information service. It will probably resemble America Online, with news, shopping, and "chat lines" or talk forums.[3]

To use these services, you need a *microcomputer*, with hard disk and printer. You also need a *modem*—as we have explained, the hardware that, when connected to your phone line, enables data from these services to be transmitted over telephone lines to your computer. Finally, you need *communications software*, so your computer can communicate via modem and interact with distant computers that have modems.

Communications software is often sold with (is bundled with) modems. Popular information services such as Prodigy, CompuServe, and America Online provide subscribers with their own software programs for going online. You can also buy communications programs as part of integrated software [✓ p. 187] packages (such as Lotus Works or Microsoft Works) or as single-purpose programs (such as Procomm Plus).

Before you can use an online information service, you need to open an account with it, using a credit card. Billing policies resemble those used by cable-TV and telephone companies. As with cable TV, you may be charged a fee for basic service, with additional fees for specialized services. In addition, the online service may charge you for the time you spend online. Finally, you will also be charged by your telephone company the same way you are charged for a regular phone call. However, most information services offer local access numbers. Thus, unless you live in a rural area, you will not be paying long-distance phone charges. All told, the typical user may pay $10–$20 a month to use an online service.

Imagine yourself one of the millions of subscribers connected to an online service. What kinds of things could you use it for? Here are some of the options:

■ *Research:* The only restriction on the amount of research you can do online is the limit on whatever credit card you are charging your time to. Depending on the online service, you can avail yourself of several encyclopedias. (*Compton's Interactive Encyclopedia* is available through Prodigy, *Grolier Academic American Encyclopedia* through CompuServe, and both through America Online.)

Many online services store unabridged text from newspapers and magazines. CompuServe's Magazine Database Plus carries full-text articles from more than 90 general-interest publications (business, science, sports, and so on). Newspaper Library contains selected full-text articles from 48 U.S. newspapers. With Prodigy you can choose from a banquet of information: book and movie/video news, contests, health reports, parenting advice, car-rental information, microwave cooking instructions, and on and on. Dow Jones News Retrieval is a collection of 46 databases, most of them directed at the business user or investor. Scientific publishers such as Elsevier are putting scientific and technical journals online to allow scientists to read articles as soon as they have been peer-reviewed and accepted and to look up other articles cited in the text, query authors, find out about new products, and track job vacancies in their field.

The information resources available online are mind-boggling, impossible to describe in this short space.

- *Electronic mail:* Many people who do not have a private e-mail system through their work can set up an electronic mailbox through a commercial online service. Also, some businesses use CompuServe, Prodigy, and others for e-mail.

- *Games:* Online computer games are extremely popular. A poll of Prodigy subscribers showed that computer games were the second most popular application for respondents in general and the first for members under 25.[4] Games may be single-player, in which you play against the computer. Or they may be multi-player, in which you play against other people, whether members of your household or individuals all over the world. Online games also offer subscribers a chance to interact and socialize.

- *Travel services:* A good travel agent is probably still one of the best deals around, because most of the services he or she provides are free to travelers. However, if you have the time to plan and plot trips, online services may be a gold mine. For instance, they allow you to play out "what if" scenarios to test various travel dates and routes for the cheapest fares. Online services use Easy Saabre or Travelshopper, streamlined versions of the reservations systems travel agents use. You can search for flights and book reservations through the computer and have tickets sent to you by Federal Express. You can also refer to weather maps, which show regions of interest. In addition, you can review hotel directories, such as the ABC Worldwide Hotel Guide, and restaurant guides, such as the Zagat Restaurant Directory.[5]

- *Shopping:* For many Americans, shopping is the national pastime. But if you're unable or unwilling to endure parking problems, limited store hours, and checkout lines, online services provide an alternative. CompuServe, for instance, offers 24-hour shopping with its Electronic Mall. This feature lists products from over 100 retail stores, discount wholesalers, specialty shops, and catalog companies. You can scan through listings of merchandise, order something on a credit card with a few keystrokes, and have the goods delivered by UPS or U.S. mail.

In some cities it's even possible to order groceries through online services. Peapod Inc. is an online grocery service serving 3,000 households in the Chicago and San Francisco areas. Peapod offers 18,000 items in the online Jewel Foodstore or Safeway, depending on the city. Users can shop by brand name, category, or store aisle, and they can use coupons. Specially trained Peapod shoppers handle each order, even selecting the best produce available. The orders are then delivered in temperature-controlled containers.

## Electronic Bulletin Board Systems

An **electronic bulletin board system (BBS)** is a centralized information source and message-switching system for a particular computer-linked interest group. There seem to be no limits to the topics of "conferences" or high-tech talk forums on bulletin boards, from bird watchers to socialists to fans of France to Star Trekkies. In many ways, BBSs resemble a workgroup's e-mail, except that they are not private in-house systems.

Public-access BBSs have become an amazing social phenomenon. By 1992, they had skyrocketed to perhaps 60,000 and become an enormous, billion-dollar industry. Once the preserve of hackers and electronics buffs, BBSs seem to be transforming American life, uniting individuals with similar interests and concerns. Indeed, says one report, the computer used as electronic connection is "making people feel intimately connected. And it's the very impersonality of the instrument that does the job."[6]

Computer bulletin boards are basically of two types—big ones operated by giant corporations, and small ones operated by individuals:

■ *Large commercial BBSs:* All the major online services, such as America Online, CompuServe, and Prodigy, operate bulletin boards. These and other online services—GEnie, Delphi—offer something for everyone. However, BBSs are only *one* of several services offered by commercial online services. And, of course, you are charged by the organization for using this particular feature.

■ *Small BBSs:* Small BBSs may be free or for-profit, but they are generally run by individuals, quite often out of their homes, and they are typically oriented toward a particular subject. BBS system operators are called **sysops.** BBSs are listed at the rate of 500–700 a month in the magazine *Boardwatch.*

Boardwatch

   An example of a large BBS is Exec-PC BBS in Elm Grove, Wisconsin, which gets more than 5,000 calls a day over 280 phone lines. Founder Bob Mahoney, who runs it with his wife Tracy and two employees, says, "Our gross revenues approach $1 million a year."[7] Most BBSs are not so profitable.

"Typically, BBSs are targeted at a particular single-issue topic," says one expert, "and online services are kind of like department stores that have a thousand different topics that are being talked about."[8]

## The Internet

The computer, modem, and telephone line that can be used to explore online services and BBSs can also be used to connect with the Internet. Whereas there may be 6 million or so users of commercial online services, there are now an estimated 25 million people worldwide using the Internet.[9] Called "the mother of all networks," the **Internet** is an international network connecting approximately 11,000 smaller networks. (See Figure 8.16.)

Created by the U.S. Department of Defense in 1969 (under the name ARPAnet), the Internet was meant to serve two purposes: (1) to share research between the military, industry, and university sources, and (2) to sustain communication in the event of nuclear attack. Today the Internet is essentially a self-governing and noncommercial community offering the following features, not just to scholars but to the general public:

■ *Information gathering:* "Try as you may," says one writer, "you cannot imagine how much data is available on the Internet."[10] There are hundreds of online databases from various universities and other research institutions and online library catalogs of all sorts. And, unfortunately, there's no directory of everything available.

   A sampling: The Library of Congress card catalog, the daily White House press releases, weather maps and weather forecasts, schedules of professional sports teams, weekly Nielsen television ratings, recipe archives, Central Intelligence Agency world map, the zip code guide, National Family Database, Project Gutenberg (offering complete text of many works of literature), Alcoholism Research Data Base, guitar chords, U.S. government addresses and phone (and fax) numbers, and *The Simpsons* archive.[11]

**Figure 8.16**
Internet: the network of all networks. *Top:* Nations with full access to the Internet worldwide computer network. *Bottom:* What's in Internet.

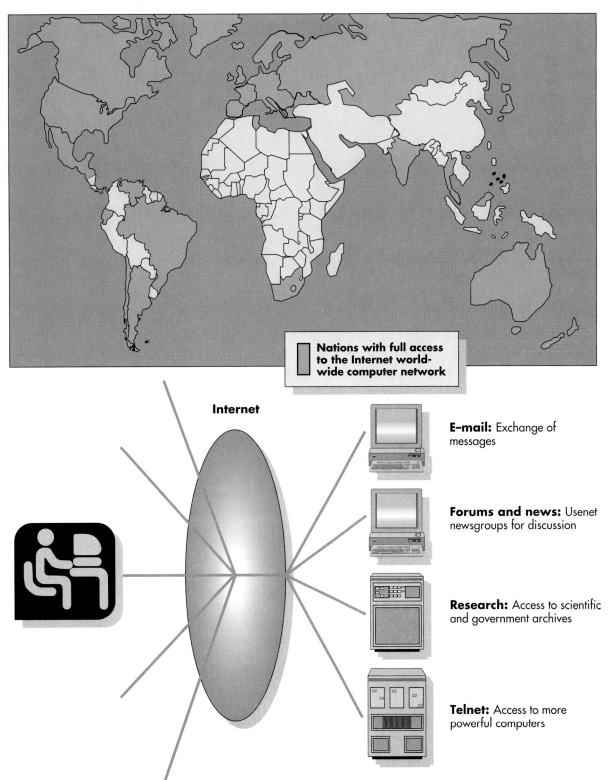

Nations with full access to the Internet world-wide computer network

**Internet**

**E–mail:** Exchange of messages

**Forums and news:** Usenet newsgroups for discussion

**Research:** Access to scientific and government archives

**Telnet:** Access to more powerful computers

■ *E-mail:* Internet electronic mail is essentially like the e-mail in a company's office—except that you can exchange messages all over the world. Internet addresses may seem a bit strange at first (for example, *president@whitehouse.gov* is the Internet address for the President of the United States), but they are not complicated.

■ *Discussion and news groups:* Usenet news groups are forums that resemble electronic bulletin boards—discussion groups carried by many Internet networks. Over 2,000 topics are carried in Usenet news groups. Users can post messages for others to read, then check back later to see what kind of responses have appeared.

In the United States, the Internet backbone (NSFNET) is maintained by the National Science Foundation (NSF). This backbone links supercomputers in San Diego; Ithaca, New York (Cornell University); Pittsburg, Pennsylvania; and Illinois with other resources to provide communications links between different research and educational institutions in the United States and around the world. Commercial companies called *service providers* maintain many of the communications lines that the Internet uses.

The information superhighway is yet to come, but the Internet provides the closest thing to it today. (For more information on the Internet, see the Clipboard at the end of this chapter.)

## Telecommuting

Today there are approximately 12 million full-time self-employed people working at home, another 12 million part-time self-employed home workers, and about 9 million employees who take office work home with them. Many people are taking advantage of fax and modem capabilities, desktop or notebook-size [✔ p. 73] microcomputers, and even cellular (portable) phones to become telecommuters. **Telecommuting** is working at home (or at another workplace) and communicating with employer, co-workers, and clients by telephone-linked computer. For many people, commuting is almost painful—fighting one's way through crowded highways, riding on packed trains and buses, taking two or more hours just getting to work and arriving "wiped out." Commuting has even made some people sick from stress, exhaustion, and exposure to pollution.

Telecommuting can spare people the stress of commuting. A telecommuter uses modems, faxes, the telephone, and other communications technologies to stay in touch with the employer—and the employer's network—sending and retrieving information as necessary. The telecommuter is fully employed by the company and receives the same salary and benefits as on-site workers. Perhaps the one major drawback of telecommuting, for some people, is the isolation of working alone.

Telecommuting even allows many people to work anywhere they choose. (See Figure 8.17.) Truckers are now often required to carry laptops with which they connect via satellite to headquarters. They can also fax reports and invoices. Real-estate salespeople may use car phones, car fax machines, pagers, and voice-activated minicassette recorders in their work. In 1994, Southwest Airlines fitted many of its planes with phones that can transmit faxes and files from passengers' laptop computers.

**Figure 8.17**
How portable technology changes time and space.

"I live and travel mostly in Alaska. I work hard in the summertime and I'm fairly recreational the rest of the year. This summer in Bristol Bay, I was logging on to The Well [electronic bulletin board] while lying in my bunk aboard the *F/V Glacier Bay* [fishing vessel]. With my PowerBook [microcomputer] on my tummy, I could log on to my favorite services, access my networks and any servers or other devices on my networks, check my e-mail, send and receive faxes, etc.

I'm often in the woods running, hiking, or biking, and almost always reachable by digital pager. My home is wired, and I maintain a dedicated phone-line link between home- and office-network zones. I've experimented with logging on from my aircraft, just for fun.

I find a digital pager quite handy for screening calls and preserving battery life on the smallest cellular phone I can find. With the combination of the PowerBook and cellular technology, I find that I very rarely need to be tied to any specific location in order to take care of business. . . ."

—Alaska salmon fisherman Blanton Forlson, in "Talking About Portables," *The Wall Street Journal,* November 16, 1992, pp. R18–R19.

## The Uses of Online Services and the Internet

In 1994, San Francisco area residents Ellen Pack and Nancy Rhine co-founded Women's WIRE (Worldwide Information Resource and Exchange) as an online service dedicated to women. Today, many women, and some men, too, are logging on from all over the country. In the conversational areas know as "conferences," they discuss matters of importance to them—their jobs, lovers, health, and homes. They also talk about politics and about the kind of online community they would like to build. They brainstorm and share information.

Clearly, Women's WIRE serves the kind of purpose for which the online universe is best suited: bringing people together. (See Figure 8.18.)

### CONNECTING WITH COMMERCIAL ONLINE SERVICES

"Conferences" or "chat boards" are only one of the features of online services, of course. The offerings are prodigious. You can learn games, obtain free software, get the latest headlines, and look up reference works. You can replay

**Figure 8.18**
Nancy Rhine and Ellen Pack started Women's WIRE, a commercial online service for women (phone: 415/615-8989, or e-mail: *info@wwire.net* or *subscribe@wwire.net*).

video and audio broadcasts, do electronic shopping, exchange e-mail, and so on. Table 8.1 rates the basic features of the principal online services: Prodigy, CompuServe, America Online, GEnie, and Delphi, as well as eWorld and Dow Jones News Retrieval.

To connect to an online service, you need a credit card, against which the service will make charges, and a telephone line. You will also need a personal computer and a modem, as well as communications software, which is usually available from the service. You also need a hard disk to store the software programs and any information you choose to download from the service. Finally, of course, you need the service's phone number.

Most online services charge a monthly fee, typically $10 to $20. In addition, most also charge for the time spent online. This is the period from the time you dial and connect to the service to the time you disconnect ("hang up"). Charges are billed to your credit card. *Warning:* Many users are surprised at their first bill, which can easily exceed $100. It's easy to get carried away when you're online, even though there may well be a "meter" on the screen that shows the mounting charges.

There are tricks to keeping the costs down, however. One is to go online only during off-hours (evenings and weekends), when the charges intended for business users are reduced. Another is to download—that is, save to your hard disk—the material you see on the display screen without bothering to look at it in detail. If, for example, you see an article title that interests you, don't stop to read the article. Just download the whole thing (save it to your hard disk) and read it later. Also, remember that the faster your modem, the less time you have to spend online to transmit data and information back and forth. Most online services now support data transmission at speeds up to 14,400 bps; some are preparing to transmit at 28,800. If you plan to spend a fair amount of time online, and have a 1,200 or 2,400 bps modem, consider upgrading to 9,600 bps or higher.

**Table 8.1**  Rating the principal online services.

| | America Online | CompuServe | Prodigy | eWorld | GEnie | Delphi Internet | Dow Jones News/Retrieval w/MCI Mail |
|---|---|---|---|---|---|---|---|
| Number of users claimed | 2,000,000 | 2,700,000[1] | 2,000,000 | 75,000 | N.A. | N.A. | 205,000 (unofficial) |
| Can use via any telecomm software | No | Yes | No | No | Yes | Yes | Yes |
| Supplies software | | | | | | | |
| DOS / Windows | Yes/Yes | Yes/Yes | Yes/Yes | No/No | Yes/Yes | Yes/Partial | Yes/Yes |
| Mac / OS/2 | Yes/No | Yes/Yes | Yes/No | Yes/No | Yes/No | No/No | No/No |
| Basic monthly fee | $9.95 | $9.95 | $9.95 | $8.95 | $8.95 | $10/$20 | None[2] |
| Free hours/month | 5 | Unlimited | 5 | 4 | 4 | 4/20 | N.A. |
| Per additional hour | $2.95 | $4.80[3] | $2.95 | $2.95 | $3.00 | $4/$1.80 | None[4] |
| Discussion groups surcharges? | No | Yes | No | No | No | No | N.A. |
| Reference database surcharges? | No | Yes | No | No | No | No | No |
| Prime-time surcharges? | None | None | None | None | $12.50/hr. | None | None |
| Free e-mail messages/month | Unlimited | 90 3-page messages | Unlimited | Unlimited | Unlimited | Unlimited | None; charged per character |
| Charge for extra e-mail | No | Yes | No | No | No | No | Yes |
| Ease of use | ★★★★★ | ★★★ | ★★★★ | ★★★★★ | ★★★ | ★★ | ★★ |
| Computer support | ★★★ | ★★★★★ | ★★★ | ★★★ | ★★★ | ★★★ | ★ |
| Business / investment info | ★★★★ | ★★★★★ | ★★★★★ | ★★★★ | ★★★ | ★★★ | ★★★★★ |
| Family orientation | ★★★★ | ★★★ | ★★★★ | ★★★★ | ★★★ | ★★★★ | ★ |
| Games and leisure | ★★★★ | ★★★★★ | ★★★★ | ★★★★ | ★★★ | ★★★★ | ★ |
| Shopping | ★★★ | ★★★ | ★★★★★ | ★★★★ | ★★★★★ | ★★★★★ | ★ |
| Quality of e-mail commands | ★★★ | ★★★★ | ★★★ | ★★★★ | ★★★★★ | ★★★ | ★★★★★ |
| Internet connection?[5] | Yes | Yes | Yes | No | No | Yes[6] | No |
| World-Wide Web browser? | No | No | Windows only | No | No | No | No |

[1]Includes users outside the United States. This is the only international service. [2]or $29.95 for 8 hours of non-prime-time, limited references use. [3]For most surcharged material. [4]$1.50 per 1,000 characters—about a screen of information; no hourly charge. [5]All offer Internet e-mail. [6]$3 per month for Internet access beyond e-mail.

*Source: San Jose Mercury News,* Computing, March 12, 1995, p. E1. (Dan Gilmore)

You will also get a separate bill from your telephone company for time spent connected via toll or long-distance phone lines. Most on-line services offer local telephone numbers for connection, and some provide toll-free (800) numbers to spare you long-distance charges. However, if you live outside populous urban and suburban areas, these cost-saving options may not exist.

Online services offer many more features than we can discuss here. How do you determine which one is best for you? Probably by reading some articles on the topic and by trying some of the services' free offers for some online time.

## CONNECTING WITH THE INTERNET

The Internet, the world's largest, fastest-growing network, was once primarily a government and research network. Today, it is experiencing expansive growth, perhaps doubling every 6–15 months. The bulk of Internet traffic is e-mail.

How do you get on the Internet? There is no master computer that everyone dials into. The Net, as it is called, is simply a web of interconnected computers around the world. Still, you can dial into the Internet from nearly anywhere on earth, as long as you have a correctly connected access computer.

### Getting Access

A network information center called *InterNIC* has been set up to serve as a clearinghouse for Internet information. To find out more, call 800/444-4345, or send e-mail to *info@internic.net*. For public access information, ask about the PDIAL list.

One thing to find out when you're looking into Internet connections is whether you will be getting *full access* or *e-mail only.* E-mail gives you virtually instantaneous worldwide communications. Full access will allow you to acquire information, software, games, pictures, and other riches.

In general, the primary providers of Internet access are the following:

■ *School or work:* The people with the easiest access to the Internet are those involved with universities and colleges, government agencies, and some commercial businesses.

Some college students can get a free account through their institution. Some campuses also allow local residents access for a monthly fee.

■ *Commercial on-line services and bulletin boards:* Many of the large commercial on-line services offer access ("gateways") to the Internet, although mostly only e-mail connections. Some electronic bulletin board systems (BBSs) also offer Internet access—but again, usually just e-mail connection.

■ *Commercial access providers:* Companies exist, called *service providers,* that will connect users to the Internet for a fee, from a few dollars an hour to thousands of dollars a year. Two basic kinds of commercial access are available: dedicated access and dial-up connections, including SLIP and PPP.

1. *Dedicated access* is designed for businesses and costs thousands of dollars. With this service, a computer in your company will have full access to the Internet. If that computer is tied to a local area network in the office, everyone on that network has access to the Internet.

2. *Dial-up connection* is the cheapest kind of Internet access. Here the commercial access provider charges a monthly and/or hourly fee for dialing into an intermediary source that then connects to the Internet. *SLIP* (serial line Internet protocol) and *PPP* (point-to-point protocol) are software programs that help connect to the Internet through your telephone line. (PPP is more sophisticated and faster than SLIP.) It is less expensive than dedicated access. However, it may still be pricey—perhaps up to a couple of hundred dollars a month. (Users must be sure that their systems are up to date enough to support the use of this software.)

### Features of the Internet

The principal features of the Internet are e-mail, file transfer, remote log-on, conferencing, and information search.

■ *E-mail:* E-mail messages on the Internet can be transmitted from one user to another often in a matter of seconds. E-mail addresses may look a bit odd, but they are not hard to understand. For example, to reach the president of the United States, you would type *president@whitehouse.gov.* The first part is the user's name—in this case, *president.* The second part is the user's computer, which follows the @ sign—in this case, *@whitehouse.* (If you were sending a message via the Internet to someone who has an e-mail box with America Online, this would be *@aol.*) The third part, following a period, is the network's "domain"—in this case, *gov* for "government." Other domains are *com* (commercial organizations, including online services such as America Online and CompuServe), *edu* (education), *mil* (military), *net* (network resources), and *org* (private organizations). A user of Delphi receiving messages via an Internet gateway would have an address of *[username]@del-phi.com.*

■ *File-transfer protocol:* If you want to copy a file from one computer to another, you need to use what is called a *file-transfer protocol,* or *FTP.* Using FTP, you can list directories of files, many of which you may access. FTP requires a user ID and possibly a password to allow access to files on a remote host system.

■ *Remote log-in:* Using the Internet protocol called *Telnet,* you can sign on to a remote computer. This feature enables you to tap into public-access files as though you were connected locally (directly). It is especially useful for perusing large databases or library card catalogs.

■ *Conferencing via Usenet:* One of the Internet's most interesting features is its news groups, or bulletin board discussion groups. For example, *Usenet* is a loose confederation of computers that exchange electronic mail and bulletin board messages. Although it overlaps with the Internet, the two are not the same. Usenet news group forums cover more than 2,000 topics. Examples are *misc.jobs.offered, rec.arts/startrek.info,* and *soc.culture.african.american.* The category called *alt news groups* offers more free-form

topics, such as *alt.rock-n-roll.metal* or *alt.internet.services.*

■ *Information searches:* Several software tools (called *gophers* or *browsers*) exist to help sift through the staggering amount of information on the Internet. Examples are *Gopher,* a campuswide service used by many colleges and universities to provide information through a simple menu display, and *Mosaic. WWW,* for *World Wide Web,* also called *The Web,* is another tool for moving from one source to another through a sophisticated graphical user interface. Other popular search tools are *Archie, Veronica, Netscape,* and *WAIS (Wide Area Information Services).* Most of these software tools are available as downloadable freeware or shareware. Off-the-shelf software packages are also available (for purchase) to assist users in navigating the Internet—examples are Internet in a Box, Internet Express, The Internet Chameleon, SuperHighway Access for Windows, and the Internet Membership Kit.

## Getting Help

For some people, getting onto and using the Internet present few problems. However, newcomers often find that the Net takes some getting used to. Fortunately, there are several books and magazines that can help you learn how to use the Internet and online services. (There are also free tutorials on the Internet, and online services offer Help information.)

### MAGAZINES

*Boardwatch Magazine.* 5970 South Vivian Street, Littleton. CO 80127. 303/973-6038 or 800/933-6038. A monthly newsletter on electronic BBSs and online information services. About $36 per year.

*Home Office Computing.* P.O. Box 51344, Boulder, CO 80321-1344. 800/ 288-7812. A monthly magazine for people with home offices. About $20 per year.

*Internet World.* P.O. Box 713, Mt. Morris, IL 61054-9965. 203/226-6967. About $30 per year for ten issues.

*On-Line Access.* 920 North Franklin #230, Chicago, IL 60610. 312/573-1700. CompuServe address *70324,343;* America Online address *OAMAG.* About $20 per year for eight issues.

## BOOKS

Eddings, J. *How the Internet Works*. Emeryville, CA: Ziff-Davis Press, 1994.

Fraase, M. *The Mac Internet Tour Guide*. Chapel Hill, NC: Ventana Press, 1994.

Hahn, H., and Stout, R. *The Internet Yellow Pages*. Berkeley, CA: Osborne McGraw-Hill, 1994.

Krol, E. *The Whole Internet User's Guide & Catalog* (2nd ed.). Sebastopol, CA: O'Reilly & Associates, 1994.

Magid, L. J. *Cruising Online: Larry Magid's Guide to the New Digital Highways*. New York: Random House, 1994.

Motley, L. *Modem USA: Second Edition, Revised.* Takoma Park, MD: Allium Press, 1994.

## CD-ROM TUTORIALS

*Atlantis Internet.* Atlantis Innovation, P.O. Box 767849, Roswell, GA 30076. 800/285-4680 or 404/642-8147.

*Hitchhiking on the Information Highway.* Moon Valley Software, 141 Suburban Road #A1, San Luis Obispo, CA 93401. 800/473-5509 or 805/ 781-3890. Walks users through the process of going on-line and getting to the Internet.

# S U M M A R Y

■ When people speak, the sound travels as *analog signals*—continuous signals that repeat a certain number of times over a certain period (frequency) at certain amplitudes (degrees of loudness). Telephone lines carry analog signals. Computers, in contrast, use *digital signals*—discontinuous (discrete) pulses of electricity (on, or 1) separated by pauses (off, or 0). (p. 262)

■ When they communicate, sending and receiving computers must use *modems* (*mod*ulate/*demo*dulate) to convert the digital signals into analog signals for transmission and then back again into digital signals for reception. Modems can be internal (built into the computer or inserted on an add-on card or board) or external (connected to the computer and the telephone by cable). (p. 263)

■ When signals are transmitted from computer to computer, patterns of bits coded to represent data are sent one bit at a time. For the receiving computer to be able to determine where one character of data ends and another starts, data is sent either asynchronously or synchronously. (p. 264)

■ In *asynchronous transmission,* each string of bits that make up a character is bracketed by control bits—a start bit, one or two stop bits, and an error check bit, or parity bit. Most microcomputers use asynchronous transmission. (p. 264)

■ In *synchronous transmission*, characters are sent as blocks with flags inserted as identifiers at the beginning and end of the blocks. This type of transmission is used by large computers to transmit huge volumes of data at high speeds. (p. 264)

■ Data communications technology must also consider the direction of data traffic: *simplex* (one way only), *half-duplex* (two-way traffic but only one direction at a time), or *full-duplex* (two-way traffic passing at the same time). (p. 265)

■ The amount of data that can be transmitted on a channel depends on the wave frequency—the cycles per second. Frequency is expressed in hertz: 1 cycle per second equals 1 hertz. The more cycles per second, the more data that can be sent through that channel. (p. 266)

■ *Bandwidth* is the difference between the highest and lowest frequencies—that is, the range of frequencies. Data may be sent not just on one frequency but on several frequencies within a particular bandwidth. Thus, the greater the bandwidth of a channel, the more frequencies it has available and hence the more data that can be sent through that channel. The rate of speed of data through the channel is expressed in bits per second (bps).

Channels that move data relatively slowly, like telegraph lines, are *narrowband* channels. Most telephone lines are *voiceband* channels, and they have a wider bandwidth than narrowband channels. *Broadband* channels (like coaxial cable, fiber-optic cable, microwave circuits, and satellite systems) transmit large volumes of data at high speeds. (p. 266)

■ The media most commonly used for communication are telephone wire (*twisted-pair*, *coaxial cable*), atmosphere (*microwave* and *satellite systems*), and *fiber-optic cable*. Each of these media differs in terms of the form of the transmitted data (electrical pulses, electromagnetic waves, or light pulses), the rate at which data moves through it, and its susceptibility to noise and "eavesdropping." (p. 267)

■ The hardware often used to communicate between computers includes modems, multiplexers, concentrators, and front-end processors:

—*Modem:* Allows the user to directly connect a computer to a telephone line. Modems can be either internal or external. (p. 276)

—*Multiplexer:* A multiplexing device that merges several low-speed transmissions into one high-speed transmission. (p. 278)

—*Concentrator:* A multiplexing device that collects data in a temporary storage area and then forwards the data when enough has been accumulated so that it can be sent economically. (p.278)

—*Front-end processor:* A multiplexing, smaller computer that is connected to a larger computer and assists with communications functions. (p. 278)

■ *Communications software* manages the transmission of data between computers or video display terminals. Communications software may also detect errors in transmission, compress/decompress transmitted data, control a remote computer, and make it possible to use your microcomputer to simulate a mainframe terminal. (p. 279)

■ For data communications to work, the hardware and software involved must adhere to certain protocols. A communications *protocol* is a set of conventions governing the exchange of data between hardware and/or software components in a communications network. (p. 280)

■ *ISDN* (Integrated Services Digital Network) is a set of international standards, or protocols, for transmitting all types of media (voice, video, and data) simultaneously over twisted-pair telephone lines. Twisted-pair lines are traditionally an analog communications medium. (p. 280)

■ Companies often set up communications *networks*, which are systems of interconnected computers, telephones, or other communications devices, and software. Networks allow users to share data and information. (p. 281)

■ Networks are categorized as follows:

—*Wide area network (WAN):* A communications network that covers a wide geographical area, such as a state or a country. (p. 281)

—*Metropolitan area network (MAN):* A communications network covering a geographic area the size of a city or suburb. (p. 281)

—*Local network:* A privately owned communications network that serves users within a confined geographical area. (p. 281)

■ The most common types of local networks are PBXs and LANs:

—*Private branch exchange (PBX):* A private or leased telephone switching system that connects telephone extensions in-house and to the outside telephone system. (p. 282)

—*Local area network (LAN):* A local network that consists of a communications link, network operating system, microcomputers or workstations, servers, and other shared hardware. (p. 282)

■ Local area networks are of two types:

—*Client-server LAN:* A LAN composed of requesting microcomputers, called *clients,* and supplying devices that provide a service, called *servers*. Different types of servers are used for different types of tasks. For example, a file server stores the programs and data files shared by the users of the LAN. Other types of servers are *database servers, print servers,* and *mail servers*. (p. 282)

—*Peer-to-peer LAN:* A LAN composed of networked microcomputers that communicate directly with one another without relying on a server. A peer-to-peer network is less expensive than a client-server network. (p. 282)

■ Local area networks are made up of several standard components (p. 284):

—Connection or cabling system

—Microcomputers with interface cards

—Network operating system

—Other shared devices

—Bridges and gateways

■ Networks can be laid out in different ways, including:

—*Star network:* All microcomputers and other communications devices are connected to a central hub, such as a file server or host computer. (p.285)

—*Ring network:* In this topology, all microcomputers and other communications devices are connected in a continuous loop. (p. 285)

—*Bus network:* In this topology, all communications devices are connected to a common channel. (p. 285)

—*Hybrid network:* In this topology, all microcomputers and communications devices are connected using a combination of the star, ring, and bus topologies. (p. 287)

—*FDDI network:* This network uses fiber-optic cable with a dual counter-rotating ring topology. (p. 287)

■ Some practical uses of communications and connectivity include:

—*Telephone-related communications services:* Voice-mail and e-mail are two telephone communications services that are very popular. (p. 287)

—*Online information services:* You can do many things with an online information service, including perform research, send/receive electronic mail, play games, make travel plans and reservations, and shop. (p. 289)

—*Electronic bulletin board systems (BBSs):* BBSs are of two types—large and small. Large BBSs include all major online services, such as America Online and CompuServe. You're charged for using the service. Small BBSs may be free or for-profit, but they are typically run by individuals. (p. 291)

—*The Internet*: The Internet is an international network connecting approximately 11,000 smaller networks worldwide through which you can perform the following types of tasks: gather information, send/receive e-mail, participate in discussion and news groups. Currently, an estimated 25 million people are using the Internet. (p. 292)

—*Telecommuting*: You are telecommuting if you work at home (or in another workplace) and have telecommunications between there and a main office. A telecommuter typically uses modems, faxes, the telephone, and other communications technologies to stay in touch with the employer and co-workers. (p. 294)

■ *Digital convergence* is the technological merger of several industries through various devices that exchange information in the electronic, or digital, format used by computers. The industries are computers, communications, consumer electronics, entertainment, and mass media/publishing.

This development signifies a shift from single, isolated technologies to a unified digital technology. This shift has given rise to the term *information superhighway,* which will be constructed mostly of fiber-optic cable. The superhighway would be a fusion of the two-way wired and wireless capabilities of telephones and networked computers with cable TV's capacity to transmit hundreds of programs. The resulting interactive digitized traffic would include movies, TV shows, phone calls, databases, shopping services, and online services. This superhighway, it is hoped, would link all homes, schools, businesses, and government organizations. (p. 273)

## KEY TERMS

## EXERCISES

**SELF-TEST**

1. List four transmission media that are used for data communications.

   a. TELEPHONE LINE

   b. COAX CABLES

   c. MICRO WAVE

   d. SATELITE , FIBER OPTIC , RADIO / INFRARED .

2. To communicate between computers across wire phone lines, you need a(n) _MODEM_ at both the sending and receiving locations.

3. Whereas computers use _digital_ signals, the telephone line can usually transmit only _ANALOG_ signals.

4. For a microcomputer to communicate with a mainframe, it must be configured with the necessary hardware and software to allow it to support _SYNCHRONOUS_ transmission.

5. A(n) _half duplex_ communications link can support two-way traffic, but data can travel in only one direction at a time.

6. Asynchronous transmission, commonly used in microcomputers, is faster than synchronous transmission. (true/false)

7. Pulses of light are sometimes used to represent data so that it can be communicated over a distance. (true/false)

8. List three popular LAN topologies.

   a. STAR

   b. RING

   c. BUS

9. A(n) _multiplexer_ optimizes the use of communications lines by allowing multiple users or devices to share one high-speed line, thereby reducing communications costs.

10. ___Full  duplex___ transmission sends data in both directions simultaneously, similar to two trains passing in opposite directions on side-by-side tracks.

11. Satellite communications systems transmit signals in the gigahertz range—billions of cycles per second. (true/false)

12. A(n) ___PROTOCOL___ is a standard set of rules for electronic communications.

13. A(n) ___NETWORK___ is a collection of data communications hardware, computers, communications software, and communications media connected in a meaningful way to allow users to share information and equipment.

14. A hybrid network is a combination of the _____, _____, and _____ network topologies.

15. The ___ELECTRONIC___ ___BULLETIN___ ___BOARD___ ___SYSTEM___ is a popular information service that allows subscribing users to place messages and advertisements into the system and also scan existing messages in the system.

16. The ___INTERNET___ is considered the "network of all networks."

17. Before you can access an on-line information service, your microcomputer must be equipped with a hardware device called a(n) ___MODEM___.

18. A(n) ___peer to peer___ LAN is one in which all microcomputers on the network communicate directly with one another without relying on a server.

19. A(n) ___WAN___ _____ network is a communications network that covers a wide geographical area, such as a state or a country.

20. ___ISDN___ is a set of international standards for transmitting voice, video, and data simultaneously as digital signals over telephone lines.

*Solutions*: (1) telephone lines, coaxial cable, microwave, satellite, fiber optics, radio/infrared waves; (2) modem; (3) digital, analog; (4) synchronous; (5) half-duplex; (6) false; (7) true; (8) star, bus, ring, hybrid, FDDI; (9) multiplexer; (10) full-duplex; (11) true; (12) protocol; (13) network; (14) star, ring, bus; (15) electronic bulletin board system; (16) Internet; (17) modem; (18) peer-to-peer; (19) wide area; (20) ISDN

## SHORT-ANSWER QUESTIONS

1. What is a communications network?
2. What are modems used for?
3. What is the function of a multiplexer?
4. Explain the difference between analog and digital signals.
5. In a network, what is the purpose of the network operating system software?
6. What is the difference between a client-server LAN and a peer-to-peer LAN?
7. What is meant by the term *protocol* as it relates to communicating between two computers?
8. What is the Internet? What is it used for?
9. Describe the difference between synchronous and asynchronous transmission modes and how they affect the speed of data transmission.
10. What is meant by the term *topology* as it relates to LANs? Give some examples.
11. What is meant by the term *telecommuting*?
12. What are the advantages of fiber-optics cable as a communications medium over other types of communications media?

## PROJECTS AND CRITICAL THINKING EXERCISES

1. Are the computers at your school or work connected to a network? If so, what are the characteristics of the network? What advantages does the network provide in terms of hardware and software support? What types of computers are connected to the network (microcomputers, minicomputers, and/or mainframes)? Specifically, what software/hardware is allowing the network to function?
2. Using current articles and publications, research the history of ISDN, how it is being used today, and what you think the future holds for it. Present your findings in a paper or a 15-minute discussion.
3. "Distance learning," or "distance education," uses electronic links to extend college campuses to people who otherwise would not be able to take college courses. College instructors using such systems are able to lecture "live" to students in distant locations. Is your school or someone you know involved in distance learning? If so, research the system's components and uses. What hardware does it use? Software? Protocols? Communications media?
4. You need to purchase a computer to use at home to perform business-related (school-related) tasks. You want to be able to communicate with the network at work (school) and the Internet so that you can use their software and access their data. Include the following in a report:
   —Description of the hardware and software used at work (school).
   —Description of the types of tasks you will want to perform at home.
   —Name of the computer system you would buy. (Include a detailed description of the computer system, such as the RAM capacity [✓ p. 83], secondary storage capacity [✓ p. 113], and modem speed.)
   —The communications software you would need to purchase or obtain.
   —A cost estimate for the system and for the online and telephone charges.
5. About the same time this text is printed, Microsoft plans to release Windows 95. Microsoft's own online service, Microsoft Network, will be bundled with Windows 95. Research and describe the main features of Microsoft Network. What types of tasks will it be used for? How will Microsoft generate revenue from Microsoft Network? Will advertising be allowed on the network? How do you think Microsoft Network will compete with other online services like CompuServe and Prodigy?

6. In an effort to reduce new construction costs, some rapidly expanding companies are allowing more and more employees to telecommute several days a week. Offices are shared by several telecommuting employees. One employee will use the office two or three days a week, and another employee will use the same office other days of the week. What advantages does the company gain from this type of arrangement? What advantages do these employees have over the traditional work environment? What are some of the disadvantages to both the company and the employees? Do you think employees' productivity will decline from telecommuting and/or sharing office space with other telecommuting employees? If so, why?

7. Talk with several people who use voice and/or e-mail on the job. How have these services improved their jobs? What other communication services do they use? Are there other services they would like to have that are not currently available to them? If so, what services and how do these employees envision the services improving the work they do?

8. There are discussion groups available on the Internet for almost any imaginable subject. Some people spend hours each day connecting to these discussion groups or "chatting" with others on the Internet. As described in the text, there are many other services available on the Internet. How do you think consumers, researchers, and others will be affected by the widespread use of the Internet? Is the Internet available at your school or work? If so, how has it changed the way you study, do research, work, etc.?

## IN THE LAB WITH MICROSOFT WINDOWS

(*Note:* If you aren't familiar with using a mouse and/or don't know how to use the Microsoft Windows graphical user interface, complete the In the Lab with Microsoft Windows exercises in Chapter 6 before proceeding.)

### Microsoft Terminal

1. In this section you will explore the Microsoft Windows Terminal. Right now, the Microsoft Windows Program Manager should be displaying.
2. DOUBLE-CLICK: Accessories group icon
   DOUBLE-CLICK: Terminal program icon
   The Terminal window should be displaying.
3. To give you an idea of some of the settings you must consider when communicating via the Windows Terminal:
   CHOOSE: Settings, Communication
   The options are gray ("not available") because "None" is selected in the Connector list box.
   CLICK: COM2 *in the Connector list box*
   To communicate with another Windows Terminal user, most of the settings in this Communications window must be the same on your computer and the remote computer.
4. To exit this dialog box:
   CLICK: Cancel button
5. Explore some of the other menu options available in the Terminal window.
6. To exit the Terminal program:
   DOUBLE-CLICK: Control-menu box *located in the upper-left corner of the Terminal window*
7. To close the Accessories group window:
   DOUBLE-CLICK: Control-menu box *located in the upper-left corner of the Accessories window*

# Chapter Topics

# CHAPTER 9

# Systems Development

No matter what your position in an organization, you will undoubtedly come in contact with a systems development life cycle (SDLC) —the process of setting up a business system, or an information system. The user always has a definite role in a systems development life cycle. If you, the user, understand its principles, you will be able to apply them to solving many types of problems, not just those in business or in computer systems.

## Preview

*When you have completed this chapter, you will be able to:*

- Explain why some systems fail

- Identify six phases of a systems development life cycle

- List some techniques for gathering and analyzing data describing the current system

- Describe the extent to which the requirements for a new information system must be defined before the system is designed

- Identify the major factors to consider in designing the input, output, and processing procedures and the storage requirements of a new system, as well as hardware and software requirements

- Describe the role of the user in the systems development life cycle

- Describe four basic approaches to implementing a new computer-based information system

**Why Is This Chapter Important?**

*An* information system *is an arrangement of human and machine components and procedures that interact to support the information or business needs of an organization and the system's users. (See Figure 9.1.) Such systems do not come prepackaged like some software applications programs; they must be custom developed.*

*The extent to which your job brings you in contact with your company's* **systems development life cycle (SDLC)**—*the formal process by which organizations build computer-based information systems—will vary depending on a number of factors. These factors can include the size of the organization, your job description, your relevant experience, and your educational background in information-processing concepts, tools, and techniques. In large companies the SDLC is usually a formal process with clearly defined standards and procedures. Although the technical aspects of each phase of the cycle will undoubtedly be handled by information specialists, users will always interface with these specialists.*

## User Participation in Systems Development

**Knowledge of systems analysis and design helps you explain your present job, improve personal productivity, and lessen risk of a project's failure.**

Following are some examples of how you, as a user, may participate in systems development:

- It may be necessary for you to explain how the current system works in your department: the manual procedures you use or what you do to support an existing computer-based system, as well as the current business terminology and purpose of the system.

- You could easily find yourself in a meeting discussing the nature of problems with the current system and how it can be improved.

- You may be required to provide systems analysts and designers with the departmental objectives and requirements that the system must meet. For instance, if you expect to have the new system produce useful reports, then you should plan to assist the information specialists in designing how these reports should look and what information or data they should contain.

- You may often be involved in the approval of projects and budgets as a member of a special steering committee.

- As the development of a new system nears completion, you will probably help evaluate and test it to ensure that it works as expected.

- You will have to help prepare some of the documentation that is accumulated during the entire process of system development.

- You may attend briefings and training sessions to learn how the new system will affect your job and what its new operating procedures will be.

- And last, but certainly not least, you will end up using the new system. This may involve preparing data for input or using information produced by the system.

In a large company the SDLC may seem like a complex process with which you have limited contact; however, your role in it is still important.

**Figure 9.1**
Components of an information system.

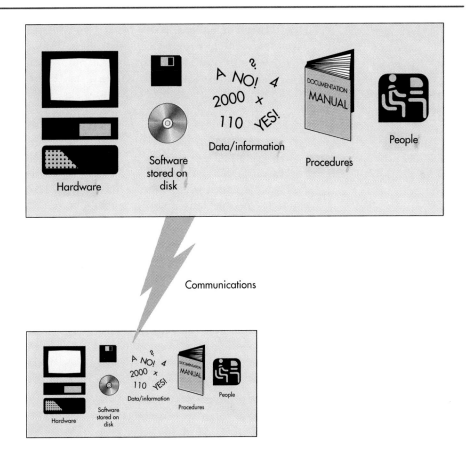

Although in a small organization you are likely to be involved in more phases of the SDLC, and your role in each phase will tend to be more detailed, you shouldn't assume that the principles of an SDLC apply only to large computer systems and applications. You may need to perform some of the basic steps in the SDLC when choosing a microcomputer, for example.

Remember: systems can fail because the components and the functions of the system are not clearly defined in terms of specific objectives and are not controlled tightly enough. In these situations, user requirements are not met, and costs greatly exceed estimates. In some cases, failure occurs because testing was inadequate. For example, not too long ago the U.S. Internal Revenue Service was unable to send tax refunds on time because it couldn't process the tax returns fast enough; the new system had not been tested beforehand in all necessary areas. These problems can be avoided through, among other things, user participation—your participation—in the system development process.

## Systems Development Life Cycle (SDLC)

The SDLC comprises six phases: (1) analyze current system; (2) define new systems requirements; (3) design new system; (4) develop new system and have users test it; (5) implement new system; and (6) evaluate performance of new system and maintain system.

Businesses and other organizations are made up of many systems and subsystems, including many manual and automated procedures. Some systems are very simple: An order entry system could be just a set of procedures for taking down a telephone order from a customer and seeing that the order is accurately entered for processing. Other systems are very complicated: a large company's payroll system involves a number of subsystems for tracking employee turnover, pay rate changes, tax exemption status, types of insurance deductions, and pension contributions, as well as overtime rates and bonuses.

In some cases, the systems development effort will be so large that dozens of people will be involved for a year or more. In other cases, a system can be set up in a relatively short time. In both extremes, however, it is equally important to follow a clearly defined process. The degree of complexity of an SDLC and the amount of effort that goes into each of its phases will vary according to the scope of the project. However, in simple and complex systems, people must interact with the system and perform the manual procedures required to feed it raw data, review the information produced, and take appropriate actions.

## Why Do Some Systems Development Projects Fail?

The chances are great that a systems development project will fail if a clearly defined SDLC isn't followed. Sometimes, however, even when companies go to the trouble to establish a formal and comprehensive SDLC, projects still fail to achieve their objectives. Why? Most failures can be traced to a breakdown in communications between the users and the data processing group and information specialists. The reasons for failure often include:

- *Inadequate user involvement:* Users must assume responsibility for making sure the analyst understands the business applications, requirements, and policies. (For example, a system may fail because major functions weren't included in the design—because users didn't make their needs known.)

- *Continuation of a project that should have been canceled:* Often it's tempting to not cancel a project because of the investment already made. Analysts should reevaluate the project at various phases to determine if it remains feasible—in other words, multiple feasibility checkpoints should be established throughout the development process.

- *The failure of two or more portions of the new system to fit together properly (called systems integration):* This often results when major portions of the systems are worked on by different groups of technical specialists who do not communicate well.

Responses to systems failure vary. Project leaders may be fired; usually the systems requirements are reassessed, and the highest-priority requirements are identified to be satisfied by a smaller system that can be more easily controlled.

## Wanted: Orderly Development Process

In most large companies, a great deal of money is allocated for information processing functions (hardware, software, and staff support). In such companies, a systems development project that costs more than $1 million is not uncommon. Hundreds, even thousands, of individual tasks may need to be performed as part of the development effort. These tasks may involve many people within an organization, often in several different organizational units. This multiplicity of effort can lead to conflicting objectives and result in a project that is difficult to coordinate. If the process of developing a system bogs down, the final product can be delayed, and the final cost can be more than double the original estimate. To avoid such difficulties, the SDLC is used as a guideline to direct and administer the activities and to control the financial resources expended. In other words, following a structured procedure brings order to the development process. In a small company the amount of money spent on project development may not be much; however, following the steps of the SDLC is no less significant. Some—but by no means all—risks of ignoring these steps include the following:

■ *The new system does not meet the users' needs.* Inaccurate or incomplete information gathered by systems analysts and designers may result in the development of software that does not do what the users need.

■ *Unnecessary hardware or too much hardware is acquired.* If personal computers and printers are sitting idle most of the time, then probably far too much money has been invested without a clear definition of how much processing power is needed.

■ *Insufficient hardware may be acquired.* For example, users may have to wait in line to use printers, or the system may have inadequate storage capacity.

■ *Software may be inadequately tested and thus may not perform as expected.* Users tend to rely heavily on the accuracy and the completeness of the information provided by the computer. However, if software is not adequately tested before it is given to users, undetected programming logic errors may produce inaccurate or incomplete information.

Different organizations may refer to the systems development life cycle by different names—such as *applications development cycle, systems development cycle,* or *structured development life cycle.* However, the general objectives will always be the same. The number of steps necessary to complete the cycle may also vary from one company to another, depending on the level of detail necessary to effectively administer and control the development of systems. One way to look at systems development is to divide it into six phases (Figure 9.2):

■ *Phase 1: Analyze current system*

■ *Phase 2: Define new systems requirements*

■ *Phase 3: Design new system*

■ *Phase 4: Develop new system and have users test it*

■ *Phase 5: Implement new system*

■ *Phase 6: Evaluate performance of new system and maintain system; when the system becomes obsolete, a planning stage is then entered to start the SDLC over again and develop a new system*

Keep in mind that, although we speak of six separate SDLC phases, one phase does not necessarily have to be completed before the next one is started. In other words, the phases often overlap. The degree of overlap usually depends on the project's size and the amount of resources committed to the project. However, work done on a subsequent phase is subject to change until the work of the preceding phase is completed.

Three groups of personnel are usually involved in an SDLC project:

1. The user group staff members (users)

2. Representatives of user management, information processing management, and system owners (management)

3. Technical staff consisting of systems analysts and programmers (information specialists)

**Figure 9.2**
The systems development life cycle. An SDLC typically includes six phases.

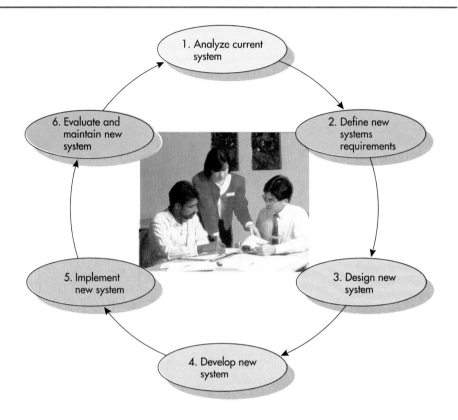

1. Analyze current system

2. Define new systems requirements

3. Design new system

4. Develop new system

5. Implement new system

6. Evaluate and maintain new system

**H**

systems analyst

The computer professional generally in charge of the SDLC is the head **systems analyst,** or *project leader.* This person, who is a member of the information systems department, studies the needs and problems of an organization and determines how computer technology—data capture, input, processing, storage, and electronic communications—interacts with data, activities, and people to deliver timely and useful information to the people who need it. The analyst often helps design the database. Systems analysts are often called systems engineers or analyst/programmers, because they usually are required to do some programming during systems development—that is, to write some of the coded computer programs. (Programming was covered in Chapter 7.) Figure 9.3 shows some of the qualifications and responsibilities of a systems analyst.

Occasionally steering committees are formed to help decide how to get started. Steering committees determine which systems development projects to work on first. A steering committee is a group of individuals from each department in an organization. It may hear reports from experts about the advantages, disadvantages, and costs of a particular project. The committee must then decide whether it is in the organization's interest to implement the project. If it decides to go ahead, the systems development life cycle proceeds.

All the detailed processes and tools used in the SDLC phases cannot be covered in one chapter of an introductory text. However, in the following sections, we provide the basic principles of the SDLC.

## Phase 1: Analyze the Current System

In the first phase of the SDLC, systems analysts conduct a preliminary analysis, determining the organization's objectives and

**Figure 9.3**
The job description for a typical systems analyst provides an example of some of the many tasks the analyst must perform and the people and departments he or she must serve.

| JOB TITLE: | Systems Analyst (multiple job levels) |
|---|---|
| REPORTS TO: | Systems Development Team Manager or Assistant Director of Systems Development |
| DESCRIPTION: | A systems analyst shall be responsible for studying the problems and needs set forth by this organization to determine how computer hardware, applications software, files and databases, networks, people, and procedures can best solve these problems and improve business and information systems. |
| RESPONSIBILITIES: | 1. Evaluates projects for feasibility.<br>2. Estimates personnel requirements, budgets, and schedules for systems development and maintenance projects.<br>3. Performs interviews and other fact gathering.<br>4. Documents and analyzes current system operations.<br>5. Defines user requirements for improving or replacing systems.<br>6. Identifies potential applications of computer technology that may fulfill requirements.<br>7. Evaluates applications of computer technology for feasibility.<br>8. Recommends new systems and technical solutions to end users and management.<br>9. Identifies potential hardware and software vendors, when appropriate.<br>10. Recommends and selects hardware and software purchases (subject to approval).<br>11. Designs system inputs, outputs, on-line dialogue, flow, and procedures.<br>12. Designs files and databases (subject to approval by Data Administration).<br>13. Writes, tests, and/or supervises applications software development.<br>14. Trains users to work with new systems and versions.<br>15. Converts operations to new systems or versions.<br>16. Supports operational applications. |
| EXTERNAL CONTACTS: | 1. Assigned end users of mainframe computers and applications.<br>2. Assigned owners (end user management) of mainframe computers and applications.<br>3. Data Administration Center personnel.<br>4. Network Administration Center personnel.<br>5. Information Center personnel.<br>6. Operations Center personnel.<br>7. Methodology/CASE expert and staff.<br>8. Computer hardware and software vendors.<br>9. Other systems analysis and development managers. |
| MINIMUM QUALIFICATIONS: | Bachelor or Master's Degree in Computer Information Systems or related field. Programming experience preferred. Prior experience with business applications considered helpful. Prior training or experience in systems analysis and design, preferably structured methods, preferred. Good communications skills—oral and written—are mandatory. |
| TRAINING REQUIREMENTS: | Analysts must complete or demonstrate equivalent backgrounds in the following in-house training courses: STRADIS Methodology and Standards, Joint Application Design (JAD) Techniques, Systems Application Architecture (SAA) Standards, Fundamentals, DB2 Database Design Techniques, CSP Prototyping Techniques, Excelerator/IS Computer Aided Design Techniques, Project Management Techniques, Microcomputer Software Tools, and Interpersonal and Communications Skills for Systems Analysts. |
| JOB LEVELS: | Initial assignments are based on programming experience and training results. The following job levels are defined:<br>Programmer/analyst: 30% analysis/design - 70% programming<br>Analyst/programmer: 50% analysis/design - 50% programming<br>Analyst: 70% analysis/design - 30% programming<br>Senior Analyst: 30% management - 60% analysis/design and 10% programming<br>Lead Analyst: 100% analysis/design or consulting |

**the nature and scope of existing problems. They then propose solutions in a report to management.**

Before a company starts to analyze its current system in detail, a company steering committee may request experts to report on a proposed new systems project. This report, often called a *feasibility study,* can be considered part of the first phase of systems development. The goal of a feasibility study is to identify as quickly as possible whether the benefits of a proposed project appear to outweigh its expected cost and disruption, based on what already is known. Because early feasibility estimates may be overly optimistic, it's usually a good idea to conduct feasibility studies at various times throughout all phases of the SDLC to determine whether to continue the project.

## Purpose of Phase 1

The main objective of Phase 1 is to gain a clear understanding of the existing system and its shortcomings, to identify existing problems, and to determine where improvements can be made. An analysis of the current system takes place regardless of whether it is manual or computer-based, and each situation (application) must be analyzed. Figure 9.4 shows a few of the problems identified in a sporting goods store's manual accounting system, as well as areas in which a computer-based system could make improvements.

Some aspects of each application within the current system that are studied include:

■ Inputs (transactions)

■ Outputs

■ File structure and storage

■ Users' requirements

■ Methods and procedures

■ Communications needs

■ Controls

■ Existing hardware and software (if any)

Improvements to systems can be defined as changes that will result in worthwhile benefits. Possibilities for improvement include:

1. Speeding up a process
2. Streamlining a process through elimination of unnecessary or duplicate steps
3. Combining processes
4. Reducing errors in input
5. Reducing redundant (duplicated) input and output
6. Improving integration of systems and subsystems
7. Simplifying customer/supplier/vendor interaction with the system
8. Cutting costs
9. Improving security

The systems analyst studies not only these individual components but also how they interact. Those users who are asked to participate in the study of users' requirements can assist the analyst by expanding their thinking about the components being studied. For example, if you were helping a systems

**Figure 9.4**
Phase 1 analysis of a sporting goods store's current accounting system. These are
only a few of the general problems and objectives that may be identified.

```
Problem Definition--Current Accounting System
The following problems have been detected in the current accounting system:

1. Because files are spread among many filing cabinets in different locations, it
   takes too long to locate the required accounting files in order to update them.
   Often a file has been misplaced, or the file contains information that belongs
   somewhere else.

2. The procedures for updating all accounting files are not clearly defined.
   Mistakes are often made when entering accounting data.

3. The files that need to be updated daily include the General Ledger, Accounts
   Receivable, Accounts Payable, and the payroll files. Because it takes so much
   time to access the files, there is never enough time to get the job done;
   consequently, the job is often done haphazardly and updated only weekly.

4. Because data is filed in several places but under different labels, it is
   difficult to obtain information from the accounting files to generate the
   following types of reports:
       Summary reports about the financial status of the company (daily, weekly,
       monthly, yearly)
       Reports about the projected growth of the company.

Objectives

The new computer-based accounting system should:

1. Reduce by 50% the amount of time required to locate the files that have to be
   updated.
2. Include built-in procedures for the user to follow when updating the accounting
   files.
3. Establish built-in controls to reduce data input errors.
4. Make it easy to update the accounting files daily.
5. Make it easy to obtain information from the accounting files to generate
   reports.
```

analyst study the existing filing system, you would have to describe everything used as a file, including not only files in file cabinets or on disk but also index card boxes, in/out boxes on your desk, the telephone book, notebook, log sheets, and materials on your shelf. In other words, anything that is used as reference for obtaining information to help you make decisions would have to be identified. The analyst will also need to know how and when you use these references/files.

*Note:* Users should keep in mind that, although systems analysts may be experts about computers and their applications, they are not as knowledgeable as the business users about the business functions they perform. It is the user's responsibility to make sure the analyst is well informed about the current system.

## Gathering Information

As you can see, the principal activities in this phase involve gathering information about the current system and then analyzing it. The analyst can use a number of techniques, including:

## Consumer Testing Software: The Alpha and the Beta

Debugging programs—whether standard or object-oriented—involves not only various internal checks but also testing them with prospective consumers. Chris Peters, general manager of the Word business unit of Microsoft Corporation, describes how this is done.

Peters says the program is first put through its paces by real users in the Alpha testing stage.

"Alpha is when you're code complete," he says. "In other words, all the features are in, but the program is still very unstable. You really haven't done any quality checking."

Alpha testing is conducted within the software company and uses sophisticated testing labs. Users are placed in rooms set up like typical offices except for the one-way windows that cover a large portion of one of the walls. Programmers sit behind the window and watch as users, probably feeling like rats in a maze, try to figure out how to use a product. Software designers use many variations on the tests, such as assigning specific tasks or taking away the users' software manuals.

The designers scrutinize almost every move a user makes during the testing sessions. Cameras record the scene, and users are sometimes asked to narrate their actions into a microphone.

(For example, "I clicked on Help to find out how to italicize a block of text. But I couldn't find the answer I needed, so I returned to my document.") Some companies compile videotapes of the users' moves and have production technicians that edit the films into the records of specific problems.

By watching these "regular guy" testers, programmers quickly learn what features are successful and which ones might die on the cutting room floor. Programmers often get a lesson in humility during the Alpha testing.

"We always screw up, basically," Peters says. "It turns out we're not really quite as smart as we thought we were."

After the problems that showed up in Alpha testing are corrected, the software is sent out to Beta testers. At this point, the software is a fairly solid product; some problems may still exist, but, for the most part, the program works. Beta testing uses feedback from users outside the software company. The testers are selected for how they represent various segments of the market, and they are asked for feedback on what they did and didn't like about the software.

Trevor Meers, "From Statistics to Shrinkwrap: The Development of Software," *PC Novice,* April 1993, pp. 33–36.

- ■ *Conducting interviews:* The analyst interviews staff members who actually perform the work and compares their perceptions of what is being done and how with the perceptions of managers, who are also interviewed. In a structured interview the analyst prepares outline forms with predetermined questions. If the questions deviate from the predetermined outline, it is called an unstructured interview.

- ■ *Reviewing policies and procedures:* The extent to which existing policies and procedures have been documented can give the analyst valuable insight into what is going on. The analyst should look over what documentation exists, thereby obtaining a picture of how current system activities are expected to operate. However, all documentation should be compared with the information obtained during interviews to determine if the documentation is up to date. Also, remember that continual new documentation of processes and decisions is necessary throughout the SDLC.

■ *Collecting sample forms, documents, memos, reports, and so on:* Collecting samples of operating documents can also help the analyst to assemble an accurate picture of current system activities. The term *document* refers to paper on which data has been recorded, including preprinted forms, handwritten forms, and computer-produced forms. The user must be sure to give the analyst copies of all documents used for data recording. In addition, the analyst studies the **organization chart,** which shows the organization's management levels and lines of authority. (See Figure 9.5.)

■ *Observing operations and office environment:* The information gathered during interviews represents what users say is being done. The existing descriptions of procedures (if any) answer the question: What should be done and how? Observing operations and the office environment will confirm the analyst's understanding of what actually exists and answer the question: What are the users actually doing?

■ *Using questionnaires to conduct surveys:* Analysts find that using questionnaires to take a survey can be useful when information must be collected from a large group of individuals. Although questionnaires take less time than personal interviews, and many responses can be collected, they must be used with care. The questions must be precisely worded so that the user completing the questionnaire understands the instruction and does not need to interpret the questions.

Needless to say, the systems analyst does not necessarily do these activities alone. Users themselves can collect data on a current system using these techniques, perhaps along with the analyst.

**Figure 9.5**
Organization chart.

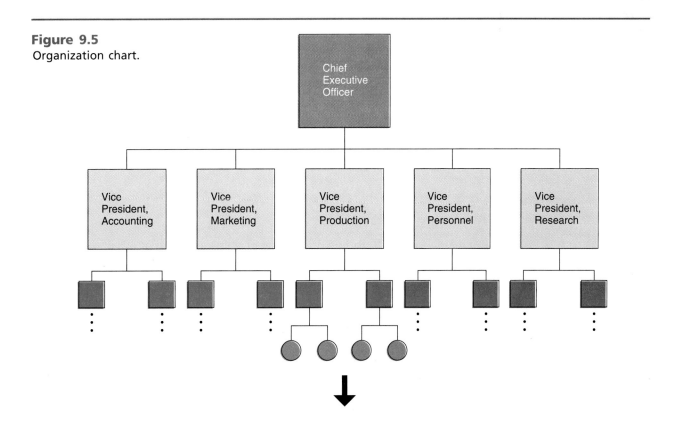

## When Systems Don't Work . . .

Some complex technological projects put enormous demands on software writers. Examples are programming for Star Wars-type missile defense or for huge video servers to handle movies-on-demand through cable-TV systems. However, consider the trials and tribulations of software contractors for the Denver International Airport (DIA) who were charged with launching an automated baggage-handling system.

When it opened on February 28, 1995, the first major U.S. airport to be built in 20 years, DIA was 16 months behind schedule and nearly $3 billion over early cost estimates. Moreover, it was far from the high-tech marvel Denver officials guaranteed would generate jobs for 100 years without spending local tax dollars.

What went wrong? Although government investigators dug into allegations of shoddy workmanship, cronyism in awarding contracts, and attempts to influence city officials, there was also the problem with the computerized baggage system.

As designed, the $193 million underground system was supposed to consist of 4,000 computer-guided carts, each carrying a single bar-coded bag, which would dash to and fro along 22 miles of little tracks, delivering 60,000 bags an hour to and from distant gates and carousels.

The goal was that passengers would virtually never have to wait at baggage-claim sections.

In early tests, however, the system was a designer's nightmare. "Carts crashed into one another, bending rails and disgorging clothes from suitcases," said a *Newsweek* account. "Others were knocked off the rails, jammed or mysteriously failed to appear when summoned."

The main culprit seemed to be software bugs, although the larger challenge was the task of automating an airport's baggage system, something never done before. In the end, DIA had to spend an extra $57 million to install a conventional baggage system as backup.

When the airport opened, the new system was used to handle only outbound bags. Arriving bags were moved by the backup system of old-fashioned tugs and carts.

*Sources:* Richard Woodbury, "The Bag Stops Here," *Newsweek,* May 16, 1994, p. 52; Dirk Johnson, "Denver May Open Airport in Spite of Glitches," *New York Times,* July 24, 1994, p. A12; B. Drummond Ayres Jr., "Mistake or Modern Marvel? Denver Airport Set to Open," *New York Times,* February 19, 1995, sec. 1, p. 12; Agis Salpukas, "Air Fares for Denver Will Rise," *New York Times,* January 30, 1995, p. C1; Louis Sahagun, "Denver's Airport Isn't the Marvel That Was Guaranteed," *San Jose Mercury News,* February 26, 1995, p. 11A, reprinted from *Los Angeles Times.*

## Analyzing Information

After the analyst has gathered information about the current system, he or she must analyze the facts to identify problems—including their causes and effects—and opportunities for improvement. Just a few of the things that the analyst determines are:

- *Minimum, average, and maximum levels of activity:* For example, when do most sales orders come in?

- *Relative importance of the various activities:* This means prioritizing the activities.

- *Redundancy of procedures:* For example, are two users entering the same sales order data at different times?

- *Unusually labor-intensive and/or tedious activities:* These are manual activities that could be computerized, like filling out forms to record sales data.

- *Activities that require extensive (complex and/or repetitive) mathematical computation:* An example is updating customer charge account balances and interest charges.

- *Procedures that have become obsolete:* Perhaps your company's licensing requirements have changed, rendering the old procedures useless.

**H**

modeling tools

The analyst can use several tools to assist in the analysis. **Modeling tools** enable the analyst to present graphic (pictorial) representations of a system, or part of a system. These tools include, among others, data flow diagrams (DFDs), systems flowcharts, connectivity diagrams, grid charts, and decision tables. Special software packages, such as Excelerator, a computer-aided software engineering (CASE) tool, automate the production of modeling tools.

- **Data flow diagrams** show the flow of data through a system and diagram the processes that change data into information. They focus on where data originates, where and how it's processed, and where it goes. (See Figure 9.6.) Data flow diagrams can be used for clarification in any

**Figure 9.6**
Data flow diagram symbols (a) and sample diagram (b). Systems analysts use these standard symbols to make data flow diagrams throughout the systems development life cycle.

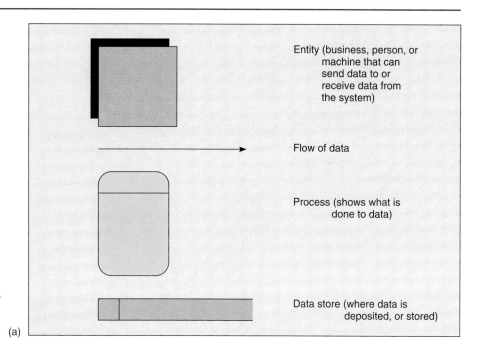

(a)

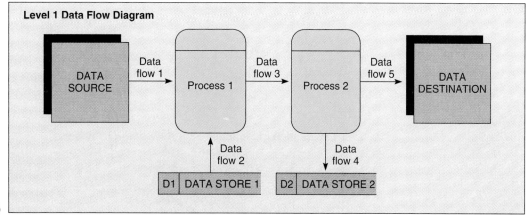

(b)

phase of the systems development life cycle. To give you an example of how data flow symbols are used, Figure 9.7 diagrams a physician's billing system.

■ **Systems flowcharts** focus not only on data flow but on all aspects of a system. They use their own special set of ANSI symbols [✔ p. 224]. (See Figure 9.8.)

■ **Connectivity diagrams** are used to map network connections of people, data, and activities at various locations. (See Figure 9.9.) These diagrams are used as the basis for designing the network and communications systems.

**Figure 9.7**
General data flow diagram of a physician's billing system.

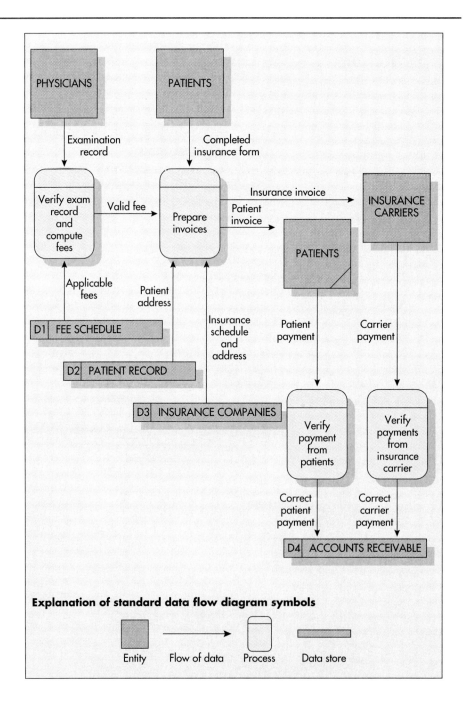

**Figure 9.8**
ANSI systems flowchart symbols.
(a) Systems flowcharts use symbols standardized by the American National Standards Institute.
(b) Example of a systems flowchart.

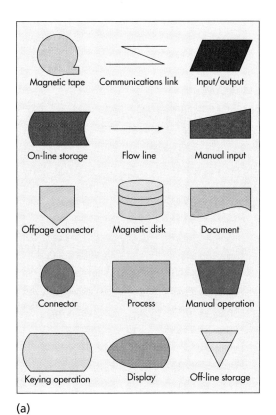

(a)

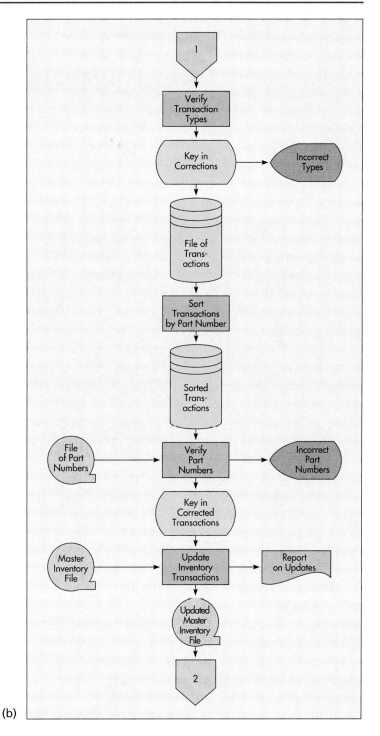

(b)

- **Grid charts** show the relationship between data on input documents and data on output documents. For example, in Figure 9.10, you can see that the data on input forms 1 and 3 is included in output forms A and B.
- **Decision tables** show the rules that apply when certain conditions occur. (See Figure 9.10.)

**Figure 9.9**
Connectivity diagram.

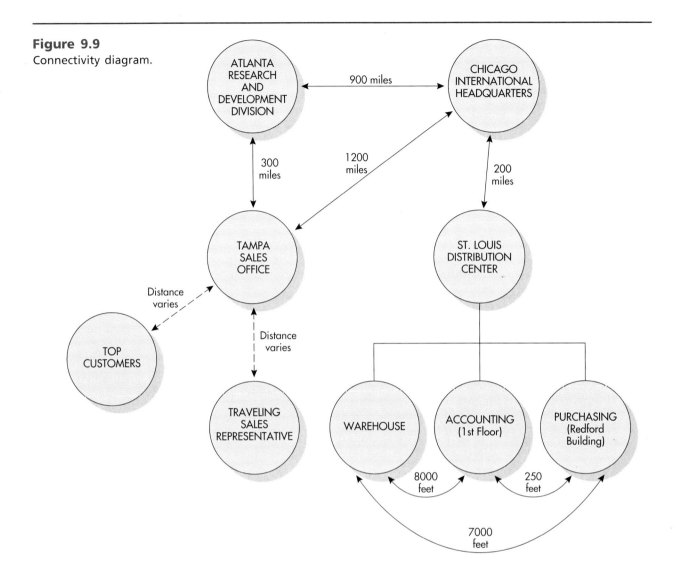

**Figure 9.10**
*Left:* Decision table; *right:* grid chart.

|  | Decision rules | | | | |
|---|:-:|:-:|:-:|:-:|:-:|
|  | **1** | **2** | **3** | **4** | **5** |
| **Conditions** If . . . | N | Y | Y | Y | N |
| And if . . . | Y | Y | N | Y | N |
| And if . . . | Y | Y | N | N | Y |
| **Actions** Then do . . . | ✓ |  |  |  |  |
| Then do . . . |  |  | ✓ |  | ✓ |
| Then do . . . |  | ✓ |  | ✓ |  |

| Forms (input) | Reports (output) | | |
|---|:-:|:-:|:-:|
|  | **Report A** | **Report B** | **Report C** |
| Form 1 | ✓ | ✓ |  |
| Form 2 |  |  | ✓ |
| Form 3 | ✓ | ✓ |  |

prototyping

■ **Prototyping** is another tool used by systems analysts to help them analyze a system and start building a new one. A prototype is essentially a small working model of the system or some aspect of it. The prototype can be set up during this phase, or a later phase, and then modified and improved during subsequent phases.

The first phase of the SDLC usually concludes with a *detailed study report* to management or the steering committee. The objectives of the Phase 1 report are to provide a clear picture of what the current system does, how it does it, and what the analysis identified as problems, causes and effects of problems, and areas where improvements can be made.

## Phase 2: Define New Systems Requirements

**In Phase 2 of the SDLC, systems analysts define the requirements of the new system in detail and evaluate alternative solutions to problems.**

In Phase 2 the analysts focus attention on what they—and the users—want the new system to do. But before designing the new system, the analysts have to define the requirements that it must satisfy. And the requirements must be defined very carefully; otherwise the new system might not end up doing what the users hope it will do.

### Purpose of Phase 2

In the second phase of the SDLC, the analyst defines the requirements for the new system in enough detail so both computer professionals and users know exactly what the new system is going to do and how the system is going to do it. Needless to say, these requirements should solve the problems identified in the first phase.

Once the requirements of a system are known, then both manual and computer-based alternatives are evaluated for new and improved systems. Among the factors affecting what alternatives should be implemented are the availability of computer hardware that is technologically suited to the business's requirements and that fits within the budget of the proposed system. Cost becomes a major factor if software must be created from scratch by a professional programmer, instead of being bought off the shelf (the "make or buy" decision).

The systems analyst uses the modeling tools and prototyping mentioned earlier to help define and graphically describe the new system's requirements and to suggest ways of fulfilling these requirements.

As we mentioned earlier, a prototype is a small-scale working model of a new system module (or of a small system). Analysts often use computer-aided software engineering and automated design tools, such as Excelerator, to create prototypes. The objective of prototyping is to get feedback from users as soon as possible; by trying out a prototype of a proposed part of a new system, users alert analysts to problems early in the SDLC.

Also, modeling and prototyping will be used throughout the entire SDLC to continually document design and development progress and to try out program and systems modules.

## Requirements That Affect Software

Once the business requirements have been defined, most systems analysts and designers focus on the *output* the system must produce. The output requirements fall into three general categories:

1. *Hardcopy output* (printed reports, special forms, and so on)
2. *Softcopy output* (displayed on video screen)
3. *Computer-usable output* (a computer file created during processing for output in one system that is also used as input to another system—for example, a file produced by the payroll system that is later used in the general ledger system)

To define the requirements for hardcopy and softcopy outputs, the analyst meets with each user who will be using each type of output to carefully identify:

■ The purpose of the output

■ The elements of information it will contain

■ How each element will be used

■ How often and how fast the output will need to be produced

In many cases, the analyst will use prototyping tools to produce forms for the user to approve.

The storage, processing, and input requirements are closely related to the output requirements. Input requirements are formulated in terms of:

■ Who will be performing the input procedure

■ The elements of data that will be entered

■ The input screens (the information displayed on the screen that tells the user what data elements to enter)

■ The control procedures to be exercised over the data entry process

Storage requirements are defined in terms of the different files that will need to be created to satisfy the processing and output requirements—for instance, (among other types of files) a master file, an inventory file, an accounts receivable file, an accounts payable file, input transaction and output/report files, and different backup files.

Processing requirements deal with processing schedules—that is, when data is to be input, when output is to be produced, and when files are to be updated—and the identification of logical and computational processing activities.

When all the software-related requirements have been defined, they are usually summarized as a part of the new systems requirements Report (described later).

### Requirements That Affect Hardware

The new system's software requirements must be defined first to determine what type of computer hardware is needed. This may involve modifying equipment already owned or buying new equipment. Hardware requirements will be discussed in more detail in Phase 4.

### Evaluating Alternative Solutions

Once the new system's requirements have been defined, the analyst should examine *alternative* approaches to satisfying the requirements. This step keeps people from jumping to conclusions and gives several options to management. For example, perhaps an expensive conversion to a computer-based system from a manual one is not really necessary! The analyst carefully weighs the advantages and disadvantages of each alternative, including how each might affect the time required to get the new system in place and its estimated cost.

### Systems Requirements Report

Phase 2 concludes with the analyst's preparation of a *systems requirements report*. The report provides the basis for the final determination of the completeness and accuracy of the new systems requirements, as well as the economic and practical feasibility of the new system. After everyone has reviewed and discussed the report, a final decision is made about whether to proceed and, if so, which alternatives to adopt. A revised schedule for project completion is also worked out. If the company is going outside its organization to hire help to develop a new system—which is called *outsourcing*—its systems requirements report may also contain a document called a *request for proposal (RFP)*. This document is used when a company wants to get bids from vendors for prices of software, hardware, programs, supplies, or service. It lists the systems requirements and any limitations.

## Phase 3: Design the New System

**In phase 3 of the SDLC, systems analysts and designers do the actual design work, often using computer-aided systems engineering tools to speed up the design process.**

The third phase of the SDLC focuses on the design of the new system. To determine how the new system will be constructed, the analyst analyzes the requirements defined in Phase 2. The activities in this phase are carried out primarily by computer specialists—that is, programmers. Users may have little direct involvement in the design phase; however, their responses are critical when a programmer needs clarification of logical or computational processing requirements. Users should also continue to be involved in the final approval of procedures that provide for user interface with the system—such as what type of dialog will show up on the video screen—and of proposed report forms, both hardcopy and softcopy. After all, the analysts can leave when their job is done; the users must live with the system!

### Purpose of Phase 3

**H**

CASE tools

Phase 3 involves two main objectives: (1) to design the new system and (2) to establish a sound framework of controls within which the new system should operate. Tools used are, among others, data flow diagrams, systems flowcharts, program flowcharts (used by programmers writing software programs), structured design and programming [✔ p. 220], and prototyping.

**Computer-aided systems engineering (CASE) tools** are also used in Phase 3. These software programs are used in any or all phases of the SDLC. (See Figure 9.11.) CASE tools provide computer-automated support for structured design techniques; they speed up the design process and improve the quality of systems development and documentation. CASE tools are built around the concept of a *project dictionary,* also called a *repository,* which stores all the requirements and specifications for all elements of data to be used in the new system. (See Figure 9.12.)

**Figure 9.11**
CASE tools are used across the entire SDLC.

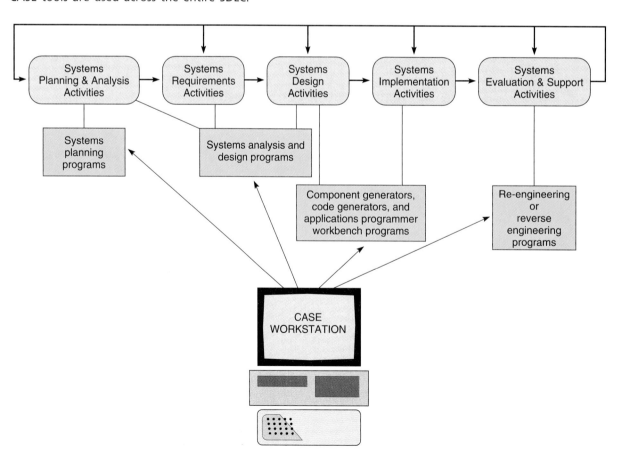

# THE CLIPBOARD

## Testing an Information System for Registered Nurses

Antelope Valley Hospital Medical Center, a full-service 361-bed district hospital located in Lancaster, Calif., has begun its process of selecting a new hospital information system. A Nursing Information Systems Task Force (NSTF) composed of nursing and ancillary directors needed to know what kind of nursing applications to suggest for purchase. They also wanted some ideas of what nursing functions, if computerized, would be beneficial to the nurses. The decision was made to conduct a four-week test on one of the nursing units of a computer-simulated Nursing Information System (NIS). . . .

The Progressive Care Unit (PCU) was chosen as the unit for the test because it is a fast-paced . . . unit with only 16 beds that has a good mix of patients with an all-RN staff.

The database was developed using 4th Dimension software by ACIUS running on Macintosh SE computers. The following decisions were made about the system's design:

- The database needed to be user friendly with limited typing because the PCU staff had never used computers;

- Only a few functions needed computerizing since it was a four-week test;

- Only the functions that would produce the most benefit in a short amount of time needed to be computerized.

The two main nursing functions were the [patient care report] and lab results reporting. . . . The PCU staff had to have two types of training. First, they had to be trained on how to use a computer. Second, they had to be trained on how to use the PCU test software. They also needed to be trained as close to the implementation date as possible to avoid forgetting what was taught. . . .

The most frequent on-line users of the PCU Test were the unit secretaries and the resource persons (RPs), who are RNs assigned to coordinate activities each shift. The staff RNs were the most frequent users of the output from the system, such as caregiver reports.

There were mixed reactions to the system. Since only a few functions were computerized, all of PCU's normal systems had to stay in place; consequently, many of the nurses felt that their workload was increased. . . .

This approach may not be suitable for every organization. The database design was very time consuming and labor intensive. The expectation of time that the system design and implementation would take was seven months, while it actually took a year and a half to complete the test. The time to design the system took 15 months.

Denise M. Overstreet, "Computer Simulation Helps Nurses Select Information Systems," *Industrial Engineering,* August 1992, p. 63.

**Figure 9.12**
Project dictionary organization. A project dictionary forms the base of a CASE tool. The dictionary is maintained on the computer and then ultimately output as documentation.

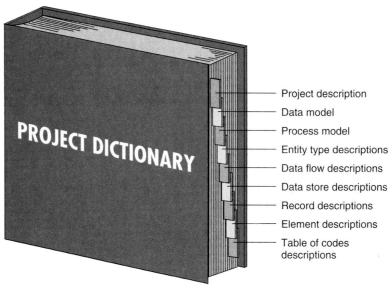

Among other outputs, CASE tools can generate:

- Graphics tools such as data flow diagrams, flowcharts, structure charts, and data models
- Reports on file contents, properties of data elements, and rules of logic
- Prototypes
- Quality analysis reports
- Programming code for writing software programs
- Project management charts
- Cost/benefit analyses

Figure 9.13 gives you an idea of how these capabilities relate to one another. In addition to Excelerator, CASE tools include, among others, Knowledgeware, Framework, AW/DOC, firstCASE, HyperAnalyst, SPQR/20, and System Architect.

## Designing New Systems Controls and Security Functions

New systems must be designed to operate within a framework of controls, a system of safeguards that protect a computer system and data from accidental or intentional damage, from input and output inaccuracies, and from access by unauthorized persons. As computer systems become easier and easier to use, and as software becomes more and more user friendly, the importance of designing adequate security controls into an information system grows. Controls involve the physical environment of the system (for example, limiting access to buildings, rooms, doors, and computer hardware), the manual procedures performed by users and computer specialists (creation of a disaster plan, documentation of procedures for distributing output), and the computer-based processing procedures (access to data, use of software, and standards for data input and verification).

**Figure 9.13**

Some computer-aided software engineering (CASE) capabilities. This figure shows how the capabilities relate to one another and to the people involved in the systems development process.

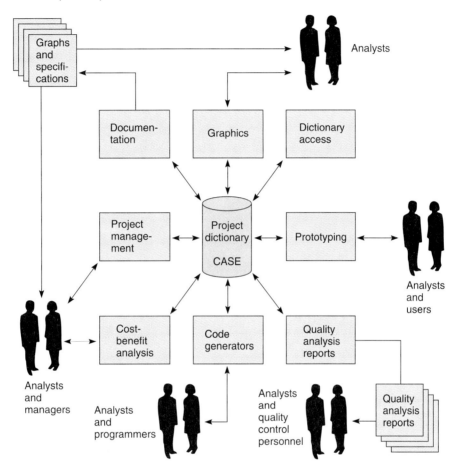

## Concluding the Design Phase

At the end of Phase 3, the analysts/designers complete, organize, and assemble the new systems design documentation by using a combination of the tools and techniques discussed earlier in the chapter. The documentation should include:

■ A complete overview of the new system as a whole

■ A description (narrative or graphic) of the major processing modules into which the system has been divided for design purposes

■ Detailed documentation describing the input, processing, and output activities in each module and submodule

■ Specifications of the storage requirements for the new system; a description of each file to be maintained in the system, including anticipated size and organization scheme/access method to be used

■ A narrative description of the controls to be used with the new system

Then systems analyst(s), users, and management meet to review the design. A decision is made to approve the design and proceed to the next phase of the SDLC—systems development—or to revise the design before continuing. Although a decision on whether to discard a project entirely would usually be made at an earlier phase, it is still possible that the project could be terminated at this time.

## Phase 4: Develop the New System and Have Users Test It

**In the fourth phase of the SDLC, hardware and software are obtained, and the new system is tested.**

A company that is changing from a manual to a computer-based system (or modifying an existing computer-based system) cannot run out and buy hardware in Phase 1 because it doesn't yet know what the new system is supposed to do. The company shouldn't make purchases during Phase 2 either because, although its requirements have been established, the new system has not yet been designed. During Phase 3, the system has been designed but not yet accepted. It's not until Phase 4 that the system is accepted and development begins. Now the company can acquire software and hardware.

### Purpose of Phase 4

During Phase 4, four major activities occur:

1. Acquire software
2. Acquire hardware
3. Train the users
4. Test the new system

### Acquire Software

If the software is not purchased off the shelf (prepackaged), it must be written by programmers. These programmers use appropriate logic-development tools, programming languages [✓ p. 198], coding procedures, and testing and documentation methods.

### Acquire Hardware

Here are some points company representatives consider when buying (or leasing) hardware:

■ If some computers have already been acquired, determine if additional units need to be compatible.

■ For a microcomputer-based system, establish the minimum amount of main memory [✓ p. 82] to satisfy the processing requirements.

■ If processing will involve extensive mathematical or graphics calculations, plan to install special math coprocessor chips [✓ p. 93] in some microcomputers.

■ Determine which video display units will need to be high resolution for certain applications like graphics. If graphics are required, graphics adapter cards and color SVGA monitors [✓ p. 163] may be required for certain computers.

■ Analyze carefully the storage requirements to help determine what size system to purchase; consider removable storage media like hard disk packs or cartridges for flexible storage capacities.

- Consider the quality, volume, and type of printed output to be produced in order to determine the types of printers required.

- Determine the delivery schedules for all equipment.

- Determine where the hardware should be installed.

- Determine how many users the system will need to support now—and in a year or two.

- Determine the amount of multitasking [✓ p. 200] required.

- Determine the type of operating system that will ensure program compatibility and efficiency.

- Evaluate computer network and other communications needs.

If using existing hardware, the new system design must be reviewed to determine if additional hardware is required. Once hardware needs have been identified, the company must determine which vendor to choose.

### Train the Users

Of course, an information system is no better than its users. Thus training is essential—the users and the computer operators must be trained to use the new hardware and software. This can often be started before the equipment is delivered; for example, the vendor may give training seminars on its own premises or provide temporary training equipment. Training is also done in Phase 5 of the SDLC. A variety of tools can be used, including instruction manuals, video tapes, live tutorials (teacher/student sessions), classes, and, in some cases, multimedia presentations.

### Test the New System

Several methods may be used to test the new system. However, a **user acceptance test** must be done to make sure the system does what users want it to do before the new system is implemented. In other words, it must be tested for *quality assurance*. Sample data must put every line of every program to the test. Also, procedures must be tested to make sure the program will support all conceivable user responses. Testing may take several months; once completed, most bugs should be eliminated.

## Phase 5: Implement the New System

**In the fifth phase of the SDLC, final operating documentation and procedures are created, files are converted, and the new system is used. Conversion to the new system may proceed in four ways: direct, parallel, phased, or pilot.**

The process of developing a new system costs a great deal of time, energy, and money. However, even a beautifully designed and developed system can fail to meet its objectives if it is not carefully implemented. In this phase, the company converts from the old system to the new system.

### Purpose of Phase 5

The implementation phase, which gets the new system up and running, involves creating the final operating documentation and procedures, converting files, and using the new system.

## Final Operating Documentation and Procedures

In the first step of getting ready to implement a new system, the analyst prepares the final operating documentation. This collection of documents (electronic and hardcopy) describes the requirements, capabilities, limitations, design, operation, and maintenance of the system. The procedures covered include entering data, making inquiries, directing processing activities, and distributing reports. The computer operators must have operating documentation that identifies the processing schedule, files to be used, and programs to be run. The data entry group must have procedures on how the input data is to be entered. The control group must have procedures for monitoring system controls and coordinating the distribution of reports. Figure 9.14 shows some elements of a documentation package.

**Figure 9.14**
Sample documentation package.

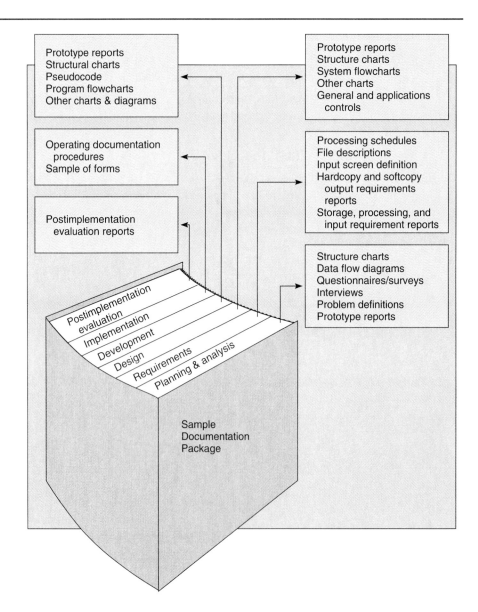

# THE CLIPBOARD

## Setting Up a Company Bulletin Board System

Many companies create BBSes [computer bulletin board systems] to establish better contact with their customers or employees. A BBS allows customers or clients to log on, check the status of orders they've placed, and ask questions about a product or service they've purchased. . . .

Some link employees at offsite locations to the company's local-area network (LAN), says Jack Rickard, editor and publisher of *Boardwatch*, a specialty online magazine. Other company BBSes are designed as sales mechanisms —for real estate offices offering listings, for instance, or for natural gas carriers conducting auctions. Still other BBSes are in business to provide publicity. Both the U.S. Olympic Committee and the National Football League have BBSes where members of the media can log on for the latest information. . . .

Before starting a BBS, you should plan carefully. It's best to do your research before investing money. Call other company BBSes to get a feeling for the online culture. Talk to BBS system operators (sysops) and ask about pitfalls you should avoid and what all is involved. . . .

BBSes can be set up for very little money, but costs can escalate quickly depending on which type of BBS software you choose, the number of phone lines you have installed, and what your application is. . . .

BBSes also take room. Most of the time it's very little room, but even the simplest BBSes need a PC and workspace. Some very large BBSes require rooms full of equipment to support multiple phone lines coming in.

But don't overestimate what's involved. The biggest mistake people make when creating a BBS that's open to the public is overestimating the number of lines needed. . . .

According to Rickard, people sometimes think you need 100 phone lines to handle 100 callers per day. In reality you can usually handle 100 callers per day with only two lines. . . .

BBSes are typically run on personal computers using the DOS, Macintosh, or Unix platforms. By far the majority of BBSes, however, are run on PCs using DOS because of the wide availability of hardware and software choices and the comparatively low cost. . . .

Assuming you've decided to go with a DOS-based BBS, your next choice is between multinode and multitasking systems. Multinode BBS software requires that you have one copy of the software for every phone line on the system. . . .

A multimode system is a good choice when you want to link remote employees to your LAN, says Rickard. Popular multinode BBS packages include *Wildcat* from Mustang Software and *PCBoard* from Clark Development. . . .

A multitasking system is a good choice if you want to do customer or client outreach. Such systems typically use more phone lines than employee BBSes. Multitasking systems are generally more economical than multinode systems when you're using multiple phone lines, especially with more than eight lines. Popular multitasking BBS software packages include *The Major BBS* from Galacticomm and *TBBS* from eSoft.

Reid Goldsborough, "Setting Up a Company Bulletin Board System," *PC Novice,* May 1994, pp. 69–72.

### Converting Files

Typically a new computer-based system cannot be used until all the manually recorded data files are converted into computer-usable form. However, sometimes the new system can be used at the same time the manual files are being converted. When a manual system is computerized, file conversion can become a monumental task. The time, effort, and cost required to design appropriate file structures and key in the data are enormous. Outside assistance may be required for large file conversion tasks. If an existing computer-based system is being changed to a new system, the files can be converted by a computer program.

### Using the New System

There are four basic approaches to implementing a new system: direct implementation, parallel implementation, phased implementation, and pilot implementation. The concepts behind the four approaches are diagrammed in Figure 9.15.

**Figure 9.15**
Four approaches to systems implementation.

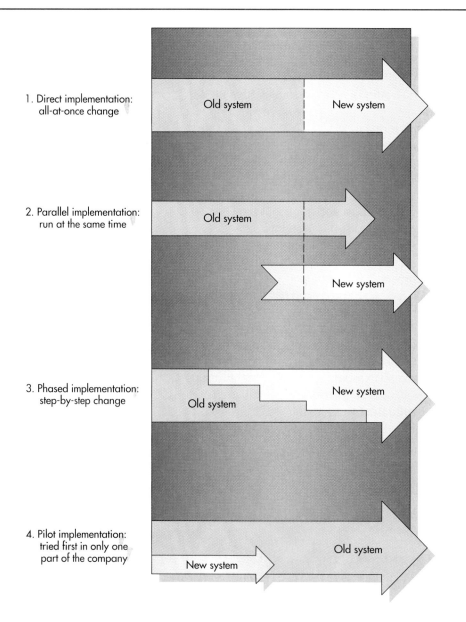

1. Direct implementation: all-at-once change

   Old system | New system

2. Parallel implementation: run at the same time

   Old system

   New system

3. Phased implementation: step-by-step change

   New system

   Old system

4. Pilot implementation: tried first in only one part of the company

   Old system

   New system

In **direct implementation,** the change is made all at once. The old system is halted on a planned date and the new system is activated. This approach is most often used for small systems or larger systems for which a systems model was previously developed and thoroughly tested. Simply halting the old system and starting up the new system is a very simple approach; however, this method carries some risks. For example, in most large systems, there are far too many variables to be adequately tested. As a result, a few unexpected errors are almost always found during the initial implementation period. These errors are much more disruptive and difficult to correct when the old system has been halted. Normal processing cannot continue until the errors are fixed.

**Parallel implementation** involves running the old system and the new system at the same time for a specified period. The results of using the new system are compared to the old system. If the performance of the new system is satisfactory, use of the old system is discontinued. This approach is the safest because operations do not have to be shut down if the new system has problems; however, it is by far the most expensive and difficult approach to coordinate. Operating two systems takes much more time and effort. In addition to operating both systems, it will be necessary to compare the output from the new system to the old system and evaluate the results.

When the parallel implementation approach is used, a formal meeting of the project development team and the users is held at the end of the trial period. The performance of the new system is discussed and a decision is reached as to whether the findings are positive enough to warrant discontinuing the operation of the old system.

Some systems are just too broad in scope or are so large that they must be implemented in phases to avoid the traumatic effect of trying to implement all the components at once. Implementation is more easily handled one phase at a time—**phased implementation.**

If a system is to be implemented at many locations in a widely dispersed company, the task can be very difficult to manage all at once. To implement the system in one location at a time—and ensure that it is working correctly before moving on to other locations—is safer. This method is called **pilot implementation.**

## Phase 6: Postimplementation Evaluation and Maintenance (Support)

**The last phase of the SDLC consists of keeping the system running through system audits and periodic evaluations. When the time and money spent on maintaining and updating a system reach a critical point, it's time to start planning a new systems development life cycle.**

Two very important activities take place after the new system has been implemented: postimplementation evaluation and systems maintenance (systems support). Ongoing **systems maintenance** involves making necessary adjustments and enhancements, or additions, to the system during the years it is used. Adjustments may be needed because, as users gain experience in using the new system, they may define additional needs. Or government reporting regulations may change, creating new requirements for a system to satisfy. Companies must remember to budget funds to pay for maintenance.

## Purpose of Phase 6

After a new system has been in operation for several months and any necessary systems maintenance has been done, a formal evaluation—called a **postimplementation evaluation**—of the new system takes place. This evaluation determines either that the new system is meeting its objectives or that certain things need to be done so that it will meet these objectives.

The end of the final step in the SDLC is marked by the preparation of a new systems evaluation report. The report summarizes the extent to which the system meets the original objectives and includes a list of enhancements to be considered for future development and implementation.

After a system has been in operation for an extended period of time, it may become obsolete. That means that the time and money involved in modernizing or altering the system may cost more than developing an entire new and better system. Time to start planning the SDLC all over again.

## What Skills Does the User Need?

Figure 9.16 reviews the points at which you, the user, may interact with the systems development life cycle. Whether or not you will need to use any of the tools and techniques for analyzing and documenting systems and their development depends on the type of organization you're with and the level of expertise you have gained. But, in most cases, you will need only a basic understanding of the life cycle used at your place of business and the objectives of each phase. You will need to develop your ability to communicate effectively with computer specialists to help your company operate efficiently and profitably. If you can't communicate your business needs clearly, your requirements may not be met by the new system.

## Suggestions for Further Reading

Brooks, F. *The Mythical Man-Month: Essays on Software Engineering*. Reading, MA: Addison-Wesley, 1982.

Kendall, K., and Kendall, J. *Systems Analysis and Design* (3rd ed.). Englewood Cliffs, NJ: Prentice Hall, 1995.

Whitten, J., Bentley, L., and Barlow, V. *Systems Design and Analysis Methods* (3rd ed.). Burr Ridge, IL: Richard D. Irwin, 1994.

**Figure 9.17**
User interaction with the systems analysis and design life cycle. This diagram reviews the points at which you, the user, may interact with systems analysts and designers.

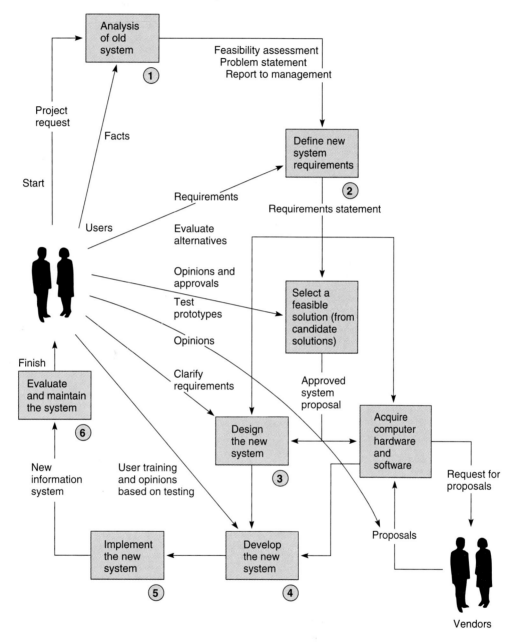

# S U M M A R Y

■ Users must participate in the systems analysis and design process because they have to explain to analysts and designers how they use the current system and what they think is wrong with it. Users also must be involved in testing new systems and have to be able to follow the charts, diagrams, and written procedures in the new systems documentation so that they will be able to use the new system effectively. (p. 310)

■ The *systems development life cycle (SDLC)* is the formal process by which organizations build manual and computer-based information systems. Systems development life cycles may be known by different names and comprise varying numbers of phases, but their principles are basically the same. (p. 311)

■ An SDLC is used as a guideline in directing and administering the activities involved in establishing business system requirements, developing the system, acquiring hardware and software, and controlling development costs. Without a reasoned approach to systems analysis and design, systems development can result in disruption of normal working procedures, acquisition of too much or too little computer hardware, development of inadequate software, misunderstood user needs and requirements, new system problems resulting from inadequate testing, and inadequate documentation for system maintenance and future modification. (p. 312)

■ An SDLC can be divided into six phases (p. 313):

   *Phase 1: Analyze* current system
   *Phase 2: Define* new systems requirements
   *Phase 3: Design* new system
   *Phase 4: Develop* new system and have users test it
   *Phase 5: Implement* new system
   *Phase 6: Evaluate* performance of and maintain (support) new system

■ In *Phase 1,* the objective is to gain a clear understanding of the existing system, including its shortcomings, and determine where improvements can be made. (p. 314)

■ To analyze the current system, analysts and users must gather information about the existing system using such techniques as interviewing; reviewing written policies and procedures; collecting sample forms, reports, and other documents, including *organization charts;* observing operations and office environment; and using questionnaires to conduct surveys. (p. 319)

■ After information about the current system has been gathered, it must be analyzed. Problems and opportunities to improve the system are identified. Systems analysts use many tools and techniques to study the system and document the analysis. Among these tools are *data flow diagrams, grid charts, decision tables, systems flowcharts, prototyping,* and *computer-aided software engineering (CASE) tools.* Phase 1 concludes with a report and presentation to management that summarizes the current systems analysis and gives a recommendation about whether or not to proceed. (p. 321)

■ *Phase 2* of the SDLC involves defining the requirements for the new system—manual as well as computer-based procedures. Requirements should be defined in the areas of input, storage, processing, and output. Defining software requirements focuses first on the output that the users will need. Phase 2 concludes with a systems requirements report. (p. 325)

■ *Phase 3* of the SDLC focuses on the technical design of the new system, using programming techniques and methods plus CASE tools and continued prototyping. Designing the new systems controls for both manual and computer-based procedures is also an important part of Phase 3. (p. 327)

■ Developing the new system, *Phase 4* of the SDLC, involves acquiring software and hardware, training users and operators, and testing the new system (*user acceptance test*). (p. 332)

■ *Phase 5* of the SDLC involves implementing the new system. This phase includes three steps (p. 333):

1. Creating final operating documentation and procedures

2. Converting files

3. Using the system

■ New systems can be implemented (p. 337):

1. All at once (*direct implementation*)

2. While the old system is still running (*parallel implementation*)

3. Step-by-step (*phased implementation*)

4. In one section of the company at a time; each section's system must be working before the next section's system is implemented (*pilot implementation*)

■ *Phase 6* of the SDLC involves postimplementation evaluation and maintenance. The evaluation determines whether or not the new system is meeting its objectives. Maintenance involves ongoing support of the system. (p. 337)

■ One reason why a new system fails is a lack of communication somewhere along the line. Thus users should understand the basics of the systems development life cycle—so that they can intelligently communicate to the information specialists the problems with the current system as it affects their jobs and their requirements for the new system.

## KEY TERMS

computer-aided software
  engineering (CASE) tools,
  p. 328
connectivity diagram, p. 322
data flow diagram, p. 321
decision table, p. 323
direct implementation, p. 337
grid chart, p. 323
modeling tools, p. 321

organization chart, p. 319
parallel implementation,
  p. 337
phased implementation,
  p. 337
pilot implementation, p. 337
postimplementation evaluation, p. 338
prototyping, p. 325

systems analyst, p. 314
systems development life
  cycle (SDLC), p. 310
systems flowchart, p. 322
systems maintenance
  (support), p. 337
user acceptance test, p. 333

## EXERCISES

### SELF-TEST

1. The process of building a small, simple model of a new information system is called ___prototype___ .

2. Name three ways of gathering data in Phase 1 of the SDLC.

   a. Interview

   b. Observe

   c. review policy & procedure

3. What are the four methods of implementing a new system?

   a. – direct

   b. – ||

   c. step by step → ∅

   d. pilot

4. The ___project___ ___dictionary___ stores all the requirements and specifications for all elements of data to be used in a new system.

5. _____Direct_____ _____implementation_____ is when the old system is halted on a given date and the new system is activated.

6. Users are never involved in systems development. (true/false) *[false circled]*

7. The modeling tool used by the systems analyst to focus on the flow of data through a system is called a(n) ___DATA___ ___FLOW___ ___DIAGRAM___.

8. The situation in which the old system and the new system are running at the same time for a specified period is called ___||___ implementation.

9. The document used by a company when it goes outside its organization to develop a new system or purchase parts of a new system is called a(n) ___request___ ___for___ ___proposal___.

10. A(n) ___business___ ___system___ supports and usually automates day-to-day business operations, whereas a(n) ___infor.___ ___system___ generates information to support decision making by managers.

11. A(n) ___organization___ ___chart___ shows an organization's levels of management and lines of authority.

12. Automated systems design and prototyping tools are called ___CASE___ _____ _____ (_____) tools

*Solutions:* (1) prototyping; (2) conduct interviews, observe operations, conduct surveys, review policies and procedures; (3) direct, phased, parallel, pilot; (4) project dictionary; (5) direct implementation; (6) false; (7) data flow diagram; (8) parallel; (9) request for proposal; (10) business system, information system; (11) organization chart; (12) computer-aided software engineering (CASE)

## SHORT-ANSWER QUESTIONS

1. What is the importance of first defining the output requirements of a proposed system?
2. Briefly describe the six phases of the SDLC.
3. What are some of the techniques used to gather data in the analysis phase of the SDLC?
4. What determines the extent to which your job brings you in contact with your company's SDLC?
5. Why is it important for users to understand the principles of the SDLC?
6. Describe the four basic approaches to implementing a new system.
7. What are computer-aided software engineering tools used for?
8. Several common tools are used for defining a new system's requirements, including modeling tools. Name some modeling tools. What are they used for?
9. Why is it important for a company to follow an orderly SDLC?
10. Why should users be included in the testing stages of a new system?

## PROJECTS AND CRITICAL THINKING EXERCISES

1. Using recent computer publications, research the state of the art of computer-aided software engineering (CASE) tools. What capabilities do these tools have? What do you think the future holds for CASE tools?
2. Designing system controls. Your company is just beginning the process of computerizing the sales order entry activities. Currently, orders are received by mail, over the phone, and at the counter when customers stop by. The plan is to key the phone orders and counter orders into the computer immediately. The orders received in the mail will be entered into the computer in groups. A typical order contains customer information (such as number, name, and address) and product information (such as product number, description, quantity ordered, and unit price).
    a. Identify possible control techniques that could be designed into the system to ensure that all sales orders are input in their entirety to the computer.
    b. Identify possible control techniques to help ensure all sales order data is accurately entered into the system.
    c. How would the control techniques for phone orders and counter orders differ from the orders received in the mail?
3. Design a system that would handle the input, processing, and output of a simple form of your choice. Use a data flow diagram to illustrate the system.
4. Interview a student majoring in computer science who plans to become a systems analyst. Why is this person interested in this field? What does he or she hope to accomplish in it? What courses must be taken to satisfy the requirements for becoming an analyst? What major changes in systems design and analysis does this person forecast for the next five years?

## IN THE LAB WITH MICROSOFT WINDOWS

(*Note:* If you aren't familiar with using a mouse and/or don't know how to use the Microsoft Windows graphical user interface, complete the In the Lab with Microsoft Windows exercises in Chapter 6 before proceeding.)

### Windows Setup

1. In this exercise, you learn how to display information about your display screen, keyboard, mouse, and network (if you're connected to one). Right now, the Microsoft Windows Program Manager should be displaying.
2. DOUBLE-CLICK: Main group icon
   DOUBLE-CLICK: Windows Setup program icon
   Information about your computer system should be displaying.
3. After reviewing the information:
   DOUBLE-CLICK: Control-menu box *located in the upper-left corner of the Windows Setup window*
4. To close the Main group window:
   DOUBLE-CLICK: Control-menu box *located in the upper-left corner of the Main window*

### Using Help

1. In this exercise, you learn how to use the Windows Help facility. The Windows Help facility is *context-sensitive*. That is, Windows displays Help information that relates to the current application and task. The procedures described in the following steps work no matter what Windows application you use. Right now, the Microsoft Windows Program Manager should be displaying.

2. Since the Program Manager is displaying, the help facility will display information related to the Program Manager.
CHOOSE: Help, Contents
You can now see a list of the topics that relate to the Program Manager. To select a topic, move the mouse pointer over a topic and then click. Notice that when you move the mouse pointer over a topic, it changes in appearance to look like a hand.
SELECT: "Start an Application"
Several other topics become available.
3. To back up to the previous list of topics:
CLICK: Back button
4. To search for information about icons:
CLICK: Search button
TYPE: icons
5. To learn how to arrange icons:
DOUBLE-CLICK: "icons, arranging"
DOUBLE-CLICK: "Arranging Windows and Icons"
Related information should be displaying.
6. Now that you've had some practice displaying help information, it's time to exit the Help facility.
DOUBLE-CLICK: Control-menu box *located in the upper-left corner of the Help window*

## Interlocking Businesses:
## A Virtual Partnership

In the Toronto, Canada, area, Anna Stahmer runs her business of management and strategic consulting on learning technologies ("learnware"). This includes a wide range of technologies—from satellite business to multimedia products and online services—for corporate training departments, schools, colleges, government, and supplier companies of learnware products. Among many other appointments, Anna also serves on the Working Group for Education and Training of the Canadian Information Highway Advisory Council.

In addition to her consulting work, Anna produces a technology publication with Lyndsay Green. They operate out of separate in-home offices to combine their consulting businesses electronically, in a "virtual partnership," to write and produce *The Training Technology Monitor.* Lyndsay has final responsibility for editing and desktop publishing, whereas Anna does the accounting and administrative and fulfillment management work. The partners share equally in identifying, researching, and writing stories and in marketing the *Monitor.* They are also frequent speakers at national and international conferences.

For writing, editing, and desktop publishing, Lyndsay uses a Macintosh Centris 660 AV, a LaserWriterPro printer, Aldus PageMaker and Microsoft Office software; for portable computing she uses an Apple Powerbook 520.

Anna uses a PC system with windows and WordPerfect 6.1. For accounting work, she uses Excel; for fulfillment management, she has built a subscriber database using Lotus Organizer. To be sure data is not lost, Anna maintains a parallel subscriber database in WordPerfect.

As a portable computer, Anna uses a Zenith Z Star 433VL PC-compatible. Lyndsay and Anna frequently exchange text, interview coding formats, and so on either by exchanging disks or by transferring files online via Maclink software. Anna often uses CompuServe for e-mail exchange and research. The partners also subscribe to the Internet and are investigating the prospect publishing the *Monitor* via the Net.

Anna and Lyndsay are continuously challenged to be at the leading edge of finding information and news stories about communications technology; maintaining contact with colleagues throughout North America, Europe, and elsewhere; and sifting, analyzing, and interpreting vast amounts of information so subscribers and clients receive the information they need in an easily readable format. Indeed, Anna and Lyndsay could be called "information agents of the future."

Anna Stahmer and Lyndsay Green, "virtual partners" in publishing *The Training Technology Monitor* in Toronto, Canada.

# Chapter Topics

# CHAPTER 10

# Database Management

Where does the power come from in a computer-based information system? Although your first answer may be "hardware and the speed with which it can process data," if you think about it a bit longer you will probably realize that the real power comes from the data. From data comes information, and access to information offers power. But the amounts of data being handled by companies with computer-based systems have grown so large in recent years that dealing with it has become a sophisticated operation.

## Preview

*When you have completed this chapter, you will be able to:*

- Describe the parts of the data hierarchy

- Explain what a database is

- Describe the difference between file management systems and database management systems

- Describe how database management systems software relates to hardware and the user

- Identify the advantages and the disadvantages of the three database models and of database management systems in general

- Explain the importance of database administration within an organization

**Why Is This Chapter Important?**

*Managers and users need information to make effective decisions. Indeed, the lifeblood of any business, no matter how large or small, is its information. The more accurate, relevant, and timely the information, the better informed people will be when making decisions. Now we turn our attention to the organization of the data that makes up the information. In general, database management concepts are the same for large computer systems and for microcomputers. As a general business user, you will most likely be using a microcomputer or a terminal to access data stored in a database. Therefore you need to understand the data hierarchy, as well as the features of a database and a database management system. Through a better understanding of database systems, you can put them to effective use in your job.*

## Overview of the Data Hierarchy

**The data hierarchy comprises bits, bytes, fields, records, and files, which are the elements of a database.**

Computers, as we have said, work on the principal that electricity may be on or off, high-voltage or low-voltage, or present or absent. Thus, individual items of data are represented by 0 for off and 1 for on. A 0 or 1 is a **bit.** A unit of 8 bits is a **byte;** it may be used to represent a letter, number, or other value, such as A, 3, or ?. Bits and bytes are the building blocks for representing data, whether it is being processed, stored, or telecommunicated.

Data can be grouped according to a hierarchy of categories, each increasingly more complex. The **data storage hierarchy** consists of the levels of stored data: bits, bytes (characters), fields, records, files, and databases. (See Figure 10.1.) Bits and bytes are what the computer hardware deals with, and you need not be concerned with them. You will, however, be dealing with characters, fields, records, files, and databases.

- *Byte (character):* A *byte* is a group of 8 bits. A **character** may be—but is not necessarily—the same as a byte. A character is a single letter, number, or special character such as ;, $, or %.

- *Field:* A **field** is a unit of data consisting of one or more characters. An example of a field is your name, your address, or your Social Security number. Note: One reason the Social Security number is often used to identify people—for good or for ill—is that, unlike many names, it is a *distinctive* (unique) field. Thus, it can be used to easily locate information about you only. Such a key is called a **key field;** this is a field that is chosen to uniquely identify a record so that it can be easily retrieved.

- *Record:* A **record** is a collection of related fields. An example of a record would be your name *and* address *and* Social Security number.

- *File:* A **file** is a collection of related records. An example of a file is collected data on everyone employed in the same department of a company, including all names, addresses, and Social Security numbers.

- *Database:* A **database** is a collection of related files. A company database might include files on all past and current employees in all departments. There would be various files for each employee: payroll, retirement benefits, sales quotas and achievements (if in sales), and so on. A database may be fairly small, contained entirely within your own personal computer. Or it may be massive, available online to you from an information service [✔ p. 289] through computer and telephone connections. Table 10.1 on page 350 reviews basic database terminology.

**Figure 10.1**

Data storage hierarchy: How data is organized. Bits are organized into bytes, bytes into fields, fields into records, records into files. Related files may be organized into a database.

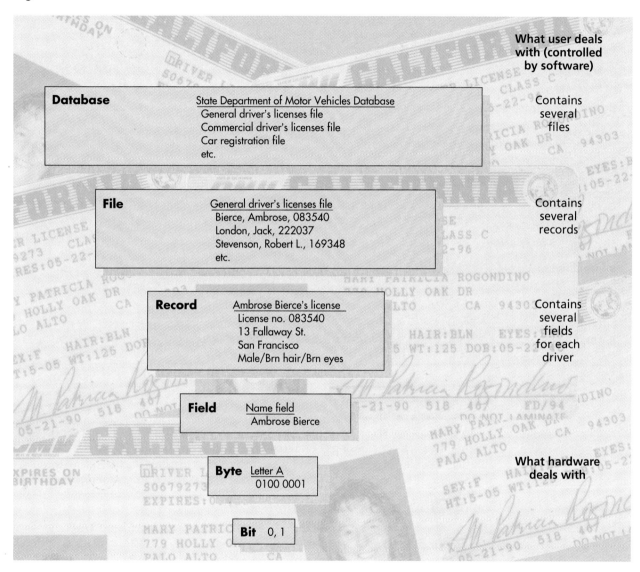

## What Is a Database Management System?

A database management system is a computer-based system for defining, creating, manipulating, controlling, managing, and using databases. A database is a collection of integrated data organized as bytes, fields, records, and files. Database management systems are replacing old file management systems and are thereby improving data integrity and independence and reducing data redundancy.

As we mentioned, a **database** is a collection of related files. It is also defined as a group of stored, integrated (cross-referenced) data elements that can be retrieved and manipulated with great flexibility to produce information. A **database management system (DBMS)** is a computer-based system whose

DBMS

**Table 10.1**   Database Terminology

**Alphanumeric (character) data:** data composed of a combination of letters, numbers, and other symbols (like punctuation marks) that are not used for mathematical calculations

**Bit:** contraction of *binary digit*; either 1 ("on") or 0 ("off") in computerized (digitized) data representation

**Byte:** a unit of 8 bits

**Character:** a single letter, number, or special character; a character may be, but isn't necessarily, the same as a byte

**Data:** the raw facts that make up information

**Database:** a large collection of stored, integrated (cross-referenced) records that can be maintained and manipulated with great flexibility; the top level in the data hierarchy

**Entity:** any tangible or intangible object or concept about which an organization wishes to store data; entities have attributes, such as name, color, and price

**Field,** or **attribute,** or **data element:** a group of related characters (an attribute is also a column of a relation in a relational database, discussed later); the second-lowest level in the data hierarchy

**File:** a group of related records; the fourth level from the bottom in the data hierarchy

**Information:** data that has value to, or that has been interpreted by, the user

**Key:** a particular field that is chosen to uniquely identify a record so that it can be easily retrieved and processed

**Numeric data:** data composed of numeric digits (numbers); used for mathematical calculations

**Record:** a group of related fields; the third level from the bottom in the data hierarchy (analogous to a tuple, or row, in a relational database, as described later)

software allows creation, maintenance, and manipulation of a database to produce relevant business or research information. By *integrated* we mean that the file records are logically related to one another so that *all* data on a topic can be retrieved by simple requests. The database management system software represents the interface between the user, and the computer's operating system [✔ p. 197] and the database. (See Figure 10.2.)

Picture a typical corporate office with a desk, chairs, telephones, and a row of file cabinets along the wall. A wide variety of business data is stored in file cabinets. If the files have been carefully organized and maintained,

**Figure 10.2**
DBMS software as interface. The database management system software is the facilitator that allows the user to access and manipulate integrated data elements in a database.

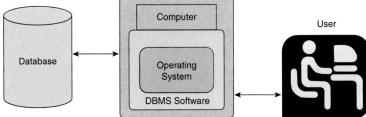

then any piece of data that needs to be retrieved can usually be located quickly and removed. However, if the data has not been properly filed, some time and effort will be expended to find it. And, regardless of how carefully the files have been organized and maintained, you will always need to retrieve related pieces of data. For example, suppose you need to review the customer files for all invoices for payments due in excess of $2,500 and prepare a simple report. How would you accomplish this task? First, you would probably go through the customer files in alphabetical order, folder by folder. You would examine each invoice in the folders to determine if the amount is in excess of $2,500 and remove and copy each invoice that meets the criterion. You would then have to refile the copies you removed (and risk misfiling them). When you had examined all the customer folders and copied all the appropriate invoices, you would then review the copies and put together your report. Imagine how much time this could take. If there are a lot of customers, you would need to spend hours, if not days.

Now let's look at the situation in a different way. The environment is the same, except you have, instead of file cabinets, a microcomputer or a terminal [✓ p. 43] and DBMS software that has access to a customer database *file.* (See Figure 10.3.) In this file a row of customer data is referred to as a *record.* An individual piece of data within a record, such as a name, is referred to as a *field.* To get the invoice data you need, you would do something like this:

■ Turn on the computer and the printer.

■ Start up the DBMS software.

■ Give the command to "open up" the customer database file stored on your disk, which is similar in concept to manually opening up the customer drawer in a file cabinet.

■ Give the command to search all the records in the database file and display copies of the records that meet your criterion (that is, the names of people with unpaid invoices greater than $2,500). If you were using dBASE IV, a popular microcomputer DBMS, the command would look something like:

```
LIST FOR_INV AMOUNT > 2500
```

**Figure 10.3**
Customer database file. This figure illustrates only a small section of our hypothetical customer file. Data stored electronically in a DBMS can be much more easily retrieved than data stored in filing cabinets.

| Customer Name | Date | Item Ordered | Quantity Ordered | Invoice Amount |
|---|---|---|---|---|
| Arthene Ng | 02/12/96 | 4065 | 6 | 2510.67 |
| Pamela Robert | 02/13/96 | 4128 | 7 | 1510.62 |
| Jeff Arguello | 02/13/96 | 4111 | 1 | 1905.00 |
| Sylvia Arnold | 02/14/96 | 4007 | 6 | 2950.93 |
| Richard Mall | 02/14/96 | 4019 | 1 | 63.55 |
| Alan Steinberg | 02/14/96 | 4021 | 3 | 1393.00 |
| Harry Filbert | 02/14/96 | 4106 | 2 | 940.56 |
| Frances Chung | 02/15/96 | 4008 | 5 | 2717.00 |
| Bruce Chaney | 02/15/96 | 4007 | 8 | 1720.00 |

Field      Record

File

If you were using SQL (Structured Query Language), the command would look like this:

```
SELECT NAME FROM CUSTOMER INV_AMOUNT FROM INVOICE
WHERE INV_AMOUNT > 2500
```

In response to this command, all the records in the file that have an invoice amount greater than $2,500 will be listed on the screen. (The SQL command would also sort the listing into alphabetical order by name.) This whole procedure would take only a few minutes for thousands of records.

The DBMS is a software tool designed to manage a large number of integrated, shared electronic "file cabinets." You describe the type of data you wish to store, and the DBMS creates the database file(s). The DBMS also provides an easy-to-use mechanism for storing, retrieving, maintaining, and manipulating the data.

In small businesses, databases may be both created and operated by the user. In moderate- to large-size businesses with minicomputer or mainframe computer systems, the corporate database is created by technical information specialists. Business users generate and extract data stored by the database management system.

## Data Management Concepts

The DBMS approach to storing and retrieving data in computer-usable form has evolved to allow users to easily retrieve and update data that is in *more than one file.* To better explain the DBMS approach and its significance, we will first describe the traditional system it evolved from—the file management system.

## File Management Systems

Computers were placed in commercial use in 1954, when General Electric purchased a UNIVAC (Universal Automatic Computer) for its research division. At first, the processing performed was straightforward. Applications software programs tended to be sequentially organized and stored in a single file on magnetic tape [✓ p. 115] that contained all the elements of data required for processing. The term **file management system** was coined to describe this traditional approach to managing business data and information. (See Figure 10.4.) However, file management systems did not provide the user with an easy way to group records within a file or to establish relationships among the records in different files. As disk storage became more cost-effective and its capacity grew, new software applications were developed to access disk-based files. The need to access data stored in more than one file was quickly recognized and posed increasingly complex programming requirements.

The most serious problems of file management systems involve:

- *Data redundancy:* In the case of **data redundancy,** the same data fields appear in many different files and often in different formats. For example, a course grades file and a tuition billing file may both contain a student's ID number, name, address, and telephone number. If data fields are repeated often in different files, storage space is wasted.

- *Updating files and maintaining data integrity:* Data redundancy creates a problem when it comes to updating files. When a data field needs to be changed—for example, student address—it must be updated in all the files in which it occurs. This is a tedious procedure. If some files are missed, data will be inconsistent. Inconsistent data leads to inaccurate information. When data is inconsistent, data integrity is not maintained—

## Figure 10.4
File management versus database management. *Top:* In the traditional file management system, some of the data elements, such as addresses, were repeated in different files. Information was not shared among files. *Bottom:* In the database management system, data elements are integrated and information is shared among different files.

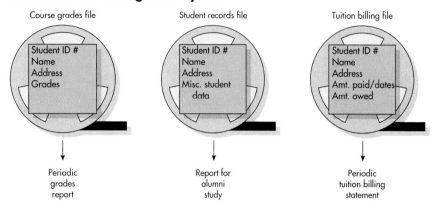

Traditional file-management system

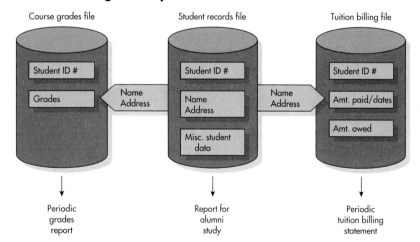

Database management system

and reports will be produced with erroneous information. **Data integrity** generally refers to the general quality of the data—that is, to its accuracy and consistency.

- *Lack of program and data independence:* Another limitation of file management systems has to do with the lack of *program independence* and *data independence*. This lack of independence means that programs must be written by programmers to use a specific file format. This process takes a programmer a large amount of time and costs a company a great deal of money for program and data file maintenance. Program and data independence means that files are organized so that business programs can be written to access data from the multiple files stored in the database. A change can be made in the program without having to change the data and vice versa.

To deal with these problems and the ever-growing demands for a flexible, easy-to-use mechanism for managing data, the concept of a database was developed.

# THE CLIPBOARD

## Using Mobile Computing and Databases in Sports

Using big sports arenas as their factory floors and games as the key gauge of market prowess, pro basketball teams are now employing computers much as other businesses do, especially companies with managers and workers who are constantly on the move.

Armed with notebook computers, fax modems, and specialized software, the teams compile scouting reports, analyze statistics, and create models to predict what players and teams might do in specific game situations. In a matter of minutes and a few keystrokes, the machines permit coaches to do work that used to take hours of laborious sorting through statistics sheets and play diagrams.

The 27 [National Basketball Association] teams are equipped with conventional Thinkpad notebooks. Recently, several teams have been experimenting with a pen-based model, the Thinkpad 700T, loaded with specialized basketball software developed by Information and Display Systems, Inc., of Jacksonville, Florida. The pen-based system allows coaches and scouts to diagram plays and store them, up to 99 plays for each of the 27 teams.

Robert Salmi is a 33-year-old assistant coach of the Knicks and one of pro basketball's self-taught computer aces. A 6-foot-7-inch former college basketball player, Mr. Salmi knew little about computers before Pat Riley, the Knicks head coach, came to him early in the 1991–92 season and told him what he wanted. . . .

Today, Mr. Salmi is comfortable with computers, speaking knowledgeably about database programs or pen-based machines. But mostly, he views the computer as a tool that saves time and that can pinpoint problems and opportunities.

For example, Mr. Riley might ask his assistant for additional statistics on their initial playoff opponents, the Indiana Pacers. . . .

The coach, Mr. Salmi says, might want to know the Pacers' won-lost record in games when they were out-rebounded, or when their guard Reggie Miller took more than 15 shots and made more than 50% in a game, or when their forward Rick Smits scored more than 20 points. Or in games when all three happened.

"Two years ago, that would have meant three or four hours of going through files and stat sheets," Mr. Salmi said. "Today, I can snap that out in five minutes."

Steve Lohr, "Electronics Replacing Coaches' Clipboards," *The New York Times,* May 5, 1993, pp. C1, C5.

## Fundamentals of Database Management Systems

DBMSs need large storage capacities, usually supplied by magnetic tape, hard disk packs, CD-ROM, and mass storage systems. DBMS software usually includes a query language, a report writer, utilities, a data dictionary, and a transaction log.

As we mentioned earlier, the term *database* describes a collection of related files that form an integrated base of data that can be accessed by a wide variety of application programs and user requests. In a database management system, data needs to be entered into the system only once. When the user instructs the program to sort data or compile a list, the program searches quickly through the data in memory (or in storage), making available needed data for the business task. The user's instructions do not change the original set of data in any way. Only authorized personnel, such as the database administrator, may change the data in the process of maintaining the database. Accessing data and maintaining the data are possible through the database management system (DBMS).

## Hardware: Storage Counts

Storage capacity is crucial to the operation of a database management system. Even the many megabytes [✓ p. 86] of hard disk storage in an efficient, modern microcomputer system can't handle the many gigabytes [✓ p. 86] of data that move through some large corporations. However, not all organizations need minicomputer- or mainframe-based database management systems. Recent advances in the speed and capacity of hard disk drives for microcomputers—plus the use of CD-ROM drives [✓ p. 129]—have made microcomputer-based database management systems possible for some organizations.

Because database files represent an important business resource, they must be protected from damage, loss, and unauthorized use. The most common way to protect the corporate database from loss or damage is to periodically make backup copies of it. In large database systems, backup copies are usually made on one or more cartridges of magnetic tape. The backup process for large corporate databases requires the involvement of computer operations specialists. The most popular form of backup for microcomputer hard disks is the tape streamer, or streaming tape unit, which is also available in cartridges. These devices are small, fast, and so easy to use that the user can perform the backup operation unassisted.

## Software: In Control

A database management system is an integrated set of software programs that provides all the necessary capabilities for building and maintaining database files, extracting the information required for making decisions, and formatting the information into structured reports. It is intended to:

■ *Make data independent of the applications programs being used, so that it is easy to access and change.* For example, you create a student database with many student records. After some time, you decide to change the structure of the student database to include phone numbers. With a DBMS you can do this and still use the application program you were using before you changed the database structure. This is possible because the data's organization is independent of the program being used.

■ *Establish relationships among records in different files.* The user can obtain all data related to important data fields. For example, the user can obtain student name and address information from the student file at the same time as viewing the student's course information (course numbers and names) from the registration file because each file has the student's Social Security number (data field) in it.

■ *Minimize data redundancy.* Because data is independent of the application program being used, most data needs to be stored only once. For example, the student data file can be accessed by both the billing application program or the student grade averaging program.

■ *Define the characteristics of the data.* Databases can be created that have data stored in them based on particular informational needs.

■ *Manage file security.* For example, the DBMS can "examine" user requests and clear them for access to retrieve data, thus keeping data safe from unauthorized access.

■ *Maintain data integrity.* Because data redundancy is minimized, file updating is made easier and data consistency is improved. The DBMS ensures that updates are properly done.

Using DBMS software, users can request that a program be run to produce information in a predefined format or extract information in a specific way. For example, if you are employed by the school's registration department, you may need to review a report of the classes that currently have space available for registration purposes. For budget purposes, the manager of the school's finance division may want to use the same data to generate a report on courses that have low enrollment.

The easiest way to view a DBMS is to think of it as a layer of software that surrounds the database files. (See Figure 10.5.) The DBMS software usually includes a query language, report writers, and utilities. Newer DBMS programs also offer graphics capabilities that make it even easier for users to run the program and graphically enhance the appearance of output reports—both hardcopy and softcopy [✓ p. 150].

**Figure 10.5**
DBMS software. The software that comprises the functions of a database management system can be thought of as a layer that surrounds the database files. Among other things, this software provides the user interface, which allows the user to interact easily with the system.

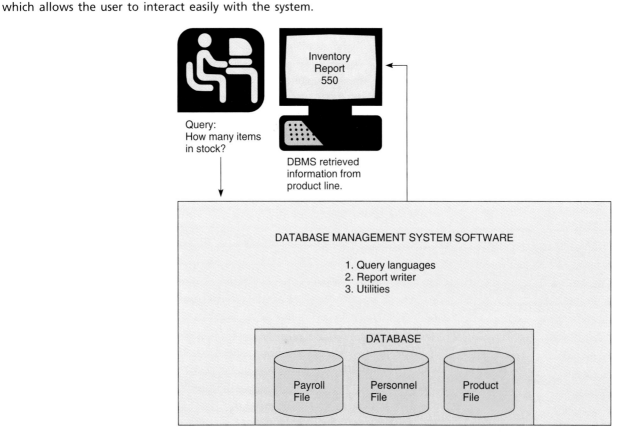

Query: How many items in stock?

Inventory Report 550

DBMS retrieved information from product line.

DATABASE MANAGEMENT SYSTEM SOFTWARE

1. Query languages
2. Report writer
3. Utilities

DATABASE

Payroll File

Personnel File

Product File

## Gigs from Gigabytes

A new computer database of food professionals can cinch careers from coast to coast.

What if all you had to do was mail in one copy of your resume to get onto a single, centralized database of North American chefs and hospitality personnel that's tapped by top restaurateurs and resources people across the country? And what if submitting that resume were free. . . .

[T]he Hosteur Network, established by the Council on Hotel, Restaurant and Institutional Education (CHRIE) and Advantage Systems of Rockville, Maryland, . . . is an electronic job matching system available to externs and executives alike, which eliminates, in the word of charter subscriber Paul Rowson of Marriott, "the job-selection lottery and resume purgatory" of current recruitment practices.

*Hosteur* is a word created by CHRIE to describe a professional who works in the hospitality and tourism industry. This new service, marketed under Alexus ProRegistry®, is continent-wide and automated, linking employers with potential job candidates who possess the type of skills needed for a wide range of professional positions in restaurants and food service, hotels and lodging, and recreation and travel services. . . .

Here's how Hosteur works: If you're looking for a new job, any job, or just wondering about the possibilities, mail in your resume (unfolded and in English only at the present time) along with a short, completed questionnaire that asks if you will commute/travel; if you have any preferred employers, a preferred salary, or language skills; and if you want the Feedback Option. . . .

Alexus scans in your resume . . . and searches for and extracts skill information, translates it into standard skill phrases, . . . and adds the phrases to its database, along with any skill phrases on your resume that could be new to the system. . . . All this high-tech processing produces a condensed, at-a-glance listing of your skills and experience, with a number.

If you or your client are looking for help, you pay an annual or per-search fee and, using your own skill-based recruitment profiles, request to see relevant candidate listings by auto-prompt on a touchtone telephone. (You can request, for example, a search for "sous chef" and "Atlanta" and "relocate" and "Trained staff" and "Spanish," etc.) Within 12 minutes, you're faxed compressed resume skills information (five listings per sheet of paper), and you can later request to be faxed the original resume of anyone who intrigues you. You contact candidates directly for interviews. . . .

For a $50 annual fee, job seekers can choose the Feedback Option, which allows them to see their summary profile, update their resume, and find out, on a quarterly basis, which companies retrieved their resumes and the names of employers who have recruited people with similar skills. . . .

[T]he goal is to get listings from the 100,000-plus students and CHRIE member colleges and universities, as well as alumni and any other candidates seeking work in the 10-million-strong hospitality and tourism industry—including students interested in internships or seasonal employment, and educators and consultants looking for short-term consulting gigs. There are even plans for the service to encompass other regions of the world as well. [Alexus ProRegistry: 301/762-5300; CHRIE: 202/331-5990]

Monica Velgos, "Gigs from Gigabytes," *Food Arts,* January/February 1995, p. 24.

### Query Language

Most users find that using a query language for data retrieval is the most valuable aspect of DBMS software. A **query language** is an easy-to-use computer language that provides access to data in a database. Traditionally, business personnel and managers rely on the information provided by periodic reports. However, this creates a problem when a decision must be made *now* and the information required to make it will not be produced until the end of the week. The objective of a query language is to provide users with a simple, natural language structure (like English) to select records from a database and produce information on demand. To be effective, a query language must allow the user to phrase requests for information in a flexible fashion. For example, take a request for inventory information. Here are some examples of questions that the user could ask using a query language when a single file is involved:

- List all items in the inventory database for which the quantity on hand equals 10. (Immediate orders would have to be placed to restock these items.)

- List all items in the database for which the quantity on hand is less than or equal to the reorder point. (This information would be used to process regular orders for restocking inventory.)

Here are examples of questions that the user could ask using a query language when more than one file is involved:

- List the names and addresses of all customers who ordered items that were out of stock and now are in stock. (This would involve using the customer order file and the inventory file and would show a listing of all customers who should be notified by mail that the items they ordered are now available for pickup.)

- List the phone numbers of customers who ordered items that were out of stock and that aren't going to be restocked. (This would also involve using both the customer order file and the inventory file and would show a listing of all phone numbers of customers who should be notified that the item they ordered will no longer be carried in inventory.)

You, the user, can learn to use a typical query language effectively with about eight hours of instruction and practice. Once you have this skill, you can prepare a special report in a few minutes instead of several days or weeks. Structured Query Language (SQL) is the most commonly used query language in database management systems.

### Report Writer

The **report writer** aspect of DBMS software simplifies the process of generating reports after querying the DBMS system for information. The procedure is fairly easy. Report headings, column headings for the items to be included in the report, as well as any totals, subtotals, or other calculations are easily specified. (See Figure 10.6.) The report form can then be saved for future use.

### Utilities

The utilities part of the DBMS software is used to maintain the database on an ongoing basis. This includes such tasks as:

- Creating and maintaining the data dictionary (described in more detail later in the chapter).

**Figure 10.6**
DBMS-generated report.

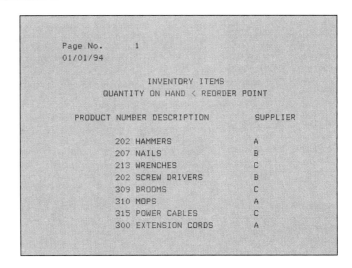

```
        Page No.      1
        01/01/94

                     INVENTORY ITEMS
              QUANTITY ON HAND < REORDER POINT

        PRODUCT NUMBER DESCRIPTION        SUPPLIER

                     202 HAMMERS          A
                     207 NAILS            B
                     213 WRENCHES         C
                     202 SCREW DRIVERS    B
                     309 BROOMS           C
                     310 MOPS             A
                     315 POWER CABLES     C
                     300 EXTENSION CORDS  A
```

- Removing records flagged for deletion. (Most DBMSs have built-in protection schemes to prevent users from accidentally deleting records.)

- Establishing control of access to portions of the database (protecting the database against unauthorized use).

- Providing an easy way to back up the database and recover data if the database is damaged.

- Monitoring performance.

- Preventing data corruption when multiple users attempt to access the same database simultaneously.

- Reorganizing the data in the database into a predefined sort order to make access quicker. This is necessary after a database has had new records added and deleted.

## Data Dictionaries and Transaction Logs

Once a DBMS has been implemented, two types of files are constantly in use besides the database files—the data dictionary and the transaction log.

The **data dictionary** is essentially a small database with information about the data and the data structure of a database. The information in the data dictionary varies from one DBMS to another. In general, the data dictionary maintains standard definitions of all data items including:

- What data are available
- Where the data are located
- Data attributes (descriptions)
- Who owns or is responsible for the data
- How the data are used
- Who is allowed to access the data for retrieval
- Who is allowed to update or change the data
- Relationships to other data items
- Security and privacy limitations

The dictionary is used constantly by the DBMS as a reference tool. (See Figure 10.7.) When an application program requests elements of data as part of

**Figure 10.7**
Data dictionary and transaction log.

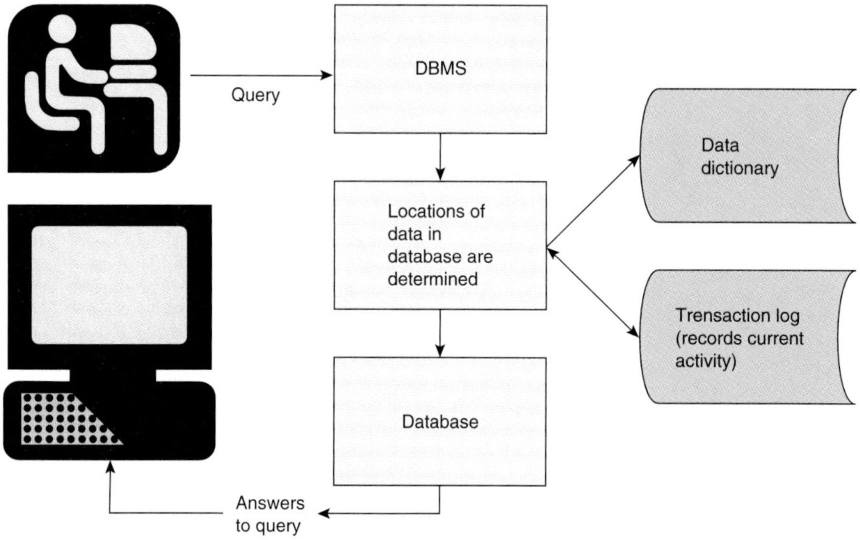


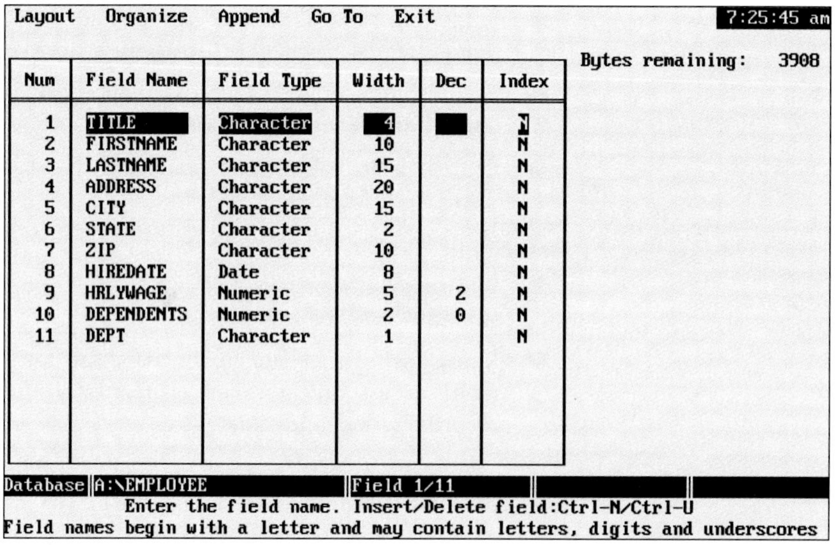

Layout Organize Append Go To Exit 7:25:45 am

Bytes remaining: 3908

| Num | Field Name | Field Type | Width | Dec | Index |
|---|---|---|---|---|---|
| 1 | TITLE | Character | 4 | | N |
| 2 | FIRSTNAME | Character | 10 | | N |
| 3 | LASTNAME | Character | 15 | | N |
| 4 | ADDRESS | Character | 20 | | N |
| 5 | CITY | Character | 15 | | N |
| 6 | STATE | Character | 2 | | N |
| 7 | ZIP | Character | 10 | | N |
| 8 | HIREDATE | Date | 8 | | N |
| 9 | HRLYWAGE | Numeric | 5 | 2 | N |
| 10 | DEPENDENTS | Numeric | 2 | 0 | N |
| 11 | DEPT | Character | 1 | | N |

Database A:\EMPLOYEE Field 1/11
Enter the field name. Insert/Delete field:Ctrl-N/Ctrl-U
Field names begin with a letter and may contain letters, digits and underscores

a query, the DBMS refers to the data dictionary for retrieving the data. The database administrator, whose job we'll discuss in more detail later, determines what the data dictionary contains.

The **transaction log** contains a complete record of all activities for minicomputers; systems for minicomputers and mainframes usually build the transaction log automatically. The transaction log is important in the reconstruction of the database after a failure and in the prevention and detection of unauthorized access.

## Types of Database Organization

**The three common database structures are hierarchical, like a family tree arrangement; network, an adaptation of the hierarchical structure; and relational, the most flexible type of database organization.**

## Using Databases in the Landscape Business

Fourteen years ago, long before computers were common in the landscaping industry, Indianapolis-based Pro Care Horticultural Services bought its first computer. Job costing for the landscape architecture company had become so labor intensive that it demanded a dedicated full-time employee. With little prepackaged software to choose from, Mitch Rolsky, then vice-president of the tiny family-owned business, brought in a consultant to write a job-costing and accounting package. After four days Rolsky decided his money would be better spent on his learning computers than on his trying to teach the consultant landscaping. . . .

Job costing had become crucial to Pro Care, because over the past 10 years the company's customers had stopped accepting bids for one big package of services and had begun demanding a menu from which to order. Pro Care had to pinpoint each cost, Rolsky says, and the new system makes that much easier. "No matter which service customers pull out, I'm profitable."

Using a database of previous jobs as a guideline, Pro Care establishes a budget before bidding on a job (such as the mowing, weeding, and mulching of a commercial building's surrounding grounds). Once that job is done, its costs are entered into the database, and Rolsky calculates his expenses and his profit. To boost margins when that customer calls for repeat service, Rolsky may send fewer workers or schedule a complementary job nearby. By tracking costs, Pro Care has lowered prices and increased profits on its current sales of $1.5 million.

Phaedra Hise, "Database Husbandry," *Inc., Annual 1994*, vol. 16, no. 13, p. 100.

---

The three most common arrangements for database management systems are *hierarchical, network,* and *relational.* (See Figure 10.8.) These three models have evolved gradually as users and computer specialists gained experience in using database management systems. They differ in terms of the cost of implementation, speed, degree of data redundancy, ease with which they can satisfy information requirements, and ease with which they can be updated.

In use since the late 1960s, the hierarchical and network database models were first developed and used principally on mainframe computers. The concepts behind the relational database model were pioneered in the early 1970s. The relational database model, which takes advantage of large-capacity direct access storage devices, was developed for mainframe and minicomputer systems but is now also used on microcomputers. The relational database model is rapidly replacing the hierarchical and network models.

### Hierarchical DBMS

hierarchical database

In a **hierarchical database,** fields or records are arranged in related groups resembling a family tree, with "child" records subordinate to "parent" records. A parent may have more than one child, but a child always has only one parent. To find a particular record, you have to start at the top with a parent and trace down the chart to the child.

**Figure 10.8**
Three types of DBMS: hierarchical, network, and relational.

**Hierarchical database:** Records are arranged in related groups resembling a family tree, with "child" records subordinate to "parent" records.

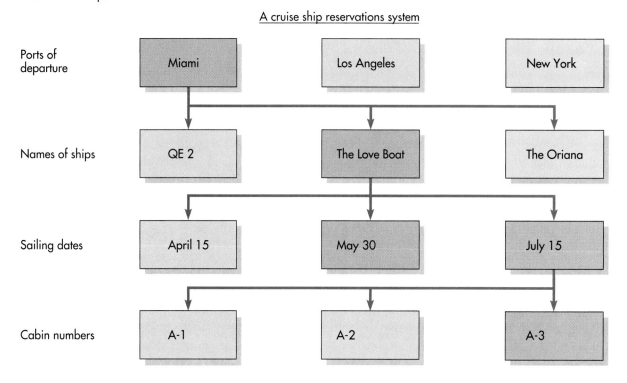

A cruise ship reservations system

Hierarchical DBMSs work well when the data elements have an intrinsic one-to-many relationship, as might happen with a reservation system. The difficulty, however, is that the structure must be defined in advance and is quite rigid. There may be only one parent per child and no relationships among the child records.

## Network Database Model

A **network database** is similar to a hierarchical DBMS, but each child record can have more than one parent record. Thus, a child record may be reached through more than one parent.

This arrangement is more flexible than the hierarchical one. However, it still requires that the structure be defined in advance. Moreover, there are limits to the number of links that can be made among records.

## Relational Database Model

The most flexible type of organization, the **relational database,** relates, or connects, data in different files through the use of a key field, or common data element. In this arrangement there are no access paths down through a hierarchy. Instead, data elements are stored in different tables made up of rows and columns. (In database jargon, the tables are called *relations,* the rows are called *tuples,* and the columns are called *attributes.*)

Within a table, a row resembles a record—for example, a car license-plate number, which is one field, and the car owner's name and address,

**Figure 10.8**
(Continued)

**Network database:** Similar to a hierarchical database, but each child record can have more than one parent record.

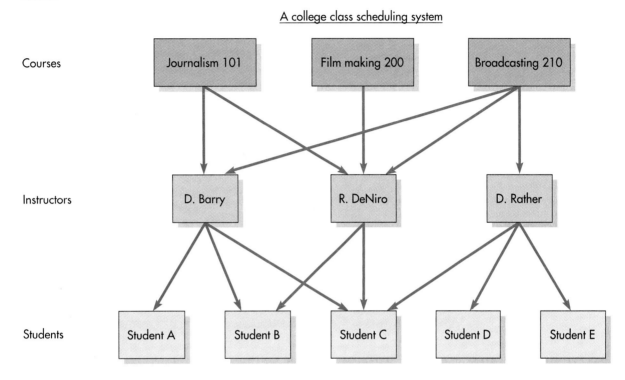

A college class scheduling system

**Relational database:** Relates, or connects, data in different files through the use of a key field, or common data element.

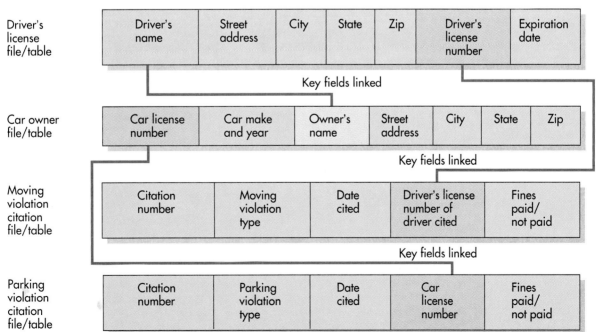

A state department of motor vehicles database

which is another field. All related tables must have a key field that uniquely identifies each row. Thus, another table might have a row consisting of a driver's license number, the key field, and any traffic violations (such as speeding) attributed to the license holder. Another table would have the driver's license number and the bearer's name and address.

In some countries (Australia, England), automatic cameras mounted on telephone poles in reduced-speed zones randomly photograph the license plates of cars traveling through and record their speeds. Through the relational database, a computer links the license-plate number to the owner's name and address and that in turn to the owner's driver's license. The bearer of the driver's license is mailed a citation requiring payment of a large fine, and the information is posted against the driver's license number.

The advantage of relational databases is that the user does not have to be aware of any "structure." Thus, they can be used with little training. Moreover, entries can easily be added, deleted, or modified. A disadvantage is that some searches can be time-consuming. Nevertheless, the relational model has become popular for microcomputer DBMSs, such as Borland's dBASE for Windows and Microsoft's Access for Windows.

## Designing a Database

**Database design is done to meet both logical and physical organizational needs. Logical design refers to what the database is (what is in it); physical design refers to how the data is organized and stored, and what storage hardware is used.**

Many users in the microcomputer environment will design a database and will actually build and implement it using a microcomputer DBMS. However, users are less involved in database design and development when the database management system is intended to be used in minicomputer and mainframe computer environments. (Users are highly involved in defining what data needs to be stored in the database, though.) In minicomputer and mainframe situations, trained and experienced information system specialists design and develop the systems.

### Matching the Design to the Organization

Most users working with microcomputer-based DBMS software focus on a very specific set of objectives and information processing needs—their own. For many small applications this is a satisfactory approach. However, the objectives must be broader when working with a large corporation, a large computer system, and more complex and sophisticated DBMS software. And the plans for the use of the database management system must be integrated with the long-range plans for the company's total information system. The information processing needs of the entire corporation must be considered to build a corporate database that facilitates collecting, maintaining, and sharing data among all organizational units. Once the general information needs have been established, the design process can proceed. This process usually comprises two distinct phases of activity—the logical design phase and the physical design phase.

### Logical Design

logical design

**Logical database design** refers to what the database is, not to how it operates; in other words, the logical design is a detailed description of the database model from the users' perspective rather than the technical perspective. The logical design of a database involves defining user information needs, analyzing data element requirements and logical groupings, considering input and output methods, finalizing the design, and creating the data dictionary. The focus is on identifying every element of data necessary to produce the required information systems reports and on the relationship among the records.

## Physical Design

Once the logical design of the database is ready, the next step is physical design. The **physical database design** specifies exactly how the data will be arranged and stored on the direct access storage devices allocated for DBMS use. The objective of the physical design is to store data so that it can be updated and retrieved as quickly and efficiently as possible. DBMS users are not involved in the physical design of the DBMS, since that is determined by the type of DBMS software they have purchased for their microcomputers or that is running on a large computer system.

## Database Administration

**Organizations usually appoint a database administrator to manage the database and related activities.**

database administrator

The effective use of a database within an organization requires a great deal of cooperation and coordination. User requirements and needs throughout an organization need to be frequently reviewed, and the overall security and integrity of the database must be ensured. Organizations working with DBMSs quickly recognized the need for a **database administrator (DBA),** an individual or a group of individuals to coordinate all related database activities and to control the database.

## Why Administrate?

As we mentioned earlier, developing and implementing a corporatewide database is a major task that requires management's complete support, substantial time from designers and users, and often large sums of money. This task needs to be coordinated. In addition, the data in the database often represents the company's most precious resource: *It must be managed well, so that it is not misused or damaged.*

## The Job of the Database Administrator (DBA)

The responsibilities for administering the database activities within an organization are usually assigned to an individual or a small group, depending on the size of the organization and the scope and complexity of the database. The database administrator has six major responsibilities.

1. *Database design:* The DBA plays a key role in both the logical and the physical design phases. He or she guides the definition of the database content and the creation of the data dictionary, as well as setting data classification and coding procedures and backup and restart/recovery procedures.

2. *Database implementation and operation:* The DBA guides the use of the DBMS on a daily basis. Among other things, this includes adding and

deleting data, controlling access to data, detecting and repairing losses, instituting restart/recovery procedures when necessary, and assigning space used on secondary storage devices.

3. *Coordination with users:* The DBA receives and reviews user requests for additional DBMS support that have been forwarded by programming analysts. The administrator establishes feasibility, resolves redundant or conflicting requests, and assists in the process of establishing priorities for the requests. In addition, the DBA is responsible for establishing and enforcing organization-wide DBMS standards for such things as techniques for accessing data, formats in which data elements will be stored, and data element names.

4. *Backup and recovery:* The DBA is responsible for preparing a plan to periodically back up the database(s) and for establishing procedures for recovery from the failure of the DBMS software or related hardware components.

5. *Performance monitoring:* The DBA constantly monitors the performance of the DBMS using specialized software to calculate and record operating statistics. If a problem occurs, such as a slowdown in responsiveness, the DBA must identify the problem and take steps to improve the performance.

6. *System security:* The DBA is responsible for designing and implementing a system that controls users' access to the database files and determines which DBMS operations can be performed, as well as which applications programs can be accessed. This system often involves the assignment of user identification codes and passwords.

Organizations with a well-organized and well-staffed database administration department can be much more successful with their database management systems than organizations without such a department.

## Advantages and Limitations of the DBMS

**A DBMS can minimize data redundancy, allow easy file updating, maximize data integrity and independence, simplify maintenance, increase user productivity and data security, and standardize data definitions. However, DBMSs require complex planning and expertise to create and maintain. They can also be expensive.**

The principal advantages of the DBMS approach include:

- *Minimization of data redundancy:* More storage becomes available when maintenance of redundant data elements among traditionally separate application files is minimized.

- *Easy file updating and maximization of data integrity:* In traditional systems in which the same element of data was kept in several different files, ensuring that all copies of the data element were updated when changes were made was a problem. When a data field needed to be changed, it had to be updated in all the files in which it occurred. If some files were missed, data became inconsistent. When data is inconsistent, data integrity is not maintained, and reports will be produced with erroneous information. Data is no longer accurate, reliable, and/or timely. DBMSs make updating files much easier and so improve the consistency of data, thus ensuring data integrity.

## Using Database Marketing to Send the Right Message at the Right Time to the Right People

. . . Arthur M. Hughes defines database marketing as "managing a computerized relational database system that collects relevant data about customers and prospects, which enables us to better service and establish long-term relationships with them."

Done right, says Hughes, databasing helps build loyalty, reduce attrition, and increase customer satisfaction and sales. "The database is used to target offerings to customers and prospects, enabling us to send the right message at the right time to the right people."

Despite its promise, many companies that should know better continue to ignore database marketing or, worse, botch the job. . . .

How serious is the problem? Several experts in the area of database marketing contend that companies without a marketing database will be out of business by, say, the year 2000. . . .

The strongest blast comes from the [chief executive officer] of a small industrial company who, after trials and tribulation, installed a marketing database and cleaned up on the competition. "You're an idiot if you don't at least use some databasing techniques," says this CEO, who, because competitors haven't caught on to his act, prefers to remain anonymous. "It can't hurt," he continues. "It's an easy way to access and segment information about your customers, which, by the way, is a good working definition of database marketing."

In a mundane industrial market where most companies rely mainly on their own sales forces or independent reps to promote their products, the CEO had the nerve to fire his own reps six years ago and, using a database to prioritize his sales effort, built strong relationships with customers via direct mail, trade shows, telesales, and ads in industry publications. "Frequency is the key," he says, revealing his promotional bias. "We call people once a quarter. I like repetition: reach and frequency."

Another critical difference from traditional selling is that those calls aren't strong-arm sales pitches. They generate orders, but they also glean information to update the database. "It's a mistake to compensate salespeople solely for selling when you should be paying them to get information about prospects and customers as well," says the CEO.

Scoffing at the notion that databasing is just for mega-corporations, the CEO argues that "it makes more sense for small companies, because the president or owner is likely to be the company's chief salesperson as well." Backed by reliable information about people genuinely interested in the company's product, the president can concentrate on the prospects and customers most likely to buy.

Martin Everett, "Know Why They Buy: Database Marketing," *Sales & Marketing Management,* December 1994, p. 66

■ *Data independence and simplification of program maintenance:* In a DBMS the programs are much more independent of the data than in traditional file processing systems. Previously, programs had to include a substantial amount of information about the format and structure of the fields and records in each file accessed. In a DBMS, this information is contained in the data dictionary.

■ *Increased user productivity:* The ability of a DBMS to respond quickly to user requests for additional information without involving the user in technical language manipulation encourages faster and more efficient work. The report generators and query languages associated with database management systems make them easy to use.

■ *Increased security:* Control of access to and use of the database is easily established. With traditional file processing systems, the data was too fragmented for effective security to be exercised.

■ *Standardization of data definitions:* Before database management systems, each application program could define similar elements of data with different names. However, the use of data dictionaries standardizes the names and descriptions of data elements.

There are disadvantages to using a database management system:

■ Database management systems are complex; extensive planning and a substantial amount of technical expertise are needed to implement and maintain a system.

■ The costs associated with the development and operation of a corporatewide DBMS can be substantial in terms of software and hardware acquisition, technical support personnel, and operations personnel.

■ The consolidation of an entire business's information resources into a DBMS can create a high level of vulnerability. A natural disaster, a fire, or even a hardware- or software-related problem can cause the loss of the current version of the database files. This could be fatal for a business unless proper precautions are taken. A very thorough framework of policies and procedures must be established to ensure that backup copies of the database files are made on a regular basis, that a transaction log is maintained, and that documentation exists for recovery procedures.

## Who Owns the Database?

**Small and large databases can all be classified as individual, company, distributed, or proprietary.**

Before ending this chapter we need to say a few words about who owns a given type of database.

The **individual database** is basically a microcomputer database used by one person. The data is usually stored on a large-capacity hard disk. A sales representative, for example, who is on the road a lot, may build and maintain an individual database of customer and sales information. (Popular microcomputer database packages are Paradox, dBASE III, dBASE IV, Quattro Pro, and FileMaker Pro. See Figure 10.9.)

The **company database (shared database)** is shared by the users of one company in one location. Company databases can be found in local area networks. The company owns the database. The data is usually stored on a minicomputer or a mainframe and managed by a database administrator. Users are linked to the database through terminals or microcomputer workstations.

The **distributed database** is shared by the users of one company, which owns the database, but the data is stored in several locations linked by a variety of communications networks [✓ p. 281].

The **proprietary database** is a huge database that functions as an information service, such as CompuServe, Prodigy, and Dow Jones News/Retrieval.

**Figure 10.9**
Popular microcomputer database packages.

The proprietor owns the database in this case. To access this type of proprietary database, the user needs a modem to hook the computer up to the service via the phone lines. (Fees are charged by the information service.) Another type of proprietary database can be "licensed" (purchased to use for a specified period of time) by computer users. For example, ABI's Business Lists-on-Disc (LOD) contains data on 9.2 million American businesses. It allows users to search for records by company name, type of business, company size, geographic area, and use of Yellow Pages ads in phone books. LOD comes on CD-ROM and works with MS-DOS [✔ p. 203] microcomputers. Such electronic database directories can be useful for direct mail, telemarketing, directory assistance, and personal sales calls.

# S U M M A R Y

■ Data in storage is organized as a hierarchy, known as the *data hierarchy* (p. 348):

1. *Byte (character)*—Group of 8 bits; a single letter, a number, or a special character.

2. *Field*—Unit of data consisting of one or more characters. A *key field* is a unique field used to search for and identify one record in a database.

3. *Record*—Group of related fields.

4. *File*—Group of related records.

5. *Database*—Collection of related files.

■ *Database management systems (DBMSs)* are comprehensive software tools that allow users to create, maintain, and manipulate an integrated base of data. (p.349)

■ *File management systems* used to be the only way of managing data and files. In these systems, data was stored in a series of unrelated files on tape or disk. The major problems associated with file management systems are (p. 352):

1. *Data redundancy.* The same data appeared in more than one file.

2. *Tedious updating procedures.* Because the same data appeared in many places, updating files was time-consuming.

3. *Poor data integrity.* If some redundant data elements were missed during file updating, data became inconsistent and caused inaccurate information to be produced.

4. *Lack of data and program independence.* Programmers could not use the data file to develop new programs because the data and the programs were restricted by existing formats. To update either the application program or the data file became a major task.

■ DBMSs were developed to (p. 355):

1. Make data independent of the programs, so that it is easy to access and change

2. Minimize data redundancy

3. Establish relationships among records in different files

4. Define data characteristics

6. Maintain data integrity

7. Provide a means of securing access to the database

8. Make it easier to access data for reports

■ DBMS software often uses a *query language* as an interface between the user and the system. This interface allows users to easily ask questions of the DBMS and obtain information to answer the questions and produce reports. (p. 358)

■ DBMS software also includes capabilities to simplify *report writing* and maintain the database (utilities) as well as to allow different application programs to use the database. (p. 358)

■ During the design of the database, a *data dictionary* is constructed that contains all the data descriptions used by the DBMS to locate and retrieve data. (p. 359)

■ The DBMS also can include a *transaction log* of current activity. This log can be used to update necessary backup copies of the database in case of failure of or damage to the operating database system. (p. 360)

■ A DBMS is usually modeled after one of three structures:

1. *Hierarchical*

2. *Network*

3. *Relational*

These models differ in terms of the cost of implementation, speed, degree of data redundancy, ease with which they can satisfy information requirements, and ease with which they can be updated.

■ The *hierarchical database model* resembles a family tree; the records are organized in a one-to-many relationship, meaning that one parent record can have many child records. Records are retrieved from the hierarchical model by starting at the root record at the top and moving down through the structure. There is no connection between separate branches. (p. 361)

■ The *network database model* is similar to the hierarchical model, but each child record can have more than one parent record, which allows relationships between records in different groups. Also, access to the database can be made from a number of points—not just from the top. (p. 362)

■ The *relational database model* is made up of many tables, called *relations*, in which related data elements are stored. The data elements are in rows, called *tuples*, and columns, called *attributes*. The main objective of the relational database model is to allow complex logical relationships between records to be expressed in a simple fashion. (p. 362)

■ In general, the hierarchical and network models are less expensive to implement and allow faster access to data. However, they are more difficult to update and aren't as effective at satisfying information requirements as the relational model can be. Relational database models are rapidly replacing the other two database models.

■ Database design usually consists of two phases: logical design and physical design. The *logical design* refers to *what* the database is as opposed to how it operates. The logical design is a detailed description of the database from the users' perspective. The *physical design* specifies exactly *how* the data will be arranged and stored on the storage devices. (p. 364)

■ The process of database design is usually carried out exclusively by specialists. However, users may have occasion to set up

small databases for microcomputers. Users also participate in defining the data during the logical design of a database for a large computer system.

■ The main responsibilities of a *database administrator* include (p. 365):

1. Guiding database design

2. Overseeing database implementation and operation

3. Coordinating users

4. Backing up and recovering files

5. Monitoring performance

6. Setting up and maintaining system security

■ In general, the main advantages of database management systems are (p. 366):

1. Minimization of data redundancy

2. Increased ease of file updating

3. Increased data independence and simplification of program and maintenance

4. Increased user productivity and efficiency

5. Increased security

6. Standardization of data definitions

■ The main disadvantages are (p. 368):

1. Complexity

2. High cost of implementation and personnel costs

3. Vulnerability of consolidated business data in a central database

■ Database ownership is *individual, company, distributed,* or *proprietary*. (p. 368)

## KEY TERMS

bit, p. 348
byte, p. 348
character, p. 348
company database, p. 368
database, pp. 348, 349
database administrator (DBA), p. 365
database management system (DBMS), p. 349
data dictionary, p. 359

data integrity, p. 353
data redundancy, p. 352
data storage hierarchy, p. 348
distributed database, p. 368
field, p. 348
file, p. 348
file management system, p. 352
hierarchical database, p. 361
individual database, p. 368
key field, p. 348

logical database design, p. 364
network database, p. 362
physical database design, p. 365
proprietary database, p. 368
query language, p. 358
record, p. 348
relational database, p. 362
report writer, p. 358
transaction log, p. 360

## EXERCISES

### SELF-TEST

1. According to the data storage hierarchy, databases are composed of:

   *(handwritten: BIT)*

   a. BYTE    d. FILE

   b. FIELD    e. DATABASE

   c. RECORD

2. An individual piece of data within a record is called a(n) ____FIELD____.

3. If an element of data in a database needs to be changed, it must be changed in *all* the files in order for data ____INTEGRITY____ to be maintained.

4. A group of related records is called a(n) ____file____.

5. *Data redundancy* means that an element of data (field) is repeated in many different files in a database. (true/false) *(true circled)*

6. The raw facts that make up information are called ____data____.

7. Microcomputers always had the storage capacity to handle database management systems. (true/false) *(false circled)*

8. If you have a collection of related records that forms an integrated base of data that can be accessed by a wide variety of applications programs and user requests, then you have a(n) ____DATA BASE____.

9. DBMS software can manage file access by "clearing" users through the use of passwords. (true/false) *(true circled)*

10. The aspect of DBMS software that simplifies the process of generating reports is called a(n) ____REPORT WRITER____.

11. The most sophisticated database model that allows complex logical relationships among records in many different files is the ____RELATIONAL____ database model.

12. A microcomputer-based database owned by one person is called a(n) ____INDIVIDUAL____ database.

13. Key fields, or candidate keys, are used to relate, or link, tables in a relational database. (true/false) *(true circled)*

14. Old file-handling methods provided the user with an easy way to establish relationships among records in different files. (true/false) *(false circled)*

15. A(n) ____QUERY____ ____LANGUAGE____ allows the user to phrase requests for information from a database in a very flexible fashion.

16. A special file in the DBMS called the _____DATA_____ _____DICTIONARY_____ maintains standard definitions of all data items within the scope of the database.

17. dBASE III, dBASE IV, and Paradox are popular microcomputer DBMS packages. (true/false)

18. Ensuring backup and recovery of a database is not one of the functions of a database administrator. (true/false)

19. The _____TRANSACTION_____ _____LOG_____ contains a complete record of all activity that affected the contents of a database during the course of a transaction period.

*Solutions:* (1) bits, bytes (characters), fields, records, files; (2) field; (3) integrity; (4) file; (5) true; (6) data; (7) false; (8) database; (9) true; (10) report writer; (11) relational; (12) individual; (13) true; (14) false; (15) query language; (16) data dictionary; (17) true; (18) false; (19) transaction log

## SHORT-ANSWER QUESTIONS

1. Why is a database management system important to many organizations?
2. What are the three main problems with old file management systems?
3. What is a query language in a DBMS?
4. What does the data dictionary in a DBMS provide?
5. What are the main limitations of a hierarchical database?
6. What is the difference between a distributed database and a proprietary database?
7. Give three main advantages of a DBMS over old file-handling approaches; give three main disadvantages.
8. Name four functions of a database administrator.
9. How is a relational database better than a hierarchical or network database?

## PROJECTS AND CRITICAL THINKING EXERCISES

1. Interview someone who works with or manages a database at your school or university. What types of records make up the database, and which departments use it? What types of transactions do these departments enact? Which database structure is used? What are the types and sizes of the storage devices? Was the software custom-written?
2. What types of databases do you think would include information about yourself? Prepare a brief summary.
3. Contact TRW Credit, P.O. Box 14008, Orange, CA 92613, and ask for a credit report in your name (the report comes from their huge database). If you are in their database, are there any mistakes in the report? If so, how do you think the incorrect data came to be in your file? (Be sure to inquire about any costs involved before you tell TRW to send the report.)
4. A number of online information services provide databases of job openings and also post users' resumes. Users with microcomputers and modems can (for a fee) scan job listings and reply electronically, with their resumes, to the groups offering jobs they are interested in. Following are a few information services that offer this job-hunting assistance.

   Adnet—through Prodigy (800/PRO-DIGY); GEnie (800/638-9636); and CompuServe (800/848-8199)
   Dialog's Career Placement Registry (800/334-2564)
   Job Information Services (JIS) (904/488-9180)

Capsule Online Job Listing (512/250-8127)
College Recruitment Database (317/872-2045)

Contact a few of these information services and request brochures and any other information on their career placement databases. Give a short report on the procedures and potential advantages involved in using such databases.

5. Look through magazines (such as *PC Computing, PC Magazine, PC World, MacWorld,* and *MacUser*) or other periodicals for microcomputer DBMS ads and articles. From your research, what DBMS software for PCs/Macs do you think is the best? How much storage capacity is required? With what type of computer system is the software compatible? What is recommended for backup? Can you store graphics? Sound? How expensive is the program?

6. How do you think you could use a microcomputer DBMS in your profession, job, or other activities? What types of data would be stored? What types of searches would you make, and what kinds of reports would you generate?

7. Companies exist today that are in the business of selling information. For example, for a fee you can purchase a list of all the businesses in your area that sell sporting goods, use IBM-compatible computers, and have 10 or more employees. The more specific your information request, the more expensive the information is. What type of database do you think would be especially valuable? What kinds of information would this database contain? What would a record look like? (Give an example.) How big do you think the database would get? Is information of the type you are describing already being sold today? How could you find out?

8. People's resistance to change, sometimes called *social inertia,* may come about simply because change is stressful to many people. Employees in organizations undergoing change from old, familiar procedures to new, computer-based procedures often resist the efforts of trainers and administrators to institute new programs. If you were a new database administrator in a large company converting to a new computer-based DBMS, what are some things you would tell people to lessen their resistance?

9. According to the Software Publisher Association, sales of educational software have increased by about 55% recently. But it can be difficult for consumers to work through the thousands of educational titles and subcategories, including astronomy, math, languages, preschool, spelling, biology, chemistry, history, and geography. To help users of educational software, Austin ProSoft offers *Edu-Ware Database on Disk,* which contains detailed information on more than 2,000 public-domain and shareware educational programs for IBM-type PCs running DOS or Windows. The database, on 3½-inch diskettes, is free. Obtain a copy and make a list of free software items that might be useful in your major.

Austin ProSoft
P.O. Box 1811
Austin TX 78767
512/323-2323

## IN THE LAB WITH MICROSOFT WINDOWS

(*Note:* If you aren't familiar with using a mouse and/or don't know how to use the Microsoft Windows graphical user interface, complete the In the Lab with Microsoft Windows exercises in Chapter 6 before proceeding.)

**Microsoft Cardfile**

1. In this section you learn how to use the Microsoft Windows Cardfile tool. You can use this tool to keep track of data such as names and addresses. In Cardfile, *a card contains a record of data*. Right now, the Microsoft Windows Program Manager should be displaying.

2. DOUBLE-CLICK: Accessories group icon
   DOUBLE-CLICK: Cardfile program icon
   The Cardfile window should be displaying.

3. Cardfile is waiting for you to type data into the first card, or record. When typing information into the first record, you must choose a command to type information into the Index field. *The records you enter will be sorted in ascending order by the contents of the Index field.*
   CHOOSE: Edit, Index
   TYPE: Lembe, Richard
   PRESS: Enter
   TYPE: 1211 Fallcrest Drive
   PRESS: Enter *to complete the address*
   TYPE: Los Angeles, CA 91111

4. To add another name and address to this file:
   CHOOSE: Card, Add
   TYPE: Arnett, Rosa
   PRESS: Enter
   TYPE: 2111 Arbing Way
   PRESS: Enter
   TYPE: San Diego, CA 92222

5. To view the list of names:
   CHOOSE: View, List
   Notice that the names are appearing in alphabetical order.
   CHOOSE: View, Card

6. On your own, add three more names and addresses using the procedure in step 4. When finished, choose View, List to see the names and addresses in alphabetical order.

7. At this point, after reviewing your work, you would normally save the address data onto the hard disk or a diskette, and then retrieve it later to add more data. We will show you the save procedure now; however, you'll cancel the SAVE command before actually saving in case you don't have a diskette available.
   CHOOSE: File, Save
   Cardfile is waiting for you to type in a name for the data. To name the address data as ADDRESS and save it onto a diskette in drive A:, for example, you would type **A:ADDRESS.** To save it onto a diskette in drive B:, you would type **B:ADDRESS.** To complete the command you would press Enter. However, to cancel the SAVE command:
   CLICK: Cancel button

8. To close the Cardfile program:
   DOUBLE-CLICK: Control-menu box *located in the upper-left corner of the Cardfile window*
   CLICK: No *when asked if you want to save your work*

9. To close the Accessories group window:
   DOUBLE-CLICK: Control-menu box *located in the upper-left corner of the Accessories window*

# Chapter Topics

# CHAPTER 11

# Information Management

To be functional, systems and databases need to be tied clearly to organizational goals, objectives, and plans. Indeed, data and systems have no meaning until they are put into the context of what an organization or a business does. To be useful as a resource—just as people and money are resources for a company—data and data processing systems must be managed according to a company's needs. Management information systems provide the means and the methods to manage the components of the computer-based information cycle—hardware, software, data/information, procedures, and people—as well as its four phases—input, processing, storage, output.

## Preview

*When you have completed this chapter, you will be able to:*

- Explain what a basic management information system is and describe its role in the organization

- Describe the levels of management, the five basic functions of managers, and the types of decisions typically made at each level

- Distinguish among transaction processing systems, management information systems for middle management, decision support systems, executive information systems, and expert systems

- Briefly describe what an information center does

- Explain the differences between centralized, decentralized, and distributed computer facilities

**Why Is This Chapter Important?**

*Information technology can ruin our lives unless we think of ways to get it under control. Without an organized approach to managing information, we may drown in an ocean of available information, unable to make decisions. Do these statements sound farfetched? They may have seemed so only a few years ago, but today, because of the fast pace of computer hardware and software development, they sound accurate. Although knowledge may be power, we must remember that information does not equal knowledge. And, for knowledge to be useful, it must be integrated into a task.*

*What should managers do to change an information technology into an intelligence technology—to put knowledge to work to assist with decision making and establishing efficient, productive, and high-quality business operations? In other words, how can users of an information system do their jobs better and not just shuffle overwhelming amounts of data and information from input to storage, from storage to processing and back to storage and on to output? The answer is: through management information systems. By understanding the principles of information management, users can help exploit technology to accomplish business and professional goals. As more and more hardware, software, and data are shared, users are becoming more and more involved in the online functioning and management of the entire information system.*

## Information Systems: What They Are, How They Work

**Computer-based information systems comprise six parts: hardware, software, data/information, procedures, communications, and people. The type of information systems found in companies vary according to the nature and the structure of the business. All information systems help organizations process data into the information they need.**

The computer-based information system comprises six parts—hardware, software, data/information, procedures, communications, and people [✓ p. 4]. The fourth component includes manual and computerized procedures and standards for processing data into usable information. A *procedure* is a specific sequence of steps performed to complete one or more information processing activities. In some organizations, these processing procedures are carried out only by users; in others they are carried out by a combination of users and the computer specialists.

If you walk into a busy discount consumer-products showroom, stand in a corner, and observe what takes place, you will probably see the following kinds of activities: Customers come in and browse around, looking at the display cases. Some customers decide to buy items and begin to fill out order forms. If they are completed properly, the order forms are taken at the counter by a clerk and placed into a *queue*—that is, in line to be processed. If an order form is not complete, the clerk asks the customer questions and completes it. Then a stock person takes the completed order forms into the stockroom or warehouse and returns with the goods. A clerk takes each order form, marks it "filled," and rings up the sale on the cash register. All these activities form a procedure that is part of the *sales order entry system*. (See Figure 11.1.)

**Figure 11.1**
This group of related procedures makes up a simple sales order entry system.

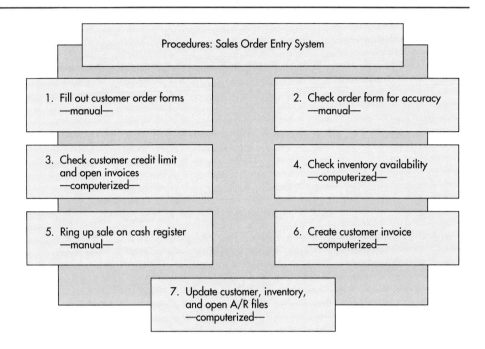

A business is made up of many procedures, grouped logically into systems. The types of information systems found in companies vary according to the nature and the structure of the business. However, the systems commonly found in many businesses include payroll, personnel, accounting, and inventory.

Businesses receive data from a variety of sources, including customers who purchase products or services, vendors from whom supplies are ordered, banks, government agencies, and insurance companies—to name just a few. Information systems help organizations process all this data into useful and complete information. One of the most important purposes of a business's information system, then, is to satisfy the knowledge requirements of management.

## What Is Management?

**Managers provide leadership and direction in planning, organizing, staffing, supervising, and controlling business activities. Each of these management functions involves making decisions. To make decisions, managers need the information provided by information systems.**

**Management** often refers to those individuals in an organization who are responsible for providing leadership and direction in the areas of planning, organizing, staffing, supervising, and controlling business activities. These five functions, which are the primary tasks of management, may be defined as follows:

1. *Planning* activities require the manager to formulate goals and objectives and develop short- and long-term plans to achieve these goals. For example, an office manager must work with top management to formulate a plan that satisfies the short- and long-term needs of the organiza-

tion for office space; the vice president of marketing must take many factors into account when planning short-term advertising campaigns and activities aimed at opening up new long-term markets.

2. Management's responsibility for *organizing* includes the development of an organizational structure and a framework of standards, procedures, and policies designed to carry out ongoing business activities. For instance, top management must decide on the type and number of divisions and departments in the company and evaluate the effectiveness of the structure; it may decide to combine the personnel and the payroll departments to save money. Office managers establish working procedures, such as "Working overtime must be approved by the department supervisor in advance."

3. *Staffing* refers to management's responsibility for identifying the personnel needs of the organization and selecting the personnel, as well as training staff. Many companies have personnel managers to take charge of these activities.

4. *Supervising* refers to management's responsibility to provide employees with the supervision, guidance, and counseling necessary to keep them highly motivated and working productively toward the achievement of company objectives. This includes the recognition of good work, perhaps through certificates or bonuses, and concrete suggestions about how to improve performance. Companywide educational seminars may also be held to upgrade employees' knowledge of the company in general or perhaps to help them deal with stress and improve their health.

5. *Controlling* refers to management's responsibility to monitor organizational and economic performance and the business environment so that steps can be taken to improve performance and profits and modify plans as necessary in response to the marketplace. This includes keeping alert to new opportunities in the marketplace and recognizing new business opportunities. Many new computer software products, for example, have been developed because software companies are ever watchful for potential markets.

Each primary management function involves making decisions, and information is required to make good decisions. Thus, to fulfill its responsibilities, management must set up information systems and subsystems. And these systems must all be designed to manage change and innovation.

## What Is a Management Information System?

A management information system provides useful, complete, and timely information to management on three levels: low-level (operational), middle (tactical), and upper (strategic). Lower management deals with decisions that affect a relatively narrow time frame and that involve details; these are called structured decisions. Middle management deals with decisions that cover a broader range of time and involve more experience. Middle managers use summary reports, exception reports, periodic reports, on-demand reports, and event-initiated reports to make semistructured decisions. Upper (top) management deals with decisions that are broad in scope and cover a wide time frame. Strategic, unstructured decisions are made at this level.

# THE CLIPBOARD

## For Strategic Decision Making—Knowing What to Know

A "database," no matter how copious, is not information. It is information's ore. For raw material to become information, it must be organized for a task, directed toward specific performance, applied to a decision. Raw material cannot do that itself. Nor can information specialists. . . .

Information specialists are toolmakers. The data users, whether executive or professional, have to decide what information to use, what to use it for, and how to use it. They have to make themselves information-literate. . . .

But the organization also has to become information-literate. It also needs to learn to ask: What information do we need in this company? When do we need it? In what form? And where do we get it? So far, such questions are being asked primarily by the military, and even there mainly for tactical, day-to-day questions. In business such questions have been asked only by a few multinationals, foremost among them the Anglo-Dutch Unilever, a few oil companies such as Shell, and the large Japanese trading companies.

The moment these questions are asked, it becomes clear that the information a business most depends on is available, if at all, only in primitive and disorganized form. For what a business needs the most for its decisions—especially its strategic ones—are data about what goes on outside of it. It is only outside the business where there are results, opportunities, and threats.

So far, the only data from the outside that have been integrated into most companies' information systems and into their decision-making process are day-to-day market data: what existing customers buy, where they buy, how they buy. Few businesses have tried to get information about their noncustomers, let alone have integrated such information into their databases. Yet no matter how powerful a company is in its industry or market, noncustomers almost always outnumber customers.

American department stores had a very large customer base, perhaps 30% of the middle-class market, and they had far more information about their own customers than any other industry. Yet their failure to pay attention to the 70% who were not customers largely explains why they are today in a severe crisis. Their noncustomers increasingly were the young, affluent, double-earner families who were the growth market of the 1980s. . . .

When it comes to nonmarket information—demographics; the behavior and plans of actual and potential competitors; technology; economics; the shifts signaling foreign-exchange fluctuations to come and capital movements—there are either no data at all or only the broadest of generalizations. Few attempts have been made to think through the bearing that such information has on the company's decisions.

Peter F. Drucker, "Be Data Literate—Know What to Know," *The Wall Street Journal,* December 1, 1992, p. A16.

A **management information system (MIS)** comprises computer-based processing and/or manual procedures that provide useful, complete, and timely information. This information must support management decision making in a rapidly changing business environment. The MIS system must supply managers with information quickly, accurately, and completely.

The approaches that companies take to develop information systems for management differ depending on the structure and management style of the organization. MIS systems enable *information resource management (IRM)*.

However, the scope of an MIS is generally companywide, and it serves managers at all three traditional levels:

1. Low-level (operational) management

2. Middle (tactical) management

3. Upper, or top (strategic), management

The primary objective of the MIS is to satisfy the need that managers have for information that is (1) *more summarized and relevant to the specific decisions that need to be made* than the information normally produced in an organization and that is (2) *available soon enough to be of value in the decision-making process.* The information flows up and down through the three levels of management and is made available in various types of reports.

## Levels of Management: What Kinds of Decisions Are Made?

Each level of management can be distinguished by the types of decisions made, the time frame considered in the decisions, and the types of report information needed to make decisions. (See Table 11.1 and Figure 11.2.)

### Lower Management

The largest level of management, **lower (operational) management,** deals mostly with decisions that cover a relatively narrow time frame. Lower management, also called *supervisory management,* actualizes the plans of middle management and controls daily operations—the day-to-day activities that keep the organization humming. Examples of a lower-level manager are the warehouse manager in charge of inventory restocking and the materials manager responsible for seeing that all necessary materials are on hand in a

---

**Table 11.1**   A Comparison of the Information Systems at the Operational, Tactical, and Strategic Management Levels

| SUMMARY CLASSIFICATION OF INFORMATION SYSTEMS | | | |
|---|---|---|---|
| **Characteristic** | **Operational** | **Tactical** | **Strategic** |
| *Frequency* | Regular, repetitive | Mostly regular | Often ad hoc (as needed) |
| *Dependability of results* | Expected results | Some surprises may occur | Results often contain surprises |
| *Time period covered* | The past | Comparative | Future |
| *Level of detail* | Very detailed | Summaries of data | Summaries of data |
| *Source of data* | Internal | Internal and external | Internal and external |
| *Nature of data* | Highly structured | Some unstructured data (semistructured) | Highly unstructured |
| *Accuracy* | Highly accurate data | Some subjective data used | Highly subjective data |
| *Typical user* | First-line supervisors | Middle managers | Top management |
| *Level of decision* | Task-oriented | Control and resource allocation oriented | Goal-oriented |

Adapted from R. Schultheis and M. Sumner, *Management Information Systems: The Manager's View,* 2nd. ed. (Homewood, IL: Richard D. Irwin, 1992), p. 329.

**Figure 11.2**

Management levels and responsibilities. *Top:* An organization has four departments: Research and Development, Production, Marketing, and Accounting and Finance. This organization chart shows the management hierarchy for just one department, Accounting and Finance. Three levels of management are shown—top, middle, and lower. The higher the manager in the organization, the more he or she must make decisions from *unstructured* information. *Bottom:* The entire organization can also be represented as a pyramid, with the four departments and three levels of management as shown. Top managers are responsible for strategic decisions, middle management for tactical decisions, and lower management for operational decisions.

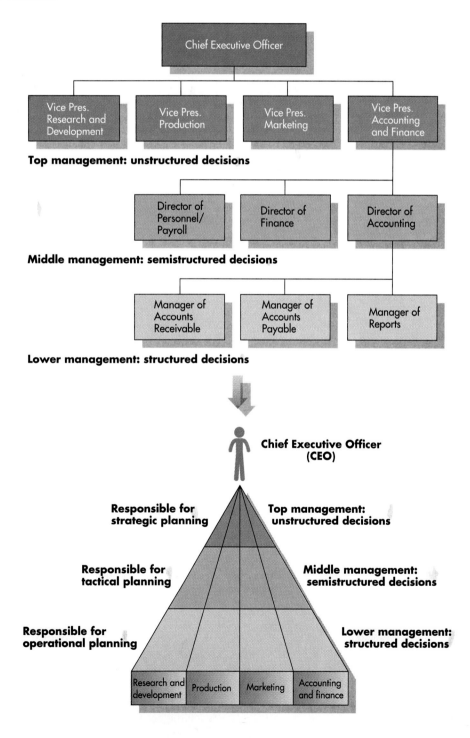

manufacturing firm to meet production needs. Most decisions at this level require easily defined information about current status and activities within the basic business functions—for example, the information needed to decide whether to restock inventory. This information is generally given in **detail reports** that contain specific information about routine activities. These reports are structured, so their form can usually be predetermined. Daily business operations data is readily available, and its processing can be easily computerized.

Managers at this level typically make structured decisions. (See Figure 11.3.) A **structured decision** is a predictable decision that can be made by following a well-defined set of predetermined, routine procedures. For example, a clothing store floor manager's decision to accept your credit card to

**Figure 11.3**

Types of information: the structured-unstructured continuum. *Top managers* need information that is unstructured. Unstructured information is summarized, less current, future-oriented; covers a broad range of facts; and is concerned with events outside as well as inside the organization. *Lower-level* managers need information that is structured. Structured information is detailed, more current, past-oriented; covers a narrow range of facts; and is concerned principally with events inside the organization. *Middle managers* require information that is both structured and unstructured.

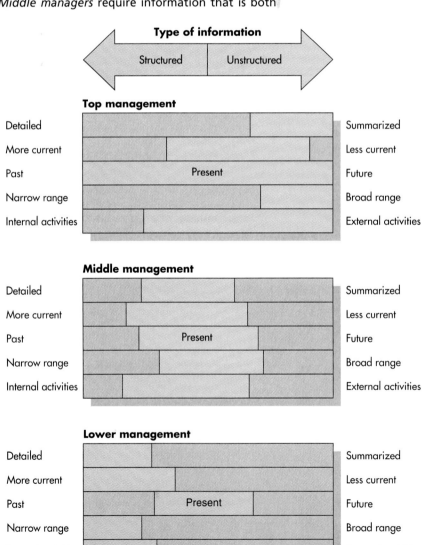

pay for some new clothes is a structured decision based on several well-defined criteria:

1. Does the customer have satisfactory identification?
2. Is the card current or expired?
3. Is the card number on the store's list of stolen or lost cards?
4. Is the amount of purchase under the cardholder's credit limit?

At this level of management, almost all the data needed to make decisions comes from within the organization. Also, decision makers at this level generally know quickly whether their decisions were correct.

### Middle Management

The **middle** level of **management** deals with decisions that cover a somewhat broader range of time and involve more experience. Some common titles of middle managers are plant manager, division manager, sales manager, branch manager, and director of personnel. The information that middle managers need involves review, summarization, and analysis of historical data to help plan and control operations and implement policy that has been formulated by upper management. This information is usually given to middle managers in two forms: (1) **summary reports,** which show totals and trends—for example, total sales by office, by product, by salesperson, and total overall sales—and (2) **exception reports,** which show out-of-the-ordinary data—for example, inventory reports that list only those items that number fewer than 10 in stock. These reports may be regularly scheduled (periodic reports), requested on a case-by-case basis (on-demand reports), or generated only when certain conditions exist (event-initiated reports).

**Periodic reports** are produced at predetermined times—daily, weekly, monthly, quarterly, or annually. These reports commonly include payroll reports, inventory status reports, sales reports, income statements, and balance sheets. **On-demand reports** are usually requested by a manager when information is needed for a particular problem. For example, if a customer wants to establish a large charge account, a manager might request a special report on the customer's payment and order history. **Event-initiated reports** usually deal with a change in conditions that requires immediate attention, such as an out-of-stock report or a report on an equipment breakdown.

Managers at the middle level of management are often referred to as *tactical decision makers* who generally deal with semistructured decisions. A **semistructured decision** is a decision that includes some structured procedures and some procedures that do not follow a predetermined set of procedures. In most cases, a semistructured decision (Figure 11.3) is complex, requiring detailed analysis and extensive computations. Examples of semistructured decisions include deciding how many units of a specific product should be kept in inventory, whether or not to purchase a larger computer system, from what source to purchase personal computers, and whether to purchase a multiuser minicomputer system. At least some of the information requirements at this level can be met through computer-based data processing.

### Top Management

The **top** level of **management** deals with decisions that are the broadest in scope and cover the widest time frame. Typical titles of managers at this level are chief executive officer (CEO), president, treasurer, controller, chief information officer (CIO), executive vice president, and senior partner. Top managers include only a few powerful people who are in charge of the four basic functions of a business—marketing, accounting and finance, production, and research and development. Decisions made at this level are unpredictable, long-range, and related to the future, not just past and/or current activities. Therefore, they demand the most experience and judgment.

A company's MIS must be able to supply information to top management as needed in periodic reports, event-initiated reports, and on-demand reports. The information must show how all the company's operations and departments are related to and affected by one another. The major decisions made at this level tend to be directed toward (1) strategic planning—for example, how growth should be financed and which new markets should be tackled first; (2) allocation of resources, such as deciding whether to build or lease office space and whether to spend more money on advertising or the hiring of new staff members; and (3) policy formulation, such as determining the company's policy on hiring minorities and providing employee incentives. Managers at this level are often called *strategic decision makers*.

Upper management typically makes unstructured decisions. (See Figure 11.3.) An **unstructured decision** is the most complex type of decision that managers are faced with. Because these decisions are rarely based on predetermined, routine procedures, they involve the subjective judgment of the decision maker. As a result, this type of decision is the hardest to support from a computer-based data processing standpoint. Examples of unstructured decisions include deciding five-year goals for the company, evaluating future financial resources, and deciding how to react to the actions of competitors.

At the higher levels of management, much of the data required to make decisions comes from outside the organization (for example, financial information about other companies). Also, managers at this level may not know for years if they made the correct decisions.

Figure 11.4 shows the areas that the three levels of management would deal with in a foods-supply business and an insurance company.

## The Role of the MIS in Business

Now that you know what we mean by *managers* and understand their need for the right kinds of information, we can go on to describe in more detail the role of the management information system. First, as we have already pointed out, an MIS must provide managers with information (reports) to help them perform activities that directly relate to their specific areas of responsibility. For example, to effectively manage marketing responsibilities, the vice president of marketing needs information about sales, competitors, and consumers. The head of the personnel department needs information about employee performance, work history, and job descriptions, among other things.

Second, a management information system must provide managers with information about the functional areas of the business so that they can coordinate their departmental activities with activities in these areas. These functional areas are usually categorized as:

- *Accounting and finance:* Keeps track of all financial activities, pays bills, issues paychecks, and produces budgets and financial forecasts

- *Production:* Makes the product

- *Marketing and sales:* Handles advertising, promotion, and sales of the product

- *Human resources (personnel):* Hires staff and handles sick leave, vacations, retirement benefits, and staff performance evaluation

**Figure 11.4**
Areas covered by the three management levels in a foods-supply business (a) and an insurance company (b).

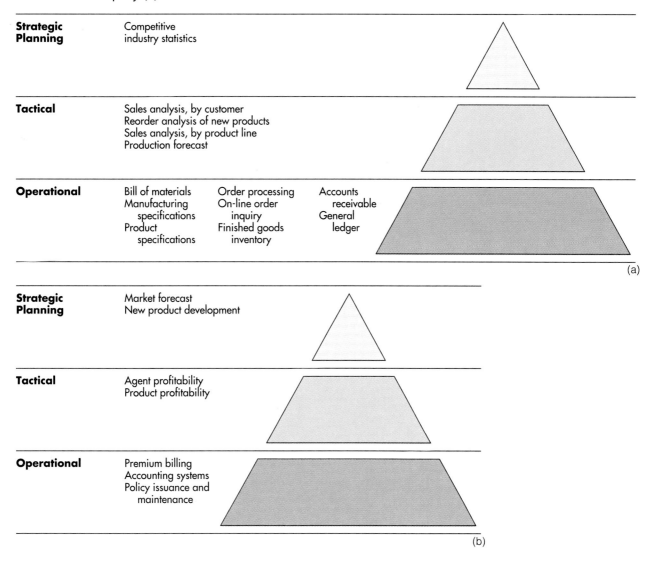

| Strategic Planning | Competitive industry statistics |
| --- | --- |

| Tactical | Sales analysis, by customer |
| | Reorder analysis of new products |
| | Sales analysis, by product line |
| | Production forecast |

| Operational | Bill of materials | Order processing | Accounts receivable |
| --- | --- | --- | --- |
| | Manufacturing specifications | On-line order inquiry | General ledger |
| | Product specifications | Finished goods inventory | |

(a)

| Strategic Planning | Market forecast |
| --- | --- |
| | New product development |

| Tactical | Agent profitability |
| | Product profitability |

| Operational | Premium billing |
| | Accounting systems |
| | Policy issuance and maintenance |

(b)

■ *Information services* (design and support of information systems): Manages systems analysis [✓ p. 314], design, and development; provides user support services

■ *Research and development:* Conducts research regarding product improvement and new products; develops and tests new products

For example, suppose that the accounting department (one functional area) has kept track of all customer invoices produced so far this year by maintaining an invoice history file. The file contains such information as:

1. Customer name

2. Customer address

3. Invoice date

4. Products sold

5. Invoice amount

## MIS Issues in Healthcare

This is a very challenging time, with provider systems integration, health care reform legislative activity, and managed care initiatives all accelerating. What are the big issues for information management professionals—especially executives—and how are they responding?

Right now, there's still a large question about what's going to happen, so people are not being very productive. They're holding off new purchases and not really looking to change their operations yet. Once the direction is set, the challenge will be to react quickly enough.

The team concept that we've looked at involves bringing communications and information management professionals, management engineers and clinicians all together. These groups will have to work well together and get things done quickly; and we'll have to work on several fronts at once to be successful.

We're hearing a lot about the hospital CIO [chief information officer] being a key member of the executive management team in hospitals. Are CIOs on that team, and are they prepared for the growing role? There are a number of examples of CIOs who are truly prepared for it and are working at that level. As in any other field, there are a lot of folks who are CIOs in name, but who really don't have the experience or strategic vision to move their organizations along; but the concept of the CIO will become increasingly important.

What is HIMSS [Healthcare Information and Management Systems Society] doing to help move the field along and develop information professionals for the new health care system? Part of what we're trying to do is give people broader focus, to include more than the traditional folks in our educational process. We are becoming more and more open to clinicians, as an integral part of the IS [information system] team. And we're trying to give people a larger focus on health care issues, as opposed to simply management engineering, information systems, or telecommunications issues. Our programs and publications are becoming more cross-pollinated. Educating our members on the goals of reform—increased access, reduced cost and increased quality—is a critical goal for us.

One of the key issues facing hospitals and health networks now is the need to integrate financial and clinical data. What are the main obstacles there? We've implemented systems separately, so clinical data has traditionally been obtained as a by-product of a financial system. I think we're going back the other way. I hope we'll see more financial data produced as a by-product of collecting clinical data, and the clinical data coming as a by-product of providing good patient care.

One area that's become sensitive is that, as medical records are automated, the lines between what the traditional medical records people do and what the information management people do are starting to blur. Is that causing confusion? How is it changing your relations with other associations? We talked with the folks at AHIMA [the American Health Information Management Association] as we looked at where the field is going, and at what role different organizations can play in helping to educate the large number of our joint members. We do have a number of crossover members: their president last year was an HIMSS member. This is an area of opportunity; it is an area that clearly has come together. We—HIMSS and AHIMA—need to work together more and more. And you'll see us collaborating more with what I'll call a smaller group of sister organizations on those kinds of things where we can support similar initiatives. The development of the computer-based record is clearly one of those things that all of us have an interest in seeing happen well.

Looking five and 10 years down the road, what big changes do you see taking place?

Our view of information and management systems will have changed; my members will have evolved to different roles, away from more traditional tasks. And you'll probably begin to see the most successful systems using teams that are multidisciplinary, looking at operations.

In five years, information and management systems activities will become mission-critical, as we move to telemedicine, for example, and that will require their skills to change. As a result, our perception of health care delivery will also change.

Mark Hagland, "Interview with John Page," Health-care Information and Management Systems Society '94 Conference Preview (Interview), *Hospitals & Health Networks,* February 5, 1994, v68 n3, p. 44(1). COPYRIGHT American Hospital Publishing Inc. 1994

To better coordinate marketing activities, the vice president of marketing (another functional area) can use this data to produce a variety of information, such as the year-to-date sales by month, a ranking of customers to whom the largest amounts of sales have been made, and an analysis of the months of highest sales. This same information could be passed along to the materials manager in production (another functional area), who can make informed decisions about when inventory levels should be raised or lowered to meet consumer demand.

But *how* do managers use information to make decisions? To understand how an MIS works, you must know something about the decision-making process.

## How Does Management Make Decisions?

**Managers may use a five-step process to make decisions. It consists of recognizing and identifying the problem and then identifying and evaluating alternatives. The manager then decides on the best alternative and takes action on the decision. Later the manager does a follow-up to evaluate the success of the decision. Each of the five steps may be affected by feedback.**

Management styles vary. Some managers follow their instincts and deal with situations on a case-by-case basis. Other managers use a more systematic and structured approach to making decisions. If we approach decision making systematically, we can view it as a process involving five basic steps, as shown in Figure 11.5 and described below. Bear in mind that feedback, or review of the gathered information, is analyzed at each step, which may necessitate revisions or a return to a previous step. For example, suppose a company decides in Step 2 to purchase one of two software packages to help with in-house publishing; at Step 3 the company discovers that one of the two software manufacturers has gone out of business. The process must return to Step 2 to evaluate other software alternatives.

### Step 1—Problem Recognition and Identification

In the first step of the decision-making process, the manager acknowledges a problem that affects the business. Take, for example, a small business like Bowman, Henderson, and Associates (BH&A), which provides training in the use of microcomputer hardware and software. The demand for training has

**Figure 11.5**
The five-step decision-making process. This recommended method of decision making for managers involves proceeding downward through five steps. At any stage, *feedback*—a review of gathered information—may require returning to any of the previous steps.

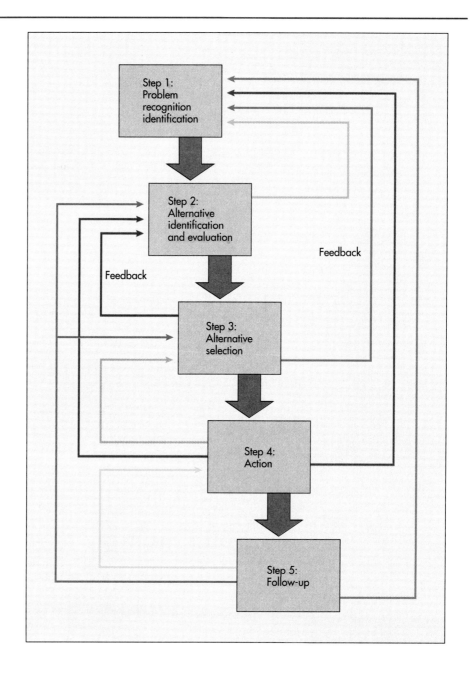

grown so fast that the staff cannot handle it, and the facilities cannot support an increase in the number of students who can be taught per session. The fact that a problem exists becomes obvious when management notices that the staff is too busy to take a day off and everyone is always running around trying to take care of last-minute details. The seriousness of the problem becomes evident when staff morale begins to drop and potential customers are turned away.

## Step 2—Identification and Evaluation of Alternatives

In the second step of the decision-making process, management considers various alternatives to solve the problem. In the case of BH&A, alternatives include (1) adding more staff and offering training in the existing facilities during expanded training hours (perhaps evenings and weekends) and

(2) adding more staff, purchasing additional equipment, and leasing additional training facilities. Once the alternative courses of action have been identified, they must be examined and compared in terms of anticipated costs and benefits.

## Step 3—Alternative Selection

When each alternative has been carefully explored, the next step is to select the one that appears to best meet the manager's objectives. The logical choice would be the alternative that offers the most benefits for the least cost. However, the manager must ensure that the chosen action is not in conflict with other activities or organizational objectives.

## Step 4—Action

Once management has decided how to solve the problem, it must act on the decision. Suppose BH&A management selected the alternative of adding more staff and scheduling the use of existing facilities for additional hours. Implementing this decision would probably involve:

1. Defining specific staff requirements and skills
2. Advertising for additional staff
3. Interviewing prospective staff members
4. Selecting the best candidates
5. Notifying existing customers of the additional staff and expanded hours
6. Scheduling the use of the facility during the new hours of operation

## Step 5—Follow-Up

In the final step of the decision-making process, management follows up on its choice of action to determine if it has been successful. Management assesses the degree to which original objectives and anticipated benefits are being achieved and takes corrective action when necessary. If the solution to the original problem has created a new problem, a new decision-making process begins to solve it.

## What Kind of Information Does Management Need to Make Decisions?

**Information provided to management must be correct, complete, current, concise, clear, cost-effective, time-sensitive, meaningful, and useful.**

Because decisions are made on the basis of information, the decision-making process is greatly affected by the scope and quality of the information provided by the MIS. This information is produced by processing data from three sources:

1. Internally generated data (produced by normal data processing systems of the business)
2. Data provided by higher or lower levels of management
3. Externally generated data (produced by sources outside the company)

Information, as required by management, has three distinct properties that vary in significance depending on the organizational level and type of decision being made:

1. Level of summarization
2. Degree of accuracy
3. Timeliness

As we mentioned in the discussion of the three management levels, the degree to which information needs to be *summarized* increases as the level of management goes up. Conversely, the lower the level of management, the more detailed the information needs to be. Top managers do not want to wade through mountains of details to make a decision. They want to be able to identify problems and trends at a glance in summary reports and exception reports; that is, they need only essential information, not nonessential details. Operational managers, however, need details on daily operations to make decisions regarding scheduling, inventory, payroll, and so on.

Of course, information must be *accurate* for wise decisions to be made. (Remember: garbage in, garbage out.) The higher the accuracy of the information, the higher the cost of the processing system. Higher costs are incurred because more controls—both manual and computer-based—must be installed to increase the accuracy of output information. Some areas such as inventory may be able to live with an accuracy rate of 90–95%, but this rate is probably too low for the accounting department, where a 5–10% error rate in dealing with money might mean substantial losses or tax problems, for example.

The *timeliness* of management information involves how soon the information is needed and whether the information is about the past, present, or future. When decisions are time-sensitive (they must be made quickly), the information system must accommodate this need. For example, whether a system is designed to use batch processing or online (real-time) processing [✓ p. 114] might be determined by how fast the information is needed by management. On the one hand, the kind of planning done by top management covers a broad time frame and requires reports that contain information covering past years as well as current performance. This type of decision making is not highly time-sensitive, so batch processing would probably be adequate. On the other hand, decisions related to banking activities may be highly time-sensitive and require online processing to provide up-to-date information.

In general, to support the making of intelligent and knowledgeable decisions, information generated at all levels of management must be:

- Correct (be accurate)
- Complete (include all relevant data)
- Current (be timely)
- Concise (include only the relevant data)
- Clear (be understandable)
- Cost-effective (be efficiently obtained)
- Time-sensitive (be based on historical, current, and/or future information and needs as required)
- Meaningful and useful

## Outside Experts Can Help

As new management thinking takes hold across North American industries, more Canadian corporations are reassessing what businesses they're in, and how they can best deliver value to their customers.

When undertaking major re-engineering initiatives, managers are increasingly aware that their information technology system and revamped business process can only be effective with well-trained end-users.

To accomplish this task—which can seem like an enormous undertaking to a business leader with an aggressive re-engineering plan—many managers are relying on a team of outside experts.

Consulting firms can offer customers a different perspective on such areas as managing change, designing business processes, and selecting the most suitable technology platform. Outside experts bring to the table specific industry knowledge, management, and re-engineering competencies critical to any large-scale re-engineering project.

To truly add value to a company's end-user training, vendors promising integrated business applications must work with consulting partners to help customers solve a myriad of complex business and technological issues.

What is decisive is how well these consulting partnerships work together as a seamless team, in collaboration with the customer's implementation team. A software vendor must build and manage a dedicated team that co-ordinates the customer, consultant and vendor relationship at each phase of the project. In some cases, this team collaborates with the customer from the very inception, defining business requirements, managing the selection process, mapping out implementation strategies and then executing those strategies to the end-users.

The combined strengths of each team member lend to the effectiveness of the implementation. This also plays a critical role when delegating responsibility or meeting the challenges the organization encounters as it re-engineers.

A software vendor must have the insight and resources to train third-party consultants on the capabilities of their product. This expands the breadth of knowledge on vendor-specific technology, which develops a well-informed group of trainers for the end-user. This additional group of trainers is a critical factor for time-sensitive implementation schedules.

It is important to gauge the knowledge of trained consultants with formal certification programs monitored by the vendors, who know their product best. Training programs should be followed by apprentice programs that monitor consultants' performance.

Software vendors can also use customer satisfaction surveys to clarify what customers need from consultants. Results of such surveys are useful for incorporating customer requirements in future implementation plans.

Finally, software vendors can leverage alliances with consulting partners to offer specialized expertise in Canadian industries. Industry specialists in both software and consulting can join to develop new functionality for a particular industry.

By identifying industry issues, vendors can be a step ahead of trends to offer customers solutions that require less customization, thereby speeding implementation cycles.

Brian Craig, "Outside Experts Can Help," *Computing Canada*, September 14, 1994, v20 n19, p.29(1).

## Types of Information Systems

**Three types of computer-based information systems provide information to the three levels of management. Transaction processing systems assist lower-level managers in making operational decisions. Management information systems help middle managers make tactical decisions. Decision support systems, executive information systems, and expert systems support top managers in making strategic decisions.**

The more structured the problem, the easier it is to develop computer-based processing support to produce the information needed to solve it. As an organization matures in its use of the computer, the extent to which it uses computers to produce information for decision making grows.

### Transaction Processing System (TPS)

**H**

TPS

Supporting day-to-day business operating activities, or *transactions,* is usually the first and most important objective of an information system. A computer-based **transaction processing system (TPS)** focuses on the operating level of a business and deals mostly with data from internal sources. (See Figure 11.6.) The management information produced by transaction information systems usually consists of detail reports of daily transactions (such as a list of items sold or all the accounting transactions that have been recorded in various ledgers and registers) or future transactions (such as lists of items that need to be ordered).

A TPS usually operates only within one functional area of a business. In other words, accounting and finance, production, marketing and sales, and research and development each has its own transaction processing information system. Database management systems [✔ pp. 183, 349] were designed to solve the problems involved with sharing computer-based files among the different functional areas. Although the reports generated by a TPS are useful to lower-level managers, they are not generally helpful to middle managers, who need more summarized information. Thus, management information systems were developed to take care of middle management's information needs.

### Management Information System (MIS)

**Management information systems (MIS),** also called *information reporting systems,* provide middle management with reports that summarize and categorize information derived from all the company databases. The purpose of the reports is to allow management to spot trends and to get an overview of current business activities, as well as to monitor and control operational-level activities. (Although the term *management information system* can be used to refer to *any* type of information system for managers, it is also used to refer specifically to *middle* management information systems.)

The scope of reports and the characteristics of their information vary according to their purpose. As you have seen, the reports can be periodic (such as income statements and balance sheets), on-demand, or event-initiated, and they can summarize information or report on exceptional events or conditions. Examples of reports generated by an MIS are sales region analyses, cost analyses, annual budgeting reports, capital investment analyses, and production schedules.

**Figure 11.6**
Three information systems for three levels of management. The pyramid shows the following: (1) The three levels of management: top, middle, and lower. (2) The four departments for each level: Research and Development, Production, Marketing, and Accounting and Finance. (3) The three kinds of computer-based information systems corresponding to each management level: top-decision support system, middle-management information system, lower-transaction processing system. (4) The kind of data required to be input for each level, and the kind of information required for output.

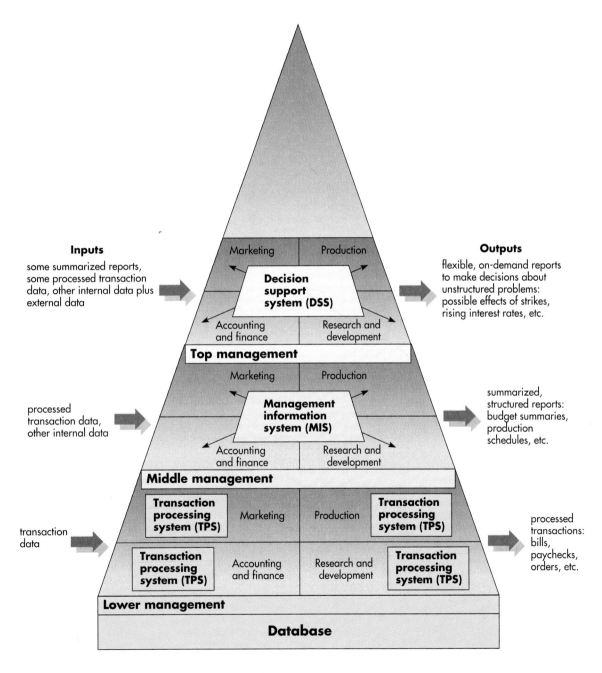

## What's the Best Method?

As we develop new business systems, the issue of training continues to be a key component in the success or failure of these systems. Experience has shown that the best system will fail if the end-user is not properly trained.

However, what is the best method for training?

Historically, training methodology evolved as a result of our technology and development methodology. Development cycles have been one to three years, methodologies and solutions have been computer-centric and often there has been a lack of continuity and commitment to the technology from the business unit.

The result is that solutions have not only been technically complex, but they have also been outdated, even prior to implementation.

In the past, training did not emphasize how the system related to the business process. Instead, the often frustrating message to end-users was that the system was the business.

Now, in the 1990s, there's a move toward object technology [✔ p. 235], client-server [✔ p. 282] and graphical user interface-based [✔ p. 204] applications. Object technology delivers quicker, more integrated development methodology and application delivery than ever before.

In the traditional approach, exhaustive analysis was performed to ensure everything was known about the challenges or problems to be solved. Then the system was designed, developed, tested and implemented, primarily by the systems people—since the technical jargon being used to explain the process was rarely understood by the end-user.

Although end-users were likely asked to input, sometimes their contributions were somehow lost between focus group discussions and the final result. End-users were asked to sign off on each of these technical documents even though they weren't intimately involved with the design, and often went through extensive and time-consuming training by systems people.

But today, input from end-users is critical at every stage. It's assumed that one can't know everything prior to designing and developing the system, so a cyclical or iterative approach is used to analyse, design and test until all the bugs are worked out.

The development to production cycle, which used to take six months to three years, can now be as little as one to three weeks and the final result is that end-users are, for the most part, already trained. End-users are involved in building the system from start to finish, so upon completion they seldom need any in-depth application training.

This is far different than in the past when systems people created applications which they had to explain to end-users. Now, if end-users have to be trained in the application, they learn from a mentor who is another end-user. Often, with this integrated development and design process, very little end-user training on the new application is really necessary.

What is more common is end-user training on how the new application interfaces with other established systems—for example, how an OS/2 application interfaces with DOS or Windows [✔ p. 203].

When training is required, those who understand the business conduct the training. The difference from the traditional methodology, which centered on the system, is that training revolves around and involves the business process and how the system enables and improves it.

Those conducting the training know the business, understand the process, and for the most part, were intimately involved in the development of the system.

Mark Winter, "What's the Best Method?," *Computing Canada*, September 14, 1994, v20 n19, p. 29(1). COPYRIGHT Plesman Publications Ltd. (Canada) 1994

## Decision Support System (DSS)

The **decision support system (DSS),** a set of special computer programs, establishes a sophisticated system to provide tools to assist managers in analyzing information from the two lower management levels and from outside the company. The analyses are used for unstructured decision making. DSSs are generally used by top management (although they support all levels of management), combine sophisticated analysis programs with traditional data access and retrieval functions, can be used by people who are not computer specialists, and emphasize flexibility in decision making. They are used to analyze unexpected problems and integrate information flow and decision-making activities. A DSS may use database management systems, query languages [✔ p. 233], financial modeling or spreadsheet programs, statistical analysis programs, report writers [✔ p. 358], and graphics programs to provide information (Table 11.2). Decision support systems do not take the place of management information systems; instead they are used together.

To reach the DSS level of sophistication in information technology, an organization must have established a transaction processing system and a management information system. But these two types of systems are not designed to handle unpredictable information and decisions well. Decision support systems are designed to handle the unstructured types of decisions— the "what if" types of decisions and analyses of special issues—that traditional management information systems were not designed to support. (See Figure 11.7.) Moreover, decision support systems provide managers with tools to help them better model, analyze, and make decisions about the information they have. Indeed, some people regard decision support systems as a separate type of information system altogether, not just an information system for top management.

Although most DSSs are designed for large computer systems, electronic spreadsheet packages and database management packages are used by many business people as tools for building a DSS for microcomputers. Spreadsheet

**Table 11.2**  Software Tools for Decision Support Systems

| DATABASE SOFTWARE | MODEL-BASED SOFTWARE | STATISTICAL- SOFTWARE | DISPLAY-BASED (GRAPHICS) SOFTWARE |
|---|---|---|---|
| dBASE IV | Foresight | SAS | ChartMaster |
| FOCUS | IFPS | SPSS | SASGRAPH |
| NOMAD II | Lotus 1-2-3 | TSAM | TELLAGRAF |
| RAMIS | Model | 1 | Presentations |
| R:base System V | Quattro Pro | | |
| DB2 | Mathematica | | |
| Oracle | Excel | | |
| Ingres | | | |
| Informix | | | |
| Paradox | | | |
| Access | | | |

**Figure 11.7**

Decision support system. These processing questions represent the types of questions a top manager might ask a DSS. (These questions would not be keyed into the computer word for word exactly as you see here; the manager would use a query language, such as SQL.)

1. If we discontinue selling baseball bats, will fewer people come into our stores?

2. If we add a new clothing line, will more people come into our stores?

3. How will offering the customers a 10% discount for all purchases totaling over $35 affect next year's net income?

4. What effect will hiring 50 additional sales employees have on the company's overall performance (i.e., profit)?

5. What effect will modernizing our stores have on sales?

software is popular among managers because it allows them to examine a variety of business situations—that is, to "see what would happen" if business conditions changed—and to make projections, or guesses, about future developments based on sophisticated computer-based data analysis. Decision support systems designed for large computer systems collect large amounts of data and analyze it in more ways and with greater efficiency than a microcomputer spreadsheet does.

Because a DSS is tailored to meet specific management information requirements, the nonmanagement user would not likely be directly involved with it. However, this type of user might be involved in gathering data to be processed by the DSS and then used as information for management.

Decision support systems generally fall into two distinct categories: general and institutional. A *general DSS* produces information that can be used in making a wide variety of management decisions. The electronic spreadsheet is an ideal tool for the development of general decision support systems for microcomputers. Large database management systems and natural languages [✓ p. 234] or query languages are used to develop decision support systems for large computer systems. An *institutional DSS* is much more industry- and function-specific. Examples include a DSS for the medical profession (including hospitals), which supports decision making in the areas of administration, patient diagnosis, determination and monitoring of drug dosages, and medical records, among other things; a DSS for the advertising profession, which supports strategy in presenting products; and a DSS for the transportation industry, which supports traffic pattern analysis.

The users of a DSS must be reasonably comfortable working with the hardware and DSS software to be effective. Many managers develop substantial skills in using some of the microcomputer-based packages such as electronic spreadsheets that can provide decision support. The software used for DSSs on large computer systems is generally too complex for people who are not computer specialists to handle; the manager would use it only on a simple level—to ask questions and obtain reports.

### DSS Software

DSS applications software is usually composed of complex instructions. As mentioned earlier, many different types of programs can make up a DSS. In most cases, it can be divided into three levels: database management systems software, query language, and specialized software or languages.

Database management software provides managers with the ability to collect, maintain, manipulate, and retrieve huge amounts of data.

A query language allows people to use software easily without having to learn countless lists of codes and procedures. This "layer" of DSS software helps managers use the database with less difficulty and perform a variety of activities such as basic mathematical operations on fields [✓ p. 348] of data contained in the database, calculation of ratios and various statistical measures, search of the database for records of a certain type, and extraction of records [✓ p. 348] for the preparation of hardcopy reports and graphic representation of data.

Specialized software or languages are used to develop decision-making models. Some organizations purchase industry-specific modeling software for such common activities as financial risk analysis and forecasting (predicting future performance and conditions). However, the most sophisticated DSS users develop their own custom-made business activity and decision-making models.

The following list identifies some of the major differences between a management information system (MIS) and a decision support system (DSS):

- MIS users *receive* reports or information from the system, whereas DSS users *interact* with the system.

- MIS users can't direct the system to support a specific decision in a specific way, whereas DSS users can.

- MISs generate information based on the past, whereas DSSs use information from the past to create scenarios for the future.

- MIS activity is initiated by middle management, whereas DSS activity is usually initiated by top management.

Although MISs and DSSs effectively process information to support managerial activities, the quantity of available information continues to grow at an alarming rate and threatens to overwhelm the users. Thus, the search for more efficient information management tools continues.

### Executive Information Systems (EIS)

An **executive information system (EIS)** is a DSS made especially for top managers and specifically supports strategic decision making. An EIS is also called an *executive support system (ESS)*. It draws on data not only from systems internal to the organization but also from those outside, such as news services and market-research databases. An EIS might allow senior executives to call up predefined reports for their personal computers, whether desktops or laptops. They might, for instance, call up sales figures in many forms—by region, by week, by fiscal year, by projected increases. The EIS includes capabilities for analyzing data and doing "what if" scenarios.

## H   Expert Systems

expert systems

An **expert system** is a set of computer programs that perform a task at the level of a human expert. (See Figure 11.8.) Expert systems are created on the basis of knowledge collected on specific topics from human experts, and they imitate the reasoning process of a human being. Expert systems have emerged from the field of artificial intelligence, which is the branch of computer science that is attempting to create computer systems that simulate human reasoning and sensation. We describe artificial intelligence in more detail in Chapter 12.

Expert systems are used by management and nonmanagement personnel to solve specific problems, such as how to reduce production costs, improve workers' productivity, or reduce environmental impact.

**Figure 11.8**
Expert system screen. This screen shows a screen from a United Airlines gate assignment expert system, which analyzes airplane traffic to assign gates to incoming air carriers.

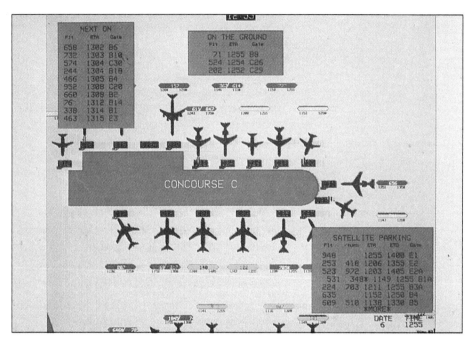

## Developing and Implementing a Management Information System

**To develop a management information system, a project development team follows the steps of the systems development life cycle.**

The task of developing and implementing any type of management information system is a formidable one, requiring a great deal of planning. Business environments change rapidly, so unless management has great foresight (and the support of good specialists and user input), an information system may be obsolete by the time it is implemented.

The successful development of a management information system requires:

■ A long- and a short-range plan for the company; a company must have plans for the future to be able to decide what to do tomorrow, next week, and next month

■ A commitment from management to allocate the personnel and resources necessary to get the job done

■ A staff of technical specialists with the skills necessary to develop the computer-based parts of the system based on user input

The most important step in undertaking the development of an MIS is forming a project development team to follow the systems development life cycle [✔ p. 310] steps of systems analysis, design, and development. The team should be made up of managers, information system users, and technical information specialists. All the team members should be familiar with the company's business objectives, current activities, and problems. And all the members must come to a general understanding of how the business operates. This task is not easy because many managers understand only how their own departments work and little, if anything, about other departments; many managers have difficulty explaining how their own departments work; and many managers, users, and computer specialists use jargon—special vocabulary and expressions—to explain what they do. Jargon is not generally understood by everyone. In a situation like this, prototyping [✓ p. 325] is often useful.

Developing a comprehensive MIS is a massive undertaking that may take years to carefully plan and coordinate. However, organizations that plan to survive the 1990s and beyond must have efficient management information systems to feed management the information it needs to be competitive.

## Information Centers

**Within an organization's MIS department, the information center offers employee training and assistance.**

troubleshooters

An **information center** is a department within a business's or organization's MIS department that offers employees hardware and software training and help in getting data from other computer systems, as well as other kinds of technical assistance. The information center is established as part of the company's information system, and the person in charge of the information center is called the **chief information officer (CIO).** The people who staff an information center are technical experts on the hardware, software, and procedures that the company is using. The staffers act as "troubleshooters"—consultants and problem solvers. However, they focus not only on technology, as they did in the earlier years of computer-based information systems, but also on the goals, productivity, and quality of the business.

The user is the person the information center was created for; the user is the only customer. If the user wants to request a computer, the information center staff will assist in identifying what kind of computer is appropriate. A user who has an operating problem with the hardware or software would call the information center for help, or for service requests and replacement parts. Information center staff also show users how to use available software to create their own customized applications and provide general training sessions for hardware and software use. In large systems with a mainframe computer, the information center will also assist users in accessing and storing data.

The information center may be a separate department that services the entire company, or each functional area—such as marketing or production— may have its own information center.

## Organizing Computer Facilities

**Computer facilities can be centralized (a single computer department); decentralized (several computer departments located in each organizational unit); or distributed (user with their own computers hooked up to a bigger computer system).**

As part of managing its information, when a company acquires a large computer system, it also usually sets up a special organizational unit, or department, to operate it. (When microcomputers are used by only one user at a time, a special department does not need to be set up to operate them—unless, of course, they are hooked up to a larger computer system.) The name of this unit may vary: Data Processing Department, Information Systems Department, or Computer Information Systems Department are common names. The computer system and related equipment plus the area set aside for the employees who staff the department are often called the *computer facility.* How a computer facility functions and how it is used within an organization tend to reflect management's organizational philosophy. You, as a user, should know how your company's computer facility is organized so that you can efficiently perform your job-related activities. There are three types of computer facilities:

1. Centralized
2. Decentralized
3. Distributed

## Centralized Computer Facilities

When an organization has established a single computer department to provide data processing and information systems services, this department is often referred to as a **centralized computer facility.** It is called centralized because it alone supplies data processing support to all other departments in the company. Entry and retrieval of data can occur either at the central facility or at terminals connected to the central facility through communications lines.

The principal advantages of the centralized processing approach are:

■ *Cost-effectiveness:* The cost effectiveness of computer hardware resources is increased because equipment is not duplicated at different locations.

■ *Coordination and control:* Processing activities are easier to coordinate and control in a centralized facility.

■ *Standards:* The ability to impose and enforce processing standards is easier in a centralized facility.

■ *Support of users:* Professional data processing personnel are located near users and so can develop a good working relationship with those they support.

In some cases, the centralized approach proves unsatisfactory because of:

■ *Lack of accountability:* In a large company, it is difficult to track and fairly allocate the costs of the computer processing facility to the many different departments based on individual departmental use. Also, departments at remote locations may feel that their information needs are not being met.

■ *Unfamiliarity:* The computer specialists responsible for the design of computer applications software can end up working in unfamiliar areas of the company. They may need a lot of time to understand the processing requirements of a new department, resulting in delays in a project. Or the result may be misunderstandings—some of the software developed fails to meet the needs of the department.

■ *Delays:* In many cases the data processing staff in centralized computer facilities have so many demands on their time that users have to wait for months (or even years) for their projects to be completed.

# THE CLIPBOARD

## The High-Tech Car Parts Salvage Yard

By applying high-tech inventory tracking to a low-tech industry, Ron Sturgeon has grown his Fort Worth-based auto-salvage business into an $8 million company and one of the industry leaders. . . .

In 1983, Sturgeon says, growth was getting out of hand. AAA Small Car World had "an awful lot of parts in stock, with sales almost doubling every year." Wrecked cars arrived at the store to be evaluated by inventory personnel, who listed the usable parts by hand on tracking sheets. Each part was labeled by hand, and a section of the label was torn off to be filed in the tiny drawers of a pharmaceutical filing cabinet. To find an alternator for a Honda, a salesperson would have to rummage through the files. "We had no automated way of tracking the fact that an alternator for a Honda might also fit an Acura," Sturgeon says. "We needed to track parts more efficiently.". . .

[In 1986] he started paying more attention to the two software vendors at the industry trade shows he attended.

After hearing the sales pitches, Sturgeon realized the developers were way ahead of him. "I didn't even know what the real possibilities were for tracking customers and financial information," he says. "They knew more about the management implications than I did." Comparing the proprietary software with off-the-shelf packages convinced Sturgeon that mass-market software wasn't well enough designed to anticipate the future needs of his growing business. So in 1987, with his company's sales at $2 million, he bit the bullet and invested $70,000 in the Checkmate inventory system. . . .

AAA Small Car World turns over about 100 cars a week. Today, when a junked car arrives at the company, the assessor tells the database that, for example, a 1991 Nissan Maxima has arrived. The database creates a report listing specific variables (like taillights with chrome bezels) and prints a sheet with a number next to each item. The assessor walks around the car with the printout, circling the parts that are usable, and then enters those parts into the car's file. The computer then prints out the labels for the parts. A process that used to take two hours now takes 15 minutes, so the parts are available to the salespeople immediately. The system also tracks prices and interchangeable parts, and tell a salesperson instantly that, say, a Honda alternator is available for a customer with an Acura. The 19 salespeople at AAA's six locations use the system simultaneously, selling and invoicing in one step. A printed invoice goes to the shipping department, and an electronic accounts-receivable form goes to accounting. As salespeople look up parts, the database tracks the number of times each part is requested by a customer, compared with the number of times that part is actually sold. If the part is requested frequently but doesn't sell, Sturgeon knows to lower the price.

Sturgeon runs formulas mercilessly, measuring everything his stores do. "Without this system we couldn't have tripled sales," he says. "We'd still be pulling pieces of paper out of file cabinets to see if we had a BMW part. That kind of limits your growth."

Phaedra Hise, "High-Tech Salvage Yard," *Inc., Annual 1994*, vol. 16, no. 13, p. 102.

■ *Costs:* Communications hardware and software costs can become high when a company's departments are spread over many distant locations.

Problems such as these have led some organizations to set up their computer facility differently. Indeed, the trend these days is away from centralized computer facilities.

## Decentralized Computer Facilities

An organization that uses a separate computer facility to service the needs of each major organizational unit has **decentralized computer facilities.** The size of each facility is determined by the processing requirements of the department it services.

The advantages of using decentralized computer facilities are:

- They are better able to meet local departmental information needs than centralized facilities are.

- They are better able to match hardware and software to local departmental needs.

- They use less sophisticated and less expensive communications hardware and software.

Although this approach solves some problems created by centralized facilities, it also creates new ones.

- The decentralized approach makes it difficult to obtain consolidated, companywide management information because each organizational unit has its own key data and information stored on its own computer system, and the various systems are not electronically linked. Because the format and content of data and information are not consistent between organizational units, the data can't be easily accessed or subjected to a simple consolidation procedure.

- The duplication of hardware, software, and personnel to run decentralized computer facilities can become an unmanageable expense.

## Distributed Computer Facility

A combination of centralized and decentralized computer facilities has been used to try to capture the advantages of both while minimizing their weaknesses. In this system, called a **distributed computer facility,** users have their own computer equipment, and one or more computer terminals are connected to a bigger system. With the growth of powerful communications networks and the decline in computer system costs, distributed systems are becoming more common.

To illustrate, let's consider a company with four divisions located in different cities throughout the country with its corporate headquarters on the West Coast. Headquarters has a large mainframe computer system, and each division has a smaller minicomputer to handle its own local processing needs. Individual users in various departments at the division level have microcomputers. The mainframe computer performs all corporate-level processing and passes pertinent data and information to each division as needed through a communications facility built into the computer systems at all locations. In many cases, several departments have microcomputer terminals connected to the minicomputer system.

In a distributed data processing environment, the corporate-level computer facility is ultimately responsible for the control and the coordination of processing activities at all company levels. This is usually accomplished through corporate-level policies and procedures, as well as by direct support from the corporate data processing department, which oversees equipment selection and systems design.

Without careful planning, the compatibility of data files can become a problem when users capture data on a microcomputer and then wish to transfer it to the central computer system. The reverse is also often true. Microcomputers use a different coding scheme for data than many larger computers do. Unless special steps are taken—adding special hardware components and using special software—data cannot be exchanged in either direction. However, when the proper steps are taken, the problem of data file compatibility is eliminated.

The principal advantages of the distributed processing approach are:

- *Increased user involvement:* The users are more directly involved in the processing activities than they would be in a centralized structure.

- *Easier cost allocation:* Computer processing costs are easier to allocate to different departments than they are in a centralized computer facility.

- *Familiarity:* The computer staff is more familiar with the activities and needs of the specific organizational unit they support than they are in a centralized setup.

- *Focus on corporate processing needs:* The central computer facility can focus more on corporate processing needs than it can when the organization uses only a centralized facility to support all its departments.

- *Fewer personnel:* There is less duplication of hardware, software, and personnel than with the decentralized approach.

- *Improved coordination:* There is more coordination between the corporate computer facility and the division-level computer facilities than with other approaches.

# S U M M A R Y

■ Management information systems are used in the areas of *planning, organizing, staffing, supervising,* and *controlling* business activities in the functional areas (departments) of *accounting and finance, production, marketing and sales, information systems,* and *research and development.* (p. 379)

■ *Management information systems*—organized standards and procedures, both computer-based and manual, for processing data into useful information—are used by three levels of management (p. 380):

1. *Lower-level (operational) management*

2. *Middle (tactical) management*

3. *Top (strategic) management*

■ The types of decisions made differ according to the level of management. Lower-level management typically makes *structured,* short-term *decisions.* Middle management, or tactical management, generally makes *semistructured decisions* based on information that is less detailed (summarized to some degree). These types of decisions have some nonquantifiable aspects to them and require some subjective judgment on the part of the decision maker. Upper management, or strategic management, typically makes *unstructured decisions,* which are the most difficult to computerize because they are made with the most subjective judgment. Unstructured decisions are broad in scope, long range, and often unpredictable and future-oriented. (p. 382)

■ Information must be made available to management in the form of reports. Operating management generally uses *detail reports* that are issued on a regular, or periodic, basis. Middle and top management use *summary reports* and *exception reports* that are issued periodically or on demand or that are initiated by an event. (p. 385)

■ Managers generally follow five steps when making decisions (p. 389):

1. *Problem recognition and identification*

2. *Identification and evaluation of alternatives*

3. *Selection of alternative*

4. *Action*

5. *Follow-up*

■ The data that managers use is generated internally (by normal data processing systems), externally (by sources outside the company), or by other levels of management. The information generated by processing the data into reports differs in level of summarization, degree of accuracy, and degree of time sensitivity, according to the management level. (p. 391)

■ A business can use three general types of management information systems to satisfy management's need for information.

1. A *transaction processing system (TPS)* supports the day-to-day operating activities and is used mostly by operating management. (p. 394)

2. A middle *management information system (MIS)* (or simply a management information system) supports the decision making of middle management with reports that summarize and categorize information derived from data generated on the transaction level. (p. 394)

3. A *decision support system (DSS)* supports the decision making of top management through sophisticated software designed to answer "what if" questions and aid in making projections. Most DSSs are designed for large computer systems, although electronic spreadsheets and database management systems software can be used to build a type of DSS for microcomputers. General decision support systems produce information that can be used to make a wide variety of management decisions. Institutional decision support systems are much more industry- and function-specific. DSS software generally uses a query language to make its use easy and specialized software languages to develop decision-making models; it also provides the manager

with the ability to retrieve and manipulate huge amounts of data. (p. 397)

■ An *executive information system (EIS)* is a DSS made especially for top managers and specifically supports strategic decision making. (p. 399)

■ Expert systems are also sometimes used by management and nonmanagement personnel to solve specific problems. An *expert system* is software consisting of knowledge and rules for using it that are gathered from human experts in particular occupations. (p. 399)

■ Users in large companies are often assisted in the use of the information system's computer facilities by staff members in the *information center*. The information center, headed by the *chief information officer (CIO)*, is part of the MIS department, and it is staffed by experts on the hardware, software, and procedures used in the company. (p. 401)

■ A *centralized computer facility* has all its equipment in one location. This equipment serves all the company's departments. (p. 402)

■ *Decentralized computer facilities* use separate computer equipment for each department in the company. (p. 404)

■ *Distributed computer facilities* combine aspects of both the centralized and decentralized facilities: Users have microcomputers with communications programs so that they may switch to the main computer from time to time. They have the choice of working independently or with the central computer. (p. 404)

## KEY TERMS

centralized computer facility, p. 402
chief information officer (CIO), p. 401
decentralized computer facilities, p. 404
decision support system (DSS), p. 397
detail report, p. 384
distributed computer facility, p. 404

event-initiated report, p. 385
exception report, p. 385
executive information system, p. 399
expert system, p. 399
information center, p. 401
lower (operational) management, p. 382
management, p. 379
management information system (MIS), pp. 381, 394

middle management, p. 385
on-demand report, p. 385
periodic report, p. 385
semistructured decision, p. 385
structured decision, p. 384
summary report, p. 385
top management, p. 385
transaction processing system (TPS), p. 394
unstructured decision, p. 386

## EXERCISES

### SELF-TEST

1. A(n) ___procedure___ is a specific sequence of steps performed to complete one or more information processing activities.

2. What are the five functions of management?

   a. PLAN

   b. ORGANIZE

   c. STAFF

   d. SUPERVISE

   e. CONTROL

3. The part of a company that assists users in using all aspects of the company's computer facilities is the ___INFORM___ ___CENTER___.

4. A(n) _MANAGEMENT_ _INFOR,_ _MIS_ _SYSTEM_ comprises computer-based processing and/or manual procedures to provide useful and timely information to support management decision making.

5. The lowest level of management is strategic management. (true/~~false~~)

6. Operating management deals with structured decisions and needs detailed information. (~~true~~/false)

7. Middle management makes _semi structure_ decisions.

8. Decision support systems are used mainly by upper management. → DSS (~~true~~/false)

9. The five steps involved in making a decision are:
   a. _Identify problem_
   b. _Alternative_
   c. _Select alternative_
   d. _Action_
   e. _Follow up_

10. Information has three properties that vary in importance depending on the decision and the decision maker. They are:
    a. _Level of summary_
    b. _Degree of accuracy._
    c. _Timeline_

11. A transaction processing system supports day-to-day business activities. (~~true~~/false)

12. A decision support system provides information analysis tools not regularly supplied by transaction processing systems and management information systems. (~~true~~/false)

13. A(n) _DECENTRALIZE_ _COMP._ _FACILITY_ has separate computer facilities for each department in the company.

14. In most companies, there are six functional areas. They are:
    a. _ACCOUNTING & FINANCE_
    b. _PRODUCTION_
    c. _MARKETING & SALES_
    d. _PERSONEL_
    e. _INFOR. SYSTEM_
    f. _RESEARCH & DEVELOPMENT_

*Solutions:* (1) procedure; (2) planning, organizing, staffing, supervising, controlling; (3) information center; (4) management information system; (5) false; (6) true; (7) semistructured; (8) true; (9) problem recognition and identification, identification and evaluation of alternatives, alternative selection, action, follow-up; (10) level of summarization, degree of accuracy, timeliness; (11) true; (12) true; (13) decentralized computer facility; (14) accounting and finance, production, marketing and sales, human resources (personnel), information systems, research and development

## SHORT-ANSWER QUESTIONS

1. What is a management information system, and what is its role in an organization?
2. What is an expert system?
3. What steps should management follow to make decisions?
4. What is a decision support system?
5. For what is a company's human resources department responsible?
6. What is an executive information system (EIS)?
7. What are transaction processing systems typically used for?
8. Describe some differences between a management information system and a decision support system.
9. What is the difference between a structured decision and a semistructured decision, and which type of decision is easier to support from a computer-based data processing standpoint?
10. What is the difference between information and knowledge? How can knowledge be made useful?
11. What does the management function of controlling deal with?

## PROJECTS AND CRITICAL THINKING EXERCISES

1. Decision support systems often take years to develop. Given this long development period, some experts argue that the system will be obsolete by the time it is complete and that information needs will have changed. Other experts argue that no alternatives exist. By reviewing current computer publications that describe management information systems, formulate an opinion about this issue.
2. Does your university/college have an information systems department that is responsible for developing and supporting all the university information systems? If so, interview a management staff member about the services and functions of the department. Can this person identify the various levels of management within the department? What kinds of user input were requested when the department was being set up? Does it use any sophisticated decision support software? What kinds of services does the department offer to students?
3. The following quote is from "The New Society of Organizations," by Peter Drucker in *Harvard Business Review* (September/October, 1992, p. 96):

    Society, community, and family are all conserving institutions. They try to maintain stability and to prevent, or at least to slow, change. But the modern organization is a destabilizer. It must be organized for innovation, and innovation, as the great Austro-American economist Joseph Schumpeter said, is "creative destruction." And it must be organized for the systematic abandonment of whatever is established, customary, familiar, and comfortable, whether that is a product, service, or process; a set of skills; human and social relationships; or the organization itself. In short, it must be organized for constant change. The organization's function is to put knowledge to work—on tools, products, and processes; on the design of work; on knowledge itself. It is the nature of knowledge that it changes fast and that today's certainties always become tomorrow's absurdities.

How do you think that managers can plan for change? What can they build into their information systems that can help them be innovative? What tools could they use?

4. As a user, how do you think you would use an information center? Would you ever want to be a CIO? Why or why not?

5. At your school, where would you go for help if you were using the computer facilities in the computer lab? In the library? The dorm? The student union? Who is in charge of these departments? What are these departments called? What kind of training was required for these positions?

## IN THE LAB WITH MICROSOFT WINDOWS

(*Note:* If you aren't familiar with using a mouse and/or don't know how to use the Microsoft Windows graphical user interface, complete the In the Lab with Microsoft Windows exercises in Chapter 6 before proceeding.)

### The Clock Tool

1. In this section you learn how to display the Microsoft Windows Clock. This tool is useful when you want the current time to display in its own window on the screen. Right now, the Microsoft Windows Program Manager should be displaying.

2. DOUBLE-CLICK: Accessories group icon
   DOUBLE-CLICK: Clock program icon
   The Clock window should be displaying. (*Note:* If the wrong time is displaying, you can use the procedure described in the next section to update the time setting.)

3. To change the display to analog:
   CHOOSE: Settings, Analog
   To change the display back to digital:
   CHOOSE: Settings, Digital

4. To display the clock even when you switch to another window:
   CLICK: Control-menu box *located in the upper-left corner of the Clock window*
   CHOOSE: Always on Top
   Now, no matter if you switch tasks, the clock will remain in plain view.

5. To reverse the command you issued in step 4:
   CLICK: Control-menu box *located in the upper-left corner of the Clock window*
   CHOOSE: Always on Top

6. To exit the Clock program:
   DOUBLE-CLICK: Control-menu box *located in the upper-left corner of the Clock window*

7. To close the Accessories group window:
   DOUBLE-CLICK: Control-menu box *located in the upper-left corner of the Accessories window*

### Changing the System Date and Time

1. If your computer is displaying the wrong system date and/or time, you can update these settings using Microsoft Windows. Right now, the Program Manager Window should be displaying.

2. DOUBLE-CLICK: Main group icon
   DOUBLE-CLICK: Control Panel program icon
   DOUBLE-CLICK: Date/Time program icon

3. Edit the date and time as needed.

4. When finished updating the date and time:
   PRESS: Enter

5. To exit the Control Panel window:
   DOUBLE-CLICK: Control-menu box *located in the upper-left corner of the Control Panel window*
6. To close the Main group window:
   DOUBLE-CLICK: Control-menu box *located in the upper-left corner of the Main window*

**The Calculator Tool**

1. In this section you learn how to use the Microsoft Windows Calculator, which you can use to perform basic and scientific calculations. Right now, the Microsoft Windows Program Manager should be displaying.
2. DOUBLE-CLICK: Accessories group icon
   DOUBLE-CLICK: Calculator program icon
   The Calculator window should be displaying.
3. To multiply, use the * symbol. To multiply 48 by 96:
   TYPE: 48
   CLICK: *
   TYPE: 96
   CLICK: =
4. The answer "4608" should be displaying.
5. To switch to Scientific view:
   CHOOSE: View, Scientific
   To switch back to the Standard view:
   CHOOSE: View, Standard
6. Practice using the Calculator tool in either Standard or Scientific view.
7. To exit the Calculator program:
   DOUBLE-CLICK: Control-menu box *located in the upper-left corner of the Calculator window*
8. To close the Accessories group window:
   DOUBLE-CLICK: Control-menu box *located in the upper-left corner of the Accessories window*

# Chapter Topics

# CHAPTER 12

# Advanced Topics

Is it really possible for computers to think like human beings? Not yet, but perhaps that time is coming. Developments in many of the different areas of artificial intelligence—robotics, natural language processing, fuzzy logic, expert systems, neural networks, virtual reality—show that computers are indeed becoming increasingly "intelligent." Professionals who are at the forefront of their disciplines make sure they are aware of new developments in computer technology.

## Preview

*When you have completed this chapter, you will be able to:*

- Define artificial intelligence and give a few examples of how it is used

- Describe how robots are used

- Define natural language and fuzzy logic

- Describe what an expert system is

- Explain what a neural network is

- Define virtual reality and describe a few of its applications

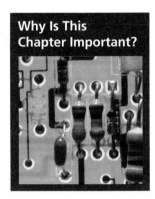

*Topics relating to artificial intelligence are receiving widespread attention from researchers, businesses, and the media. In this chapter, we describe why so much interest is focused on these areas and how you can expect to be affected by the research done in these areas now and in the future.*

## Artificial Intelligence (AI)

**The field of artificial intelligence (AI) attempts to develop machines that emulate human activities and functions. AI includes the area of robotics, perception systems, natural language processing, expert systems, neural networks, virtual reality, and fuzzy logic, as well as building computers that can pass the Turing Test.**

You're having trouble with your new software program. You call the "help desk" at the software maker. Do you get a busy signal or get put on hold to listen to music for several minutes? Technical support lines are often swamped, and waiting is commonplace. Or, to deal with your software difficulty, do you find yourself dealing with . . . other software?

This event is not unlikely. Programs that can walk you through a problem and help solve it are called expert systems. As the name suggests, these are systems that are imbued with the knowledge by a human expert. Expert systems are one of the most useful applications of an area known as *artificial intelligence.*

AI

**Artificial intelligence (AI)** is a group of related technologies used in an attempt to develop machines to emulate human-like qualities, such as learning, reasoning, communicating, seeing, and hearing. AI evolved from early attempts to write programs that would allow computers to compete with humans in games such as chess and to prove mathematical theorems.

### What Is AI Supposed to Do?

The aim of AI is to produce a generation of systems that will be able to communicate with us by speech and hearing, use "vision" (scanning) that approximates the way people see, and be capable of intelligent problem solving. In other words, AI refers to computer-based systems that can mimic or simulate human thought processes and actions. Some of the primary areas of research within AI that are of particular interest to business users are robotics, natural language processing, fuzzy logic, expert systems, neural networks, and virtual reality.

### Robotics

robotics

**Robotics** is a field that attempts to develop machines that can perform work normally done by people. The machines themselves, of course, are called robots. According to *Webster's Ninth New Collegiate Dictionary,* a **robot** is an automatic device that performs functions ordinarily ascribed to human beings or that operates with what appears to be almost human intelligence. It derives from the Polish word *robotnik,* which means "slave."

All robots are preprogrammed. That is, they can only respond to situations for which they have been specifically programmed. (See Figure 12.1.) The most extensive uses of robots so far have been in automobile manufac-

**Figure 12.1**
Robots. HelpMate robot helps with mundane chores at Stanford University.

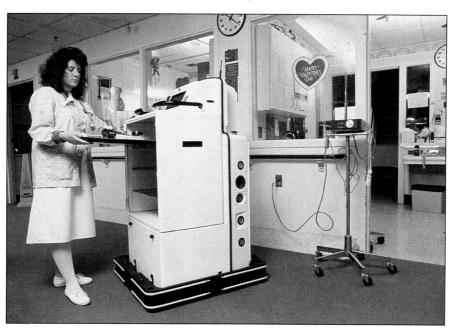

turing or in dangerous environments. Dante II, for instance, is an eight-legged, 10-foot-high, satellite-linked robot used by scientists to explore the inside of Mount Spurr, an active volcano in Alaska.[1]

### Perception Systems

Robots that emulate the human capabilities of sight, hearing, touch, and smell, and then respond based on the new information are called **intelligent robots,** or **perception systems.** (See Figure 12.2.) One future application of intelligent robotics is a machine that is small enough to be swallowed. It will be able to scan intestinal walls with a miniature camera, searching for possible tumors, and send the images to a doctor watching a monitor. Then, under instructions from the doctor, it will take a tissue sample. Obviously, this robot is very sensitive to touch.

Robot vision has already been successfully implemented in many manufacturing systems. To "see," a computer measures varying intensities of light; each intensity has a numbered value that is compared to a template of intensity patterns stored in memory. One of the main reasons for the importance of vision is that production-line robots must be able to discriminate among parts. General Electric, for example, has Bin Vision Systems, which allows a robot to identify and pick up specific parts in an assembly-line format.

Another area of interest is the "personal" robot, familiar to us from science fiction. Existing personal robots exhibit relatively limited abilities, and whether a sophisticated home robot can be made cost-effective is debatable. B.O.B. (Brains On Board) is a device sold by Visual Machines that can speak (using prerecorded phrases), follow people around using infrared sensors, and avoid obstacles by using ultrasonic sound. Software will allow the robot to bring its owner something to drink from the refrigerator. Another type of personal robot is the Spimaster, built by Cybermotion. This security robot patrols up to 15 miles per shift, collecting video images and recording data. If it

**Figure 12.2**
Perception systems. *Right:* A vision system. *Below:* A touch system that inserts objects into various parts of machinery.

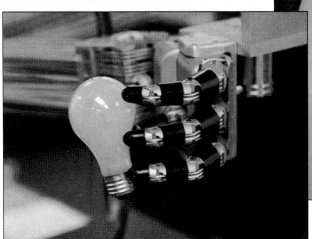

senses a problem, it heads for the trouble zone and sounds alarms on-site and at security headquarters.

The performance limitations of personal robots reflect the difficulties in designing and programming intelligent robots. In fact, we have just begun to appreciate how complicated such mundane tasks as recognizing a can of Pepsi in the refrigerator can be. Another concern is that, if a robot does in fact become intelligent, what would stop it from deciding that work is something to avoid?

### Natural Language Processing

Natural languages are ordinary human languages, such as English. (A second definition is that they are programming languages, called fifth-generation languages, that give people a more natural connection with computers.) **Natural language processing** is the study of ways for computers to recognize and understand human language, whether in spoken or written form. The primary difficulty in implementing this kind of communication is the sheer complexity of everyday conversation. For example, we readily understand the sentence "The spirit is willing, but the flesh is weak." One natural language processing system, however, understood this sentence to mean "The wine is agreeable, but the meat has spoiled." It also understood the phrase "out of sight, out of mind" to mean "blind idiot." It turns out that the system must have access to a much larger body of knowledge than just a dictionary of terms. People use their world knowledge to help them understand what another person is saying. For example, we know the question "Coffee?" means "Do you want a cup of coffee?" But a computer would have difficulty understanding this one-word question.

**H**

Turing test

Alan Turing, a famous British mathematician, proposed many years ago a method by which the intelligence—or natural language processing capacity—of a computer can be tested. The **Turing test** is a test or game for determining whether a computer is considered to possess "intelligence" or "self-awareness." (See Figure 12.3.) In this test, a person is seated in front of two computer terminals; one terminal is directed by a computer and the other is directed by a human (through a keyboard). The subject is supposed to hold conversations (using a keyboard) with each terminal and then guess which

---

**Figure 12.3**

The Turing test. In this test, a human judge converses via computer terminal with two entities in another location. One is a human being, the other a computer program. The task of the judge is to figure out whether the "intelligence" he or she is conversing with is human or not. Often the computer just gives itself away by being illogical, as in this "conversation."

"**Computer:** As a psychoanalyst, I am familiar with discussing such marital troubles with you as the patient on the couch. If you don't have a bad marriage just pretend that you do. Please start with 'My wife . . .' or 'My husband . . .'
**Judge:** Ok, I'll pretend I have a bad marriage. Let's say the reason is because he never picks up his dirty underwear. Is this marriage irreparable?
**Computer:** Well, if you think I'm hopeless, you can always just swear at me."
—Judith Anne Gunther, "An Encounter with A.I.," *Popular Science*, June 1994, pp. 90–93.

# T H E   C L I P B O A R D

## Virtual Therapy

At a conference, Ralph Lamson put on a virtual reality (VR) helmet and entered a new world. As a technician guided him through the novel landscape, he found himself on top of a tall building, which happened to be his greatest fear. "I could have taken off the helmet, but I decided to wait and see what happened," he recalls. He ventured to the edge of the building and, looking down, forced himself to cope with the scary sensations. That single experience carried over, helping him conquer his fear of heights. To Lamson, a psychologist and therapist, the next step was obvious: He decided to see if the same technique would work for others.

He contacted a VR company, Division Incorporated of Redwood City, California, which agreed to design a virtual environment enabling acrophobia sufferers to confront their terrors head-on. In the acro-land scenario, virtual explorers start off in a cafe, go through a doorway, and step onto an elevated patio. They walk across a narrow plank that appears to be several stories above the ground, until they reach a suspension bridge spanning a large body of water.

The environment certainly seemed realistic to the 36 patients Lamson recruited at Kaiser Permanente, the San Rafael HMO [health maintenance organization] where he practices. Acrophobes conducted the VR tour standing up and, at times, their legs wobbled. Occasionally they grew dizzy, reaching for something to grasp onto. Yet they plowed bravely ahead. Overall, the experiment—possibly the first clinical study using VR—was a stunning success. After one virtual therapy session, 91% of the subjects were able to attain new heights, such as walking across the Golden Gate Bridge. . . .

Why does it work? Because the virtual environment seems "real and unreal," Lamson thinks. "You would immediately know this is a computer-generated environment, but your sensory reactions seem real just the same. The truth is, ordinary reality is too real for these people. Thus technology offers a step before reality— a place where they can confront and work through their fears." The approach involves the lowering of the stress response. "You can see it in the heart rate and blood pressure measurements [monitored continuously during the VR excursions]," explains Lamson, who plans soon to offer virtual therapies for claustrophobia [fear of narrow, closed spaces] and agoraphobia [fear of open areas, fear of going out of the house].

. . . VR has Lamson reconsidering the traditional reliance on talk therapy. "It now appears in most cases people won't need prolonged therapy to overcome conditions like acrophobia. With VR, they can work on the fears directly, in a way no talk therapy can match." . . .

Steve Nadis, "Virtual Therapy," *Omni*, March 1995, p. 20.

one is run by a human. Hugh Loebner, a New York businessman, with support from the National Science Foundation and the Alfred P. Sloane Foundation, has offered a $100,000 prize for the first computer system that can pass the Turing test by fooling the subject into thinking he or she is communicating with a person. In November of 1991 a competition based on the Turing test was held in Boston's Computer Museum. Five out of ten judges were fooled by a computer program called PC Therapist III, from Thinking Software, Inc., which won a $1,500 prize. The $100,000 prize is still up for grabs!

The U.S. Postal Service is currently using a language-processing system that was developed by Verbex to speed up the sorting and delivery of mail

## Talking to Robots Made Easy

If you think programming your VCR is difficult, pity the poor souls who must give robots their instructions. Factory automation has simplified and streamlined assembly lines, yet programming the robots that work in the factories is still a labor-intensive task, involving writing and rewriting thousands of lines of computer code for each new job. Now software created by researchers at Carnegie Mellon University promises to make the effort much easier by using colorful icons to represent actions.

Onika, a graphical user interface created by grad student Matthew Gertz, 27, enables anyone who can use a personal computer to program a robot by simply lining up the proper icons on a computer screen. The edges of each icon are shape- and color-coded so only icons that logically follow each other fit together, like puzzle pieces, preventing you from making a mistake. For example, if you tried to place the icon for "open grip" next to the icon with the house on it, which represents the starting, or "home," position, your program would not work. You would be missing the crucial "move to" icon that would need to come before the "home" icon.

The secret to Onika's simplicity is Chimera, its underlying computer operating system for robots. Chimera is an example of object-oriented programming, widely used to create software for corporate networks and databases but rarely used in manufacturing. A conventional computer program is a set of instructions for manipulating a particular set of data; changing the instructions or the data usually requires rewriting the entire program. Object-oriented programming packages pieces of the data and its related instructions into discrete "objects" that embody a certain task, such as "open grip." Because these objects, represented in Onika by icons, are self-contained, they can be reused and assembled into a host of configurations with only minor alterations.

Chimera and Onika were developed in the laboratory of Carnegie Mellon professor Pradeep Khosla, who is taking two years off to manage manufacturing technology programs at the federal government's Advanced Research Projects Agency. Says he: "People on the factory floor who don't even know how to write computer code will be able to make changes quickly. Ultimately, this will reduce the cost of making products." About 200 Onika icons are already stored in electronic libraries on the Internet [✓ p. 292], where they're used by universities and government research labs.

$K^2T$ of Pittsburgh, a Carnegie Mellon spin-off, is developing commercial versions of Onika and Chimera, which should be available in about a year. Meanwhile, Ph.D. candidate Gertz is still putting his own finishing touches on Onika. He's planning to have an icon that triggers a robot to dance to Tchaikovsky's "Waltz of the Flowers" completed in time for his doctoral defense.

Alison L. Sprout, "Talking to Robots Made Easy," *Fortune,* October 31, 1994, p. 240.

that doesn't include a zip code. After the human mail sorter reads the address into a microphone, the computer responds in an electronic voice with the correct zip code.

Most existing natural language systems run on large computers; however, scaled-down versions are now available for microcomputers. Intellect, for example, is the name of a commercial product that uses a limited English vocabulary to help users orally query databases [✓ p. 348] on both mainframes and microcomputers. One of the most successful natural language systems is LUNAR, developed to help users analyze the rocks brought back from the moon. It has access to extensive detailed knowledge about geology in its knowledge database and answers users' questions.

## Fuzzy Logic

fuzzy logic

One relatively new concept being used in the development of natural languages is fuzzy logic. Classical logic has been based on either/or propositions. For example, to evaluate the phrase "The cat is fat," classical logic requires a single cutoff point to determine when the cat is fat, such as a specific weight for a certain length. It is either in the set of fat cats or it is not. However, "fat" is a vague, or "gray," notion; it's more likely that the cat is "a little fat." **Fuzzy logic** is a method of dealing with imprecise data and vagueness, with problems that have many answers rather than one. Unlike traditional "crisp" digital logic, fuzzy logic is more like human reasoning: it deals with probability and credibility. That is, instead of being simply true or false, a proposition is *mostly* true or *mostly* false, or *more* true or *more* false.

A frequently given example of an application of fuzzy logic is in running elevators. How long will most people wait for an elevator before getting antsy? About a minute and a half, say researchers at the Otis Elevator Company. The Otis artificial intelligence division has done considerable research into how elevators may be programmed to reduce waiting time.[2] Ordinarily when someone on a floor in the middle of a building pushes the call button, the system will send whichever elevator is closest. However, that car might be filled with passengers, who will be delayed by the new stop (perhaps making them antsy). Another car, however, might be empty. In a fuzzy-logic system, the computer assesses not only which car is nearest but also how full the cars are before deciding which one to send.

Artificial intelligence has the potential to solve many problems; however, it may create some as well. For example, some people think that AI is dangerous because it does not address the ethics of using machines to make decisions nor does it require machines to use ethics as part of the decision-making process. In spite of these concerns, AI has been used to develop yet another system—the expert system—to support decision making in many areas, including the business environment.

## Expert Systems: Human Expertise in a Computer

We described expert systems in Chapter 11, Information Management, in relation to its uses by management and nonmanagement personnel to solve specific problems, such as how to reduce production costs or improve workers' productivity. In this section we describe expert systems in more detail. As you may recall from Chapter 11, an *expert system* is set of computer programs that performs a task at the level of a human expert. To expand on that definition, an **expert system** is an interactive computer program that can apply rules to input in such a way as to generate conclusions. The program helps users solve problems that would otherwise require the assistance of a human expert. *It is important to emphasize that expert systems are designed to be users' assistants, not replacements.*

An expert system solves problems that require substantial expertise to understand. The system's performance depends on the body of facts (knowledge) and the heuristics (rules of thumb) that are fed into the computer. Knowledge engineers gather, largely through interviews, the expert knowledge and the heuristics from human experts in the field for which the computer-based system is being designed to support decisions—fields such as medicine, engineering, or geology. (For example, in the field of medicine, one question that might be asked of an expert system is whether one treatment is better for a patient than another one.) The responses recorded during the interviews are codified and entered into a knowledge base that can be used by a computer. An expert system has the capacity to store the collection of knowledge and manipulate it in response to user inquiries; in some cases, it can even explain its responses to the user.

An expert system has three major program components (Figure 12.4):

- *Knowledge base:* A **knowledge base** is an expert system's database of knowledge about a particular subject. This includes relevant facts, information, beliefs, assumptions, and procedures for solving problems. The basic unit of knowledge is expressed as an IF-THEN-ELSE rule ("IF this happens, THEN do this, ELSE do that"). Programs can have as many as 10,000 rules. A system called ExperTAX, for example, which helps accountants figure out a client's tax options, consists of over 2,000 rules.

- *Inference engine:* The **inference engine** is the software that controls the search of the expert system's knowledge base and produces conclusions. It takes the problem posed by the user of the system and fits it into the rules in the knowledge base. It then derives a conclusion from the facts and rules contained in the knowledge base.

- Reasoning may be by a forward chain or backward chain. In the forward chain of reasoning, the inference engine begins with a statement of a problem from the user. It then proceeds to apply any rule that fits the problem. In the backward chain of reasoning, the system works backward from a question to produce an answer.

- *User interface:* The user interface is what appears on the display screen for the user to interact with. It gives the user the ability to ask questions and get answers. It also explains the reasoning behind the answer.

### Expert Systems at Work

One of the most famous expert systems—an older system now being replaced by updated ones—is MYCIN, a system that diagnoses infectious diseases and recommends appropriate drugs. For example, bacteremia (bacteria in the blood) can be fatal if it is not treated quickly. Unfortunately, traditional tests for it require 24 to 48 hours to verify a diagnosis. However, MYCIN provides physicians with a diagnosis and recommended therapy within minutes.

**Figure 12.4**

Components of an expert system. The three components are the user interface, the inference engine, and the knowledge base.

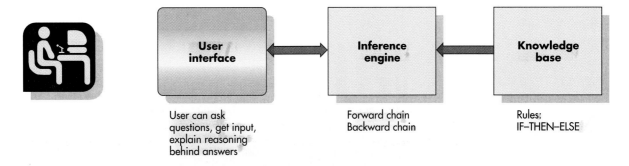

## Visionaries Picture the Information Superhighway

Leslie Crawford, of PC World magazine, asked some movers and shakers for their views about the Information Superhighway. Here is what they had to say:

"Videoconferencing and video on demand will fund the building of the highway. But when I think of opportunity, I think of an incredible breadth of applications, in areas like medical diagnosis or education. I think that when people are empowered to get access to information on these networks it will have profound, positive effects for every area of work and home life."
—William Gates, chair and CEO, Microsoft

"The digital superhighway is much more than a highway system. It's actually the construction of an entirely new virtual continent in which the highway runs. In the future, we will live part of our lives in cyberspace, in the world of virtual reality. We could bequeath few gifts to future generations more important than getting this right. It's critically important to balance public and private interests, much as it's very important to do so in land use, where even private landowners have certain obligations to the public."
—Jaron Lanier, "father" of virtual reality

"A full-access universal network is really what we're talking about—broadband, fully interactive, bidirectional, and universally available. I see it happening in the next three to five years."
—John C. Malone, president and CEO, TCI

"The information highway is going to take its place among other important home appliances: the telephone, the computer, the VCR, the stereo, and yes, the radio. Why? Because there is no substitute for being there, out there, working, traveling, mingling, greeting, meeting, learning . . . as Lyndon Johnson used to say, pressing the flesh."
—Michael D. Eisner, CEO, Walt Disney Company

"It's the kitchen sink condensed into one home-office mobile apparatus that is connected to the world by the various technologies—a multimedia device as simple as your remote control. It will revolutionize and expedite the educational process, free up valuable land that can be restored to its natural state, reduce the frequency of ground and air travel (and thus pollution), and deliver three-dimensional pictures and sound, enabling people to spend less time doing mundane things and more time thinking. . . ."
—Shelley Duvall, Think Entertainment

"All this may seem more like science fiction than reality. Indeed, in the history of the world, it has been only a few hundred years since gunpowder transformed human warfare and less than a century since television connected the world. But just as those inventions brought us to the twentieth century, so will digital information transmit us into the next, transforming everything from how we learn to how we work."
—Albert Gore, vice president of the United States

"The digital superhighway will be as important an underpinning for the new global economy as the interstate highway system, international jet airports, television, and the telephone system were for the industrial age."
—John Sculley, former chair and CEO, Apple Computer and Spectrum Information Technologies

"As we are poised to cross the threshold of a new century, Time Warner Cable's vision is an electronic superhighway into the home. Customers will have access to a wide range of entertainment, information, education, and communication services."
—Gerald Levin, chair and CEO, Time Warner

Leslie Crawford, "Visionaries Picture the Superhighway," PC World, February 1994, p. 139.

To use MYCIN, the physician enters data on a patient; as the data is being entered, MYCIN asks questions (for example, "Is patient a burn patient?"). As the questions are answered, MYCIN's inference engine "reasons" out a diagnosis: "IF the infection is primary bacteria AND the site of the culture is a gastrointestinal tract, THEN there is evidence (0.7) that the identity of the organism causing the disease is Bacteroides." The "0.7" means that MYCIN "thinks" there is a 7 out of 10 chance that this diagnosis is correct. This pattern closely follows that of human thought; much of our knowledge is inexact and incomplete, and we often reason using odds (such as "There's a 40% chance it's going to rain") when we don't have access to complete and accurate information.

Gensym Corporation's G2 Real-Time Expert system is used in Mrs. Baird's Bakery (a large independent bakery in Fort Worth) for scheduling and monitoring the production of baked goods. The system takes care of scheduling such tasks as ingredient mixing and oven operations—don't plan on finding a burned cookie at Mrs. Baird's!

The Residential Burglary Expert System (REBES) is an expert system that uses certain rules of thumb to help a detective investigate a crime scene. REBES, which acts like a partner to the detective, might ask "Did the intruder search the entire house? If so, an accomplice might be involved" or "Was valuable jewelry taken but cheaper jewelry left behind? If so, thieves may be professionals/repeaters."

Examples of other expert systems are XCON, a system that puts together the best arrangement of Digital Equipment Corporation (DEC) computer system components for a given company; DENDRAL, a system that identifies chemical compounds; PROSPECTOR, a system that evaluates potential geological sites of oil, natural gas, and so on; and DRILLING ADVISOR, a system that assists in diagnosing and resolving oil-rig problems.

## Building an Expert System

Capturing human expertise for the computer is a time-consuming and difficult task. **Knowledge engineers** are trained to elicit knowledge (for example, by interview) from experts and build the expert system. The knowledge engineer may program the system in an artificial intelligence programming language, such as LISP or PROLOG, or may use system-building tools that provide a structure. Tools allow faster design but are less flexible than languages. An example of such a tool is EMYCIN, which is MYCIN without any of MYCIN's knowledge. A knowledge engineer can theoretically enter any knowledge (as long as it is describable in rules) into this empty shell and create a new system. The completed new system will solve problems as MYCIN does, but the subject matter in the knowledge base may be completely different (for example, car repair).

Expert systems are usually run on large computers—often dedicated artificial intelligence computers—because of these systems' gigantic appetites for memory; however, some scaled-down expert systems (such as the OS/2 [✓ p. 206] version of KBMS, Knowledge Base Management System) run on microcomputers. Negotiator Pro from Beacon Expert Systems, Inc., for IBM and Apple Macintosh computers, helps executives plan effective negotiations with other people by examining their personality types and recommending negotiating strategies. Scaled-down systems generally do not have all the capabilities of large expert systems, and most have limited reasoning abilities. LISP and PROLOG compilers [✓ p. 223] are available for microcomputers, as are some system-building tools such as EXPERT-EASE, NEXPERT, and VP-Expert, which allow relatively unsophisticated users to build their own expert system. Such software tools for building expert systems are called *shells*.

## Work in the Information Society in 2010

Information technology—infotech for short—consists primarily of computing combined with telecommunications and networking. Infotech also includes expert systems, imaging, automation, robotics, sensing technologies, and mechatronics (microprocessors embedded in products, systems, and devices). These interconnected technologies are moving out of the office and across the landscape to reshape how workers do their jobs. . . . By the year 2010, infotech will effect many positive changes. . . .

- Farmers will become farm managers. Farmers will primarily work indoors, where information will come to them. Farmers will oversee extensively automated smart farms. Sensing technologies will feed data into computers, which will analyze soil conditions, plant health, degree of ripeness, fertilizer mix, and moisture content. . . .

- Police officers will be well-armed—with information. The bane of police officers' existence—paperwork—will be transformed by electronics. Police officers and detectives will hunt for clues in databases instead of searching door to door. DNA sampling will supplement fingerprints. Automated traffic-management systems will smooth traffic flows and identify offenders. . . .

- Utility workers will oversee automated operations. Automation will eventually make jobs such as meter reading obsolete. Instead of human meter readers, utility supercomputers will exchange data with traditional meters or with buildings' energy-management systems.

  In utility plants, workers will use virtual reality in overseeing automated operations: A worker will manipulate an image of a part needing repair while tele-operated robots and equipment carry out the worker's commands. . . .

- Consultants will provide fast and timely advice. The management consultant . . . will benefit from computer networks, personal communicators, videoconferencing, e-mail, and faxes. . . .

  Artificial-intelligence software agents, or "knowbots," will search through networks of databases for the desired information. . . .

  Salespeople will pioneer the mobile office. . . . Sales vehicles will be equipped with portable cellular phones with voice recognition, digital faxes, notebook computing, and perhaps built-in videoconferencing capability.

  Images will become increasingly important for selling. Customers will want to see what they are buying and then try it out by using simulations. . . .

- Scientists expand their horizons. . . .

  A key in 2010 will be videoconferencing and groupware—software that enables workers in different locations to share the same information on their computer screens. The longer-range goal will be technologies allowing scientists to work on problems simultaneously. . . .

- Doctors will team up. . . . Consulting with colleagues and expert-system assistants will become routine. Expert systems will supplement and enhance the physician's skills, filling knowledge and skill gaps, providing advice for complicated procedures, and doing routine diagnoses. . . .

  Infotech will also link physicians in remote areas with nearby high-tech centers. . . .

- Factory workers guide robots. . . .

  Designing, monitoring, and maintaining the automated systems will be primary functions of factory workers or engineers. . . .

  Computer-aided design and computer-assisted manufacturing systems will tie all branches of a factory into design. . . .

- Pilots become flight supervisors. The chief functions of the future pilot will be to coordinate the plane's on-board technologies with air-traffic control and headquarters and to reassure passengers during flight. . . .

- Teachers facilitate learning. . . . Teachers will act as intermediaries between students and the world of information, helping students draw on resources around the globe. . . .

    The artificial-intelligence tutor will become a valuable assistant, providing the individualized instruction that a teacher with 20 or more pupils does not have the time for.

Andy Hines, "Jobs and Infotech: Work in the Information Society," *The Futurist,* January-February 1994, pp. 9–14.

### Implications for Business

Expert systems are becoming increasingly important to business and manufacturing firms. However, it is difficult to define what constitutes "expertise" in business. Unlike some other areas—notably math, medicine, and chemistry—business is not made up of a specific set of inflexible facts and rules. Some business activities, however, do lend themselves to expert system development. DEC has developed several in-house expert systems, including ILPRS (which assists in long-range planning) and IPPMS (which assists in project management).

Another issue that inhibits the use of expert systems in business is that businesses want systems that can be integrated into their existing computer systems. Many existing expert systems are designed to run in a stand-alone mode. Furthermore, who will use the expert system? Who will be responsible for its maintenance? Who will have authority to add and/or delete knowledge in the expert system? What are the legal ramifications of decisions made by an expert system? These and other questions will have to be answered before expert systems are fully accepted in the business environment.

Cost is also a factor. Associated costs include purchasing hardware and software, hiring personnel, publishing and distribution costs (if the expert system is used at more than one location), and maintenance costs, which are usually more than the total of any costs already incurred. The costs can easily run into the many thousands of dollars. However, over the last few years, the number of implementations of expert systems has exploded from the hundreds to the thousands as businesses realize the benefits of better performance, reduced errors, and increased efficiency. In addition, less expensive micro-based tools are becoming increasingly powerful and available to businesses.

### Neural Networks

**H**

neural networks

Artificial intelligence and fuzzy logic principles are also being applied to the development of neural networks. **Neural networks** use physical electronic devices or software to mimic the neurological structure of the human brain.

The human brain has about 100 billion neurons, or brain cells. However, these cells do not act as "computer memory" sites. No cell holds a picture of your dog or the idea of happiness. You could eliminate any cell—or even a few million—in your brain and not alter your "mind."

Where do memory and learning lie? In the connections between cells. These connections are called *synapses,* and they constitute about 40% of the brain mass. Using electrical pulses, the neurons send "on/off" messages along the synapses.

Computer-based neural networks work according to the same principle, using special AI software and complicated fuzzy-logic processor chips to take inputs and convert them to outputs with a kind of logic similar to human logic. (See Figure 12.5.)

Ordinary computers mechanically obey instructions according to set rules. However, neural-network computers, like children, learn by example, problem solving, and memory by association. The network "learns" by fine-tuning its connections in response to each situation it encounters. (In the brain, learning takes place through changes in the synapses.) If you're teaching a neural network to speak, for example, you train it by giving it sample words and sentences, as well as the pronunciations. The connections between the electronic "neurons" gradually change, allowing more or less current to pass.

Electronic neurons are primitive representations of real ones. However, neural networks are still startlingly "intelligent." One neural network learned how to pronounce a 20,000-word vocabulary overnight. At first the network sounded like a child, groping for the right sounds, then gradually mastering words and sentences.

Recently, using software from a neural network producer, Intel introduced a neural network chip that contains many more transistors than the Pentium, its newest microcomputer chip. Other chip makers are also working on neural network chips. Over the next few years, these chips will begin to bring the

**Figure 12.5**

Neural network. A neural network is a web of densely interconnected processing elements, called *neurons,* or *nodes,* because of their functional resemblance to the basic nerve cells of the human brain. Like their biological counterparts, the neurons in a neural network can send information to, and receive information from, thousands of fellow processors at once.

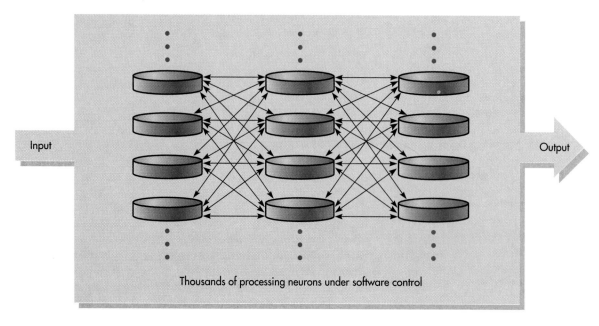

Thousands of processing neurons under software control

# THE CLIPBOARD

## Wetware: Linking the Human Brain with Computers

Virtual telepathy is probably generations away (if it ever happens), but researchers are currently experimenting with devices that might someday evolve into a kind of wetware [the linking of the human brain and computers]. Scientists are trying to create computer images through electrodes attached to the brain, arm or facial muscles. These systems work by translating the electrical signals generated by the nervous system into patterns that the computer can read. The research helps increase computer access for disabled people who could substitute a blink of an eye or the twitch of a cheek for fingers on the keyboard. . . .

The BioMuse computer from BioControl Systems, a company in Palo Alto, Calif., processes signals from muscles, eyes and brains, according to cofounder Anthony Lloyd. His partners are an engineer and a neurophysiologist. An armband or sweatband picks up the electrical signals. The BioMuse isn't reading the user's mind in the science-fiction sense; it turns the body's electrical impulses into digital data that the computer understands. Ultimately, the company hopes, the BioMuse could allow users to control the computer through thinking. The computer could interpret thought patterns as different commands, depending on the software that's used with it, Lloyd says.

Another small company, IBVA Technologies, Inc., in New York, says its Interactive Brainwave Visual Analyzer transforms brain waves, again collected through a device that looks like a headband, into many forms, including music. As you become angry, for example, your brain waves change and the notes corresponding to particular patterns shift as well. It's a cousin of biofeedback, says Helen Meschkow, IBVA's sales manager. She says in future incarnations, the machine might be used to turn your whole house into a kind of mood ring. If you come home feeling stressed, the machine would translate that tension into a command to lower the lights and turn on soothing music.

Barbara Kantrowitz, "Computers as Mind Readers," *Newsweek*, May 30, 1994, p. 68.

---

power of these silicon "brains" not only to your PC but also to such tasks as automatically balancing shifting laundry loads in washing machines.

Many experts expect that soon all computers will have neural network chips. They'll serve as information-filtering tools on your PC, and adjust to your needs. For example, they will sort your electronic mail [✓ p. 288] in order of your priorities and automatically select online news items you would want and store them for you to read later.

Here are two examples of how neural networks have been used so far:

■ Using a PC and a $195 neural network program from California Scientific Software of Nevada City, California, Don Emmons, a professional better, recently picked the winning horse in 17 out of 22 races at a track in Detroit. He gathered data on the various horses' past performances and fed it into the program.

■ The Montgomery County Court House in Norristown, Pennsylvania, uses a neural network to save $40,000 a year in fees for unneeded jurors. With two previous years' data on juror use and the next day's trial schedule, the system provides an immediate readout of the number of jurors required. The jurors, who had been alerted 30 days ahead of time, are called only if they are needed.

## Virtual Reality

**H**

virtual reality

Want to take a trip to the moon? Be a race car driver? See the world through the eyes of an ocean-bottom creature or your cat? Without leaving your chair, you can experience almost anything you want through the form of AI called virtual reality (VR). **Virtual reality** is a kind of computer-generated artificial reality that projects a person into a sensation of three-dimensional space. (See Figure 12.6.) In virtual reality, the user is inside a world instead of just observing an image on the screen. To put yourself into virtual reality, you need the following interactive sensory equipment:

- *Headgear:* The headgear (one type is Eyephones) has two small video display screens, one for each eye, that create the sense of three-dimensionality. Headphones pipe in stereophonic sound or even "3-D" sound. Three-dimensional sound makes you think you are hearing sounds not only near each ear but also all around you.

- *Glove:* The glove (such as the DataGlove) has sensors that collect data about your hand movements.

- *Software:* Software (such as Body Electric) gives the wearer of this special headgear and glove the interactive sensory experience that feels like an alternative to real-world experiences.

**Figure 12.6**

Virtual reality. *Top:* Man wearing interactive sensory headset and glove. When the man moves his head, the 3-D stereoscopic views change. *Middle left:* What the man is looking at—a simulation of an office. When the man moves his glove, sensors collect data about his hand movements. The view then changes so that the man feels he is "moving" over to the bookshelf and "grasping" a book. *Right:* Glove.

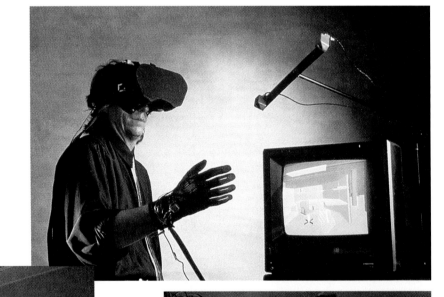

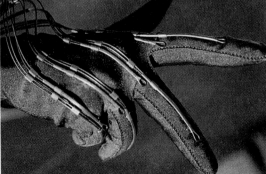

## Envisioning
## the Impossible

Like a true hacker, Stewart McSherry sleeps until noon and spends most nights awash in the glow of a CRT. But while McSherry works in a back-room studio at Silicon Graphics Inc., he's not designing wicked-fast hardware. He's laboring over virtual glass sculptures, bending light with silicon chips.

McSherry started out studying computer science and art in college. He moved on to design outdoor laser shows, then tried commercial animations—flying TV logos. He is now the first artist-in-residence at SGI, where he pursues his dream of melding art into technology, no strings attached. His job is simply "to build impossible things." He has a room of SGI machines with so much graphical horsepower, "I can't keep them busy most of the time." This despite the fact that his final creations can take days to render.

McSherry uses computers to chase art into more abstract modes than a painter or glassmaker ever could. This piece began as primitive shapes that he stretched and deformed. McSherry then added textures and color and placed light sources inside the shapes. The final picture traces hundreds of thousands of rays of light to create a world that McSherry hopes, someday, to cast in glass.

Kevin Kelly, *Wired* magazine, February, 1995, p. 95.

Aside from entertainment, artificial reality can provide instructional simulation situations to help people learn to exercise skills under varying conditions —skills such as driving, flying, outer space operations, police work, and disaster management, to name but a few. Architects are currently using virtual reality systems to allow clients to "test" their houses—walk through them and try out room sizes and designs—before building plans are finalized. Medical schools are starting to use virtual reality to teach surgical procedures to medical students. VIRTUS VR allows microcomputer users to create and explore rooms, checking out furniture arrangements before moving their real furniture into their living room. (See Figure 12.7.)

**Figure 12.7**
With VIRTUS VR software, microcomputer users can try different furniture arrangements and color combinations.

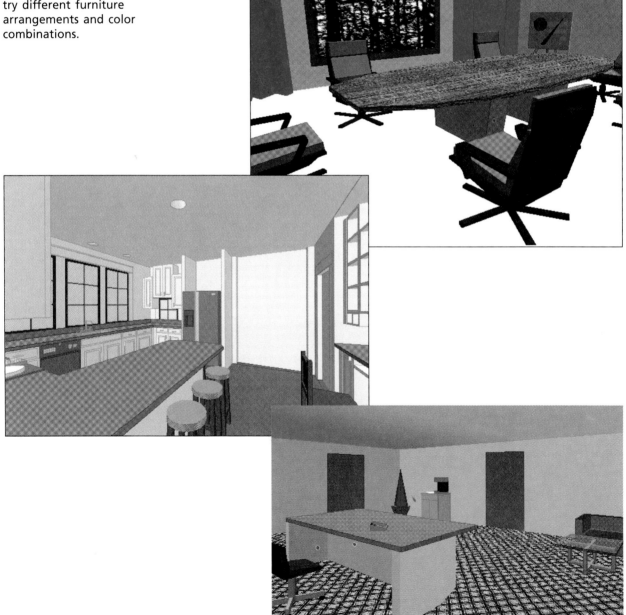

# S U M M A R Y

- *Artificial intelligence (AI)* is basically the science of making machines do what humans can do. The following are some of the primary areas of research within AI: robotics, natural language processing, fuzzy logic, expert systems, neural networks, and virtual reality. (p. 414)

- A *robot* is an automatic device that performs activities normally performed by human beings. Robots that emulate the human capabilities of sight, hearing, touch, and smell, and then respond based on the new information are called *intelligent robots* or *perception systems*. (p. 414)

- The goal of *natural language processing* is to enable a computer or robot to communicate with the user in the user's native language. (p. 416)

- The *Turing test* is used to determine the "intelligence" of a computer; if an operator is fooled into thinking that he or she is dealing with another human being instead of a computer, the computer passes the test. (p. 417)

- *Fuzzy logic* is used along with natural language in artificial intelligence products. This type of logic allows for partial membership in a set, instead of restricting the logic to "either/or" propositions. (p. 420)

- *Expert systems,* an application of artificial intelligence, are also used in the business world to aid in the support of decision making. An expert system is a collection of knowledge (and rules for using it, or heuristics) gathered by knowledge engineers from human experts and fed into a computer system. (p. 420)

- *Neural networks* use AI principles, fuzzy logic, and special microprocessors to simulate the activity of the human brain. (p. 425)

- *Virtual reality* enables the user to experience a computer-generated environment; in other words, the user feels like he or she is actually experiencing an environment rather than just looking at it on the screen. (p. 428)

## KEY TERMS

artificial intelligence (AI), p. 414
expert system, p. 420
fuzzy logic, p. 420
inference engine, p. 421
intelligent robot, p. 415

knowledge base, p. 421
knowledge engineer, p. 423
natural language processing, p. 416
neural network, p. 425
perception system, p. 415

robot, p. 414
robotics, p. 414
Turing test, p. 417
virtual reality, p. 428

## EXERCISES

### SELF-TEST

1. _____Robot_____ is an automatic device that performs functions that are ordinarily performed by a human being.

2. The goal of ___natural___ ___language___ ___processing___ is to enable the computer to communicate with the user in the user's native language.

3. ___UNINTELLIGENT___ robot cannot respond to a situation for which it has not been specifically programmed.

4. ___Expert___ ___System___, which are based on a body of facts collected from human experts, help to solve problems that require substantial expertise to understand.

5. ___NEURAL___ ___NETWORK___ is a computer-based system that attempts to mimic the activities of the human brain.

6. A new concept being used in the development of natural language processing is ___FUZZY___ ___LOGIC.___, which doesn't base decisions on either/or propositions.

7. A form of AI that lets you experience almost anything, such as viewing the world through the eyes of a monkey, is called ___VIRTUAL___ ___REALITY___.

8. A robot that can hear, see, smell, and touch is referred to as a(n) ___INTELLIGENT___ ___ROBORT.___.

9. Some popular areas of research within ___A___ ___I___ are robotics, natural language processing, fuzzy logic, expert systems, neural networks, and virtual reality.

10. To experience virtual reality, you need headgear, a glove, and software. (true/false)

*Solutions:* (1) robot; (2) natural language processing; (3) unintelligent; (4) expert systems; (5) neural network; (6) fuzzy logic; (7) virtual reality; (8) intelligent robot [perception system]; (9) artificial intelligence; (10) true

## SHORT-ANSWER QUESTIONS

1. What is meant by the term *artificial intelligence*?
2. What is natural language processing?
3. What is an expert system?
4. Describe the relationship between the Turing test and research into artificial intelligence and natural language processing.
5. What is meant by the term *virtual reality*? What are some of the things you can do with it?
6. What do you need in order to experience virtual reality?
7. What are the three main components of an expert system?
8. Why is it so expensive to develop an expert system?
9. What inhibits many companies from using expert systems?
10. What characteristics does an intelligent robot, or perception system, have?

## PROJECTS AND CRITICAL THINKING EXERCISES

1. Research virtual reality in current computer magazines and other popular periodicals such as *Time* and *Newsweek*. What do you think of this new technology? What would you use it for? How could it be applied in educational settings?
2. During the rest of the 1990s you can expect expert systems to be used for the monitoring and control of a growing number of complex systems. Research what expert systems are currently being used and then focus on one that is of particular interest to you. Who developed the expert system? How long did it take? What are the hardware requirements for supporting the expert system? How is the expert system updated? Who uses the expert system and how is information retrieved from it?
3. Artificial intelligence professional societies provide a variety of published material as well as symposia, workshops, conferences, and related services and activities for those involved in various AI fields. The societies offer

432

publications and notices intended to keep members up to date on developments in the field. They also lobby elected officials on computer-related issues, provide scholarships, and develop educational videos and television shows. Following are four AI-related societies:

American Association for Artificial Intelligence (AAAI)—the premier AI society 415/328-3123

Association for Computing Machinery (ACM)—for computing professionals of all types 817/776-6876

Institute of Electrical and Electronics Engineers (IEEE)—for engineers of all kinds 202/785-0017

International Association of Knowledge Engineers (IAKE)—a relatively new group for AI practitioners 301/231-7826

Contact these societies and request information on activities, services, and fees. Obtain some of their publications and give a short report. If possible, obtain a video presentation to show to the class.

4. One branch of expert system technology is called *intelligent tutoring systems (ITS)*. Some of these systems are designed to teach students about certain subjects such as geometry or solving quadratic equations. What might be some advantages of using ITS? Some disadvantages? Do you think that intelligent tutoring systems will ever replace human teachers? Why or why not?

## IN THE LAB WITH MICROSOFT WINDOWS

(*Note:* If you aren't familiar with using a mouse and/or don't know how to use the Microsoft Windows graphical user interface, complete the In the Lab with Microsoft Windows exercises in Chapter 6 before proceeding.)

### Paintbrush

1. In this section you learn how to use the Microsoft Paintbrush tool, which is used for creating drawings. Right now, the Program Manager window should be displaying.
2. DOUBLE-CLICK: Accessories group icon
   DOUBLE-CLICK: Paintbrush program icon
   The Paintbrush window should be displaying.
3. To type the current date and your name in the upper-left corner of the screen:
   CLICK: "abc" tool *located on the left side of the screen*
   CLICK: *near the upper-left corner of the blank area*
   TYPE: [*current date*]
   PRESS: Enter
   TYPE: [*your name*]
4. To create a drawing:
   CLICK: paintbrush tool *in the second column*
5. In the white area below the current date and your name, draw the word of your choice by dragging the mouse (for example, "hello").
6. To change the background color:
   CLICK: paintbrush tool *in the left column*
   CLICK: green *located on the palette on the bottom of the screen*
   CLICK: *on the white area of your drawing*
   The background color should have changed to green.
7. On your own, practice using some of the other Paintbrush tools and colors that are available to you for creating drawings. (*Note:* To draw thicker lines, click a different line in the lower-left corner of the Paintbrush window.)

8. Keep the following in mind as you work with Paintbrush:
   a. To clear the screen so you can create a new drawing:
      CHOOSE: <u>F</u>ile, <u>N</u>ew
      CLICK: <u>N</u>o *when asked if you want to save*
      (*Note:* You're clicking "No" because we don't know if you have access to a data disk.)
   b. If your computer is connected to a printer, you can print a drawing:
      CHOOSE: <u>F</u>ile, <u>P</u>rint
      PRESS: Enter
9. To exit the Paintbrush program:
   DOUBLE-CLICK: Control-menu box *located in the upper-left corner of the Paintbrush window*
   CLICK: <u>N</u>o *if you're asked whether you want to save*
10. To close the Accessories group window:
    DOUBLE-CLICK: Control-menu box *located in the upper-left corner of the Accessories window*

# Chapter Topics

# CHAPTER 13

# Ethics, Privacy, and Security

A computer system consists not only of software, hardware, data/information, and procedures, but also of people—the users of the computer system. Because computer systems are the products of human effort, we cannot trust them any more than we trust people. People can use computer systems for both good and bad purposes, and they may appreciate them or be suspicious of them when they use them. But regardless of how they use them or how they feel about them, most people realize that computers have changed the way we live. The deeper that computer technology reaches into our lives, the more questions we should be asking ourselves. For example: What are the consequences of the widespread presence of computer technology? Is computer technology creating more problems than it's solving? In the following sections we examine some critical issues related to the widespread use of computers.

## Preview

*When you have completed this chapter, you will be able to:*

- Discuss the issue of computers and the unethical invasion of privacy through the use of databases and networks

- Discuss the major laws passed in the United States to protect citizens' privacy and prevent the misuse of computers

- Describe copyright matters that relate to software and network piracy, plagiarism, and ownership

- Describe how computers can alter the perceived "truth" of art and journalism

- Describe the major threats to computers and communications systems

- Describe some methods for securing a computer and communications system

*"How did they get my name?" "I've just been denied a job on the basis of an error-ridden credit report!" "My employer got hold of my medical records!" "Someone used my social security number to set up some fraudulent accounts!" "Can XYZ Inc. really sell data on my financial history to that marketing organization?" "Someone took a copyrighted photograph of mine, changed it slightly, and had it printed without my permission in a famous magazine!" "Fred wants to copy my word processing software, since he can't afford to buy his own. Do you think I should let him?"*

*Such questions and comments are heard frequently these days. Unfortunately, their answers and solutions are heard less often. Indeed, many people are not aware of the extent of the problems relating to the ethical uses of computer technology, let alone the rights and duties they may have in using it. If you are to be a responsible member of the Information Age, you need to know about:*

- *Computers and privacy*
- *Intellectual property rights*
- *Truth in art and journalism*
- *The threats to computers and communications systems*
- *Security issues relating to computers and communications systems*

## Computers and Privacy

**Users of information technology must weigh standards of behavior and conduct in several areas. One important area relates to ethics and personal privacy. Information about people that is stored in databases must be protected from misuse, and electronic "spying" must be controlled.**

One definition of **ethics** is that it is a set of moral values or principles that govern the conduct of an individual or a group. People in most countries agree that they are entitled to the right of **privacy**—the right of people not to reveal information about themselves, the right to keep personal information, such as credit ratings and medical histories, from getting into the wrong hands. The right of privacy from an electronic "invasion" into the realm of personal data has become a serious ethical issue.

Some of the computer-related privacy issues involve the use of large databases and electronic networks and the enactment of certain laws.

### Databases

Large organizations around the world are constantly compiling information about most of us. The number of online databases in 1975–1980 was approximately 400; in 1990 the number was 4,465, with 70% of those based in the United States. In the United States, Social Security numbers are routinely used as key fields [✔ pp. 139, 348] in databases for organizing people's employment, credit, and tax records. As part of the billing process, telephone companies compile lists of the calls made, the numbers called, the time the calls were made, and so on. Using a special telephone directory called a *reverse directory* that lists telephone numbers followed by the names of the number holders, governmental authorities and others can easily get addresses of and other details about the persons we call. Credit card companies keep similar records.

Professional data gatherers, or "information resellers," collect personal data and sell it to fund-raisers, direct marketers, and others. In the United States, even some motor-vehicle departments sell the car-registration data they store. From this database, companies have been able to collect names, addresses, and other information about the majority of American households. Some privacy experts estimate that the average person is on 100 mailing lists and in 50 databases at one time. (See Figure 13.1.)

This invasion of privacy raises three issues:

1. How do you feel about personal information being spread without your consent? What if a great deal of information about your shopping habits and your income—collected without your consent—were made available to any small or large business that wanted it? Until they dropped the project in 1990, Lotus Development Corporation and Equifax were preparing to do just that.

   On highways and bridges in some states—Texas, Louisiana, and Oklahoma, for example—toll-collecting systems read special tags affixed to cars. When a car passes through a toll plaza, a machine records the tag's ID number and then, at the end of the month, bills the driver for tolls. The states say that the system cuts down on traffic and smog. But privacy advocates say the system could also give state government a powerful new tool to monitor its citizens; it will know when they're gone and which way they've traveled.

   What if you discovered that your employer was using your medical records to make decisions about placement, promotion, and firing? A survey done in the United States in 1988 found that half of the Fortune 500 companies were using employee medical records to make these decisions.

2. How do you feel about the spread of inaccurate information? Mistakes made in one computer file may find their way into other computer files. For example, many people find that their credit records contain errors. And even if you get the mistake corrected in one file, it may not be corrected in other files.

   Robert Ellis Smith, a U.S. lawyer, was worried enough about inaccuracy in the collection and dissemination of personal information to do something about it. In the early 1970s, as the use of computers became widespread, he worried that government and businesses could know too much about an individual's life and lifestyle. And what they knew quickly became a commodity for marketers. Smith said: "What I soon discovered was that there was often not any need for the information that was being collected, or respect for its accuracy." Smith has successfully been party to a suit against TRW, a major U.S. credit-reporting company. The result of the suit is to make it easier for consumers to correct errors in their credit reports. TRW has agreed to set up toll-free numbers for consumers to call with credit report questions. It will also make its reports easier to read and create a set of strict new rules for handling consumer complaints about credit report errors.

   However, credit-reporting companies also do background investigations on individuals for potential employers. Their reports are sometimes incorrect, and the result is that, for no valid reason, the applicant is not hired. To prevent this, consumer groups advocate the following:

   —*Improved accuracy:* Credit bureaus should take responsibility for correcting mistakes, no matter where the data came from, and they should inform other credit reporters of errors.

**Figure 13.1**
Junk mail: how your name gets on mailing lists. Lists are compiled from two principal sources about you: List brokers use public information sources. List brokers use commercial transactions in which you have been involved. Compilers and brokers then sell your name to each other and to various direct mailers.

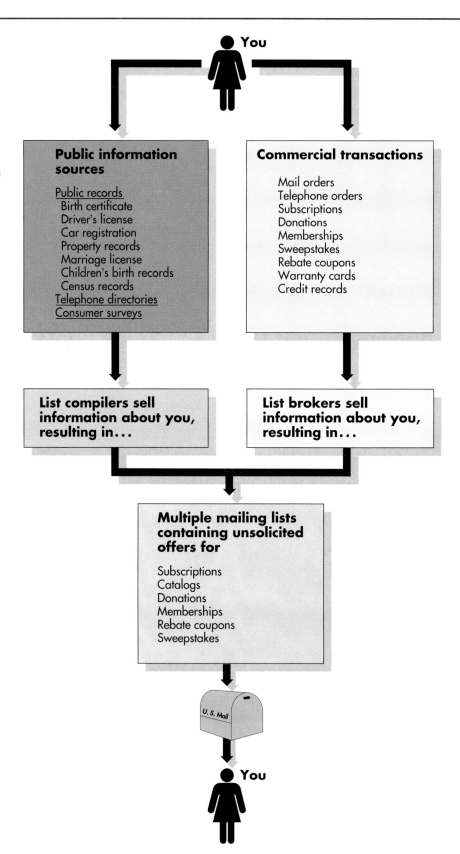

—*Free reports:* Consumers should be entitled to a free copy of their credit reports once a year, not just when they are denied credit.

—*Privacy protection:* Consumers should be given a clear chance to prevent sales of personal data to marketers.

—*Improved service:* Credit-denial notices should include a list of consumers' rights. Investigations of errors should take 30 days, tops.

—*Better enforcement:* The Federal Trade Commission should be given more power to penalize U.S. credit reporters for violating the law.

Fortunately, U.S. law allows its citizens to gain access to records about themselves that are held by credit bureaus and by governmental agencies (we'll discuss this in more detail later).

3. How do you feel about anonymous individuals and large companies profiting from the personal activities that make up your life? "Whose life is it, anyway?"

## Electronic Networks

Imagine you use your company's electronic mail system [✓ p. 288]—or an electronic bulletin board service [✓ p. 291]—to send people a political message that includes some unflattering remarks against a particular group. Later you learn supervisors have been spying on your exchange or that the electronic bulletin board service has screened your messages and not sent them.

In the United States, some legislation has been introduced to control unannounced electronic "spying"—**electronic surveillance**—by supervisors. For example, one proposed law would require employers to provide prior written notice of electronic monitoring and supply some sort of audible or visual signal to alert employees that monitoring was occurring. However, most commercial electronic bulletin board services commonly restrict libelous, obscene, and offensive material through the use of electronic surveillance.

Many people believe that, in a nation linked by electronic mail, there has to be fundamental protection against other people reading or censoring messages or taking action because of their contents. Indeed, in October 1991, in a case involving CompuServe, a federal court in New York ruled that a computer network (information service) company is not legally liable for the contents of the information it disseminates. But some people think that there has to be a limit on the potentially libelous, offensive, or otherwise damaging contents of some messages, in spite of any existing rights to free speech and freedom from censorship. For example, the Prodigy information service network has a policy of prescreening its members' public notes. It warns its members that it won't carry messages that are obscene, profane, or otherwise offensive. But who determines exactly what is "obscene," "profane," or "offensive"?

## Rules and Laws on Privacy

In the 1970s, the Department of Health, Education, and Welfare developed a set of five Fair Information Practices. These rules have since been adopted by a number of public and private organizations. The practices also led to the enactment of a number of laws to protect individuals from invasion of privacy. (See Figure 13.2.) Perhaps the most important law is the Federal Privacy Act, or Privacy Act of 1974. The **Privacy Act of 1974** prohibits secret personnel files from being kept on individuals by government agencies or their contractors. It gives individuals the right to see their records, see how the data is used, and correct errors. Another significant piece of legislation was the Freedom of Information Act, passed in 1970.

## Figure 13.2

The five Fair Information Practices and important federal privacy laws. The Fair Information Practices were developed by the U.S. Department of Health, Education, and Welfare in the early 1970s. They have been adopted by many public and private organizations since.

### Fair Information Practices

1. There must be no personal data record-keeping systems whose existence is a secret from the general public.

2. People have the right to access, inspect, review, and amend data about them that is kept in an information system.

3. There must be no use of personal information for purposes other than those for which it was gathered without prior consent.

4. Managers of systems are responsible and should be held accountable and liable for the reliability and security of the systems under their control, as well as for any damage done by those systems.

5. Governments have the right to intervene in the information relationships among private parties to protect the privacy of individuals.

### Important Federal Privacy Laws

*Freedom of Information Act (1970):* Gives you the right to look at data concerning you that is stored by the federal government. A drawback is that sometimes a lawsuit is necessary to pry it loose.

*Fair Credit Reporting Act (1970):* Bars credit agencies from sharing credit information with anyone but authorized customers. Gives you the right to review and correct your records and to be notified of credit investigations for insurance employment. A drawback is that credit agencies may share information with anyone they reasonably believe has a "legitimate business need." Legitimate is not defined.

*Privacy Act (1974):* Prohibits federal information collected about you for one purpose from being used for a different purpose. Allows you the right to inspect and correct records. A drawback is that exceptions written into the law allow federal agencies to share information anyway.

*Family Educational Rights and Privacy Act (1974):* Gives students and their parents the right to review, and to challenge and correct, students' school and college records; limits sharing of information in these records.

*Right to Financial Privacy Act (1978):* Sets strict procedures that federal agencies must follow when seeking to examine customer records in banks; regulates financial industry's use of personal financial records. A drawback is that the law does not cover state and local governments.

*Privacy Protection Act (1980):* Prohibits agents of federal government from making unannounced searches of press offices if no one there is suspected of a crime.

*Cable Communications Policy Act (1984):* Restricts cable companies in the collection and sharing of information about their customers.

*Computer Fraud and Abuse Act (1986):* Allows prosecution of unauthorized access to computers and databases. A drawback is that people with legitimate access can still get into computer systems and create mischief without penalty.

*Electronic Communications Privacy Act (1986):* Makes eavesdropping on private conversations illegal without a court order.

*Computer Security Act (1987):* Makes actions that affect the security of computer files and telecommunications illegal.

*Computer Matching and Privacy Protection Act (1988):* Regulates computer matching of federal data; allows individuals a chance to respond before government takes adverse actions against them. A drawback is that many possible computer matches are not affected, such as those done for law-enforcement or tax reasons.

*Video Privacy Protection Act (1988):* Prevents retailers from disclosing video-rental records without the customer's consent or a court order.

## How to Get Your Files, and Information on Privacy-Related Issues

It is possible to find out some of the information that various organizations have been gathering about you and storing away on their databases. In all cases, you should be able to get the same files that are made available to others. Just call or write a letter to the following places, and they'll tell you what to do to get this or related information.

### CREDIT INFORMATION

*Equifax Credit Information Services*
Box 740241, Atlanta, GA 30374-0241;
800/685-1111.
Cost: $3 in Maine and Montana, $5 in Maryland, $10 in Massachusetts, free in Vermont, $8 in all other states.

*TRW Consumer Complimentary Report*
(This is the address to use if you have *not* been denied credit in the past 60 days.)
Box 2350, Chatsworth, CA 91313-2350;
214/235-1200 (Dallas HQ).
Cost: Free (one credit report per year).

*TRW Consumer Assistance Center*
(This is the address to use if you *have* been denied credit in the past 60 days.)
Box 749029, Dallas, TX 75374; 214/235-1200.
Cost: Free (one credit report per year).

*Trans Union Corp.*
Box 7000, North Olmsted, OH 44070;
216/779-2378.
Cost: Free if you've been denied credit within the past 60 days; otherwise, $15 for an individual-account record, $30 for a joint-account.

*The three major credit bureaus are allowed to sell some information about you to direct marketers. The law allows you to exempt yourself from such promotions if you contact the bureaus.*

*TRW Target Marketing Division, Mail Preference Service*
901 N. International Parkway, Suite 191,
Richardson, TX 75081; 800/353-0809.

*Equifax Options*
Equifax Marketing Decision Systems, Inc.,
P.O. Box 740123, Atlanta, GA 30374-0123;
800/219-1251

*Trans Union*
555 W. Adams Street, 8th Floor, Chicago, IL
60661; 800/241-2858.

### MEDICAL INFORMATION

*Medical Information Bureau*
Box 105, Essex Station, Boston, MA 02112;
617/426-3660.
Cost: Free.

### CRIMINAL RECORD INFORMATION

*Federal Bureau of Investigation*
(Use this address if you don't have a criminal record but think you might have been under FBI investigation at some point in your life.)
Attn: Freedom of Information Section, 10th St. and Pennsylvania Ave., NW, Washington, DC 20535; 202/324-5520.
Cost: First 100 pages are free; $0.10 for each additional page.

*Federal Bureau of Investigation*
(This is the address to use if you have a criminal record.)
Identification Div., Rm. 10104, 10th St. and Pennsylvania Ave., NW, Washington, DC 20535.
Cost: $17.

### SOCIAL SECURITY INFORMATION

*Social Security Administration*
Wilkes-Barre Data Operations Ctr., Box 20,
Wilkes-Barre, PA 18767-0020; 800/772-1213.
Cost: Free.

### PRIVACY AND JUNK-MAIL MATTERS

*Privacy Rights Clearing House*
Center for Public Interest Law, University of San Diego, 5998 Alcala Park, San Diego, CA 92110-2492; 800/773-7748 or 619/298-3396. A non-profit organization that offers fact sheets on junk mail and other privacy issues.

*Stop Junk Mail Association*
3020 Bridegway #150, Sausalito, CA 94965; 800/827-5549. This association offers a mailing-list name-deletion service for its members, and it lobbies on behalf of postal privacy rights.

*Direct Marketing Association, Mail Preference Service*
P.O. Box 9008, Farmingdale, NY 11735. Many merchants and mail-order outfits belong to this association. One letter to the DMA should take you off their mailing lists.

*Direct Marketing Association, Telephone Preference Service*
P.O. Box 9014, Farmingdale, NY 11735-9014. Write if you want to reduce those annoying tele-marketing calls.

**MATTERS CONCERNING SOFTWARE PIRACY AND COMPUTER THREATS**

*Canadian Alliance Against Software Theft*
800/263-9700

*Computer Emergency Response Team (CERT)*
CERT Coordination Center, Software Engineering Institute, Carnegie-Mellon University, Pittsburgh, PA 15213-3890; 412/268-7090; CERT@CERT.ORG. A 24-hour hotline for the U.S. CERT Coordination Center, designed to combat threats from hackers, crackers, and viruses.

---

*The European Commission's proposal would:*
▶ Prevent companies from keeping personal data or ID numbers without the person's O.K.
▶ Let consent be withdrawn at any time and permit damage suits if such privacy rights are infringed
▶ Require file-keepers to set up a security system to bar unauthorized access
▶ Ban electronic profiles of individuals based on what they buy or do through computer networks
▶ Bar transmission of data to countries without similar protections

**Figure 13.3**
Proposed European privacy standards.

The **Freedom of Information Act** allows ordinary citizens to have access to data gathered about them by federal agencies. Most privacy laws regulate only the behavior of government agencies or government contractors. For example, the *Computer Matching and Privacy Protection Act* of 1988 prevents the government from comparing certain records to try to find a match. This law does not affect most private companies.

Banking and credit are two private industries for which there are federal privacy laws on the books. The **Fair Credit Reporting Act of 1970** allows you to have access to and gives you the right to challenge your credit records. If you have been denied credit, this access must be given to you free of charge. The **Right to Financial Privacy Act of 1978** sets restrictions on federal agencies that want to search customer records in banks.

Since the late 1970s, seven European nations have enacted a patchwork of data protection laws. But Italy, Belgium, Spain, Portugal, and Greece have passed none. The matter of data protection and privacy remains one of the many barriers to a Europe that is a truly unified economic entity. If the European nations were to adopt a single privacy standard (Figure 13.3), however, current thinking is that it could be stricter than U.S. and Canadian laws.

## Intellectual Property Rights

**Ethics in the Information Age also concerns intellectual property rights, especially software and network piracy, plagiarism, and ownership of images and sounds.**

Information technology has presented legislators and lawyers—and you—with some new ethical matters regarding rights to intellectual property. **Intellectual property** consists of the products of the human mind, tangible or intangible. There are three methods of protecting intellectual property. They are *patents* (as for an invention), *trade secrets* (as for a formula or method of doing business), or *copyrights*.

Of principal interest to us is copyright protection. A **copyright** is a body of law that prohibits copying of intellectual property without the permission of the copyright holder. The law protects books, articles, pamphlets, music, art, drawings, movies, and other expressions of ideas. It also protects computer software.

A copyright protects the *expression* of an idea but not the idea itself. Thus, others may copy your idea for, say, a new shoot-em-up video game but not your particular variant of it. Copyright protection is automatic and lasts a minimum of 50 years; you do not have to register your idea with the government (as you do with a patent) in order to receive protection.

These matters are important because the Digital Age has made the act of copying far easier and more convenient than in the past. Copying a book on a photocopying machine might take hours, so people felt they might as well buy the book. Copying a software program onto another diskette might take just seconds. Digitization threatens to compound the problem. For example, current copyright law doesn't specifically protect copyright material online. Says one article:

> Copyright experts say laws haven't kept pace with technology, especially digitization, the process of converting any data—sound, video, text—into a series of ones and zeros that are then transmitted over computer networks. Using this technology, it's possible to create an infinite number of copies of a book, a record, or a movie and distribute them to millions of people around the world at very little cost. Unlike photocopies of books or pirated audiotapes, the digital copies are virtually identical to the original.[1]

Three copyright-related matters deserve our attention: software and network piracy, plagiarism, and ownership of images and sounds.

- *Software and network piracy:* It may be hard to think of yourself as a pirate (no sword or eye patch) when all you've done is make a copy of some commercial software for a friend. However, from an ethical standpoint, an act of piracy is like shoplifting the product off a store shelf—even if it's for a friend.

    **H**

    software piracy

    **Piracy** is theft or unauthorized distribution or use. A type of piracy is to appropriate a computer design or program. This is the piracy that Apple Computer claimed in a suit (since rejected) against Microsoft and Hewlett-Packard, saying that items in its interface, such as icons and windows, had been copied. **Software piracy** is the unauthorized copying of copyrighted software. One way is to copy a program from one diskette to another. Another is to download a program from a network and make a copy of it. **Network piracy** is using electronic networks to distribute unauthorized copyrighted materials in digitized form. Record companies, for example, have protested the practice of computer users' sending unauthorized copies of digital recordings over the Internet [✓ pp. 292, 298].[2]

    The easy rationalization is to say that "I'm just a poor student, and making this one copy isn't going to cause any harm." But it is the single act of software piracy multiplied millions of times that is causing the software publishers a billion-dollar problem. They point out that the loss of revenue cuts into their budget for offering customer support, upgrading products, and compensating their creative people. Piracy also means that software prices are less likely to come down; if anything, they are more likely to go up.

    In time, anti-copying technology may be developed that, when coupled with laws making the disabling of such technology a crime, will reduce the piracy problem. Regardless, publishers, broadcasters, movie studios, and authors must be persuaded to take chances on developing

# THE CLIPBOARD

## Scary Thoughts About Stolen Chips

"Computer chips are the dope of the 90s," Sgt. Jim McMahon is saying. "They're easier to steal than dope. Worth more money than dope. And for the people who steal them, here's the best part: Once stolen, they're almost untraceable."

It's a Monday morning in May, and McMahon, head of the High-Tech Crime Unit of the San Jose Police Department, is standing outside an evidence room at headquarters. . . .

McMahon . . . lifts a computer chip that sits nearby. The tiny silicon unit has been implanted in a PGA, the prong-and-grid array that plugs into a computer. Ready for action, the chip and its PGA are smaller and thinner than a Saltine cracker.

McMahon flips the assembly between his fingers. "On the street," he says, "the most valuable chips are worth between $400 and $600. And do you see any marks on this? Any serial numbers? I don't. Neither do the robbers. The guys who make them keep it that way."

Thanks to an $80 billion annual boom in silicon-chip-equipped technology—automobiles, computers, medical equipment, children's toys, magazine ads, and even greeting cards use them—demand has never been greater. . . .

A wave of "takeover style" robberies began in 1991, and it has washed over every corner of the computer industry. From Osaka, Japan, to Portland, Oregon, bands of heavily armed men have forced their way into factories, stealing chips and beating one or two of the witnesses to secure a fearful silence. . . .

"The chips change hands 8 to 15 times within 72 hours after they've been stolen,"
McMahon says. "They may go overseas or out of town by FedEx or UPS. They're incredibly hard to track." At each step in the chain, the price of the chips rises until their value nears that of the marketplace. Then, with everyone having made money and the chips carrying a price that seems legitimate, new receipts are drawn up, and the chips are sold into the lawful marketplace. . . .

"Despite the attributes black-market dealers of computer chips claim their wares have," McMahon says, "the quality of these batches of chips is often less than perfect."

Many times, he says, computer chips haven't been tested when they're stolen, or, even worse, during the helter-skelter of the robbery, batches of faulty chips may be mixed with fully functional ones. And since all 486 chips look the same to the human eye, the only certain way to find out is to test them, a step not all companies take, since they assume their vendors haven't sold them duds.

"This is where things get scary," says McMahon, "since many chips these days are purchased for uses other than personal computers.

"Do you want a faulty, black-market chip running the navigation system on your commercial aircraft?" he asks. "How about the blood-temperature machine in a surgical lab when you're going under the knife?"

Donovan Webster, "Chips Are a Thief's Best Friend," *The New York Times Magazine,* September 18, 1994, pp. 54–59.

online and multimedia [✓ pp. 58, 72, 133] versions of their intellectual products. Such information providers need to be able to cover their costs and make a reasonable return. If not, says one writer, the information superhighway [✓ p. 273] will remain "empty of traffic because no one wants to put anything on the road."[3]

■ *Plagiarism:* **Plagiarism** is the expropriation of another writer's text, findings, or interpretations and presentation of it as one's own. Information technology puts a new face on plagiarism in two ways. On the one hand, it offers plagiarists new opportunities to go far afield for unauthorized copying. On the other hand, the technology offers new ways to catch people who steal other people's material.

Electronic online journals are not limited by the number of pages, and so they can publish papers that attract a small number of readers. In recent years, there has been an explosion in the number of such journals and of their academic and scientific papers. This proliferation may make it harder to detect when a work has been plagiarized, since few readers will know if a similar paper has been published elsewhere.[4]

Yet information technology can also be used to identify plagiarism. Scientists have used computers to search different documents for identical passages of text. In 1990, two "fraud busters" at the National Institutes of Health alleged after a computer-based analysis that a prominent historian and biographer had committed plagiarism in his books. The ensuing uproar shook the academic community for four years. The historian, who said the technique turned up only the repetition of stock phrases, was later exonerated in a scholarly investigation.[5]

■ *Ownership of images and sounds:* Scanners, digital cameras, digital samplers, and computers make it possible to alter images and sounds to be almost anything you want. What does this mean for the original copyright holders? An unauthorized sound snippet of James Brown's famous howl can be electronically transformed by digital sampling into the background music for dozens of rap recordings.[6] Images can be appropriated by scanning them into a computer system, then altered or placed in a new context.

The line between artistic license and infringement of copyright is not always clear-cut. In 1993, a Federal appeals court in New York upheld a ruling against artist Jeff Koons for producing ceramic art of some puppies. It turned out that the puppies were identical to those that had appeared in a postcard photograph copyrighted by a California photographer.[7] But what would have been the judgment if Koons had scanned in the postcard, changed the colors, and rearranged the order of the puppies?

In any event, to avoid lawsuits for violating copyright, a growing number of artists who have recycled material have taken steps to protect themselves. This usually involves paying flat fees or a percentage of their royalties to the original copyright holders.

## Truth in Art and Journalism

**Ethics also concerns the matter of altering sound and visual originals without making it clear that this has been done.**

The ability to manipulate digitized images and sounds has brought a new tool to art but a big new problem to journalism. How can we now know that what we're seeing or hearing is the truth? Consider the following:

■ *Manipulation of sound:* Frank Sinatra's 1994 album *Duets* pairs him through technological tricks with singers like Barbra Streisand, Liza Minnelli, and Bono of U2. Sinatra recorded solos in a recording studio. His singing partners, while listening to his taped performances on earphones, dubbed in their own voices. This was done not only at different times but often, through distortion-free phone lines, from different places. The illusion in the final recording is that the two singers are standing shoulder to shoulder.

Newspaper columnist William Safire loves the way "digitally remas-tered" recordings recapture great singing he enjoyed in the past. However, he called *Duets* "a series of artistic frauds." Said Safire, "The question raised is this: When a performer's voice and image can not only be edited, echoed, refined, spliced, corrected, and enhanced—but can be transported and combined with others not physically present—what is a performance? . . . Enough of additives, plasticity, virtual venality; give me organic entertainment."[8] Another critic said that to call the disk *Duets* seemed wrong. "Sonic collage would be a more truthful description."[9]

Some listeners feel that new technology changes the character of a performance for the better—that the sour notes and clinkers can be edited out. Others, however, think the practice of assembling bits and pieces in a studio drains the music of its essential flow and unity.

Whatever the problems of misrepresentation in art, however, they pale beside those in journalism. Could not a radio station edit a stream of digi-tized sound to achieve an entirely different effect from what actually happened?

■ *Manipulation of photos:* When O.J. Simpson was arrested on suspicion of murder, the two principal newsmagazines both ran pictures of him on their covers.[10] *Newsweek* ran the mug shot unmodified, as taken by the Los Angeles Police Department. *Time,* however, had the shot redone with special effects as a "photo-illustration" by an artist working with a computer. Simpson's image was darkened so that it still looked like the photo but, some critics said, with a more sinister cast to it.

Should a magazine that reports the news be taking such artistic license? Should *National Geographic* in 1982 have moved two Egyptian pyramids closer together so that they would fit on a vertical cover? Was it even right for *TV Guide* in 1989 to run a cover showing Oprah Winfrey's head placed on Ann-Margret's body?

The potential for abuse is clear. "For 150 years, the photographic image has been viewed as more persuasive than written accounts as a form of 'evidence,'" says one writer. "Now this authenticity is breaking down under the assault of technology."[11] Asks a former photo editor of *The New York Times Magazine,* "What would happen if the photograph appeared to be a straightforward recording of physical reality, but could no longer be relied upon to depict actual people and events?"[12]

Many editors try to distinguish between photos used for commercial-ism (advertising) versus journalism, or for feature stories versus news sto-ries. However, this distinction implies that the integrity of photos applies only to some narrow definition of news. In the end, it can be argued, tampered photographs pollute the credibility of all of journalism.

**H**

morphing

■ *Manipulation of video:* The technique of morphing, used in still photos, takes a quantum jump when used in movies, videos, and television com mercials. In **morphing,** a film or video image is displayed on a computer screen and altered pixel by pixel, or dot by dot. The result is that the image metamorphoses into something else—a pair of lips into the front of a Toyota, for example.

Morphing and other techniques of digital image manipulation have had a tremendous impact on film making. Director and digital pioneer Robert Zemeckis (*Death Becomes Her*) compares the new technology to the advent of sound in Hollywood.[13] It can be used to erase jet contrails from the sky in a western and to make digital planes do impossible stunts. It can even be used to add and erase actors. In *Forrest Gump,* many scenes involved old film and TV footage that had been altered so that the Tom Hanks character was interacting with historical figures.

Films and videotapes are widely thought to be somewhat accurate versions of reality (as evidenced by the reaction to the amateur videotape of the Rodney King beating by police in Los Angeles). Thus, the possibility of digital alterations raises some real problems. One is the possibility of doctoring videotapes supposed to represent actual events. Another concern is for film archives: Because videotapes suffer no loss in resolution, there are no "generations." Thus, it will be impossible for historians and archivists to tell whether the videotape they're viewing is the real thing or not.[14]

Information technology increasingly is blurring humans' ability to distinguish between natural and artificial experience, say Stanford University communication professors Byron Reeves and Clifford Nass.[15] For instance, they have found that showing a political candidate on a large screen (30 or 60 inches) makes a great difference in people's reactions. In fact, you will actually like him or her more than if you watch on a 13-inch screen. "We've found in the laboratory that big pictures automatically take more of a viewer's attention," said Reeves. "You will like someone more on the large screen and pay more attention to what he or she says but remember less." (This is why compelling TV or computer technology may not aid education.) Our visual perception system, they find, is unable to discount information—to say that "this is artificial"—just because it is symbolic rather than real.

If our minds have this inclination anyway, how can we be expected to exercise our critical faculties when the "reality" is not merely artificial but actively doctored?

# THE CLIPBOARD

## Public Policy Issues in Building the Canadian Information Highway

Publishers need to be aware of policy issues that affect publishing over networks. In Canada, Industry Canada is taking the lead on these issues for government and has appointed members to a National Advisory Council to advise the prime minister regarding the issues in developing an information highway. The council is considering, among others, the following policy issues.

■ How fast should the advanced network infrastructure be built? How will network improvements be financed?

■ How should copyright and intellectual property be addressed?

■ What controls, if any, should be placed on the information that is put on the network?

■ How can the information highway be used to improve government services to the public?

■ How can the personal privacy and security of information be protected?

From Dr. Dorothy Phillips, "Writing for the Networks," *WRITE94 Proceedings,* Vancouver, BC, June 16–18, 1994. [Hosted by the University of British Columbia Continuing Studies, 5997 Iona Dr., Vancouver, BC V67 1Z1, Canada. 604/222-5251.]

## Threats to Computers and Communications Systems

**Information technology can be disabled by a number of occurrences. It may be harmed by people, procedural, and software errors; by electromechanical problems; and by "dirty data." It may be threatened by natural hazards and by civil strife and terrorism. Criminal acts perpetrated against computers include theft of hardware, software, time and services, and information; and crimes of malice and destruction. Computers may be harmed by viruses. Computers can also be used as instruments of crime. Criminals may be employees, outside users, hackers, crackers, and professional criminals.**

There will probably always be a need for paper towels or the equivalent. That is because there will always be household accidents and mistakes—spills, messes, leaky pipes. Similarly, accidents and other disasters will probably disable computer and communications systems from time to time, as they have in the past. What steps should we take to minimize them, and how should we deal with them when they do happen?

Here we discuss the following threats to computers and communications systems:

■ Errors and accidents

■ Natural and other hazards

■ Crimes against information technology

■ Crimes using information technology

■ Viruses

### Errors and Accidents

ROBOT SENT TO DISARM BOMB GOES WILD IN SAN FRANCISCO, read the headline.[16] Evidently, a hazardous-duty police robot started spinning out of control when officers tried to get it to grasp a pipe bomb. Fortunately, it was shut off before any damage could be done. Most computer glitches are not so spectacular, although they can be almost as important.

In general, errors and accidents in computer systems may be classified as people errors, procedural errors, software errors, electromechanical problems, and "dirty data" problems.

■ *People errors:* Recall that one part of a computer system is the people who manage it or run it. For instance, Brian McConnell of Roanoke, Virginia, found that he couldn't get past a bank's automated telephone system to talk to a real person. This was not the fault of the system so much as of the people at the bank. McConnell, president of a software firm, thereupon wrote a program that automatically phoned eight different numbers at the bank. People picking up the phone heard the recording, "This is an automated customer complaint. To hear a live complaint, press. . . ."[17] Quite often, what may seem to be "the computer's fault" is human indifference or bad management.

■ *Procedural errors:* Some spectacular computer failures have occurred because someone didn't follow procedures. Consider the 2½-hour shutdown of NASDAQ, the nation's second largest stock market. NASDAQ is so automated that it likes to call itself "the stock market for the next 100 years." In July 1994, NASDAQ was shut down by an effort, ironically, to make the computer system more user-friendly. Technicians were phasing in new software, adding technical improvements a day at a time. A few days into this process, the technicians tried to add more features to the software, flooding the data-storage capability of the computer system. The result was a delay in opening the stock market that shortened the trading day.[18]

■ *Software errors:* We are forever hearing about "software glitches" or "software bugs." A **software bug** is an error in a program that causes it to malfunction. (See Figure 13.4.)

An example of a somewhat small error is the one a school employee in Newark, New Jersey, made in coding the school system's master scheduling program. When 1,000 students and 90 teachers showed up for the start of school at Central High School, half the students had incomplete or no schedules for classes. Some classrooms had no teachers while others had four instead of one.[19]

An example of a large number of software errors is the set of errors behind the delay in launching the automatic baggage system for the new Denver International Airport. Consisting of 4,000 computer-guided baggage carts and 22 miles of tracks, the system was supposed to be able to shuttle 60,000 bags an hour around the airport. However, in its first test, carts crashed into each other, others went off the rails, and others didn't appear when summoned.[20]

Especially with complex software, there are always bugs, even after the system has been thoroughly tested and "debugged." However, there comes a point in the software development process where debugging must end. That is, the probability of the bugs disrupting the system is considered to be so low that it is not worth searching further for them.

■ *Electromechanical problems:* Mechanical systems, such as printers, and electrical systems, such as circuit boards, don't always work. They may be

---

**Figure 13.4**
Software error. A software error caused automatic teller machines to deduct more than they should from customers' accounts.

"In one of the biggest computer errors in banking history, Chemical Bank mistakenly deducted about $15 million from more than 100,000 customers' accounts on Tuesday night, causing consternation among its customers around the New York area.

The problem stemmed from a single line in an updated computer program installed by Chemical on Tuesday in its Somerset, N.J. computer center that caused the bank to process every withdrawal and transfer at its automated teller machines twice. Thus a person who took $100 from a cash machine had $200 deducted, although the receipt only indicated a withdrawal of $100. . . .

[T]he obvious suspect was a small section of new software that had been installed as part of a year-long effort by Chemical to improve the software it uses to operate its A.T.M.'s.

The problem line of the computer program was meant to be 'dormant,' until further changes in the system were made. . . . What it did, however, was to send an electronic carbon copy of every A.T.M. withdrawal and transfer that was made to a second computer system used for processing paper checks. That meant money was deducted from customers' accounts once by the A.T.M. system and then a second time by the check system."

—Saul Hansell, "Cash Machines Getting Greedy at a Big Bank," *The New York Times,* February 18, 1994, pp. A1, C16.

faultily constructed, get dirty or overheated, wear out, or become damaged in some other way. Power failures (brownouts and blackouts) can shut a system down. Power surges can burn out equipment.

Whatever the reason, whether electromechanical failure or another problem, computer downtime is expensive. A survey of about 450 information system executives picked from Fortune 1,000 companies found that companies on average suffer nine 4-hour computer-system failures a year. Each failure cost the company an average of $330,000. Because of them, companies were unable to deliver a service, complete production, earn fees, or retrieve data. Moreover, employees lost productivity because of idle time.[21]

■ *"Dirty data" problems:* When keyboarding a research paper, you undoubtedly make a few typing errors (which, hopefully, you clean up). Typos are also a fact of life for all the data-entry people around the world who feed a continual stream of raw data into computer systems. A lot of problems are caused by this kind of "dirty data." **Dirty data** is data that is incomplete, outdated, or otherwise inaccurate.

A good reason for having a look at your records—credit, medical, school—is so you can make any corrections to them before they cause you complications.

# THE CLIPBOARD
## 'Net Terrorism

Late fall of 1994, 20,000 Internet users received racist or homophobic e-mail from a Texas A&M university professor's address. The message began: "Free money can be yours if you are an 80-IQ, welfare mother producing illegitimate offspring at 9-month intervals starting at age 13."

The message went on to criticize Jews, gays, and other minority groups and then described a shortwave radio program produced by the National Alliance, a white supremacist organization.

Professor Grady Blount, whose e-mail address was used for the hate mail, was bombarded with angry replies from people who thought that he was the bigot. Actually, a hacker somehow got Blount's password and accessed his account to do the deed. Only a University of Wisconsin-Milwaukee instructor who received the hate mail didn't jump to accuse Blount.

UWM computer science professor Leonard Levine wrote to Blount: "I was just wondering if you were in fact the originator or if you were a victim, too. The Internet is a busy place, and there are mean folks all over."

Blount was pleased to receive mail from somebody who didn't assume him guilty from the start. He wrote: "Out of the approximately 500 responses I've gotten to this prank, yours is the first to wonder aloud if anyone would be stupid enough to do what this hacker did. Thanks, I'm really feeling beaten on right now. I'm getting death threats because of this clown, and none of our computer people wants to talk about it. But it isn't going away. This thing is apparently still sprawling all over the Internet, and I've developed the rap as the super-racist from South Texas. Very sad indeed. Where are the cyberfuzz when you need them?"

The so-called cyberfuzz—whoever they are—have not caught the culprit.

*Online Access,* February 1995, p. 28.

## Natural and Other Hazards

Some disasters do not merely lead to temporary system downtime, they can wreck the entire system. Examples are natural hazards, and civil strife and terrorism.

■ *Natural hazards:* Whatever is harmful to property (and people) is harmful to computers and communications systems. This certainly includes natural disasters: fires, floods, earthquakes, tornadoes, hurricanes, blizzards, and the like. If they inflict damage over a wide area, as did Florida's 1992 Hurricane Andrew, natural hazards can disable all the electronic systems we take for granted. Without power and communications connections, automatic teller machines, credit-card verifiers, and bank computers are useless.

■ *Civil strife and terrorism:* We may take comfort in the fact that wars and insurrections seem to take place in other parts of the world. Yet we are not immune to civil unrest, such as the so-called Rodney King riots that wracked Los Angeles in 1992. Nor are we immune, apparently, to acts of terrorism, such as the February 1993 bombing of New York's World Trade Center. In the latter case, companies found themselves frantically moving equipment to new offices and reestablishing their computer networks.

## Crimes Against Computers and Communications

An **information-technology crime** can be of two types. It can be an illegal act perpetrated *against* computers or telecommunications. Or it can be the use of computers or telecommunications to accomplish an illegal act. Here we discuss the first type.

Crimes against information technology include theft—of hardware, of software, of computer time, of cable or telephone services, of information. Other illegal acts are crimes of malice and destruction. Some examples are as follows:

■ *Theft of hardware:* Stealing of hardware can range from shoplifting an accessory in a computer store to removing a laptop or cellular phone from someone's car. Professional criminals may steal shipments of microprocessor chips off a loading dock or even pry cash machines out of shopping-center walls.

   A particularly interesting case was the theft in December 1990 of a laptop computer from the car of a British officer. It happened to contain U.S. General Norman Schwarzkopf's preliminary military plans for the invasion of Iraq. Fortunately, the war plans were not compromised by the event.

   Theft of computers has become a major problem on many campuses. Often the thieves, who may be professionals, don't take the peripheral devices, only the system unit.[22]

■ *Theft of software:* Stealing of software can take the form of physically making off with someone's diskettes, but it is more likely to be copying of programs. (See Figure 13.5.) Software makers secretly prowl electronic bulletin boards in search of purloined products, then try to get a court order to shut down the bulletin boards.[23] They also look for companies that "softlift"—buy one copy of a program and make copies for as many computers as they have. Many pirates are reported by co-workers or fellow students to the "software police," the Software Publishers Association. The SPA has a toll-free number (800/388-7478), on which anyone can report illegal copying, to initiate antipiracy actions. In mid-1994, two New

**Figure 13.5**
Example of user license prohibiting copying—Microsoft Word.

**This Microsoft License Card is your proof of license.**
**Please treat it as valuable property.**

**Proof of License**

# Microsoft License Agreement

**This is a legal Agreement between you (either an individual or an entity), the end user, and Microsoft Corporation. If you do not agree to the terms of this Agreement, promptly return this product to the place you obtained it for a full refund.**

MICROSOFT SOFTWARE LICENSE

1. GRANT OF LICENSE. The Microsoft License Agreement (the "License") grants you the following rights with respect to the Microsoft software program identified above (the "SOFTWARE"):

(a) <u>Server And/Or Workstation Software</u>. If this product package includes SOFTWARE designated as Server software, you may use such Server software on a single computer system (i.e., a network server). If this product package includes SOFTWARE designated as Workstation software, you may use such Workstation software on a single computer or workstation. If any licensed copy of the Workstation software is permanently installed on the hard disk or other storage device of a computer (other than a network server) and one person uses that computer more than 80% of the time it is in use, then that person may also use the Workstation software on a portable or home computer.

(b) <u>Microsoft Add Paks (MAPs) and Multiple Workstation Packages</u>. If this product package is an MAP or a multiple workstation package, you may make additional copies of Workstation software (whether made from SOFTWARE included in this package or previously acquired) so that the total number of copies in your possession under this License equals the number of Workstations authorized above. Each such additional authorized copy may be used on a single computer.

(c) Mail Gateway Packages. If this product package includes SOFTWARE designated as "Gateway" SOFTWARE you may use such Gateway SOFTWARE on any single computer connected to a single terminal (i.e. a single CPU) acting as a Microsoft Mail Gateway computer as described in the user documentation included in this product package. If this product package includes SOFTWARE designated a "Gateway Access," "Gateway Post Office," and/or "Message Service" SOFTWARE you may use such portion(s) of the SOFTWARE on a single CPU which is acting as a Microsoft Mail "post office" as described in the user documentation included in this product package.

(d) <u>Transfer</u>. You may transfer the SOFTWARE licensed under this Microsoft License Agreement to another computer as often as you like, provided that it is removed from the computer from which it is transferred.

(e) <u>Notice to Users.</u> You shall inform all users of the SOFTWARE of the terms and conditions of the Microsoft License Agreement.

For the purposes of this Section, "use" means loading the software into RAM, as well as installation on a hard disk or other storage device. You may access the SOFTWARE from a hard disk, over a network, or any other method you choose so long as you otherwise comply with the License.

2. COPYRIGHT. The SOFTWARE is owned by Microsoft or its suppliers and is protected by United States copyright laws and international treaty provisions. Therefore, you must treat the SOFTWARE like any other copyrighted material (e.g., a book or musical recording) <u>except</u> that you may either (a) make one copy of the SOFTWARE solely for backup or archival purposes, or (b) transfer the SOFTWARE to a single hard disk provided you keep the original solely for backup or archival purposes. You may not copy the written materials accompanying the SOFTWARE.

3. OTHER RESTRICTIONS. This Microsoft Software License Card is your proof of license to exercise the rights granted herein and must be retained by you. You may not rent or lease the SOFTWARE, but you may transfer your rights under this Microsoft License Agreement on a permanent basis provided you transfer this Microsoft Software License Card, all copies of the SOFTWARE and all written materials, and the recipient agrees to the terms of this Agreement. You may not reverse engineer, decompile, or disassemble the SOFTWARE. Any transfer of the SOFTWARE must include the most recent update and all prior versions.

4. DUAL MEDIA SOFTWARE. If this product package contains Server or Gateway SOFTWARE on both 3-1/2" and 5-1/4" disks, then you may use only the disks appropriate for your single computer. You may not use the other disks on another computer or loan, rent, lease, or transfer them to another user except as part of the permanent transfer (as provided above) of all SOFTWARE and written materials.

England college students were indicted for allegedly using the Internet to encourage the exchange of copyrighted software.[24]

Another type of software theft is copying or counterfeiting well-known software programs (DOS, Windows, Seventh Guest). These pirates often operate in Taiwan, Mexico, Russia, and various parts of Asia and Latin America. In some countries, more than 90% of U.S. microcomputer software in use is thought to be illegally copied.[25]

■ *Theft of time and services:* The theft of computer time is more common than you might think. Probably the biggest use of it is people using their employer's computer time to play games. Some people also run sideline businesses.

Theft of cable and telephone services has increased over the years. Cable TV Montgomery reported it lost $12 million a year to pirates using illegal set-top converter boxes. Under federal law, a viewer with an illegal decoder box can face up to 6 months in jail and a $1,000 fine.[26]

For years "phone phreaks" have bedeviled the telephone companies. More recently, they have found ways to get into company voice-mail [✓ p. 287] systems, then use an extension to make long-distance calls at the company's expense.[27] They have also found ways to tap into cellular phone networks and dial for free.[28] In 1992, a ring of young men gained access to a widely used computer network called Tymnet and the private network of Bank of America.[29] From there they broke into more computer networks.

■ *Theft of information:* In 1992, "information thieves" were caught infiltrating the files of the Social Security Administration, stealing confidential personal records, and selling the information.[30] Thieves have also broken into computers of the major credit bureaus and stolen credit information. They have then used the information to charge purchases or have resold it to other people. On college campuses, thieves have snooped on or stolen private information such as grades.

■ *Crimes of malice and destruction:* Sometimes criminals are more interested in abusing or vandalizing computers and telecommunications systems than in profiting from them. For example, a student at a Wisconsin campus deliberately and repeatedly shut down a university computer system, destroying final projects for dozens of students. A judge sentenced him to a year's probation, and he left the campus.[31] In 1988 a student at an upstate New York university unleashed a program that jammed several thousand computers across the country. In 1989 a young man going under the name Phiber Optik took offense at some remarks made by a journalist. He retaliated by downloading the journalist's credit history and displaying it online for all to see.[32] Phiber Optik was one of a ring of "hackers"—a subject we take up shortly.

## Crimes Using Computers and Communications

Just as a car can be used to assist in a crime, so can a computer or communications system. For example, in 1990, the Internal Revenue Service instituted electronic filing, enabling taxpayers to speed their returns via computer and get quicker refunds. In 1994, the IRS reported that the system had been used by crooks to defraud the government of $15 million. The IRS has more difficulty catching fraudulent refund claims from electronic returns than from traditional paper returns.[33] The proliferation of desktop publishing [✓ p. 180] has also caused a boom in the counterfeiting of fraudulent checks, as criminals use inexpensive microcomputers with sophisticated graphics capabilities for illegal purposes.[34]

Investment fraud has also come to cyberspace. Many people now use online services to manage their stock portfolios through brokerages hooked into the services. Scam artists have followed, offering nonexistent investment deals and phony solicitations and manipulating stock prices.[35]

Information technology has also been used simply to perpetrate mischief. In 1993, a wild rumor about gang violence swept the bulletin board systems around San Jose, California. The rumor claimed that teenagers seeking to join gangs were driving at night with their headlights off. Then, as part of a supposed gang initiation rite, the teenagers shot well-meaning motorists who flashed their headlights at them.[36] In the same year, three students at a Wisconsin campus faced disciplinary measures after distributing bogus e-mail messages, one of which pretended to be a message of resignation sent by the university's chancellor.[37]

## Viruses

Viruses are a form of high-tech maliciousness. Computer **viruses** are "deviant" programs that can cause destruction to computers that contract them. They are passed in two ways. The first way is via an infected diskette, such as one you get from a friend or a repair person, although it might also be a sales demo disk or even (in 3% of cases) a shrink-wrapped commercial disk. The second way is via a network, such as files downloaded from an electronic bulletin board or as e-mail.

The virus then usually attaches itself to your hard disk. It might then display annoying messages ("Your PC is stoned—legalize marijuana") or cause Ping-Pong balls to bounce around your screen and knock away text. More seriously, it might add garbage to or erase your files or destroy your systems software [✓ p. 10, 175, 197]. It may evade your detection and spread its havoc elsewhere.

Viruses may take several forms. The two principal ones are the boot-sector virus and file viruses, but there are others.[38]

■ *Boot-sector virus:* The boot sector is that part of the system software containing most of the instructions for booting, or powering up, the system. The boot sector virus replaces these boot instructions with some of its own. Once the system is turned on, the virus is loaded into main memory [✓ pp. 82, 93, 112] before the operating system. From there it is in a position to infect other files.

Any diskette that is used in the drive of the computer then becomes infected. When that disk is moved to another computer, the contagion continues.

■ *File virus:* File viruses attach themselves to executable files—those that actually begin a program. (These files have the extensions .com and .exe.) When the program is run, the virus starts working, trying to get into main memory and infecting other files.

■ *Worm:* The worm spreads by replicating itself. It travels through networks to different computer systems, then makes many copies of itself, wasting vast amounts of computer time.

■ *Logic bomb:* Logic bombs, or simply bombs, differ from other viruses in that they are set to go off at a certain date and time. A disgruntled programmer for a defense contractor created a bomb in a program that was supposed to go off two months after he left. Designed to erase an inventory tracking system, the bomb was discovered only by chance.

■ *Trojan horse:* The Trojan horse covertly places illegal, destructive instructions in the middle of a legitimate program, such as a computer game. Once you run the program, the Trojan horse goes to work, doing its damage while you are blissfully unaware.

■ *Polymorphic virus:* A polymorphic virus, of which there are several kinds, can mutate and change form just as human viruses can. These are especially troublesome because they can change their profile, making existing antiviral technology ineffective.

■ *Virus mutation engines:* A virus mutation engine allows programmers to actually create polymorphic viruses. One, called Virus Creation Laboratory, has a user interface with pull-down menus [✓ p. 178], making it easy for even novices to create their own viruses.[39]

## The Computer-Security Professional

The profession of computer-security expert was practically nonexistent 15 years ago, when businesses did not think about the need to safeguard their computer systems. Today, an estimated 10,000 U.S. computer-security experts work on staff at corporations or hire themselves out as consultants, and the number jumps yearly by about 25%. "At any given time, we are trying to find candidates for 20 to 30 companies," says Cameron Carey, president of Computer Security Placement Service in Northborough, Massachusetts.

Typically, a computer-security expert advises companies how to best guard their data. He or she evaluates protective software programs and researches the new ways that computer viruses, disgruntled employees, and industrial spies might slip around the precautions in place.

The demand for security consultants has so far been greatest at banks, brokerage houses, and airlines, all of which would be paralyzed without the data stored in their computer systems.

A bachelor's degree in computer science provides the basic tools of the computer-security expert, but only a few U.S. schools, such as George Washington University and Idaho State University, have courses that cover computer detective work.

Michelangelo virus

There have been many strains of viruses in recent years, some of them quite well known (Stoned, Jerusalem, Lehigh, Pakistani Brain). Most famous was Michelangelo, so named because it was programmed to erase hard disks on the artist's birthday, March 6, 1992. Michelangelo was supposed to cause a million computers to crash, but on March 7 it was found that only a few thousand were damaged. Does this mean that the threat was oversold—mainly by makers of antivirus software?[40] **Antivirus software** scans a computer's hard disk, diskettes, and main memory to detect viruses and, sometimes, to destroy them. (See Figure 13.6.) Since the Michelangelo scare, the appearance of polymorphic viruses, virus mutation engines, and other new forms shows that this threat must still be taken seriously.

### Computer Criminals

What kind of people are perpetrating most of the information-technology crime? Over 80% may be employees, and the rest are outside users, hackers and crackers, and professional criminals.

- *Employees:* "Employees are the ones with the skill, the knowledge, and the access to do bad things," says Donn Parker, an expert on computer security at SRI International in Menlo Park, California. "They're the ones, for example, who can most easily plant a 'logic bomb.' . . ." Dishonest or disgruntled employees, he says, pose "a far greater problem than most people realize."[41] The increasing use of laptops off the premises, away from the eyes of supervisors, concerns some security experts. They worry that dishonest employees or outsiders can more easily intercept communications or steal company trade secrets.

**Figure 13.6**
Antivirus software screen, showing that the anti-virus software has scanned 20% of the hard disk for viruses.

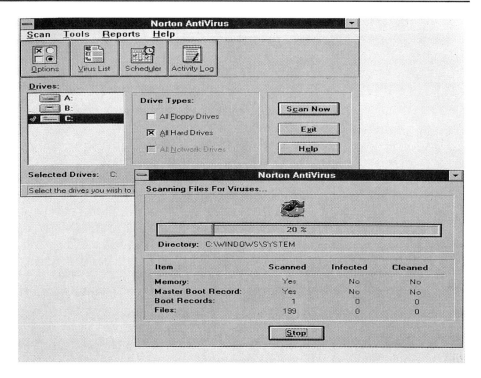

Workers may use information technology for personal profit or steal hardware or information to sell. They may also use it to seek revenge for real or imagined wrongs, such as being passed over for promotion. Sometimes they may use the technology simply to demonstrate to themselves that they have power over people. This may have been the case with a Georgia printing-company employee convicted of sabotaging the firm's computer system. As files mysteriously disappeared and the system randomly crashed, other workers became so frustrated and enraged that they quit.

■ *Outside users:* Suppliers and clients may also gain access to a company's information technology and use it to commit crimes. With both, this becomes more a possibility as electronic connections become more commonplace.

■ *Hackers and crackers:* **Hackers** are people who gain unauthorized access to computer or telecommunications systems for the challenge or even the principle of it. For example, Eric Corley, publisher of a magazine called *2600: The Hackers' Quarterly,* believes that hackers are merely engaging in "healthy exploration." In fact, by breaking into corporate computer systems and revealing their flaws, he says, they perform a favor and a public service. Such unauthorized entries show the corporations the leaks in their security systems.[42]

■ **Crackers** also gain unauthorized access to information technology but do so for malicious purposes. (Some observers think the term *hacker* covers malicious intent, also.) Crackers attempt to break into computers and deliberately obtain information for financial gain, shut down hardware, pirate software, or destroy data.

The tolerance for "benign explorers"—hackers—has waned. Most communications systems administrators view any kind of unauthorized access as a threat, and they pursue the offenders vigorously. Educators try to point out to students that universities can't provide an education for everybody if hacking continues.[43] The most flagrant cases of hacking are met with federal prosecution. A famous instance involved five young New York-area men calling themselves the Masters of Deception who had broken into numerous information systems.[44]

■ *Professional criminals:* Members of organized crime rings don't just steal information technology. They also use it the way that legal businesses do—as a business tool, but for illegal purposes. For instance, databases can be used to keep track of illegal gambling debts and stolen goods. Drug dealers have used pagers as a link to customers. Microcomputers, scanners, and printers can be used to forge checks, immigration papers, passports, and driver's licenses. Telecommunications can be used to transfer funds illegally.

As information-technology crime has become more sophisticated, so have the people charged with preventing it and disciplining its outlaws. Campus administrators are no longer being quite as easy on offenders and are turning them over to police. Industry organizations such as the Software Publishers Association are going after software pirates large and small. (Commercial software piracy is now a felony, punishable by up to five years in prison and fines of up to $250,000 for anyone convicted of stealing at least 10 copies of a program, or more than $2,500 worth of software.) Police departments as far apart as Medford, Massachusetts, and San Jose, California, now have police patrolling a "cyber beat." That is, they cruise online bulletin boards looking for pirated software, stolen trade secrets, child molesters, and child pornography.[45]

In 1988, after the last widespread Internet break-in, the U.S. Defense Department created the Computer Emergency Response Team (CERT). Although it has no power to arrest or prosecute, *CERT* provides round-the-clock international information and security-related support services to users of the Internet. Whenever it gets a report of an electronic snooper, whether on the Internet or on a corporate e-mail system, CERT stands ready to lend assistance. It counsels the party under attack, helps them thwart the intruder, and evaluates the system afterward to protect against future break-ins.[46, 47]

## Security: Safeguarding Computers and Communications

**Information technology requires vigilance in security. Four areas of concern are identification and access, encryption, protection of software and data, and disaster-recovery planning.**

Wouldn't it be great to have a tool that tracks down friends and colleagues anywhere in cyberspace? Actually, such a tool already exists. Called Finger, it is a kind of "telephone directory" for the Internet.

With Finger, people connected to the Internet anywhere in the world can frequently find out your name and electronic-mail address. They can also discover whether you're working online at your computer and even the exact location from which you are logging in. In addition, they can tell how long it's been since you last checked your e-mail and who has sent you mail.

Now that you know how versatile Finger is, you might have some second thoughts. Do you really want people to be able to check up on you this closely? Others are also concerned about Finger. Some are worried about the privacy implications, others about its use as an aid to breaching computer security. The way Finger works cannot be altered by individuals; it requires systemwide changes. For example, most campus computer-system administrators have kept some version of the tool intact for the convenience of users on local networks. This allows neighbors to get information about each other. However, Finger cannot be used by outsiders not directly connected to the campus system—a safeguard against crackers.[48]

And so we see the ongoing dilemma of the Digital Age—balancing convenience against security. **Security** is a system of safeguards for protecting information technology against disasters, systems failure, and unauthorized access that can result in damage or loss. We consider four components of security:

- Identification and access

- Encryption

- Protection of software and data

- Disaster-recovery planning

## Identification and Access

Are you who you say you are? The computer wants to know.

There are three ways a computer system can verify that you have legitimate right of access. Some security systems use a mix of these techniques. The systems try to authenticate your identity by determining (1) what you have, (2) what you know, or (3) who you are.

- *What you have—cards, keys, signatures, badges:* Credit cards, debit cards, and cash-machine cards all have magnetic strips or built-in computer chips that identify you to the machine. Many require you to display your signature, which someone may compare as you write your signature. Computer rooms are always kept locked, requiring a key. Many people also keep a lock on their personal computers. A computer room may also be guarded by security officers who must see an authorized signature or a badge with your photograph before letting you in.

  Of course, credit cards, keys, and badges can be lost or stolen. Signatures can be forged. Badges can be counterfeited.

- *What you know—PINs, passwords, and digital signatures:* To gain access to your bank account through an automatic teller machine (ATM), you key in your PIN. A **PIN,** or **personal identification number,** is the security number known only to you that is required to access the system. Telephone credit cards also use a PIN. If you carry either an ATM or a phone card, *never* carry the PIN written down elsewhere in your wallet (even disguised).

  A **password** is a special word, code, or symbol that is required to access a computer system. Passwords are one of the weakest security links, says AT&T security expert Steven Bellovin. Passwords can be guessed, forgotten, or stolen. To reduce a stranger's guessing, Bellovin recommends never choosing a real word or variations of your name or birthdate or those of your friends or family. Instead you should mix letters, numbers, and punctuation marks in an oddball sequence of no fewer than eight characters.[49]

  Skilled hackers may break into national computer networks and detect passwords as they are being used. Or they pose on the telephone as computer technicians to cajole passwords out of employees. They may even find access codes in discarded technical manuals in trash bins.[50]

  A new technology is the digital signature, which security experts hope will lead to a world of paperless commerce. A **digital signature** is a string of characters and numbers that a user signs to an electronic document being sent by his or her computer. The receiving computer performs mathematical operations on the alphanumeric string to verify its validity.

**H**

digital signature

Kevin Mitnick, 31, stood in the federal courtroom, his hands cuffed—unable, for the first time in more than two years, to feel the silky click of computer keys. He glanced over at Tsutomu Shimomura, the computer-security expert whose extraordinarily well-guarded personal computer Mitnick had allegedly broken into on Christmas Day. Shimomura, playing Pat Garrett to Mitnick's Billy the Kid, had taken his revenge by tracking the wily hacker across cyberspace—through the Internet, through local and long-distance phone companies and at least two cellular phone carriers—until he finally traced him to his hideout in an apartment complex in Raleigh, North Carolina. . . .

Across the country, computer-network security experts were talking a lot, . . . calling the entire Mitnick affair a watershed moment—not for what it proves about the hacker but for what it says about the systems he hacked. At a time when American businesses are frantic to set up shop on the computer networks, those networks—and the telecommunications systems that carry their traffic—are turning out to be terminally insecure. One of the things Mitnick is believed to have stolen from Shimomura's computer is a set of utility programs—the electronic equivalent of a locksmith's toolbox—that would make, in the hands of a determined hacker, a potent set of burglar's tools. Given the speed with which such programs can be duplicated and transmitted, it must now be assumed that they have been distributed widely throughout the computer underground.

From Joshua Quittner, "Cracks in the Net," *Time*, February 27, 1995, p. 34.

The system works by using a *public-private key system*. That is, the system involves a pair of numbers called a private key and a public key. One person creates the signature with a secret private key, and the recipient reads it with a second, public key. "This process in effect notarizes the document and ensures its integrity," says one writer.[51]

For example, when you write your boss an electronic note, you sign it with your secret private key. (This could be some bizarre string beginning 479XY283 and continuing on for 25 characters.) When your boss receives the note, he or she looks up your public key. Your public key is available from a source such as an electronic bulletin board, the Postal Service, or a corporate computer department. If the document is altered in any way, it will no longer produce the same signature sequence.[52, 53]

■ *Who you are—physical traits:* Some forms of identification can't be easily faked—such as your physical traits. Biometrics tries to use these in security devices. **Biometrics** is the science of measuring individual body characteristics.

For example, before a number of University of Georgia students can use the all-you-can-eat plan at the campus cafeteria, they must have their hands read. As one writer describes the system, "a camera automatically compares the shape of a student's hand with an image of the same hand pulled from the magnetic strip of an ID card. If the patterns match, the cafeteria turnstile automatically clicks open. If not, the would-be moocher eats elsewhere."[54]

Besides handprints, other biological characteristics read by biometric devices are fingerprints, voices, the blood vessels in the back of the eyeball, and the lips. (See Figure 13.7.)

Some computer security systems have a "call-back" provision. In a **call-back system,** the user calls the computer system, punches in the password and hangs up. The computer then calls back a certain preauthorized number. This measure will block anyone who has somehow got hold of a password but is calling from an unauthorized telephone.

## Encryption

PGP is a computer program written for encrypting computer messages—putting them into secret code. **Encryption,** or enciphering, is the altering of data so that it is not usable unless the changes are undone. In other words, the data is transformed so as to be unreadable to anyone without a secret decryption key, usually a mathematical algorithm. PGP (for pretty good privacy) is so good that it is practically unbreakable; even government experts can't crack it.[55] (This is because it uses a two-key method similar to that described earlier for digital signatures.)

Encryption is clearly useful for some organizations, especially those concerned with trade secrets, military matters, and other sensitive data. However, from the standpoint of our society, encryption is a two-edged sword. For instance, police in Sacramento, California, found that PGP blocked them from reading the computer diary of a convicted child molester and finding links to a suspected child pornography ring. *Should* the government be allowed to read the coded e-mail of its citizens? What about its being blocked from surveillance of overseas terrorists, drug dealers, and other enemies?

**Figure 13.7**
Biometrics: biological characteristics read by security devices.

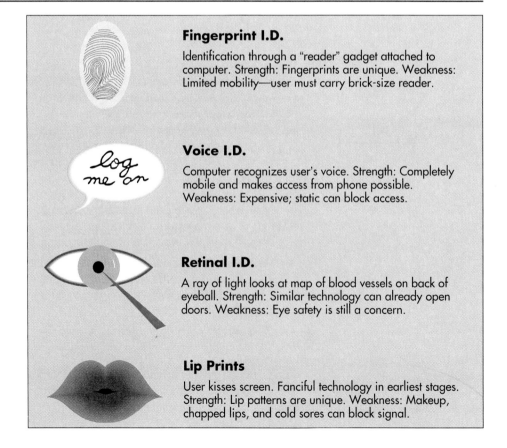

**Fingerprint I.D.**

Identification through a "reader" gadget attached to computer. Strength: Fingerprints are unique. Weakness: Limited mobility—user must carry brick-size reader.

**Voice I.D.**

Computer recognizes user's voice. Strength: Completely mobile and makes access from phone possible. Weakness: Expensive; static can block access.

**Retinal I.D.**

A ray of light looks at map of blood vessels on back of eyeball. Strength: Similar technology can already open doors. Weakness: Eye safety is still a concern.

**Lip Prints**

User kisses screen. Fanciful technology in earliest stages. Strength: Lip patterns are unique. Weakness: Makeup, chapped lips, and cold sores can block signal.

The issue of encryption came to a head in 1994 with the so-called Clipper chip. The Clinton administration supported a proposed voluntary encryption standard that would make it possible for anyone to keep messages private. The system would work as follows: Government agencies and private companies, such as banks and credit agencies, would use a special microchip, the "Clipper chip," in telephones and other equipment. The chip could be used to scramble communications so they could not be read by hackers, criminals, and spies.

The new wrinkle, however, was that the Clipper would use mathematical formulas developed by the super-secret National Security Agency and would remain classified. Mathematical keys that unscramble coded data would be kept by two independent government agencies. One suggestion was that these "escrow agencies" might be the National Institute of Standards and Technology and the automated systems division of the Treasury Department. Before proceeding with any eavesdropping, law-enforcement agencies would have to obtain court orders for wiretapping before the "escrow agencies" would grant them access to these keys. In other words, users of the Clipper could encrypt all their messages—but the government could still open a "trap door" and listen in. Many critics objected that because such investigation targets as foreign powers and criminals would use other means of encryption, the trap door was not justified.[56, 57] In July 1994, the government backed down from implementing the Clipper chip as a data-encryption standard.[58, 59]

## Protection of Software and Data

Organizations go to tremendous lengths to protect their programs and data. As might be expected, this includes educating employees about making backup disks, protecting against viruses, and so on.

Other security procedures include the following:

- *Control of access:* Access to online files is restricted only to those who have a legitimate right to access—because they need them to do their jobs. Many organizations have a transaction log [✔ p. 360] that notes all accesses or attempted accesses to data.

- *Audit controls:* Many networks have *audit controls,* which track which programs and servers were used, which files opened, and so on. This creates an *audit trail,* a record of how a transaction was handled from input through processing and output.

- *People controls:* Because people are the greatest threat to a computer system, security precautions begin with screening of job applicants. That is, resumes are checked to see if people did what they said they did. Another control is to separate employee functions, so that people are not allowed to wander freely into areas not essential to their jobs. Manual and automated controls—input controls, processing controls, and output controls—are used to check that data is handled accurately and completely during the processing cycle. Printouts, printer ribbons, and other waste that may yield passwords and trade secrets to outsiders is disposed of through shredders or locked trash barrels.

## Disaster-Recovery Plans

A **disaster-recovery plan** is a method of restoring information processing operations that have been halted by destruction or accident. "Among the countless lessons that computer users have absorbed in the hours, days, and weeks after the [New York] World Trade Center bombing," wrote one reporter, "the most enduring may be the need to have a disaster-recovery plan. The

# THE CLIPBOARD

## Ten Security Tips for PC Users

■ *Password security:* Choose strong passwords. Never use your name or the name of a loved one, or even a word in the dictionary. Use a mix of alphanumeric characters, but make it easy to remember.

■ *Social engineering:* The hacker's most effective tool isn't technological at all—it's the manipulation of humans. Be suspicious of unfamiliar requests, whether over the phone or via mail [or e-mail]. Never disclose your password or details of your computer system to strangers whose motives, need to know, or identity you cannot verify.

■ *Credit card security:* Don't send your credit card number "in the clear" (that is, without encryption) over the Internet.

■ *Terminate connections:* Don't leave modem lines or Internet connections open when you're not using them. Turn off your computer when you leave it.

■ *Anti-virus defense:* Install anti-virus scanning software and use it unceasingly.

■ *Access control and encryption:* Consider using a PC security package that demands passwords for computer access and encrypts data resident on the hard disk.

■ *Physical security:* Consider installing key-locked diskette drive security devices to prevent unauthorized access via diskette.

■ *Backup:* Make frequent backups of vital data and store it in a different physical locale from the computer.

■ *Buy smart:* When buying operating systems or applications software, inquire about available security features. At the very least, does the package offer password protection? Does it offer an encryption option? If it is a product to be used by more than one person, does it offer access control so you can decide who sees what?

■ *Ask about security:* In the workplace, ask your manager or network administrator about the company's information security policies and procedures for users.

Source: Computer Security Institute, San Francisco. Printed in the *San Francisco Examiner,* February 19, 1995, p. B-3.

second most enduring lesson may be this: Even a well-practiced plan will quickly reveal its flaws."[60]

Mainframe computer systems are operated in separate departments by professionals, who tend to have disaster plans. Mainframes are usually backed up. However, many personal computers, and even entire local area networks [✔ p. 282], are not backed up. The consequences of this lapse can be great. It has been reported that, on average, a company loses as much as 3% of its gross sales within eight days of a sustained computer outage. In addition, the average company struck by a computer outage lasting more than 10 days never fully recovers.[61]

A disaster-recovery plan is more than a big fire-drill. It includes a list of all business functions and the hardware, software, data, and people to support those functions. It includes arrangements for alternate locations, either hot sites or cold sites. A *hot site* is a fully equipped computer center, with everything needed to resume functions. A *cold site* is a building or other suitable environment in which a company can install its own computer system. The disaster-recovery plan includes ways for backing up and storing programs and data in another location, ways of alerting necessary personnel, and training for those personnel.

How fancy should the alternate arrangements be? The best way to judge is to figure out how long it would take to duplicate the present arrangements. "At the World Trade Center," said an executive with a company offering recovery services, "traders had two or three terminals on each desk. That is a lot of communications to duplicate."[62]

## Suggestions for Further Reading

Cheswick, W. *Firewalls and Internet Security: Repelling the Wily Hacker.* Reading, MA: Addison-Wesley, 1994. AT&T's security expert describes how to build a "firewall," or electronic security, against unauthorized access to computer systems.

*Child Safety on the Information Highway,* Interactive Services Association and the National Center for Missing and Exploited Children. 800/843-5678.

Kane, P. *The Data Recovery Bible.* New York: Brady Books, 1993.

Larson, E. *The Naked Consumer: How Our Private Lives Become Public Commodities.* New York: Viking Penguin, 1994. A two-year investigation into how consumers "shed" information about themselves and what to do about it.

*Privacy Times,* P.O. Box 21501, Washington, D.C. 20009; 202/829-3660. This is a bi-weekly, 10-page newsletter.

Rothfeder, J. *Privacy for Sale: How Computerization Has Made Everyone's Private Life an Open Secret.* New York: Simon & Schuster, 1992. The author shows how the average person's personal records can be tapped with relative ease.

Schneier, B. *E-Mail Security: How to Keep your Electronic Messages Private.* New York: Wiley, 1995.

*Stop Junk Mail Forever.* Good Advice Press, P.O. Box 78, Elizabeth, NY 12523.

# S U M M A R Y

■ *Ethics* refers to a set of moral values or principles that govern the conduct of an individual or a group. (p. 438)

■ People in most countries agree that they are entitled to the right of *privacy*—the right of people not to reveal information about themselves, the right to keep personal information, such as credit ratings and medical histories, from getting into the wrong hands. (p. 438)

■ The development of computers and large electronic databases has facilitated the collection of information about individuals. In the past, this information has been sold to marketing groups without the individual's consent. Many people believe this is an unethical practice. (p. 439)

■ The information that is collected about individuals and is then transmitted to credit-reporting companies is often error-ridden, causing people to be denied loans and jobs, in addition to causing other problems. (p. 439)

■ Seemingly private information about individuals, such as medical records, has been disseminated to employers and others and used to make decisions about which the individuals may know nothing. (p. 439)

■ Consumer groups are trying to correct the problems involving data collection and dissemination and make information sellers more responsible by advocating (p. 439):

1. *Improved accuracy:* Information sellers must correct mistakes in the data, no matter where it came from.

2. *Free reports:* At the request of an individual, information sellers must provide a copy of the individual's report for free once a year.

3. *Protect privacy:* Companies that sell data must give an individual a clear chance to prevent sales of personal data to marketers.

4. *Improved service:* Credit denial notices should include a list of consumers'

rights. Investigations of errors should take no more than 30 days.

5. *Better enforcement:* Credit reporters should be penalized for violating the law.

■ The use of electronic communications and information networks has also raised ethical concerns about the censorship of some messages and the *electronic spying* on message contents by supervisors in companies and directors of information services. (p. 441)

■ The United States has passed several major laws in an attempt to protect individual privacy and regulate the selling of information. (p. 441)

■ Computers have given birth to *copyright* issues, including the following (p. 445):

—*Software and network piracy:* Software piracy is theft or unauthorized distribution or use of copyrighted or patented material. Network piracy is using electronic networks to distribute unauthorized copyrighted material in digitized form.

—*Plagiarism:* Plagiarism is the expropriation of another writer's text, findings, or interpretations and presentation of them as one's own.

—*Ownership of images and sound:* Computers make it possible to alter images and sounds. Who owns the copyright to the altered image? Many artists have protected themselves by paying a flat fee or a royalty to the original copyright holder.

■ When computers edit sound, photos, and video, there are other issues worth considering. For instance, it is becoming more and more difficult to distinguish between altered and unaltered photos, video, and recordings. (p. 447)

■ Many threats to computers and communications systems exist including:

—*Errors and accidents:* Computer errors and accidents occur for a number of

466

reasons including people errors, procedural errors, software errors (*software bugs*), electromechanical problems, and *dirty data* problems (that is, data that is inaccurate). (p. 450)

—*Natural and other hazards:* Some disasters can ruin a computer system including natural hazards such as fires, floods, earthquakes, and the like. Also, civil strife and terrorism can cause much unrest, causing companies to move entire computer networks to a different location. (p. 453)

—*Crimes against information technology:* Crimes *against* information technology include theft of hardware, theft of software, theft of time and services, theft of information, and crimes of malice and destruction. (p. 453)

—*Crimes using information technology:* Computer fraud is alive on computer networks. For example, scam artists offer nonexistent investment deals. Or lies spread via a network, such as a "bogus" e-mail message about a local gang ritual, may cause people to act on the misinformation and get hurt. (p. 455)

—*Viruses:* Computer viruses are "deviant" programs that can cause destruction to computers that contract them. The principal types of viruses are *boot-sector viruses* and *file viruses.* (p. 456)

—*Computer criminals:* Computer criminals are people who perpetrate information-technology crime. Over 80% of computer criminals are employees. The rest are outside users, *hackers* and *crackers*, and professional criminals. (p. 457)

■ Information technology requires vigilance in security. *Security* is a system of safeguards for protecting information technology against disasters, systems failure, or unau-

thorized access that can result in damage or loss. Four approaches to adding security to a computer system are (p. 459):

1. *Identification and access*—Before you are allowed access to a computer:

   —You must use the appropriate card, key, signature, or badge.

   —You must know the correct PIN, password, or have the matching digital signature.

   —Your "characteristics" must match those that the computer is expected to find.

2. *Encryption*—Encryption is the altering of data so that it is not usable unless the changes are undone. Encryption is particularly useful for organizations concerned with trade secrets, military matters, and other sensitive data. (p. 462)

3. *Protection of software and data*—Companies go to great lengths to protect their software and data. One method they use is to control access to the computer system. In addition, companies use *audit controls* to track which programs and servers were used, which files opened, and so on, and *people controls,* including extensive job screening and restricted access to other departments in the company. (p. 463)

4. *Disaster-recovery plans*—A disaster-recovery plan is a method of restoring information processing operations that have been halted by destruction or accident. It includes a list of all business functions and all elements (hardware, software, data, people) that support those functions. In addition, a good plan includes arrangements for an alternative location for the computer center. (p. 463)

## KEY TERMS

antivirus software, p. 457
biometrics, p. 461
call-back system, p. 462
copyright, p. 445
cracker, p. 458
digital signature, p. 460
dirty data, p. 452
disaster-recovery plan, p. 463
electronic surveillance, p. 441
encryption, p. 462
ethics, p. 438
Fair Credit Reporting Act of
  1970, p. 444

Freedom of Information Act
  of 1970, p. 444
hacker, p. 458
information-technology
  crime, p. 453
intellectual property, p. 444
morphing, p. 448
network piracy, p. 445
password, p. 460
personal identification
  number (PIN), p. 460
piracy, p. 445
plagiarism, p. 446

privacy, p. 438
Privacy Act of 1974, p. 441
Right to Financial Privacy Act
  of 1978, p. 444
security, p. 460
software bug, p. 451
software piracy, p. 445
virus, p. 456

## EXERCISES

### SELF-TEST

1. _____Ethic_____ is a set of moral values or principles that govern the conduct of an individual or a group.

2. The Privacy Act of 1974 prohibits secret personnel files from being kept on individuals by government agencies or their contractors. It gives individuals the right to see their records, see how the data is used, and correct errors. (true/false)

3. ____Electronic____ ____Surveillance____ involves the electronic monitoring by a supervisor of employees' work performance.

4. The U.S. Freedom of Information Act of 1970 gives citizens the right to look at data concerning themselves that is stored by the U.S. government. (true/false)

5. _____Piracy_____ is theft or unauthorized distribution or use.

6. CERT provides round-the-clock international information and security-related support services to users of the Internet. (true/false)

7. ____HACKER____ are people who gain unauthorized access to a computer system for fun; ____CRACKER____ gain unauthorized access for malicious purposes.

8. Computer ____Security____ is the protection of information, hardware, and software from unauthorized use as well as from damage.

9. ____ENCRYPTION____, or enciphering, is the altering of data so that it is not usable unless the changes are undone.

10. ____Dirty____ ____Data____ is data that is incomplete, outdated, or otherwise inaccurate.

11. ____Intellectual____ ____Property____ consists of the products of the human mind, tangible or intangible.

468

12. _____NETWORK_____ _____PIRACY_____, _____ is using electronic networks to distribute unauthorized copyrighted materials in digitized form.

13. _____PLAGIARISM_____ is the expropriation of another writer's text, findings, or interpretations and presentation of it as one's own.

14. Computer _____VIRUS_____ are "deviant" programs that can cause destruction to computers that contract them.

*Solutions:* (1) ethics; (2) true; (3) electronic surveillance; (4) true; (5) piracy; (6) true; (7) hackers, crackers; (8) security; (9) encryption; (10) dirty data; (11) intellectual property; (12) network piracy; (13) plagiarism; (14) viruses

## SHORT-ANSWER QUESTIONS

1. List five things that consumer groups believe credit-reporting companies should do to better serve customers.
2. What does the Privacy Act of 1974 do?
3. Define *information technology crime* and give a few examples.
4. Define *ethics.*
5. What is meant by the term *intellectual property?*
6. What is data encryption used for?
7. What four methods can be used to secure a computer system?
8. What is a computer virus? Describe the two main types of computer viruses.
9. Describe five types of errors and accidents that may affect a computer system.
10. What danger might exist in electronically manipulating photos and other illustrations?
11. What is software piracy?

## PROJECTS AND CRITICAL THINKING EXERCISES

1. What's your opinion about the issue of free speech on an electronic network? Research some recent legal decisions in various countries, as well as some articles on the topic, and then give a short report about what you think. Should the contents of messages be censored? If so, under what conditions?
2. Data encryption technology continues to improve. Explore the "state of the art" in encryption technology. What is AT&T and VLSI Technology's role? Do the National Security Agency, FBI and other government agencies still prefer "Clipper chip" technology over newer encryption technologies? Why? Why not?
3. *Privacy for Sale,* by Jeffrey Rothfeder (Simon & Schuster, 1992), catalogs major and minor "horror stories" from the recent annals of America's constantly growing computer state. For example, one man, who did not smoke or drink and who was in good health, was shocked when he was told by an insurance company that he would have to pay an exorbitant premium for disability insurance. Why? Because he was an alcoholic, the insurance company said. The man, who was not an alcoholic, finally discovered that the source of the misinformation was a little-known Massachusetts company that is said to control the largest collection of medical records in the United States.

   Mr. Rothfeder gives some specific suggestions for protecting personal information. Obtain a copy of his book from the library or a bookstore, and prepare a short report on some of the major privacy issues he identifies and his suggestions for protecting privacy.

4. Contact the Software Publishers Association, 1730 M Street, NW, #700, Washington, DC 20036 (202/452-1600) and the Adobe Softawareness Hotline (1-800/525-6111). Ask for guidelines and literature on keeping software legal. Give a short report based on the information you receive.
5. Contact Computer Professionals for Social Responsibility, and report on their membership requirements. What is the focus of their activities?

CPSR
P.O. Box 717
Palo Alto, CA 94301
415/322-3778

6. In your opinion, have people become less ethical with the invention and widespread use of computers and related technology, or is some unethical behavior just more obvious now because news can travel so much faster and farther? Explain your answer.

## IN THE LAB WITH MICROSOFT WINDOWS

(*Note:* If you aren't familiar with using a mouse and/or don't know how to use the Microsoft Windows graphical user interface, complete the In the Lab with Microsoft Windows exercises in Chapter 6 before proceeding.)

### Checking for Viruses

1. In this section you learn how to use the Microsoft Windows Anti-Virus tool, which enables you to detect and then remove viruses from your computer system. Right now, the Program Manager window should be displaying.
2. DOUBLE-CLICK: Microsoft Tools group icon
   DOUBLE-CLICK: Anti-Virus program icon
   The Microsoft Anti-Virus window should be displaying.
3. If you have access to a formatted data diskette that contains data, insert it in drive A:.
4. To see if any viruses exist on the diskette in drive A:
   CLICK: A: *in the Drives area*
   CLICK: Detect
   When the Anti-Virus program is finished checking the diskette, you'll see summary information in the Statistics window. If the "Infected" column contains all zeros, then your diskette is fine. (*Note:* If your diskette contains some infected areas, press Enter and then click the "Detect and Clean" button to delete any viruses.)
   PRESS: Enter *to exit the Statistics window*
5. To exit the Anti-Virus program:
   DOUBLE-CLICK: Control-menu box *located in the upper-left corner of the Anti-Virus window*
6. To close the Microsoft Tools group window:
   DOUBLE-CLICK: Control-menu box *located in the upper-left corner of the Microsoft Tools window*

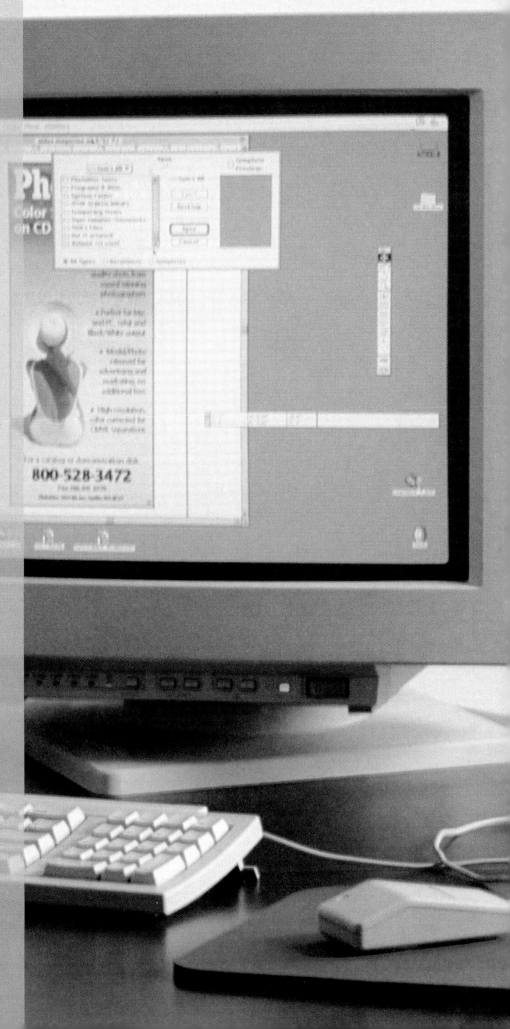

# Chapter Topics

# CHAPTER 14

# Purchasing and Maintaining a Microcomputer System

As you can imagine, it's easy to spend a few thousand dollars on a microcomputer system! Given this substantial investment, carefully consider your processing needs before pulling out your checkbook. Don't pay for things you don't need, and remember to maintain your microcomputer properly so that it will have a long and problem-free life.

## Preview

*When you have completed this chapter, you will be able to:*

- Explain what should be considered before purchasing a microcomputer system

- Maintain a microcomputer system on a daily basis so that you can rely on it over time

- Explain some of the health concerns associated with frequent computer use, and describe some of the ergonomic options open to users

- Describe some of the options open to the environmentally aware computer user

- Read a computer ad and explain what the terms mean

*Many different microcomputers—with different features and processing capabilities—exist on the market today. If you, or your company, are in the market to purchase a microcomputer you should consider carefully your processing needs. Not only should you define your software and hardware requirements clearly before you purchase a microcomputer system, but you should also investigate the company from which you are buying the computer to make sure it will offer support in the long run.*

*Despite the substantial investment they have made, many users treat their microcomputers no more carefully than they do a desktop calculator or a telephone. For example, microcomputers are very sensitive to temperature changes. But temperature is only one factor that will affect the life of your computer. We'll cover others.*

*In this chapter we provide you with the basic information that will help you purchase a microcomputer system and maintain it over time.*

## Purchasing a System: What to Consider

**Applications software needs should be determined before hardware is purchased. Make sure you have enough RAM to run your applications. IBM PCs and IBM clones are essentially the same; Macintoshes have a different CPU chip and run different software.**

"You need a 300 MB hard disk." "You must purchase a PostScript laser printer." "By all means, purchase *this* word processing package." Purchasing a microcomputer system involves doing some research, listening to a lot of advice, and ultimately making a number of different purchasing decisions. Many people will buy hardware and software on just the recommendation of a friend. Although recommendations are helpful, if you don't do additional research, you may find yourself spending more for a system that offers features you will never use.

In this section we provide advice on choosing software and hardware to support your processing needs and explain what to consider before you purchase a particular brand of microcomputer or a microcomputer **clone**—that is, a microcomputer that is virtually identical to and compatible with the brand of computer it is copying. In addition, we describe some factors that should affect where you purchase a microcomputer system.

### What Software and Hardware Will You Need?

If you are a first-time buyer of a microcomputer, you should choose your applications software *first,* after you identify your processing needs. (See Figure 14.1.) For example, do you want to generate documents? Budgets? Graphics? In color? Will others use the computer? If so, what are their processing needs? Depending on your needs, you will purchase one or more applications software packages.

Once your applications software requirements have been determined, choose the compatible hardware models and systems software [✔ p. 197] that will allow you to use your applications software efficiently and expand your system if necessary. (Often the systems software is included with the computer.)

The documentation (user's manual) that accompanies the applications software you purchase will list the minimum hardware requirements necessary to

**Figure 14.1**
If possible, choose your
software first, after you have
determined processing needs.
Then choose hardware that will
run your chosen software.

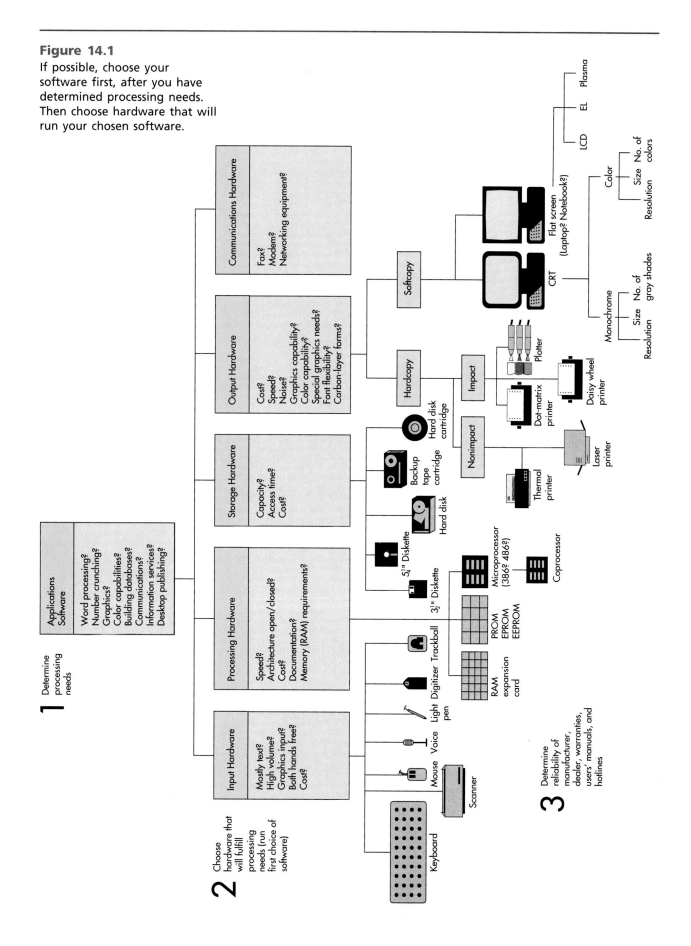

run the software. For example, your microcomputer must have a minimum of 4 MB RAM [✔ pp. 82, 93, 112] to run most of the software applications on the market today—many programs require 8–16 MB RAM. And if your objective is to output graphics, you must make sure that your software is compatible with the printer you want to use; that is, make sure the software contains the *printer driver* [✔ p. 196] (software instructions) that tells the software how to communicate with your printer. Unless you plan on purchasing an obscure printer, such as one sold by a small computer company with few sales, the software you use will most likely support the printer you want to use.

By choosing your applications software first, you will ensure that all your processing requirements will be satisfied: you won't be forced to buy a software package that is your second choice simply because your first software choice wasn't compatible with the hardware or systems software already purchased.

When you go to work in an office, chances are that the computer hardware and systems software will already be in operation, so if you have to choose anything, it will most likely be applications software to help you do your job. If you do find yourself in a position to choose applications software, make sure not only that it will satisfy the processing requirements of your job, but also that it is compatible with your company's hardware and existing software.

## PC Clones: A Good Bet?

Yes, usually. If you ask some important questions before making a purchase, you will end up with a compatible system for a good price.

- Is the microcomputer accompanied by proper and adequate documentation? This is extremely important. If your microcomputer needs to be repaired or upgraded, the computer technician will want to look at the technical documentation that accompanies your system. No matter what the price, if the system comes without documentation, you should not buy it.

- Is the ROM chip [✔ pp. 95, 98] a known PC compatible? If the answer is "yes," then you will be able to run all the software (generally) that is written for the microcomputer your machine is a clone of.

- Are the characteristics of the motherboard—the main circuit board—similar to those of the PC's motherboard? If they are, then PC adapter boards [✔ p. 96] (such as expanded memory or video adapter boards) will work in the clone.

- Is the system covered by a warranty? The system should be covered by at least a 12-month warranty. Many computers are covered for 24–36 months. If something fails during that time, the manufacturer should repair it at no cost.

- If the system fails after the warranty period, will parts be available? The manufacturer should service your computer after the warranty period expires. In other words, watch out for fly-by-night manufacturers.

Companies have conducted studies that prove their computers are 100% compatible with the microcomputer they are cloning. This type of information is useful to the microcomputer clone buyer; ask your dealer about such studies.

Because IBM microcomputers are very popular in the business environment, computer makers often manufacture IBM clones and sell them with their own manufacturing label. (See Figure 14.2.) Don't think that a microcomputer with an IBM label is better than an IBM clone—clones are some-

**Figure 14.2**
The Compaq Deskpro computer on the right is a clone of the IBM computer on the left.

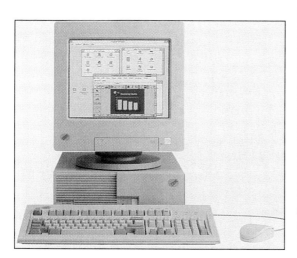

times more powerful and typically are less expensive than the machines they copy. As a result, IBM clones have become extremely popular and have achieved a niche of their own in the marketplace. When IBM makes a change in its microcomputer line, you can be sure that other compatibles, or clones, will appear that incorporate those changes.

## Macintoshes

Since Apple Computer introduced the Macintosh microcomputer in 1983, it has remained popular with many people who were impressed with its "user-friendly" graphic interface [✓ p. 204]. In contrast to pre-Windows IBM PCs, the Macintosh was not command-oriented; in other words, users worked with icons, menus, and the mouse to issue commands instead of having to memorize many DOS commands [✓ p. 203] and type them in on the computer. However, the Macintosh was not—and still is not—used in business as much as the IBM and IBM clones.

Then, with the introduction in 1985 of Adobe's PostScript page description language [✓ p. 155] for the Mac, desktop publishing was essentially invented. Thus the Macintosh line of microcomputers became essential to many types of people in publishing, design, illustration, and typesetting. Although desktop publishing programs—such as Quark XPress and PageMaker—are now available for the IBM, the high-end Quadra and the Power Mac are still preferred by many people in desktop publishing and related areas. (See Figure 14.3.)

Basically, the Mac can do anything the IBM can do, and many people still insist it's easier to use than IBM microcomputers—even those with Windows. It's getting easier to swap files between the two systems—with extra, inexpensive software all Macs can accept diskettes formatted on an IBM PC. (Macs with System 7 operating system software include this special software.) Newer Macs have a diskette drive called a *Superdrive,* which can handle diskettes formatted on an MS-DOS machine. The new Power Mac has two kinds of chips to enable the computer to support both Mac- and PC-based programs; and, as with all Macs, networking capability is built in. However, this system is still relatively expensive.

**Figure 14.3**
High-end Quadra and Power Mac. Press two keys on the Power Mac, and you can switch from Macintosh programs into a Windows environment and use PC programs.

## Where to Go

The following three factors should greatly influence where you purchase a microcomputer:

1. The company's reputation
2. The warranty agreement
3. The price

Since each of these factors influences the others, they can't be described independently. If a local computer store has been in business for a few years, you can be reasonably confident that it has tested the waters and won't go out of business. When deciding where to purchase a computer, consider the following:

■ Manufacturers generally support warranties on computers sold through dealers. Should anything happen to the computer in 6–12 months, parts and labor are covered by the manufacturer's **warranty,** or agreement between the manufacturer (and sometimes the seller) and purchaser. If a computer has a problem, you will likely experience it in the first 6–12 months anyway, so this warranty is a fair deal. If a computer is sold through someone other than an authorized dealer—computers sold in this way are referred to as *gray-market computers*—many manufacturers ignore the manufacturer's warranty.

■ When purchasing a computer from a local store, you have a convenient place to take the computer if it needs to be serviced. However, even if you purchase a computer from a mail-order company, you can often pack up the computer in its original box and send it back to the company for service.

■ When you purchase from a local computer company, you have the advantage of establishing personal contacts at the computer store should you have questions about your system.

You can also purchase a microcomputer and peripheral equipment from a mail-order company for a substantial discount. Make sure the hardware you purchase is supported by a warranty before purchasing it. Computer magazines all contain advertisements for mail-order companies. Although many mail-order companies have solid reputations, some don't. Do the following homework before buying from a mail-order company:

- Check back issues of the magazine to see if the advertisement has been running regularly. If it has, the company has been paying its bills.

- Check the ad for a street address. If no street address exists—only a P.O. box—it is possible that the company may be a temporary operation.

- Compare the prices offered by different mail-order companies. If the price you are eyeing is more than 25% lower than the competition, you might be looking at something that is too good to be true.

- Make sure the system's price includes all the features and peripherals that you want. For example, make sure the price includes a monitor and a keyboard.

- As mentioned previously, make sure the system you purchase is covered by a manufacturer's warranty. Some major computer manufacturers don't honor warranties on computers sold through mail-order companies.

- Pay by credit card. If you have an unresolved complaint about the product, U.S. federal law says that the credit card company can't bill you if you report your complaint to them promptly.

- In addition, you may want to check with the Better Business Bureau or local consumer protection department in the company's area to find out more details about the company.

## Other Practical Considerations

Following are a few more guidelines that will help you in choosing a microcomputer system:

1. Determine the maximum amount of money you can spend. *Don't spend money on fancy functions you don't need or may never use!*

2. After you decide what you want the system to do for you and have chosen your software, determine what the minimum hardware requirements are to run the software. These requirements are listed in the documentation that accompanies each software program. Pay special attention to RAM requirements.

3. Determine if any of your hardware needs to be portable.

4. To ensure the possibility of upgrading the computer in the future, choose one designed with open architecture, for insertion of expansion cards [✓ p. 96], or sufficient interfaces (ports) [✓ p. 99] for hooking up the peripheral devices you need.

5. Determine if your system must be compatible with another system—either in your office or in another context—or with software you or your colleagues are already using. If so, be sure to choose compatible hardware, and make sure that any systems software that comes with the computer is compatible also.

6. If possible, buy everything (computer, keyboard, monitor, printer, and so on) at one place, so you have to make only one phone call to ask questions and solve problems.

7. If you purchase from a local computer store, use the computer for a while before you decide to purchase it. Take special care to make sure you're comfortable with the keyboard and monitor.

**Figure 14.4**

Shopping for a CD-ROM drive.

No new computer, at home or work, is complete until it can handle CD-ROMs. And to handle a CD-ROM, your computer needs a CD-ROM drive.

Many of the latest programs for PCs and Macs come on CD-ROMs because a CD-ROM can hold as much as hundreds of floppy disks. It's a lot cheaper to ship a big program on a single CD-ROM instead of dozens of floppies. And sometimes CDs are necessary. Some multimedia programs with sound (which takes up a lot of disk space), color pictures (which take up even more disk space), and video (so huge that a floppy can hold only a few seconds) can fit only on CD-ROMs.

How do you choose a CD-ROM drive?

It's easy if you're looking at new computers. All the built-in CD-ROM drives in today's PCs and Macs are at least "double-speed, multi-session, Photo-CD compatible" drives. Double-speed is OK—not ideal but OK.

What about buying a drive to add to your computer?

Be forewarned that this is tougher than you might think. Lots of add-on drives are sold and then returned because the hook-up was too complex or buggy. Still, if you want to use all those new CD-ROMs and can't afford a whole new computer, this is your only choice.

Here's what you ask for:

1. Go for the right speed (how fast the drive moves information from disk to computer). Avoid single-speed, which won't do multimedia. If you can afford only $100 to $150, get double-speed, which handles text, sound, and animation reasonably well. Video is somewhat restricted. Avoid triple-speed, which offers some improvement but has been leapfrogged by the next level. For $250 to $350 you can get quad-speed, which handles on-screen video and multimedia well.

2. Decide whether to buy an internal or an external drive. Internal models plug inside the main computer case. An external drive sits in its own little box and connects by cable to the back of the computer. Internal drives cost less but are harder to hook up.

3. SCSI connections [✓ p. 100] are best. Macs come with SCSI; you just need to specify that you want Mac cables and software with your drive. (Mac CD-ROM drives cost more than PC drives.) Most PCs do not have SCSI ports. But many sound boards do have a SCSI socket built in. If you don't have one, get a SCSI interface board (card). If you need to buy a sound board or interface board with your drive, you're getting a "kit," and that can cost more.

4. Ask about guarantees, warranties, tech support, and so on. You want easy installation, with a manual, chart, and even a videotape. Then you want to be able to call when you need to get help.

5. Get a "caddieless" drive. Some CD-ROM drives require that you put each CD-ROM disk into a "caddie," a little plastic holder that protects the CD-ROM disk from dust. Others let you just plop the CD-ROMs onto a tray that then slides into the drive.

6. Ask about audio-only features. CD-ROM drives can play audio CDs. You'll want a utility program that lets you change volume and choose tracks. Better yet, get a drive that also has front-panel buttons and dials so you can play music without calling up any utility program. Then you can just press Play, Skip Track, and so on, as you would with a typical CD audio player. Also look for a headphone jack, so you can spare others from loud music or wacky sounds.

7. Check on Photo-CD compatibility, if you want your drive to be able to read the picture on Kodak Photo-CD disks. Even if you don't think you'll use Photo-CDs, this standard guarantees other kinds of performance that some multimedia titles depend on.

If you can afford to wait awhile before purchasing a CD-ROM drive, do so. Soon CD-ROM "jukeboxes" will be available, which will hold six or seven disks at a time.

Adapted from Phillip Robinson, "Shopping for a CD-ROM Drive?", *San Jose Mercury News,* Sunday, February 12, 1995, p. 2F.

8. Determine how much secondary storage [✓ p. 113] you will need and buy accordingly. (This includes CD-ROM capacity. See Figure 14.4.)

9. Determine if you need color in either hardcopy or softcopy output.

10. Determine your most common output needs. For example, will you need to print out forms with many carbon layers? Will you be outputting mostly business letters or internal memos? Will you also need to output graphics? Fancy color brochures? (See Figure 14.5.)

11. Determine your communications needs: Are fax-modem capabilities sufficient, or will you also need to access a network?

12. Decide what file backup method you will use—diskettes? hard disk cartridges? tape?

13. Determine what scanning capabilities you need. (See Figure 14.6.)

14. Determine sound output needs. (See Figure 14.7.)

See the end of the chapter for a portable checklist that you can take with you when you decide to purchase a microcomputer. To help you further, Figure 14.8 interprets a few hardware and software ads to start you on the way to understanding them. Table 14.1 lists popular computer magazines and periodicals you can consult for more detailed information on buying hardware and software than we can offer here.

## Maintaining a System

**Factors to monitor in order to properly maintain a computer system include temperature, length of time the computer is left on, power surges and supply, and dust and pollutants.**

A microcomputer system presents a sizable investment—from a few hundred to a few thousand dollars. Even so, many users don't take care of this investment, which leads to system abuse and failures. Most microcomputer problems can be prevented by regular maintenance. Maintaining a system properly —on an ongoing basis—is easy, and will pay for itself many times over by reducing hardware malfunctions and data loss and increasing the life of your computer.

In this section you will learn how to maintain your microcomputer system by following some simple procedures and words of advice.

### Temperature

Computer systems should be kept in an environment with as constant a temperature as possible. In cold climates, where office temperatures are controlled by an automatic thermostat causing warmer temperatures during the day and much cooler temperatures at night, microcomputers tend to have the most system failures. The ideal room temperature for microcomputers ranges from 60 to 90 degrees Fahrenheit when the system is on and from 50 to 110 degrees when the system is off. But maintaining a constant temperature in an environment is more important than the number of degrees.

The following problems can eventually occur if a microcomputer system is subjected to substantial temperature changes in short amounts of time:

■ The chips inside the system unit can work their way out of their sockets in the system boards. In addition, the chip connectors can corrode more quickly so that they become brittle and crack.

**Figure 14.5**
Shopping for a printer.

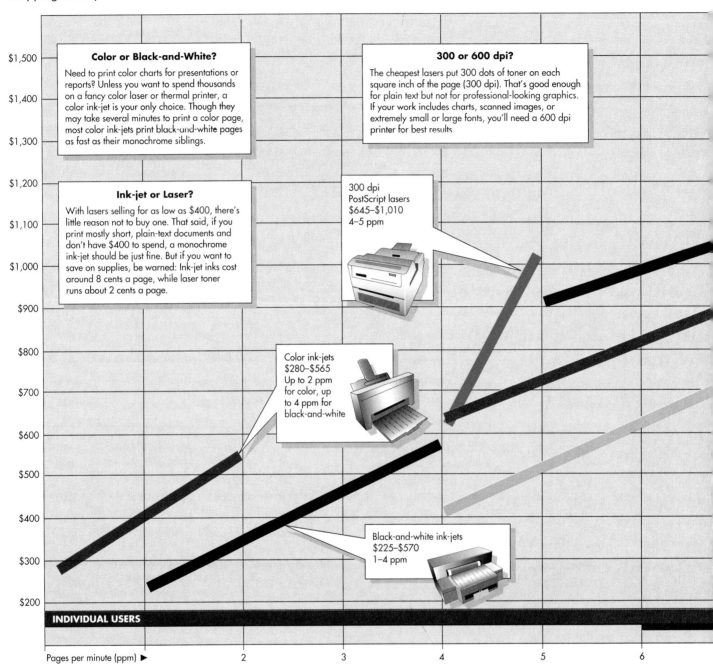

**Color or Black-and-White?**

Need to print color charts for presentations or reports? Unless you want to spend thousands on a fancy color laser or thermal printer, a color ink-jet is your only choice. Though they may take several minutes to print a color page, most color ink-jets print black-and-white pages as fast as their monochrome siblings.

**300 or 600 dpi?**

The cheapest lasers put 300 dots of toner on each square inch of the page (300 dpi). That's good enough for plain text but not for professional-looking graphics. If your work includes charts, scanned images, or extremely small or large fonts, you'll need a 600 dpi printer for best results.

**Ink-jet or Laser?**

With lasers selling for as low as $400, there's little reason not to buy one. That said, if you print mostly short, plain-text documents and don't have $400 to spend, a monochrome ink-jet should be just fine. But if you want to save on supplies, be warned: Ink-jet inks cost around 8 cents a page, while laser toner runs about 2 cents a page.

300 dpi
PostScript lasers
$645–$1,010
4–5 ppm

Color ink-jets
$280–$565
Up to 2 ppm
for color, up
to 4 ppm for
black-and-white

Black-and-white ink-jets
$225–$570
1–4 ppm

INDIVIDUAL USERS

Pages per minute (ppm) ▶

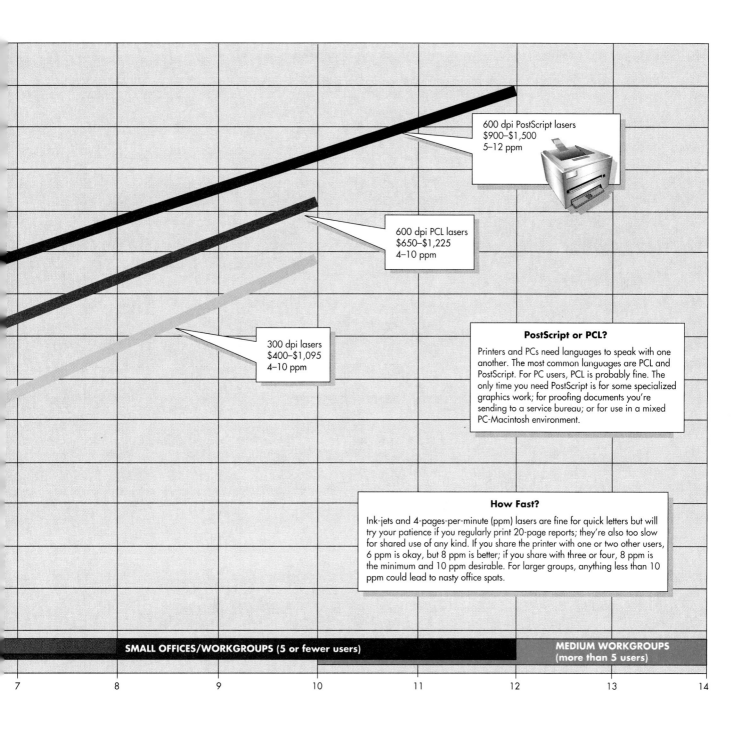

600 dpi PostScript lasers
$900–$1,500
5–12 ppm

600 dpi PCL lasers
$650–$1,225
4–10 ppm

300 dpi lasers
$400–$1,095
4–10 ppm

**PostScript or PCL?**

Printers and PCs need languages to speak with one another. The most common languages are PCL and PostScript. For PC users, PCL is probably fine. The only time you need PostScript is for some specialized graphics work; for proofing documents you're sending to a service bureau; or for use in a mixed PC-Macintosh environment.

**How Fast?**

Ink-jets and 4-pages-per-minute (ppm) lasers are fine for quick letters but will try your patience if you regularly print 20-page reports; they're also too slow for shared use of any kind. If you share the printer with one or two other users, 6 ppm is okay, but 8 ppm is better; if you share with three or four, 8 ppm is the minimum and 10 ppm desirable. For larger groups, anything less than 10 ppm could lead to nasty office spats.

**SMALL OFFICES/WORKGROUPS (5 or fewer users)**          **MEDIUM WORKGROUPS
(more than 5 users)**

7        8        9        10        11        12        13        14

## Figure 14.6
Different scanners for different applications. Desktop publishing, OCR, and other jobs require different scanner features.

*dpi = dots per inch. The more dots per inch a scanner produces, the higher the resolution and the better the image quality.

†Scanners that store images as shades of gray rather than in color are *gray-scale scanners*. These scanners, which cost less than color scanners, usually incorporate up to 256 shades of gray.

‡OCI = optical character recognition. OCR software translates scanned images of text (which are actually only *images* of the text) into actual, editable text.

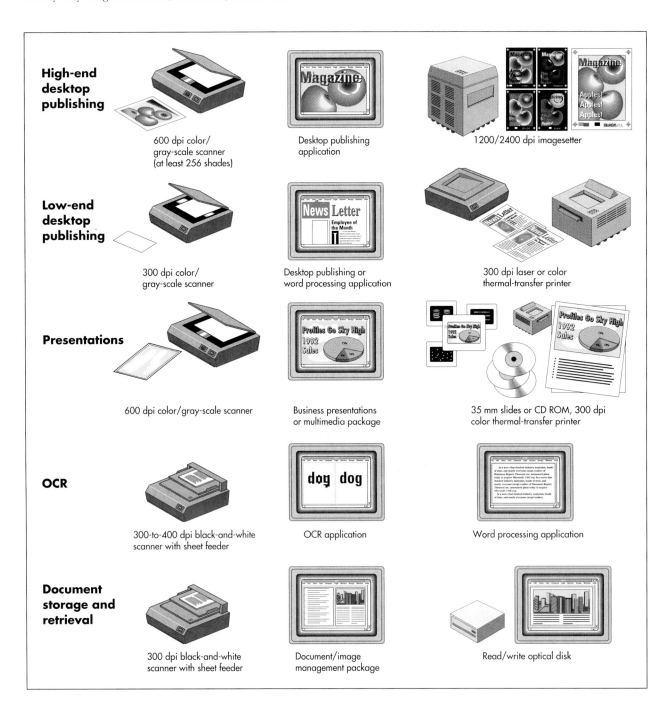

**Figure 14.7**

Elements of audio. When it comes to computer sound, you often must know something in order to ask something. Many beginning computer users have heard about the wondrous things possible when sound is used on the PC, but a majority don't know where to start asking questions. They could blindly query sales-people, but retailers may not have the patience to explain or may try to sell products the customer doesn't really need. Here's a chance to bone up on audio.

**Q: What is a sound board?**
**A:** The sound board, or sound card, is a circuit board providing enhanced sound quality over what computers produce with the basic PC speaker. PCs lacking sound boards typically produce only elec-tronic beeps or somewhat muffled sound effects. Sound boards allow high-quality music, realistic sound effects, and the recording and manipulation of sounds. If you want to work with sound, you'll need one.

The sound board uses an expansion slot inside the computer. On the circuit board are a record-ing mechanism, an amplifier, an analog/digital [✓ pp. 262, 263] converter, some type of synthesizer chip, and a MIDI processor. [MIDI = musical instrument digital interface, a protocol that allows a synthesizer to send signals to another synthesizer or to a computer, or a computer to a musical instrument, or a computer to another computer.] External connectors on the exposed end of the board may include a line input for devices like boombox stereos, a speaker connection, a MIDI connection, a microphone connection, a volume dial, and usually a joystick port [✓ p. 99].

**Q: What is Sound Blaster compatibility?**
**A:** Sound Blaster is the dominant sound board stan-dard created by Creative Labs. The Sound Blaster standard is as commonplace as the PC (IBM) compat-ibility standard in computers. Most sound boards on the market conform to Sound Blaster's specifications instead of soliciting support for their own boards.

Games typically list something like "sound board (Sound Blaster)" among their system requirements. Game players can avoid headaches in most cases by buying a Sound Blaster-compatible board. Users planning to work mainly with music can worry less about Sound Blaster-compatibility and concentrate on cards that are General MIDI compatible and have feature wave table technology.

**Q: How are sounds recorded and stored in a computer?**
**A:** Computers are strictly digital devices, meaning they recognize only the specific values 1 and 0. Humans live in an analog world in which we recognize ever-changing, infinitely variable values.

Sounds consist of rapid fluctuations in air pressure caused by vibrations. Microphones convert the variations in air pressure into corresponding variations in electrical voltage levels. The sound board's analog/digital converter samples the electrical audio levels to create a digital version. (*Sam-pling* is the process of taking very rapid measurements, or samples, of a sound wave.) The samples represent the wave's amplitude over narrow time spans. The more samples taken, the more accu-rately the wave can be reconstructed during playback. Recording sound with computers is often referred to as "digitizing" or "sampling." Sample files usually carry the .wav file extension and are often called *wave files*.

**Q: What is a sampling rate?**
**A:** *Sampling rate* is the number of times a sound wave is sampled per second. The higher the sam-pling rate, the more accurate the reproduction and the better the sound quality. Sounds are typi-cally recorded at 11 kilohertz (kHz), 22 kHz, or 44 kHz. (*Kilohertz* represents 1,000 hertz, or 1,000 cycles per second.) Listeners can distinguish a clear difference in sound quality among the three sampling rates.

**Q: What is the difference between 8-bit and 16-bit sound?**
**A:** During the purchasing process, you're likely to hear about 8-bit and 16-bit sound boards. For technical reasons, 8-bit sound is analogous to radio music, while 16-bit sound is like that of a CD. Note that 16-bit samples (files) require twice as much storage space as 8-bit samples. Both 8-bit and 16-bit playback and recording are available on most current sound boards. The 16-bit playback is critical for quality sound. However, 8-bit sound is sufficient for many home microcomputer users.

**Figure 14.7** (continued)

**Figure 14.8**
Interpreting hardware and software ads.

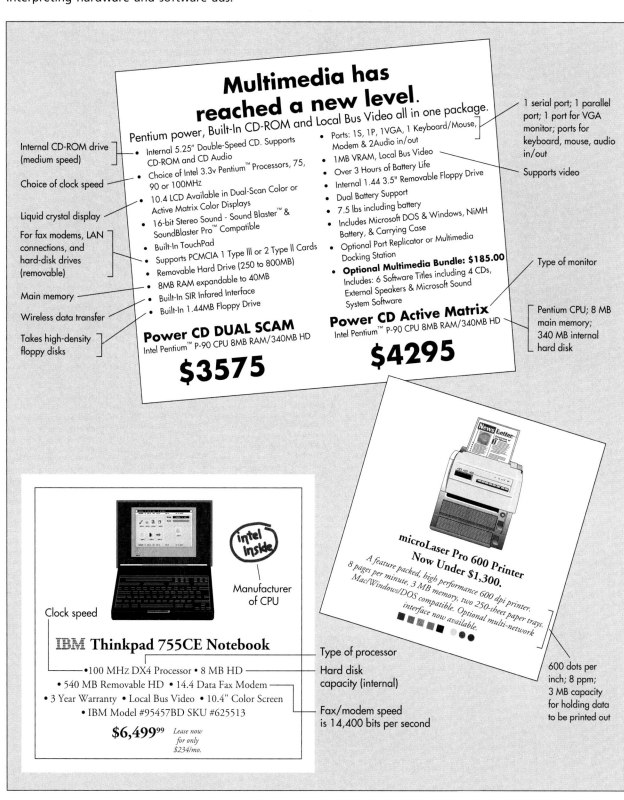

**Figure 14.8** (continued)

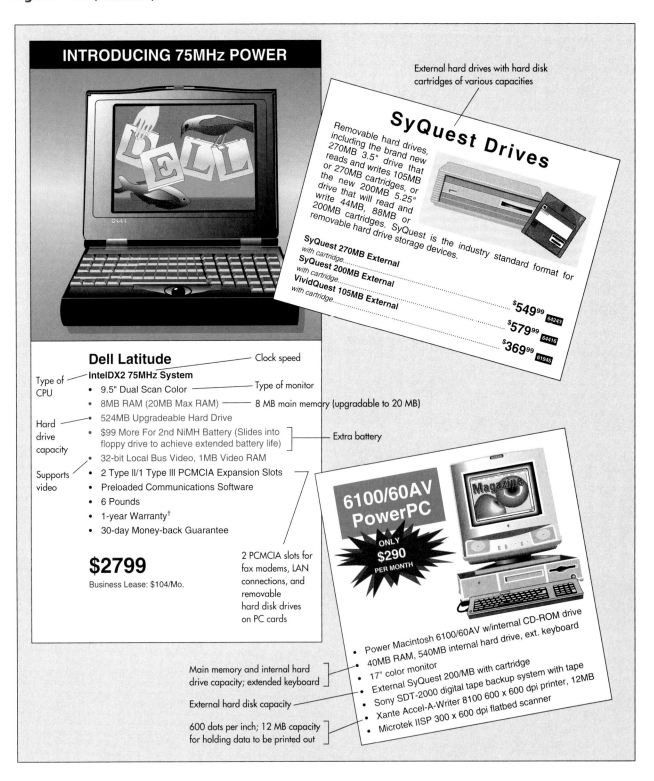

INTRODUCING 75MHz POWER

External hard drives with hard disk cartridges of various capacities

# SyQuest Drives

Removable hard drives, including the brand new 270MB 3.5" drive that reads and writes 105MB or 270MB cartridges, or the new 200MB 5.25" drive that will read and write 44MB, 88MB or 200MB cartridges. SyQuest is the industry standard format for removable hard drive storage devices.

SyQuest 270MB External
with cartridge..................................................... $549⁹⁹   64243
SyQuest 200MB External
with cartridge..................................................... $579⁹⁹   64416
VividQuest 105MB External
with cartridge..................................................... $369⁹⁹   61945

## Dell Latitude

Clock speed

Type of CPU — IntelDX2 75MHz System

- 9.5" Dual Scan Color — Type of monitor
- 8MB RAM (20MB Max RAM) — 8 MB main memory (upgradable to 20 MB)
- 524MB Upgradeable Hard Drive

Hard drive capacity

- $99 More For 2nd NiMH Battery (Slides into floppy drive to achieve extended battery life) — Extra battery
- 32-bit Local Bus Video, 1MB Video RAM

Supports video

- 2 Type II/1 Type III PCMCIA Expansion Slots
- Preloaded Communications Software
- 6 Pounds
- 1-year Warranty†
- 30-day Money-back Guarantee

## $2799

Business Lease: $104/Mo.

2 PCMCIA slots for fax modems, LAN connections, and removable hard disk drives on PC cards

# 6100/60AV PowerPC

ONLY $290 PER MONTH

- Power Macintosh 6100/60AV w/internal CD-ROM drive
- 40MB RAM, 540MB internal hard drive, ext. keyboard
- 17" color monitor
- External SyQuest 200/MB with cartridge
- Sony SDT-2000 digital tape backup system with tape
- Xante Accel-A-Writer 8100 600 x 600 dpi printer, 12MB
- Microtek IISP 300 x 600 dpi flatbed scanner

Main memory and internal hard drive capacity; extended keyboard

External hard disk capacity

600 dots per inch; 12 MB capacity for holding data to be printed out

**Table 14.1**
Alphabetized List of Popular Computer Magazines and Periodicals

| PERIODICAL AND PUBLISHER | TELEPHONE |
| --- | --- |
| *BBS* (Callers Digest) | 800-822-0437 |
| *Byte* (McGraw-Hill) | 800-257-9402 |
| *CD-ROM Today* (GP) | 415-696-1661 |
| *Computer Currents* (IDG) | 508-820-8118 |
| *ComputerLife* (Ziff) | 800-926-1578 |
| *Computer Shopper* (Ziff) | 800-274-6384 |
| *Computerworld* (IDG) | 800-669-1002 |
| *Electronic Entertainment* (Infotainment World) | 800-770-3248 |
| *Family PC* (Ziff and Disney) | 800-413-9749 |
| *Home Office Computing* (Scholastic) | 800-288-7812 |
| *HomePC* (CMP) | 800-829-0119 |
| *Information Week* (CMP) | 516-562-5000 |
| *Infoworld* (IDG) | 415-572-7341 |
| *Internet World* (Mecklermedia) | 203-226-6967 |
| *MacHomeJournal* (MacHome Journal) | 800-800-6542 |
| *MacUser* (Ziff) | 800-627-2247 |
| *MacWeek* (Ziff) | 415-243-3500 |
| *Macworld* (IDG) | 800-524-3200 |
| *News Media* (Hypermedia) | 415-573-5170 |
| *Online Access* (Chicago Fine Print) | 800-36-MODEM |
| *PC Computing* (Ziff) | 800-365-2770 |
| *PC Magazine* (Ziff) | 800-289-0429 |
| *PC Novice* (Peed) | 800-582-2600 |
| *PC Today* (Peed) | 800-424-7900 |
| *PC Week* (Ziff) | 800-451-1032 |
| *PC World* (IDG) | 800-825-7595 |
| *Publish* (IDG) | 800-685-3435 |
| *Windows Magazine* (CMP) | 516-562-5948 |
| *Windows Sources* (Ziff) | 800-364-3414 |
| *Wired* (Wired Ventures) | 800-SO-WIRED |

■ Hard disks suffer from dramatic changes in temperature, which can cause read/write [✓ p. 119] problems. If a new hard disk drive has been shipped in a cold environment, manufacturers usually recommend that users wait for a few hours to a day before operating the hard disk.

These problems are caused by the expansion and contraction that naturally occurs when materials are heated and then cooled. The bottom line is that changes in temperature are stressful for microcomputer systems. Therefore, don't place your system near heating vents, in direct sunlight, or directly in front of cold-air blasts. If you use removable hard disk cartridges that have been in a cold car, for example, let them—and your computer—return to room temperature before you use them.

## Turning the Computer On/Off

Sudden changes in temperature can cause lasting damage to a computer system. When a computer system is turned on, it is subjected to the most extreme change in temperature—computers are relatively cool when they are off and become quite warm when they are turned on. For this reason, the fewer times a system has to be turned on, the longer it will remain in good working order. Ideally, keep the system on all day so that it is turned on and off only once each day.

One myth that we would like to dispel is that leaving a microcomputer system on will wear down a hard disk. By running a hard disk continuously, you are greatly reducing any stress on the drive due to temperature variations. This will reduce the potential of any read/write failures that are caused by such variations and increase the life of the drive.

If you do leave your system on for long periods without using it, turn the monitor off; otherwise make sure that the screen automatically goes blank after a few minutes if the keyboard or other input device isn't used. Most manufacturers now include this feature with their computer systems—if not, special software is available that will do this for you. If you have an old screen that doesn't go blank, the phosphors on the screen can burn, leaving a permanent image on the screen. The monitors in airports that display flight information still sometimes show these phosphor-burn effects. Some software includes a screen-saver utility; screen saver programs may also be purchased separately—for example, Flying Toasters and Monty Python's Complete Waste of Time screen savers featuring figures from the Ministry of Silly Walks or Floating Elephants.

## Plugging in the System

Many users plug a number of different system components into one power strip that contains a number of different plug outlets. (See Figure 14.9.) However, certain types of equipment, including coffee makers, laser printers, and copy machines, can cause voltage spikes (surges of electricity), which can do damage to a computer that is connected to the same line. Therefore, it's best to keep your computer on a line separate from other equipment, including your printer. If you must connect peripheral equipment on the same power line, turn on that equipment before turning on the computer. Make sure your circuits will bear the load. (See Figure 14.10.)

If your computer is in an environment that is susceptible to power surges or power outages, you should plug your system into a surge suppressor or uninterruptible power supply. (See Figure 14.11.) **Surge suppressors** are devices into which you can plug your microcomputer system, and which in turn are connected to the power line. Costing between $20 and $200, surge suppressors help protect the power supply and other sensitive circuitry in

**Figure 14.9**
Multiplug extender.

your computer system from voltage spikes. An **uninterruptible power supply (UPS)** is also used to protect your hardware from the damaging effects that a power surge can have on your computer system. In addition, should you lose power, a UPS will keep your system running for around 8–30 minutes, providing you with plenty of time to save your work and shut the system down. The cost of a UPS system is determined by the amount of time it can continue to provide power to your computer system after the power has been cut off. Prices are around $100.

**Figure 14.10**
How many amps does your equipment need? Be sure your circuits will bear your equipment load.

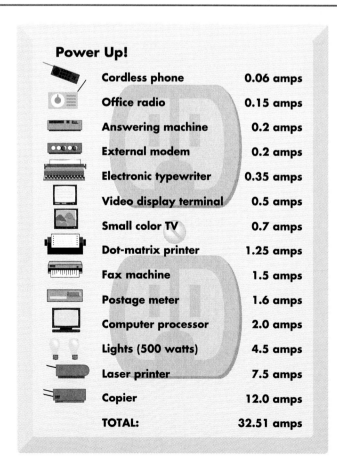

**Power Up!**

| | |
|---|---|
| Cordless phone | 0.06 amps |
| Office radio | 0.15 amps |
| Answering machine | 0.2 amps |
| External modem | 0.2 amps |
| Electronic typewriter | 0.35 amps |
| Video display terminal | 0.5 amps |
| Small color TV | 0.7 amps |
| Dot-matrix printer | 1.25 amps |
| Fax machine | 1.5 amps |
| Postage meter | 1.6 amps |
| Computer processor | 2.0 amps |
| Lights (500 watts) | 4.5 amps |
| Laser printer | 7.5 amps |
| Copier | 12.0 amps |
| **TOTAL:** | **32.51 amps** |

**Figure 14.11**
(a) Uninterruptible power supply (UPS); (b) surge suppressor.

(a)

(b)

Some industry experts say that the electrical distribution infrastructure in North America will be overtaxed by the year 2000. Thus surge suppressors soon will not provide enough protection for computer users against blackouts and brownouts. As a result, UPSs will increase in popularity and perhaps soon will be "bundled" (packaged with) microcomputers and will have longer battery lives than they have now.

## Dust and Pollutants

As an experiment, when your computer is on, light a match in front of a diskette drive and notice where the smoke goes. The smoke is inhaled by the system unit!

Most microcomputers are configured with a fan inside the system unit. The fan is mounted near the power supply and causes air to be drawn into the system unit through any possible opening and then blown out. Systems are designed this way to allow even cooling of the microcomputer system. Unfortunately, in this process dust, smoke, and any other pollutants in the air are drawn into the system unit. Over time these particles will insulate the system unit and prevent it from cooling properly. In addition, some of these particles can conduct electricity, causing minor electrical shorts in the system. (However, be sure not to block the vents; otherwise the system will overheat.)

Diskette drives are especially susceptible to dust and other pollutants because they provide a large hole through which air flows. The read/write heads [✔ p. 119] in the disk drive won't work accurately if they are contaminated with foreign particles. (Hard disks aren't at risk because they are stored in airtight containers.) For this reason, many companies enforce "No Smoking" policies in rooms where computers are present.

If you want to clean the diskette drives in your computer system (the read/write heads can become dusty over time, and dust can reduce the reliability with which they can store and retrieve data), an easy method does exist. You must first purchase a head-cleaning disk from a local computer store. Head-cleaning disks come in two basic styles—that is, wet or dry. The wet-cleaning disk uses a liquid cleaning agent that has been squirted onto the disk, and the dry-cleaning disk uses an abrasive material that has been put onto the cleaning disk. Most computer professionals recommend using the wet system, because the dry system can actually damage the read/write heads of the disk if it is used too often. To use a cleaning disk, simply put it into the disk drive and run a program (that is stored on the disk) to make the disk spin. When the disk spins in the disk drive, the read/write heads touch the surface of the cleaning disk and are wiped clean. In a clean (smoke-free) office environment, diskette drives should be cleaned about once a year. (Some technical professionals recommend cleaning the diskette drives twice a year.) In a smoking environment, diskette drives should be cleaned every 3–6 months.

The diskette drives aren't the only system components that should be cleaned periodically. If a microcomputer system is operated in a dirty environment, such as on the floor of a lumber shop, it should also be cleaned every 3–6 months. But in most office environments, the cleaning should be done every one to two years. You can either clean the appropriate components yourself or hire a professional to clean them for you. If you aren't familiar with the process of cleaning a microcomputer, hire a professional.

## Other Practical Considerations

Shocks and vibrations are bad for computer disk drives. Therefore, you should also keep the following considerations in mind:

- Never place an impact printer (dot-matrix or daisy wheel printer) [✔ p. 152] on the same surface as the computer.

- Don't drop or throw objects onto the surface on which the computer is located.

- If you place your system unit on the floor to free up desk space, make sure it's not in a place where you will accidentally kick it or people will bump into it.

- Don't move a laptop or notebook computer when the hard disk drive is working (while the HD light is on).

## Backing Up Your Microcomputer System

**Users should always back up their work regularly, protecting it against loss in case of power outage or other problems. Backup should be done on removable media, such as tape cartridges.**

The scenario: You've stored a year's worth of client information on your hard disk. You are able to retrieve client information easily onto the screen. You have confidence in your computer system—until the hard disk crashes. The read/write heads fall onto the surface of the disk, making the disk unusable and causing the loss of all the data stored on the disk! Well, at least you have a backup copy of your client files. What? You don't?

One of the most important tasks in maintaining a microcomputer system is to make copies, or a *backup,* of your data files. A popular rule of thumb is to never let the time between backups go longer than the amount of data it represents that you are willing to lose in a disk disaster. Depending on the amount of activity on a system, hard disks should be backed up at the end of each day or each week. All managers should make sure that office policies include backup procedures.

## Procedures

You must decide how often you want to back up data. Do you want to back up the entire hard disk or simply the files that have been changed since the last backup? Perhaps you want to make daily copies of the files that have been changed and, at the end of the week, make a backup copy of the entire disk, including software and data files. Whatever the procedures, they should be defined clearly and followed routinely.

Also, remember that backup must be done on **removable media**—storage media that can easily be removed from the system and stored in another place. Some businesses configure microcomputers with two hard disks. The first hard disk is the work disk on which all the current processing activities and updated files are stored. The second hard disk is used as a backup disk—the contents of the first disk are copied onto the second. This is not advisable. Suppose the microcomputer system is subjected to a massive power surge? The contents of *both* disks will be destroyed. Or suppose the entire microcomputer system is stolen? Once more, you won't have any backup files.

Once data has been backed up, it is important to clearly label and date the backup media.

*Note:* Wise microcomputer users also back up their operating system software files on diskettes and keep them handy in case the hard disk operating system files develop problems. (You can't use your applications software without the system software.) Your systems software documentation will tell you which files to back up and how to do it.

## Hardware and Software

Diskettes are still used in some cases as backup media. All microcomputer systems come with at least one diskette drive, so without a substantial hardware investment in a **dedicated backup system**—hardware and software used *only* for backup purposes—the user can back up the contents of a hard disk onto removable media (diskettes). Backup software for diskette systems is available that assists in the backup process, prompting the user to "insert a new diskette, please" when one diskette becomes full. However, using diskettes to back up a hard disk is slow.

Magnetic tape is the more commonly used storage medium for backing up hard disks. With a hard disk of 40 MB or higher, a reliable tape storage unit is a good investment. (See Figure 14.12.) Tape backup units can easily support 250 MB or more per tape and are fast and accurate. Once you decide to purchase a tape backup unit, you must decide what software to purchase to run the tape system. Many tape backup manufacturers write their own software. In addition to your specific needs, you should be sure that the software offers the following capabilities:

- Files can be backed up individually or all at once.
- Several backups can be copied onto a single tape.
- A backup can span more than one tape.
- The backup data can be verified to ensure that it was recorded reliably on the tape.

By paying special attention to the temperature of your system, the number of times you turn it on and off, how it is plugged in, the quality of the air surrounding the system, and routine backup procedures, you will increase the life of your computer system.

**Figure 14.12**
Magnetic tape is often used for backing up hard disks. This photo shows an internal cartridge tape unit and an external unit. The tape cartridge is inserted in the slot on the front.

## Ergonomics: Health Issues

**Ergonomics, the science of human-comfort engineering, concerns itself with preventing some common computer-related health problems, such as eye, back, and neck strain; repetitive strain injury (RSI); and annoying noise and stress.**

Even though the cost of computers has decreased significantly, they are still expensive. Why have them, then, unless they can make workers more effective? Ironically, in certain ways computers may actually make people less productive. Many of the problems that affect productivity are commonly experienced by people working in data-entry-intensive positions, such as clerks and word processors. However, such problems may also be experienced by anyone whose job involves intensive use of the computer. As a result, interest in ergonomics has been increasing, and greater effort is being made to avoid health risks. Basically, **ergonomics** is the science of human-comfort engineering—especially comfort in the area of computer use.

### Physical Health

Sitting in front of a screen and using a keyboard for long periods may lead to eyestrain, headaches, back pain, and repetitive strain injury. Of course, adopting such commonsense measures as taking frequent rest breaks and using well-designed computer furniture can alleviate some of the discomfort. However, other suggestions have also proven useful. (See Figure 14.13.)

1. *Avoid eyestrain and headache.* The use of computer screens requires focusing the eyes on items at a closer range than our eyes are designed for. Focusing on the screen at this close range for long periods of time can cause eyestrain, headaches, and double vision. To avoid these prob-

**Figure 14.13**
The ergonomic work office.

**HEAD** Directly over shoulders, without straining forward or backward, about an arm's length from screen.

**NECK** Elongated and relaxed.

**SHOULDERS** kept down, with the chest open and wide.

**BACK** Upright or inclined slightly forward from the hips. Maintain the slight natural curve of the lower back.

**ELBOWS** Relaxed, at about a right angle.

**WRISTS** Relaxed, and in a neutral position, without flexing up or down.

**KNEES** Slightly lower than the hips.

**CHAIR** Sloped slightly forward to facilitate proper knee position.

**SCREEN** At eye level or slightly lower.

**FINGERS** Gently curved.

**KEYBOARD** Best when kept flat (for proper wrist positioning) and at or just below elbow level. Computer keys that are far away should be reached by moving the entire arm, starting from the shoulders, rather than by twisting the wrists or straining the fingers. Take frequent rest breaks.

**FEET** Firmly planted on the floor. Shorter people may need a footrest.

lems, take a 15-minute break every hour or two. Minimize reflected glare on the screen by keeping the screen away from windows and other sources of bright light. (If necessary, purchase an antiglare screen or a glare shield for your existing screen.) In general, bigger monitors cause less eye strain than small ones, particularly in graphics-intensive applications, and smaller dot pitches [✔ p. 162] are easier on the eyes. The screen should be three to four times brighter than room light. In addition, the computer screen, the keyboard, and anything you are reading while typing should all be positioned at the same distance from your eyes—about 20–24 inches away. Clean the screen of dust from time to time.

2. *Avoid back and neck pain.* Make sure equipment is adjustable. You should be able to adjust your chair for height and angle, and the chair should have good back support. The monitor should be able to tilt and swivel, and the keyboard should be detachable (so you can place it on your lap, for example).

3. *Avoid effects of electromagnetic fields.* VDTs generate electromagnetic field (EMF) emissions, which can pass through the human body. Even though the fact has not been proved, some observers believe that EMF emissions could be involved in miscarriages and possibly some cancers. [In the United States, the Environmental Protection Agency (EPA) and the Federal Drug Agency (FDA) are studying this issue.] For this reason,

older monitors should be replaced with new, low-emission monitors or shielded with special snap-on screen covers. Also, try to sit 2 feet away from your monitor and at least 3 feet away from neighboring monitors.

4. *Avoid repetitive strain injury (RSI).* **Repetitive strain injury**—also known as *repetitive motion injury* and *cumulative trauma disorder*—is the name given to a number of injuries resulting from fast, repetitive work. (See Figure 14.14.) RSI causes neck, wrist, hand, and arm pain. The recent publicized increase in RSI problems is mainly the result of increasing computer keyboard use and bar-code scanner [✔ p. 51] use

**Figure 14.14**
RSI diagram.

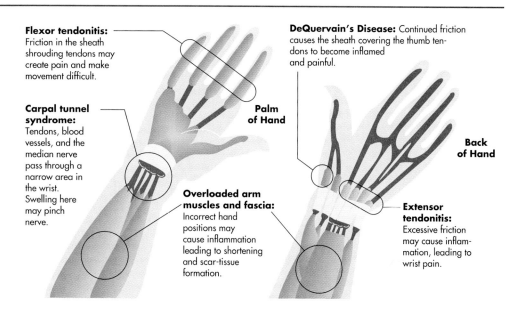

**Flexor tendonitis:** Friction in the sheath shrouding tendons may create pain and make movement difficult.

**Carpal tunnel syndrome:** Tendons, blood vessels, and the median nerve pass through a narrow area in the wrist. Swelling here may pinch nerve.

**Palm of Hand**

**DeQuervain's Disease:** Continued friction causes the sheath covering the thumb tendons to become inflamed and painful.

**Back of Hand**

**Overloaded arm muscles and fascia:** Incorrect hand positions may cause inflammation leading to shortening and scar-tissue formation.

**Extensor tendonitis:** Excessive friction may cause inflammation, leading to wrist pain.

Gently pull thumb down and back until you feel the stretch. Hold for 5 seconds.

Grasp fingers and gently bend back wrist. Hold for 5 seconds.

Massage inside and outside of hand with thumb and fingers.

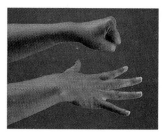

Clench fist tightly, then release, fanning out fingers. Repeat five times.

Gently massage hands; press palm down to stretch underside of forearm; press fist down to stretch top side of forearm. Hold positions for at least 10 seconds.

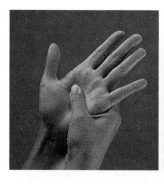

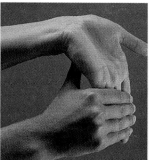

(for example, a clerk grasping items in the grocery cart and moving them past the bar-code scanner mounted in the counter at the super-market).

An RSI called *carpal tunnel syndrome* is particularly common among people who use computers and certain types of scanners intensively. In the United States, it afflicts some 230,000 workers annually, and the medical bill for treating carpal tunnel syndrome is about $805 million per year. This syndrome involves damage to nerves and tendons in the hands. RSI is basically caused by four factors:

- *Repetition and duration*—Prolonged, constant, and repetitious movements such as typing irritate tendons and nerve casings, causing them to swell.
- *Force*—The harder a person strikes the keys, the more likely he or she is to suffer injury.
- *Joint angle*—Flexing, raising, or twisting hands to reach the keys constricts the carpal tunnel (pinches the medial nerve running through the wrist).
- *Prolonged constrained posture*—Holding any position without moving puts excessive strain on muscles and tendons.

For some victims, the pain of carpal tunnel syndrome is so intense that they cannot open doors or shake hands. Left untreated, this syndrome can cause atrophied muscles and permanent nerve damage. To avoid RSI, take frequent short rest breaks instead of infrequent long ones. Or try using User Friendly Exercises software, distributed by PM Ware, which will time exercise intervals and display reminders as well as exercise instructions. Experts also advise getting plenty of sleep and exercise, maintaining appropriate weight, sitting up straight, and learning stress-management techniques.

You might also try one of the new ergonomically sound keyboards like The Vertical, the MI Key, or the DataHand. (See Figure 14.15.) (Although not enough testing has been done to indicate that such keyboards prevent RSI, many users find them more comfortable to use than traditional keyboards.)

## Mental Health

Computers often create mental/psychological irritants that can turn out to be counterproductive.

1. *Avoid noise.* Computer users sometimes develop headaches and experience tension from being exposed to noisy impact printers and to the high-pitched, barely audible squeal produced by some computer monitors. Indeed, some people, particularly women, who hear high-frequency sounds better than men do, may be affected by the noise even when they are not conscious of hearing it. Sound-muffling covers are available for some printers. However, to avoid ending up in a high-tension state because of monitor squealing, the advice again is to take frequent short rest breaks.

2. *Avoid stress from electronic supervision.* Research shows that workers whose performance is supervised electronically suffer more health problems than do those watched by human supervisors. For instance, a computer may monitor the number of keystrokes a data entry clerk completes in a day or the time a customer-service person takes to handle a call. Such monitoring may force a pace that leads to RSI problems and mental stress. One study found that electronically supervised employees reported great boredom, high tension, extreme anxiety, depression, anger, and severe fatigue.

**Figure 14.15**
Ergonomically sound keyboard by Kinesis Corporation.

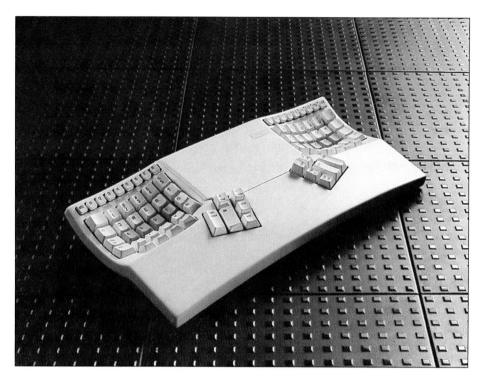

## The Environmentally Aware Computer User

**Many options exist for the computer user to avoid waste and contribute to recycling.**

These days, we hope everyone is environmentally aware. As you may imagine, computer hardware and software manufacturers use resources that often end up—in one form or another—in a garbage dump. Every year, an estimated 12 million laser printer [✓ p. 153] toner cartridges get dumped in the trash, along with dot-matrix printer ribbons, laptop and notebook computer batteries, and paper from fax machines and all types of printers.

What can you do to help prevent waste and contribute to the recycling effort?

- *Recycle used printer toner cartridges:* Hewlett-Packard (800/752-0900), Canon (800/962-2708), and Lexmark (800/848-9894) all provide postage-paid mailers so you can return your toner cartridges for recycling. Qume (800/421-4326) pays about $5 plus shipping per cartridge.

- *Recycle batteries:* Laptop and notebook computers often use nickel cadmium batteries; cadmium is a toxic heavy metal that should never reach a garbage landfill. Buy your computer from a company that will accept used batteries.

- *Consider buying a "green" printer:* Some new laser printers, like the Ecosys from Kyocera, don't use toner cartridges but instead need only to have the toner itself refilled.

■ *Use a plain-paper fax machine:* Although they are more expensive than the fax machines that use specially coated paper (that tends to curl), fax machines that can print out on regular sheets of paper are better for the environment because their paper can be recycled.

■ *Refill ink-jet printer cartridges and re-ink dot-matrix and daisy wheel printer ribbons:* Once you get the hang of it (or hire someone else to do it), the savings are worthwhile. Call Computer Friends (800/547-3303) or the International Cartridge Recycling Association (202/857-1154) for information.

■ *Reduce paper use, recycle what you use, and purchase recycled paper:* Contact the National Office Paper Recycling Project (202/223-3088) for information about what types of paper are not recyclable.

■ *Buy CD-ROM reference works* instead of traditional bound reference books like encyclopedias, atlases, etc. (saves paper).

■ *Don't trash obsolete software:* Contact the manufacturer for permission to give it to a school or to charity. (For example, WordPerfect Corporation will send you a new license that you can give to a school along with your old software. More than 70,000 copies of the WordPerfect word processing program have been donated to schools this way.) Or buy software from companies that recycle outdated software disks. Alternatively, send outdated disks to Greendisk in Redmond, Washington, for recycling.

■ *Recycle hardware:* IBM, Hewlett-Packard (916/785-7124), and Compaq (800/524-9859) will pay postage/freight and recycle many types of computer hardware, including batteries. Or you can donate used hardware to schools or other groups that can't afford to buy new items.

■ Try to buy a computer made of *recyclable plastic* (check the documentation or ask the vendor).

■ Try to buy "green" computer products with the seal of approval from the *Computer Users for Social Responsibility.*

■ *Buy a computer that has a "sleep mode.* This type of computer reduces power consumption by going into a state of "rest" when it is not being actively used (however, it is still on). A PC that uses sleep mode is estimated to use about *half* the power that a regular PC does when both are on all day and turned off at night. Sleep mode microcomputers also run cooler and need no fan—thus they are quieter. (PCs that conserve energy and therefore demand fewer natural resources have an Energy Star designation from the U.S. Environmental Protection Agency.)

## Additional Resources

### Used Computer Brokers
American Computer Exchange, 800/786-0717 or 404/250-0050
Boston Computer Exchange, 800/262-6399 or 617/542-4414
Damark, 800/729-9000
National Computer Exchange, 800/NACOMEX or 212/614-0700

### Higher Education Discounts
*Some manufacturers offer higher-education prices (usually discounted) on their products.*

COMPUTERS
Apple Computer, 800/776-2333
AST Research, 800/876-4AST
AT&T, 800/229-7055

Compaq, 800/888-5912
Dell, 800/759-1240

PRINTERS
Epson, 800/BUY-EPSON

DISK DRIVES
Gateway 2000, 800/846-2059

**Used Software**
*If you're buying a used computer, you may also want to consider buying used software.
(Also, older PCs may not be able to run new versions of software.) Recycled Software
ensures that all the programs they sell are complete and free of computer viruses. They
include all the disks and manuals. They will ship you a replacement if the disks are
defective. They do not buy software whose licensing agreement prohibits its sale or
transfer. Here are some programs that have been for sale. Call to find out about new
ones.*

Microsoft Word for DOS 2.1; $25 (list price $450)
Lotus 1-2-3 for DOS 1.1; $75 (list price $495)
R:Base 2.11 ; $30 (list price $795)
Norton Utilities 6.01; $40 (list price $179)
MS-DOS 5.0; $25 (list price $99)

Recycled Software
P.O. Box 266
Kings Mills, OH 45034
800/851-2425; 513/459-1435

*Purple Mountain Computers also sells used software.*

Purple Mountain Computers
15600 NE 8th St. #A3-412
Bellevue, WA 98008
206/399-8700

**Groups Accepting Used Computers**
Gifts in Kind America
700 North Fairfax St. #300
Alexandria, VA 22314
703/836-2121

CONNECT
Technical Development Corporation
30 Federal St., 5th Floor
Boston, MA 02110
617/728-9151

Information Technology Resource Center
59 East Van Buren #2020
Chicago, IL 60605-1219
312/939-8050

Plugged In
1923 University Ave.
East Palo Alto, CA 94303
800/225-PLUG

The National Christina Foundation
591 West Putnam Ave.
Greenwich, CT 06830
203/622-6000

Detwiler Foundation Computer for School Program
470 Nautilus St. # 300
La Jolla, CA 92037
619/456-9045

Nonprofit Computer Exchange
Fund for the City of New York
121 Sixth Ave., 6th Floor
New York, NY 10013
212/925-5101

CompuMentor
89 Stillman St.
San Francisco, CA 94107
415/512-7784

The Shareware Project
410 Townsend St. #408
San Francisco, CA 94107
415/543-0500

# S U M M A R Y

- If possible, when purchasing a new computer system, decide on your software requirements before your hardware components. (p. 474)

- When purchasing a computer, consider buying a PC clone. However, make sure that the microcomputer (p. 476):

  —is accompanied by good documentation

  —contains a ROM chip that is a known PC compatible

  —contains a motherboard that is similar to those used in PCs

  —is covered by at least a 12-month warranty

  Also, make sure that parts will be available after the warranty period.

- Consider the following factors when deciding where to purchase a computer (p. 478):

  1. The company's reputation

  2. The warranty agreement

  3. The price

- To maintain your computer system over time (p. 481):

  1. Keep the computer in an environment with as constant a temperature as possible.

  2. Try to turn the computer on and off as little as possible. When you turn on a computer, it is subjected to a severe temperature change, which can wear a computer down over time.

  3. If your work environment is susceptible to power surges, consider plugging your system into a *surge suppressor* or an *uninterruptible power supply (UPS)*.

  4. Keep your computer in a clean-air environment. Smoke and dust particles can damage your computer by conducting electricity, causing electrical shorts in the system. If possible, clean the computer at least once a year.

  5. One of the most important tasks in maintaining a microcomputer is to make copies, or a backup, of your data files. Back your data up onto diskettes or onto magnetic tape.

- To avoid the aches and pains associated with constant computer use, consider the following (p. 495):

  1. *To avoid eyestrain,* take a 15-minute break every hour or two. Also, to minimize reflected glare on the screen, keep your computer away from windows and other sources of bright light.

  2. *To avoid back and neck pain,* make sure the equipment you use is adjustable. That is, you should be able to adjust your chair for height and angle, tilt and swivel your monitor, and detach your keyboard.

  3. *To avoid the effects of electromagnetic fields,* consider replacing an old monitor with a newer, low-emission, monitor.

  4. *To avoid repetitive strain injury (RSI),* which refer to pains associated with the neck, wrist, hand, and arm, consider the following:

     —Prolonged, constant, and repetitious movements, such as typing, irritate tendons and nerve casings, causing them to swell.

     —The harder a person strikes the keys, the more likely he or she is to suffer injury.

     —Flexing, raising, or twisting hands to reach the keys can pinch a nerve running through your wrist.

     —Holding any position without moving puts excessive strain on muscles and tendons.

## EXERCISES

To end this last chapter, explain what the following system descriptions mean.

1. New Mac IIVX 5/80 W/CD, PowerPC upgradable, 680330-32 MHz with 68882 math coproc.: $1,099.
2. NEC Versa M and Versa P, two Type II or one Type III PCMCIA slot, removable hard drive and floppy drive, MS-DOS, Windows 3.1, Pentium 75, 540 MB HD, active matrix: $5,389.
3. Apple PowerBook Duo 210, 4/80, 68030/25 MHz, grayscale screen: $699.
4. Compaq Prolinea Desktop, 4 MB RAM expandable to 100 MB, 3.5" floppy drive, local bus graphics, 486DX2/66, Pentium upgradable, Energy Star compliant, MS-DOS 6.0, Windows 3.1, 525 MB HD: $1,639.
5. Zenith Z-Noteflex Multimedia Notebook, user upgradable processor, memory, hard drive, and display, 4 MB/8 MB RAM exp. to 24 MB, 32-bit VESA local bus video, built-in 16-bit stereo sound with speaker and microphone, integrated trackball, two Type II or one Type III PCMCIA slot, MS-DOS, Windows, 3-year warranty, 486DX4/100, 9.5" active matrix, 520 MB HD: $4,989.
6. Okidata ML 380 dot-matrix 24-pin, 192 cps: $219.
7. Comtrade Multimedia Tornado 4X, 16-bit stereo sound card, 2 amplified stereo speakers, MS-DOS, Windows, Microsoft Works, EnCarta CD, quad-speed CD-ROM drive, 16 MB RAM plus 256 K cache, 730 MB hard drive, 1 floppy drive ( 3.5" or 5.25"), PCI local bus, 2 serial ports, 1 parallel port, 1 game port, enhanced 101-key keyboard, mouse, Pentium-100, 14,400 fax modem, 1280 × 1024 monitor: $3,000.
8. Dell Dimension 466D workstation, Intel DX2 66 MHz, 4 MB RAM, 260 MB hard drive, 128 K cache, 3.5" diskette drive, MS-DOS 6.2, Windows 3.1, mouse: $1,299.
9. Gateway 2000 16-bit CD-quality sound card, compatible with Sound Blaster cards, with MIDI game port, microphone and stereo connections, 2 speakers: $99.
10. Hewlett-Packard 4P LaserJet printer, 600 dpi, PCL 5, 45 resident fonts, 2 MB standard memory and 3 SIMM slots available for additional memory or PostScript fonts, includes parallel cable: $999.

# Portable Checklist for Buying a Microcomputer System

*Copy this list and take it along when you're shopping for a microcomputer system.*

### Price Range (including peripherals)

_____ up to $1,000     _____ up to $2,000     _____ up to $3,000

_____ up to $4,000     _____ up to $5,000     _____ more than $5,000

### Uses (Software Needed)

*(Note: All applications software chosen must run with compatible systems software.)*

_____ Writing letters and reports; preparing professional papers (word processing software)

_____ Personal finance; budgeting and planning; taxes (spreadsheet software)

_____ Programming (programming language, such as BASIC, COBOL, Pascal, C, FORTRAN)

_____ Business applications; finance management, accounting, planning, scheduling, inventory and sales management (spreadsheet, DBMS, and/or graphics software)

_____ Entertainment (software games)

_____ Education (tutorial software)

_____ Mailing lists (word processing software; DBMS software)

_____ Publishing newsletters and brochures (word processing, graphics, desktop publishing software)

_____ Multimedia programs (_____ for presentation or reference; _____ for creating your own presentations)

_____ Information retrieval from public information services (communications software)

_____ Personal record-keeping (desktop management software)

_____ Creating art and graphics for use in published materials (graphics and desktop publishing software)

_____ Communications software

_____ CAD/CAM software

_____ Networking software (_____ needs to be compatible with other networks?)

_____ Anti-virus software

_____ Conversion software for cross-platform use (IBM–Macintosh)

_____ Data compression (_____ other utilities)

TOTAL projected cost for software $_____

**Hardware**

*(Check your chosen software's documentation for minimum hardware requirements and compatibility restrictions; when no requirements are given in the documentation, check your own preferences.)*

1. _____ System must be compatible with other systems? (Y/N)

   If yes, what kind: _____

2. _____ Uses what kind of systems software?

3. _____ How much main memory do I need?

   _____ 4 MB; _____ 8 MB; _____ 16 MB;

   _____ more (how much?)

4. _____ 16-bit processor; _____ 32-bit processor

   (number of bits that the microprocessor needs to handle at

   once) (check the bus architecture: _____ ISA;

   _____ EISA; _____MCA; _____ PCMCIA)

5. _____ _____ 25 MHz (clock speed); _____ 33 MHz;

   _____ 50 MHz; than 50 MHz

6. _____ Microcomputer must be portable? (Y/N) (laptop; notebook)

7. _____ Monochrome screen; _____ color screen (_____ RAM

   requirements; _____ low emission?)

8. _____ VGA; _____ Super VGA; _____ Other (screen resolu-

   tion, or clarity of image)

9. _____ Number of colors or gray shades (make sure you get appropri-

   ate software driver to support number of colors you want)

10. _____ Screen can tilt and swivel? (Y/N)

11. _____ Size of screen (appropriate to resolution?)

12. _____ System cabinet can be put on floor to save desk space? (Y/N)

13. _____ Detachable keyboard?

14. _____ QWERTY keyboard; _____ other keyboard (_____

    silent keys; _____ keys that "click")

15. _____ Numeric keypad?

16. _____ Number of required function keys

17. _____ Voice input?

18. _____ Single diskette drive; _____ dual diskette drive;

    _____ 3½ inch disks; _____ Do you need a

    5¼-inch drive?

19. _____ hard disk: 80 MB; 120 MB; 240 MB; _____ MB

20. _____ Tape backup

21. _____ Surge suppressor; _____ uninterrupted power supply

22. _____ Mouse; _____ trackball (_____ with palm support?)

23. _____ Dot-matrix printer; _____ laser printer; _____ inkjet printer; _____ color capability; _____ graphics capability; _____ multiple-form capability; _____ font availability (what kind? resident? cartridge? soft?); _____ speed; _____ noise level; _____ quality of text output; _____ PostScript support needed?

24. _____ Modem (_____ internal; _____ external); _____ 2,400 bps; _____ 9,600 bps; _____ 14,400 bps; _____ 28,800 bps; _____ error correction? _____ data compression?

25. _____ Fax (_____ internal; _____ external; _____ handle photos?)

26. _____ Scanner ( _____ color? _____ gray-scale? _____ slides? _____ photos?)

27. _____ Is system upgradable? How easy is it to upgrade?

28. _____ Any special needs? (such as voice output/braille input for a blind person, special keyboards for a disabled person)

29. _____ Do you need a CD-ROM drive?

30. _____ Any other multimedia hardware needs?

Identify: _____

_____

_____

_____

*(Note: If you need sound and video capability, make sure the sound card is compatible with the software you plan to use. Sound and video cards use different standards.)*

TOTAL projected cost for hardware $_____

## Support

Investigate the following:

1. Manufacturer's reputation and length of time in business
2. Dealer's reputation and length of time in business
3. Warranties
4. Quality of documentation (user's manuals): easy to follow? detailed?
5. Hotline availability to solve problems in emergencies
6. Location and availability of repair services
7. Availability of training
8. Will dealer install?

As a simple guide, we recommend the following minimum requirements for a microcomputer system:

- At least 4 MB RAM (8 MB is preferable)

- VGA or SVGA monitor (some multimedia programs require SVGA monitors)

- 486SX (33 MHz) or higher CPU

- *At least* 80 MB hard disk drive storage capacity (multimedia programs require greater storage capacity)

- Mouse

- Both 5¼-inch and 3½-inch diskette drives (One or two 3½-inch diskette drives)

- Modem (fax/modem combination preferable)

- Surge protector

- Keyboard (usually included)

- Extra expansion slots

- Upgradable RAM

- CD-ROM drive, if multimedia programs will be used

- Sound card, speakers, and driver software, if multimedia programs will be used

- Your need for a video capability, printer, scanner and other peripherals depends on what you intend to do with your system.

# *Appendix:*
## Key Dates in the History and Future of Information Processing*

| YEAR | EVENT |
|---|---|
| **Less than 100,000 years ago** | Homo sapiens begin using intelligence to further goals. |
| **More than 5000 years ago** | The abacus, which resembles the arithmetic unit of a modern computer, is developed in the Orient. |
| **3000–700 B.C.** | Water clocks are built in China in 3000 B.C., in Egypt approx. 1500 B.C., and in Assyria 700 B.C. |
| **2500 B.C.** | Egyptians invent the idea of thinking machines: citizens turn for advice to oracles, which are statues with priests hidden inside. |
| **427 B.C.** | In the *Phaedo* and later works Plato expresses ideas, several millennia before the advent of the computer, that are relevant to modern dilemmas regarding human thought and its relation to the mechanics of the machine. |
| **approx. 420 B.C.** | Archytas of Tarentum, a friend of Plato, constructs a wooden pigeon whose movements are controlled by a jet of steam or compressed air. |
| **approx. 415 B.C.** | Plato founds the Academy for the pursuit of science and philosophy in a grove on the outskirts of Athens. It results in the fertile development of mathematical theory. |
| **387 B.C.** | Theaetetus, a member of Plato's Academy, creates solid geometry. |
| **293 B.C.** | Euclid, also a member of Plato's Academy, is the expositor of plane geometry. He writes the *Elements,* a basic mathematics textbook for the next 2000 years. |
| **c. 200 B.C.** | In China artisans develop elaborate automata, including an entire mechanical orchestra. |
| **725** | A Chinese engineer and a Buddhist monk build the first true mechanical clock, a water-driven device with an escapement that causes the clock to tick. |
| **1540, 1772** | The technology of clock and watch making results in the production of more elaborate automata during the European Renaissance. Gianello Toriano's mandolin-playing lady (1540) and P. Jacquet-Droz's child (1772) are famous examples. |
| **1617** | John Napier invents Napier's Bones, of significance to the future development of calculating engines. |
| **1642** | Blaise Pascal perfects the Pascaline, a machine that can add and subtract. It is the world's first automatic calculating machine. |
| **1694** | Gottfried Wilhelm Leibniz, an inventor of calculus, perfects the Leibniz Computer, a machine that multiplies by performing repetitive additions, an algorithm still used in modern computers. |
| **1726** | Jonathan Swift, in *Gulliver's Travels,* describes a machine that will automatically write books. |
| **1805** | Joseph-Marie Jacquard devises a method for automating weaving with a series of punched cards. This invention will be used many years later in the development of early computers. |
| **1821** | Charles Babbage is awarded the first gold medal by the British Astronomical Society for his paper "Observations on the Application of Machinery to the Computation of Mathematical Tables." |
| **1821** | Michael Farraday, widely recognized as the father of electricity, reports his discovery of electromagnetic rotation and builds the first two motors powered by electricity. |
| **1822** | Charles Babbage develops the Difference Engine, but its technical complexities exhaust his financial resources and organizational skills. He eventually abandons it to concentrate his efforts on a general-purpose computer. |
| **1829** | The first electromagnetically driven clock is constructed. |
| **1832** | Charles Babbage develops the principle of the Analytical Engine, which is the world's first computer; it can be programmed to solve a wide variety of logical and computational problems. |
| **1835** | Joseph Henry invents the electrical relay, a means of transmitting electrical impulses over long distances. The relay serves as the basis for the telegraph. |

---

* Adapted from Raymond Kurzweil, *The Age of Intelligent Machines,* Cambridge, Mass.: Massachusetts Institute of Technology, 1990, pp. 465–483.

**1837**    Samuel Finley Breese Morse patents his more practical version of the telegraph, which sends letters in codes consisting of dots and dashes.

**1843**    Ada Lovelace, Lord Byron's only legitimate child and the world's first computer programmer, publishes her own notes with her translation of L. P. Menabrea's paper on Babbage's Analytical Engine.

**1846**    Alexander Bain uses punched paper tape to send telegraph messages, greatly improving the speed of transmission.

**1847**    George Boole publishes his first ideas on symbolic logic. He will develop these ideas into his theory of binary logic and arithmetic—a theory that is still the basis of modern computation.

**1854**    An electric telegraph is installed between Paris and London.

**1855**    William Thomson develops a successful theory concerning the transmission of electrical signals through submarine cables.

**1861**    San Francisco and New York are connected by a telegraph line.

**1864**    Ducos de Harron develops a primitive motion-picture device in France.

**1866**    Cyrus West Field lays a telegraph cable across the Atlantic Ocean.

**1876**    Alexander Graham Bell's telephone receives U.S. Patent 174,465, the most lucrative patent ever granted.

**1879**    G. Frege, one of the founders of modern symbolic language, proposes a notational system for mechanical reasoning. This work is a forerunner to predicate calculus, which will be used for knowledge representation in artificial intelligence.

**1885**    Boston is connected to New York by telephone.

**1886**    Alexander Graham Bell, with a modified version of Thomas Alva Edison's phonograph, uses wax discs for recording sound.

**1888**    William S. Burroughs patents an adding machine. This machine is modified four years later to include subtraction and printing. It is the world's first dependable key-driven calculator and will soon win widespread acceptance.

**1888**    Heinrich Hertz experiments with the transmission of what are now known as radio waves.

**1888**    The first commercial roll-film camera is introduced.

**1890**    Herman Hollerith, incorporating ideas from Jacquard's loom and Babbage's Analytical Engine, patents an electromechanical information machine that uses punched cards. It wins the 1890 U.S. Census competition, with the result that electricity is used for the first time in a major data processing project.

**1894**    Guglielmo Marconi builds his first radio equipment, which rings a bell from 30 feet away.

**1896**    A sound film is first shown before a paying audience in Berlin.

**1896**    Herman Hollerith forms the Tabulating Machine Company, which will become IBM.

**1897**    Alexander Popov, a Russian, uses an antenna to transmit radio waves, and Guglielmo Marconi, an Italian, receives the first patent ever granted for radio. Marconi helps organize a company to market his system.

**1899**    The first recording of sound is made magnetically on wire and on a thin metal strip.

**1900**    Herman Hollerith introduces an automatic card feed into his information machine to process the 1900 census data.

**1900**    The entire civilized world is connected by telegraph, and in the United States there are more than 1.4 million telephones, 8000 registered automobiles, and 24 million electric light bulbs. Edison's promise of "electric bulbs so cheap that only the rich will be able to afford candles" is thus realized. In addition, the Gramophone Company is advertising a choice of five thousand recordings.

**1901**    Marconi, in Newfoundland, receives the first transatlantic telegraphic radio transmission.

**1904**    John Ambrose Fleming files a patent for the first vacuum tube, a diode.

**1906**    Reginald Aubrey Fessenden invents AM radio and transmits by radio waves to wireless operators on U.S. ships off the Atlantic Coast. The transmission includes a Christmas carol, a violin trill, and for the first time the sound of a human voice.

**1907**    Lee De Forest and R. von Lieben invent the amplifier vacuum tube, known as a triode, which greatly improves radio.

| | |
|---|---|
| **1911** | Herman Hollerith's Tabulating Machine Company acquires several other companies and changes its name to Computing-Tabulating-Recording Company (CTR). In 1914 Thomas J. Watson is appointed president. |
| **1913** | Henry Ford introduces the first true assembly-line method of automated production. |
| **1913** | A. Meissner invents a radio transmitter with vacuum tubes. Radio-transmitter triode modulation is introduced the following year, and in 1915 the radio-tube oscillator is introduced. |
| **1921** | Czech dramatist Karel Capek popularizes the term *robot,* a word he coined in 1917 to describe the mechanical people in his science-fiction drama *R.U.R. (Rossum's Universal Robots).* His intelligent machines, intended as servants for their human creators, end up taking over the world and destroying all mankind. |
| **1923** | Vladimir Kosma Zworkin, the father of television, gives the first demonstration of an electronic television-camera tube, using a mechanical transmitting device. He develops the iconoscope, an early type of television system, the following year. |
| **1924** | Thomas J. Watson becomes the chief executive officer of CTR and renames the company International Business Machines (IBM). IBM will become the leader of the modern industry and one of the largest industrial corporations in the world. |
| **1925** | Vannevar Bush and his co-workers develop the first analog computer, a machine designed to solve differential equations. |
| **1926** | The era of talking motion pictures is introduced by *The Jazz Singer,* starring Al Jolson. |
| **1928** | John von Neumann presents the minimax theorem, which will be widely used in game-playing programs. |
| **1928** | Philo T. Farnsworth demonstrates the world's first all-electronic television, and Vladimir Zworkin receives a patent for a color television system. |
| **1929** | FM radio is introduced. |
| **1930** | Vannevar Bush's analog computer, the Differential Analyzer, is built at the Massachusetts Institute of Technology (MIT). It will be used to calculate artillery trajectories during World War II. |
| **1932** | Radio Corporation of America (RCA) demonstrates a television receiver with a cathode-ray picture tube. In 1933 Zworkin produces a cathode-ray tube, called the iconoscope, that makes high-quality television almost a reality. |
| **1937** | Building on the work of Bertrand Russell and Charles Babbage, Alan Turing publishes "On Computable Numbers," his now-celebrated paper introducing the Turing machine, a theoretical model of a computer. |
| **1937** | The Church-Turing thesis, independently developed by Alonzo Church and Alan Turing, states that all problems solvable by a human being are reducible to a set of algorithms, or more simply, that machine intelligence and human intelligence are essentially equivalent. |
| **1940** | John V. Atanasoff and Clifford Berry build an electronic computer known as ABC. This is the first electronic computer, but it is not programmable. |
| **1940** | The 10,000-person British computer war effort known as Ultra creates Robinson, the world's first operational computer. It is based on electromechanical relays and is powerful enough to decode messages from Enigma, the Nazis' first-generation enciphering machine. |
| **1941** | Konrad Zuse, a German, completes the world's first fully programmable digital computer, the Z-3, and hires Arnold Fast, a blind mathematician, to program it. Fast becomes the world's first programmer of an operational programmable computer. |
| **1943** | The Ultra team builds Colossus, a computer that uses electronic tubes 100 to 1000 times faster than the relays used by Robinson. It cracks increasingly complex German codes and contributes to the Allies' winning of World War II. |
| **1944** | Howard Aiken completes the first American programmable computer, the Mark I. It uses punched paper tape for programming and vacuum tubes to calculate problems. |
| **1945** | Konrad Zuse develops Plankalkul, the first high-level language. |
| **1946** | John Tukey first uses the term *bit* for binary digit, the basic unit of data for computers. |
| **1946** | John von Neumann publishes the first modern paper on the stored-program concept and starts computer research at the Institute for Advanced Study in Princeton. |

| | |
|---|---|
| **1946** | John Presper Eckert and John W. Mauchley develop ENIAC, the world's first fully electronic, general-purpose (programmable) digital computer. It is almost 1000 times faster than the Mark I and is used for calculating ballistic-firing tables for the Army. |
| **1946** | Television enters American life even more rapidly than radio did in the 1920s. The percentage of American homes having sets jumps from 0.02% in 1946 to 72% in 1956 and more than 90% by 1983. |
| **1947** | William Bradford Schockley, Walter Hauser Brittain, and John Ardeen invent the transistor, a minute device that functions like a vacuum tube but switches current on and off at much faster speeds. It launches a revolution in microelectronics, bringing down the cost of computers and leading to the development of minicomputers and powerful new mainframe computers. |
| **1949** | Maurice Wilkes, influenced by Eckert and Mauchley, builds EDSAC, the world's first stored-program computer. Eckert and Mauchley's new U.S. company brings out BINAC, the first American stored-program computer, soon after. |
| **1950** | The U.S. census is first handled by a programmable computer, UNIVAC, developed by Eckert and Mauchley. It is the first commercially marketed computer. |
| **1950** | Alan Turing's "Computing Machinery and Intelligence" describes the Turing test, a means for determining whether a machine is intelligent. |
| **1950** | Commercial color television begins in the United States; transcontinental black-and-white television is inaugurated the following year. |
| **1950** | Claude Elwood Shannon writes a proposal for a chess program. |
| **1951** | EDVAC, Eckert and Mauchley's first computer that implements the stored-program concept, is completed at the Moore School at the University of Pennsylvania. |
| **1952** | The CBS television network uses UNIVAC to correctly predict the election of Dwight D. Eisenhower as president of the United States. |
| **1952** | The pocket-size transistor radio is introduced. |
| **1952** | The 701, IBM's first production-line electronic digital computer, is designed by Nathaniel Rochester and marketed for scientific use. |
| **1955** | IBM introduces its first transistor calculator, with 2200 transistors instead of the 1200 vacuum tubes that would otherwise be required. |
| **1955** | The first design is created for a robot-like machine for industrial use in the United States. |
| **1955** | Allen Newell, J. C. Shaw, and Herbert Simon develop IPL-II, the first artificial intelligence (AI) language. |
| **1955** | The beginning space program and the military in the United States, recognizing the need for computers powerful enough to steer rockets to the moon and missiles through the stratosphere, fund major research projects. |
| **1956** | The first transatlantic telephone cable begins to operate. |
| **1956** | FORTRAN, the first scientific computer programming language, is invented by John Backus and a team at IBM. |
| **1956** | MANIAC I, the first computer program to beat a human being in a chess game, is developed by Stanislaw Ulam. |
| **1956** | Artificial intelligence is formally named at a computer conference at Dartmouth College. |
| **1958** | Jack St. Clair Kilby invents the first integrated circuit. |
| **1958** | John McCarthy introduces LISP, an early (and still widely used) AI language. |
| **1958–1959** | Jack Kilby and Robert Noyce independently develop the chip, which leads to much cheaper and smaller computers. |
| **1959** | Dartmouth's Thomas Kurtz and John Kemeny find an alternative to batch processing: timesharing. |
| **1959** | Grace Murray Hopper, one of the first programmers of the Mark I, develops COBOL, a computer language designed for business use. |
| **1960** | About 6000 computers are in operation in the United States. |
| **1962** | A U.S. company markets the world's first industrial robots. |
| **1962** | The first department of computer science offering a Ph.D. is established at Purdue University. |

| 1962 | D. Murphy and Richard Greenblatt develop the TECO text editor, one of the first word processing systems, for use on the PDP1 computer at MIT. |
|---|---|
| 1963 | AI researchers of the 1960s, noting the similarity between human and computer languages, adopt the goal of parsing natural-language sentences. Susumo Kuno's parsing system reveals the great extent of syntactic and semantic ambiguity in the English language. Kuno's system is tested on the sentence "Time flies like an arrow." |
| 1963 | John McCarthy founds the Artificial Intelligence Laboratory at Stanford University. |
| 1964 | IBM solidifies its leadership of the computer industry with the introduction of its 360 series. |
| 1964 | Daniel Borrow completes his doctoral work on Student, a natural-language program that can solve high-school-level word problems in algebra. |
| 1964 | Gordon Moore, one of the founders of Fairchild Semiconductor Corporation, predicts that integrated circuits will double in complexity each year. His statement will become known as Moore's law and will prove true for decades to come. |
| 1964 | Marshall McLuhan's *Understanding Media* foresees electronic media, especially television, as creating a "global village" in which "the medium is the message." |
| 1965 | John G. Kemeny develops the programming language BASIC at Dartmouth College. |
| 1965 | Raj Reddy founds the Robotics Institute at Carnegie-Mellon University. The institute becomes a leading research center for AI. |
| 1965 | The DENDRAL project begins at Stanford University, headed by Bruce Buchanan, Edward Feigenbaum, and Nobel laureate Joshua Lederberg. Its purpose is to experiment on knowledge as the primary means of producing problem-solving behavior. The first expert system, DENDRAL, embodies extensive knowledge of molecular-structure analysis. Follow-up work, carried out through the early 1970s, produces Meta-DENDRAL, a learning program that automatically devises new rules for DENDRAL. |
| Mid-1960s | Computers are beginning to be widely used in the criminal justice system. |
| Mid-1960s | Scientific and professional knowledge is beginning to be codified in a machine-readable form. |
| 1967 | Seymour Papert and his associates at MIT begin working on LOGO, an education-oriented programming language that will be widely used by children. |
| 1967 | The software business is born when IBM announces it will no longer sell software and hardware in a single unit. |
| 1968 | The film *2001: A Space Odyssey,* by Arthur C. Clarke and Stanley Kubrick, presents HAL, a computer that can see, speak, hear, and think like its human colleagues aboard a spaceship. |
| 1968 | The Intel Corp. is founded. Intel will grow to become the dominant manufacturer of microprocessors in the U.S. computer industry. |
| 1970 | The floppy disk is introduced for storing data in computers. |
| 1970 | Harry Pople and Jack Myers of the University of Pittsburgh begin work on Internist, a system that aids physicians in the diagnosis of a wide range of human diseases. |
| 1971 | Kenneth Colby, Sylvia Weber, and F. D. Hilf present a report on PARRY, a program simulating a paranoid person, in a paper entitled "Artificial Paranoia." The program is so convincing that clinical psychiatrists cannot distinguish its behavior from that of a human paranoid person. |
| 1971 | The first microprocessor is introduced in the United States. |
| 1971 | The first pocket calculator is introduced. It can add, subtract, multiply, and divide. |
| 1971 | Direct telephone dialing on a regular basis begins between parts of the United States and Europe. |
| 1971 | Daniel Bricklin and Software Arts, Inc. release the first electronic spreadsheet for PCs, VisiCalc. The program helps launch the personal computing era by showing the convenience with which information can be handled on a desktop. |
| 1973 | Alain Colmerauer presents an outline of PROLOG, a logic-programming language. The language will become enormously popular and will be adopted for use in the Japanese Fifth-Generation Program. |
| 1974 | The first computer-controlled industrial robot is developed. |

| | |
|---|---|
| **1974** | Edward Shortliffe completes his doctoral dissertation on MYCIN, an expert system designed to help medical practitioners prescribe an appropriate antibiotic by determining the precise identity of a blood infection. Work to augment this program with other important systems, notably TEIRESIAS and EMYCIN, will continue through the early 1980s. TEIRESIAS will be developed in 1976 by Randall Davis to serve as a powerful information-structuring tool for knowledge engineers. EMYCIN, by William van Melle, will represent the skeletal structure of inferences. |
| **1974** | The SUMEX-AIM computer communications network is established to promote the development of applications of artificial intelligence to medicine. |
| **1975** | Benoit Mandelbrot writes "Les objets fractals: Forme, hasard, et dimension," his first long essay on fractal geometry, a branch of mathematics that he developed. Fractal forms will be widely used to model chaotic phenomena in nature and to generate realistic computer images of naturally occurring objects. |
| **1975** | Medicine is becoming an important area of applications for AI research. Four major medical expert systems have been developed by now: PIP, CASNET, MYCIN, and Internist. |
| **1975** | The Defense Advanced Research Programs Agency launches its Image Understanding Program to stimulate research in the area of machine vision. |
| **1975** | More than 5000 microcomputers are sold in the United States, and the first personal computer, with 256 bytes of memory, is introduced. |
| **1970s** | The role of knowledge in intelligent behavior is now a major focus of AI research. Bruce Buchanan and Edward Feigenbaum of Stanford University pioneer knowledge engineering. |
| **1976** | Kurzweil Computer Products introduces the Kurzweil Reading Machine, which reads aloud any printed text that is presented to it. Based on omnifont character-recognition technology, it is intended to be a sensory aid for the blind. |
| **1976–1977** | Lynn Conway and Carver Mead collaborate on a collection of principles for VLSI design. Their classic textbook *Introduction to VLSI Design* is published in 1980. VLSI circuits will form the basis of the fourth generation of computers. |
| **1977** | Steven Jobs and Stephen Wozniak design and build the Apple computer. |
| **1977** | Voyagers 1 and 2 are launched and radio back billions of bytes of computerized data about new discoveries as they explore the outer planets of our solar system. |
| **1977** | The Apple II, the first personal computer to be sold in assembled form, is successfully marketed. |
| **1978** | Total computer units in the United States exceed a half million. |
| **1979** | In a landmark study published in the *Journal of the American Medical Association* by nine researchers, the performance of MYCIN is compared with that of doctors on 10 test cases of meningitis. MYCIN does at least as well as the medical experts. The potential of expert systems in medicine becomes widely recognized. |
| **1979** | Ada, a computer language developed for use by the armed forces, is named for Ada Lovelace. |
| **1979** | Pac Man and other early computerized video games appear. |
| **1979** | Hayes markets its first modem, which sets the industry standard for modems in years to come. |
| **Early 1980s** | Second-generation robots arrive with the ability to precisely effect movements with five or six degrees of freedom. They are used for industrial welding and spray painting. |
| **Early 1980s** | The MYCIN project produces NeoMYCIN and ONCOCIN, expert systems that incorporate hierarchical knowledge bases. They are more flexible than MYCIN. |
| **1981** | Desktop publishing takes root when Xerox brings out its Star Computer. However, it will not become popular until Apple's Laserwriter comes on the market in 1985. Desktop publishing provides writers and artists an inexpensive and efficient way to compose and print large documents. |
| **1981** | IBM introduces its Personal Computer (PC). |
| **1982** | Compact-disk players are marketed for the first time. |
| **1982** | A million-dollar advertising campaign introduces Mitch Kapor's Lotus 1-2-3, an enormously popular spreadsheet program. |

| | |
|---|---|
| **1982** | With over 100,000 associations between symptoms and diseases covering 70% of all the knowledge in the field, CADUCEUS, an improvement on the Internist expert system, is developed for internal medicine by Harry Pople and Jack Myers at the University of Pittsburgh. Tested against cases from the *New England Journal of Medicine,* it proves more accurate than humans in a wide range of categories. |
| **1983** | Six million personal computers are sold in the United States. |
| **1984** | Apple Computer, Inc., introduces the Macintosh. |
| **1984** | RACTER, created by William Chamberlain, is the first computer program to author a book. |
| **1984** | Waseda University in Tokyo completes Wabot-2, a 200-pound robot that reads sheet music through its camera eye and plays the organ with its ten fingers and two feet. |
| **1984** | Optical disks for the storage of computer data are introduced, and IBM brings out a mega-RAM memory chip with four times the memory of earlier chips. |
| **1984** | Hewlett-Packard brings high-quality printing to PCs with its LaserJet laser printer. |
| **1985** | The MIT Media Laboratory creates the first three-dimensional holographic image to be generated entirely by computer. |
| **1985** | Aldus Corp. introduces PageMaker for the Macintosh, the first desktop publishing software. |
| **Mid 1980s** | Third-generation robots arrive with limited intelligence and some vision and tactile senses. |
| **1986** | Dallas police use a robot to break into an apartment. The fugitive runs out in fright and surrenders. |
| **1986** | Electronic keyboards account for 55.2% of the American musical keyboard market, up from 9.5% in 1980. This trend is expected to continue until the market is almost all electronic. |
| **1986** | Technology for optical character recognition represents a $100-million-dollar industry that is expected to grow to several hundred million by 1990. |
| **1986** | New medical imaging systems are creating a mini-revolution. Doctors can now make accurate judgments based on views of areas inside our bodies and brains. |
| **1986** | Using image processing and pattern recognition, Lillian Schwartz comes up with an answer to a 500-year-old question: Who was the Mona Lisa? Her conclusion: Leonardo da Vinci himself. |
| **1986** | Russell Anderson's doctoral work at the University of Pennsylvania is a robotic ping-pong player that wins against human beings. |
| **1986** | The best computer chess players are now competing successfully at the senior master level, with HiTech, the leading chess machine, analyzing 200,000 board positions per second. |
| **1987** | Computerized trading helps push New York Stock Exchange (NYSE) stocks to their greatest single-day loss. |
| **1987** | Current speech systems can provide any one of the following: a large vocabulary, continuous speech recognition, or speaker independence. |
| **1987** | Japan develops the Automated Fingerprint Identification System (AFIS), which enables U.S. law enforcement agencies to rapidly track and identify suspects. |
| **1987** | There are now 1900 working expert systems, 1200 more than last year. The most popular area of application is finance, followed by manufacturing control and fault diagnosis. |
| **1988** | Computer memory today costs only $10^{-8}$ of what it did in 1950. |
| **1988** | The population of industrial robots has increased from a few hundred in 1970 to several hundred thousand, most of them in Japan. |
| **1988** | In the U.S. 4,700,000 microcomputers, 120,000 minicomputers, and 11,500 mainframes are sold in this year. |
| **1988** | W. Daniel Hillis's Connection Machine is capable of 65,536 computations at the same time. |
| **1988** | Warsaw Pact forces are at least a decade behind NATO forces in artificial intelligence and other computer technologies. |

| | |
|---|---|
| **1989** | Computational power per unit of cost has roughly doubled every 18 to 24 months for the past 40 years. |
| **1989** | The trend from analog to digital continues to revolutionize a growing number of industries. |
| **Late 1980s** | The core avionics of a typical fighter aircraft uses 200,000 lines of software. The figure is expected to grow to about 1 million in the 1990s. The U.S. military as a whole uses about 100 million lines of software (and is expected to use 200 million in 1993). Software quality becomes an urgent issue that planners are beginning to address. |
| **Late 1980s** | The computer is being recognized as a powerful tool for artistic expression. |
| **Early 1990s** | A profound change in military strategy arrives. The more developed nations increasingly rely on "smart weapons," which incorporate electronic copilots; pattern recognition techniques; and advanced technologies for tracking, identification, and destruction. |
| **Early 1990s** | Continuous speech systems can handle large vocabularies for specific tasks. |
| **Early 1990s** | Computer processors operate at speeds of 100 mips. |
| **1990s** | Significant progress is made toward an intelligent assistant, a decision-support system capable of a wide variety of administrative and information-gathering tasks. The system can, for example, prepare a feasibility report on a project proposal after accessing several databases and "talking" to human experts. |
| **1990s** | Reliable person identification, using pattern-recognition techniques applied to visual and speech patterns, replaces locks and keys in many instances. |
| **Late 1990s** | An increasing number of documents never exist on paper because they incorporate information in the form of audio and video pieces. |
| **Late 1990s** | Media technology is capable of producing computer-generated personalities, intelligent image systems with some human characteristics. |
| **1999** | The several-hundred-billion-dollar computer and information-processing market is largely intelligent by 1990 standards. |
| **2000** | Three-dimensional chips and smaller component geometries contribute to a multi-thousandfold improvement in computer power (compared to that of a decade earlier). |
| **2000** | Chips with more than a billion components appear. |
| **2000** | The world chess champion is a computer. |
| **Early 2000s** | Translating telephones allow two people across the globe to speak to each other even if they do not speak the same language. |
| **Early 2000s** | Speech-to-text machines translate speech into a visual display for the deaf. |
| **Early 2000s** | Exoskeletal robotic prosthetic aids enable paraplegic persons to walk and climb stairs. |
| **Early 2000s** | Telephones are answered by an intelligent telephone-answering machine that converses with the calling party to determine the nature and priority of the call. |
| **Early 2000s** | The cybernetic chauffeur, installed in one's car, communicates with other cars and sensors on roads. In this way it successfully drives and navigates from one point to another. |
| **Early 21st century** | Computers dominate the educational environment. Courseware is intelligent enough to understand and correct the inaccuracies in the conceptual model of a student. Media technology allows students to interact with simulations of the very systems and personalities they are studying. |
| **Early 21st century** | The entire production sector of society is operated by a small number of technicians and professionals. Individual customization of products is common. |
| **Early 21st century** | Drugs are designed and tested on human biochemical simulators. |
| **Early 21st century** | Seeing machines for the blind provide both reading and navigation functions. |
| **2010** | A personal computer has the ability to answer a large variety of queries, because it will know where to find knowledge. Communications technologies allow it to access many sources of knowledge by wireless communication. |
| **2020–2050** | A phone call, which includes highly realistic three-dimensional holographic moving images, is like visiting with the person called. |
| **2020–2070** | A computer passes the Turing test, which indicates human-level intelligence. |

# Glossary

**access time** Average time to locate instructions or data from **secondary (auxiliary) storage** device and transfer to computer's **main memory (RAM).**

**active-matrix display** Type of **flat-panel display** in which each pixel on the screen is controlled by its own transistor; active-matrix screens are brighter and sharper than **passive-matrix** screens.

**Ada** High-level programming language developed by Department of Defense for military systems; supports real-time procedures, automatic error recovery, and flexible input and output operations.

**addressing scheme** Computer design feature that determines amount of main memory CPU can control at any one time.

**algorithm** Well-defined rules or step-by-step procedures for solving a problem; may include diagrams.

**alphanumeric data** Data that can include letters, digits, and special symbols such as punctuation marks; it cannot be mathematically manipulated. *Compare* **numeric data.**

**American National Standards Institute (ANSI)** Organization that develops standards for all high-level programming languages.

**American Standard Code for Information Interchange (ASCII)** Pronounced "*as*-key." Standard 8-bit code used in data communications, microcomputers, and many minicomputers; 128 valid characters can be formulated with ASCII.

**amplitude** Size of voltage or magnitude of wave form in data or voice transmission.

**analog signal** Signal that is continuously varying and represents a range of frequencies; the traditional telephone system is based on analog signals. *See* **digital signal.**

**analytical graphics** Graphical forms used to make numerical data easier to understand; the most common analytical graphics forms are bar chart, line chart, pie chart. Analytical graphics are usually spreadsheet-based; that is, they are created using a **spreadsheet** software package. *Compare* **presentation graphics.**

**ANSI** *See* **American National Standards Institute.**

**antivirus software** Utility program that scans disks and detects viruses before they can cause damage.

**applications generator** Software system that generates computer programs in response to user's needs. The system consists of precoded modules that perform various functions. The user selects the functions he or she needs, and the applications generator determines how to perform the tasks and produces the necessary instructions for the software program.

**applications software** Program or programs designed to carry out a specific task to satisfy a user's specific needs—for example, calculate payroll and print out checks. *Compare* **systems software.**

**arithmetic/logic unit (ALU)** Part of the computer's central processing unit (CPU) that performs all arithmetic and logical (comparison) functions.

**arithmetic operations** The operations of addition, subtraction, multiplication, division, and exponentiation.

**artificial intelligence (AI)** Field of study concerned with using computer hardware and software to simulate human thought processes such as imagination and intuition.

**ASCII** *See* **American Standard Code for Information Interchange.**

**assembler** Software that translates **assembly language** into **machine language.**

**assembly language** Language using low-level symbolic abbreviations to represent machine-language instructions. Assembly language is specific to different makes and models of computers. Assembly languages are also known as **second-generation languages.** *Compare* **machine language; procedural language.**

**asynchronous transmission** In data communications, sending one character or **byte** (eight bits) at a time, each byte preceded by a "start" bit and followed by one or two "stop" bits and an error check bit (or parity bit). An inexpensive and widely used but relatively slow form of data communication. Also called *start-stop transmission.*

**audio input device** Device that records or plays analog sound and translates it into digital signals for storage and processing. Examples are audio boards and MIDI boards.

**automated teller machine (ATM)** *See* **financial transaction terminal.**

**auxiliary storage** *See* **secondary storage.**

**backup** Tape or diskette that is a duplicate (copy) of another form of storage.

**backup file** Copy of file made to ensure data and programs are preserved if original file is damaged or destroyed.

**band printer** *See* **line printer.**

**bandwidth** In data transmission, the difference between the highest and lowest **frequencies**—that is, the range of frequencies. Data may be sent on several frequencies within one bandwidth. Different types of transmission equipment—for example, microwave and radio—operate within different bandwidths.

**bar code** Code made up of a series of variable-width vertical lines that can be read by a **bar-code reader.** Bar codes are used to identify retail sales items, such as groceries, books, and clothing.

**bar code reader** Input scanning device for reading the light and dark bar codes (stripes) on products that represent their inventory stock numbers or product numbers. The scanner analyzes the bars for width and spacing and translates this data into electrical signals for the computer. Two types of scanners are the handheld wand and the countertop scanner.

**BASIC (Beginner's All-Purpose Symbolic Instruction Code)** High-level (procedural) interactive programming language designed to teach users how to program on microcomputers.

**batch** Group of documents or transactions intended for input to the computer all at once, in a controlled fashion.

**batch processing** Method of processing whereby data is collected over several days or weeks and then processed all at one time, as a batch.

**belt printer** *See* **line printer.**

**binary code** Scheme for encoding data using binary digits.

**binary digit (bit)** In binary notation, either 1 or 0. The digit 1 represents an "on" electrical (or magnetic) state; the digit 0 represents an "off" state. A group of adjacent bits (usually eight bits) constitutes a **byte,** or single character.

**binary system** Number system with only two digits: 0 and 1. *See also* **binary digit.**

**biometrics** In computer security, pertains to the use of specific human characteristics that reflect unique personal attributes—such as fingerprints, eye blood vessel prints, voice prints, lip prints—to identify people who are allowed access to a computer system.

**bit** *See* **binary digit.**

**bit-mapped display (graphics)** CRT screen display system in which each possible dot is controlled by a single character in memory. Also known as *dot-addressable* or *all-points addressable* display.

**bits per second** Unit used to measure **modem** transmission speeds—for example, some modems operate at 28,800 bps.

**boot** To turn on the computer and start the automatic loading of software instructions.

**bpi** Bits per inch; *see* **recording density.**

**bps** *See* **bits per second.**

**bridge** Communications interface (hardware and software) that allows similar networks to communicate. *Compare* **gateway.**

**G.1**

**bug**   Programming error.

**bundled**   Components of a system are sold together for a single price, as with software **suites**. *Compare* **unbundled.**

**bus**   An "electronic highway" or communications path linking several devices and parts of the **central processing unit (CPU).**

**bus network**   Communications **network** in which all messages are transmitted to the entire network (whose ends are not connected to form a circle), traveling from the sender in both directions along the cable until a message reaches the computer for which it was intended. A central computer is not required to control activity.

**byte**   A group of contiguous (adjacent) bits, usually 8 bits, that form a character.

**C**   **High-level programming language** introduced by Bell Laboratories for use in writing systems software. Though complex to learn, C can be used on a variety of machines.

**cache memory**   Special high-speed memory area that the CPU can quickly access; it comprises a small area of RAM created in addition to the computer's main memory (RAM); a copy of the most frequently used data and instructions is kept in the cache so the CPU can look in the cache first—which makes the computer run faster. Cache memory is usually located right on the 386 or 486 microprocessor chip.

**call-back system**   In some security systems, the user calls the computer system, punches in a password, and hangs up. The computer then calls back on a preauthorized line.

**card dialer**   *See* **Touch-Tone device.**

**card reader**   Device that translates the holes in punched cards into electrical signals, which are input to the computer; is also another name for a **Touch-Tone device,** also known as a *card dialer.*

**cartridge-tape unit**   Device that reads **magnetic tape** in cassette form; often used as alternative type of **secondary storage** to **hard disk** and as backup storage for hard disks. The most popular tape cartridges use 1/4-inch tape in reels up to 1,000 feet long. *See also* **tape streamers.**

**cathode-ray tube (CRT)**   Electronic display screen used with computer terminals and desktop PCs to display data and information; also called *video display screen*. *Compare* **flat-panel display.**

**CD-ROM**   *See* **compact disk/read-only memory.**

**centralized computer facility**   A single computer department in a company established to provide sole data processing support to all other departments.

**central processing unit (CPU)**   The "brain" of the computer; the part of the computer composed of electrical circuitry directing most of the computer system's activities. The CPU consists of the **control unit** and the **arithmetic/logic unit (ALU),** connected by a **bus.**

**chain printer**   *See* **line printer.**

**character**   *See* **byte.**

**character box**   Fixed location on a video display screen where a standard character can be placed. Most screens can display 80 characters of data horizontally and 25 lines vertically, or 2,000 character boxes (called *character-mapped display*)—the number the electron gun can target. The more **pixels** that fit into a character box, the higher the resolution of the resulting image. Each character box is "drawn" according to a prerecorded template stored in **read-only memory (ROM).**

**character-mapped display**   *See* **character box.**

**characters per second (cps)**   Measure of speed of printers and other output devices.

**check bit**   *See* **parity bit.**

**chief information officer (CIO)**

**child record**   In hierarchical database, record subordinate to parent record. *Compare* **parent record.**

**chip**   Integrated circuit made of a semiconductor (silicon) and containing electronic components; can be as little as 1/4-inch square.

**CISC**   *See* **complex instruction set computing.**

**client-server LAN**   **Local area network** consisting of requesting microcomputers (clients) and supplying devices that provide a service (servers).

**clock**   Device in **CPU** that synchronizes all operations in a **machine cycle**; clock speed is measured in **megahertz.**

**clone**   Product or idea that is a duplicate or copy of another; used to refer to a microcomputer that closely resembles the operation of an IBM microcomputer

**closed architecture**   Attribute of computers that cannot be upgraded by the use of expansion cards; the user cannot open the **system unit**. *Compare* **open architecture.**

**coaxial cable**   Type of thickly insulated copper wire for carrying large volumes of data—80 times more than **twisted-pair cable.** Often used in local networks connecting computers in a limited geographic area.

**COBOL (COmmon Business Oriented Language)**   **High-level programming language** for business. Its commands and **syntax** use common human language (for example, English). COBOL is most appropriate for business applications.

**codec techniques**   Refers to compression/decompression techniques; compression (software-controlled) removes redundant data elements so that files take up less storage. Decompression returns the data to a state appropriate for display or other output.

**code-oriented**   Refers to **desktop publishing**; **page description software** that displays all the formatting codes on the screen, thus preventing the user from seeing what the page will actually look like when it is printed out. *Compare* **WYSIWYG.**

**color display screen**   Display screen that can display up to 16.7 million colors, depending on the type of screen and adapter board. *See also* **CGA, VGA, SVGA, XGA.**

**color dot-matrix printer**   **Dot-matrix printer** that uses multicolored ribbons to produce color output.

**color graphics adapter (CGA)**   Expansion card plugged into **expansion slot** in **system cabinet** that allows compatible **monitor** to display **bit-mapped graphics;** must be used with appropriate software; monitor displays four colors as well as monochrome images.

**common carrier**   *See* **public network.**

**communications**   Electronic transfer of information from one location to another.

**communications software**   Programs that allow users to access software and data from a computer in a remote location and to transmit data to a computer in a remote location.

**compact disk (CD)**   Optical disk that stores laser-recorded data in digital form; *CD* usually refers to an audio disk.

**compact disk/read-only memory (CD-ROM)**   Optical disk whose data is laser-recorded by the disk manufacturer; the user cannot change it or write on the disk—the user can only "read" the data. *Compare* **erasable optical disk; write once, read many (WORM).**

**company database (shared database)**   Database shared by the users of one company in one location.

**compatibility**   Capability of operating together; can refer to different models of computers, different types of hardware peripherals, and various systems and applications software—not all software is compatible with all computers and other types of hardware, and not all types of hardware are compatible with one another. Incompatibility can often be overcome with the use of **modems** and/or special hardware and software.

**compiler**   Computer program that translates a **high-level language** program (**source code**) into **machine-language** instructions (**object code**) all at once. *Compare* **interpreter.**

**complex instruction set computing (CISC)** Microprocessor chip design used in most of today's **microprocessor chips.** *Compare* **reduced instruction set computing (RISC).**

**compression** *See* **codec techniques.**

**computer** Data processing device made up of electronic and electromechanical components that can perform computations, including arithmetic and logical operations. Also known as **hardware.** By itself, a computer has no intelligence.

**computer-aided design (CAD)** The use of a computer and special graphics software to design products.

**computer-aided engineering (CAE)** The use of a computer and special software to simulate situations that test product designs.

**computer-aided manufacturing (CAM)** The use of computers to control manufacturing equipment; includes **robots.**

**computer-aided software engineering (CASE)** Software tools used to automate systems design, development, and documentation.

**computer-based information system** Computer system for collecting data, processing it into information, and storing the information for future reference and output. The system consists of five components: hardware, software, data/information, procedures, and people. It has four major phases of activity: input, processing, output, and storage.

**computer generation** One of four phases of computer development; the term is used to delineate major technological developments in hardware and software.

**computer graphics** *See* **analytical graphics; presentation graphics.**

**computer output microfilm/microfiche (COM) system** Equipment that captures computer output on microfilm or microfiche.

**computer professional** Person with formal education in technical aspects of computers—for example, a programmer, a systems analyst, or a computer operator.

**computer system** System of hardware, software, procedures, and people for converting data into information.

**concentrator** Communications device that multiplexes (combines) low-speed communications lines onto one high-speed line; it is more "intelligent" than a **multiplexer** because it can store communications for later transmission.

**connectivity** When one computer is set up to communicate with another computer system, connectivity becomes the sixth system element, after hardware, software, data/information, procedures, and people; it describes the manner in which the systems are connected.

**connectivity diagram** Chart used in information systems design that identifies parts of a network and shows how they will be connected.

**controller** Device that allows multiple terminals and printers to share a communications link but that also controls and routes transmissions and performs error checks and other functions; used in place of a **multiplexer.**

**controller card** Circuit board that allows the **CPU** to work with the computer's various peripheral devices.

**control program** *See* **supervisor.**

**control (logic) structure** Used in structured programming to solve problems in programming logic. There are three control structures: **sequence, selection** (if-then-else), and **iteration** (or looping; do-while).

**control unit** Part of the **CPU** that reads, interprets, and sees to the execution of software instructions.

**conventional memory** The first 640 K of RAM (main memory). *Compare* **expanded memory, extended memory, upper memory.**

**coprocessor chip** Special integrated circuit designed to speed up numeric processing. It can be added to a computer after manufacture.

**cps** *See* **characters per second.**

**CPU** *See* **central processing unit.**

**cracker** A programmer who gains access to a system without authorization.

**CRT** *See* **cathode-ray tube.**

**cursor** Indicator on video display screen that shows where data will be entered next.

**cursor-movement keys** Computer keyboard keys, usually marked with arrows, that are used to move the **cursor** around the display screen.

**custom software** Software created specially for the purchaser. *Compare* **off-the-shelf software.**

**cylinder** All the tracks in a disk pack with the same **track** number, lined up, one above the other. The **read/write heads** in a disk pack move together and so are always on the same cylinder at the same time.

**daisy wheel printer** **Impact printer** with plastic or metal disk with typeface impressions of characters on outside tips of spokes; the print character is forced against ribbon and paper.

**data** Raw, unevaluated facts, concepts, or instructions; after processing, data becomes **information.**

**data access area** Exposed part of a **disk,** through which the **read/write head** inside the disk drive "reads" and "writes" data from and to a disk.

**database** Large group of stored, integrated (cross-referenced) data that can be retrieved and manipulated to produce information.

**database administrator (DBA)** Person who coordinates all related activities and needs for a corporation's **database.** A DBA has six major responsibilities: (1) database implementation, (2) coordination with user, (3) backup, (4) recovery, (5) performance monitoring, and (6) system security.

**database management system (DBMS) software (database manager)** Comprehensive software tool that allows users to create, maintain, and manipulate an integrated base of business data to produce relevant management information. A DBMS represents the interface between the user and the computer's **operating system** and **database;** allows storage of large amounts of data that can be easily cross-indexed, retrieved, and manipulated to produce information for management reports.

**data bus** Electronic communication link that carries data between components of the computer system.

**data compression** *See* **codec techniques.**

**data dictionary** Reference **file** in a **DBMS** that stores information about data and information that is essential to the management of that data and information as a resource.

**data disk** Diskette that holds data, not programs.

**data file** *See* **file.**

**data flow diagram** Graphic representation of flow of data through a system; standard **ANSI** symbols are used to represent various activities such as input and processing.

**data independence** Attribute of data that is stored independent of applications programs being used, so that it is easy to access and change.

**data integrity** Attribute of data that describes its accuracy, reliability, and timeliness; that is, if data has integrity, then it is accurate, reliable, and timely.

**data (information) processing** Operations for refining, summarizing, categorizing, and otherwise manipulating data into a useful form for decision making.

**data manipulation language (DML)** Program that is part of **DBMS** software and that effects input to and output from the **database** files; the technical instructions the make up the input/output routines in the DBMS.

**data processing** The computer-based manipulation of raw data to produce useful information; includes such processes as summarizing, classifying, refining, and comparing.

**data redundancy**  Attribute of data that describes how often the same data appears in different files, often in different formats; a high degree of data redundancy makes updating files difficult.

**data storage hierarchy**  The levels of data stored in a computer file: (1) **files** (broadest level), (2) **records,** (3) **fields,** (4) **bytes,** and (5) **bits** (narrowest level).

**data transfer rate**  Time required to transfer data from disk into a computer's **main memory (RAM).**

**DBMS**  *See* **database management system software.**

**debug**  To detect, locate, and remove all errors in a computer program.

**decentralized computer facility**  Separate computer facilities, established to service the needs of each major department or unit in an organization.

**decision table**  Modeling tool used by systems analysts that shows the rules that apply when certain conditions occur.

**decision support system (DSS)**  A computer-based information system for assisting managers (usually high-level managers) in planning and decision making. A DSS may use **database management systems, query languages,** financial modeling or **spreadsheet** programs, statistical analysis programs, **report generators,** and/or **graphics** programs o provide information. A DSS may be general or institutional.

**decision table**  A chart that lists all contingencies to be considered in the description of a problem, with corresponding actions to be taken; sometimes used instead of flowcharts to describe operations of a program.

**dedicated fax machine**  *See* **fax machine.**

**dedicated line**  Communication line created or leased by a company for its own transmission purposes. *See also* **point-to-point line.**

**default disk drive**  The disk drive that is automatically affected by commands unless the user specifies another drive.

**demodulation**  Process of using communications hardware to convert **analog signals** sent over a telephone line into **digital signals** so that they can be processed by a receiving computer.

**desk checking**  Proofreading a printout of a newly written program; part of testing new programs.

**desktop accessory**  Software package that provides an electronic version of office tools such as calendar, clock, card file, calculator, notepad.

**desktop computer**  *See* **microcomputer.**

**desktop publishing software**  Programs that enable user to use a **microcomputer, scanners,** and a desktop-sized **laser printer** to combine files created by different software applications packages to produce high-quality publications.

**desktop terminal**  A **keyboard** and a **video display screen** connected to a central computer but fitting on top of the user's desk.

**detail report**  Computer-produced report for **operating** (lower-level) **management** that contains specific information about routine activities; such reports are highly structured and their form is predetermined.

**dialog box**  Interactive message box that appears on the computer screen and that contains a set of choices or questions for the user; appears when the executing program needs to collect information from the user.

**digital**  Refers to communications signals or information that is represented in a binary (two-state) way. *See also* **binary system.**

**digital convergence**  *See* **information superhighway.**

**digital signal**  Signal that is discontinuous and discrete; it consists of bursts that form a transmission pattern. Computers communicate with each other in streams of bits transmitted as digital (binary) signals—a series of on and off electrical pulses. *See* **analog signal.**

**digital signature**  String of characters and numbers that a user signs to an electronic document being sent by his or her computer. The receiving computer performs mathematical calculations on the string to verify its validity.

**digitizer (digitizing tablet)**  Input device that can be moved over a drawing or a photograph thereby converting the picture to computerized data that can be stored, printed out, or shown on a video display screen.

**direct access storage and retrieval**  Situation in which records are stored and retrieved in any order. The computer can go directly to the desired data. Also called *random access. Compare* **sequential storage.**

**direct-connect modem**  Modem that directly connects computer to telephone line. An internal direct-connect modem is placed inside the computer, an external direct-connect modem is outside the computer.

**direct entry**  Data input that uses nonkeyboard input devices such as **card readers** and **scanning devices.** *Compare* **keyboard entry.**

**direct implementation**  One of four approaches to systems implementation; the change is made all at once, with the old system being halted at the same time the new system is activated. *Compare* **parallel implementation; phased implementation; pilot implementation.**

**direct (random) file organization**  **Secondary storage** method whereby data is stored in no particular sequence; data is accessed according to **key fields.** *Compare* **sequential file organization.**

**dirty data**  Data that is incomplete, outdated, or otherwise inaccurate.

**disaster-recovery plan**  Method of restoring information processing operations that have been halted by destruction or accident.

**disk**  A revolving platter on which data and programs are stored in the form of spots representing electrical "on" and "off" states; direct access storage device.

**disk cartridge**  Form of **secondary storage** consisting of a 5¼- or 3½-inch cartridge containing one or two platters and enclosed in a hard plastic case; the cartridge is inserted into the disk drive much like a music tape cassette.

**disk drive**  Device into which a **diskette** (floppy disk), **hard disk,** or **disk pack** is placed for storing and retrieving data.

**disk drive gate**  Door of disk drive, which must be closed for the read/write operation to be performed. (Not all computers' disk drives have gates—for example, the Apple Macintosh.)

**diskette**  Thin plastic (Mylar) disk enclosed in paper or plastic that can be magnetically encoded with data; originally 8 inches in diameter, standard diskettes are now 5¼ or 3½ inches. (Diskettes used to be known as *floppy disks,* but now some of them are covered by rigid plastic and are no longer "floppy."); direct access storage device. (3½-inch diskettes are now much more common than 5¼-inch diskettes.)

**disk operating system (DOS)**  **Systems software** for microcomputers; Microsoft's **MS-DOS** and IBM's **PC-DOS** have become the industry standard for IBM PC microcomputers; **OS/2** and **Warp** are used on IBM's PS/2 Series microcomputers; the **Macintosh operating system** and **System 7** are used on Apple microcomputers; **Windows NT** and **Windows 95** are used on newer IBM-type microcomputers; **Unix** is used on larger machines. These disk operating systems are not generally mutually compatible.

**distributed computer facility**  **Centralized computer facility** and **decentralized computer facility** combined; users have own computer equipment, but some computer **terminals** are connected to a bigger computer in a remote location.

**distributed database**  Database shared by the users of one company, which owns the database, but the data is stored in several locations linked by a variety of communications networks.

**documentation**  Written description of a system's or a software package's parts and procedures; can come in the form of a user's manual that tells the user how to operate a piece of hardware or run a particular software program, or it can be a large collection of volumes and printouts to be used by programmers and computer operators.

**DOS** *See* **disk operating system.**

**dot-matrix printer Impact printer** using pin-like hammers to strike a ribbon against paper in computer-determined patterns of dots, making possible a variety of type styles and graphics.

**dot pitch** Refers to the amount of space between **pixels;** the closer the dots, the crisper the image.

**double-density** *See* **recording density.**

**double-sided disk** Disk(ette) that stores data on both sides.

**double-sided disk drive** Disk drive with **read/write heads** for both top and bottom surfaces of a disk.

**do while Pseudocode** logic statement; directs the computer to repeat an activity as long as a particular condition exists. *See also* **iteration.**

**drive A (A:)** Designation for the first **disk(ette) drive** in a microcomputer; the program diskette is usually inserted in this drive, which is often the left-hand or the upper drive.

**drive B (B:)** Designation for the second **disk(ette) drive** in a microcomputer; the data diskette is usually inserted in this drive, which is often the right-hand or the lower drive.

**drive C (C:)** Designation for the **hard disk** drive in a microcomputer.

**drive gate** *See* **disk drive gate.**

**drive bay** Slot on opening in the computer cabinet in which the disk drive is installed.

**driver** Also called a *device driver,* a program that links a peripheral device to the **operating system;** basic drivers come with the operating system, and new drivers (usually on diskette) are installed when new peripheral devices are added to the system. Peripherals (such as a mouse or CD-ROM drive) will not run without the appropriate drivers.

**drum printer** *See* **line printer.**

**DSS** *See* **decision support system.**

**dumb terminal** A **terminal** that is entirely dependent on the computer system to which it is connected; it cannot do any processing on its own and is used only for data input (using the keyboard) and retrieval (data is displayed on the monitor). *Compare* **intelligent terminal; smart terminal.**

**EBCDIC** *See* **Extended Binary Coded Decimal Interchange Code.**

**E-cycle** *See* **execution cycle.**

**electroluminescent (EL) display** Type of **flat-panel display** with light-emitting layer of phosphor and two sets of electrodes surrounding the phosphor layer—one side forming vertical columns (usually 512), the other side forming horizontal rows (usually 256). To form a pixel on the screen, current is sent to row-column intersection, and the combined voltages cause the phosphor to glow at that point.

**electronic banking** Service enabling customers to access banking activities from home or private office via a terminal or personal computer connected to their telephones.

**electronic bulletin board service (BBS) Online information service** that can be reached via computer connected to telephone lines that allows user to place or read messages from other users.

**electronic communications** Movement of voice and data over short and long distances, such as by telephone or microwave, through the use of computers and communications hardware and software.

**electronic shopping** Service through which users can order merchandise by using microcomputers and electronic communications to browse through products listed on remote databases.

**electronic spreadsheet** *See* **spreadsheet software.**

**electronic surveillance** Use of special hardware and software to monitor people working on a computer system.

**electrostatic plotter** Special-purpose output device for reproducing computer-produced drawings. The plotter produces images on specially treated paper with small dots of electrostatic charges, and the paper is then run through a developer to make the image appear.

**e-mail (electronic mail)** Transmission and storing of messages by computers and telecommunications.

**encryption** The conversion of data into a "secret" code to ensure privacy.

**erasable optical disk Optical storage** disk whose data can be changed and erased. *Compare* **compact disk/read-only memory (CD-ROM); write once, read many (WORM).**

**ergonomics** The study of the relationships between people and their work environments; involves the design of products that are easy to use by people; also called *human engineering.*

**event-initiated report** Report generated for **middle management** only when certain conditions exist, such as changes requiring immediate attention (for example, equipment breakdown).

**exception report** Report generated for **middle management** that shows out-of-the-ordinary data—for example, inventory reports listing only items numbering fewer than 10 in stock.

**execution cycle (E-cycle)** Activity in **CPU** that includes execution of instruction and subsequent storing of result in a **register.** *See also* **instruction cycle; machine cycle.**

**executive information system MIS** software designed to make gathering information easy for top-level executives.

**executive (desktop) workstation** *See* **workstation.**

**expanded memory** In a microcomputer, main memory (RAM) that has been added to exceed the usual 640 K maximum; it consists of an add-on memory board and special driver software; generally used in compatible 8088 microcomputers. (**Extended memory** is used in later-model computers.)

**expansion card (board)** Circuit board that plugs into a socket on a computer's **system board** and that adds a new capability or more memory to the computer system.

**expansion slot** In a microcomputer that has **open architecture,** an area within the **system cabinet** where expansion cards—such as color graphics adapter cards and expanded memory cards—can be inserted and plugged into the computer's circuitry.

**expert system** Kind of software consisting of knowledge and rules for using it gathered from human experts in a particular occupation. One of the first practical applications of **artificial intelligence,** it consists of (1) a **natural language** interface with the user, (2) a **knowledge base,** (3) an **inference machine** to solve problems and make logical inferences, and (4) an explanation module to explain the conclusions to the user.

**Extended Binary Coded Decimal Interchange Code (EBCDIC)** Pronounced "eb-see-dick." The most popular code used for IBM and IBM-compatible mainframe computers.

**extended graphics array (XGA) Video display adapter** that supports up to 16.7 million colors at very high resolution.

**extended memory** In a microcomputer, all memory over 1 megabyte. Extended memory is available only in 80286 and later-model microcomputers.

**external modem Modem** that is outside the microcomputer and uses its own power supply; it is connected to the computer by a cable.

**fax** A faxed item. *See* **fax machine.**

**fax machine** Short for *facsimile machine,* a type of **scanner** externally connected to the computer that "reads" text and graphics and transmits them over telephone lines to a computer with a **fax modem** or to another fax machine. (Dedicated fax machines do nothing but send and receive fax documents.)

**fax modem**  Modem that can send and receive fax transmissions that is installed as circuit board inside the computer's system cabinet; cannot scan paper documents, as a fax machine can.

**fiber optics communications**  Form of computer communications in which signals are converted to light form and fired by laser in bursts through thin (2,000ths of an inch) insulated glass or plastic fibers. Nearly 1 billion bits per second can be communicated through a fiber optic cable.

**field**  Group of related characters (bytes) of data. *See* **data storage hierarchy.**

**fifth-generation language**  *See* **natural language.**

**file**  Group of related **records.** A file may contain data (data file) or software instructions (program file). *See* **data storage hierarchy.**

**file management system**  *See* **flat-file data management system.**

**filename extension**  One to three characters added to a file name to aid in file identification. The file name and the extension are separated by a dot.

**filename length**  Convention specified by different **operating systems**—for example, DOS specifies one to eight characters in file names.

**file server**  A high-speed computer, usually a microcomputer, with large-capacity storage, that stores data and programs shared by users on a network of terminals.

**file updating**  A factor in **data redundancy** and **data integrity;** when an element of data in a **database** needs to be updated (changed), it must be updated in *all* files that contain it.

**financial transaction terminal**  **Terminal** used in banking activities to access a central computer. It may be an automated teller machine (ATM) or specialized terminal used by bank tellers.

**first-generation language**  *See* **machine language.**

**fixed disk**  Magnetic disk for **secondary storage** that cannot be removed from the disk drive.

**flash memory**  Small, lightweight, fast memory circuitry on credit-card-size units (PC cards) that can take the place of hard disk drives. Their small size and low power consumption will allow portable computers to shrink even more (perhaps to 2 pounds for a complete microcomputer) and run for days on a single battery charge, instead of for hours. Flash memory cards may also be used to simulate RAM.

**flat-file database management system**  DBMS software that can deal with data in only one file at a time; cannot establish relationships among data elements stored in different files.

**flat-panel display**  Type of display screen used on portable computers; they are much thinner, weigh less, and use less power than **CRTs.** *See* **electroluminescent display; gas plasma display; liquid crystal display.**

**floating point**  Scientific form of notation used to handle large numbers; the decimal point is allowed to move around, or "float."

**floppy disk**  *See* **diskette.**

**flops**  One of three units of measuring processing speeds; stands for floating-point operations per second.

**flowchart**  *See* **program flowchart.**

**font**  A complete assortment or set of all the characters (letter, numbers, punctuation, and symbols) of a particular typeface in a particular size.

**formatting**  (1) Directing the computer to put magnetic **track** and **sector** pattern on a disk to enable the disk to store data or information. Also known as *initializing.* (2) In **word processing,** the alteration of text by addition of underlining or boldface, change of margins, centering of headings, and so on.

**FORTRAN (FORmula TRANslator)**  One of the first **high-level languages;** used for technical and scientific applications, primarily on minicomputers and mainframes.

**fourth-generation language (4GL)**  Nonprocedural programming language that allows nonprofessional computer users to develop software. *See* **applications generator; query language; report generator.** *Compare* **high-level language.**

**frame**  Row of magnetic spots and spaces (1s and 0s) recorded across the width of a magnetic tape.

**freeware**  Software provided by a vendor at no charge.

**frequency**  Number of times a transmission signal repeats the same cycle (fluctuates) in a second. Frequency is expressed in **hertz;** the higher the frequency, the more data is transmitted per second.

**front-end processor**  Computer used in a computer center to handle data transmission and communications from outside terminals and devices to allow the main computer to concentrate solely on processing applications as quickly as possible.

**full-duplex transmission mode**  Communications transmitted in both directions simultaneously.

**function keys**  Specialized keys on a microcomputer **keyboard** for performing specific tasks with applications software; the keys are used differently with each applications package; they are labeled F1, F2, F3, and so on.

**fuzzy logic**  In **artificial intelligence,** a mathematical technique of dealing with imprecise data and vagueness, with problems that have many solutions rather than one.

**gas plasma display**  Type of **flat-panel display;** uses three pieces of glass sandwiched together. The inner layer has numerous small holes drilled in it. The outer two layers are placed on both sides of the middle one, and the holes are filled with a gas mixture, usually a mixture of argon and neon. Both outer layers of glass have a thin grid of vertical and horizontal wires. A **pixel** appears at a particular intersection when the appropriate horizontal and vertical wires are electrified.

**gateway**  Communications interface (computer and software) that connects two different types of networks and performs **protocol** conversion. *Compare* **bridge.**

**GB**  *See* **gigabyte.**

**gigabyte (GB)**  One billion bytes.

**graphics coprocessor**  Specialized processor **chip** installed on the **motherboard** that helps the **CPU** process graphics-related calculation more quickly.

**graphics monitor (terminal)**  Screen that can display both **alphanumeric data** and graphics; different types can display one-, two-, or three-dimensional graphics. *Compare* **alphanumeric monitor (terminal).**

**graphics software**  Programs that allow the user to present information in pictorial form, often with text. *See* **analytical graphics; presentation graphics.**

**graphic(al) user interface**  Software feature that allows user to select **menu** options by choosing an **icon** that corresponds to a particular processing function; makes software easier to use, and typically employs a **mouse.** Examples are the **Macintosh Operating System, Warp,** and **Microsoft Windows.**

**gray-scale monitor**  Monitor that can display many shades of gray; 256 shades, for example.

**gray-scale scanner**  Scanner that can "read" many shades of gray—such as those in a black-and-white photograph—and input the data to the computer system.

**grid chart**  Chart that shows the relationship between documents used for input and documents that are output.

**groupware**  Applications software used on a **network** and serves a group of users.

**hacker**  A skilled computer enthusiast who works alone and is obsessed with learning about programming and exploring the capabilities of computer systems.

**half-duplex transmission mode**  Two-way data communications in which data travels in only one direction at a time.

**hand-held scanner**  Small input device used to scan printed documents on a limited basis to input the documents' contents to a computer.

**hand-held terminal**  Small portable **terminal** that users can carry with them to hook up to a central computer from remote locations, often via telecommunications facilities. Most portable terminals are connected to the central computer by means of telephone lines. These terminals have **modems** built into them that convert the data being transmitted into a form suitable for sending and receiving over the phone lines.

**hardcopy**  Output recorded on a tangible medium (generally meaning that you can touch it) such as paper or microfilm. *Compare* **softcopy.**

**hard disk (drive)  Direct access secondary storage** device consisting of a rigid metal platter connected to a central spindle; the entire unit, including the **read/write heads,** is enclosed in a permanently sealed container. Hard disks store much more data than do **diskettes.**

**hard disk cartridge**  One or more hard disks and **read/write head** enclosed in a plastic case. The case is inserted into an external unit connected to the computer.

**hard-sectored disk  Hard disk** or **diskette** that always has the same number and size of **sectors,** as determined by the manufacturer. *Compare* **soft-sectored disk.**

**hardware**  Electronic and electromechanical computer components: input, storage, processing, communications, and output hardware. *See also* **computer.** *Compare* **software.**

**head crash**  Problem that occurs when the surface of a disk drive's **read/write head** comes into contact with the disk surface, causing the loss of data on the disk.

**Help menu**  Software **menu** that offers a choice of **Help screens,** specific instructions on how to perform tasks.

**Help screen**  On-screen instruction regarding the use of the software.

**hertz**  Measure of **frequency,** or number of transmission wave cycles per second.

**hierarchical database**  Type of **database** organization in which data is arranged into related groups resembling a family tree, with **child records** subordinate to **parent records.** A parent record can have many child records, but each child record can have only one parent record. The record at the highest level, or top of the "tree," is called the *root record.*

**hierarchical network  Star networks** configured into a single multilevel system, with a single large computer controlling all network activity. However, a computer connected into the main computer can have a star network of devices connected to it in turn. Also known as *tree network.*

**hierarchy chart**  *See* **structure chart.**

**high-level language**  Third-generation programming language designed to run on different computers with few changes—for example, **COBOL, FORTRAN,** and **BASIC.** Most high-level languages are considered to be procedure-oriented because the program instructions comprise lists of steps, or procedures, that tell the computer not only what to do but how to do it. Also known as *procedural language.*

**hub**  Round opening in the center of a diskette, which enables the disk to fit over a spindle in the disk drive.

**hybrid network**  Combination of **star, ring,** and **bus networks.**

**hypertext**  Software that links basic file units (text and graphics) with one another in creative ways. The user typically sees index-type "cards" and "card stacks" on the screen as well as other pictorial representations of file units and combination choices; card and stack contents can be determined by the user or supplied in an **off-the-shelf software** package

**I-cycle**  *See* **instruction cycle.**

**icon**  Pictorial representation of a software function or a peripheral device, such as a disk drive or a printer; used in **graphical user interfaces.**

**imaging system**  Sophisticated scanning system for converting text and graphics into digital form for storage in a computer system and later manipulation. Imaging systems are used in **desktop publishing** and **multimedia.**

**impact printer**  Output device that makes direct contact with paper, forming the print image by pressing an inked ribbon against the paper with a hammer-like mechanism. Impact printers are of two types. *See* **daisy-wheel printer; dot-matrix printer.**

**indexed sequential file organization**  Method of secondary storage file organization whereby records are stored sequentially but with an index that allows both sequential and direct (random) access. Used almost exclusively with random access microcomputer storage devices to provide maximum flexibility for processing. *See also* **direct access storage and retrieval; sequential file organization.**

**index hole**  Hole in protective jacket enclosing **diskette** that enables the disk to be positioned over a photoelectric sensing mechanism. Each time the disk revolves, a hole in the disk passes under the index hole in the jacket and activates a timing mechanism that determines which portion of the disk is over or under the **read/write heads.**

**Industry Standard Architecture (ISA)  Bus** standard developed for the IBM PC.

**inference machine**  Program component of an **expert system;** the software that controls the search of the system's **knowledge base** and produces conclusions.

**information**  Raw **data** processed into usable form by the computer. It is the basis for decision making.

**information center**  Department staffed by experts on the hardware, software, and procedures used in the company; the experts help users in all matters relating to computer use. In companies without a mainframe, it is often called a *personal computer support center.*

**information reporting system**  *See* **management information system.**

**information service**  *See* **online information service.**

**information superhighway**  Refers to the fusion of two-way wired and wireless communications capabilities with cable TV's capacity to transmit hundreds of programs. This superhighway would link all homes, schools, businesses, government agencies, and service and research organizations.

**information system**  An organization's framework of standards and procedures for processing data into usable information; it can be manual or computer-based. *See also* **computer-based information system.**

**initializing**  *See* **formatting.**

**ink-jet printer  Nonimpact printer** that resembles **dot-matrix printer** in that it forms images or characters with dots. The dots are formed not by hammer-like pins but by droplets of ink fired through holes in a plate.

**input controls**  Manual and computerized procedures to safeguard the integrity of input data, ensuring that all such data has been completely and accurately put into computer-usable form.

**input hardware  Hardware** used to input data to a computer system; examples are keyboards and mice, light pens, and digitizers (direct-entry devices).

**input/output bus**  Computer **bus** that links the **CPU** to every hardware device.

**input/output (I/O) operations**  Instructions provided by a program for inputting data into **main memory (RAM)** and for outputting information.

**input phase**  First phase of activity in the **computer-based information system,** during which data is captured electronically—for example, via a **keyboard** or a **scanner**—and converted to a form that can be processed by a computer.

**input screen**  On a **video display screen,** a kind of format that is a combination of displayed text and pictorial data that identifies the elements of data to be entered and in which order they are to be entered. Input screens allow data entry operators to verify visually all data being entered.

**installation** Use of a special software program provided with applications software for installing the software on the hard disk and configuring it for use.

**instruction(s)** Set of characters (code) directing a data processing system to perform a certain operation. *See also* **software.**

**instruction cycle (I-cycle)** In the **CPU,** the operation whereby an instruction is retrieved from **main memory (RAM)** and is decoded, alerting the circuits in the CPU to perform the specified operation.

**integrated circuit** *See* **chip.**

**integrated software** Software combining several applications into a single package with a common set of commands. **Word processing,** electronic **spreadsheets, database management systems, graphics,** and **data communications** have been combined in such packages.

**integrated workstation** *See* **executive workstation.**

**intelligent robot** Robot that emulates the human capabilities of sight, hearing, touch, and smell and that responds based on the data it receives.

**intelligent terminal** Terminal that can be used to input and retrieve data as well as do its own processing; in addition to the keyboard, monitor, and communications link, an intelligent terminal also includes a processing unit, storage capabilities, and software; microcomputers are often used as intelligent terminals. *Compare* **dumb terminal; smart terminal.**

**interactivity** Describes computer systems or software that actively involve the user in asking and answering on-screen questions and in responding directly to software requests.

**internal memory** *See* **main memory.**

**internal modem** Modem that is inside a microcomputer; it is located on a circuit board plugged into an expansion slot and draws power directly from the computer's power supply. No special cable is required. *Compare* **external modem.**

**international network** Network providing intercontinental voice and data communications, often using undersea cable or satellites.

**International Standards Organization (ISO)** Organization working to develop standards for programming languages, communications, and compatibility among computers.

**Internet** International wide area network consisting of a large number of smaller networks of all types that connect organizations in industry, education, government, and research.

**interpreter** Language processor that converts high-level program instructions into **machine language** one instruction statement at a time. *Compare* **compiler.**

**iteration (do-while) control structure** In **structured programming,** the structure that allows an activity to be repeated (iterated) as long as a certain condition remains true. Also known as a *loop.*

**joystick** Input pointing device that consists of a vertical handle like a gearshift lever mounted on a base with one or two buttons used to control the cursor on the screen and to issue commands.

**K** *See* **kilobyte.**

**key** *See* **key field.**

**keyboard** Device resembling typewriter keyboard for entering data and computer-related codes. Besides standard typewriter keys, it has special **function keys, cursor-movement keys, numeric keys,** and other special-purpose keys.

**keyboard entry** Inputting data using a **keyboard.** *Compare* **direct entry.**

**key field (key)** Unique element of data contained in each **record** used to identify the record and to determine where on

the disk the record should be stored or retrieved using the **direct access storage and retrieval method.**

**kilobyte (K)** 1,024 bytes.

**knowledge base** Component of an **expert system;** the database of knowledge about a particular subject

**knowledge engineer** Experts who are trained to elicit information (knowledge) from experts in a particular subject in order to build an **expert system.**

**language translator (processor)** Program that translates **high-level languages** and **assembly languages** into **machine language.** Also known as *translator.*

**laser printer** Output device in which a laser beam is directed across the surface of a light-sensitive drum to record an image as a pattern of tiny dots. As with a photocopying machine, the image is then transferred to the paper a page at a time.

**laptop computer** Microcomputer using **flat-screen technology** that is small enough to beheld on a person's lap.

**license** The document that comes with software that authorizes the software purchaser to run the product on his or her computer; *see also* **software piracy.**

**light pen** Pen-shaped input device consisting of a light-sensitive photoelectric cell that, when touched to a video display screen, is used to signal the screen position to the computer.

**line printer** Nonserial impact output device in which a whole line of characters is printed practically at once. Includes band (belt) printers, drum printers, and print-chain printers, in which a printable character is located on a band (belt), drum, or print chain, with a separate print hammer for each print position across the width of the paper guide. As the band, drum, or print chain revolves around the print line, the hammers are activated as the appropriate characters pass in front of them.

**liquid crystal display (LCD)** Used as a **flat-panel display** screen in some laptop microcomputers. LCD uses a clear liquid chemical trapped in tiny pockets between two pieces of glass. Each pocket of liquid is covered both front and back by thin wires. When current is applied to the wires, a chemical reaction turns the chemical a dark color, thereby blocking light. The point of blocked light is the **pixel.**

**local network** Privately owned communications network that serves users within a confined geographic area—such as an office, a building, or a group of buildings.

**local area network (LAN)** Local network connected by wire, cable, or fiber optics link that serves parts of a company located close to each other, generally in the same building or within two miles of one another. LANs allow workers to share hardware, software, and data.

**logical database design** Detailed description of database model from business rather than technical perspective; it involves defining user information needs, analyzing data element requirements and logical groupings, finalizing the design, and creating the **data dictionary.** Every element of data necessary to produce required management information system reports is identified and the relationship among records is specified.

**logical operations** Operations consisting of three common comparisons: equal to, less than, and greater than. Three words used in basic logical operations are AND, OR, and NOT.

**logical record** Record defined by user according to logic of the program being used; it is independent of the **physical records.**

**logic error** In programming, an error caused by incorrect use of **control structures,** incorrect calculation, or omission of a procedure.

**loop** *See* **iteration (do-while) control structure.**

**lower management** *See* **operational management.**

**low-level programming language** *See* **assembly language.**

**machine cycle** In the **CPU** during processing, the **instruction cycle** and the **execution cycle** together, as they apply to one instruction.

**machine language** The language the **CPU** understands; data and instructions are represented as **binary digits.** Each type of computer responds to a unique version of machine language, such as **ASCII** or **EBCDIC.** Also known as **first-generation language.**

**Macintosh operating system** **Disk operating system** designed by Apple Computers for the Apple Macintosh microcomputer.

**macro** Applications software feature that allows users to use a single keystroke or command to initiate a series of predetermined keystrokes or commands. The use of macros saves time.

**magnetic-ink character recognition (MICR)** Data entry technology used in processing checks; it involves the electronic reading of numeric characters and special symbols printed on checks with magnetic ink.

**magnetic tape** Plastic tape with a magnetic surface for storing data in a code of magnetized spots; tape is a **sequential storage** medium.

**mainframe computer** After the **supercomputer,** the most powerful type of computer; it is usually housed in a controlled environment and can support many powerful peripheral devices and the processing requirements of hundreds of users.

**main memory** Computer's primary storage area, where data and instructions are held for immediate access by the **CPU;** main memory is **volatile**—when the power is turned off, all data and instructions in memory are lost unless they have been permanently recorded on a **secondary storage medium.** Also known as *internal memory* and *RAM (random access memory).*

**management** Individuals responsible for providing leadership and direction in an organization's areas of planning, organizing, staffing, supervising, and controlling of business activities. Management may be low-level (operating or supervisory), middle-level, and upper-level (strategic). *See also* **middle management; operational management; upper management.**

**management information system (MIS)** Computer-based processing and/or manual procedures within a company to provide useful and timely information to support decision making on all three levels of management; at the **middle management** level, also called *information reporting system.*

**mass storage system** System for storing enormous amounts of data; it may consist of as many as 2,000 honeycomb-like cells that hold data cartridges with magnetic tape, each of which can store 50 MB of data. Each cartridge may be retrieved individually and positioned under a special read/write head for data transfer.

**master file** File used to store data permanently for access and updating. *Compare* **transaction file.**

**math coprocessor** Specialized processor **chip** installed on the motherboard that helps the **CPU** process mathematical calculations more quickly.

**MB** *See* **megabyte.**

**medium** (*pl.* **media**) Type of material on which data is recorded—for example, paper, magnetic tape, or magnetic disk.

**megabyte (MB)** 1,000 kilobytes (K)—approximately 1 million characters.

**megahertz (MHz)** One million hertz; a measure of speed at which computers perform operations; clock speed.

**memory** *See* **main memory.**

**menu** List of command options (choices) displayed on the screen.

**menu-driven** Describes a software program that offers varying levels of menus, or lists of choices displayed on the screen, to the user to lead him or her through the program function; menus may also include small descriptive pictures, or **icons.**

**merging** Bringing together information from two different files.

**metropolitan area network (MAN)** Communications network that covers an area the size of a city or suburb.

**Micro Channel Architecture (MCA)** 32-bit **bus** standard used in IBM PS/2 microcomputers.

**microcomputer** Small, general-purpose computer system that uses a microprocessor chip as its **CPU.** It can usually be used by only one person at one time; can be used independently or as a **terminal.** Also known as *personal computer, desktop computer.*

**microprocessor** **Integrated circuit** (chip) containing the **CPU** circuitry for a microcomputer.

**Microsoft Windows** Microsoft Corp.'s **graphic user interface** systems software for DOS-based microcomputers; newest version is **Windows 95.**

**Microsoft Windows NT** Version of **Microsoft Windows** systems software for recent IBM-type computers; uses a **graphic user interface** and has networking capabilities, among other advanced functions

**microwave system** Communications technology using the atmosphere above the earth for transmitting signals point to point from tower to tower. Such systems are extensively used for high-volume as well as long-distance communication of both data and voice in the form of electromagnetic waves similar to radio waves but in a higher frequency range. Microwave signals are said to be "line-of-sight" because they cannot bend around the curvature of the earth.

**middle management** Level of management dealing with decisions that cover a broader range of time and are less structured than decisions made by **operational management.** However, middle management deals with decisions that are more time specific and more structured than decisions made by **upper,** or strategic, **management.**

**millions of instructions per second (MIPs)** One of three ways in which processing speeds are measured.

**minicomputer** Computer that is similar to but less powerful than a **mainframe computer;** it can support 2–50 users and computer professionals.

**MIPs** *See* **millions of instructions per second.**

**MIS** *See* **management information system.**

**modeling tools** Program and systems design tools such as **computer-aided software engineering (CASE), pseudocode, structure chart, data flow diagram, systems flowchart,** and so on.

**modem** Device for translating **digital signals** from a computer into **analog signals** for transmission over telephone lines and then back into digital signals again for processing (a modem must be hooked up at each end of the transmission). Modem stands for MOdulate/DEModulate.

**Modula-2** **High-level programming language** that is an improvement of **Pascal;** it is better suited for business use than Pascal and can be used as an applications software development tool.

**modulation** Process of converting **digital signals** from a computer into **analog signals** so that data can be sent over a telephone line.

**module** In **top-down programming design,** a small, easy-to-work-with unit in a program that has only a single function, a single entry, and a single exit point. Also known as *subroutine.*

**monitor** Device for viewing computer output. Also known as **cathode-ray tube (CRT); screen; video display screen.**

**monochrome display screen** Device for viewing text and in some cases graphics in a single color, commonly green or amber. *Compare* **color display screen.**

**morphing** Alteration of a displayed film or video image pixel by pixel so that the image changes into something else.

**motherboard** Main circuit board in a microcomputer system. It normally includes the **microprocessor chip** (or **CPU**), **main memory (RAM)** chips, all related support circuitry, and the **expansion slots** for plugging in additional components. Also known as a *system board.*

**mouse** Handheld input device connected to a microcomputer by a cable; when the mouse is rolled across the desktop, the **cursor** moves across the screen. A button on the mouse allows users to make **menu** selections and issue commands.

**mouse pointer** Symbol on the screen controlled by the **mouse;** usually an arrow or a pointing finger.

**MPC machine** Multimedia personal computer that adheres to standards set by the Multimedia PC Marketing Council.

**MS-DOS** *See* **disk operating system.**

**multidrop line** Communications line that connects many devices; usually leased. *Compare* **point-to-point line.**

**multifunction device** Hardware that combines several functions, such as printing, scanning, copying, and faxing.

**multimedia system** Sophisticated software and hardware that combines basic text and graphics along with animation, video, music, and voice.

**multiplexer** Device that allows several terminals to share a single communications line.

**multiprocessing** Activity in which an **operating system** manages simultaneous execution of programs with two or more **CPU**s. This can entail processing instructions from different programs or different instructions from the same program. *Compare* **multitasking.**

**multiprogramming** *See* **multitasking.**

**multitasking** Activity in which more than one task or program is executed at a time. A small amount of each program is processed, and then the **CPU** moves to the remaining programs, one at a time, processing small parts of each. Also known as *multiprogramming.*

**natural language** Programming language designed to resemble human speech. Similar to **query language,** it eliminates the need for user to learn specific vocabulary, grammar, or **syntax.** Examples of natural languages are Clout for microcomputers and Intellect for mainframes. Also known as *fifth-generation language.*

**NetWare** Manufactured by Novell, Inc.; the most popular operating system for microcomputer-based **local area networks.**

**network** Collection of data communications hardware, computers, communications software, communications media, and applications software connected so that users can share information and equipment. *See also* **international network; local area network; private network; public network; ring network; star network; token ring network.**

**network database** Type of **database** organization similar to **hierarchical database model** but allowing multiple **one-to-many relationships;** each **child record** can have more than one **parent record.** Access to the database can be from a number of points, not just the top.

**neural network** Field of **artificial intelligence** in which electronic devices and software mimic the neurological structure of the human brain.

**nonimpact printer** Output device that does not make direct contact with paper when it prints. *See* **ink-jet printer; laser printer; thermal printer.** *Compare* **impact printer.**

**nonprocedural language** Programming language that allows programmers and users to specify what the computer is supposed to do without having to specify *how* the computer is supposed to do it. *See also* **fourth-generation language.** *Compare* **procedural language.**

**nonvolatile storage** Type of storage that is relatively permanent—such as data saved to disk or tape; that is, computer instructions and data are not lost when the power is turned off. *Compare* **volatile storage.**

**notebook computer** Portable computer that weighs 4–7.5 pounds and is roughly the size of a thick notebook.

**NuBus** Apple 32-bit **bus** standard used in recent-model Macintosh microcomputers.

**numeric data** Data that can be mathematically manipulated. *Compare* **alphanumeric data.**

**numeric keys (keypad)** The keys labeled 0–9 on the computer **keyboard;** used to enter numbers for mathematical manipulation.

**object** Block of preassembled code used in **object-oriented programming.**

**object code** **Machine-language** code that results from the translation of higher-language **source code.**

**object-oriented programming (OOP)** Programming method that combines data with instructions for processing that data into an independent **object** that can be re-used in other programs.

**object code** Program consisting entirely of machine-language instructions. *Compare* **source code.**

**object linking and embedding (OLE)** Software feature that allows the integration of different applications programs; the user can, for example, embed in a word-processed document an illustration created in a graphics program.

**off-the-shelf software** **Applications software** that can be purchased in a computer store, as opposed to software that is custom-written by a programmer.

**on-demand report** Report requested by **middle management** on a case-by-case basis.

**one-to-many relationship** In a **hierarchical database model,** the parent-child relationship between two record types; one **parent record** has many **child records.**

**online processing** Method of processing whereby input data is processed immediately, not stored temporarily in a **transaction file** for later processing; anything in a computer system that is on-line is linked up to current processing operations.

**online information service** Commercial organization that provides subscribers with access to databases, electronic meeting places, **electronic bulletin board services,** and other electronic services such as shopping.

**open architecture** Attribute of computers that can be upgraded by the use of expansion cards, such as **expanded memory;** the user can open the **system cabinet** and insert the expansion cards in the computer's **expansion slots.** *Compare* **closed architecture.**

**open wire** Earliest type of telephone line, composed of unsheathed, uninsulated copper wires strung on telephone poles.

**operating management** The lowest level of management in an organization; operating managers deal mostly with **structured decisions** covering a relatively narrow time frame, actualizing the plans of **middle management** and controlling daily operations. Also known as *supervisory management.*

**operating system (OS)** Master set of programs to allow computer to direct its own resources and operations; in microcomputers, called a *disk operating system.*

**Operating System/2 (OS/2)** IBM and Microsoft microcomputer **systems software** intended to take advantage of 80286 and 80386 microprocessors (such as in the IBM PS/2 Series microcomputers) and support multitasking and software applications requiring up to 16 MB of main memory (RAM); used in conjunction with Presentation Manager and Microsoft Windows; newest version is called **Warp.**

**operating system command** Internal or external command that allows users to manage disks and disk files. *See* **external command instructions; internal command instructions.**

**operating systems software** Program that starts up the computer and functions as the principal coordinator of all hardware components and applications software programs. *See* **internal command instructions.**

**operational management** Low-level manager who typically makes **structured decisions** regarding daily business operations.

**operator (technical) documentation** Documentation prepared during systems development that will aid future operators in running and maintaining the system.

**optical card**  Plastic, laser-recordable, wallet-size card that stores digital personal data than can be read by an optical card reader.

**optical character recognition (OCR)**  Input device that reads hardcopy data from source documents into computer-usable form; such devices use light-sensitive equipment to read bar codes, optical marks, typewritten characters, and handwriting.

**optical disk**  Removable disk on which data is written and read through the use of laser beams.

**optical mark**  Mark made by special pencil on form meant to be read by an **optical mark reader.**

**optical mark reader**  Device that reads data recorded on preprinted sheets with special pencil and converts it into computer-usable form.

**optical mark recognition (OMR)**  *See* **optical mark reader.**

**optical storage**  **Secondary storage** technology using a high-power laser beam to burn microscopic spots in a disk's surface coating. Data is represented by the presence and the absence of holes in the storage locations (1s and 0s). A much lower-power laser beam is used to retrieve the data. Much more data can be stored in this way than with traditional storage media and it is faster and cheaper.

**organization chart**  Chart that shows the levels of management within an organization, as well as the functions.

**output**  Computer-produced text, graphics, or sound in **hardcopy** or **softcopy** form that can be used immediately by people, or computer-produced data stored in computer-usable form for later use by computers and people.

**output file**  Data that is processed and then output in the form of a **file** to be used by another person or program at a later time.

**output hardware**  Hardware used to produce **softcopy** output (monitor display) and **hardcopy** output (from printers and plotters, for example).

**output phase**  A phase of activity in the **computer-based information system** during which the user is provided with all the necessary information to perform and manage day-to-day business activities and make decisions. Output can be provided for immediate use or for storage by the computer for future use.

**page description language (PDL)**  Part of **desktop publishing software;** it allows the **laser printer** to combine text and graphics from different files on a single page.

**page printer**  *See* **laser printer.**

**palmtop computer**  Pocket PC small enough to hold in one hand.

**parallel implementation**  One of four approaches to systems implementation; the old system and new system are run at the same time for a specified period, then the old system is discontinued when the new system is judged satisfactory. *Compare* **direct implementation; phased implementation; pilot implementation.**

**parallel port**  Socket on the **system unit** for attaching peripheral devices that transmit 8 bits simultaneously; used mainly for connecting printers.

**parallel processing**  Using many processors (**CPU**s) to process data simultaneously, thus speeding up processing.

**parent record**  In **hierarchical database model,** the **record** higher in the structure than a **child record.** Each child can have only one parent—that is, each record may have many records below it but only one record above it, a **one-to-many relationship.** Deletion of a parent record automatically deletes all child records.

**parity bit (check bit)**  An extra (ninth) **bit** attached to the end of a **byte;** it is used as part of an error-checking scheme: Computers are designed to use either an odd-parity scheme or an even-parity scheme, in which the total number of 1s in each byte, including the parity bit, must add up to an odd number or an even number.

**Pascal**  **High-level programming language** for large and small computer systems; developed to teach programming as a systematic and structured activity. It has strong mathematical and scientific processing capabilities.

**passive-matrix display**  Type of **flat-panel display** whereby a transistor controls a whole row or column of **pixels;** passive-matrix displays are not as bright or as sharp as **active-matrix displays** but are less expensive.

**PC-DOS**  *See* **disk operating system.**

**PCI** 64-bit **bus** standard used in Pentium-based microcomputer systems.

**PCMCIA (PC cards)**  *See* **Personal Computer Memory Card International Association.**

**peer-to-peer LAN**  **Local area network** in which all microcomputers communicate directly with one another without relying on a **server.**

**pen-based computing (pen computer)**  Handheld computer in which special software interprets handwriting done directly on a special type of computer screen. As the computer interprets the handwriting, it displays what was written on the screen in a computer typeface. Users can edit what they have entered and give commands by circling words, checking boxes, and using symbols developed by the manufacturer.

**perception system**  *See* **intelligent robot.**

**periodic report**  Report for **middle management** produced at predetermined times—for example, payroll report, inventory status report.

**personal computer (PC)**  *See* **microcomputer.**

**Personal Computer Memory Card Association (PCMCIA)**  The organization that developed the **bus** standard that allows recent-model portable computers to accept credit-card size peripherals (such as added RAM, modem, or disk storage) called PC cards inserted in slots in the computer.

**personal digital assistant (PDA)**  Pocket PC that is handheld and pen-controlled.

**personal information manager**  Software package that provides **word processing, database manager,** and **desktop accessory** capabilities.

**phased implementation**  One of four approaches to systems implementation: a system is so large it is implemented one phase at a time. *Compare* **direct implementation; parallel implementation; pilot implementation.**

**Photo CD**  Format developed by Eastman Kodak to store photos digitally on optical disk.

**physical database design**  In design of a **database,** the stage following the **logical design.** Physical design involves specifying how best to store data on the **direct access storage devices** so that it can be updated and retrieved quickly and efficiently.

**pilot implementation**  One of four approaches to system implementation in which, in a widely dispersed company, the system is introduced at one location at a time. *Compare* **direct implementation; parallel implementation; phased implementation.**

**piracy**  *See* **software piracy.**

**pixels**  Picture elements; dots that make up a picture; glowing phosphors on a **cathode ray tube (CRT)** screen. Small pixels provide greatest image clarity (**resolution**).

**PL/1 (Programming Language 1)**  **High-level,** general-purpose **programming language** for computation and heavy-duty file handling. Primarily used on minicomputers and mainframes.

**plotter**  Output device used to create **hardcopy** drawings on paper in a variety of colors. *See also* **electrostatic plotter; pen plotter; thermal plotter.**

**pocket PC (handheld PC)**  Personal computer that weighs 1 pound or less.

**pointing device**  Nonkeyboard data entry device that moves cursor and sends command messages to computer—such as a **dig-**

**itizing tablet, mouse, joystick, light pen,** and **touch screen.**

**point-of-sale (POS) terminal**  Input/output device (**smart terminal**) used like a cash register to print sales transaction receipt and to send sales and inventory data to a central computer for processing.

**point-to-point line**  Communications line that directly connects the sending and the receiving devices; if it is a *switched line,* it is disconnected when transmission is finished; if it is a *dedicated line,* it is always established. *Compare* **multidrop line.**

**port**  Electrical interconnection—for example, on a microcomputer, the point where the printer is plugged into the computer. Different ports are used for the mouse, the modem, and other peripheral devices.

**portable terminal**  Input/output device that users can carry with them to remote locations and connect via telecommunications lines to a central computer. **Dumb terminals** can send and receive data to and from the main computer; **smart terminals** permit some data to be entered and edited before the connection to the main computer.

**postimplementation evaluation**  In systems design, a formal evaluation of a new system after operation for several months and after systems maintenance has been done to determine if the system is meeting its objectives.

**PostScript**  **Page description language** that has become a standard on many laser printers.

**power supply**  Source of electrical power to components housed in the **system unit** of a microcomputer.

**presentation graphics**  Graphical forms that go beyond simple **analytical graphics** (bar charts, line charts, pie charts); sophisticated presentation graphics software allows the user to function as an artist and combine free-form shapes and text.

**primary storage**  *See* **main memory.**

**print-chain printer**  *See* **line printer.**

**printer**  Output device that prints characters, symbols, and sometimes graphics on paper. *See also* **impact printer; nonimpact printer.**

**private branch exchange (PBX)**  **Local network** that connects telephone extensions within a company's physical location (in-house).

**private network**  **Network** supporting voice and data communications needs of a particular organization.

**procedural language**  *See* **high-level language.**

**procedures**  In an information system, specific sequence of steps performed to complete one or more information processing activities.

**procedures manual**  Written **documentation** of noncomputer-based and computer-based procedures used in a computer-based data processing system.

**processing**  The computer-based manipulation of **data** into **information.**

**processing hardware**  Circuitry used to process data into information; *see also* **central processing unit, microprocessor, system unit.**

**processing phase**  The second phase of activity in the **computer-based information system,** during which all the number and character manipulation activities are done that are necessary to convert the **data** into an appropriate form of **information.**

**processing registers**  In the **CPU,** the registers holding data or instructions being acted on. Their size determines the amount of data that can be processed in a single cycle.

**program**  Group of related instructions that perform specific processing tasks.

**program disk**  Disk that holds programs, not data.

**program files**  Programs stored on magnetic disk or tape.

**program flowchart**  Diagram using standard **ANSI** symbols to show step-by-step processing activities and decision logic needed to solve a programming problem.

**program independence**  Attribute of programs that can be used with data files arranged in different ways—for example, some with the date first and expense items second and others with expense items first and date second. Program dependence means that a separate program has to be written to use each differently arranged data file.

**programmable keys**  *See* **function keys.**

**programmable read-only memory (PROM)**  Type of **read-only memory (ROM)** chip in which data or program instructions are not prerecorded when it is manufactured; thus, users can record their own data or instructions, but once the data has been recorded, it cannot always be changed.

**programming language**  Code used to write instructions for the computer; there are five generations of programming languages.

**program testing**  Procedures carried out during program development to **debug** programs and otherwise check their reliability.

**project dictionary**  Stores all the requirements and specifications for all elements of data to be used in a new system.

**project management software**  Applications software used to plan, schedule, and control the people, time, costs, and resources required to complete a project on time.

**proprietary database**  Large database that functions as an information service—for example, CompuServe, Prodigy, and Dow Jones News/Retrieval. The proprietor owns the database.

**proprietary operating system**  **Operating system** developed for only one brand of computer.

**protocol**  In electronic communications, formal rules for communicating, including those for timing of message exchanges, the type of electrical connections used by the communications devices, error detection techniques, methods required to gain access to communications channels, and so on.

**protocol converter**  Specialized intelligent **multiplexer** that facilitates effective communications between microcomputers and the main computer system.

**prototyping**  In systems analysis and design, the process of building a small-scale working model of a new system, or part of a new system, in order to get feedback from users as quickly as possible. **Report generators, applications generators, DBMS (database management) software,** and **CASE (computer-aided software engineering)** software may be used as prototyping tools.

**pseudocode**  "Fake" code; programming code not actually entered into the computer that uses modified human language statements (instead of flowchart symbols) to represent program logic. It is more precise in representing logic than regular, idiomatic English human language but does not follow a specific syntax. It uses four statement keywords to portray logic: IF, THEN, ELSE, and DO.

**public domain software**  Software entirely in the public domain—that is, it carries no copyrights—and carries no restrictions.

**public network**  **Network** providing subscribers with voice and data communications over a large geographical area. Also known as *common carrier, specialized common carrier.*

**pull-down menu**  List of command options, or choices, that are displayed from the top of the screen downward when its title is selected from the menu bar. Pull-down menus can be opened by keystroke commands or by "clicking" (pressing) the mouse button while pointing to the title and then dragging the mouse pointer down.

**quad(ruple)-density**  *See* **recording density.**

**QWERTY**  Term that designates the common computer **keyboard** layout, whereby the first six letters of the first row of lettered keys spell "QWERTY".

**query language**  **Fourth-generation programming language** that allows users to ask questions about, or retrieve information from, database files by forming requests in normal human language statements. Learning the specific grammar, vocabulary, and **syntax** is usually a simple task. The definitions for query language and for **database management systems software** are so similar that they are usually considered to be the same.

**RAID storage system**  Redundant array of inexpensive disks; **secondary storage** system (direct access) used with large computer systems. Consists of more than 100 5¼-inch disk drives in a single cabinet, sending data to the computer along several parallel paths simultaneously.

**RAM** *See* **random access memory.**

**random access** *See* **direct access storage and retrieval.**

**random access memory (RAM)**  The name given to the integrated circuits (**chips**) that make up main memory, which provides **volatile** temporary storage of data and program instructions that the **CPU** is using; data and instructions can be retrieved at random, no matter where they are located in main memory. RAM is used for storing **operating system** software instructions and for temporary storage of **applications software** instructions, input data, and output data.

**raster scan rate**  Measure of number of times per second the image on a video display screen can be refreshed—that is, "lit up" again. Because the phosphors hit by the electron beam do not glow very long, the beam must continuously sweep the screen. With a low raster scan rate, the screen will seem to flicker.

**read**  Refers to the when data represented digitally on disk is copied and converted by the read/write head to electronic signals and transmitted to **RAM.**

**read only**  Refers to a disk that cannot be written on and whose data cannot be erased; the contents can only be "read."

**read-only memory (ROM)**  Type of memory in which instructions to perform operations critical to a computer are stored on integrated circuits (chips) in permanent, **nonvolatile** form. The instructions are usually recorded on the chips by the manufacturer. *Compare* **random access memory (RAM).**

**read/write head**  Recording mechanism in **secondary storage** devices that "reads" (accepts) the magnetic spots of data and converts them to electrical impulses and that "writes" (enters) the spots on the disk. Most disk drives have two read/write heads to access the top and bottom surfaces of a disk simultaneously.

**real-time processing**  Immediate processing; each transaction is fully processed when input, and there is immediate feedback (action can be taken right away). All related computer files affected by the transaction are updated immediately, and printed output can be produced on the spot. *Compare* **batch processing.**

**record**  Collection of related fields. *See also* **data storage hierarchy.**

**recording density**  Number of **bits** per inch (bpi) that can be written onto the surface of a magnetic disk. Disks and drives use one of three kinds of recording densities: (1) single-density, (2) double-density, or (3) quad-density. The higher the density number, the more data a disk can hold. Only older systems use single-density.

**reduced instruction set computing (RISC)**  Refers to **microprocessor chip** constructed to run faster than standard **CISC** chips by operating with fewer instructions.

**register**  Temporary storage location within the **CPU** that quickly accepts, stores, and transfers data and instructions being used immediately. An instruction that needs to be executed must be retrieved from **main memory (RAM)** and placed in a register for access by the ALU (**arithmetic/logic unit**). The larger the register (the more **bits** it can carry at once), the greater the processing power.

**removable-pack hard disk system**  **Secondary storage** system with 6-20 hard disks aligned above one another in a sealed case.

The entire pack can be inserted into and removed from compatible units connected to the computer.

**relational database**  Type of database organization in which many tables (called *relations*) store related data elements in rows (called *tuples*) and columns (called *attributes*). The structure allows complex logical relationships between records to be expressed in a simple fashion. Relational databases can cross-reference data and retrieve data automatically, and data can be easily added, deleted, or modified. Data can be accessed by content, instead of address, which is the case with **hierarchical database** and **network database models.**

**relational operation**  Operation comparing two elements of data to determine if one element is greater than, less than, or equal to the other.

**removable media**  Diskettes, hard disk cartridges, and optical disk cartridges that can be removed from their drives.

**repetitive strain injury (RSI)**  Name given to a number of injuries resulting from fast, repetitive work—such as typing on a computer keyboard.

**report generator (writer)**  Fourth-generation language similar to **query language**, which allows users to ask questions of a **database** and retrieve information from it for a report. The user cannot alter the contents of the database file but has great control over the appearance of the output.

**request for proposal**  Part of the systems requirement report of phase 2 of the systems development life cycle; companies going outside their own organizations for help in developing a new system use it to request bids from vendors for prices of software, hardware, programs, supplies, and/or services.

**resolution**  Clarity of the image on the **video display screen.**

**retrieving**  In **word processing,** obtaining previously created documents from a storage device and placing them in **main memory (RAM).**

**ring network**  Electronic communications **network** in which messages flow in one direction from a source on the loop to a destination on the loop. Computers in between act as relay stations, but if a computer fails, it can be bypassed.

**RISC** *See* **reduced instruction set computing.**

**robot**  Automatic device that performs functions ordinarily ascribed to humans or that operates with what appears to be almost human intelligence; in the field of **artificial intelligence (AI),** produced to assist in industrial applications, such as **computer-aided manufacturing (CAM).**

**robotics**  Field of **artificial intelligence** that attempts to develop machines that can perform work normally done by people (robots).

**ROM** *See* **read-only memory.**

**RPG (report program generator)**  High-level programming language designed to help small businesses generate reports and update files easily. It can be used to solve clearcut and relatively simple problems.

**satellite system**  In electronic communications, a system that uses solar-powered satellites in stationary orbit above the earth to receive, amplify, and retransmit signals. The satellite acts as a relay station from microwave stations on the ground (called *earth stations*).

**saving**  Activity of permanently storing data from a microcomputer's **main memory (RAM)** (primary storage) on disk or tape (**secondary storage**).

**scanner (scanning device)**  Hardware device that "reads" text and graphics and converts them to computer-usable form; scanners "read" copy on paper and transmit it to the user's computer screen for manipulation, output, and/or storage.

**screen** *See* **monitor.**

**screen utility**  Applications software utility, RAM-resident, used to increase the life of the computer video screen.

**scrolling**  Activity of moving text up or down on the video display screen; can be done with the mouse, the arrow keys, or in other ways.

**SCSI port** Socket on the **system unit** that provides an interface for transferring data at high speeds between the computer and compatible peripheral devices such as CD-ROM drives and backup tape units.

**search and replace** In **word processing,** the activity of automatically searching for and replacing text in a document.

**secondary storage** Any storage device designed to retain data and instructions in permanent form. Secondary storage is **nonvolatile:** data and instructions remain intact when the computer is turned off. Also called *auxiliary storage. Compare* **primary storage.**

**second-generation language** *See* **assembly language.**

**sector** One of several wedge-shaped areas on a hard disk or diskette used for storage reference purposes. The point at which a sector intersects a **track** is used to reference the data location. *See* **hard-sectored disk; soft-sectored disk.**

**seek time** In a disk drive, the time required for the drive to position the **read/write heads** over the proper **track.**

**selection (if-then-else) control structure** In **structured programming,** the **control structure** that allows a condition to be tested to determine which instruction(s) will be performed next.

**semiconductor** Material (often silicon) that conducts electricity with only a little ("semi") resistance; impurities are added to it to form electrical circuits. The integrated circuits (**chips**) in the **main memory (RAM)** of almost all computers today are based on this technology.

**semistructured decision** Decision typically made at the **middle-management** level that, unlike **structured decisions,** must be made without a base of clearly defined informational procedures.

**sequence control structure** In **structured programming,** the **control structure** that specifies that all events take place in sequence, one after the other.

**sequential file organization (storage)** Method of file recording and storage in which data is retrieved one record at a time in the sequence in which it was recorded on the storage medium; to find one particular record, the system must work through all preceding records.

**server** *See* **file server.**

**serial port** Socket in the **system unit** for connecting a peripheral device, such as a modem or a mouse, that transmits data one bit after the other (serially). *Compare* **parallel port.**

**setting time** In a disk drive, the time required to place the **read/write heads** in contact with the disks.

**shareware** Software distributed on request for an evaluation period, after which the user pays a registration fee or returns the software. After the user pays the registration fee—or licensing fee—he or she is usually sent documentation, and, in some cases, additional support and notification of updates.

**simplex transmission mode** Communications transmission in which data travels only in one direction at all times.

**single-density disk** *See* **recording density.**

**single-sided disk** Diskette that stores data on one side only.

**smart card** Credit card-sized personal transaction computer that can be inserted into special card-reading **point-of-sale terminals.** Smart cards have memory chips containing permanent records that are easily updated each time the card is used. The transaction data stored on the card can later be read into the computer to update the user's bank records.

**smart terminal** Terminal that can be used to input and retrieve data and also do some limited processing on its own, such as editing or verifying data. *Compare* **dumb terminal; intelligent terminal.**

**softcopy** Output produced in a seemingly intangible form such as on a video display screen or provided in voice form. *Compare* **hardcopy.**

**soft-sectored disk** Disk that is marked magnetically by the user's computer system during **formatting,** which determines the size and number of **sectors** on the disk. *Compare* **hard-sectored disk.**

**software** Electronic instructions that tell the computer what to do and when and how to do it. Frequently made up of a group of related programs. The two main types of software are **applications software** and **systems software.** Most software is written by programmers in high-level programming languages.

**software development cycle** Orderly process of identifying an organization's applications software requirements and developing the appropriate software.

**software package** **Applications software** and **documentation** usually created by professional software writers to perform general business functions.

**software piracy** Unauthorized copying of software disks for personal use.

**sound-output device** Digital audio circuit board and software that produce digitized sounds, ranging from beeps and chirps to music.

**source code** Program written in **high-level programming language.** Source code must be translated by a **language processor** into **object code** before the program instructions can be executed by the computer.

**spelling checker** In **word processing,** programs that check a document for spelling errors.

**spreadsheet software** Software program enabling user to create, manipulate, and analyze numerical data and develop personalized reports involving the use of extensive mathematical, financial, statistical, and logical processing. The user works with an electronic version of the accountant's traditional worksheet, with rows and columns, called a *spreadsheet.*

**spreadsheet-based graphics** *See* **analytical graphics.** *Compare* **presentation graphics.**

**star network** Electronic communications **network** with a central unit (computer or **file server**) linked to a number of smaller computers and/or terminals (called *nodes*). The central unit acts as traffic controller for all nodes and controls communications to locations outside the network.

**start-stop transmission** *See* **asynchronous transmission.**

**status report** Management report used to supply data and information on the state of something, such as the number of items in inventory; it is a form of output.

**storage hardware** Devices that accept and hold computer instructions and data in a form that is relatively permanent, commonly on magnetic disk or tape or on optical disk.

**storage phase** Phase of activity in the **computer-based information system,** during which data, information, and processing instructions are stored in computer-usable form, commonly on magnetic disk or tape or on optical disk; stored data can be processed further at a later date or output for the user in **softcopy** or **hardcopy** form.

**strategic decision maker** Manager in **upper management** who makes **unstructured decisions**—unpredictable and long-range, not just about past and/or current activities. Such decisions tend to be directed toward strategic planning, allocation of resources, and policy formulation.

**structure chart** In systems analysis, a chart for diagramming the breakdown of **modules** in a program. Also known as *hierarchy chart.*

**structured decision** Predictable decision that can be made about daily business activities by following a well-defined set of routine procedures; typically made by **operational management.**

**structured design** A **top-down design** system to ensure that agreement is reached as early as possible on major program design decisions. Its goals are simplicity, refinement by level, and modularity. *See also* **module.**

**structured programming** Method of programming using **top-down design** and **three control structures** (that is, **sequence, selection, iteration**) to break down main functions into smaller **modules** for coding purposes.

**structured walkthrough** In programming, a the method whereby a group of programmers meet to review a program designed by another programmer in order to identify what is not clear or workable.

**stub testing** Process by which several high-level **modules** in a program are tested before the program is designed for the rest of the lower-level modules; the objective is to eliminate as many errors as possible without having to write the whole program first. A stub is an unprogrammed module.

**subnotebook computer** Portable computer that weighs 2.5–4 pounds (smaller than a **notebook** computer).

**suite** Group of different applications software programs **bundled** and sold for one price.

**summary report** Report for **middle management** that reviews, summarizes, and analyzes historical data to help plan and control operations and implement policy formulated by **upper management.** Summary reports show totals and trends.

**supercomputer** The largest and most powerful computer; it is about 50,000 times more powerful than a **microcomputer** and may cost as much as $20 million. Supercomputers are housed in special rooms; the next most powerful computer is the **mainframe.**

**superconductor** A not-yet-developed material to be used for integrated circuits (**chips**); this material would conduct electricity faster (with less or no resistance) and with less heat output than semiconductors.

**super video graphics array (SVGA)** **Video display adapter** plugged into **expansion slot** in **system cabinet** that allows compatible monitor to display **bit-mapped graphics** in color; must be used with appropriate software; displays up to 256 colors at a very high **resolution.**

**supervisor** The "captain" of the **operating system,** it remains in a microcomputer's main memory and calls in other parts of the operating system as needed from **secondary storage** and controls all other programs in the computer. In a **multitasking** environment, a supervisor coordinates the execution of each program. Also known as *control program.*

**supervisory management** *See* **operating management.**

**surge suppressor** Device that protects electrical equipment from being damaged by surges of high voltage; the computer is plugged into the surge suppressor, which is plugged into the wall socket.

**SVGA** *See* **super video graphics array.**

**switched line** **Point-to-point communications line** that is disconnected when transmission is finished.

**synch bits** Header and trailer bytes inserted as identifiers at beginnings and ends of blocks of coded data; used in **synchronous transmission.**

**synchronous transmission** Form of transmitting groups of characters as blocks with no start and stop bits between characters. Characters are sent as blocks with header and trailer bytes (called **synch bits**) inserted as identifiers at the beginnings and ends of blocks. Synchronous transmission is used by large computers to transmit huge volumes of data at high speeds. *Compare* **asynchronous transmission.**

**syntax** Rules and patterns required for forming programming language sentences or statements that tell the computer what to do and how to do it.

**syntax error** In programming, an error resulting from incorrect use of the rules of the language the program is being written in.

**sysop** Short for *system operator;* person who runs an online information system or an electronic bulletin board.

**system board** *See* **motherboard.**

**system cabinet** *See* **system unit**.

**system clock** *See* **clock.**

**systems analyst** Computer professional generally in charge of the **systems development life cycle;** person responsible for the development of an information system.

**systems development life cycle (SDLC)** Formal process by which organizations build **computer-based information systems.** Participants are users, information processing staff, management of all departments, and computer specialists. The SDLC is used as a guide in establishing a business system's requirements, developing the system, acquiring hardware and software, and controlling development costs. It is generally divided into six phases: (1) analyze current system; (2) define new system requirements; (3) design new system; (4) develop new system and have users test it; (5) implement new system; and (6) evaluate performance of and maintain new system.

**systems flowchart** **Systems development** modeling tool used to diagram and document design of a new system and present an overview of the entire system, including data flow (points of input, output, and storage) and processing activities.

**systems maintenance (support)** The phase after a new system has been implemented when adjustments must be made (correction of minor processing errors).

**systems requirement report** Report concluding the second phase of the **systems development life cycle;** it enables managers to determine the completeness and accuracy of the new system requirements, as well as the economic and practical feasibility of the new system; it may also include a request for proposal for prices of software, hardware, supplies, and/or services from vendors.

**systems software** Programs that are the principal interface between all hardware, the user, and applications software.

**systems test** Phase of testing all programs and related procedures for operating a new system.

**system unit** Main computer system cabinet in a microcomputer, which usually houses the power supply, the motherboard, and some storage devices.

**tactical decision maker** **Middle-level manager** who generally deals with **semistructured decisions.**

**tape streamer** Storage method in which data is written onto a tape in one continuous stream, with no starting or stopping, no IBGs (interblock gaps) or IRGs (interrecord gaps). Tape cassettes are often used as backup storage for hard disks

**TB** *See* **terabyte.**

**telecommuting** Working at home or another workplace and communicating with employer, co-workers, and clients by telephone-linked computer.

**teleconferencing** Electronic linkage of several people who participate in a conversation and share displayed data at the same time.

**terabyte (TB)** One trillion bytes.

**terminal** Input/output device; it typically consists of a **video display screen,** a **keyboard,** and a connecting cable. A dumb terminal is entirely dependent for all its capabilities on the computer system to which it is connected; it cannot do any processing of its own. A smart terminal is able to do some editing and storage of data without interacting with the central computer system, but it cannot be used for programming. An intelligent terminal can input and receive data, as well as allow users to edit and program.

**terminal emulation software** Software that allows a modem-equipped PC to perform as a terminal in a large computer system and tap into it, for example, for research purposes.

**thermal plotter** Plotter that uses heated pens and heat-sensitive paper to output two-color images.

**thermal transfer printer** **Nonimpact printer** that uses heat and colored waxes to produce an image. The print mechanism heats the surface of chemically treated paper, producing dots as characters. No ribbon or ink is used.

**thesaurus** Software program that provides a list of words both similar to and opposite to the meaning of a selected word in a document.

**third-generation language** *See* **high-level language.**

**timesharing** System that supports many user stations or terminals simultaneously. A **front-end processor** may be used to schedule and control all user requests entering the system from the **terminals,** enabling the main computer to concentrate solely on processing.

**token ring network** Electronic communications **network** in which each computer obtains exclusive access to the communications channel by "grabbing" a "token" and altering it before attaching a message. This altered token acts as a message indicator for the receiving computer, which in turn generates a new token, freeing up the channel for another computer. Computers in between the sender and the receiver examine the token and regenerate the message if the token is not theirs. Thus, only one computer can transmit a message at one time.

**top-down design** In **structured programming** and systems design, the act of identifying the main functions of a program and then breaking them into smaller units (**modules**).

**top management** *See* **upper management.**

**touch screen** Video display screen sensitized to receive input from touch of a finger.

**Touch-Tone device** Input device hooked up to the telephone line for the purpose of running credit card checks; the device sends data to a central computer, which then checks the data against its files and reports credit information back to the store. Also called *card dialer* or *card reader.*

**track** (1) On **magnetic tape** a channel of magnetic spots and spaces (1s and 0s) running the length of the tape. (2) On **disks,** a track is one of the circular bands.

**track density** Number of **tracks** on magnetic medium. Common track densities are 48 tracks per inch (tpi) and 96 tpi. Track density affects capacity.

**trackball** Essentially an upside-down **mouse.** The ball is held in a socket on the top of the stationary device; instead of moving the ball by rolling the device around on the desktop, the user moves the ball with his or her fingers.

**transaction file** Temporary storage file in which data is stored in computer-usable form until needed for processing. *Compare* **master file.**

**transaction log** Complete record of activity affecting contents of a **database** during transaction period. This log aids in rebuilding database files if they are damaged.

**transaction processing system (TPS)** Information system supporting day-to-day business operating activities or transactions; usually the first and most important objective of an information system. A computer-based transaction information system operates at the lowest level of a business and usually within only one functional area of a business—marketing, accounting and finance, production, or research and development. Also called an *operations information system (OIS)* or an *electronic data processing (EDP) system.*

**translator** *See* **language processor.**

**tree network** *See* **hierarchical network.**

**Turing test** Test devised by Alan Turing for determining whether a computer possesses "intelligence."

**twisted-pair cable** Insulated pairs of wires twisted around each other; they are often packed into bundles of a thousand or more pairs, as in telephone lines.

**unbundled** Components of a system sold at separate prices. *Compare* **bundled.**

**uninterruptible power supply (UPS)** Equipment used to pro-

tect your computer hardware from power surges; in addition, if the power goes out, a UPS will keep the system running for around 8–30 minutes, providing time to save work and shut the system down.

**UNIX Operating system** initially created for **minicomputers;** it provides a wide range of capabilities, including **virtual storage, multiprogramming,** and **timesharing.**

**unstructured decision** Decision rarely based on predetermined routine procedures; involves the subjective judgment of the decision maker and is mainly the kind of decision made by **upper management.** Unstructured decisions are supported by management information systems in the form of highly summarized reports covering information over long time periods and surveying activities outside as well as inside the company.

**upper (top) management** The level of management dealing with decisions that are broadest in scope and cover the longest time frame. Top managers include only a few powerful people who are in charge of the four basic functions of a business: (1) marketing, (2) accounting and finance, (3) production, and (4) research and development. A manager at this level is also known as a *strategic decision maker. Compare* **middle management; operating management.**

**upper memory** Microcomputer memory located between 640 kilobytes and 1 megabyte of **RAM.**

**user** Person receiving the computer's services; generally someone without much technical knowledge who makes decisions based on reports and other results that computers produce. *Compare* **computer professional.**

**user acceptance test** During phase 4 of the **systems development life cycle,** testing the new system—before it is implemented—to make sure it does what the users want it to do.

**utility programs** Programs often built into systems software to support, enhance, or expand existing programs—examples are screen savers, data recovery, backup, data compression, disk defragmentation, and antivirus programs.

**VESA (Video Electronics Standard Association)** 32-bit **bus** standard that connects peripherals directly to the microprocessor; used with most 80486 systems.

**VGA** *See* **video graphics array.**

**video adapter port** Socket on the **system unit** used to connect the video display screen outside the computer to the **video display adapter** card inside the system unit.

**video display adapter** Also called a *graphics adapter card;* circuit board in the **system unit** that determines the display screen's resolution, number of colors, and how fast images appear. (The card and the monitor must be compatible models.)

**video display screen** Device for viewing computer output. Two main types are **cathode-ray tube (CRT)** and **flat screen.**

**video graphics array (VGA)** Video **display adapter** card plugged into **expansion slot** in **system cabinet** that allows compatible monitors to display **bit-mapped graphics** in color; must be used with appropriate software; displays 16 colors.

**video RAM** Type of **RAM** that stores display images for the monitor.

**virtual memory** Operating system element that enables the computer to process as if it contained almost an unlimited supply of **main memory.** It enables a program to be broken into modules, or small sections, that can be loaded into main memory when needed. Modules not currently in use are stored on high-speed disk and retrieved one at a time when the operating system determines that the current module has completed executing. Also known as *virtual storage.*

**virtual reality** Three-dimensional, computer-generated simulation of reality (artificial reality) with which users can interact using special gloves and a headset.

**virtual storage** *See* **virtual memory.**

**virus** Software **bugs** created intentionally by some programmers, usually by "hackers," that consist of pieces of computer code (either hidden or posing as legitimate code) that, when downloaded or run, attach themselves to other programs or files and cause them to malfunction or "crash."

**voice input device** Input device that converts spoken words into electrical signals by comparing the electrical patterns produced by the speaker's voice to a set of prerecorded patterns. If a matching pattern is found, the computer accepts it as a part of its standard "vocabulary" and then activates and manipulates displays by spoken command. Also known as *voice recognition system*.

**voice mail** Electronic voice-messaging system that answers callers with a recording of the user's voice and records messages. Messages can be forwarded to various locations; local telephone companies provide voice mail services; voice mail systems are also used within companies.

**voice output device** Hardware and software that produce computer-synthesized "spoken" output.

**voice recognition system** *See* **voice input device.**

**volatile storage** Form of storage in which data and instructions are lost when the computer is turned off. *Compare* **nonvolatile storage.** *See also* random access memory (RAM).

**wand** *See* **bar code reader.**

**Warp** *See* **Operating System/2.**

**wide area network (WAN)** Communications network that covers a wide geographic area, such as a state or a country.

**window** Most **video display screens** allow 24–25 lines of text to be viewed at one time; this portion is called a *window*. By moving (scrolling) text up and down the screen, other windows of text become available.

**Windows** *See* **Microsoft Windows.**

**Windows 95** *See* **Microsoft Windows.**

**word** Group of bits that can be manipulated or stored at one time by the CPU; the more bits in a word, the faster the computer.

**word processing** Preparation of text for creating, editing, or printing documents.

**word processing software** Program enabling user to create and edit documents: inserting, deleting, and moving text. Some programs also offer formatting features such as variable margins and different type sizes and styles, as well as more advanced features that border on **desktop publishing.**

**word wrap** In **word processing,** when the **cursor** reaches the right-hand margin of a line it automatically returns (wraps around) to the left-hand margin of the line below and continues the text; the user does not have to hit a key to make the cursor move down to the next line.

**wordsize** The size of a **register** is referred to as **wordsize.** In general, the larger the register, the more bits (larger **words**) can be processed at once.

**workstation** A sophisticated and powerful microcomputer used by one person at a time for specialized applications such as **computer-aided design** and **computer-aided engineering.**

**WORM (write once, read many)** **Optical disk** whose data and instructions are imprinted by the disk manufacturer but whose content is determined by the buyer; after the data is imprinted, it cannot be changed. *Compare* **compact disk/read-only memory (CD-ROM); erasable optical disk.**

**write** Refers to when electronic data is processed by the computer and recorded onto disk or tape. *Compare* **read.**

**write-protect notch** On a **diskette,** a notch in the protective cover that can be covered to prevent the **read/write head** from touching the disk surface so that no data can be recorded or erased.

**WYSIWYG (what you see is what you get)** **Page description software** that allows the user to see the final version of a **desktop publishing** document on the screen before it is printed out. *Compare* **code-oriented.**

**XGA** *See* **extended graphics array.**

# Index

# Notes

## Chapter 1

1. Sandra D. Atchison, "The Care and Feeding of 'Lone Eagles,'" *Business Week*, November 15, 1993, p. 58.

2. Susan N. Futterman, "Quick-Hit Research of a Potential Employer," *CompuServe Magazine*, September 1993, p. 36.

3. Susan Kuchinskas, "Online Services Make Themselves at Home," *San Francisco Examiner*, November 7, 1993, pp. F-1, F-6.

## Chapter 2

1. David Gelernter, quoted in Associated Press, "Bombing Victim Says He's Lucky to Be Alive," *San Francisco Chronicle*, January 28, 1994, p. A15.

2. Zachary Coile, "'Free' Computer Revolution Now Has a Price Tag," *San Francisco Examiner*, January 30, 1994, p. B-3.

3. John Pierson, "Do-It-Yourself Grocery Checkout," *The Wall Street Journal*, January 31, 1994, p. B1.

4. Burr Snyder, "A Calling to Collect," *San Francisco Examiner*, February 27, 1994, pp. E-1, E-10.

5. William M. Bulkeley, "Get Ready for 'Smart Cards' in Health Care," *The Wall Street Journal*, May 3, 1993, p. B7.

6. Julie Schmit, "The Ticket to Ride: Smart Cards," *USA Today*, January 11, 1994, p. 1B.

7. Bulkeley, 1993.

8. Associated Press, "Sprint Unveils Voice-Activated Phone Card," *San Francisco Chronicle*, January 6, 1994, p. D2.

9. David Haskin, "Speech Recognition: Closer Than You Think," *Windows Sources*, September 1993, p. 46.

10. Jerry Adler, "The Miracle of the Keys," *Newsweek*, December 23, 1991, p. 67.

## Chapter 3

1. Katherine Murray, revised by Doug White and Tony Shafer, *Introduction to Personal Computers*, 4th ed. (Carmel, IN: Que Corp., 1993), p. 108.

2. Peter H. Lewis, "PC Buyers Will Soon Face Choices among Work Stations," *The New York Times*, February 14, 1993, sec. 3, p. 8.

3. Michael Allen, "Workstations Go from Desk Jobs to Role Once Played Solely by Supercomputers," *The Wall Street Journal*, August 11, 1992, p. B1.

4. Steve Lohr, "Midsized I.B.M. Line Upgraded," *The New York Times*, September 7, 1993, p. C1.

5. Adam Bryant, "Small Computer Maker Counts on Discontent," *The New York Times*, October 7, 1992, p. C18.

6. Laurie Hays, "IBM Tries to Keep Mainframes Afloat against Tide of Cheap, Agile Machines," *The Wall Street Journal*, August 12, 1993, pp. B1, B7.

7. Peter Nulty, "When to Murder Your Mainframe," *Fortune*, November 1, 1993, pp. 109–120.

8. John Markoff, "A Remade I.B.M. Reinvents the Mainframe," *The New York Times*, January 29, 1993, pp. C1, C5.

9. Richard Preston, "The Mountains of Pi," *The New Yorker*, March 2, 1992, pp. 36–67.

10. John W. Verity and Julie Flynn, "Call It Superbig Blue," *Business Week*, June 29, 1992, pp. 74–75.

11. John Markoff, "A Crucial Linkup in the U.S. Data Highway," *The New York Times*, September 30, 1992, p. C6.

12. Suzanne Weixel, *Easy PCs*, 2nd ed. (Indianapolis: Que Corp., 1993), p. 19.

13. Earle J. Robinson, "PCMCIA Redefines Mobile Computing," *PC/Computing*, July 1993, pp. 238–252.

## Chapter 4

1. Adam Bryant, "Text! Video! Sound! In a Gizmo Now," *The New York Times*, October 11, 1992, sec. 3, p. 10.

2. Evan I. Schwartz, "CD-ROM: A Mass Medium at Last," *Business Week*, July 19, 1993, pp. 82–83.

3. William M. Bulkeley, "Publishers Deliver Reams of Data on CDs," *The Wall Street Journal*, February 22, 1993, p. B6.

4. Bulkeley, 1993.

5. James Coates, "CD-ROM Movie as Big as Your Imagination," *The Australian*, March 22, 1994, p. 45.

6. Peter H. Lewis, "Besides Storing 1,000 Words, Why Not Store a Picture Too?" *The New York Times*, October 11, 1992, sec. 3, p. 8.

7. "Gargantua's 'Lossless' Compression," *The Australian*, March 22, 1994, p. 32; reprinted from *The Economist*.

8. Peter Coy, "Invasion of the Data Shrinkers," *Business Week*, February 14, 1994, pp. 115–116.

9. "Gargantua's 'Lossless' Compression," 1994.

10. Steve Lohr, "Record Store of Near Future: Computers Replace the Racks," *The New York Times*, May 12, 1993, pp. A1, C5.

11. Tom Adams, quoted in Lohr, 1993, p. A1.

12. Paul M. Eng, Robert D. Hof, and Hiromi Uchida, "It's a Whole New Game: The Hards vs. the Cards," *Business Week*, June 8, 1992, pp. 101-103.

13. John Markoff, "An Advanced Technology to Read Data," *The New York Times*, August 20, 1993, p. C3.

14. David P. Hamilton, "NEC Physicists Develop Method to Store and Erase Information Using Atoms," *The Wall Street Journal*, June 3, 1993, p. B5.

## Chapter 5

1. Jim Seymour, *On the Road: The Portable Computing Bible* (New York: Brady, 1992), pp. 184–185.

2. Peter H. Lewis, "So the Computer Talks. Does Anyone Want to Listen?" *The New York Times*, October 4, 1992, sec. 3, p. 9.

3. Diana Berti, quoted in Timothy L. O'Brien, "Aided by Computers, Many of the Disabled Form Own Businesses," *The Wall Street Journal*, October 8, 1993, pp. A1, A5.

## Chapter 6

1. David Kirkpatrick, "Groupware Goes Boom," *Fortune*, December 27, 1993, p. 100.

2. Gary McWilliams, "Lotus 'Notes' Get a Lot of Notice," *Business Week*, March 29, 1993, pp. 84–85.

3. Kirkpatrick, 1993, pp. 100–101.

4. Steve Lohr, "Microsoft Seeks to Pad Wide Lead in PC Suites," *The New York Times*, October 15, 1993, p. C3.

5. Allan Freedman, *The Computer Glossary*, 6th ed. (New York: AMACOM, 1993), p. 406.

6. Walter S. Mossberg, "Organizer Program Takes a Leaf from Date Books," *The Wall Street Journal*, January 21, 1993, p. B1.

7. Stacey Richardson, quoted in: Peter H. Lewis, "Pairing People Management with Project Management," *The New York Times*, April 11, 1993, sec. 3, p. 12.

8. Bernie Ward, "Computer Chic," *Sky*, April 1993, pp. 84–90.

9. Peter H. Lewis, "Champion of MS-DOS, Admirer of Windows," *The New York Times*, April 4, 1993, sec. 3, p. 11.

10. Ed Bott, "Inside Windows 4.0," *PC/Computing*, March 1994, pp. 124–139.

11. Peter H. Lewis, "A Strong New OS/2, with an Uncertain Future," *The New York Times*, June 20, 1993, sec. 3, p. 8.

12. Steve Lohr, "Standard Set for Unix Interface," *The New York Times*, August 31, 1993, p. C4.

13. Tom Moran, "Apple Tells Its Software Future," *Macworld*, June 1994, pp. 36–37.

14. Peter H. Lewis, "Newest Netware Challenges Customers," *The New York Times*, March 28, 1993, sec. 3, p. 8.

## Chapter 7

1. Alan Freedman, *The Computer Glossary*, 6th ed. (New York: AMACOM, 1993).

2. Freedman, 1993.

## Chapter 8

1. L. R. Shannon, "Conversing On Line With Older Americans," *The New York Times*, October 19, 1993, p. B7.

2. Mike Branigan, "The Cost of Using an Online Service," *PC Novice*, January 1992, pp. 65–71.

3. Richard Brandt and Amy Cortese, "Bill Gates's Vision," *Business Week*, June 27, 1994, pp. 57–62.

4. Larry Magid, *Cruising Online: Larry Magid's Guide to the New Digital Highways* (New York: Random House, 1994).

5. Del Jones, "On-line Services Best for Leisure Trips," *USA Today*, December 27, 1993, p. 5B.

6. "The Warming of the Workplace," *Psychology Today*, May/June 1992, p. 10.

7. Bob Mahoney, quoted in Keay Davidson, "Wild About Computer Bulletin Boards," *San Francisco Examiner*, April 18, 1993, pp. B-1, B-3.

8. Marshall Toplansky, quoted in Jennifer Larson, "Telecommunications and Your Computer," *PC Novice*, March 1993, pp. 14–19.

9. Peter H. Lewis, "You Can't Roller-Skate on Electronic Highway," *The New York Times*, June 28, 1994, p. B8.

10. Rick Tetzeli, "The Internet and Your Business," *Fortune*, March 7, 1994, pp. 86–96.

11. David Landis, "Exploring the Online Universe," *USA Today*, p. 4D.

*Chapters 9, 10, 11*

No notes

*Chapter 12*

1. Charles Petit, "8-Legged Robot to Crawl Into Volcano," *San Francisco Chronicle*, July 28, 1994, p. A3.

2. Jeanne B. Pinder, "Fuzzy Thinking Has Merits When It Comes to Elevators," *The New York Times*, September 22, 1993, pp. C1, C7.

*Chapter 13*

1. Barbara Kantrowitz, Andrew Cohen, and Melinda Lieu, "My Info Is NOT Your Info," *Newsweek*, July 18, 1994, p. 54.

2. Teresa Riordan, "Writing Copyright Law for an Information Age," *The New York Times*, July 7, 1994, pp. C1, C5.

3. David Edelson, "What Price Superhighway Information?" (letter), *The New York Times*, January 16, 1994, p. 16.

4. David L. Wheeler, "Computer Networks Are Said to Offer New Opportunities for Plagiarists," *The Chronicle of Higher Education*, June 30, 1993, pp. A17, A19.

5. Denise K. Magner, "Verdict in a Plagiarism Case," *The Chronicle of Higher Education*, January 5, 1994, pp. A17, A20.

6. Robert Tomsho, "As Sampling Revolutionizes Recording, Debate Grows Over Aesthetics, Copyrights," *The Wall Street Journal*, November 5, 1990, p. B1.

7. William Grimes, "A Question of Ownership of Images," *The New York Times*, August 20, 1993, p. B7.

8. William Safire, "Art Vs. Artifice," *The New York Times*, January 3, 1994, p. A11.

9. Hans Fantel, "Sinatra's 'Duets': Music Recording or Wizardry?" *The New York Times*, January 1, 1994, p. 13.

10. Cover, *Newsweek*, June 27, 1994; cover, *Time*, June 27, 1994.

11. Jonathan Alter, "When Photographs Lie," *Newsweek*, July 30, 1990, pp. 44–45.

12. Fred Ritchin, quoted in Alter, 1990.

13. Robert Zemeckis, cited in Laurence Hooper, "Digital Hollywood: How Computers Are Remaking Movie Making," *Rolling Stone*, August 11, 1994, pp. 55–58, 75.

14. Woody Hochswender, "When Seeing Cannot Be Believing," *The New York Times*, June 23, 1992, pp. B1, B3.

15. Kathleen O'Toole, "High-Tech TVs, Computers Blur Line Between Artificial, Real," *Stanford Observer*, November-December 1992, p. 8.

16. Associated Press, "Robot Sent to Disarm Bomb Goes Wild in San Francisco," *The New York Times*, August 28, 1993, p. 7.

17. "Frustrated Bank Customer Lets His Computer Make Complaint," *The Los Angeles Times*, October 20, 1993, p. A28.

18. Arthur M. Louis, "Nasdaq's Computer Crashes," *San Francisco Chronicle*, July 16, 1994, pp. D1, D3.

19. Joseph F. Sullivan, "A Computer Glitch Causes Bumpy Start in a Newark School," *The New York Times*, September 18, 1991, p. A25.

20. Richard Woodbury, "The Bag Stops Here," *Time*, May 16, 1994, p. 52.

21. John Abell, "Computer Crashes Costing Corporate America Plenty," *San Francisco Examiner*, August 30, 1992, p. E-14.

22. David L. Wilson, "Devastating Wave of Computer Theft Pushes Universities to Compare Notes and Search for Ways to Boost Security," *The Chronicle of Higher Education*, June 9, 1993, pp. A17-A18.

23. G. Pascal Zachary, "Software Firms Keep Eye on Bulletin Boards," *The Wall Street Journal*, November 11, 1991, p. B1.

24. Thomas J. DeLoughry, "2 Students Are Arrested for Software Piracy," *The Chronicle of Higher Education*, April 20, 1994, p. A32.

25. Suzanne P. Weisband and Seymour E. Goodman, "Subduing Software Pirates," *Technology Review*, October 1993, pp. 31–33.

26. Mark Robichaux, "Cable-TV Pirates Become More Brazen, Forcing Industry to Seek New Remedies," *The Wall Street Journal*, May 7, 1992, pp. B1, B8.

27. John J. Keller, "Hackers Open Voice-Mil Door to Others' Phone Lines," *The Wall Street Journal*, March 15, 1991, pp. B1, B3.

28. John J. Keller, "Thanks to Hackers, Cellular Phone Firms Now Face Crime Wave," *The Wall Street Journal*, June 14, 1991, pp. A1, A5.

29. Anthony Ramirez, "5 Charged in Huge Computer Break-Ins," *The New York Times*, July 9, 1992, p. A7.

30. William Barnhill, "'Privacy Invaders,'" *AARP Bulletin*, May 1992, pp. 1, 10.

31. David L. Wilson, "Gate Crashers," *The Chronicle of Higher Education*, October 20, 1993, pp. A22–A23.

32. Mary B. W. Tabor, "Urban Hackers Charged in High-Tech Crime," *The New York Times*, July 23, 1992, pp. A1, A12.

33. Katherine Rizzo, "Hi-Tech Tax Cheats Bilk IRS," *San Francisco ErChronicle*, July 19, 1994, p. A9.

34. Saul Hansell, "New Breed of Check Forgers Exploits Desktop Publishing," *The New York Times*, August 15, 1994, pp. A1, C3.

35. David Einstein, "Crooks Swindle On-Line Investors," *San Francisco Chronicle*, July 1, 1994, pp. B1, B2.

36. Steve Rubenstein, "San Jose Police Tryu to Stop Computer-Sent Gang Slaying Rumors," *San Francisco Chronicle*, September 22, 1993, p. A22.

37. Jeremy L. Milk, "3 U. of Wisconsin Students Face Punishment for Bogus E-Mail Messages," *The Chronicle of Higher Education*, October 20, 1993, p. A25.

38. Jeffrey Hsu, "Computer Viruses, Technological Poisons," *PC Novice*, October 1993, pp. 41–43.

39. Peter H. Lewis, "The Virus: Threat or Menace," *The New York Times*, June 15, 1993, p. B6.

40. Lewis, 1993.

41. Donald Parker, quoted in William M. Carley, "Rigging Computers for Fraud or Malice Is Often an Inside Job," *The Wall Street Journal*, August 27, 1992, pp. A1, A5.

42. Eric Corley, cited in Kenneth R. Clark, "Hacker Says It's Harmless, Bellcore Calls It Data Rape," *San Francisco Examiner*, September 13, 1992, p. B-9; reprinted from *Chicago Tribune*.

43. Wilson, October 20, 1993.

44. Tabor, 1992.

45. Timothy Ziegler, "Elite Unit Tracks Computer Crime," *San Francisco Chronicle*, May 27, 1994, pp. A1, A17.

46. John Markoff, "Keeping Things Safe and Orderly in the Neighborhoods of Cyberspace," *The New York Times*, October 24, 1993, sec. 4, p. 7.

47. Joshua Cooper Ramo, "A SWAT Team in Cyberspace," *Newsweek*, February 21, 1994, p. 73.

48. David L. Wilson, "Convenience vs. Security on the Internet," *The Chronicle of Higher Education*, July 13, 1994, pp. A15–A17.

49. Steven Bellovin, cited in Jane Bird, "More than a Nuisance," *The Times* (London), April 22, 1994, p. 31.

50. Anthony Ramirez, "How Hackers Find the Password," *The New York Times*, July 23, 1992, p. A12.

51. Robert Lee HJotz, "Sign on the Electronic Dotted Line," *Los Angeles Times*, October 19, 1993, pp. A1, A16.

52. William M. Bulkeley, "Electronic Signatures Boost Security of PCs," *The Wall Street Journal*, June 7, 1993.

53. Stephen Wildstrom, "Digital Signatures That Can't Be Forged," *Business Week*, July 4, 1994, p. 13.

54. Eugene Carlson, "Some Forms of Identification Can't Be Handily Faked," *The Wall Street Journal*, September 14, 1993, p. B2.

55. William M. Bulkeley, "Popularity Overseas of Encryption Code Has the U.S. Worried," *The Wall Street Journal*, April 28, 1994, pp. A1, A7.

56. Peter H. Lewis, "Of Privacy and Security: The Clipper Chip Debate," *The New York Times*, April 24, 1994, sec. 3, p. 5.

57. Lawrence J. Magid, "Clipper Won't Clip Crooks' Wings," *San Jose Mercury News*, May 22, 1994, p. 1F.

58. John Markoff, "An Administration Reversal on Wiretapping Technology," *The New York Times*, July 21, 1994, p. C1.

59. Stephen H. Wildstrom, "Data Privacy: A Win for Business," *Business Week*, August 8, 1994, p. 11.

60. John Holusha, "The Painful Lessons of Disruption," *The New York Times*, March 17, 1993, pp. C1, C5.

61. The Enterprise Technology Center, cited in "Disaster Avoidance and Recovery Is Growing Business Priority," special advertising supplement in *LAN Magazine*, November 1992, p. SS3.

62. John Painter, cited in Holusha, 1993.

## *Photo Credits*

*Page 3* (a) IBM, (b) Sun, (c–f) IBM; *5* Hewlett-Packard; *9* Hayes Microcomputer Products; *11* Comp USA; *13* (a) Cray Research, (b) IBM, (c) Digital Equipment Corp., (d) Apple Computer, (e) Sun; *21* (a–c) IBM Archives, (d–e) Smithsonian Institution, (e) IBM Archives; *22* Unisys Archives; *26* Aspen Photography; *28* (left) Steve Webster, Apple Computer, (right) Microsoft Corp.; *29* (top) Frank Pryor, Apple Computer, (bottom) BellSouth; *43* Microsoft Corp.; *44* (Figure 2.4) IBM, (inset) Micros Hospitality Information Systems; *44* (Figure 2.5) The Image Works; *45* (top) Micros Corp., (middle) Kensington, (bottom) Thrustmaster; *48* (left) Boston Chicken, (right) AT&T Global Info/Solution; *49* FTG Data Systems; *49* (left) Calcomp, (right) Hewlett-Packard; *50* EO Computers, (right) Apple Computer; *52* (top left, bottom left) NCR, (middle) FedEx Corp., (bottom right) IBM; *54* (Figure 2.15) NEC; *54* (Figure 2.16) BellSouth; *55* Brilliant Color Cards; *70–71* (left to right) NEC, Sun, NEC, NEC, Apple Computer, Omnibook, Sharp, Toshiba, Apple Computer, Digital Equipment Corp., IBM, Cray Research; *72* IBM, (inset) Toshiba; *75* (left) Sun, (middle) Universal Studios, (right) Reuters/Bettmann; (Figure 3.4) *76* Digital Equipment Corp.; *76* (Figure 3.5) IBM; *77* Cray Research; *82* (top) IBM, (bottom) Intel; *101* Hayes Microcomputer Products, Inc.; *116* (Figure 4.2) IBM; *116* (Figure 4.3) Irwin; *117* (Figure 4.4) Exabyte; *117* (Figure 4.5) IBM; *121* IBM; *127* SyQuest; *128* NCR Corp.; *130* (left) Panasonic Personal Computer Co., (right) NEC; *132* (bottom right) Greenlar/The Image Works; *138* Paul Higon/NYT Pictures; *152* Canon; *154* Hewlett-Packard; *155* Hewlett-Packard; *157* Tektronix; *158* (Figure 5.8) Hewlett-Packard; *158* (Figure 5.9) Okidata; *174* Q Software, SousChef 3.1; *175* Comp USA/Gerry Kahn; *192* (left) Autodesk; (right) IBM; *267* AT&T; *270* Newfoundland Telephone Co.; *272* Sprint; *277* Hayes Microcomputer Products, Inc.; *279* Randall/The Image Works; *295* Brian K. Williams, (inset) Apple Computer; *369* Frank Bevans Photography; *400* United Airlines Gate Assignment Display System; *415* Transitions Research Corp.; *428* Peter Menzel; *429* Stewart McSherry; *430* Virtus WalkThrough Pro; *458* Symantec; *477* (left) IBM, (right) Compaq; *478* Apple Computer; *480* NEC Technologies, Inc.; *485* Creative Labs, Inc.; *491, 492, 495, 496, 497* Frank Bevans Photography; *499* Kinesis.

## *Text Credits*

*Figure 9.3* from Whitten, Jeffrey L., Bently, Lonnie D., & Barow, Victor M. *Systems Analysis & Design Methods* (Third Edition). Burr Ridge, IL: Irwin, 1994; *Figures 14.5, 14.6* adapted from Patrick Marshall, *PC World,* April 1992, p. 191.

*Page 17* (Clipboard) from *PC Novice,* Peed Corporation, 120 West Harvest Drive, Lincoln, NE 68521. For subscription information, please call 800-582-2600. *19* (Clipboard) reprinted with permission of *The Wall Street Journal,* © 1993 Dow Jones & Company, Inc. All rights reserved worldwide. *28* (Figure 1.15 quote) from *Newsweek,* October 11, 1993, and © 1993, Newsweek, Inc., All rights reserved. Reprinted with permission. *29* (Figure 1.16 quote) reprinted with permission of *The Wall Street Journal,* © 1993 Dow Jones & Company, Inc. All rights reserved worldwide. *42* (Clipboard) excerpt reprinted with permission of *Datamation* magazine, January 7, 1994 © 1994 by Cahners Publishing Company. *47* (Clipboard) reprinted with permission of *The New Republic.* *74* (Clipboard) © 1994 Time Inc. All rights reserved. *80* (Clipboard) © 1994 Time Inc. All rights reserved. *90, 98* (Clipboard) from *PC Novice,* Peed Corporation, 120 West Harvest Drive, Lincoln, NE 68521. For subscription information, please call 800-582-2600. *124* (Clipboard) *New York Times, 138* reprinted with permission of Cox News Service. *159* Boyd & Fraser Publishing Co. *187, 194* (Clipboard) *PC Novice,* Peed Corporation, 120 West Harvest Drive, Lincoln, NE 68521. For subscription information, please call 800-582-2600. *194* (Clipboard) *PC Novice,* Peed Corporation, 120 West Harvest Drive, Lincoln, NE 68521. For subscription information, please call 800-582-2600. *199* reprinted with permission of Jeffrey Henning (e-mail: 74774.157@compuserve.com). *227* reprinted with permission from Microsoft Corporation. *238* copyright © 1994 by Scientific American, Inc. All rights reserved. *294* (Clipboard) *PC Novice,* Peed Corporation, 120 West Harvest Drive, Lincoln, NE 68521. For subscription information, please call 800-582-2600. *295* (Figure 8.17 quote) reprinted by permission of *The Wall Street Journal,* © 1992 Dow Jones & Company, Inc. All rights reserved worldwide. *296* (Clipboard and photo) reprinted with permission of the *San Francisco Chronicle.* *329* (Clipboard) reprinted with permission from *Industrial Engineering,* Marcel Dekker, Inc., New York. *335* (Clipboard) *PC Novice,* Peed Corporation, 120 West Harvest Drive, Lincoln, NE 68521. For subscription information, please call 800-582-2600. *354* (Clipboard) *New York Times. 357* (Clipboard) *Food Arts. 361* (Clipboard) reprinted with permission, *Inc. Annual 1994.* Copyright 1994 by Goldhirsh Group, Inc., 38 Commercial Wharf, Boston, MA 02110. *367* (Clipboard) reprinted with permission of *Sales and Marketing Management. 381* (Clipboard) reprinted by permission of *The Wall Street Journal,* © 1992 Dow Jones & Company, Inc. All rights reserved worldwide. *388* (Clipboard) reprinted from *Hospitals & Health Networks,* Vol. 68, No. 3, by permission, February 5, 1994. Copyright 1994, American Hospital Publishing, Inc. *393* (Clipboard) reprinted with permission of *Computing Canada,* Plesman Publications Ltd., Willowdale, Ontario. *403* (Clipboard) reprinted with permission, *Inc. Annual 1994.* Copyright 1994 by Goldhirsh Group, Inc., 38 Commercial Wharf, Boston, MA 02110. *418* (Clipboard) reprinted by permission of *Omni,* 1995, Omni Publications International, Ltd. *419* (Clipboard) © 1994 Time Inc. All rights reserved. *427* (Clipboard) from *Newsweek,* May 30, 1994 and © 1994, Newsweek, Inc. All rights reserved. Reprinted by permission. *424* (Clipboard) reproduced with permission from *the Futurist,* published by the World Future Society, 7910 Woodmont Avenue, Suite 450, Bethesda, Maryland 20814. *446* (Clipboard) *New York Times. 452* (Clipboard) reprinted with permission of *Online Access, 464* (Clipboard) Computer Security Institute, San Francisco. *480* (Figure 14.4) reprinted with permission of Phillip Robinson. *485* (Figure 14.7), *PC Novice,* Peed Corporation, 120 West Harvest Drive, Lincoln, NE 68521. For subscription information, please call 800-582-2600.